THE NATIONAL UNDERWRITER COMPANY

COMMERCIAL GENERAL LIABILITY COVERAGE GUIDE, 11th EDITION

Donald S. Malecki, CPCU, David Thamann, J.D., CPCU, ARM

The ISO Commercial General Liability form is the backbone of most commercial insurance programs. That's why virtually every insurance professional must be able to navigate it confidently. *Commercial General Liability Coverage Guide* is the only professional resource that traces the coverage provisions of the ISO CGL form from the 1986 (in some cases earlier editions) to the most recently released form.

This practical guide has proven itself as the gold-standard for handling CGL coverage. With a focus on real-world application, the book has been a perpetual best seller since the first edition was published in 1985. Now in its 11th edition, this singular reference extends the long-standing tradition of continuous improvement by adding three new chapters:

- Introduction to Umbrella Coverage

- Umbrella Liability Coverage Form CU 00 01 04 13

- Excess Liability Coverage Form CX 00 01 04 13

Commercial General Liability Coverage Guide also includes the Umbrella Form and Excess Form themselves along with fully updated case law and a revised case law index.

In addition to the all-new material, expert authors Donald S. Malecki and David Thamann have fully reviewed and revised (where necessary) the entire book. The 11th edition contains everything you've come to expect from this industry-standard CGL resource, including:

- Original discussion and expert analyses supported by up-to-date, multi-jurisdictional case law

- The real-life examples that make this book the most practical CGL resource

- Analyses of endorsement that may be used to tailor coverage

- Highlights of the major changes seen in the 2013 ISO CGL form and analysis of how they affect coverage

Only *Commercial General Liability Coverage Guide* enables you to master the Commercial General Liability form, navigate all the major policy provisions, correctly interpret policy language, and keep your focus on practical applications to real-world situations.

For customer service questions or to place additional orders, please call 1-800-543-0874.

11th Edition

Commercial General Liability Coverage Guide

Commercial Lines Series

Donald S. Malecki, CPCU
David D. Thamann, J.D., CPCU, ARM

The National Underwriter Company

Copyright © 2013, 2012, 2005, 2001, 1998, 1997, 1996, 1994, 1992, 1990, 1986, 1985 by
THE NATIONAL UNDERWRITER COMPANY
4157 Olympic Blvd.
Suite 225
Erlanger, KY 41018

First Edition, June 1985
Second Edition, January 1986
Second Printing, June 1986
Third Edition, August 1990
Fourth Edition, August 1992
Fifth Edition, December 1994
Sixth Edition, May 1996
Second Printing, January 1997
Third Printing, January 1999
Fourth Printing, November 1999
Seventh Edition, October 2001
Second Printing, March 2004
Eighth Edition, March 2005
Second Printing, June 2007
Ninth Edition, September 2011
Tenth Edition, May 2013
Eleventh Edition, January 2015

International Standard Book Number: 978-1-941627-43-3
Library of Congress Control Number: 2014959671

Printed in the United States of America

ABOUT SUMMIT PROFESSIONAL NETWORKS

Summit Professional Networks supports the growth and vitality of the insurance, financial services and legal communities by providing professionals with the knowledge and education they need to succeed at every stage of their careers. We provide face-to-face and digital events, websites, mobile sites and apps, online information services, and magazines giving professionals multi-platform access to our critical resources, including Professional Development; Education & Certification; Prospecting & Data Tools; Industry News & Analysis; Reference Tools and Services; and Community Networking Opportunities.

Using all of our resources across each community we serve, we deliver measurable ROI for our sponsors through a range of turnkey services, including Research, Content Development, Integrated Media, Creative & Design, and Lead Generation.

For more information, go to http://www.SummitProfessionalNetworks.com.

ABOUT THE NATIONAL UNDERWRITER COMPANY

The National Underwriter Company is a Summit Professional Network.

For over 110 years, The National Underwriter Company has been the first in line with the targeted tax, insurance, and financial planning information you need to make critical business decisions. Boasting nearly a century of expert experience, our reputable Editors are dedicated to putting accurate and relevant information right at your fingertips. With *Tax Facts*, *Tools & Techniques*, *National Underwriter Advanced Markets*, *Field Guide*, *FC&S®*, *FC&S Legal* and other resources available in print, eBook, CD, and online, you can be assured that as the industry evolves National Underwriter will be at the forefront with the thorough and easy-to-use resources you rely on for success.

The National Underwriter Company Update
Service Notification

This National Underwriter Company publication is regularly updated to include coverage of developments and changes that affect the content. If you did not purchase this publication directly from The National Underwriter Company and you want to receive these important updates sent on a 30-day review basis and billed separately, please contact us at (800) 543-0874. Or you can mail your request with your name, company, address, and the title of the book to:

The National Underwriter Company
4157 Olympic Boulevard, Suite 225
Erlanger, KY 41018

If you purchased this publication from The National Underwriter Company directly, you have already been registered for the update service.

National Underwriter Company Contact Information

To order any National Underwriter Company title, please

- call 1-800-543-0874, 8-6 ET Monday – Thursday and 8 to 5 ET Friday

- online bookstore at www.nationalunderwriter.com, or

- mail to The National Underwriter Company, Orders Department, 4157 Olympic Blvd, Suite 225, Erlanger, KY 41018

About the Author

Donald S. Malecki, CPCU

The insurance world in general and the National Underwriter Company in particular have lost a colleague and a friend. Don Malecki passed away on Friday, December 12th.

Don was a recognized insurance and risk management expert who spent over fifty years in the business as a writer, consultant, and expert witness. Don began his career as a fire underwriter and later as a supervising casualty underwriter. He began his writing career when he joined the staff of the *Fire, Casualty, and Surety (FC&S) Bulletins*, the National Underwriter Company, in 1966. Don left the National Underwriter Company in 1984 to start his own consulting practice, a practice in which he contributed his every working hour toward understanding the insurance business, and sharing that understanding and knowledge with all those seeking his guidance. Don was a recognized expert witness who was called upon numerous times over his career to testify in courts around the country as to the history and meaning of insurance policy language. Don was also an author and co-author of many books on insurance and risk management. He was past president of the Cincinnati Chapter of Chartered Property Casualty Underwriters (CPCU) and a member of the Society of Risk Management Consultants.

It is safe to say that Don Malecki was a giant in the insurance industry, a man who dedicated his life's work to learning and teaching about insurance coverage and risk management. Don will be greatly missed by those who benefitted in the past and still benefit now from his sharing of his time and knowledge, and he will be especially missed by those who knew him and worked with him. God Bless.

About the Publisher

Kelly B. Maheu, J.D., is Managing Director of the Professional Publishing Division of The National Underwriter Company, a Division of Summit Professional Networks. Kelly has been with The National Underwriter Company since 2006, serving in editorial, content acquisition, and product development roles prior to being named Managing Director.

Prior to joining The National Underwriter Company, Kelly worked in the legal and insurance fields for LexisNexis®, Progressive Insurance, and a Cincinnati insurance defense litigation firm.

Kelly has edited and contributed to numerous books and publications including the Personal Auto Insurance Policy Coverage Guide, Cyberliability and Insurance, The National Underwriter Sales Essentials Series, and The Tools and Techniques of Risk Management for Financial Planners.

Kelly earned her law degree from The University of Cincinnati College of Law and holds a BA from Miami University, Ohio, with a double major in English/Journalism and Psychology.

Editor–Author

David D. Thamann, J.D., ARM, CPCU, is the managing editor of the *FC&S Bulletins*® and has been an *FC&S* editor since 1987. Before joining the National Underwriter Company, he was a claims supervisor and senior underwriter for American Druggists Insurance Company, a commercial property lead underwriter for Transamerica Insurance, and a commercial package underwriter for CNA and Safeco Insurance companies.

Mr. Thamann graduated from Salmon P. Chase College of Law and Xavier University.

The publications he wrote or contributed to include *Business Auto Coverage Guide, Personal Auto Coverage Guide, Workers Compensation Guide*, and *Commercial General Liability Supplement*, all published by The National Underwriter Company. Mr. Thamann also writes articles for *Claims* magazine, InsWorld, and ProducersWEB. He is a speaker or presenter at various insurance related seminars and meetings.

Editorial Services

Connie L. Jump, Manager, Editorial Operations
Emily Brunner, Editorial Assistant

Table of Contents

Introduction

In 1986, insurers began using a new series of general liability forms and endorsements. These forms and endorsements were developed by Insurance Services Office (ISO) to replace the 1973 edition of the comprehensive general liability coverage part and related forms and endorsements. An immediate concern of risk managers and insurance personnel was how the 1986 forms, particularly the two commercial general liability coverage forms that were the nucleus of the new program, differed from the 1973 forms.

The first and second editions of this text addressed that concern by describing the two new coverage forms and explaining how they differed from the 1973 comprehensive general liability coverage part and broad form comprehensive general liability endorsement (which was commonly attached to the CGL coverage part).

A third edition was necessitated by ISO's introduction of revised commercial general liability (CGL) coverage forms, effective March 1, 1990, in most jurisdictions. This text refers to those forms as the 1990 CGL coverage forms, even though the forms are dated 11/88 (November 1988), the date that ISO originally set for their effective date. The considerable gap between the date on the forms and their actual effective date was largely the result of negotiations between ISO and the National Association of Insurance Commissioners on various features of the revised forms.

A fourth edition of *Commercial General Liability* was prepared to add analysis of further modifications proposed by ISO for introduction in 1992. These changes were implemented in only a few states partly because some of the changes affecting coverage for defense costs assumed by the insured under a contract were controversial.

A fifth edition was published to include further changes introduced in 1993. These changes were more readily accepted by regulators than the 1992 changes. Because of the controversial nature of the 1992 revisions, they were not incorporated into the new CGL forms containing the 1993 changes. In those jurisdictions that accepted both the 1992 and the 1993 revisions, the 1992 changes could be added to the 1993 form by use of a standard amendatory endorsement.

The sixth edition of *Commercial General Liability* described further changes that were filed in thirty-five states plus the District of Columbia in 1995. Because these forms became effective in most states in 1996, they are referred to in this text as the 1996 forms. Although many of the changes made to the 1996 forms are editorial and do not have a substantial effect on coverage, some of the 1996 changes do affect coverage. In fact, most of the 1992 changes (with some modifications) have been included in the 1996 forms.

Like the earlier editions, the sixth edition continued to compare the CGL coverage forms to the 1973 general liability program, since some insurers still used the older forms. Two years after the 1996 policy revisions were introduced, ISO introduced some additional revisions; the major ones affecting the pollution exclusion and Coverage B-Personal and Advertising Injury. Since, with the exception of the latter two revisions, most other amendments were minor, a supplement was issued instead of another edition of the book.

The seventh edition discussed not only the 1986, 1990, 1992, 1993, 1996 and 1998 versions of the CGL forms, but also the revisions that took effect in December 2001 in the majority of states and in other states in early 2002. Many comparisons with the 1973 CGL form were eliminated in the seventh edition because these forms are seldom used today and most practitioners are no longer familiar with them as a point of comparison. However, comparisons to the 1973 CGL form and broad form CGL endorsement continue to be made when such references are helpful in understanding the current CGL forms.

The eighth edition encompasses not only the preceding editions back to 1986, but also two revisions earmarked for 2004 and one revision to be effective in 2005.

The first of the two 2004 revisions became effective in July, 2004. This revision involved some of the additional insured endorsements that, according to ISO, were being interpreted by the courts to provide coverage for the sole fault of the additional insured even when the named insured remained blameless. A new contractual limitation endorsement also was introduced that, as an underwriting tool, could be used to make contractual liability coverage correspond to the coverage of these revised additional insured endorsements.

The second set of changes took effect in December, 2004, and involves numerous amendments to endorsements and two new coverage parts: electronic data liability coverage and product withdrawal and recall coverage.

The 2005 changes, though largely editorial, introduce two exclusions. The first one is mandatory and targets violators of unsolicited facsimiles under the Telephone Consumer Protection Act of 1991, and violators of unsolicited e-mail messages under the CAN-SPAM Act of 2003.

The ninth edition discusses the preceding editions back to 1986 (and in some cases, earlier), along with the revisions introduced in the 2004, 2005 and 2007 CGL forms. Where necessary, the implications and potential problem areas of the 2007 revisions are also discussed.

The 2007 changes are for the most substantive even though some are restrictions. They involve Coverage B – personal and advertising injury liability; the supplementary payment provision regarding the exclusion of attorneys' fees or expenses taxed against the insured; the "tightening up" of two endorsements involving the employment-related practices exclusion and the abuse or molestation exclusion; and the introduction of some new endorsements to enable insurers to provide coverage in the area of completed operations for snowplowing, real estate operations, and coverage for the use of canoes and rowboats.

The tenth edition traces the coverage provisions of the ISO CGL form from the 1986 (and earlier) edition to the most recently released form from April 2013. As a broad overview, the 2013 revisions involve the following:

Five exclusions that are built into the occurrence and claims-made coverage forms: (1) liquor liability; (2) aircraft, auto or watercraft; (3) electronic data; (4) recording and distribution of material or information in violation of law; and (5) material published with knowledge of falsity and material published prior to the policy period.

The other insurance condition.

Definitions of auto and mobile equipment.

Two liquor liability coverage forms

Railroad protective liability coverage form

Two pollution liability coverage forms

Electronic data liability coverage form

The following multi-state endorsements:

Limited product withdrawal endorsement CG 04 36; Electronic data liability endorsement CG 04 37;

Additional Insured—Concessionaires Trading Under Your Name CG 20 03; Additional Insured—Controlling Interest CG 20 05; Additional Insured--Engineers, Architects, or Surveyors CG 20 07; Additional

Insured—Users Of Golfmobiles CG 2 08; Additional Insured—Owners, Lessees Or Contractors—Scheduled Person or Organization CG 20 10; Additional Insured—Managers Or Lessors of Premises CG 20 11; Additional Insured—State Or Government Agency Or Subdivision Or Political Subdivision—Permits Or Authorizations CG 20 12; Additional Insured—State Or Governmental Agency Or Subdivision Or Political Subdivision—Permits Or Authorizations Relating To Premises CG 20 13; Additional Insured—Vendors CG 20 15; Additional Insured—Mortgagee, Assignee Or Receiver CG 20 18; Additional Insured—Executors, Administrators, Trustees Or Beneficiaries CG 20 23; Additional Insured—Owners Or Other Interest From Whom Land Has Been Leased CG 20 24; Additional Insured—Designated Person Or Organization CG 20 26; Additional Insured—Co-Owner Of Insured Premises; Additional Insured—Lessor Of Leased Premises CG 20 27; Additional Insured—Lessor Of Leased Equipment CG 20 28; Additional Insured—Grantor Of Franchise CG 20 29; Oil Or Gas Operations—Nonoperating, Working Interests CG 20 30; Additional Insured—Engineers, Architects Or Surveyors CG 20 31; Additional Insured—Engineers, Architects Or Surveyors—Not Engaged By The Named Insured CG 20 32; Additional Insured—Owners, Lessees Or Contractors—Automatic Status When Required In Construction; CG 20 33; Additional Insured—Lessor Of Leased Equipment—Automatic Status When Required In Lease Agreement With You CG 20 34; Additional Insured—Grantor Of Licenses—Automatic Status When Required By Licensor CG 20 35; Additional Insured—Grantor Of Licenses CG 20 36; Additional Insured—Owners, Lessees Or Contractors—Completed Operations CG 20 37; and Additional Insured—State Or Governmental Agency Or Subdivision Or Political Subdivision—Permits Or Authorizations CG 29 35.

Revision To Amendment Of Liquor Liability Endorsements: CG 21 50 and CG 21 51 applicable to the CGL Coverage Part; and CG 29 52 and CG 29 53 applicable to the Products-Completed Operations Coverage Part; Exclusion--Failure To Supply CG 22 50; Pesticide Or Herbicide Applicator Coverage Endorsements CG 22 64 and CG 28 12; Lawn Care Services Coverage Endorsement CG 22 93; Druggists Endorsement CG 22 69; Real Estate Property Managed CG 22 70; Colleges Or Schools (Limited Form) Endorsement CG 22 71 and Colleges Or Schools Endorsement CG 22 72; Waiver Of Governmental Immunity Endorsement CG 24 14; Amendment Of Coverage Territory—Worldwide Coverage CG 24 22; Amendment Of Coverage Territory—Additional Scheduled Counties CG 24 23; Amendment Of Coverage Territory—Worldwide Coverage With Specific Exceptions CG 24 24; Amendment of Insured Contract Definition CG 24 26; Limited Contractual Liability—Railroads CG 24 27;

Exclusion—Designated Professional Services CG21 16; Exclusion—Financial Services CG 21 52; Exclusion--Funeral Services CG 21 56;

Exclusion—Counseling Services CG 21 57; Exclusion—Professional Veterinarian Services CG 21 58; Exclusion—Diagnostic Testing Laboratories CG 21 59; Exclusion—Inspection, Appraisal And Survey Companies CG 22 24; Exclusion—Professional Services—Blood Banks CG 22 32; Exclusion—Testing Or Consulting Errors Or Omissions CG 22 33; Exclusion—Construction Management Errors And Omissions CG 22 34; Exclusion—Products And Professional Services (Druggists); Exclusion—Products And Professional Services (Optical And Hearing Aid Establishments) CG 22 37; Exclusion—Camps Or Campgrounds CG 22 39; Exclusion—Engineers, Architects Or Surveyors Professional Liability CG 22 43; Exclusion—Services Furnished By Health Care Providers CG 22 44; Exclusion—Specified Therapeutic Or Cosmetic Services CG 22 45; Exclusion—Insurance And Related Operations CG 22 48; Druggists CG 22 69; Colleges Or Schools (Limited Form) CG 22 71; Colleges Or Schools CG 22 72; Professional Liability Exclusion—Computer Software CG 22 75; Professional Liability Exclusion—Health Or Exercise Clubs Or Commercially Operated Health Or Exercise Facilities CG 22 76; Professional Liability Exclusion—Computer Data Processing CG 22 77.

The following newly introduced multi-state endorsements:

Introduction Of Primary And Noncontributory—Other Insurance Condition Endorsement CG 20 01; Introduction of Additional Insured—Owners, Lessees Or Contractors—Automatic Status For Other Parties When Required In Written Construction Agreement CG 20 38; Introduction Of Total Pollution Exclusion For Designated Products Or Work Endorsement CG 21 99; Introduction Of Liquor Liability—Bring Your Own Alcohol Establishments Endorsement CG 24 06; Introduction Of Amendment Of Personal And Advertising Injury Definition Endorsement CG 24 13; and Introduction Of Designated Location(s) Aggregate Limit Endorsement CG 25 14.

The April 2013 ISO CGL forms are reproduced in this book, along with prior CGL forms.

The eleventh edition encompasses all of the preceding information and adds discussions of the ISO Commercial Liability Umbrella Policy and the Commercial Excess Liability Coverage form. An umbrella liability policy has a net effect of providing the insured with an "umbrella" of liability protection over the insured's primary liability insurance.

The first chapter on umbrella coverage offers an introductory discussion of commercial umbrella liability insurance. The next chapter presents a general overview and analysis of the Commercial Liability Umbrella

Policy, CU 00 01 04 13. The last chapter has a discussion and analysis of the Commercial Excess Liability Coverage form, CX 00 01 04 13.

These forms are reproduced in this book.

Long considered the industry's CGL gold-standard, the **Commercial General Liability Coverage Guide** delivers discussions supported by case law, practice-based examples that make the analysis immediately applicable, examination of the endorsements that may be used to tailor coverage, and more.

For customer service questions or to place additional orders, please call 1-800-543-0874.

Overview of CGL Coverage Forms

The current commercial general liability program consists of two coverage forms and a multitude of endorsements. By combining a coverage form and applicable endorsements with a declarations page and the ISO common policy conditions form, an insurer assembles a CGL *coverage part* that can be issued as a monoline policy or combined with one or more other coverage parts (such as commercial property, commercial crime, or inland marine) in a commercial package policy.

The current CGL coverage forms, designated CG 00 01 and CG 00 02, differ from one another only with respect to their coverage triggers. Form CG 00 01 has an occurrence trigger, whereas form CG 00 02 has a claims-made trigger. Apart from their different coverage triggers (which will be described in detail in this text), CG 00 01 and CG 00 02 are the same. Both forms provide the following coverages:

- Coverage A—Bodily Injury and Property Damage Liability

- Coverage B—Personal and Advertising Injury Liability

- Coverage C—Medical Payments

- Supplementary Payments (applicable to Coverages A and B)

In addition to the two CGL coverage forms, ISO maintains a series of miscellaneous commercial liability coverage forms. These forms can be used to provide the following coverages:

- Owners and contractors protective liability

- Liquor liability

- Railroad protective liability

- Products/completed operations liability

- Pollution liability

- Analysis of these forms is beyond the scope of this text.

Note on the Claims-Made Form

When the 1986 CGL coverage forms were first introduced, there was a widespread fear, in the midst of the liability insurance crisis of the mid-1980s, that insurers would offer only the claims-made form to most insureds. Contrary to expectations, the claims-made form has seen only limited use since its introduction. Despite the sparing use of the claims-made form to date, this latest edition of *Commercial General Liability* continues to devote a full chapter to management of the claims-made form, for two reasons.

First, the claims-made form will always be used for some risks, regardless of market conditions. Proper handling of the claims-made form is a complex subject. Unless presented with sufficient explanation, the subject cannot be adequately understood by those who need to understand it.

Second, insurers may be more likely to use the claims-made form if history repeats itself in the form of another liability insurance crisis. Many insurance and risk professionals who have not had to deal with claims-made policies may need a thorough explanation of how to handle the claims-made CGL coverage form.

Chapter 1

Coverage A—Bodily Injury and Property Damage Liability

Bodily injury and property damage liability coverage is provided as Coverage A of the commercial general liability (CGL) coverage forms. Coverage A consists of two sections: insuring agreement and exclusions.

Insuring Agreement

Under the Coverage A insuring agreement, the insurer agrees to pay those sums that the insured becomes *legally obligated* to pay as *damages* because of *bodily injury* or *property damage* to which the insurance applies. In addition, the bodily injury or property damage must be caused by an *occurrence* that takes place in the *coverage territory*. Each of the italicized terms above is discussed in more detail in this chapter.

The insuring agreement also sets forth the coverage trigger that applies to each form. Form CG 00 01 contains an occurrence trigger, and CG 00 02 contains a claims-made trigger. The coverage triggers of the CGL coverage forms are described briefly in this chapter; a more detailed explanation of the coverage triggers is in Chapter 4.

While there are liability policies that are only activated when the legal obligation to pay is determined by a court, such is not the case with the standard CGL forms. Yet, there are differences of opinion. In insurance custom and practice, the phraseology "legally obligated to pay" does not mean that adjudication can only be resolved by a court. In fact, many insurers would prefer not to get involved in litigation because the cost of defense often can far exceed the cost of indemnity. On the other hand, there are cases, such as *Bacon v. American Insurance Co., 330 A.2d 389*, (1974) where it was held that the policy term "legally obligated to pay" required the presentation of proofs in a court of competent jurisdiction and a finding by the court or jury of liability." The answer, therefore, is not definitive.

Finally, the insuring agreement expresses the insurer's duty to defend the insured. Accordingly, this chapter describes the defense coverage provided by Coverage A. Because of their logical relationship to defense coverage, the supplementary payments section of the CGL coverage forms is also described in this chapter. The supplementary payments also apply to Coverage B, the subject of Chapter 2.

1

Meaning of Legally Obligated

The expression legally obligated connotes legal responsibility that is broad in scope. It is directed at civil liability, rather than criminal liability, the latter being against public policy to insure. Civil liability can arise from either unintentional (negligent) or intentional tort, under common law, statute, or contract.

The Coverage A insuring agreement does not contain the statement, found in the 1973 general liability policy, that the insurer will "pay on behalf of the insured." The absence of that language should not, however, be taken to mean that the CGL coverage forms are indemnity policies, that is, policies that pay the insured only after the insured has paid the injured party. The current insuring agreement does not use the word indemnify, nor does it express any requirement that the insured must pay the injured party first. The insurer's promise to "pay those sums that the insured becomes legally obligated to pay" requires only that the insured have an *obligation* to pay.

"Damages Because of"

Damages comprise those sums of money that the law imposes as compensation, such as medical and funeral expenses, loss of services, lost wages, and pain and suffering resulting from bodily injury, and repair bills and other forms of retribution for damage to property or its loss of use. Unless otherwise prohibited by law, damages may also include punitive damages. The fact that "damages" is not defined in CGL policies has made it the focal point in litigation dealing with environmental cleanup costs. Insureds have maintained that the costs associated with remediating contamination damage to property constitute damages. Insurers, on the other hand, have maintained that the term in question embraces any legal damages, or, in other words, the costs associated with actions at law, rather than actions in equity. An action in equity seeks an equitable remedy. For example, injunctive relief proceedings, one form of action in equity, deal with the required performance or prohibition of an act and therefore do not directly involve money damages, but these proceedings do involve costs and expenses in litigating them.

Yet the courts have interpreted damages in insurance policies independently of the legal and equitable distinction that has been asserted by insurers. Examples are nuisance actions, situations involving the mitigation of damage to restore property, and actions that have alleged a combination of injunctive relief and damages in an otherwise covered claim or suit.[1]

The phraseology "damages because of," as used in the CGL policy insuring agreement, conveys a broad promise that is sometimes overlooked.

The pertinent part of the insuring agreement in which this phraseology appears reads: "We will pay those sums that the insured becomes legally obligated to pay as damages because of 'bodily injury' or 'property damage' to which this insurance applies."

In light of this wording, all damages flowing as a consequence of bodily injury or property damage would be encompassed by the insurer's promise, subject to any applicable exclusion or condition. This includes purely economic damages, as long as they result from otherwise covered bodily injury or property damage.

For example, absent some allegation of physical bodily harm potentially covered by a liability policy, there may be no coverage for allegations of emotional distress or mental anguish, depending on the law of the jurisdiction involved. In fact, the debate over whether emotional distress or mental anguish equates with bodily injury in the absence of physical bodily harm has long persisted. However, if a claimant sustains bodily injury or personal injury that is deemed to be covered by the policy, there should be no question that all damages for emotional distress or mental anguish flowing as a consequence from the bodily injury or personal injury should also be covered.

Likewise, loss of investments or profits and goodwill are not considered to be property damage, because the definition of property damage requires physical injury to tangible property. However, these damages, when associated with and flowing as a consequence of otherwise covered property damage, would also be covered.

"Bodily Injury" and "Property Damage"

"Bodily injury," as defined in the CGL coverage forms, remains relatively unchanged from predecessor forms. It means:

Bodily injury, sickness or disease sustained by a person, including death resulting from any of these at any time.

It has been said that when "bodily injury" is stated to mean bodily injury, it is an attempt to use words that need no further explanation, and it would be an imposition on insurers to require them to provide insureds with "an unnecessary lexicon" [*Cotton States Mutual Ins. Co. v. Crosby, 260* S.E.2d 860 (Ga. 1979)]. In its usual sense of the word, however, bodily injury means hurt or harm to the human body by contact of some force and any resulting pain and suffering, sickness or disease, as well as death.

A definite uncertainty is whether bodily injury encompasses mental or emotional harm. Some courts have held that the term "bodily injury" is ambiguous and, therefore, includes emotional distress, whereas others courts have rejected such arguments. Much will depend on the facts. One thing for certain, however, is that there is no consensus. But, if, as a result of bodily injury, mental or emotional injury follows as a consequence, the liability policy generally covers such injury.

The definition of property damage has changed since introduction of the 1986 forms. To understand the transition of this definition, it is helpful to restate the definitions as they appeared in the 1986 forms and again with the 1990 and subsequent editions.

1986 CGL Policy Definition

    a.   Physical injury to tangible property, including all resulting loss of use of that property; or

    b.   Loss of use of tangible property that is not physically injured.

Within Insuring Agreement 1.c. there is an additional explanation:

"Property damage" that is loss of use of tangible property that is not physically injured shall be deemed to occur at the time of the "occurrence" that caused it.

1990 and subsequent editions of the CGL Policy

    a.   Physical injury to tangible property, including all resulting loss of use of that property. All such loss of use shall be deemed to occur at the time of the physical injury that caused it; or

    b.   Loss of use of tangible property that is not physically injured. All such loss of use shall be deemed to occur at the time of the "occurrence" that caused it.

Under the 1986 forms, loss of use of tangible property resulting from physical injury to that tangible property is covered at any time it occurs following the physical injury. So, for example, loss of use of tangible property in 2002 resulting from physical injury to that tangible property in 2000 would be covered by the 2000 policy under the wording of Part (1) of the property damage definition in the 1986 policy. This application is reinforced by the fact that the CGL policy also covers "damages because of" property damage and that loss of use of tangible property physically injured, as a consequence, would fall into that category.

This contrasts with the wording found in Part a. of the property damage definition of the 1990 forms and as it exists today in subsequent policy editions, where loss of use resulting from physical injury to tangible property is deemed to occur at the time of the injury that caused it. It has been said that injury or damage generally is simultaneous with an occurrence, but that is not necessarily the case in every instance. However, not to complicate matters, assume that work was performed on a building in 2000. Defects in the construction cause windows to leak, damaging some contents in 2001. As a result of that physical injury to tangible property, there is loss of use of that part of the building in 2002, while repairs are pending and while repairs are being made. For purposes of applying coverage, loss of use would relate back to the policy year 2001, the date the water damage occurred.

In theory, there should be little difference in the application of coverage between the 1986 and 1990 editions. However, by stating under both of these editions that loss of use and the occurrence causing it must take place during the policy period, coverage may be difficult to ascertain or even be eliminated where the occurrence is in one policy period and loss of use is in another.

Interestingly, the property damage definition wording of the 1986 and 1990 CGL forms, requiring that both the occurrence and the loss of use occur during the policy period, produces a result similar in some ways to the progressive injury exclusion (so-called Montrose endorsements, named after the 1995 case of *Montrose Chemical Corp. v. Admiral Insurance Company*, 913 P.2d 878) that is now part of the standard CGL insuring agreements. The *Montrose* case and its consequences will be discussed in more detail in Chapter 4. However, it needs to be mentioned here that the purpose of the progressive injury exclusion is to preclude coverage in future policies for continuous or progressive injury or damage once it is known to exist. This is also the general idea behind the wording of the property damage definition stating that the loss of use of tangible property is deemed to occur at the time of the occurrence that caused it.

Reference to physical injury suggests that the tangible property must sustain some form of visible harm or impairment. However, even if loss or theft of property is not considered to be physical injury to tangible property, the insured may still be able to recover on the ground that there is "loss of use of tangible property not physically injured." For example, see *Travelers Insurance Co. v. De Bothuri and P.L.A. Inc., 465 So.2d 662 (Fla. App. 1985)*. A major coverage obstacle, however, is the damage to property exclusion j.(4) dealing with property damage to personal property in the care, custody or control of the insured. Depending on the facts, however, coverage is still possible despite the exclusion. See *Empire Associates, et al., v. North River Ins. Co., 637 N.Y.S. 2d 417 (A.D. 1 Dept. 1996)*, where the care, custody or control exclusion was held not to apply to theft of jewelry from insureds' tenant's deposit box where the insureds did not maintain duplicate keys to these boxes.

Some insurers now specifically exclude money, securities, and other valuables from coverage under liability policies, or liability for loss to tangible property from theft. If other courts were to follow the decision of *Advanced Network, Inc. v. Peerless Ins. Co.*, 119 Cal. Rptr.3d 17 (2010), these kinds of exclusion might be unnecessary. This was an action for damages for "loss of use" of property within the meaning of a CGL policy. The insurer argued, and the court agreed, that the replacement of cash stolen by the named insured's employee from one of its clients, a credit union, was not "loss of use" but, instead, "loss of" the property and, therefore, not covered.

The 2001 revision of the CGL policy added the following language to the definition of "property damage":

> For purposes of this insurance, electronic data is not tangible property.

> As used in this definition, electronic data means information, facts or programs stored as or on, created or used on, or transmitted to or from computer software, including systems and applications software, hard or floppy disks, CD-ROMS, tapes, drives, cells, data processing devices or any other media which are used with electronically controlled equipment.

The tendency of some people to view computer data as intangible property is rooted in the premise that tangible property must possess some physical property capable of being touched, and they believe that computer data does not exhibit such characteristics. However, once information travels from thought process to a computer disk as data, it can be viewed and edited and then printed onto paper or conveyed via email or computer-generated facsimiles. From this perspective, many insureds would view electronic data as being tangible property.

Whether it was this perspective of insureds about viewing electronic data as tangible property or the fact that a policy definition is not an equivalent of an exclusion, ISO introduced a new exclusion, designated as exclusion p. in the 2004 edition of the CGL coverage form. This exclusion buttressed the intent that liability for loss of electronic data, however caused, is not intended to be covered by the basic policy provisions. Exclusion p. is discussed later in this chapter.

Caused by "Occurrence"

A basic requirement of both CG 00 01 and CG 00 02 is that the bodily injury or property damage must be caused by an occurrence, which both forms define as follows:

"Occurrence" means an accident, including continuous or repeated exposure to substantially the same general harmful conditions.

The definition of this term in the CGL coverage forms differs from the definition in the 1973 policy. Reference in the 1973 policy to "bodily injury or property damage neither expected nor intended from the standpoint of the insured" does not appear in the current definition. Instead, the current forms treat intentional harm through an exclusion that is described later in this chapter. Reference to "the same general harmful conditions" in the current definition is taken in part from the limits of liability section of the 1973 policy, which reads: "For purposes of determining the limit of the company's liability, all bodily injury and property damage arising out of continuous or repeated exposure to substantially the same general conditions shall be considered as arising out of one occurrence."

Despite the change in the wording of the occurrence definition, the effect is intended to be the same as in the 1973 policy. Thus, whether it can be said that bodily injury or property damage is *caused by an occurrence* still hinges on fortuity. It does not matter whether the event is sudden and definite in time or place, or one that is continuous or repeated and difficult to pinpoint within a specific time-frame. What really matters is whether the bodily injury or property damage results without the insured's foresight or anticipation.[2]

"Coverage Territory"

Under the CGL coverage forms, an occurrence must take place within the coverage territory in order for bodily injury and property damage to be covered under Coverage A, and an offense must take place within the coverage territory in order for personal and advertising injury to be covered under Coverage B. This is a significant requirement, particularly with regard to products liability, that did not apply to earlier editions. Thus, a trigger of coverage is both where the occurrence happens and where the resulting injury or damage occurs. It is obviously important, therefore, to understand the meaning of "coverage territory." Until the 2001 CGL revision, "coverage territory" remained unchanged from when first introduced in 1986. The 2001 changes primarily affect Coverage B— Personal and Advertising Injury, to take into consideration the worldwide loss exposures arising out of e-commerce.

"Coverage territory" means:

a.   The United States of America (including its territories and possessions), Puerto Rico and Canada;

b. International waters or airspace, but only if the injury or damage occurs in the course of travel or transportation between any places included in a. above; or

c. All other parts of the world if the injury or damage arises out of:

   (1) Goods or products made or sold by you in the territory described in a. above;

   (2) The activities of a person whose home is in the territory described in a. above, but is away for a short time on your business; or

   (3) "Personal and advertising injury" offenses that take place through the Internet or similar electronic means of communication;

   provided the insured's responsibility to pay damages is determined in a "suit" on the merits, in the territory described in a. above or in a settlement we agree to.

The effects of the above definition are as follows:

*   Reference to injury in c. above is intended to include not only bodily injury but also personal and advertising injury, the subject of Coverage B.

*   Regarding products liability coverage, the coverage territory is worldwide, provided (1) the goods or products are made or sold by the named insured in the basic coverage territory, even though sold for use or consumption abroad; (2) the occurrence takes place in the covered territory; (3) bodily injury or property damage occurs during the policy period; and (4) is caused by an occurrence. This means that if a defective component product was made in a foreign country, and it was determined that the occurrence happened there, no coverage would apply under the CGL form for bodily injury or property damage arising from that defective product, despite having met the other preceding conditions. Conversely, if the occurrence were determined to have happened at the time of injury or damage, and the other conditions are met, coverage should apply, unless an exclusion is applicable. See *ACE American Ins. Co., v. RC2 Corporation, Inc., et al., 600 F.3d 763 (2010)*, where the occurrence was determined to happen in the U.S., rather than in China, but the foreign CGL policy only applied to bodily injury or property damage taking place outside of the U.S.

*   In contrast, the policy territory of the 1973 CGL policy provided international coverage for products only if they were sold for use

or consumption in the basic coverage territory (the United States, Puerto Rico, and Canada), but without the additional requirement, unlike subsequent editions, that the occurrence also must happen in the covered territory. Although the 1986 and later CGL coverage forms provide a broader territorial definition for overseas products than the 1973 policy did, apart from the occurrence restriction, the insured who makes or sells products for overseas use or consumption is still likely to want broader coverage than that found in current CGL forms to cover suits filed outside the basic coverage territory. Those businesses involved in foreign exposures on a limited basis may be able to expand their coverage with one of three endorsements introduced in 2001 amending the coverage territory, which are discussed in Chapter 6.

- Although products and completed operations are combined for purposes of defining the elements of the products-completed operation hazard, completed operations are not covered on a worldwide basis. Like the 1973 CGL policy, the current CGL forms do not cover injury or damage resulting from the insured's completed operations that occurs outside the basic coverage territory.

- The coverage territory for occurrences or offenses involving the activities of a person for whose acts the insured may be responsible is worldwide, provided the person's home is within the basic coverage territory (i.e., that part of the coverage territory described in part a. above) and the person is away only for a short time. In the case of *Caci International Incorporated, et al. v. St. Paul Fire & Marine Ins. Co., 566 F.3d 150 (4th Cir. 2009)*, the named insured argued that "short time" being an undefined term was ambiguous and therefore should be construed in its favor. In disagreeing, the court stated that the word "short" has an ordinary everyday meaning: "brief" or "lasting only a short period of time," and that travel outside the coverage territory for several weeks would defy the common understanding of "short." The court added that "short time" naturally covered a brief, discrete event, such as a several day business trip abroad.

- While personal and advertising injury coverage requires that the offense be committed in the coverage territory during the policy period, the resulting injury has no territorial restriction. For purposes of offenses taking place through the Internet, the CGL policy's territorial scope is worldwide. Likewise, personal and advertising offenses committed by a person while in a foreign jurisdiction are within the coverage territory so long as that person resides in one of the places identified in part a.

- Until the 2001 policy revision, the problem has been in determining where an offense takes place if an injury is sustained outside the coverage territory. Because the Internet has no boundaries, finding an answer would have been difficult, if not impossible. With the 2001 revision of the coverage territory, the task of determining where the offense takes place is no longer a concern. Coverage now applies, for purposes of an offense involving personal and advertising injury, because of the Internet or other similar electronic means of communication, on a worldwide basis.

- Although a certain amount of coverage is on a worldwide basis, the insured's responsibility to pay damages must be determined in a suit on the merits in the basic coverage territory. Whether it necessarily must be the original suit (a requirement under the 1973 CGL policy) that is filed against the insured is not readily apparent. A literal reading of the policy wording reveals no such requirement. It therefore is conceivable that a suit originally filed in a foreign country could be dismissed (without prejudice) and refiled later in the coverage territory.

- Under pre-1986 CGL forms, there was a question whether claims within foreign jurisdictions were covered. The basis for that position is that the terms of the 1973 CGL policy stated that the insurer may investigate and settle any such claim it deemed expedient. If the claim materialized into a lawsuit then arguably the original suit was required to be brought within the policy territory.

In 1986 and subsequent editions of CGL forms, the insurer's obligation to investigate and settle claims is at the insurer's discretion. However, it would not be in the best interest of the insurer (and the insured) if the insurer were to ignore the investigation of any claim wherever it occurs. In fact, it could be construed as a failure on the part of the insurer to mitigate damages arising from a claim. Thus, it would appear that if an insurer decides to settle a claim outside the coverage territory, the claim should be covered for at least three reasons:

1. There is no specific policy provision that precludes such an obligation;

2. The insured's legal obligation to pay damages can arise from a claim or a suit; and

3. The term "suit" is defined in 1986 and subsequent policy editions, but the term "claim" is not defined in these policies connoting a difference between the two.

Coverage Triggers

In form CG 00 01, Coverage A applies to bodily injury or property damage that occurs during the policy period. This is the so-called occurrence coverage trigger, also used in the 1973 CGL policy. Simply stated, the policy in effect at the time injury or damage occurs is the policy that covers resulting damages, even if a claim is not made until long after the policy expires.

In form CG 00 02, Coverage A is subject to a claims-made coverage trigger. Coverage applies only to injury or damage for which a claim is first made during the policy period. In addition, the injury or damage for which a claim is made must have occurred on or after the retroactive date, if any, shown in the policy declarations.

Prior to introduction of form CG 00 02 in 1986, a claims-made trigger had not been used in standard general liability forms. It was added to CGL forms to give insurers an appropriate form for insuring risks that could incur long-tail liability losses, that is, injury or damage that does not result in a claim until long after the injury or damage occurs. An example is a claim, made today, for injury that is considered to have occurred when the claimant was exposed to the insured's product several years ago. Typically, an insurer does not want to cover long-tail risks under an occurrence policy, because the insurer will be liable for claims made at any later time due to injury or damage that occurs during the policy period. Another problem (from the insurer's point of view) with the occurrence trigger is that injury occurring over several years (as in the case of long-term exposure to a substance such as asbestos) may be covered under all policies in effect during those years, allowing the insured to stack the per-policy limits.

In 1999, ISO introduced a mandatory endorsement (CG 00 57) that modified the Coverage A insuring agreement of the occurrence CGL form to eliminate coverage for injury or damage known to the insured before the policy period began. The language of the endorsement was incorporated in the occurrence form with the 2001 CGL revision. This language, commonly referred to as the Montrose provision after a California court case, is discussed in Chapter 4 as part of the provisions that define the occurrence coverage trigger.

In contrast with the operation of the occurrence trigger, when the claims-made form is used, a claim is payable only under the policy in effect when the claim is first made. Once that policy period ends, the insurer will be aware of all claims it must pay under that policy, unless additional claims are reported during an *extended reporting period*, that is, an additional period for reporting of claims after the policy period ends.

Despite the advantages of claims-made coverage to insurers, it is generally avoided by insureds. In fact, apart from the excess and surplus lines markets, the ISO claims-made forms are not widely used, presumably in part because of the generous five-year tail coverage which is available. Because of the retroactive date and the various options for extended reporting periods, arranging claims-made coverage is often complicated and can result in coverage gaps. Accordingly, an in-depth explanation of the claims-made trigger (which also applies to Coverage B of the 1990 and 1993 versions of form CG 00 02) is provided in Chapter 4 of this text.

Duty to Defend—Allocation

It has been a well-known fact since the introduction of standard general liability policy provisions in 1941 that the duty to defend is broader than the duty to pay. Insurers, in other words, have been required to defend the insured against all allegations and assume the costs of defense for even those allegations clearly not covered by the policy. In fact, these earlier policies, until the 1986 forms were introduced, stated that the insurer's duty to defend applied "even if any of the allegations of the suit are groundless, false or fraudulent."

When the standard ISO 1986 forms were introduced, the insurer's right and duty to defend was stated this way:

> We will have the right and duty to defend the insured against any "suit" seeking those damages. . We may at our discretion investigate any "occurrence" and settle any claim or "suit" that may result ....

The above wording remains to this very day despite numerous revisions to the forms. However, what may have been overlooked with the introduction of the 1986 forms was the elimination of the phraseology "groundless, false or fraudulent." It was mentioned in this text in the early editions that, while that explicit statement no longer appeared in current CGL forms, it would not matter since the insurer still has "the right and duty to defend the insured against any `suit' seeking damages." If "any" is given its literal meaning, the statement should encompass groundless, false, or fraudulent suits as well as legitimate ones. Thus, absence of the prior wording should not be interpreted to mean that the insurer was relieved of the duty to defend groundless, false, or fraudulent suits against the insured.[3]

Of course, the complaint must have contained at least one allegation that was potentially within coverage. It was not necessary that all of the allegations came within the scope of coverage. It became generally recognized that if some part of the damages sought were covered, the insurer had to defend, but had no obligation to pay damages not covered by the policy.

There has been continuous dialogue over the years that defense costs far exceeded the payment of damages and that something had to be done about it. One of the approaches to reducing the costs of defense espoused by insurers was allocation. This comes as no surprise for those insurers that feel that all claims need to be adjudicated by the courts, instead of paid when coverage appears to be applicable. This concept of allocating defense costs between covered and noncovered claims has been around for many years. Directors and officers liability policies, for example, have long sought to allocate defense costs between covered and noncovered claims.

What may have encouraged insurers to allocate defense costs between covered and noncovered claims was the case of *United States v. United States Fidelity & Guaranty Co.*, 601 F.2d 1136 (10th Cir. 1979). This case dealt with an architectural and engineering firm that purchased a CGL policy subject to a professional services exclusion. When two suits were filed in 1971 against the firm alleging bodily injuries resulting from the performance of professional services, the CGL insurer denied both defense and coverage.

The U.S. Court of Appeals for the 10th Circuit held that the insurer was obligated to defend its insured because it was unclear whether the exclusion of professional services applied to the duty to defend as well as to the duty to pay. The court explained that "if the insurance company wants to protect itself in this type of situation, it should be clearly stated that the exclusion clause applies to both the duty to pay and the duty to defend."

Citing the above case, ISO issued a memorandum in 1991 advising insurers that if they do not want to defend a suit alleging damages not covered by the policy, they should clearly state their intentions in the policy. As a result, insurers began to issue endorsements with wording attempting to make this subject clear. It was not until the 1996 CGL policy revisions that the following specific wording first appeared within the insuring agreement of standard forms:

> However, we will have no duty to defend the insured against any "suit" seeking damages for "bodily injury" or "property damage" to which this insurance does not apply.

On its face, this wording may not appear to limit the defense obligation since case law still requires that the insurer defend the entire action if even one cause of action is potentially covered. As a result, some insurers began to also reserve their right of reimbursement of defense costs. Some courts, however, have held that if an insurer desires reimbursement of such costs in defending suits that have no potential for coverage, the issuance of a reservation of rights is insufficient. One such case where the court held that an insurer was not entitled to be reimbursed for defense costs, absent an express provision in the insurance policy is *American Foreign Insurance Co., et al. v. Jerry's Sport Center, Inc., 2A.3d 526 (Pa.2010).*

To combat these kinds of court decisions, ISO has made available Interline endorsements dealing with defense costs in Illinois (IL 01 62) and Wyoming (IL 01 14). Entitled Changes—Defense Costs, these endorsements state that if an insurer provides defense and later determines that any allegations are not covered, it has a right of reimbursement. This right of reimbursement, however, applies only to defense costs incurred after the insured has been notified by a reservation of rights that there may not be coverage, and that the insurer is reserving its rights to terminate defense and to seek reimbursement of the defense costs incurred.[4]

These revisions by ISO indicate an intent to pursue the right to allocate dating back to its deletion in 1986 of the "groundless, false, or fraudulent" wording.

One of the commonly cited cases upholding allocation in an insurer's favor is *Buss v. The Superior Court of Los Angeles County, 939 P.2d 766 (1997).* This case is not a good one to rely on because of all the allegations cited, only one allegation was potentially covered. The CGL policy also did not contain the wording above that was introduced by ISO in its 1996 CGL forms. However, the insurer did include in its reservation of rights a statement to the effect that the insurer expressly reserves its rights to be "reimbursed and/or an allocation of attorneys' fees and expenses," if it were determined that there was no coverage under the policy. Also, the attorney defending the case was instructed by the insurer to keep specific records of time allocable to the covered claim as opposed to the claims not covered.

In this case, the court held that with respect to claims for which there never was any potential for coverage, the insurer could recover costs shown by a preponderance of evidence to be fairly reasonably allocable solely to the noncovered claim or claims. The court also held that an insurer's unilateral reservation of rights to recoup defense costs could not, in absence of policy wording to that effect, justify a claim for the recovery of such costs prior to a determination of noncoverage. This is an important point, because of the policy language introduced by ISO in 1996. In policies expressly stating that there is no defense obligation for claims not covered by the policy and omitting the "groundless, false, or fraudulent" wording found in earlier policies, there now seems to be an argument for the allocation of defense costs expended on noncovered claims even before a case is over, subject to possible arguments of ambiguity in policy wording.

What has been discussed here relative to Coverage A—Bodily Injury and Property Damage Liability also applies to Coverage B—Personal and Advertising Injury Liability.

Relationship of Defense Costs to Limits of Insurance

The defense provisions stated above are followed by two conditions. The first of these states that "the amount [the insurer] will pay for damages is limited as described in Section III—Limits of Insurance." Although the various limits of insurance that apply to the CGL coverage forms will be discussed in Chapter 5, a key point of this condition is that policy limits are applicable only to *damages*. Thus, all other covered costs in connection with a covered claim against the insured, including expenses incurred to defend the insured, are payable in addition to the applicable limits of insurance.

The second condition states that the insurer's "right and duty to defend end when we have used up the applicable limit of insurance in the payment of judgments or settlements under Coverage A or B or medical expenses under Coverage C." As noted above, the limits of insurance apply only to damages; all other costs, including defense, are payable in addition to the limits. However, once the applicable limit of insurance has been paid, the insurer's duty to defend is intended to cease.

There is one notable exception to the fact that defense costs are payable in addition to policy limits. First introduced with the 1992 and 1996 revisions, and now applying to all subsequent policy editions, is the statement, as part of the contractual liability exclusion, that the insurer will pay defense costs that the insured assumes under an insured contract. However, any payment the insurer makes for defense costs assumed under contract are payable *within the applicable limits of insurance*. To reinforce this provision, the defense provisions in the 1992 and 1996 forms state that the insurer has the right and duty to defend only *the insured* against suits seeking covered damages. Prior editions stated that the insurer had the right and duty to defend *any* suit seeking damages covered under the policy. The coverage for defense costs assumed under contract is discussed in more detail later in this chapter in connection with the contractual liability exclusion.

Definition of "Suit"

The word "suit" in the defense provision was first defined in the 1986 policy provisions. In the 1992 and 1996 amendments, the definition of suit was broadened to include arbitration proceedings and other alternative dispute resolution proceedings to which any insured—not just the named insured—submits. The latest version reads as follows:

Suit" means a civil proceeding in which damages because of "bodily injury", "property damage" or "personal and advertising injury" to which this insurance applies are alleged. "Suit" includes:

a.   An arbitration proceeding in which such damages are claimed and to which the insured must submit or does submit with our consent; or

b.   Any other alternative dispute resolution proceeding in which such damages are claimed and to which the insured submits with our consent.

One reason why the definition of suit was introduced was to encompass arbitration proceedings and other techniques for resolving disputes, such as minitrials and pretrial mediations. These techniques, advocated by insurers as a less costly alternative to court proceedings, have become increasingly popular ways to resolve claims against the insured.

Another possible reason for adding the definition of suit was to preclude coverage for insureds seeking protection under their CGL policies following receipt of notice from a governmental agency that they were potentially responsible parties to an environmental incident. Such notice is commonly referred to as a PRP letter. Insurers have maintained that a PRP letter or other notice is not the equivalent of a lawsuit and therefore have denied insureds the benefit of any defense. The courts, however, are split on this subject. Adding the definition of suit appears to be the method chosen to end those kinds of disputes.

Supplementary Payments

Closely related to the insurer's duty to defend are the supplementary payments that the insurer promises to make in addition to paying damages. These payments, which apply to both Coverage A and Coverage B, are expressed in the 2007 CGL forms as follows:

We will pay, with respect to any claim we investigate or settle, or any "suit" against an insured we defend:

a.   All expenses we incur.

b.   Up to $250 for cost of bail bonds required because of accidents or traffic law violations arising out of the use of any vehicle to which the Bodily Injury Liability Coverage applies. We do not have to furnish these bonds.

c.   The cost of bonds to release attachments, but only for bond amounts within the applicable limit of insurance. We do not have to furnish these bonds.

d.   All reasonable expenses incurred by the insured at our request to assist us in the investigation or defense of the claim or "suit", including actual loss of earnings up to $250 a day because of time off from work.

e.   All court costs taxed against the insured in the "suit". However, these payments do not include attorneys' fees or attorneys' expenses taxed against the insured.

f.   Prejudgment interest awarded against the insured on that part of the judgment we pay. If we make an offer to pay the applicable limit of insurance, we will not pay any prejudgment interest based on that period of time after the offer.

g.   All interest on the full amount of any judgment that accrues after entry of the judgment and before we have paid, offered to pay, or deposited in court the part of the judgment that is within the applicable limit of insurance. These payments will not reduce the limits of insurance.

In most respects, these supplementary payments provisions are the same, in effect, as those of the 1973 general liability policy. The few differences are noted below.

Unlike the 1973 version, the current supplementary payments do not include coverage for expenses incurred by the named insured for first aid to others at the time of an accident. However, the medical payments section of the current forms does specifically cover reasonable expenses for first aid administered at the time of an accident. A difference between the two ways of covering first aid expenses is that the current approach requires the insured to have purchased medical payments coverage, while the old approach provides the coverage automatically, as long as the insured has liability coverage.

Moreover, under the current forms, the payment of first aid expenses reduces the applicable limits of liability, whereas the 1973 provision applied in addition to policy limits. The applicable limits of liability with respect to the current medical payments coverage are a per-person limit applicable only to medical payments, an each occurrence limit for both medical payments and bodily injury/property damage liability, and a "general aggregate" limit. (These limits are described more thoroughly in Chapter 5.)

The loss of earnings provision allows up to $250 per day for loss of earnings because of time off from work. The loss of earnings provision in the 1973 form limited recovery to $25 per day. The 1986, 1990, and 1993 CGL forms limit recovery to $100 per day.

Paragraph e. of the supplementary payments section pertains to costs taxed against the insured. Previous editions of the CGL forms simply declared that supplementary payments included "all costs taxed against the insured in the suit." The December 2007 edition now states that "all court costs taxed against the insured in the suit" are considered supplementary payments. Moreover, the revised form declares that "these payments do not include attorneys' fees or attorneys' expenses taxed against the insured." What this means is that the attorneys' fees and expenses of opposing counsel that may be taxed against the insured, such as is common with civil rights suits, are not covered. What insurers maintain they intend to cover under the supplementary payments provision are the costs of defense, including fees and expenses of the attorney selected by the insurer to handle the defense of the insured.

Considering that opposing attorneys' fees and expenses taxed against insureds are being held as covered by the courts, this change would appear to be a restriction as opposed to the provision being replaced. The problem for insurers is that by excluding opposing attorneys' fees and attorneys' expenses as supplementary payments, it simply means that these fees and expenses will be viewed by insureds and some courts as damages the insurer is legally obligated to pay because of injury or property damage.

The current provision respecting interest on judgments applies not only to interest accruing after entry of the judgment but also to prejudgment interest awarded against the insured. Until 1984, when ISO introduced in many states an amendatory endorsement for general liability forms providing prejudgment interest coverage, standard liability forms provided for postjudgment interest only.

The current supplementary payments provisions are silent as to the cost of premiums on appeal bonds required in any suit defended by the insurer, an item that was specifically covered under the 1973 provisions. The absence of a provision regarding appeal bonds should probably not be construed as an indication that the CGL coverage forms relieve the insurer of the obligation to pay for appeal bonds in all cases. And, more importantly, the absence of an appeal bond provision should not be interpreted as relieving the insurer of the duty to pursue an appeal if there are reasonable grounds for an appeal.

A case in point is *Cathay Mortuary (Wah Sang), Inc. v. United Pacific Ins. Co.*, 582 F. Supp. 650 (N.D. Cal. 1984). In this case a United States district court held that "there is a general consensus that an insurer is obligated to pursue an appeal on behalf of its insured where there are reasonable grounds for appeal." Moreover, the court held that the insurer's duty to pursue post-trial remedies, including appeal, was "part and parcel of the general duty to defend," and was not attributable to the provision regarding payment for the cost of appeal bonds.

Consequently, if an insurer, under the current forms, is obliged to pursue an appeal by virtue of its general duty to defend, payment for appeal bonds required in conjunction with that appeal would seem to be inseparable from the insurer's duty to pay for the other costs associated with the appeal.

An insurer's failure to pursue an appeal when there are reasonable grounds for appeal can subject the insurer "to liability for both the costs of defense and any adverse judgment the insured suffers, even when the judgment was rendered on a theory not within the policy coverage." (*Kapelus v. United Title Guarantee Co.*, 93 Cal. Rptr. 278 (1971), as quoted in the Cathay Mortuary case.)

Defense of the Indemnitee
Costs within or Outside the Policy Limit?

In 1992, ISO proposed that the defense costs assumed under an "insured contract" would be considered damages and therefore payable as part of the policy limit, rather than in addition to the limit of insurance. ISO also proposed that the insurer express no right or duty to defend the indemnitee, the person or organization whose liability is being assumed under contract by the insured (who is the indemnitor). This proposal created a great deal of controversy. In fact, not all insurers implemented this proposal but instead continued to defend the indemnitee in order to maintain some control over the suit.

In the 1996 CGL revision, new provisions were inserted into the Supplementary Payments provision of the CGL and other coverage forms. These provisions provide that, if the indemnitee and the insured ask the insurer to conduct and control the defense of the indemnitee, the insurer will defend an indemnitee of the insured if the indemnitee is named in a suit against the insured, and pay the defense costs of the indemnitee in addition to the policy's limit of insurance, if the following conditions are met:

1. The suit against the insured also names an indemnitee of the insured as a party to the suit.

2. The suit against the indemnitee must seek damages for which the insured has assumed liability in an "insured contract."

3. The insurance provided under the policy applies to such liability assumed by the insured.

4.   The obligation to defend, or the cost of the defense of, the indemnitee has also been assumed by the insured in the same contract.

5.   The allegations in the suit and information known about the occurrence are such that no conflict appears to exist between the insured's interests and the indemnitee's interests. The indemnitee and the insured must agree that the insurer can assign the same counsel to defend both parties.

6.   The indemnitee agrees in writing to:

   a.   cooperate with the insurer in the investigation, settlement or defense of the suit;

   b.   immediately send the insurer copies of any demands, notices, summonses or legal papers received in connection with the suit;

   c.   notify any other insurer whose coverage is available to the indemnitee;

   d.   cooperate with the insurer in coordinating other applicable insurance available to the indemnitee; and

   e.   provide the insurer with written authorization to: (i) obtain records and other information related to the suit; and (ii) conduct and control the defense of the indemnitee in such suit.

Legal costs unquestionably have become an increasingly heavy burden on insurance companies and often represent a highly disproportionate amount compared to the damages payable by the insurer. It therefore is understandable that insurers are seeking ways to reduce these kinds of costs. But these conditions create so many obstacles that this particular approach is destined for failure.

The question is what the effect is if one of the conditions is not met. It should be pointed out that there are many ways in which these conditions will not be met. One of the common ways involves so-called third-party-over actions (discussed under Exclusion E—Employers Liability later in this chapter) where indemnitees, alone, are the ones named in a suit. Also, it is not unusual to find a dispute between the indemnitor and indemnitee as to the degree of liability assumed. Adversarial relationships are common. In any event, if one of the above conditions is not met, the answer to the question is that defense costs assumed by the indemnitor (insured) in an insured contract, assuming coverage otherwise applies, will be paid subject to the policy's limit of insurance, and not in addition to the limits of insurance. The provisions of the CGL form that describe the coverage for defense costs assumed under an insured contract are described later in this chapter, under Exclusion B—Contractual Liability.

In a growing number of instances, hold harmless and indemnity agreements are reinforced by additional insured endorsements. Assuming the proper endorsement is attached to the named insured's (indemnitor's) CGL policy and applies in a given claim or suit, the foregoing conditions dealing with defense costs within limits may not be applicable. The reason is that, at least from the standpoint of defense for additional insureds, defense costs are in addition to policy limits. One of the exceptions where additional insured status may not solve this issue is when the hold harmless and indemnity agreement is broader in scope than the additional insured endorsement. The rule is that the indemnitee is to be provided the broader of the two coverages, that is, contractual liability or additional insured status.

The reason contractual liability coverage may be broader than additional insured coverage is that under ISO additional insured endorsements, at least, the most coverage the additional insured can obtain is for partial fault. This is so, because the additional insured endorsement hinges on coverage where injury or damage is caused in whole or in part by the named insured's acts or omissions. Contractual liability coverage, on the other hand, can cover even the sole fault of the indemnitee (additional insured), if no limitation endorsement, i.e., CG 21 39 or CG 24 26.is attached. Whether sole fault coverage is permitted, however, depends on the applicable anti-indemnity statute. Many such statutes hold both sole and partial negligence to be void and unenforceable but do not affect the validity of insurance. Both the additional insured endorsements and the contractual liability limitation endorsements are discussed in Chapter 6.

Exclusions

The bodily injury and property damage liability insurance provided in Coverage A of the CGL coverage forms is subject to several exclusions. With some important exceptions, these exclusions achieve the same effect as the exclusions found in the 1973 general liability policy and relevant portions of the broad form comprehensive general liability endorsement. For example, the watercraft exclusion of the current CGL coverage forms contains an exception providing coverage for nonowned boats less than twenty-six feet long, which was previously expressed as a separate coverage in the broad form liability endorsement. Similarly, many of the former broad form property damage provisions are incorporated into the current exclusions instead of being stated in a separate endorsement.

The most significant items found in the current exclusions are an almost total exclusion of pollution liability, clarifications and liberalizations in the scope of property damage coverage with respect to the insured's work or products, and amendments in contractual liability coverage. These and other changes in the exclusions are discussed in the order in which the exclusions appear in the CGL coverage forms.

In the 1993 and later editions of the CGL forms, all of the Coverage A exclusions carry a descriptive title. For example, exclusion a. is entitled "Expected or Intended Injury." This change may have helped to clarify that it is not an intentional act that is excluded, but rather an intentional injury or result of such act. The titles of the other exclusions are included in the subheadings that follow.

Exclusion A—Expected or Intended Injury

Exclusion a. of the CGL coverage forms is derived from the 1973 form's definition of occurrence and from the extended bodily injury coverage of the broad form CGL endorsement. The current exclusion reads as follows:

This insurance does not apply to:

"Bodily injury" or "property damage" expected or intended from the standpoint of the insured. This exclusion does not apply to "bodily injury" resulting from the use of reasonable force to protect persons or property.

It might appear that the term occurrence in the insuring agreement of the CGL coverage forms would be sufficient to preclude coverage for such claims or suits as are excluded here, especially if occurrence is interpreted to include fortuitous events only. The exclusion, however, clarifies that deliberate or intentionally caused bodily injury or property damage is not deemed to be accidental.

As noted above, it is the intentional *injury*, rather than the intentional *act*, that is excluded. This exclusion therefore does not rule out protection of an insured who commits an intentional act, unless it can be proved that the consequences of the act could have been expected. In many cases, it is likely to be a question of fact for a court to decide, unless the insurance company's investigation reveals solid ground on which to pay or deny the claim.

The exception to this exclusion duplicates the extended bodily injury coverage of the broad form liability endorsement. While it may be recognized that a person has the right to use reasonable force to protect his or her person or property, this exception grants an important clarification of coverage. Although coverage may apply in absence of the clarification, the insurer is less likely to deny coverage for a claim or suit alleging such an intentional act when the policy specifically provides coverage. This does not mean that coverage will be granted automatically. The bodily injury must have been prompted by a threat of harm and must have resulted from the exercise of *reasonable* force. What is reasonable will depend on the circumstances. (Note that the exception does not include property damage resulting from the use of reasonable force.)

Exclusion B—Contractual Liability

Exclusion b. approximates the blanket contractual liability coverage available under the broad form general liability endorsement formerly added to the 1973 general liability policy. By use of an endorsement (CG 21 39), the scope of contractual liability coverage under the current CGL coverage forms can be reduced to the *incidental contracts* coverage provided under the 1973 policy without the broad form endorsement.

The current version of exclusion b. reads:

This insurance does not apply to:

"Bodily injury" or "property damage" for which the insured is obligated to pay damages by reason of the assumption of liability in a contract or agreement. This exclusion does not apply to liability for damages:

(1) That the insured would have in the absence of the contract or agreement; or

(2) Assumed in a contract or agreement that is an "insured contract", provided the "bodily injury" or "property damage" occurs subsequent to the execution of the contract or agreement. Solely for the purposes of liability assumed in an "insured contract", reasonable attorney fees and necessary litigation expenses incurred by or for a party other than an insured are deemed to be damages because of "bodily injury" or "property damage", provided:

(a) Liability to such party for, or for the cost of, that party's defense has also been assumed in the same "insured contract"; and

(b) Such attorney fees and litigation expenses are for defense of that party against a civil or alternative dispute resolution proceeding in which damages to which this insurance applies are alleged.

An addition to exception (2) above, providing payment of defense expenses for which the insured has assumed liability in an insured contract, is discussed under the section entitled "Defense of the Indemnitee Costs Within or Outside the Policy Limit?"

Liability in Absence of Contract

The contractual liability exclusion clearly states that it does not apply if the insured would be liable for damages in the absence of any contract or agreement. This exception makes coverage certain in situations that would otherwise be a source of conflict between insurance companies and their insureds.

An example is an insured contractor who agrees to hold harmless and indemnify a railroad owner for any bodily injury or property damage arising out of the project, regardless of whether the contractor is otherwise liable. This is not an insured contract if such injury occurs within fifty feet of the railroad, due to the railroad protective exclusion (discussed later in these pages). However, if the insured would have been liable in absence of the contract— that is, the insured's own negligence caused the accident—the insured will nevertheless be covered, in spite of the railroad protective exclusion.

Meaning of "Insured Contract"

The second exception to the contractual liability exclusion states that the exclusion does not apply to liability assumed under an "insured contract." The definition of insured contract includes the following:

a. A contract for a lease of premises. However, that portion of the contract for a lease of premises that indemnifies any person or organization for damage by fire to premises while rented to you or temporarily occupied by you with permission of the owner is not an "insured contract";

b. A sidetrack agreement;

c. Any easement or license agreement, except in connection with construction or demolition operations on or within 50 feet of a railroad;

d. An obligation, as required by ordinance, to indemnify a municipality except in connection with work for a municipality;

e. An elevator maintenance agreement;

f. That part of any other contract or agreement pertaining to your business (including an indemnification of a municipality in connection with work performed for a municipality) under which you assume the tort liability of another to pay damages because of "bodily injury" or "property damage" to a third person or organization. Tort liability means a liability that would be imposed by law in absence of any contract or agreement.

The contracts itemized in parts a. through e. are comparable to the definition of incidental contract in the 1973 general liability policy (without the broad form endorsement), except that the definition in the 1986 and later versions of the CGL form does not require that the contract be in writing. Thus, the 1986 and later editions of the CGL form cover both written and oral agreements. However, the 1990 and later editions require that the insured contract must have been executed before the bodily injury or property damage occurred. Despite this requirement, court decisions go both ways.

Items a. through e. do not limit insured contracts to those under which the named insured assumes the liability of another. They, of course, can involve tort liability assumed but that is not mandatory. Thus, the CGL forms cover liability assumed by any insured under a contract described in items a. through e. However, coverage for any contract of a type not described in items a. through e. is restricted to the named insured's assumption of another entity's tort liability, that is, "a liability that would be imposed by law [on the other entity] in the absence of any contract or agreement."

The restriction of item f. to assumptions of the tort liability of another may be intended to strengthen the position, affirmed by a number of courts, that "liability assumed by the insured under any contract refers to liability incurred when one promises to indemnify or hold harmless another, and does not refer to liability that results from breach of contract" [as stated by the Alaska Supreme Court in *Olympic, Inc. v. Providence Washington Ins. Co.*, 648 P.2d 1008 (Alaska 1982)]. The failure of an insured to have the CGL policy endorsed to name an additional insured as promised by contract is an example of a breach of contract. However, it is possible not only for the same act to constitute both a breach of contract and a tort but also for an allegation of breach of contract to be brought about by tort and be covered by the policy. See, for example, the landmark case of *Vandenberg v. Superior Court of Sacramento County*, 88 Cal. Rptr. 2d 366 (1999). (In this case, the breach of contract was claimed to have caused property damage.)

An important and often misunderstood point is that part d. above allows coverage of obligations to indemnify a municipality as required by ordinance. For example, a contractor constructing sidewalks for the owner of property in a particular city may be required by ordinance to indemnify the city for claims made against the city for injury arising in some way from the contractor's work. The contractor's obligation to indemnify the city is covered under this provision unless the work is being performed *for the city*. But, even if the work is being performed for the city, the insured may still have coverage for the obligation by virtue of part f. of the definition. Since the 1990 revisions, part f. specifically includes "an indemnification of a municipality in connection with work performed for a municipality," as long as the obligation is an assumption of the municipality's tort liability to pay damages because of bodily injury or property damage to a third party.

Since an escalator is not an elevator, the question is how are contracts involving the assumption of liability for their maintenance handled? If the owner of an escalator assumes the sole or partial tort liability of a company that maintains escalators, coverage would apply under item f., assuming the assumption is not otherwise void and unenforceable under any anti-indemnity statute. If no tort liability is assumed, however, coverage would apply as a premises-operations hazard.

What "Insured Contract" Does Not Include

Following item f. of the definition of "insured contract" are the exclusions shown below.

Paragraph f. does not include that part of any contract or agreement:

(1) That indemnifies a railroad for "bodily injury" or "property damage" arising out of construction or demolition operations, within 50 feet of any railroad property and affecting any railroad bridge or trestle, tracks, roadbeds, tunnel, underpass or crossing;

(2) That indemnifies an architect, engineer or surveyor for injury or damage arising out of:

   (a) Preparing, approving, or failing to prepare or approve maps, shop drawings, opinions, reports, surveys, field orders, change orders, or drawings and specifications; or

   (b) Giving directions or instructions, or failing to give them, if that is the primary cause of the injury or damage;

(3) Under which the insured, if an architect, engineer or surveyor, assumes liability for injury or damage arising out of the insured's rendering or failing to render professional services, including those listed in (2) above and supervisory, inspection, architectural or engineering activities.

The 1986 and 1990 editions of the CGL form also exclude "that part of any contract or agreement ... That indemnifies any person or organization for damage by fire to premises rented or loaned to you." In the 1993 and later editions of the policy, a comparable exclusion is located under item a. (pertaining to leases of premises) of the definition of insured contract. In either case, the purpose is to clarify that contractual liability coverage does not apply to the exposure covered by fire damage legal liability coverage, which (as discussed later in this chapter) is subject to a separate limit of insurance rather than the full each occurrence limit.

Railroad Protective Exclusion

Railroad companies frequently require contractors or others who are to perform work on, above, or otherwise within fifty feet of the railroad to hold the railroad company harmless for any claims or suits that may arise in connection with the work, even if the contractor would not otherwise be liable. Item (1) of the above clauses, sometimes called the railroad protective liability exclusion, expresses the insurer's intent not to cover liability arising under such hold harmless agreements (unless the insured would have been liable in the absence of the agreement, as stated under the contractual liability exclusion).

Although the same exposure is addressed in item c. of the definition of insured contract, that provision relates only to easement or license agreements. The provision expressed in item (1) above applies only to contracts described in item f. of the definition of insured contract.

(Note that in the 1986 and 1990 editions of the CGL coverage forms, the railroad protective exclusion applied to that part of a contract that indemnifies *any person or organization*, rather than just a *railroad*, as in later editions). Whenever work is conducted on or within the proximity of railroad property, the railroad owner will likely impose a broad indemnification agreement and require the contractor to procure a separate railroad protective liability policy for the benefit of the railroad. Even if a separate railroad protective liability policy is purchased by the contractor for the railroad, the contractor should still seek to have paragraph (1) deleted from its CGL policy, if possible. The reason is to protect the contractor in the event the insurer providing the railroad protective policy decides to bring a subrogation action against the insured.

Subrogation against the contractor buying the railroad protective policy for the benefit of the railroad may appear to be a remote possibility, but it happened under an owners and contractors protective liability (OCP) policy (which is similar in many ways to the railroad protective policy) in the case of *Rome v. Commonwealth Edison Co.*, 401 N.E.2d 1032 (Ill. App. 1980). An Illinois court permitted the OCP insurer to subrogate against the contractor who purchased the OCP policy for the project owner because the parties did not agree that the insurance would satisfy the obligation to indemnify.

As a general rule, an insurer cannot subrogate against its own insured. Thus, it may be difficult for the insurer of the railroad protective policy to subrogate against the contractor who purchases the policy for the railroad if the same insurer also writes the contractor's CGL insurance. However, many insurers do not issue railroad protective liability policies, even though a standard ISO coverage form is available (CG 00 35). Thus, the insurer providing the railroad protective policy may be different from the insurer providing the contractor's CGL insurance, opening the door to a subrogation action against the insured contractor.

Deletion of the railroad protective exclusion is therefore recommended whenever an insured is required (1) to purchase a railroad protective liability policy; (2) to sign an indemnification agreement with a railroad; or (3) to fulfill both of the preceding items. Endorsement CG 24 17, Contractual Liability—Railroads, is the ISO endorsement for effecting this change. This endorsement provides coverage if the railroad requires the assumption of tort liability based on its sole fault. In 2005, ISO introduced endorsement CG 24 27 Limited Contractual Liability—Railroads. This reduces the sole negligence coverage of the railroad to coverage for injury or damage caused in whole or in part by the named insured or those acting on its behalf.

Professional Liability Exclusion

The exclusions contained in clauses (2) and (3) are both aimed at eliminating contractual liability coverage for injury or damage resulting from professional errors or omissions of architects, engineers, or surveyors.

- Clause (2) excludes coverage when the insured (who may or may not be an architect, engineer, or surveyor) agrees to indemnify an architect, engineer, or surveyor for injury or damage arising out of the itemized services.

- Clause (3) excludes coverage when the insured is an architect, engineer, or surveyor and assumes liability for injury or damage arising out of its rendering or failure to render professional services for others, including the itemized services.

The purpose of these exclusions is to prevent the insurer from covering losses that should be insured under a professional liability policy. Note that this exclusion applies to "injury" or "damage," rather than "bodily injury" or "property damage." Injury and damage can have wide application, since they are broader in scope than bodily injury or property damage. The purpose for using the words injury or damage is not clear, given the fact that Coverage A only insures bodily injury and property damage liability in the first place.

Not to confuse the situation, but let's assume a CGL policy is issued to an architect, engineer or surveyor and no professional services exclusion applies. This means that the CGL policy covers professional services but only to the extent of bodily injury, property damage and personal and advertising injury. If the architect, engineer or surveyor were to agree to hold harmless, defend and indemnify a project owner for injury or damage arising solely out of the professional's work, coverage should apply because the professional here has not assumed the tort liability of anyone and this exclusion applies only to item f. dealing with tort liability assumed. In other words, when the named insured under a CGL policy is an architect, engineer or surveyor who agrees to hold harmless, defend and indemnify another party to the agreement, because of the professional's sole fault, the professional's CGL coverage remains intact. This is so because (1) the agreement is not an "insured contract, and (2) the liability of the professional for its own negligence would exist even in the absence of any contract or agreement. This assumes there is no professional liability exclusion.

What may beg the question here is what coverage applies for liability in the absence of any contract or agreement. The answer is that it does not really matter under a CGL policy. For purposes of categorizing the coverage and claims for underwriting or claims statistical purposes, the appropriate coverage is premises-operations.

One of the perennial problems with the similar exclusions under the broad form liability endorsement, a problem that will probably continue under the current forms, is the gray area between professional and nonprofessional services. In one case, for example, an engineering firm sought coverage under its general liability policy for property damage liability resulting from the digging of a trench for the laying of pipes. The insurer denied coverage by maintaining that such activity was in the performance of "engineering services" and "the preparation or approval of maps, plans, ... surveys, designs or specifications." The Texas Court of Appeals, however, ruled for the insured. It did so for two reasons. In the court's opinion, the locating of underground pipes was not an activity included within the term "engineering services," and the latter term was ambiguous in that it was not defined. The case is *Aetna Fire Underwriters Ins. Co. v. Southwestern Engineering Co.*, 626 S.W.2d 99 (Tex. App. 1981).

However, in another case the professional services exclusion in a CGL form was held to preclude coverage; this case is *Natural Gas Pipeline Co. of America v. Odom Offshore Surveys, Inc.*, 889 F.2d 633 (5th Cir. 1989). The U.S. Court of Appeals in the 5th Circuit held that the professional liability exclusion barred coverage for damage to a natural gas pipeline caused by the negligence of the insured's employees in misdirecting the placement of a boat's anchor.

One of the ways commonly advocated to avoid such problems is to purchase both professional liability and general liability insurance from the same insurer. In reality, however, it is often impossible to obtain general liability insurance from the same insurer that provides the professional liability policy.

Defense Costs Assumed under Contract

One of the amendments proposed by ISO in 1992 was the following language, added to the contractual liability exclusion:

> Solely for the purposes of liability assumed in an "insured contract", reasonable attorney fees and necessary litigation expenses incurred by or for a party other than an insured are deemed to be damages because of "bodily injury" or "property damage" provided:
>
> (a) Liability to such party for, or for the cost of, that party's defense has also been assumed in the same "insured contract"; and
>
> (b) Such attorney fees and litigation expenses are for defense of that party against a civil or alternative dispute resolution proceeding in which damages to which this insurance applies are alleged.

Because this provision covers defense costs assumed under an insured contract, it was represented by ISO as being a broadening of contractual liability coverage since many insurers previously considered the CGL policy to cover only *damages* (and not *defense costs*) assumed under an insured contract. However, some insurers apparently interpreted the policy to cover defense costs before the new language was introduced—and, moreover, to cover an indemnitee's defense costs in addition to the limits of insurance. Because the new language considers defense costs assumed under contract to be damages, they are payable *within* the limits. In this respect, some viewed the new language to be a restriction of existing coverage.

Because of its controversial nature, only a handful of states approved this 1992 change. When the same change was reintroduced as part of the 1996 revisions, it was approved by many states. However, the 1996 and later editions of the CGL policy contain additional provisions described earlier in this chapter under the heading "Supplementary Payments." The additional provisions provide that when the indemnitee and the insured are codefendants (and if several other conditions exist), the insurer will pay the defense costs of both parties in addition to policy limits.

It is important to note that the defense costs provision in the contractual liability exclusion applies only to indemnitees who are not also additional insureds. Thus, one way for indemnitees of the insured to sidestep this provision is to request and obtain additional insured status. They will then be entitled to defense coverage in addition to the limits of insurance regardless of whether they are codefendants with the named insured.

Exclusion C—Liquor Liability

Exclusion c. of the CGL coverage forms excludes:

"Bodily injury" or "property damage" for which any insured may be held liable by reason of:

(1) Causing or contributing to the intoxication of any person;

(2) The furnishing of alcoholic beverages to a person under the legal drinking age or under the influence of alcohol; or

(3) Any statute, ordinance or regulation relating to the sale, gift, distribution or use of alcoholic beverages.

This exclusion applies only if you are in the business of manufacturing, distributing, selling, serving or furnishing alcoholic beverages.

This exclusion has primarily the same intent as the one that applies under the 1973 liability policy: to exclude liquor liability under common law, as well as under statute, be it a dram shop act or an alcoholic beverage control act. Apart from that similarity, there are some notable differences.

Conspicuous by its absence from the 1986 and later editions of the CGL form is the prior exclusion of coverage for owners or lessors of premises used by others for purposes of liquor businesses. The fact that owners or lessors of premises are now covered, when they are not engaged in the liquor business, eliminates the problem of requiring liquor liability insurance of tenants and naming premises owners as additional insureds.

Also absent from the current CGL coverage forms is a separate host liquor liability coverage, which in the broad form general liability endorsement is intended to be nothing more than a clarification of what the liquor liability exclusion does not encompass. It seems likely that a separate host liquor liability provision was not included in the current forms because it is too often confused as some kind of extra protection, particularly since it is provided under the broad form endorsement, which requires an additional premium. In fact, there have been some cases in which liquor vendors who were without separate liquor liability coverage attempted to find coverage under the host liquor provision. In one case, for example, a vendor maintained that because his license restricted liquor sales to 49 percent of the restaurant's total revenue, his liquor operation was only incidental to the insured's business. The insured lost his argument. The case is *Heritage Ins. Co. of America v. Cilano*, 433 So. 2d

1334 (Fla. App. 1983). The applicability of the liquor liability exclusion hinges on the meaning of the phrase "in the business of." Since that phrase is not defined, it could present a problem for insurers and insureds alike. In one case, the New Hampshire Supreme Court held that the word *business* means "any regular activity that occupies one's time and attention, with or without a direct profit motive." In a narrow sense, it means "an activity with a direct profit motive." Since the word *business* was considered to be ambiguous, a club was granted coverage despite the liquor liability exclusion. The case is *Laconia Rod & Gun Club v. Hartford Accident and Indemnity Co.*, 459 A.2d 249 (N.H. 1983).

Another common attack on the CGL policy's liquor exclusion relates to the endorsement, Products-Completed Operations Redefined CG 24 07, which is required for a liquor establishment that sells food and beverages for consumption on and away from the business. Some liquor establishments have maintained that this endorsement creates an ambiguity. The effect of this endorsement is to redefine the policy's definition of the "products-completed operations hazard" to encompass not only bodily injury or property damage that occurs away from the named insured's premises, after the product has been relinquished to others, but also injury or damage that occurs on the named insured's premises after the product has been relinquished to others. In the case of *B.L.G. Enterprises, Inc. d/b/a The Alley Bar v. First Financial Ins. Co.*, 491 S.E. 2d 695 (S.C. App. 1977), the court stated that this endorsement left undisturbed the policy's exclusion of coverage for an intoxicated patron who left the premises and caused injury to himself and to others.

Despite the foregoing cases, owners or operators of liquor establishments would be well advised to obtain liquor liability insurance. Whether organizations that hold special events where liquor is sold need special insurance is a question that is difficult to answer. If they require a permit, there is a good chance they should have liquor liability insurance.

In any event, the inference may now be made that if a person or organization is not in the business (whatever that means) of manufacturing, distributing, selling, or furnishing alcoholic beverages, it will have protection by exception to this exclusion. The coverage that is intended to be provided should correspond to those events commonly cited as being covered by host liquor liability insurance.

In 1988, Insurance Services Office proposed changes to the CGL coverage forms that would have modified the liquor liability exclusion substantially. While ISO defended the modification as a means of distinguishing between a social host and a purveyor of alcoholic beverages, the Risk and Insurance Management Society (RIMS) and other parties opposed the change. Following public hearings by the National Association of Insurance Commissioners (NAIC) and meetings between ISO and NAIC, ISO agreed to leave the existing 1986 liquor liability exclusion intact and, as part of 1990 CGL amendments, offer the revised exclusion as an optional endorsement entitled Amendment of Liquor Liability Exclusion, CG 21 50.

The amended exclusion contains parts (1), (2), and (3) of the regular liquor liability exclusion quoted above, plus the following:

This exclusion applies only if you:

(1)   Manufacture, sell or distribute alcoholic beverages;

(2)   Serve or furnish alcoholic beverages for a charge whether or not such activity:

    (a)   Requires a license;

    (b)   Is for the purpose of financial gain or livelihood; or

(3)   Serve or furnish alcoholic beverages without a charge, if a license is required for such activity.

The amended exclusion avoids the troublesome question of whether an insured is in the business of selling alcoholic beverages. For example, the exclusion applies in any situation, even a social gathering, when the insured serves alcoholic beverages for a charge. If the insured is required to have a license to serve alcoholic beverages, the exclusion applies even if the beverages are served free of charge.

In the 1990 CGL amendments, ISO also introduced a new endorsement that contains the exclusion just described but allows coverage for activities specifically described in the endorsement. An advantage of this endorsement over the regular liquor liability exclusion in the CGL form is that the endorsement allows the insured to be certain of coverage for the described event instead of having to depend on the insurer's interpretation of whether the insured is in the business of serving alcoholic beverages. The endorsement, Amendment of Liquor Liability Exclusion—Exception for Scheduled Activities (CG 21 51), allows the underwriter to assess the risk connected with the event to be covered and charge an additional premium for the specified event.

Note that in light of some court decisions holding for coverage involving liquor-related accidents, ISO is revising this exclusion in the April 2013 edition of the CGL form to preclude coverage even if the claims against any insured allege negligence or other wrongdoing. The cases cited by ISO that have been the impetus for this change are as follows.

In *Penn-America Insurance Co. v. Peccadillos*, 27 A.3d 259 (Pa. Super. Ct. 2011), the court ruled that the insurer had a duty to defend its named insured under a CGL policy when the named insured was alleged to have continued to serve alcohol to visibly intoxicated patrons and then ejected them from the premises in an inebriated condition that resulted in an auto accident with deaths and injuries.

In *McGuire v. Curry*, 766 N.W.2d 501 (SD, 2009), the court ruled that the employer could be held liable for the actions of its underage employee when the employer allowed its underage employee unsupervised and unrestricted access to alcoholic beverages.

Briefly, the insurer, in the case of *Essex Insurance Co. v. Café Dupont, LLC*, 674 F. Supp. 2d 166 (USDC, DC, 2009), issued a CGL policy to a nightclub operator who was sued because of a liquor-related incident. After being served and permitted to consume alcoholic beverages, the customer drove off in his auto, despite being intoxicated or at least appearing to be intoxicated, and was involved in an accident, seriously injuring another motorist. The suit filed by the legal guardian of the injured motorist against the nightclub operator sought $15 million in compensatory damages and $5 million in punitive damages. The nightclub operator also purchased a liquor liability policy but it was not in force at the time of this incident.

The insurer that issued the CGL policy to the nightclub operator denied coverage and defense and later filed a declaratory judgment action. One of the CGL policy's exclusions that was the "Achilles heel" of the nightclub operator precluded coverage for "any act or omission by the insured or any employee of any insured that respects providing or failing to provide transportation, detaining or failing to detain any person, or any act of assuming or not assuming responsibility for the wellbeing, supervision or care of any person allegedly under or suspected to be under the influence of alcohol." The nightclub operator argued that the foregoing exclusion only applied to injuries to the person under or suspected to be under the influence of alcohol. The court disagreed and said that was an unreasonable interpretation. The court went on to explain that "[a]lthough the exclusion only covers failure to provide transportation ... detain anyone ... or ...assum[e] responsibility for the wellbeing of an intoxicated person, it applies to any injury, loss or damage that might arise as a result." The court also stated it would not seek out ambiguity where none exists.

As the result of these cases, ISO is adding to its liquor liability exclusion verbiage which will in effect (as noted previously) preclude coverage even if claims allege negligence or other wrongdoing in:

- the supervision, hiring, employment, training or monitoring of others; or

- providing or failing to provide transportation with respect to any person that may be under the influence of alcohol.

Note that ISO does have liquor liability coverage forms, CG 00 33 (occurrence) and CG 00 34 (claims-made). These forms provide liquor liability coverage to the extent an underwriter is willing to provide it. A great deal of this type coverage is written in the excess and surplus lines market.

Bring Your Own Bottle (BYOB) Exposures

Some restaurants, instead of selling and serving alcoholic beverages, allow patrons to bring their own bottles. Restaurants in this category that permit bringing in bottles of alcoholic beverages sometimes will charge a corkage fee, require that the beverages be poured and served by restaurant employees, and may charge for the mixers and ice. From time to time, producers have questioned underwriters about whether these practices of restaurants are subject to the liquor liability exclusion. This question is being answered with the response of another revision to the liquor liability exclusion which ISO states is a broadening of coverage.

The revision states: for purposes of this exclusion, permitting a person to bring alcoholic beverages on your premises, for consumption on your premises, whether or not a fee is charged or a license is required for such activity, is not by itself considered the business of selling, serving or furnishing alcoholic beverages.

It must be remember that even if the BYOB exposure is an expressed exception to the liquor liability exclusion, a liquor-related accident can still preclude coverage as illustrated in the case of *Simmon v. Homatas*, 925 N.E.2d 1089 (IL, 2010). In addition, as mentioned later with reference to the multi-state endorsements, when any one of the Amendment Of Liquor Liability Exclusion Endorsements is issued (namely, CG 21 50, CG 21 51, CG 29 52 and CG 29 53), the exclusion will also apply even if an insured permits any person to bring any alcoholic beverages on the named insured's premises for consumption on the premises.

These revisions dealing with the liquor liability exclusion affect both the CGL occurrence form (CG 00 01) and claims-made form (CG 00 02), as well as the Products/Completed Operations Liability occurrence form (CG 00 37) and claims-made form (CG 00 38).

Exclusion D—Workers Compensation and Similar Laws

The workers compensation exclusion deals with a number of employment-related statutory coverages. The exclusion applies to:

Any obligation of the insured under a workers' compensation, disability benefits or unemployment compensation law or any similar law.

Use of the word "obligation" in the above exclusion means that no coverage applies when (1) an insured has such statutory coverage and it applies to a loss or (2) an insured should have obtained the statutory protection that applies to a loss. Note also that this exclusion applies to the insured (which includes the named insured), rather than the named insured only. While a disability benefits law applies to nonemployment disability, it is still considered to be an employment-related law, because only those who are employed can generally qualify for the coverage in those states that mandate it. The same criterion applies to unemployment insurance.

Exclusion E—Employers Liability

Employers liability insurance is a necessary complement to workers compensation coverage and both are generally available under one statutory form of protection, except in monopolistic-fund states.

Before the exclusion itself is discussed, it may be worthwhile to review the reasons why employers liability insurance is still considered necessary. They are as follows:

- Workers compensation insurance may be elective, rather than compulsory, for certain types of employment. Employers liability insurance gives the employer both defense cost and indemnification coverage against liability for injury to exempt employees.

- Employers who are sued by members of an employee's family for loss of consortium (i.e., loss of companionship, comfort, and affection) may be required to pay damages even though the disabled employee has collected benefits under workers compensation coverage.

- Employers can become involved in suits called third-party-over or simply third-party actions. These actions arise when an injured employee sues a negligent third party (regardless of workers compensation benefits received), and the third party, in turn, impleads the employer. The employer, in such a case, must look to employers liability insurance (or stopgap coverage in monopolistic-fund states), unless the employer assumed the liability of the third party. In that instance, the CGL contractual liability coverage, rather than employers liability coverage, is the applicable coverage.

The employers liability exclusion of the current CGL forms reads as follows:

"Bodily injury" to:

(1)   An "employee" of the insured arising out of and in the course of:

    (a)   Employment by the insured; or

    (b)   Performing duties related to the conduct of the insured's business; or

(2)   The spouse, child, parent, brother or sister of that "employee" as a consequence of Paragraph (1) above.

This exclusion applies:

(1)   Whether the insured may be liable as an employer or in any other capacity; and

(2)   To any obligation to share damages with or repay someone else who must pay damages because of the injury.

This exclusion does not apply to liability assumed by the insured under an "insured contract".

Part (1)(a) of this exclusion is intended to prevent an insurer from having to cover the liability of any insured because of injury sustained by its employee that would or should be covered by employers liability insurance. This exclusion is not limited to employees of the named insured; it applies to employees of any party that qualifies as an insured under the policy, including an additional insured.

With the 1993 revision of the CGL policy, the terms "employee" and "leased worker" were defined in order to provide coverage for employee leasing arrangements (see Chapter 5). Because the term "employee" is defined to include a "leased worker," the 1993 and later editions of the CGL policy exclude bodily injury sustained by a leased worker defined in part as a person leased to the insured for purposes of performing duties related to the conduct of the insured's business. This is the rationale for part (1)(b) of the above exclusion. However, not within the scope of this exclusion are "temporary workers," whose employment is on a day-to-day or short-term basis, and "volunteer workers," a newly defined term of the 2001 edition meaning in part a person who is not an employee of the named insured.

When the definition of "temporary worker" was introduced by ISO in 1993, few believed that the newly introduced term would lead to litigation. The linchpin or problem with that definition is that part of the definition reading "Temporary worker means a worker who is furnished to an entity ...." Some courts have held that "furnished to" is ambiguous, but not all courts agree. In light of many disputes over that term and the lack of consensus, primarily falling on ambiguity, it would not be surprising if ISO were to revisit that definition in the future. The second part of the exclusion eliminates coverage for claims or suits by spouses or other close relatives against employers as a consequence of bodily injury sustained by employees. The apparent rationale for this part of the exclusion is to clarify that such claims or suits must be filed under the employers liability portion of the workers compensation policy. Although earlier editions of employers liability insurance did not state that coverage applied to these consequential damages, the current workers compensation and employers liability policy does.

Dual Capacity Claims

The employers liability exclusion is stated to apply whether the insured is liable as an employer or in any other capacity. The phrase "in any other capacity" is intended to encompass claims or suits against employers under the so-called dual capacity doctrine.

The dual capacity doctrine holds that an employer normally shielded by the exclusive remedy of workers compensation laws may still be answerable for additional damages in tort. This type of claim can occur when the employer is judged to occupy a second capacity that constitutes an exposure that is common to the public in general, rather than to one's employment. A simplified example of an event to which this doctrine might apply is the injury that occurs to an employee of an insured beer distributor while the employee is stocking the insured's product on a vendor's shelves.

If the dual capacity doctrine applied in the above example, the employee would have two sources of recovery from the employer. The first would be under the employer's workers compensation insurance, since the injury arose out of and during the course of employment. The second source of recovery would be a lawsuit against the employer, such as any other member of the public could file against the employer. In other words, the injury, or the exposure thereto, is not necessarily peculiar to employment. It is an exposure to which the employee would have been equally exposed, apart from his or her employment, as a consumer of the product.

Since the workers compensation and employers liability policy is now recognized as the only source of coverage for such suits by employees against employers, whether under the dual capacity doctrine or otherwise, the intent of the employers liability exclusion of the CGL coverage forms should be clear.

Third-Party-Over Actions

The last part of the employers liability exclusion deals with third-party-over actions. The reason third-party-over actions are excluded under the current forms is that coverage for such actions is available under employers liability insurance, with one exception. This exception is when such liability is assumed by the insured under a contract. In that event, coverage applies under the CGL coverage form subject of course to the scope of that coverage for liability assumed under an insured contract.

Assume, for example, that an insured agrees to hold harmless and indemnify another party for liability stemming from the insured's negligence, including injury to employees of the insured. An employee of the insured is injured during the course of employment and collects benefits under the insured's workers compensation insurance. The employee then sues the third party for whom work was performed. When the third party demands that the employer hold it harmless against the employee's suit, coverage should apply under the insured's contractual liability coverage of the insured's CGL policy. In the absence of a contractual assumption by the employer, coverage for a third-party-over action would apply under the employers liability portion of the workers compensation policy.

Exclusion F—Pollution

Without a doubt, the CGL provision that has changed the most, in terms of number of times and in scope, is the pollution exclusion. It was once referred to as the "absolute pollution exclusion" in 1986 when it was first introduced because it eliminated coverage in most situations for bodily injury and property damage resulting from pollutants, and it totally excluded the costs of cleaning up pollutants. It was not too long thereafter that amendments were introduced to this exclusion, first to strengthen and then to liberalize it in a number of ways.

To gain a better perspective on how this exclusion has changed and the significance of the changes, each of the changes is discussed briefly later in these pages through numbered notes on an exhibit entitled "A Chronology of Changes Affecting the Pollution Exclusion." It is first necessary to understand why the pollution exclusion was first introduced with standard forms and why problems were encountered with it.

Background

The first standard pollution exclusion was introduced in 1970. Originally added to general liability policies by endorsement, the 1970 pollution exclusion was later incorporated into the standard 1973 CGL coverage part. However, the first application for approval of a pollution exclusion to the Maryland Insurance Department came in October 1981. Approval was granted in January 1983.[5]

According to its drafters, the exclusion was introduced for two reasons:

1. To make clear that the policy's definition of "occurrence" was not to categorize all pollution or contamination damage as being expected or intended by the insured.

2. To clarify that bodily injury or property damage resulting from pollution or contamination was excluded, even if accidental, unless the discharge, dispersal, release or escape was both sudden and accidental.[6]

However, when the definition of occurrence was taken into consideration in liability actions stemming from gradual pollution, the courts found that the exclusion either was "temporal" or "nontemporal" in nature.

To be considered temporal, the word "sudden" would be required to have one meaning and that is a temporal aspect of immediacy; that is, the characteristic of being swift, abrupt, quick, instantaneous, etc.

The problem for some insurers has been that when dictionary definitions of *sudden* are consulted, all are not limited to the temporal aspect and, instead, also consider *sudden* to mean unanticipated and unforeseen. As a result, the courts in some of these cases have agreed that when the word *sudden* is defined in both a temporal and nontemporal way, it is considered to be ambiguous and construed in the insured's favor.

Another aspect of this exclusion concerns the alleged polluter who seeks payment for the costs of cleaning up the source of contamination on the polluter's own property. The question is: where does the polluter's own property end? Some say at the water table or at the level where property is considered to be within the domain of natural resources. In one of the leading cases on this subject, coverage was held to apply, despite the exclusion of property damage to property owned by the insured (exclusion j.1), for two reasons:

1. The cleanup costs were deemed to be necessary to prevent further damage to third parties.

2. If steps had not been taken to clean up the premises, the insurer would have sustained additional losses.

The case is *Bankers Trust Co. v. Hartford Accident and Indemnity Co.*, 518 F. Supp. 371 (S.D.N.Y. 1981), decided by the United States district court for the southern district of New York. For a time since this exclusion was introduced in 1986, it addressed this problem by totally excluding the costs of cleaning up pollutants. However, since 1998, certain exceptions apply to the exclusion of cleanup costs.

The imposition of liability under a variety of federal and state laws also is a target of the pollution exclusion, particularly enforcement under the Comprehensive Environmental Response Compensation and Liability Act (CERCLA) of 1980, also known as Superfund; the Superfund Amendments and Reauthorization Act of 1986, referred to as SARA; and the Resource Conservation and Recovery Act (RCRA) of 1976. Alleged polluters, especially those who are or were involved in the handling of wastes, are commonly looking to their CGL policies for protection in the wake of suits filed against them by the federal government. Because the 1970 pollution exclusion has not lived up to insurers' expectations, the action to implement a broader exclusion and a buy-back procedure was viewed as the only way to keep insurers from having to pick up all the costs prompted by the pollution claims and suits.

The wording of exclusion f. in the CGL policy is found in the accompanying exhibit along with information as to when the exclusion was amended. An explanation of the rationale for the changes follows the exhibit. The 1986 and subsequent versions of this exclusion can be found in the appendices to this text.

A Chronology of Changes
Affecting the Pollution Exclusion (f.)

BI and PD Exclusion 1986

1998(1)

(1) "Bodily injury" or "property damage" arising out of the actual, alleged or threatened discharge, dispersal, seepage, migration, release or escape of "pollutants":

At or from the Premises
1998 (2)

(a) At or from any premises, site or location which is or was at any time owned by or occupied by, or rented or loaned to, any insured. However, this subparagraph does not apply to:

Heating Equipment Coverage
1997

(i) "Bodily injury" if sustained within a building and caused by smoke, fumes,

Cooling and Dehumidifying
Equipment Coverage
2004 (3)

vapor or soot pro-
duced by or originat-
ing from equipment
that is used to heat,
cool, or dehumidify
the building, or equip-
ment that is used to
heat water for personal
use, by the building's
occupants or their
guests;

Owner as Additional Insured
1998 (4)

(ii) "Bodily injury" or
"property damage"
for which you may
be held liable, if
you are a contrac-
tor and the owner or
lessee of such prem-
ises, site or location
has been added to
your policy as an
additional insured
with respect to your
ongoing operations
performed for that
additional insured at
that premises, site
or location and such
premises, site or
location is not and
never was owned
or occupied by, or
rented or loaned to,
any insured, other
than that additional
insured; or

Hostile Fire Coverage
1986 (5)

(iii) "Bodily injury" or
"property damage"
arising out of heat,
smoke or fumes from
a "hostile fire";

Waste Treatment Site
1986 (6)

(b) At or from any premises, site or location is or was at any time used by or for any insured or others for the handling, storage, disposal, processing or treatment of waste;

Transported, Handled
Processed, etc. 1986 (7)

(c) Which are or were at any time transported, handled, stored, treated, disposed of, or processed as waste by or for: (1) Any insured; or (2) Any person or organization for whom you may be legally responsible; or

At the Job Site While Work
Is in Progress 1998 (8)

(d) At or from any premises, site or location on which any insured or any contractors or subcontractors working directly or indirectly on any insured's behalf are performing operations if the "pollutants" are brought on or to the premises, site or location in connection with such operations by such insured, contractor or subcontractor. However, this subparagraph does not apply to

Mobile Equipment Exception
1996 (9)

(i) "Bodily injury" or "property damage" arising out of the escape or fuels, lubricants or other operating fluids which are needed to perform the normal electrical, hydraulic or mechanical functions necessary for the operation of "mobile equipment"

Mobile Equipment Exception 1996 (9) (Continued)

or its parts, if such fuels, lubricants or other operating fluids escape from a vehicle part designed to hold or receive them. This exception does not apply if the "bodily injury" or "property damage" arises out of the intentional discharge, dispersal or release of the fuels, lubricants or other operating fluids, or if such fuels, lubricants or other operating fluids are brought on or to the premises, site or location with the intent to be discharged, dispersed or released as part of the operations being performed by such insured, contractor or subcontractor;

Contractors' Operations Vapor Coverage 1998 (10)

(ii) "Bodily injury" or "property damage" sustained within a building and caused by the release of gases, fumes or vapors from materials brought into that building in connection with operations being performed by you or on your behalf by a contractor or subcontractor; or

Hostile Fire Coverage 1986 (11)

(iii) "Bodily injury" or "property damage" arising out of heat, smoke or fumes from a "hostile fire"

Professional Cleanup
Exclusion 1986 (12)

(e) At or from any prem-
ises, site or location on
which an insured or any
contractors or subcon-
tractors working direct-
ly or indirectly on any
insured's behalf are per-
forming operations if the
operations are to test for,
monitor, cleanup, remove,
contain, treat, detoxify or
neutralize, or in any way
respond to, or assess the
effects of, "pollutants."

(2) Any loss, cost or expense arising out of any:

Cleanup Exclusion
1998 (13)

(a) Request, demand, order
or statutory or regulato-
ry requirement that any
insured or others test for,
monitor, cleanup, remove,
contain, treat, detoxify or
neutralize, or in any way
respond to, or assess the
effects of "pollutants"; or

Cleanup Exclusion
1986 (14)

(b) Claim or suit by or on
behalf of a governmen-
tal authority for dam-
ages because of testing
for, monitoring, cleaning
up, removing, containing,
treating, detoxifying, or
neutralizing or in any way
responding to or assessing
the effects of "pollutants."

Cleanup Exclusion
Exceptions 1998 (15)

However, this subparagraph does not
apply to liability for damages because of
"property damage" that the insured would
have in the absence of such request,
demand, order or statutory or regulatory
requirement or such claim or "suit" by
or on behalf of a governmental authority.

The pollution exclusion as introduced with the 1986 CGL policy provisions has been restructured extensively and expanded to the point where it would be difficult to determine what has changed without the above chronology and a brief explanation of amendments below.

(1) This first subparagraph is one of the few remaining originals. However, even this part was amended in 1998 with the reference to the term "pollutants" in quotes to show that its meaning is to be found in the definitions section of the CGL forms rather than at the end of the exclusion, as has been the case since 1986.

(2) With the exception of the second sentence, this, too, is one of the few remaining original provisions. The second sentence was added in 1998, as part of the reconstruction process. Prior to this change, amendments to the exclusion were simply added in an unorganized fashion making it difficult to determine when a particular provision applied. This second sentence is a prelude to three exceptions specifically applicable to subparagraph f.(1)(a).

(3) This is the first exception to subparagraph f.(1)(a) and applies to bodily injury if sustained within a building and caused by smoke, fumes, vapor, or soot from equipment used to heat that building. This exception is meant to clarify the point that the CGL forms apply to a claim for bodily injury suffered by someone who has been adversely affected by smoke or fumes from a heater. For example, if a customer of the insured is injured or dies from carbon monoxide seeping from the insured's furnace, the CGL form will respond to a subsequent claim. Note that the furnace (or any other equipment to heat the building) need not be owned by the insured. One question was whether this exception was broad enough to encompass bodily injury by persons who acquire the so-called Legionnaires Disease. To the extent that this disease is caused by vapor from air-conditioning systems, there was room for argument, given that heating systems also commonly include air-conditioning.

To avoid these types of arguments and, according to ISO, at the request of agents and insurers, this building heating exception was clarified with the 2004 CGL revisions to include cooling and dehumidifying equipment, since both are said to have similar exposures to building heating equipment insofar as emitting various toxins. What may not have been anticipated with this latest change is that with humidity comes the possibility for the growth of mold, which would then likely be covered in light of this revision.

(4) The second exception was introduced in 1998 as a broadening of coverage and applies when the named insured is a contractor. Prior to this change, the pollution exclusion was triggered if pollutants escaped or were released from a premises or site owned or occupied by any insured. Assume, for purposes of illustration, that the named insured contractor is working on a building site and the owner of the site requires that it be listed as an additional insured on the contractor's CGL policy. While work is being performed, pollutants leak from the site and damage an adjoining premises. The owner of the adjoining premises files suit against the contractor and the site owner, who in turn looks to the contractor for protection as an additional insured. Prior to this change in 1998, the exclusion could have been interpreted to exclude a claim from the adjoining property owner because the additional insured owned the site and the pollution came from there.

The situation is now changed. The fact that the additional insured owns the site from which escaping pollutants have harmed a third party will not prevent the named insured contractor from receiving coverage under his or her CGL policy, if the named insured is held to be liable for the damage. The relationship of the additional insured, as owner or lessee of the work site and as an additional insured on the contractor's CGL form, no longer has an effect on the question of coverage for the named insured contractor. Note, however, that this exception applies only to additional insured status during ongoing operations, not within the "products-completed operations hazard."

(5) The third exception is for bodily injury or property damage arising out of heat, smoke or fumes from a hostile fire. This is not new to CGL forms, but the exception has been moved so that its relationship with subparagraph f.(1)(a) is made clearer. It also applies by exception to d.(iii). Basically, the exception means, for example, that if someone were to be injured from smoke from a fire billowing from the named insured's warehouse containing herbicides, pesticides, and other contaminants, the CGL form would apply to a bodily injury claim made against the insured, notwithstanding the pollution exclusion.

(6), (7) These two subparagraphs remain unchanged since they were introduced in 1986. They flatly exclude any bodily injury or property damage emanating from waste treatment sites, as well as while being transported, handled, treated, stored, disposed of, or processed as waste by the insured or by anyone for whom the named insured may be legally responsible.

(8) This subparagraph 1.(d) is sometimes overlooked. It is an original provision but was amended in 1998 with the addition of the last sentence. This is a significant subparagraph because some coverage applies by exception for bodily injury or property damage arising out of the named insured's products and completed operations. This exclusion does not contain any statement that products and completed operations are excepted from the exclusion. However, under certain circumstances, coverage can be inferred from the language of the exclusion. Thus, if the exclusion does not encompass bodily injury or property damage under a particular set of circumstances, then the bodily injury or property damage is covered, subject of course to all other policy provisions.

To illustrate, say the named insured sells and installs carpeting. If, after being installed by the named insured in a customer's home, a particular lot of carpeting emits vapors that cause bodily injury to the home owner, the injury claim would not be excluded by any provision of the pollution exclusion. The vapors, although they are pollutants, were not discharged at the named insured's premises or at a waste handling site [subparagraphs (1)(a) and (b)]; they were not transported or handled as waste [subparagraph (1)(c)]; and they were not discharged at a site at which the insured or any contractors are performing operations [subparagraph (1)(d)]. Subparagraph (1)(d), because it uses only present tense verbs ("premises ... on which any insured or any contractors or subcontractors working directly or indirectly on any insured's behalf are performing operations"), seems capable of excluding bodily injury or property damage that occurs only while operations are being performed and should therefore not be applicable to bodily injury or property damage that occurs after work is completed.

In fact, as noted in (10) below, at least two court cases have upheld coverage for injuries arising from the emission of toxic fumes from carpeting, undoubtedly leading to the introduction of a provision permitting coverage in these instances.

However, coverage for products and completed operations does not apply in all instances. For example, completed operations in the nature of waste disposal are clearly excluded by subparagraph (1)(b).

In addition to products and completed operations, another area where some coverage can be inferred from the exclusionary wording of 1(d) is where its subparts (d)(i) and (d)(ii) do not apply. Thus, if a pollution loss results under conditions not described in (d)(i) or (d)(ii) and the location is not otherwise excluded by sections (a), (b), or (c) of the pollution exclusion, then the loss may be covered—including cleanup costs as addressed in part (2) of the exclusion.

To illustrate, assume that the insured is an independent contractor working on a building project away from its own premises. If the insured negligently causes the release of pollutants that were brought to the work site by the owner or by another contractor who is not working on behalf of the insured, resulting damages for bodily injury or property damage (and cleanup costs) should be covered by the contractor's CGL form. The exclusion would apply, however, if the pollutants had been brought to the work site by the insured or by a contractor or subcontractor working on behalf of the insured, or if the insured's operation from which the pollution resulted had been for purposes of testing for, monitoring, cleaning up, etc., of pollutants.

(9) Subparagraph (d)(i) was introduced in 1996 to make clear that the pollution exclusion does not apply to bodily injury or property damage arising out of the escape of fuels, lubricants or other operating fluids which are needed to perform the normal electrical, hydraulic or mechanical functions necessary for the operation of mobile equipment or its parts, if such fuels, etc., escape from a vehicle part designed to hold, store or receive them. This exception does not apply if the fuels, lubricants or other operating fluids are intentionally discharged, dispersed or released, or if such fuels, lubricants or other operating fluids are brought on or to the premises, site, or location with the intent to be discharged, dispersed or released as part of the operations being performed by such insured, contractor, or subcontractor.

(10) Subparagraph (d)(ii) was added as an exception to the pollution exclusion in 1998. This makes clear what might have been subjected to argument under subparagraph (1)(d). A probable rationale for this addition is that actual cases on point were being ruled against insurers. In *Garfield Slope Housing Corp. v. Public Service Mutual Insurance Co.*, 973 F. Supp. 326 (E.D. N.Y. 1997), a former owner of an apartment sued the building apartment manager, alleging she was injured by fumes from new hallway carpet that had been installed and removed while she still lived in the apartment. The court held for coverage despite a pollution exclusion, because the policy could reasonably be construed as applying to environmental pollution and not applying to claims based on carpet fumes. Moreover, the court said, "the kind of injuries

to which a reasonable insured might expect smelly carpet to give rise—that is, aggravation, inconvenience, annoyance, etc.—are plainly not those that would typically implicate a liability policy."

In the later case of *Freidline v. Shelby* Insurance Company, 739 N.E.2d 178 (Ind. App. 2000), occupants of an office building filed suit against an insured carpet installer alleging they were harmed by toxic fumes from substances used to install carpeting. The court held that the pollution exclusion was ambiguous because while the policy's definition of pollutants included the word "fumes," it did not include carpet glue or any other substance used to install carpet. The insurer would prefer that the emphasis of this claim be on fumes, the court explained, but the plaintiffs did not complain of injury because of fumes but rather by fumes coming from substances used to install carpeting.

(11) See note (5) for an explanation of this subparagraph.

(12) Subparagraph 1 (e) is also one of the original provisions introduced with the 1986 exclusion. Specifically precluded from coverage is any bodily injury or property damage emanating from operations in any way related to the testing, monitoring, cleanup, removal, containment, treatment, detoxifying, neutralizing, or in any way assessing the effects of pollutants. So, for example, if a contractor were hired to perform a Phase II environmental task, no coverage would apply for bodily injury or property damage emanating from that work.

(13), (14) and (15) Before the 1998 revisions, commercial general liability insurance utilizing standard ISO wording did not apply to any loss, cost or expense arising out of any request, demand or order that any insured test for, monitor, cleanup, treat, or in any way respond to or assess the effects of pollutants. The revised CGL forms add that the insurance also does not apply to a "statutory or regulatory requirement" that any insured cleanup or in any way respond to the effects of pollutants.

The words "request," "demand," and "order" signify an action on the part of some entity that forces the insured to cleanup a pollution spill. However, there may be some statute or regulation on the books that would require the insured to cleanup a pollution spill, but, for whatever reason, no entity has taken the initiative to demand action on the part of the insured. The insured could clean up the spill and then present the bill to the insurer and say, "there was no actual demand or order for us to clean up the spill, but there is a regulation that holds us responsible and requires us to clean up our mess, so we did, and there is no applicable wording in the pollution exclusion that covers this situation. Please pay the bill." With the revised wording of this cleanup exclusion, the insurer is now saying that the CGL forms will not cover the cleanup expenses of the insured, even if the insured was acceding to some regulatory wording instead of responding to a demand or order. In effect, the exclusion's wording expands application of the exclusion such that it no longer requires a request, demand or order that the insured cleanup in order to trigger the exclusion's application. Under the revised wording, so long as a statute, ordinance, or regulation dictating a cleanup obligation of any kind exists (however obscure), that statute, once located will be the basis of excluding coverage here.

This part of the pollution exclusion has another change worth noting. There has been some confusion when it came to the relationship between cleanup costs and property damage. On the one hand, the insured may be liable for property damage due to a release or escape of pollutants and, through an exception of the pollution exclusion, have insurance coverage for that property damage. On the other hand, some insurers argued that the insured has no coverage for cleanup costs. And, the cleanup costs exclusion was being interpreted by some to dispute or void any property damage coverage, a finding not supported by clear policy wording. So, where does paying for property damage end and cleanup costs for polluted property begin?

The 1998 revision clarifies this issue by declaring that the cleanup costs section of the pollution exclusion does not apply to liability for property damage that the insured would have anyway. In other words, if the insured is liable for property damage due to a pollution spill, and has insurance coverage due to an exception to the pollution exclusion, the CGL form should pay for the property damage, and there should be no denial of coverage with an assertion that the property damage is a cleanup cost and thus not covered.

Note that the revisions, as propounded by ISO and discussed above, are stated to apply only to coverage for bodily injury and property damage liability; there is no reference to personal and advertising injury liability. However, personal and advertising injury coverage does have a pollution exclusion, as discussed in a later chapter. Interestingly too, despite the many cases involving noise pollution, as well as injury through electromagnetic exposure, the pollution exclusion does not address these types of risk.

Pollution Coverage Options

ISO has prepared a number of endorsements for modifying exclusion f. to provide various levels of pollution liability coverage, or to exclude the pollution liability exposure entirely. The bad news is that there are not many insurers that are willing to provide coverage enhancements despite the availability of the endorsements. Generally, insureds in need of broader coverage need to seek out specialty line insurers for buy-back environmental impairment insurance.

However, the following paragraphs describe briefly the purpose for each of the ISO standard endorsements:

(1) **Pollution Liability Extension Endorsement (CG 04 22).** When this endorsement is attached, subparagraph (1) of exclusion f., dealing with bodily injury and property damage is deleted.

(2) **Limited Pollution Liability Extension Endorsement (CG 24 15).** This endorsement expands coverage in two ways. First, the pollution exclusion is modified so as to not apply to bodily injury or property damage from premises owned, occupied, rented or loaned to the named insured. The second way the exclusion is modified is to provide coverage at locations at which the insured is performing operations that could be described as nonenvironmental in nature. Coverage also applies to cleanup costs other than as mandated by law. As this endorsement states, the exclusion for cleanup costs does not apply to liability for sums the insured becomes legally obligated to pay as damages because of property damage that the insured would have in the absence of such request, demand, order, or statutory or regulatory requirement, or by such claim or suit by or on behalf of a governmental authority.

(3) **Pollution Liability Coverage Part (CG 00 39).** This coverage form is for designated sites. Written on a claims-made basis, it provides coverage for bodily injury and property damage resulting from covered "pollution incidents," as defined in this coverage part, including cleanup costs as may be required by law. To obtain coverage in the event of voluntary cleanup costs, it would be necessary to attach the Voluntary Cleanup Costs Reimbursement (CG 28 33), which is only available with this coverage Part.

(4) **Pollution Liability Coverage Part [Limited] (CG 00 40).** This coverage form has the same coverage characteristics as the preceding coverage part, except that it does not provide coverage for cleanup costs as may be required by law.

(5) **Underground Storage Tank Policy, Designated Tanks (CG 00 42).** This policy provides two coverages: The first liability coverage applies in the event of bodily injury or property damage sustained by third parties and caused by an underground storage tank incident. The second coverage applies for corrective action costs the insured is obligated to pay in response to EPA requirements, because of an underground storage tank incident.

(6) **Total Pollution Exclusion (CG 21 49).** This endorsement is stated to apply to bodily injury and property damage which would not have occurred in whole or in part but for the actual, alleged or threatened discharge, dispersal, seepage, migration, release or escape of "pollutants" any time. Also precluded are cleanup costs whether done voluntarily or through governmental order.

(7) **Total Pollution Exclusion with a Hostile Fire Exception (CG 21 55).** Despite an absolute pollution exclusion, it is advisable to obtain the hostile fire exception, which insurers are not reluctant to provide. In fact, it would be advisable to also obtain the building heating equipment exception. If that is possible, then the endorsement listed below, (CG 21 65), would be applicable. Otherwise, this one (CG 21 55) needs to be issued.

(8) **Total Pollution Exclusion with a Building Heating, Cooling and Dehumidifying Equipment Exception and a Hostile Fire Exception (CG 21 65).** This endorsement is applicable only when the insurer is willing to modify its absolute pollution exclusion with both exceptions. This endorsement's title was amended with the 2004 revisions to include reference to the cooling and dehumidifying equipment exception. Thus, this endorsement, although entitled as being a total exclusion, makes an exception for bodily injury produced by or originating from equipment used not only to heat but also to cool or dehumidify the building.

(9) **Pollution Exclusion—Named Peril Limited Exception for a Short-Term Pollution Event (CG 04 28).** This endorsement affects subparagraphs (a) and (d). Furthermore, the discharge, dispersal, escape, etc., of pollutants must begin, end, and be reported within a certain period stated in this endorsement. Also, coverage only applies for injury or damage due to certain named perils, such earthquake, collapse, windstorm, vandalism, and overturn of tanks. In light of the 2004 CGL policy revisions, this endorsement also provides coverage, through an exception in sub-subparagraph (i), for bodily injury produced by or

originating from equipment used not only to heat but also to cool or dehumidify the building.

(10) **Pollution Exclusion—Limited Exception for a Short-Term Pollution Event (CG 04 29).** This endorsement is similar to the preceding one, except that it is not limited to certain named perils. Coverage, instead, applies regardless of the circumstances, but only for a short period of time. Also, the bodily injury and property damage must not be a repeat or resumption of a previous discharge that occurred within the 12 months prior to the repeat or resumption of the discharge. In light of the 2004 CGL policy revisions, this endorsement also provides coverage, through an exception in sub-subparagraph (i), for bodily injury produced by or originating from equipment used not only to heat but also to cool or dehumidify the building.

(11) **Pollution Exclusion—Limited Exception for Designated Pollutant(s) (CG 04 30).** This endorsement adds an exception to subparagraphs (1)(a) and (1)(d) of exclusion f. for any release or escape of a pollutant specifically scheduled on this endorsement. This allows the owner of premises where certain pollutants are stored a limited amount of coverage that would not otherwise be available without this endorsement. However, this endorsement and its exception do not apply to the discharge, dispersal, etc. of a pollutant listed in the schedule of this endorsement which takes place while such pollutant is being (a) transported, handled, stored, treated, disposed of, or processed as waste; or (b) transported or stored for others.

(12) **Total Pollution Exclusion (CG 21 98).** This endorsement was introduced in 2007 and is available for use with Products-Completed Operations Liability Coverage Form CG 00 37 (occurrence form) and Form CG 00 38 (claims-made). The problem with this endorsement is that many products are potentially a pollutant or contain a pollutant. The insured will still be charged a rate for the sale of the product but may not have coverage at the time of the claim. In fact, what begs a question here is, when did the product become a pollutant? As long as there is no claim, it is a product. When a claim arises, however, the product then becomes a pollutant and is not covered.

(13) **Extended Reporting Period Endorsement (CG 28 01).** If the policy is cancelled or not renewed for any reason other than for nonpayment of premium, the insured may be able to purchase an extended reporting period for one year, if the insurer is willing, with the issuance of this endorsement.

(14) **Insurance Site Definition (CG 28 02).** When this endorsement is issued, it modifies the "insured site" definition in the pollution liability coverage form to include coverage for the liability of contractors working the premises of others.

(15) **Exclusion—Underground Storage Tank Incidents (CG 29 78).** When the named insured owns or operates underground storage tanks that come within the scope of federal regulation, bodily injury, property damage, environmental damage and cleanup costs caused by underground storage tank incidents are excluded.

Exclusion G—Aircraft, Auto or Watercraft

Since 1986, this exclusion has undergone several revisions. The first two concerned negligent entrustment and contractual assumptions. The third one, introduced in 2001, deals with what is referred to as negligent supervision or hiring. The fourth revision, found in the 2004 edition of the CGL policy, makes an exception for injury or damage arising out of the operation of machinery or equipment attached to a land vehicle under conditions that are discussed later in this chapter.

The last revision (April 2013) affects the last exception to exclusion g. Under paragraph (5) in the exception, there is a reference to the operation of machinery or equipment that is attached to, or part of, a land vehicle that would qualify under the definition of mobile equipment if it were not subject to a compulsory or financial responsibility law or other motor vehicle insurance in "the state" where it is licensed or principally garaged. In light of the fact that the ISO filings also are available in the District of Columbia, Puerto Rico, Guam, and the U.S. Virgin Islands, the word "state" is being deleted.

This revision affects both the CGL occurrence form (CG 00 01) and claims-made form (CG 00 02), along with the Pollution Liability Limited Coverage Form Designated Sites (CG 00 40); Exclusion—Volunteer Workers (CG 21 66); and Principals Protective Liability Coverage (CG 28 07).

The current exclusion reads as follows:

"Bodily injury" or "property damage" arising out of the ownership, maintenance, use, or entrustment to others of any aircraft, "auto" or watercraft owned or operated by or rented or loaned to any insured. Use includes operation and "loading or unloading."

This exclusion applies even if the claims against any insured allege negligence or other wrongdoing in the supervision, hiring, employment, training or monitoring of others by that insured if the "occurrence" which caused the "bodily injury" or "property damage" involved the ownership, maintenance, use or entrustment to others of any aircraft, "auto" or watercraft that is owned or operated by or rented or loaned to any insured.

This exclusion does not apply to:

(1)   A watercraft while ashore on premises you own or rent;

(2)   A watercraft you do not own that is:

    (a)   Less than 26 feet long; and

    (b)   Not being used to carry persons or property for a charge;

(3)   Parking an "auto" on, or on the ways next to, premises you own or rent, provided the "auto" is not owned by or rented or loaned to you or the insured; or

(4)   Liability assumed under any "insured contract" for the ownership, maintenance or use of aircraft or watercraft.

(5)   "Bodily injury" or "property damage" arising out of:

    (a)   the operation of machinery or equipment that is attached to, or a part of, a land vehicle that would qualify under the definition of "mobile equipment" if it were not subject to a compulsory or financial responsibility law or other motor vehicle insurance law where it is licensed or principally garaged; or

    (b)   the operation of any of the machinery or equipment listed in paragraph **f.(2)** or **f.(3)** of the definition of "mobile equipment".

The addition of *entrustment* to the exclusion appears to be more of a preventive measure, since most of the cases involving negligent entrustment of vehicles concern homeowners policies. While not all insureds have been successful in obtaining coverage for negligent entrustment, it can be a means to obtaining protection when no other insurance exists for a loss. The way a negligent entrustment claim usually arises is this: an owner of an auto lends it to a person who is a careless or an incompetent motorist. Following a claim stemming from the use of the auto, the owner, along with the permissive user, is sued. Since the owner does not have auto insurance, he or she looks to the personal liability coverage of the homeowners policy and maintains that coverage applies there. Despite an exclusion for the ownership, maintenance, or use of a motor vehicle, some courts have ruled for coverage. In doing so, the courts maintained that the resulting liability had nothing to do with the ownership, maintenance, or use of the auto, but, instead, with its negligent entrustment, or the insured's negligence in granting permission to use the vehicle, which is not excluded.

The second paragraph of this exclusion was new to the 2001 edition of the CGL form and is said by ISO to be a clarification that could result in a reduction of coverage in states where courts have ruled that the previous exclusion is inapplicable to negligent supervision and kindred claims.

One such case is *Pablo v. Moore*, 995 P.2d 460 (Mont. 2000), which involved an accident that occurred when a truck driven by a paving company's employee struck the rear end of an auto. The auto's occupants sued the paving company alleging in part that the owner was negligent in hiring, training, and supervising its employee. The owner sought coverage under its CGL policy. The insurer argued that this policy was not intended to cover the injuries sustained in this accident, since the injuries arose out of the use of an auto, and this exclusion precluded coverage. The court ruled against the insurer because the auto exclusion did not clearly and unambiguously exclude negligent hiring, training or supervision.

It is unclear whether this revised exclusionary language is broad enough to be all-encompassing. For example, one of the allegations in the above case was negligent failure to warn of a known danger. The paving company's owner drove past the accident site about ten minutes before the accident occurred and saw a large cloud of dust created by a state highway broom truck that obscured visibility. The allegation was that the paving company's owner was negligent in failing to use his cellular phone to notify his employee of the hazardous road condition. Currently, the only specific reference in CGL policies for a failure to warn is within the definitions of "your product" and "your work." Additional reference to failure to warn may be necessary in the auto exclusion, given the possibility of failure to warn being raised as an allegation in future claims involving autos.

Like the 1973 exclusion, the current one flatly excludes aircraft liability. (However, note the exception below.)

The current watercraft exclusion tracks with the 1973 general liability policy exclusion and the nonowned watercraft coverage provided in the broad form liability endorsement. Thus, coverage applies (1) if the watercraft is on shore on premises that the named insured owns or rents or (2) if the watercraft is not owned by the named insured, is less than twenty-six feet in length, and is not used to carry passengers or property for hire.

Exception (3) of the current exclusion achieves the same effect as a comparable portion of the 1973 exclusion: the policy covers liability arising out of the parking of autos on or adjacent to premises owned or rented by the named insured. However, the coverage does not apply if the auto is owned by or rented or loaned to any insured. Thus, the coverage is intended primarily for the parking of customers' autos, as when the insured provides valet parking services. Because of the care, custody, or control exclusion, to be discussed later in this chapter, the insured is not covered for damage to the car being parked. Garagekeepers coverage is needed to insure that exposure.

Under exception (4) of the current exclusion, coverage is provided for liability assumed under any insured contract for the ownership, maintenance, or use of aircraft or watercraft—but not an auto. In contrast, the contractual liability coverage of the broad form liability endorsement does not exclude auto liability. An insured with the current CGL form can cover auto liability assumed under contract through the business auto coverage form.

The last exception to exclusion g., under paragraph (5), refers to the operation of: machinery or equipment that is attached to, or part of, a land vehicle that would qualify under the definition of "mobile equipment" if it were not subject to a compulsory or financial responsibility law; or any of the equipment as listed in paragraphs f.(2) and f.(3) of the definition of "mobile equipment." That definition is examined in more detail below, but here it will suffice to say that paragraphs f.(2) and (3) of the definition relate to certain types of mobile equipment—cherry pickers, air compressors, pumps, generators, etc.—that are permanently attached to self-propelled vehicles. The definition merely states that such vehicles are to be considered as autos. Paragraph (5) of the exclusion makes it clear that operation of the equipment attached to such vehicles is not excluded, even though the vehicle to which the equipment is attached is an auto and therefore subject to the auto exclusion.

To illustrate, say that while a cherry picker mounted on a truck is being used by the insured to clear tree branches away from power lines, a large branch falls and damages a passing auto. A resulting liability claim against the insured would not be subject to the auto exclusion, since the damage arose out of the operation of the equipment attached to the vehicle. If, instead, the truck on which the cherry picker is mounted became involved in an intersection accident on the way to the next work site, coverage for the claim under the insured's CGL form would be precluded by the auto exclusion. The insured would need to have auto liability insurance on the vehicle in order to be covered for its operation.

Meaning of "Auto" and "Mobile Equipment"

The April 2013 CGL coverage forms define the word "auto" as follows:

"Auto" means:

a.   A land motor vehicle, trailer or semitrailer designed for travel on public roads, including any attached machinery or equipment; or

b.   Any other land vehicle that is subject to a compulsory or financial responsibility law or other motor vehicle insurance law where it is licensed or principally garaged.

However, "auto" does not include "mobile equipment."

Before one can determine more precisely what an auto may or may not be, the definition of "mobile equipment" must also be considered.

"Mobile equipment" means any of the following types of land vehicles, including any attached machinery or equipment:

a.   Bulldozers, farm machinery, forklifts and other vehicles designed for use principally off public roads;

b.   Vehicles maintained for use solely on or next to premises you own or rent;

c.   Vehicles that travel on crawler treads;

d.   Vehicles, whether self-propelled or not, maintained primarily to provide mobility to permanently mounted:

     (1)   Power cranes, shovels, loaders, diggers or drills; or

     (2)   Road construction or resurfacing equipment such as graders, scrapers or rollers;

e.   Vehicles not described in a., b., c. or d. above that are not self-propelled and are maintained primarily to provide mobility to permanently attached equipment of the following types:

     (1)   Air compressors, pumps and generators, including spraying, welding, building, cleaning, geophysical exploration, lighting and well servicing equipment; or

     (2)   Cherry pickers and similar devices used to raise or lower workers;

f.   Vehicles not described in a., b., c. or d. above maintained primarily for purposes other than the transportation of persons or cargo.

     However, self-propelled vehicles with the following types of permanently attached equipment are not "mobile equipment" but will be considered "autos":

     (1)   Equipment designed primarily for:

          (a)   Snow removal;

          (b)   Road maintenance, but not construction or resurfacing;

          (c)   Street cleaning;

> (2) Cherry pickers and similar devices mounted on automobile or truck chassis and used to raise or lower workers; and
>
> (3) Air compressors, pumps and generators, including spraying, welding, building cleaning, geophysical exploration, lighting and well servicing equipment.
>
> However, "mobile equipment" does not include land vehicles that are subject to a compulsory or financial responsibility law or other vehicle insurance law where it is licensed or principally garaged. Land vehicles subject to a compulsory or financial responsibility law or other motor vehicle insurance law are considered "autos."

The above definition of mobile equipment is both longer and more detailed than its counterpart in the 1973 CGL policy. To qualify as mobile equipment under the 1973 policy, a land vehicle, whether or not self-propelled, must come within one of four categories. The current definition entails six such categories and several subcategories. The apparent reason for the more detailed approach of the current definition is to state more precisely the types of vehicles that will be given mobile equipment status (and, hence, automatic coverage), rather than leaving the matter of status to interpretation that fosters both arguments and varying results, as is the case with the 1973 policy.

Paragraphs a. through c. of the current mobile equipment definition are quite straightforward and seldom result in misunderstandings. The remaining parts of the definition do sometimes create confusion and are therefore analyzed below.

Paragraph d. includes vehicles that might otherwise be considered "autos" if they were not being maintained primarily to provide mobility to the types of permanently mounted equipment described in subparts (1) and (2) of the exclusion. In addition, paragraph f. includes vehicles not described in paragraphs a, b, c, or d that are maintained primarily for purposes other than the transportation of persons or cargo. This open-ended description could include, for example, a truck maintained primarily to provide mobility to any of various types of mobile equipment not described in paragraph d. However, paragraph f. goes on to clarify that self-propelled vehicles with other types of permanently attached equipment are not mobile equipment but will be considered autos. See subparts (1), (2), and (3) of paragraph f.

It is important to note that subparts (1), (2), and (3) of paragraph f. do not eliminate CGL coverage for the listed types of equipment; they eliminate CGL coverage only for the vehicles to which the mobile equipment is attached. Thus, the CGL policy covers the operation of the attached equipment (for example, spraying equipment while being used at a job site) but does not cover the operation of the vehicle to which the mobile equipment is attached (unless the CGL policy is endorsed to do so). The ISO business auto coverage form covers the vehicle exposure if the vehicle qualifies as a covered auto under the particular policy, and it specifically excludes the operation of the attached equipment.

The types of equipment under subsections (1), (2), and (3) of paragraph f. are primarily those that were the subject of controversy under the 1973 policy. When the definition of mobile equipment was first introduced to general liability policy provisions in 1966, some insurers were reluctant to give mobile equipment status to certain vehicles that in the absence of the definition of mobile equipment would have been rated as automobiles. An example is a truck whose sole purpose is to provide mobility to building cleaning equipment permanently attached to the truck. As the definition of mobile equipment reads in the 1973 CGL policy, the truck should be covered automatically under the CGL policy rather than rated separately under the insured's automobile policy.

Indicative of the kind of problems under the 1973 definition of mobile equipment was a case that involved a pickup truck to which welding equipment was bolted and welded. The insured had an automobile policy, which did not list this truck, and a comprehensive general liability policy. Both policies were with different insurers. When claim was made under the liability policy, the insurer denied it on the ground that the truck was not maintained for the sole purpose of providing mobility to the welding equipment, since the truck was also used for the insured's personal use.

In construing the definition of mobile equipment, a Louisiana appeals court hearing this case held that the truck was a type of equipment covered by the liability policy. The court's rationale was that a land vehicle is mobile equipment if it is designed (i.e., structurally suited) or maintained (i.e., functionally suited) for the sole purpose of providing mobility to the equipment attached to it. The case is *Doty v. Safeco Ins. Co.*, 400 So. 2d 718 (La. App. 1981). Because of paragraph f. of the current definition, the vehicle involved in this case would clearly appear to be an auto under the current CGL forms, rather than mobile equipment, and would need to be insured under an automobile policy.

Paragraph e. of the mobile equipment definition gives mobile equipment status to vehicles that are not self-propelled and are maintained primarily to provide mobility to permanently attached equipment of the types specified. Liability coverage would apply here to both the existence and operations exposures of such equipment. However, when equipment in this category is being transported by an auto, the equipment is covered under the insured's business auto coverage form, rather than under either of the CGL coverage forms, because of exclusion h. (see below), which excludes mobile equipment while being transported by an auto owned or operated by or rented or loaned to any insured.

2004 Revision Affecting Mobile Equipment

The last paragraph of the definition of mobile equipment, added with the 2004 revisions, attempts to make clear that a land vehicle that is subject to compulsory or financial responsibility or other motor vehicle insurance laws is not intended to be considered as mobile equipment and, therefore, is not covered for its over-the-road exposures under the CGL policy.

The reference to compulsory insurance laws in the new wording includes laws requiring insurers to offer or provide uninsured motorists (UM) coverage. Since becoming mandatory in many states for both personal and commercial auto risks, UM coverage has become a thorn in the side of many insurers, particularly those issuing the CGL policy. These insurers often are required to pay for UM claims involving injuries sustained by operators of mobile equipment. The intent has been to cover mobile equipment exposures under general liability provisions since standard forms were introduced in 1941. In fact, with the 1966 CGL policy provisions, a condition entitled *financial responsibility laws* was added in order to certify registered mobile equipment under financial responsibility laws of states and Canadian provinces.

This condition was eliminated with the 1973 CGL policy, and an endorsement—Motor Vehicle Laws, CG 99 01 11 85—was introduced with the 1986 CGL forms to replace the condition. Prior to this endorsement, coverage, when applicable, was automatic. In other words, the burden was on the insurer to provide coverage to mobile equipment involved in accidents on public roads. With the introduction of CG 99 01 in 1986, the burden shifted to the named insured to request the motor vehicle laws endorsement when an exposure arose.

Apparently, uninsured motorists, no-fault, and kindred coverages were still being required by some courts to be provided by the CGL form, despite the absence of this endorsement request. So, CG 99 01 was withdrawn and the CGL form was revised in 2004, so that mobile equipment and other land motor vehicles subject to compulsory or financial responsibility laws or other motor vehicle insurance laws are no longer covered by the CGL policy but, instead, are considered to be autos.

Exclusion H—Mobile Equipment

Although mobile equipment is generally insured under the CGL forms, there are two situations, set forth in the following exclusion, when mobile equipment is not covered. The exclusion applies to:

"Bodily injury" or "property damage" arising out of:

(1)   The transportation of "mobile equipment" by an "auto" owned or operated by or rented or loaned to any insured; or

(2)   The use of "mobile equipment" in, or while in practice for, or while being prepared for, any prearranged racing, speed, demolition, or stunting activity.

The reason for part (1) of the current exclusion is that mobile equipment while being transported is considered to be part of the auto and therefore covered by the insured's auto policy, if any. The reason for part (2) of the exclusion is to exclude exposures that are particularly hazardous and require specialized insurance if those excluded events are to be undertaken.

Exclusion I—War

The 1973 general liability policy war exclusion applied to:

"Bodily injury" or "property damage" due to war, whether or not declared, or any act or condition incident to war. War includes civil war, insurrection, rebellion or revolution. This exclusion applies only to liability assumed under a contract or agreement.

Although this exclusion had not, in the past, been the subject of much scrutiny, insurance buyers should not have been surprised to eventually see an expansion of the war risk exclusion, particularly in light of the terrorist attack on the World Trade Center on September 11, 2001.

ISO introduced three war endorsements in 2002 that expanded the war exclusion beyond contractually assumed liability to eliminate coverage for bodily injury or property damage arising out of any type of war or warlike action. One such endorsement, CG 00 62, was developed for use with the CGL coverage forms. Endorsement CG 00 63 was to be used with the Owners and Contractors Protective Liability (OCP) coverage form. And, endorsement CG 00 64 was designed for use with the liquor liability, pollution liability, railroad protective liability, and underground storage tank coverage forms.

With its 2004 commercial liability changes, ISO withdrew these endorsements and replaced the prior war exclusion with the new exclusionary wording that eliminates coverage for:

"Bodily injury" or "property damage", however caused, arising, directly or indirectly, out of: _

(1)   War, including undeclared or civil war;

(2)   Warlike action by a military force, including action in hindering or defending against an actual or expected attack, by any government, sovereign, or other authority using military personnel or other agents; or

(3)   Insurrection, rebellion, revolution, usurped power, or action taken by governmental authority in hindering or defending against any of these.

Exclusion J—Damage to Property

Exclusion j. of the current CGL forms is a combination of the care, custody, or control and alienated premises exclusions of the 1973 general liability policy and various exclusions in the broad form property damage (BFPD) provisions. When the 1986 CGL forms were introduced, ISO prepared a chart comparing the then new occurrence form with the 1973 occurrence form. On the subject of property damage, including broad form property damage coverage, the chart stated that the "Exclusions have been completely rewritten and clarified with no change in overall scope of coverage."[7] There are, however, some new twists to the exclusions as found in the current forms, such as the following:

1.   Limitation of the care, custody, or control exclusion to *personal* property;

2.   Elimination of the exception allowing coverage for damage to property in the care, custody, or control of the insured resulting from use of elevators;

3.   Amendment of the alienated premises exclusion with respect to speculative building;

4.   Limitation of the "faulty workmanship" exclusion to ongoing operations; and

5.   A limitation on coverage for mitigation costs to prevent further damage to property of others.

These and other differences between the 1973 and post-1986 versions of the exclusions are discussed in more detail following quotation of exclusion j.

The current version of the exclusion applies to the following.

"Property damage" to:

(1)   Property you own, rent, or occupy, including any costs or expenses incurred by you, or any other person, organization or entity, for repair, replacement, enhancement, restoration or maintenance of such property for any reason, including prevention of injury to a person or damage to another's property;

(2)   Premises you sell, give away or abandon, if the "property damage" arises out of any part of those premises;

(3)   Property loaned to you;

(4)   Personal property in the care, custody or control of the insured;

(5)   That particular part of real property on which you or any contractors or subcontractors working directly or indirectly on your behalf are performing operations, if the "property damage" arises out of those operations; or

(6)   That particular part of any property that must be restored, repaired or replaced because "your work" was incorrectly performed on it.

Paragraphs (1), (3) and (4) of this exclusion do not apply to "property damage" (other than damage by fire) to premises, including the contents of such premises, rented to you for a period of seven or fewer consecutive days. A separate limit of insurance applies to Damage To Premises Rented To You as described in Section III—Limits of Insurance.

Paragraph (2) of this exclusion does not apply if the premises are "your work" and were never occupied, rented or held for rental by you.

Paragraphs (3), (4), (5) and (6) of this exclusion do not apply to liability assumed under a sidetrack agreement.

Paragraph (6) of this exclusion does not apply to property damage included in the products-completed operations hazard.

Paragraph (1)—Insured's Property

Paragraph (1) of exclusion j. corresponds to exclusion k(1) of the 1973 general liability policy. Since the word "property" is not qualified, this exclusion applies to both real and personal property that the named insured owns, rents, or occupies. The purpose of the exclusion is to avoid covering an exposure that can be insured by some form of property insurance. The only exception to the exclusion, stated at the end of the Coverage A exclusions, is for damage by fire to premises while rented to the named insured or temporarily occupied by the named insured with permission of the owner, thus providing fire legal liability coverage.

The portion of paragraph (1) that follows "Property you own, rent or occupy" was added in the 2001 CGL revision. This phraseology, which ISO refers to as a clarification, precludes costs incurred by the named insured or by others to repair, replace, enhance, restore or maintain property the named insured owns, rents or occupies for any reason, including the prevention of injury to a person or damage to another's property.

The basis for this new wording is *Aetna Insurance Co. v. Aaron*, 685 A.2d 858 (Md. App. 1996), which involved a suit brought by a condominium association against one of its unit owners for costs the association incurred to repair the unit owner's glass enclosure in order to prevent damage to another unit owner. ISO's explanation is that the CGL policy is not intended to pay for expenses incurred for repairs, etc. made on the insured's own property for any reason. The exclusion is primarily aimed at insureds involved in environmental situations where the insureds apply for coverage for the costs incurred in cleaning up their property because a pollutant has or is threatening to harm the natural resources. There is a good argument for coverage in the absence of this additional wording

Paragraph (2)—Alienated Premises

Paragraph (2) corresponds to exclusion l. of the 1973 liability policy, commonly referred to as the alienated premises exclusion. Its purpose is to preclude coverage for damage to property that has been sold, given away, or abandoned. For example, say the insured sells a building with a fire hazard that is neither disclosed by the insured nor clearly visible to the purchaser. If the building sustains fire damage as a result of the undisclosed hazard, the insured will have no protection in the event he or she is sued. However, the exclusion does not reach bodily injury and damage to property other than the alienated premises.

One of the problems with this part of exclusion j. is that in some cases it can create an ambiguity. An example is where an insured and a subcontractor construct a dwelling. The insured occupies the dwelling for one year and then sells it. Following sale, it is partially damaged because of a defect in the work of the subcontractor. The question is: Did the damage arise out of the premises sold? Or did the property damage arise out of the work performed on behalf of the insured? It would seem that but for the construction work in the first place, the property damage would not be within the scope of the premises alienated (premises you sell) exclusion j. (2), but instead, the subject of coverage in light of the exception to the "damage to your work" exclusion l. This exception states that the damage to your work exclusion does not apply "if the damaged work or the work out of which the damage arises was performed on your behalf by a subcontractor."

The main difference between the 1973 and current versions of the exclusion is that the current one is subject to an exception stating that the exclusion does not apply if the premises are *your work* and were never occupied, rented, or held for rental by the named insured. The definition of "your work" is quoted later but may be briefly defined for present purposes to mean work or operations performed by or on behalf of the named insured. This exception makes it clear that the exclusion does not apply to houses or other real estate built on speculation, as long as the builder never occupied the property, rented it, or held it for rental. Thus, a completed house built on speculation has the same coverage under the current CGL forms as one built under contract with a property owner, and cannot be flatly excluded by the alienated premises exclusion, as sometimes happened under the 1973 policy despite the fact that the loss would otherwise be covered by the insured's BFPD coverage.

Paragraph (3)—Property Loaned to Named Insured

Paragraph (3), excluding "property loaned to you," is wording found on current CGL forms. While both real and personal property loaned to the named insured could, depending on the circumstances, be reached by paragraphs (1) and (4) of exclusion j., this additional wording is likely to tie up any loose ends.

Paragraph (4)—Care, Custody, or Control

Paragraph (4) is the counterpart to the 1973 care, custody, or control exclusion. However, the current version applies only to personal property, whereas the 1973 version could apply to either real or personal property. Moreover, the current exclusion does not retain the former reference to property "as to which the insured is for any purpose exercising physical control." Nor does it have any exception, as the 1973 version does, providing coverage for property damage (other than to the elevator itself) arising out of the use of an elevator at the insured's premises. Consequently, an insured under the current CGL forms needs to arrange some other form of insurance to cover personal property of others in its care, custody, or control that can be damaged by use of its elevators, if such coverage is desired. Exclusion j. of the current CGL forms does, however, contain an exception of liability assumed under a sidetrack agreement, which applies to paragraphs (3) through (6) of the exclusion. A similar exception applies to the 1973 care, custody, or control exclusion and to comparable BFPD exclusions.

The fact that the care, custody, or control exclusion applies only to personal property should not be taken to mean that the insured has coverage for real property in its care, custody, or control in every case. Apart from the portions of exclusion j. already discussed, which can apply to real property in certain situations, parts (5) and (6) of the same exclusion can also apply to real property.

Before addressing parts (5) and (6), however, it should be pointed out that when BFPD coverage was added to the 1973 comprehensive general liability policy, the care, custody, or control exclusion of the liability policy was deleted in its entirety. In place of the deleted exclusion, BFPD coverage imposed a number of more specific exclusions. The retention in the current CGL forms of the care, custody, or control exclusion as respects personal property perhaps explains why some of these BFPD exclusions have no specific counterparts in the current forms. The exclusions omitted from the BFPD endorsement relate to the following:

- Property entrusted to the insured for storage or safekeeping;

- Property while on the insured's premises for purposes of having operations performed on it;

- Tools or equipment while being used by the insured; and

- Property in the insured's custody that is to be installed, erected, or used in construction by the insured.

It is problematical to say whether the current approach will result in more or less coverage than was available under the BFPD provisions. However, it seems possible that the blanket exclusion of personal property in the care, custody, or control of the named insured could have a wider scope of application than the separate, more specific BFPD exclusions.

In the 1986 edition of the CGL coverage forms, the care, custody, or control exclusion applies to personal property of the named insured ("you"). This means that the exclusion does not apply to personal property in the care, custody, or control of other (unnamed) insureds under the policy. The 1990 and later versions of this exclusion apply to property damage to "personal property in the care, custody, or control of the insured."

The 1998 revision declared that paragraphs (1), (3) and (4) of this exclusion do not apply to premises and contents of such premises that are rented to the named insured for a period of seven or fewer consecutive days. For example, if an employee of the named insured rents a hotel room on a business trip and negligently causes damage to the room or its contents, the named insured's CGL form will provide property damage coverage for the insured.

This coverage revision does not refer to damage by fire to premises rented to the named insured; that loss exposure is already covered under the fire damage, or fire legal liability, clause of the CGL forms, which will be discussed at the end of this chapter. However, the same limit, called the "damage to premises rented to you limit" in the 1998 and later editions, applies to both the coverage described in the paragraph above and fire legal liability coverage. Whether the damage is caused by fire or some other negligent action on the part of the insured, the insurer will pay no more than the "damage to premises rented to you limit" shown on the declarations page.

Paragraph (5)—Property Being Worked On

The counterpart to paragraph (5) of exclusion j. is the BFPD exclusion of the following:

... that particular part of any property not on premises owned by or rented to the insured, (i) upon which operations are being performed by or on behalf of the insured at the time of the property damage arising out of such operations, or (ii) out of which any property damage arises.

The only substantive difference between paragraph (5) and the BFPD exclusion is the limitation of paragraph (5) to *real property*.

The purpose of paragraph (5) and its BFPD counterpart is to exclude only "that particular part" of property on which work is being performed by or on behalf of the insured. For example, say that a subcontractor is erecting steel beams in a building. One of the beams falls while being attached and damages the work of the general contractor and other subcontractors. The general contractor, if held responsible for the loss, should be protected under its policy for damage caused by the beam, but coverage should not be expected for damage to the beam that fell.

If considered real property, the beam is excluded as "that particular part of real property..." If considered personal property, because it was not yet attached to the realty, paragraph (6), as discussed below, would presumably exclude coverage for the fallen beam.

Paragraph (6)—Faulty Workmanship

Paragraph (6) of exclusion j. is derived from the BFPD exclusion of damage "to that particular part of any property, not on premises owned by or rented to the insured, the restoration, repair or replacement of which has been made necessary by faulty workmanship *thereon* by or on behalf of the insured (emphasis added)." The versions of this "faulty workmanship" exclusion found in the BFPD provision and in the 1986 and later editions of the CGL coverage forms differ in at least two ways.

First, the BFPD exclusion applies only to property away from premises owned by or rented to the insured, while the current exclusion applies to work being performed either on or off the insured's premises. This should not amount to a significant difference in coverage, however, since BFPD coverage is subject to an exclusion of damage to property on the insured's premises for purposes of having operations performed on such property. This exclusion has not been carried forward into the current CGL forms, but they achieve much the same effect through their exclusion of damage to personal property in the care, custody, or control of the insured. Thus, both BFPD coverage and the current CGL forms will ordinarily exclude an entire piece of personal property (not merely "that particular part") that is on the insured's premises (i.e., in the insured's care) for purposes of having work performed on it by the insured. The chief applicability of the current faulty workmanship exclusion should therefore be to property away from the insured's premises.

If the insured is working on personal property away from his or her own premises, coverage for damage to other than "that particular part" will depend on whether the entire piece of property is in the insured's care, custody, or control. If the entire piece of personal property is in the insured's care, custody, or control, damage to the entire piece of property is excluded by the care, custody, or control exclusion. If the rest of the property is not in the insured's care, custody, or control, then only paragraph (6) applies, and the insured is covered for the entire loss except for "that particular part" whose replacement was required because of faulty workmanship. Since the current care, custody, or control exclusion applies only to personal property, real property the insured is working on is never subject to that exclusion.

A second way in which paragraph (6) differs from its BFPD counterpart is that it is specifically stated not to apply to property damage within the products-completed operations hazard. This does not mean that the insured therefore has coverage for damage to his or her own completed work in every case; on the contrary, exclusion l., discussed later in this chapter, defines the scope of coverage for damage to work within the products-completed operations hazard. However, the exception of completed work from paragraph (6) does eliminate from the current CGL forms the uncertainty under BFPD provisions of whether the faulty workmanship exclusion applies only to ongoing operations or to completed operations as well. In cases involving faulty work of subcontractors, it is to the insured's benefit not to have the faulty workmanship exclusion apply. This issue is discussed in more detail along with exclusion l.

A court decision involving broad form property damage coverage that has application to the 1986 and subsequent CGL forms is *National Union Fire Insurance Company of Pittsburgh, PA v. Structural Systems Technology, Inc.*, 756 F. Supp. 1232 (E.D. Mo. 1991). Briefly, the facts are as follows: SST contracted with Gillette Company for the erection of a 2,000 foot broadcasting tower. The land on which the tower was to be erected was owned by a married couple who leased it to Gillette. SST contracted with a subcontractor (L&RT) for diagonal rods to be used in the tower. SST also contracted with KIRX, Inc. to redesign the tower to accommodate an antenna and transmission line. After SST installed the television transmission equipment onto the tower and the television station began transmitting, defects were discovered in the tower. It was determined that the cracks were attributed to the work of the subcontractor (L&RT). While SST employees were repairing the tower and replacing the diagonal rods of the subcontractor, the tower collapsed and all equipment was destroyed.

All parties involved were sued for damages involving destruction of the tower, its transmission line, antenna system and associated equipment, diminution in the value of the station, and lost profits. The insurer of SST's commercial general liability policy denied defense and indemnification of damages based on "damage to your product" exclusion k., "damage to your work" exclusion l., and broad form property damage exclusions j. (4), (5), and (6).

Since the tower was considered to be real property, the court held that the "damage to your product" exclusion k. was inapplicable. Other reasons why this exclusion was inapplicable were that the tower was constructed by SST and not manufactured by it, and the other equipment furnished by SST was not "sold, handled, distributed or disposed of" by SST. (Within this context, "handle" meant to "deal or trade in," rather than to touch.)

Likewise "damage to your work" exclusion l. was held to be inapplicable because, at the time of the collapse, the only work being performed was the repair by SST of the tower with the replacement rods, which were not considered to be "your work" (SST's work) but rather the work of the subcontractor, L&RT. Furthermore, the damage to your work exclusion l. does not apply if the damaged work or work out of which the damage arises was performed on the named insured's behalf by a subcontractor. The insurer argued that this exception to exclusion l. did not apply because the supplier of the diagonal rods was a material man rather than a subcontractor. However, this argument of the insurer also was overruled.

Regarding the damage to property exclusion, the court held as follows:

- With respect to exclusion j.(5): this exclusion applies to the tower if it is determined that the collapse arose out of the actual repair operations, as opposed to out of the alleged defective rods. The insurer therefore had the obligation to defend because of the potential for coverage. However, if it is determined that the collapse arose out of the tower, exclusion j.(5) will apply and the insurer will have no obligation to pay damages. However, the destruction of other equipment, for example, transmission lines and antenna system, are not excluded by j.(5) because they were not real property.

- With respect to exclusion j.(6): the tower was not excluded because the damage fell within the products-completed operations hazard exception. Such exception applied here, the court explained, since the work being conducted was treated as completed in that the work of SST was characterized as "service, maintenance, correction, repair or replacement." The other equipment alleged to have been damaged was not excluded because it was not being restored, repaired, or replaced.

- With respect to diminution in value of property and lost profits: To the extent there is property damage coverage, both diminution in value of property and lost profits are covered.

Exclusion K—Damage to "Your Product"

The exclusion of damage to the named insured's products applies to:

"Property damage" to "your product" arising out of it or any part of it.

The extent to which this exclusion may apply to property damage, whether it involves physical injury to tangible property or loss of use of tangible property that has not been physically injured, hinges on the meaning of "your product." This term is defined as follows:

"Your product":

a. Means:

    (1) Any goods or products, other than real property, manufactured, sold, handled, distributed or disposed of by:

       (a)   You;

       (b)   Others trading under your name; or

       (c)   A person or organization whose business or assets you have acquired; and,

   (2)   Containers (other than vehicles), materials, parts or equipment furnished in connection with such goods or products.

  b.   Includes:

   (1)   Warranties or representations made at any time with respect to the fitness, quality, durability, performance or use of "your product," and,

   (2)   The providing of or failure to provide warnings or instructions.

  c.   Does not include vending machines or other property rented to or located for the use of others but not sold.

The specific exception of real property under part a. makes it clear that work performed by contractors on buildings, structures, and other realty is not considered to be the named insured's product. Some insurers have used the injury to products exclusion of the 1973 general liability policy (or the fictitious work/product exclusion) to deny completed operations losses that would otherwise have been covered under the insured's BFPD coverage. Similar denials of coverage under the current CGL forms are clearly incorrect.

Another noteworthy provision is a.(1c). Since the current CGL forms, like the broad form liability endorsement, automatically cover mergers and acquisitions for ninety days (see Chapter 5), all the exposures that confront the purchased or acquired firm are relevant, including liability for products previously sold by the acquired firm. Provision a.(1c) makes it clear that the current CGL forms cover that products exposure. Whether a successor is liable for damage caused by a product sold by the predecessor does not have a clear-cut answer.[8]

The fact that "your product" includes warranties and representations does not mean that product warranty insurance is being provided, as some insureds might like to believe. If coverage is to apply, there must be bodily injury or property damage resulting from such warranty or representation— other than to the product itself.

However, there should be coverage for physical damage to another entity's product in which the insured's product has been incorporated as a component. Naturally, the cost of the insured's own product (the component) would not be payable, due to exclusion k. If the other entity's product is not physically injured, but is merely rendered unusable because of the insured's component, coverage for the product (exclusive of the insured's component product) will depend on whether exclusion m. of the current CGL forms, dealing with "impaired property," applies to the loss. Exclusion m. is discussed later in this chapter.

In 1990, the definition of "your product" was amended to include "the providing of or failure to provide warnings or instructions." This provision was added in response to court decisions upholding coverage— despite policy exclusions of the products-completed operations hazard— for products liability suits alleging the manufacturer's failure to provide warnings. The rationale for coverage was that the products exclusion did not specifically preclude coverage for liability stemming from the failure of a manufacturer to provide warnings or instructions for its product.

One of the earlier cases to uphold coverage for this reason is *Cooling v. United States Fidelity & Guaranty Company*, 269 So. 2d 294 (La. App. 1972). This action arose when the insured sold diesel engines and failed to warn the buyer about the adequacy of safety devices that would have made the engines safer to operate. As a result of an accident and injury, the insured was sued based on the failure to warn constituting actionable negligence. The court ruled in favor of the insured because of the absence of an express exclusion in the policy for injuries arising out of the failure of the insured to warn that machinery it sold could have been operated more safely with additional equipment. For later cases, see *American Trailer Service, Inc. v. The Home Insurance Company*, 361 N.W.2d 918 (Minn. App. 1985); *Chancler v. American Hardware Mutual Insurance Company*, 694 P.2d 1301 (Ida. App. 1985) *rev'd* 712 P.2d 542; and *Keystone Spray Equipment, Inc. v. Regis Insurance Company*, 767 A.2d 572 (Pa. Super. 2000).

The 1990 policy amendment concerning the failure to warn is directed at those instances when the CGL form is endorsed specifically to exclude the products-completed operations coverages. Its purpose is to put an end to the loophole that has allowed some insureds to obtain coverage despite a specific exclusion of the products-completed operations hazard. When products liability is not excluded, the 1990 addition clarifies that products suits based on failure to warn are subject to the aggregate limit that applies to products and completed operations.

Exclusion L—Damage to "Your Work"

Exclusion l. of the current CGL forms eliminates coverage for:

> "Property damage" to "your work" arising out of it or any part of it and included in the "products-completed operations hazard."

This exclusion does not apply if the damaged work or the work out of which the damage arises was performed on your behalf by a subcontractor.

Since the term "your work" is an integral part of that exclusion, it must be understood as well. It is defined as follows:

"Your work" means:

a.   Means:

(1)   Work or operations performed by you or on your behalf; and,

(2)   Materials, parts or equipment furnished in connection with such work or operations.

b.   Includes:

(1)   Warranties or representations made at any time with respect to the fitness, quality, durability, performance or use of "your work" and,

(2)   The providing of or failure to provide warnings or instructions.

In 1990, the definition of "your work" was amended to include "the providing of or failure to provide warnings or instructions" for the same reason as that phrase is included in the definition of "your product." Refer to "Exclusion K—Damage to Your Product" for the rationale of this phrasing.

Since the injury to work performed exclusion applies only to the products-completed operations hazard, it is important to quote that term's definition here as well. The definition is similar, but not identical, to the definitions of "products hazard" and "completed operations hazard" of the 1973 liability provisions. The 2001 and the current version of the definition is quoted below.

"Products-completed operations hazard":

a.   Includes all "bodily injury" and "property damage" occurring away from premises you own or rent and arising out of "your product" or "your work" except:

(1)   Products that are still in your physical possession; or

(2)   Work that has not yet been completed or abandoned. However, "your work" will be deemed completed at the earliest of the following times:

(a)   When all of the work called for in your contract has been completed.

    (b)   When all of the work to be done at the job site has been completed if your contract calls for work at more than one job site.

    (c)   When that part of the work done at a job site has been put to its intended use by any person or organization other than another contractor or subcontractor working on the same project.

Work that may need service, maintenance, correction, repair or replacement, but which is otherwise complete, will be treated as completed.

    b.   Does not include "bodily injury" or "property damage" arising out of:

    (1)   The transportation of property, unless the injury or damage arises out of a condition in or on a vehicle not owned or operated by you, and that condition was created by the "loading or unloading" of that vehicle by any insured;

    (2)   The existence of tools, uninstalled equipment or abandoned or unused materials;

    (3)   Products or operations for which the classification listed in the Declarations or in a policy schedule states that products-completed operations are subject to the General Aggregate Limit.

The injury to work performed exclusion of the 1973 general liability forms eliminates coverage for property damage to work performed by or on behalf of the insured arising out of the work or any part of it, including materials, parts, and equipment furnished in connection therewith. That exclusion differs from exclusion l. of the current forms in two noteworthy ways.

First, the current exclusion applies only to work within the products-completed operations hazard, whereas the 1973 exclusion applies to either completed work or work in progress. However, exclusion j. of the current forms, as discussed earlier, does apply to work in progress.

The second, perhaps more significant difference between the 1973 exclusion and the current one is that the current one is clearly stated not to apply if the damaged work or the work out of which the damage arises was performed by a subcontractor. Thus, with respect to completed operations, if the named insured becomes liable for damage to work performed by a subcontractor—or for damage to the named insured's own work arising out of a subcontractor's work—the exclusion should not apply to the resulting damage. Neither, apparently, should any exclusion apply to the named insured's liability for damage to a subcontractor's work out of which the damage to other property arises. If, for example, a subcontractor's faulty wiring causes an entire building to burn and the general contractor is sued for the entire loss by the building owner, the general contractor's CGL coverage form should cover his liability for the entire amount of the loss, including the cost of the failed wiring. If, instead, the loss had originated in work performed by the general contractor, the general contractor would be covered only for damage to work performed by subcontractors; there would be no recovery for any work performed by the named insured (general contractor).

As discussed more fully in Chapter 6, this exception to exclusion l., concerning damage to work performed by subcontractors, was the leading reason construction defects were held to be covered under the policies of general contractors. To combat many of these types of cases, ISO introduced two endorsements in 2001, discussed in Chapter 6. One of these endorsements is applicable on a blanket basis (CG 22 94), and the other is a site-specific exclusion (CG 22 95).

Even though these two endorsements are available to eliminate coverage for damage to work performed by subcontractors on the named insured's behalf, some insurers have tried to eliminate coverage without issuing either one of those two endorsements. One way is to argue that the exception to the exclusion only applies to work performed on the named insured's behalf by a subcontractor and the one who was performing work was a materialman instead. (See *National Union Fire Ins. Co. of Pittsburgh, PA v. Structural Systems Technology, Inc., discussed earlier in this chapter.*) The second, and perhaps more important way, is for insurers to deny coverage by maintaining that defective work is neither an occurrence nor property damage, regardless of who does the work. By taking this approach, it is unnecessary to take into consideration this or any other exclusion of the CGL policy, since both an occurrence and the presence of property damage are necessary before considering exclusions. Although some courts of states have accepted this argument of insurers, other states, such as Arkansas, Colorado, Hawaii, and South Carolina, have enacted statutes aimed at the restrictive interpretations of the courts. In essence, these statutes, require insurers to interpret the term "occurrence" to include faulty work. As a result, while defective work is itself excluded, damages flowing from defective work are still considered to be a covered occurrence. In the meantime, some insurers are offering buy-back coverage in those states where the courts have ruled that the result of defective work is not an occurrence and where statutes have not been enacted. However, this coverage, for the most part is inferior. Other insurers have taken the approach of issuing endorsements, without additional charge, making clear that damages from defective work are still considered to be a covered occurrence.

The previous BFPD provisions, when arranged to include completed operations coverage, have a similar effect, which is accomplished by deletion of the injury to work performed exclusion found in the 1973 general liability forms. In its place, the BFPD provisions substitute a similar exclusion, but without any reference to work performed on behalf of the named insured. When read in isolation, this exclusion allows for the same scope of coverage as found under the current injury to work performed exclusion.

However, insurers have frequently cited the separate faulty workmanship exclusion (discussed earlier with reference to paragraph (6) of exclusion j.) to deny BFPD coverage for damage to a subcontractor's failed work from which the injury to other property arose. In the current CGL forms, paragraph (6) of exclusion j.—the counterpart to the BFPD faulty workmanship exclusion—is clearly stated not to apply to work within the products-completed operations hazard and thus precludes the possibility of its being applied to a completed operations loss.

Paragraph (5) of exclusion j. also seems inapplicable to most completed operations claims, due not to a specific exception but to its own wording: "That particular part of real property on which you or any contractors or subcontractors working directly or indirectly on your behalf are performing operations." If the named insured or subcontractors are performing operations on the property at the time of the loss, it is quite unlikely that the operations will have been "completed" at the same time.

If the named insured becomes liable for damage to its subcontractor's work before operations are completed, one or more subparts of exclusion j. may apply to the claim, as discussed earlier. That is, if a subcontractor's faulty electrical work caused the building to burn before completion, paragraphs (5) and (6) of exclusion j. would eliminate coverage for the faulty electrical work. Damage to other real property arising out of the faulty work would not be excluded. Coverage for damage to personal property arising out of the faulty work would depend on whether other subparts of exclusion j.—such as the exclusion of personal property in the insured's care, custody, or control—are applied to the loss.

Exclusion M—Damage to Impaired Property or Property Not Physically Injured

Exclusion m. is comparable to the so-called failure-to-perform exclusion of previous general liability forms, yet may come to be known as the "impaired property" exclusion, due to its use of that term as introduced in 1986.

The failure-to-perform exclusion has had a controversial history since it was first introduced under standard policy provisions in 1966. The first version contained an exception for active malfunctioning that was difficult to understand, and it worked to the detriment of insurers. The second version, introduced in 1973, has proved to be somewhat clearer, but it is not quite as "tight" as insurers might have wanted. The current version of the exclusion seems to address two weaknesses of previous CGL policies. These weaknesses are discussed subsequently.

The current exclusion applies to:

"Property damage" to "impaired property" or property that has not been physically injured, arising out of:

(1) A defect, deficiency, inadequacy or dangerous condition in "your product" or in "your work"; or,

(2) A delay or failure by you or anyone acting on your behalf to perform a contract or agreement in accordance with its terms.

This exclusion does not apply to the loss of use of other property arising out of sudden and accidental physical injury to "your product" or "your work" after it has been put to its intended use.

The policy definitions of "your product" and "your work" are quoted and explained earlier in this chapter, in connection with exclusions k. and l. The definition of impaired property is as follows:

"Impaired property" means tangible property, other than "your product" or "your work," that cannot be used or is less useful because:

a.   It incorporates "your product" or "your work" that is known or thought to be defective, deficient, inadequate or dangerous; or

b.   You have failed to fulfill the terms of a contract or agreement;

if such property can be restored to use by:

a.   The repair, replacement, adjustment or removal of "your product" or "your work"; or

b.   Your fulfilling the terms of the contract or agreement.

The effect of the 1986 and later versions of the exclusion is largely the same as that of the 1973 version. However, the 1973 version applies only to *loss of use* of tangible property which has not been physically injured or destroyed resulting from…, whereas the current one applies to property damage to "impaired property" *or* to property (not merely its loss of use) that has not been physically injured.

While the definition of impaired property, like the entire 1973 exclusion, is aimed at *loss of use* of property that has not been physically injured, the other part of the current lead-in language—the reference to "property that has not been physically injured"—transcends loss of use, and in that respect it enlarges the scope of the current exclusion.

The purpose of the impaired property exclusion is to exclude damages or costs or both associated with tangible property that cannot be used, or is made less useful, because (1) it incorporates the named insured's product or work, or (2) the named insured fails to fulfill the terms of a contract—but only if that property can be restored to use by the repair, removal, or replacement of the work or product or by fulfilling the terms of the contract.

To understand the application of the impaired property exclusion, one must read the exclusion and definition of impaired property in concert. In doing so, one should note the following:

- The exclusion acknowledges that the incorporation of a defective product or work into other property constitutes property damage.

- The exclusion is inapplicable if the property damage amounts to loss of use of other tangible property arising from the sudden and accidental physical injury to the named insured's product or work; or conversely, the exclusion is applicable if the loss of use of other tangible property does not arise from the sudden and accidental physical injury to the named insured's product or work.

- If the property damage did not arise from sudden and accidental physical injury to the named insured's product or work and the property damage was due to the incorporation of such work or product: (1) if the damaged property can be corrected or fixed through the repair, removal or replacement of the named insured's product or work, then such property damage is excluded; or (2) if the damaged property cannot be corrected or fixed through the repair, removal, or replacement of the named insured's product or work, then the impaired property exclusion does not apply and the property damage is covered.

- If the property damage did not arise from the sudden and accidental physical injury to the named insured's product or work, and the resulting loss of use is due to breach of contract, (1) if the other property can be restored to use by full performance of the contract, then the property damage is excluded; or (2) if the other property cannot be restored to use by full performance of the contract, then the impaired property exclusion does not apply and the property damage is covered.

Based on the above principles, the following are some examples dealing with the mechanics of this exclusion:

(1)   A contractor's careless work on an underground storage tank causes the contents to leak into the ground. The impaired property exclusion would not apply because the loss of the tank's contents cannot be restored to use by the repair, removal or replacement of the tank.

(2)   A manufacturer's machine part component, when added to another manufacturer's product, causes the machine to fail to work properly. The impaired property exclusion should apply to the machine's loss of use, because the machine can be restored to use with the repair, removal or replacement of the defective component.

(3)   Defective roof insulation work of one contractor causes corrosion damage to the roofing work of another contractor thus necessitating the replacement of the insulation and roof. The impaired property exclusion should not be applicable because the resulting corrosion damage to property of others cannot be eliminated through the repair, removal or replacement of the defective roof insulation.

(4)   Lumber used to build houses is discovered to be defective and presents the high probability that the houses may become unsafe in time. The owners not only sustain loss of use of their houses because of the potentially unsafe condition, but also diminution in the value of the property.

Whether the impaired property exclusion applies in this last instance is a question that cannot be answered. The ultimate question is whether the houses can be restored to use with the repair or replacement of lumber. In theory, the answer is yes. But for all practical purposes the answer is likely to be no, because it may require the dismantling or destruction of the houses in order to restore them to use. The answer also becomes one of economics; that is, whether the required restoration can be done reasonably and economically.

It is uncertain whether the impaired property exclusion will succeed in its objectives or fail like its predecessor exclusions. The impaired property exclusion's track record in the courts thus far is better than its predecessor exclusions but, more often than not, courts hold the current exclusion to be inapplicable when insurers rely on it to deny coverage. Part of the problem may be that it is cited by insurers more often than it should be, or it may be too difficult to understand.[9]

Among the cases to be considered is *Gaylord Chemical Corporation v. Propump, Inc.*, 753 So. 2d 349 (La. App. 2000). This case arose when a newly purchased pump did not perform according to its specifications. The purchaser sought refund of the entire price, lost profits, and additional expenses incurred due to the pump's failure to perform properly, as well as damage to its physical plant and loss of use of some of its other equipment. As to the impaired property exclusion raised by the insurer, the court held that it was inapplicable to physical injury to the pump purchaser's plant, equipment, or other property. The exclusion, the court said, applied only if the property was not physically injured or the claimed damages were solely for loss of use of that property.

Another case is *Federated Mutual Insurance Company v. Grapevine Excavation, Inc.*, 197 F.3d 720 (5th Cir. 1999). Here, a general contractor was hired by Wal-Mart to construct a parking lot at its store. The general contractor hired a subcontractor to perform the excavation, backfilling and compacting work. Six months after the work was completed, Wal-Mart discovered that the selected fill materials provided and installed by the subcontractor failed to meet specifications and, as a result, had caused damage to the work of the general contractor. The subcontractor's insurer denied coverage for a number of reasons, including the impaired property exclusion. The court, in ruling for coverage, held that the impaired property exclusion was inapplicable because the asphalt paving could not be "restored to use" by "the repair, replacement, adjustment or removal" of the underlying defective fill and therefore could not be considered impaired property.

In *Shade Foods, Inc. v. Innovative Products Sales & Marketing, Inc.*, 78 Cal. App. 4th 847 (2000), the impaired property exclusion was held to be inapplicable where cereal nut clusters, found to contain wood splinters, could not be restored to use.

In *Dorchester Mutual Fire Insurance Company v. First Kostas Corporation, Inc.*731 N.E.2d 569 (Mass. App. Ct. 2000), the contractor, while painting the exterior of a house, caused lead paint chips and dust to go inside the house. As a result, the homeowners sent a demand letter to the contractor claiming that the latter's activities caused them to hire a hazardous waste cleanup company, vacate the premises, and conduct tests of family members and pets for lead levels. The contractor's insurer denied coverage by raising several exclusions including the impaired property exclusion. The court held the impaired property exclusion to be applicable because there was no injury to property apart from the incorporation of the contractor's faulty work and no coverage applied for damage to property that was not physically injured and arose from a "defect, deficiency, inadequacy, or dangerous condition" in the contractor's work.

In *Standard Fire Ins. Co. v. Chester-O'Donley & Associates, Inc.*, 972 S.W.2d 1 (Tenn. App. 1998), the issue was over the loss of use of a building occasioned by the installation of a faulty heating system. The court stated that the exclusion is intended to target situations where a defective product, after being incorporated into the property of another, must be replaced or removed at great expense, thereby causing loss of use. However, the court said that the exclusion does not apply if there is damage to property other than the insured's work or if the insured's work cannot be repaired or replaced without causing physical injury to other property.[10]

For an example of how the current exclusion might operate in a particular situation, say that the insured installs a heating and ventilation system in a new building. If the system later proves to be defective, resulting in loss of use of the building while the system is being repaired or replaced, the insurer can cite the portion of the exclusion relating to "impaired property" in denying coverage for a resulting loss-of-use claim against its insured.

There is an exception to the exclusion, however. The exclusion does not apply to loss of use of other property (i.e., property other than the insured's product or work) due to sudden and accidental physical injury to the named insured's product or work after it has been put to its intended use. Returning to the above example, if the system's heat exchanger suddenly and accidentally ruptured, the resulting loss of use of the rest of the building would be insured, assuming no other policy provision stood in the way of coverage.

Exclusion N—Recall of Products, Work, or Impaired Property

Exclusion n. is commonly referred to as the sistership liability exclusion. The sistership liability exclusion derives its name from occurrences in the aircraft industry where enormous loss-of-use claims resulted from the grounding of all airplanes of the same type because one of the planes crashed and its "sister ships" were suspected of having a common defect. Anticipating similar situations with respect to virtually any type of product or work, insurers added a so-called sistership exclusion to general liability policies in 1966.

The purpose of the exclusion was, and is, to preclude coverage for the costs incurred because products have to be recalled or withdrawn from the market or from use because of a known or suspected defect or deficiency. While the exclusion may have more applicability to products, it also applies to work performed by or on behalf of the insured. The current version of this exclusion precludes coverage for:

> Damages claimed for any loss, cost or expense incurred by you or others for the loss of use, withdrawal, recall, inspection, repair, replacement, adjustment, removal or disposal of:
>
> 1) "Your product";
>
> 2) "Your work"; or
>
> 3) "Impaired property";
>
> if such product, work, or property is withdrawn or recalled from the market or from use by any person or organization because of a known or suspected defect, deficiency, inadequacy, or dangerous condition in it.

This current exclusion is considerably more detailed than the 1973 version in an apparent attempt to close some of the gaps created by court interpretations. One of the more notable stopgaps is that the current exclusion applies whether the damages claimed for loss, cost, or expense are incurred by the named insured or by others.

In a number of cases, the previous exclusion has been held not to apply if the actual withdrawal of the product is performed by organizations other than the named insured. With specific reference to "damages claimed for any loss, cost or expense incurred by you *or others*" (emphasis added), the new exclusion may apply as was originally intended.

Note that this exclusion applies to loss of use, withdrawal, recall, etc., of "your product," "your work," or "impaired property." The definition of impaired property is quoted earlier in this chapter, under the discussion of exclusion m.

Exclusion O—Personal and Advertising Injury

When the 1986 edition of standard CGL forms was introduced, the term "personal injury" was newly defined to mean "injury, other than bodily injury, arising out of one or more of the following offenses ..." This specific reference to bodily injury as being outside the scope of personal injury coverage caught the eye of some commentators who noted a potential problem with this wording. These commentators reasoned that if bodily injury resulted from a personal injury offense (for example, bodily injury resulting from a scuffle between a store's security guard and one of the store's customers during a false arrest), the insured storeowner might not be fully covered. The allegation of false arrest would be the subject of Coverage B, but the resulting bodily injury claim would not, because the personal injury definition precluded bodily injury. If any coverage were to be applicable to bodily injury, it would have had to be under Coverage A of the policy. However, these same commentators pointed out that there could be situations when bodily injury still might not be covered in light of policy exclusion (a), dealing with expected or intended injury, that is, the allegation that the security guard expected the injury to happen based on his or her conduct.

As a result of these concerns, ISO made two revisions to its CGL forms in 1998. One was to specifically include, under Coverage B, consequential bodily injury arising out of the covered offenses, and the other was to exclude, from Coverage A, the type of consequential bodily injury now covered under Coverage B. The exclusion, designated exclusion o., reads as follows:

"Bodily injury" arising out of "personal and advertising injury".

By including consequential bodily injury in the revised definition of "personal and advertising injury" (discussed in Chapter 2), potential problems in applying coverage for bodily injury resulting from an offense should be reduced.

Exclusion P—Electronic Data

In the 2004 revision of the CGL form, ISO added an exclusion pertaining to damages arising out of the loss of, loss of use of, damage to, corruption of, inability to access, or inability to manipulate electronic data. This exclusion also contains a broad definition of electronic data. This exclusion was added to reinforce the 2001 modification that excluded electronic data (as defined) from the CGL definition of property damage.

Closer scrutiny of this exclusion reveals that considerably more than simply loss to electronic data is being excluded. For example, the term "damages" in that exclusion is not a defined term in the CGL forms. It therefore can include damages for physical injury to tangible property, loss of use of tangible property not physically injured, and also bodily injury.

Assume the following two scenarios: While working in a health care facility, a contractor damages electronic data that controls a life support system with potentially deadly consequences. Or, heavy equipment on a customer's premises short circuits, damaging electronic data controlling production machinery safety devices resulting in a worker's serious injury. In both of these scenarios, coverage could be argued to be excluded. What is equally, if not more so, an eye-opener, is the reference in exclusion p. to "damages arising out of." The words "arising out of," as used in this exclusion, could encompass any injury or damage arising out of the corruption of, inability to access, or inability to manipulate electronic data.

Understandably, insurers have to be concerned about the developments of e-commerce, including electronic data, given the growth in this technology and its far-reaching exposures to loss. Not to be overlooked, however, are also the concerns of insurance buyers who cannot afford to retain these risks. Chapter 6 discusses some of the forms endorsements dealing with electronic data. In fact, at the time exclusion p. was introduced in 2004, ISO introduced an Electronic Data Liability Coverage Form (CG 00 65).

When exclusion p. was introduced, it was criticized as being overly broad in scope, because it appeared to preclude loss to simply more than electronic. For example, with the term "damages" not being defined, the exclusion is said to be so broad and encompassing as to also preclude damages for physical loss or damage to tangible property, loss of use of tangible property not physically injured, and also bodily injury.

In light of requests to modify this exclusion, the April 2013 revision includes the following statement: "However, this exclusion does not apply to liability for damages because of bodily injury." Given the uncertainty about the exposures of electronic data liability, it is understandable that a broad exclusion be introduced. With a better learning curve and with no frequency to speak of, other than for property damage, the time is ripe for this change dealing with bodily injury.

This revision affects the CGL occurrence form (CG 00 01) and claims-made form (CG 00 02), along with the Products/Completed Operations Liability occurrence form (CG 00 37) and claims-made form (CG 00 38); Owners and Contractors Protective Liability Coverage Form—Coverage For Operations Of Designated Contractor (CG 00 09); Pollution Liability Coverage Form Designated Sites (CG 00 39); Pollution Liability Limited Coverage Form Designated Sites (CG 00 40); and Underground Storage Tank Policy Designated Tanks (CG 00 42).

Exclusion Q—Distribution of Material in Violation of Statutes

This exclusion was originally conceived as an endorsement (CG 00 67). It was introduced in 2005 by ISO to exclude bodily injury or property damage arising out of any action or omission that violates or is alleged to violate the TCPA, the CAN-SPAM Act of 2003, or any other similar statute, ordinance, or regulation that prohibits or limits the sending, transmitting, communicating, or distribution of material or information. The December 2007 revision of the CGL form incorporated the endorsement wording into the CGL form itself. Endorsement CG 00 67 has been withdrawn from use by ISO.

The wording of the exclusion in the previous CGL form is as follows:

"Bodily injury" or "property damage" arising directly or indirectly out of any action or omission that violates or is alleged to violate:

(1) The Telephone Consumer Protection Act (TCPA), including any amendment of or addition to such law; or

(2) The CAN-SPAM Act of 2003, including any amendment of or addition to such law; or

(3) Any statute, ordinance or regulation, other than the TCPA or CAN-SPAM Act of 2003, that prohibits or limits the sending, transmitting, communicating or distribution of material or information.

This exclusion is revised in the April 2013 edition of the CGL form; the revision affects both coverage A and coverage B. It is being revised through the incorporation into the exclusion of endorsement CG 00 68 (now withdrawn from use by ISO) that was used to exclude coverage for the recording and distribution of material or information, such as by telephone, facsimiles and email, in violation of law; in other words, bodily injury, property damage and personal and advertising injury arising out of any action or omission violating or alleged to have violated certain consumer protection statutes.

The exclusion revises paragraph (3) as follows: The Fair Credit Reporting Act (FCRA), and any amendment of or addition to such law, including the Fair and Accurate Credit Transactions Act (FACTA). And, a fourth paragraph is added: Any federal, state, or local statute, ordinance or regulation, other than the TCPA, CAN-SPAM Act of 2003, or FCRA and their amendments and additions, that addresses, prohibits, or limits the printing, dissemination, disposal, collecting, recording, sending, transmitting, communicating or distribution of materials or information.

This change affects the CGL occurrence form (CG 00 01) and claims-made form (CG 00 02).

Fire Damage Coverage

The final provision of the Coverage A exclusions is a statement that exclusions c. through n. do not apply to "damage by fire to premises while rented to you or temporarily occupied by you with permission of the owner," thus providing what the CGL forms call "fire damage" coverage, which is the same thing as fire legal liability coverage. A special limit of insurance applies to this coverage, as is discussed in Chapter 5.

The applicability of fire legal liability coverage when the insured has agreed by contract to be liable for fire damage to rented premises is discussed earlier in this chapter, with exclusion b. Briefly, if the insured would have been liable for fire damage to rented premises in the absence of any contract or agreement, fire damage coverage will apply; and this is true even if the insured had also agreed by contract to be responsible for such damage. In essence then, the insured is covered for fire damage to rented premises resulting from the insured's negligence. However, if there are no grounds for liability other than a contract or agreement, fire damage coverage does not apply, because of exclusion b and the definition of "insured contract".

Reference to the term "rented" in the final provision of the Coverage A exclusions may, in some jurisdictions, be argued to require a transfer of money between a tenant and landlord before this coverage becomes effective. However, tenants are sometimes granted occupancy privileges for consideration other than rental monies, such as the performance of managerial or janitorial duties. To acknowledge this practice, the CGL coverage forms were amended in 1993 to encompass such arrangements. The provision as amended in the 2001 forms reads:

Exclusions c. through n. do not apply to damage by fire to premises while rented to you or temporarily occupied by you with the permission of the owner. A separate limit of insurance applies to this coverage as described in Section III—Limits of Insurance.

The revised wording also encompasses situations when there is no consideration paid as long as the premises are occupied with permission of the owner or, presumably, the owner's agent. A corresponding change also has been made in the Limits of Insurance section pertaining to the fire damage limit.

Endnotes

1.   See, for example, *Garden Sanctuary, Inc. v. Insurance Company of North America*, 292 So.2d 75 (1974); *City of Ypsilanti v. Appalachian Ins. Co.*, 547 F. Supp. 823 (1983); and Doyle v. Allstate Ins. Co., 154 N.Y.S.2d 10 (1956).

2.   "Occurrence," FC&S, Casualty & Surety Vol., Public Liability M.12; also, "Construction and Application of Provision of Liability Insurance Policy Expressly Excluding Injuries Intended or Expected by Insured," American Law Reports 4th, p.957

3.   Required when a CGL policy is issued in New York is endorsement CG 01 63 04 09, New York Changes—Commercial General Liability Coverage Form which, among other provisions, reintroduces reference to the "groundless, false or fraudulent" phraseology. As mentioned, insurers may be able to obtain reimbursement for defense costs incurred on

allegations ultimately deemed not to be covered, but they still have the obligation to defend all allegations.

4. Whether a countrywide endorsement will be made available to handle defense costs (as is the case in Illinois and Wyoming) is likely to depend on what course the issue of reimbursement of defense costs takes in the near future and whether such a filing would be approved.

5. *Bentz v. Mutual Fire Marine & Inland Insurance Co.*, 575 A.2d 795 (Md. App. 1990).

6. Memorandum to letter from Insurance Rating Board to Ohio Insurance Department dated May 8, 1970.

7. The fact that there is no change in the overall scope of broad form property damage means that the January 29, 1979 memorandum issued by ISO to explain application of broad form property damage can still be relied upon conceptually.

8. For a review of court decisions on this matter, *see* "Liability of Successor Corporation for Injury or Damage Caused by Product Issued by Predecessor," 66 American Law Reports 3d (The Lawyers Co-Operative Publishing Co., Rochester; and Bancroft-Whitney Co., San Francisco, 1975), p. 824

9. See, for example, Pete Ligeros and Donald S. Malecki, "Impaired Property Exclusion: Using Discretion to Make It Work," Claims Magazine, Nov. 1994, p. 58.

10. The court in this case also referred to an earlier edition of the present text, which gave an illustration of how the impaired property exclusion would apply to a defective heating and ventilation system.

Chapter 2

Coverage B—Personal and Advertising Injury Liability

Advertising liability insurance for organizations other than advertising agencies was probably first introduced for use in the United States with umbrella liability policies in the 1940s. The first standardized form for providing advertising liability coverage with the comprehensive general liability policy was the broad form comprehensive general liability endorsement, introduced in 1976. Personal injury liability coverage, packaged with advertising injury liability coverage in the broad form liability endorsement, had been available since at least the late 1950s when multi-peril package policies were first offered. When the simplified commercial general liability coverage forms were introduced in 1986, personal and advertising injury liability coverage was included as Coverage B. It then became an integral part of the coverage form instead of being an optional coverage added by endorsement. It was not until the growth of litigation over the meaning of advertising injury liability coverage in the late 1980s and the 1990s that advertising injury liability coverage was widely recognized as an important addition to liability policies.

In large part because of the litigation over advertising injury liability coverage, Coverage B of the CGL coverage forms has undergone many changes since those forms were introduced in 1986. The emergence of e-commerce exposures potentially covered under personal and advertising injury liability coverage prompted additional changes in the 2001 CGL revision. This chapter examines the most current provisions for Coverage B and also traces significant changes that have been made to the Coverage B provisions since the 1986 forms were introduced. Where appropriate, this chapter also makes some comparisons to the personal and advertising injury liability coverage of the pre-1986 broad form liability endorsement.

Insuring Agreement

The CGL coverage forms provide personal and advertising injury liability coverage under the insuring agreement that follows.

> We will pay those sums that the insured becomes legally obligated to pay as damages because of "personal and advertising injury" to which this insurance applies. We will have the right and duty to defend the insured against any "suit" seeking those damages. However, we will

have no duty to defend the insured against any "suit" seeking damages for "personal and advertising injury" to which this insurance does not apply. We may, at our discretion, investigate any offense and settle any claim or "suit" that may result. But:

(a)   The amount we will pay for damages is limited as described in Section III—Limits of Insurance; and

(b)   Our right and duty to defend end when we have used up the applicable limit of insurance in the payment of judgments or settlements under Coverages A or B or medical expenses under Coverage C.

No other obligation or liability to pay sums or perform acts or services is covered unless explicitly provided for under Supplementary Payments – Coverages A and B.

In several ways, this insuring agreement resembles the Coverage A insuring agreement described in detail in Chapter 1. The principal difference is that the Coverage B agreement covers damages because of personal and advertising injury instead of damages because of bodily injury and property damage. The policy definition of personal and advertising injury is therefore a key provision for Coverage B and is discussed in detail in a separate section that follows. Notably, the Montrose provisions that apply to the Coverage A insuring agreement are not included in the Coverage B insuring agreement.

Insurer's Duty to Defend

The Coverage B provisions relating to defense are essentially the same as under Coverage A of the CGL coverage forms. The insurer's duty to defend ends when the applicable limit of insurance has been used up in payment of damages under Coverage A or B or medical expenses under Coverage C. If, for example, earlier claims under Coverages A and C have used up the general aggregate limit, the insured would have no defense coverage for a subsequent Coverage B claim, even though no other claim had been made under Coverage B during the policy period. In addition to the general aggregate limit, Coverage B is subject to the "personal and advertising injury limit," which is the most the insurer will pay in damages for all personal and advertising injury sustained by any one person or organization. Both of these limits will be discussed in more detail in Chapter 5.

Coverage Triggers

When introduced in 1986, form CG 00 01 and form CG 00 02 both had the same coverage trigger for Coverage B. The policy in effect when the offense was committed was the policy that covered the resulting advertising or personal injury. For all practical purposes, this trigger operated like the occurrence trigger of Coverage A in form CG 00 01. Consequently, in form CG 00 02, the Coverage B "offense committed" trigger was inconsistent with the claims-made trigger that applied to Coverage A of that form. In the 1990 CGL revision, ISO eliminated this inconsistency by giving Coverage B of form CG 00 02 a claims-made trigger that applies in the same way as the claims-made trigger for Coverage A of that form. (Chapter 4 will describe in detail the claims-made trigger applicable to both Coverages A and B of form CG 00 02.)

Application of the offense-committed trigger, like the occurrence trigger, is ordinarily uncomplicated. Although there is usually not much difficulty in determining when libel, slander, or other personal and advertising injury offenses were committed, there can be difficulty in determining when an alleged offense of malicious prosecution was committed.

Malicious prosecution refers to an offense committed when a person or entity files an action against a person or entity maliciously and without the probable cause necessary to sustain the allegations being made. This offense typically occurs in the context of a retaliation by a person or entity against a third party and often arises in the heat of anger or for competitive reasons.

In a footnote to the case of *Downey Venture, et al., v. LMI Insurance Co. 78 Cal. Rptr. 2d 142 (1998)*, the court noted that malicious prosecution has roots dating back to the 10th and 11th century, in Anglo Saxon courts, where the price for losing a suit was the loss of one's tongue. The footnote went on to explain that courts have long recognized the chilling effect of malicious prosecution actions because of their potential impact on an ordinary citizen's willingness to report a crime or pursue his or her legal rights.

The majority of jurisdictions hold that the applicable policy is the one in effect when the action alleged to constitute malicious prosecution was filed. The minority hold that it is the policy in effect at the time when that action terminates in favor of the party alleging malicious prosecution. The rationale for this difference is explained in the two cases noted below.

In *Consulting Engineers, Inc. v. Insurance Company of North America*, 710 A.2d 82 (Pa. Super. 1998), the issue was whether two insurance companies were required to defend and indemnify the insured for damages flowing from the tort of wrongful use of civil proceedings. The basis of the dispute was that the suit alleged to be wrongful was commenced by the insured prior to the policy periods of both insurers, although the action continued after those two policies came into effect. The court held that both insurers had no obligation where the action was initially commenced prior to the time coverage under the policies commenced.

In *Harbor Insurance Co. v. Argonaut Insurance*, 211 Cal. Rptr. 902 (1985), the court held that the offense of malicious prosecution was committed upon initiation of the underlying action and rejected the notion that the offense was a continuing one. What made this case unusual was that it was the various insurers involved who proposed that malicious prosecution be deemed a continuing offense over the duration of the malicious prosecution action so that any obligation to indemnify could be apportioned among each of the insurers.

Definition of Personal and Advertising Injury

Before the 1998 CGL revision, Coverage B contained separate definitions for personal injury and advertising injury. In the 1998 revision, the definitions were modified in response to court decisions that had run adverse to insurers' interests, and the two definitions were combined into a single definition of personal and advertising injury in order to make the Coverage B provisions less complicated. Additional, but minor, revisions were made to the 2001 definition, which begins:

"Personal and advertising injury" means injury, including consequential "bodily injury", arising out of one or more of the following offenses...

The lead-in language to the current definition states that it includes bodily injury that occurs as a consequence of any of the listed personal and advertising injury offenses. An example of such consequential bodily injury is that which can result when a tenant is injured during a wrongful eviction of that tenant from the named insured's apartment building. The definitions of advertising injury and personal injury that preceded the combined definition of personal and advertising injury excluded bodily injury, which could be covered only under Coverage A. That approach was dropped in the 1998 revision, addressing the possible result that consequential bodily injury could in many cases be excluded under Coverage A because of the intentional injury exclusion.

The lead-in language is followed by paragraphs a. through g., which list and describe the specific offenses included in the definition. The paragraphs are quoted in turn below, with interspersed commentaries.

False Arrest, Detention or Imprisonment; Malicious Prosecution

a.   False arrest, detention or imprisonment;

b.   Malicious prosecution;

The first two paragraphs of the definition include false arrest, detention, or imprisonment; and malicious prosecution. These same offenses were covered in the personal and advertising injury liability coverage of the broad form liability endorsement, and they have remained unchanged in the simplified CGL coverage forms since they were introduced in 1986.

Wrongful Eviction, Wrongful Entry, Invasion of Right of Private Occupancy

c.   The wrongful eviction from, wrongful entry into, or invasion of the right of private occupancy of a room, dwelling or premises that a person occupies, committed by or on behalf of its owner, landlord or lessor.

To understand the full effect of the above provision, it is helpful to contrast this provision with earlier versions of the provision that appeared in the 1986 CGL forms and the personal and advertising injury liability coverage of the broad form liability endorsement. The comparable provision of the broad form liability endorsement applied to "wrongful entry or eviction or other invasion of the right of private occupancy." When the 1986 forms were introduced, reference to "other invasion of the right of private occupancy" was dropped, limiting coverage to "wrongful entry into, or eviction of a person from, a room, dwelling or premises that the person occupies." Thus, a complaint alleging personal injury resulting from the insured's invasion of the claimant's right of private occupancy by some means other than wrongful entry or eviction, although covered under the pre-1986 forms, would not, presumably, be covered by the 1986 CGL forms.

The potential difference between the pre-1986 and the 1986 language for this offense can be illustrated by considering the case of *Town of Goshen v. Grange Mutual Ins. Co.*, 424 A.2d 822 (N.H. 1980). The question in this case was whether a town's personal injury liability endorsement provided defense coverage against a landowner's allegation that the town had created economic hardships that destroyed viability of the owner's land development project.

The endorsement covered the usual personal injury offenses, including "wrongful entry or eviction or other invasion of the right of private occupancy." The insurer, pointing to the absence of allegations of any invasion, intrusion, or interference by any person or thing upon the owner's land, took the position that the allegations in the owner's complaint did not come within the policy coverage for the offense quoted above.

Holding that tangible interference with physical property itself is not necessary to constitute invasion of the right of private occupancy, the court decided that the insurer was liable for defending its insured. Had the covered offense been only "wrongful entry ... or eviction," as in the 1986 CGL forms, without any mention of "other invasion of the right of private occupancy," it seems quite possible that the court would not have found in favor of coverage.

In the 1990 CGL revision, "invasion of the right of private occupancy" was added to the definition of personal injury. However, unlike the pre-1986 version of the definition, the personal injury definition in the 1990 edition of the CGL policy uses the following, more restrictive wording:

> c.   The wrongful eviction from, wrongful entry into, or invasion of the right of private occupancy of a room, dwelling or premises that person occupies by or on behalf of its owner, landlord or lessor.

Presumably, the 1990 language (which remained unchanged in the 1993 and 1996 CGL forms) limits coverage to cases in which the alleged wrongful eviction, wrongful entry, or other invasion of the right of private occupancy was from, into, or of a place already occupied by the claimant. Thus, the 1990 revision broadened the 1986 language to cover invasion of the right of private occupancy but clarified that the definition does not include situations in which someone does not have legal possession to property but seeks to obtain such possession.

Two additional court cases illustrate the problem that the current language is apparently intended to solve. In both cases, courts upheld coverage for property owners' alleged discrimination under the personal injury coverage phrase "or other invasion of the right of private occupancy." In *Drought v. Nawrocki*, 444 N.W.2d 65 (Wisc. App. 1989), which involved the pre-1986 language, the court held that a liability policy's reference to "other invasion of the right of private occupancy" was ambiguous and therefore covered a suit against the insured for violation of a state housing law dealing with discrimination. In *Gardner v. Romano*, 688 F. Supp. 489 (E.D. Wisc. 1988), the insurer was required to defend, under its personal injury coverage for "other invasion of the right of private occupancy," a federal civil rights action by prospective tenants who were refused occupancy to an apartment by its owner because of racial discrimination.

To summarize, the 1990 and later versions of paragraph c. are meant to restrict coverage solely to situations where a claimant has a legal right to occupancy already possessed, and the alleged tortfeasor is the property's owner, landlord, or lessor. In other words, paragraph c. is intended to be limited to a landlord and tenant relationship and thus would not cover, for example, the removal of a business invitee (as opposed to a tenant) from the insured's premises, because the term "eviction" connotes a landlord and tenant relationship.

Although that may be ISO's intent, coverage may not necessarily be restricted to that intent. A case on point is *Insurance Company of North America v. Forrest City Country Club*, 819 S.W.2d 296 (Ark. App. 1991). The insurer in this case urged the court to strictly construe eviction as a term limited to interference with a tenant's enjoyment of the property. The court, however, disagreed with the insurer, stating that, while the term eviction has been defined as meaning "interference with a tenant's enjoyment of premises," the word "evict", as used in its popular sense also means to merely force out or to eject. The policy, therefore, was held to be ambiguous from the court's perspective.

In 1998, ISO amended the wording of part c. of the definition of personal and advertising injury to include the word appearing in bold (emphasis added):

c.   The wrongful eviction from, wrongful entry into, or invasion of the right of private occupancy of a room, dwelling or premises that a person occupies, **committed** by or on behalf of its owner, landlord or lessor.

Prior to this change, the wording of paragraph c. was not clear because it was uncertain whether it was the wrongful eviction or entry that had to be committed by or on behalf of the owner, landlord, or lessor; or if the room, dwelling, or premises wrongfully entered or from which a third party was evicted had to be occupied by that third party by or on behalf of the owner, landlord, or lessor. The added word clarifies that the wrongful eviction or entry must be committed by or on behalf of the owner, landlord, or lessor.

Reference to a person in c. (and d., see below) raises the question whether these provisions can also include an organization. A case that answers that question and may have an impact on coverage in some jurisdictions is *Mirpad, et al. v. California Insurance Guaranteee Association*, 34 Cal. Rptr. 3d 136 (Ct. App. 2d Dist. Div. 3, 2005). The California court of appeal, in overruling the trial court, held here in a case involving wrongful eviction under a CGL policy that coverage for a "person" did not include an organization. Among some of the reasons expressed by the court of appeal in concluding that a "person," as used in the context of "wrongful eviction"refers solely to a natural person, and not also to an organization are the following:

- Places from which the eviction must take place are where people live, i.e., from a room, dwelling or premises that a person occupies;

- If a person were to be interpreted to include an organization, the word "organization," in the often repeated phrase "person or organization" would become redundant and surplusage; and

- The CGL policy discretely uses the term "organization" 12 times and the phrase "person or organization" 20 times.

Fortunately for insureds, there have been other cases that have not followed the precedent of the Mirpad case. One such case is *Supreme Laundry Service, L.L.C. v. Hartford Casualty Ins. Co.*, 521 F.3d 743 *(U.S. Ct. App. 7th Cir. 2008)*, where the court held the language distinguishing between "persons" and "organizations" to be ambiguous.

Slander, Libel, Disparagement

d. Oral or written publication, in any manner, of material that slanders or libels a person or organization or disparages a person's or organization's goods, products or services.

In the pre-1998 editions of the CGL coverage forms, the paragraph quoted above was included in both the personal injury and advertising injury definitions. The only change that ISO has made to this item since the introduction of the 1986 CGL forms is the addition of the phrase "in any manner," which was added in the 2001 revision. This change clarifies that publication of slanderous or libelous material on the Internet or CD-ROM, for example, is within the definition of personal or advertising injury.

The paragraph under discussion includes three related offenses: slander, libel, and disparagement. Slander and libel are two types of defamation, a tort that refers to harming a person's or organization's reputation by publication of a false statement. Originally, libel was defamation that occurred through written or printed material, and slander was defamation that was conveyed by speech. Libel now includes various media such as pictures, cartoons, signs, statues, and motion pictures. An accepted legal definition of disparagement of goods is "a statement about a competitor's goods which is untrue or misleading and is made to influence or tends to influence the public not to buy" (*Black's Law Dictionary*, 6th edition). By their traditional legal definitions, libel and slander are applicable only to the defaming of a person or an organization, whereas disparagement of goods, products, or services relates to statements about the goods, products, or services themselves.

Violation of a Person's Right of Privacy

e. Oral or written publication, in any manner, of material that violates a person's right of privacy.

This paragraph, like the preceding one, was included in both the personal injury and advertising injury definitions in the pre-1998 CGL coverage forms. The only change that this paragraph has undergone since 1986 is the addition of the phrase "in any manner" in 2001. Violation of a person's right of privacy can occur in various ways, such as public disclosure of private facts or unauthorized release of confidential information. Thus, many types of insureds are well advised to have coverage against this offense.

Unauthorized Use, Infringement

f.   The use of another's advertising idea in your "advertisement"; or

g.   Infringing upon another's copyright, trade dress or slogan in your "advertisement".

These advertising injury offenses underwent substantial change in the 1998 CGL revision. Until the 1998 CGL revision, these offenses were expressed in the CGL coverage forms as follows:

c.   Misappropriation of advertising ideas or style of doing business; or

d.   Infringement of copyright, title or slogan.

According to ISO, it omitted the reference to "style of doing business" from the new paragraph f. because that language has been the subject of coverage disputes. ISO replaced "style of doing business" with the term "trade dress" under new paragraph g. ISO has described trade dress as "the totality of elements in which a product or service is packaged or presented."[1] *Black's Law Dictionary* (6th edition) defines "trade dress" as: "the total appearance and image of a product, including features such as size, texture, shape, color, graphics, and even particular advertising and marketing techniques used to promote its sale." The term trade dress, under certain facts, may thus encompass the misappropriation of a style of doing business, something ISO apparently is seeking to avoid by having deleted specific reference to "misappropriation of style of doing business."

ISO's stated reason for omitting the word "title" from new paragraph g. was that some court cases involving the prior Coverage B language had held the term "title" to include "infringement of trademark," an offense that ISO never intended to be covered under personal and advertising injury liability coverage of the CGL policy. ISO also expressed the opinion in its filing circular for the 1998 changes that the phrase "infringement of copyright" is broad enough to encompass infringement of publication titles, such as titles of books or songs.[2]

Because the pre-1998 CGL forms included paragraphs c. and d. (as shown above) in the definition of advertising injury only (and not in the definition of personal injury), the described offenses were covered only when committed in the course of advertising the named insured's goods, products, or services. In the 1998 and later forms, paragraphs f. and g. of the new definition similarly restrict coverage to offenses committed in the named insured's advertisement. The definition of advertisement that was added to the 1998 CGL forms is as follows.

"Advertisement" means a notice that is broadcast or published to the general public or specific market segments about your goods, products or services for the purpose of attracting customers or supporters.

With the 2001 revision, the following qualification was added to the definition of advertisement to clarify that material placed on the Internet will, under the circumstances described, be considered an advertisement.

For purposes of this definition:

a.   Notices that are published include material placed on the Internet or on similar electronic means of communication; and

b.   Regarding web-sites, only that part of a web-site that is about your goods, products or services for the purposes of attracting customers or supporters is considered an advertisement.

Exclusions

In the 1986, 1990, 1992, and 1993 editions of the CGL coverage forms, Coverage B had four exclusions that applied to both personal injury and advertising injury liability, and another four exclusions that applied only to advertising injury. In the 1996 CGL revision, two exclusions were added with the intent of eliminating coverage for any claim resulting from pollution, including cleanup costs. In 1998, when the prior definitions of personal injury and advertising injury were combined into a single definition of personal and advertising injury, the Coverage B exclusions were extensively revised and reformatted.

Again in 2001, the exclusions were reformatted to show a short name for each exclusion (as in the Coverage A exclusions) and expanded to address emerging e-commerce issues. The Coverage B exclusions from the CGL forms are discussed below, with comparisons to the prior Coverage B exclusions. The exclusions are discussed in the order in which they appear in the coverage forms.

Exclusion A—"Knowing Violation of Rights of Another"

"Personal and advertising injury" caused by or at the direction of the insured with the knowledge that the act would violate the rights of another and would inflict "personal and advertising injury".

The broad form liability endorsement contained an exclusion of advertising injury "arising out of any act committed by the insured with actual malice." This exclusion was omitted from the simplified CGL coverage forms when they were introduced in 1986, perhaps because the drafters felt that it would be extremely difficult for insurers to deny coverage on the basis of an exclusion requiring the insurer to prove malice on the part of the insured.

In the 1998 CGL revision, ISO added the exclusion quoted above the preceding paragraph. The new exclusion is worded very differently from the earlier exclusion of malicious acts, but both exclusions have a similar intent: to prevent the insurer from having to pay for injury caused intentionally by the insured. To understand this exclusion, one needs to keep in mind that Coverage B covers the insured against certain described offenses (such as libel and slander) that result from intentional acts (such as publishing a report or making a public statement). The present exclusion is aimed at eliminating coverage only in situations when the insured commits a personal and advertising injury offense knowing that the act will violate another's rights and be injurious. The exclusion thus should not be considered to be an intentional acts exclusion. Personal and advertising injury resulting from an intentional act of the insured is covered if the insured did not know that the act would violate the rights of another person or organization and cause injury.

Exclusion B—"Material Published with Knowledge of Falsity"

Personal and advertising injury arising out of oral or written publication, in any manner, of material, if done by or at the direction of the insured with knowledge of its falsity.

The broad form liability endorsement contained an exclusion similar to the one quoted above, which has remained virtually unchanged since it was included in the 1986 CGL forms. Although more narrowly focused than exclusion a., exclusion b. shares the same basic purpose of preventing the insurer from having to pay for injury resulting from acts that the insured knew were capable of causing injury. See, for example, *Chrysler Insurance Co. v. Greenspoint Dodge of Houston, Inc.*, 297 S.W.2d 248 (TX, 2009), which involved a suit for defamation coverage. The court of appeals concluded that this exclusion did not apply to the corporation because no corporate officer knew that the defamatory statements, made by other corporate employees, were false. On petition for review, however, it was held that a corporation's knowledge is not limited to what officers know, but may include other employees' knowledge, if they are corporate vice-principals, such as the corporation's general manager, comptroller, and used car sales manager. In *GTE Sw., Inc. v. Bruce*, 998 S.W.2d 605 (TX, 1999), it was stated that "A vice-principal represents the corporation in its corporate capacity and includes persons who have authority to employ, direct, and discharge servants of the master, and those to whom a master has confided the management of the whole or a department or division of his business."

Exclusion b. is aimed mainly at libel, slander, and disparagement claims, in instances where the insured knew that the material being made public was false. Exclusion a. can apply to a wider range of claims.

Note that in 2001, ISO introduced a revision that included the phrase "in any manner" in the appropriate provisions of Coverage B, such as with libel, slander and disparagement. This change was intended to clarify that publication of slanderous or libelous material via the Internet or CD-ROM was within the definition of personal and advertising injury. To be consistent with the foregoing, exclusion b. in the newly revised CGL form dealing with material published with knowledge of falsity likewise now includes the phrase "in any manner."

This revision dealing with exclusion b. of Coverage B affects both the CGL occurrence form (CG 00 01) and claims-made form (CG 00 02).

Exclusion C—"Material Published Prior to Policy Period"

"Personal and advertising injury" arising out of oral or written publication, in any manner, of material whose first publication took place before the beginning of the policy period.

This exclusion, like exclusion b., has not been materially changed since it was included in the 1986 CGL forms, and the broad form liability endorsement contained a similar exclusion. The exclusion has two versions. The version quoted above appears in form CG 00 01, which has the offense committed trigger for Coverage B, described earlier in this chapter. Another version of the exclusion appears in form CG 00 02, which has a claims-made trigger for Coverage B. The claims-made version of the exclusion applies to publications that first take place before the policy's retroactive date (if any).

Although this exclusion has been included in personal injury forms since 1950, its use has taken on more importance as more use of the Internet brings about more liability involving the publication of material. The purpose of this exclusion is to prevent the current policy from having to pay claims arising out of material published before the current policy period (or before a claims-made policy's retroactive date)—even if publication might have continued into the current policy period. In the absence of such an exclusion, an insured might argue successfully that all policies in effect while material was published should apply to any personal and advertising injury claims arising out of that material—a result that insurers have gone to great lengths in their policy drafting to avoid.

One of the cases that dealt with this exclusion is *Superperformance International v. Hartford Casualty Co. Ins. Co.*, 203 F. Supp. 2d 587 (E.D. Va., 2002). The named insured, Superperformance, was sued for allegedly having infringed on the trademark rights of the plaintiffs. Several months later, it purchased a commercial general liability policy with an effective date of March 9, 2001. On August 24, 2001, subsequent to the issuance of that policy, the plaintiffs filed an amended complaint. The named insured then tendered the defense of the amended complaint to its insurer which promptly denied coverage. The court ruled against the named insured, in part based on the exclusion applicable where the offense arises out of material first published prior to the policy's issuance. The court rejected the notion that there was a duty to defend the second complaint, given that allegations were the same as in the initial complaint with minor exceptions.

Note that the 2013 revised CGL form adds the phrase "in any manner" to the exclusion just as in exclusion b.

Exclusion D—"Criminal Acts"

"Personal and advertising injury" arising out of a criminal act committed by or at the direction of the insured.

Before the 1998 CGL revision, Coverage B contained an exclusion of injury "arising out of the willful violation of a penal statute or ordinance committed by or with the consent of the insured." In the 1998 revision, ISO adopted a new exclusion that applied to personal and advertising injury "arising out of a criminal act committed by or at the direction of any insured." ISO believed that the new exclusion was a "more concrete and somewhat broader exclusion" than its predecessor.[3]

The 2001 version of the exclusion was modified to refer to a criminal act committed by or at the direction of "the" insured, instead of "any" insured. The difference between "the insured" and "any insured" can be crucial to coverage. "The insured" is properly interpreted to mean only the insured against whom a claim is being made, whereas "any insured" could be anyone who qualifies as an insured under the policy even if not the insured against whom a claim is being made.[4]

To illustrate how coverage could depend on this wording, say that the named insured is sued by a person who alleges that the named insured's employee committed an act that constituted personal and advertising injury and was also a criminal act. Although the employee is an insured under the policy, he is not the insured against whom a claim is being made. Thus, the possibility that the employee committed a criminal act does not bring the claim within the exclusion that appears in the 2001 forms. However, the 1998 version of the exclusion could apply, since the employee, though not the insured being sued, qualifies as *any* insured.

Exclusion E—"Contractual Liability"

"Personal and advertising injury" for which the insured has assumed liability in a contract or agreement. This exclusion does not apply to liability for damages that the insured would have in the absence of the contract or agreement.

This exclusion has not changed since it was introduced in the 1986 CGL forms, and a similar exclusion was contained in personal and advertising injury liability coverage of the broad form liability endorsement. Exclusion e. is comparable in purpose to the contractual liability exclusion that applies to Coverage A, but the Coverage B exclusion does not have any exception for liability assumed under an insured contract as defined in the policy. Thus, unless the insured would be liable in the absence of the contract, Coverage B does not extend coverage for personal and advertising injury liability that the insured assumes under a contract, even though the contract is one of those included in the policy definition of insured contract. Unless an organization can obtain coverage for this exposure under an endorsement or an independently filed form, the organization should carefully review all hold harmless and indemnity agreements it enters into to make sure that they don't make the organization responsible for any type of injury that does not fall within the CGL policy definitions of bodily injury and property damage, because those are the only types of injury for which the CGL policy provides contractual liability coverage.

Exclusion F—"Breach of Contract"

Personal and advertising injury arising out of a breach of contract, except an implied contract to use another's advertising idea in your "advertisement".

The earlier editions of the CGL coverage forms all contain an exclusion of advertising injury arising out of a breach of contract, and the broad form liability endorsement also contained such an exclusion. A basic purpose of this exclusion is to clarify that personal and advertising injury liability coverage is not intended to cover products liability actions based on breach of warranty.

The version of the exclusion quoted above the preceding paragraph first appeared with the 1998 CGL revision. The only thing about the current exclusion that has changed from earlier editions is the exception to the exclusion. The change in wording corresponds to the omission of "misappropriation of advertising ideas" from the 1998 definition of "personal and advertising injury." The new exception to the exclusion—"an implied contract to use another's advertising idea"—corresponds to the new covered offense ("the use of another's advertising idea") that replaced "misappropriation of advertising ideas" in the definition of "personal and advertising injury." (An implied contract is an agreement that is legitimately inferred from the conduct of the parties or by the law as a matter of reason and justice.)

Exclusion G—"Quality or Performance of Goods— Failure to Conform to Statements"

"Personal and advertising injury" arising out of the failure of goods, products or services to conform with any statement of quality or performance made in your "advertisement."

This exclusion has been included in the CGL coverage forms since they were introduced in 1986. The last four words of the version quoted above were added as part of the 1998 CGL revision when the personal injury and advertising injury definitions were combined into one. The exclusion is aimed at preventing insurers from having to pay claims made by consumers who are disappointed with the quality or performance of the insured's goods, products, or services. The exclusion is somewhat comparable in intent to the failure to perform exclusion that existed in the 1973 comprehensive general liability policy and the impaired property exclusion under Coverage A of the current CGL coverage forms.

Exclusion H—"Wrong Description of Prices"

"Personal and advertising injury" arising out of the wrong description of the price of goods, products or services stated in your "advertisement."

This exclusion has been part of the CGL coverage forms since they were introduced in 1986, and the broad form liability endorsement contained a similar exclusion. The exclusion clarifies that there is no coverage for claims alleging (for example) that the insured should be compelled to sell a $4,999 product at the erroneously advertised price of $4.99.

Exclusion I—"Infringement of Copyright, Patent, Trademark or Trade Secret"

"Personal and advertising injury" arising out of the infringement of copyright, patent, trademark, trade secret or other intellectual property rights. Under this exclusion, such other intellectual property rights do not include the use of another's advertising idea in your advertisement."

However, this exclusion does not apply to infringement, in your "advertisement", of copyright, trade dress or slogan.

The broad form liability endorsement that preceded the simplified
CGL coverage forms contained an exclusion of advertising injury arising
out of infringement of trademark, service mark, or trade name, other than
titles or slogans. This exclusion was omitted from the 1986 simplified CGL
coverage forms, perhaps on the assumption that these types of infringement
did not need to be excluded because they were not specifically covered
by the new definitions of personal injury and advertising injury. However,
some court decisions found that Coverage B of the simplified CGL forms
covered trademark infringement because the definition of advertising injury
included "infringement of ... title." As discussed earlier in this chapter,
ISO has eliminated "infringement of ... title" from the new definition
of personal and advertising injury. In addition, ISO added the exclusion
quoted above this paragraph with its 2001 CGL revision.

The first sentence of the first part of this exclusion was clarified in
2007 with the addition of the second sentence to clarify the fact that "the
use of another's advertising idea in your advertisement" is still included in
the definition of personal and advertising injury. Exclusion (i), according to
ISO, also will not be used to deny personal and advertising injury coverage
to an insured should a claim arise against it based on the use of another's
idea in the named insured's advertisements.

The exception to the exclusion is important because it restores coverage
for infringement of copyright, trade dress, or slogan that occurs in the
named insured's advertisement. Outside of the named insured's advertising
activities, infringement of copyright, trade dress, or slogan is excluded. And
in all situations—even those involving advertising—infringement of patent,
trademark, trade secret, or other intellectual property rights is excluded.

Exclusion J—"Insureds in Media and Internet Type Businesses"

"Personal and advertising injury" committed by an insured whose
business is:

(1)   Advertising, broadcasting, publishing or telecasting;

(2)   Designing or determining content of web-sites for others; or

(3)   An Internet search, access, content or service provider.

However, this exclusion does not apply to Paragraphs 14. a., b. and c.
of "personal and advertising injury" under the Definitions Section.

For purposes of this exclusion, the placing of frames, borders or links,
or advertising, for you or others anywhere on the Internet, is not by

itself, considered the business of advertising, broadcasting, publishing or telecasting.

The pre-1998 editions of the CGL forms contain an exclusion of advertising injury arising out of "[a]n offense committed by an insured whose business is advertising, broadcasting, publishing or telecasting." The rationale behind this exclusion is that an insured in one of the listed businesses is more appropriately insured against advertising injury under a separate advertisers liability policy handled by specialist underwriters. When ISO combined the separate definitions of personal injury and advertising injury in the 1998 CGL revision, the exception pertaining to paragraphs a., b., and c. of the personal and advertising injury definition was added to the exclusion. Adding this exception made clear that the exclusion did not apply to covered offenses (false arrest, false detention, false imprisonment, and malicious prosecution) that had formerly been included in only the personal injury definition (which was not subject to the exclusion).

The other portions of current exclusion j. were added in the 2001 CGL revision as part of ISO's effort to address e-commerce issues. With the growth of e-commerce, new types of businesses came into existence that, like conventional advertisers and publishers, were highly exposed to advertising liability. Thus, the 2001 version of the exclusion applies also to Web site designers and various types of Internet-related businesses, subject to the exception contained in the exclusion's final paragraph, which describes various Internet activities (such as placing Web site links) that, in and of themselves, are not considered to be the business of advertising, broadcasting, publishing, or telecasting.

Exclusion K—"Electronic Chatrooms or Bulletin Boards"

"Personal and advertising injury" arising out of an electronic chatroom or bulletin board the insured hosts, owns, or over which the insured exercises control.

This exclusion appeared in the 2001 CGL revision as part of ISO's effort to address e-commerce issues. Firms that conduct these excluded activities will need to find appropriate coverage under the e-commerce policies that some insurers are now offering. (Note that ISO does have an e-commerce policy, EC 00 10 11 09. It is named the Information Security Protection Policy.)

Exclusion L—"Unauthorized Use of Another's Name or Product"

"Personal and advertising injury" arising out of the unauthorized use of another's name or product in your email address, domain name or metatag, or any other similar tactics to mislead another's potential customers.

ISO added this exclusion in its 2001 CGL revision to address yet another loss exposure that has arisen with the development of e-commerce.

Exclusion M—"Pollution"

"Personal and advertising injury" arising out of the actual, alleged or threatened discharge, dispersal, seepage, migration, release or escape of "pollutants" at any time.

Exclusion N—"Pollution-Related"

Any loss, cost or expense arising out of any:

(1)   Request, demand, order or statutory or regulatory requirement that any insured or others test for, monitor, cleanup, remove, contain, treat, detoxify or neutralize, or in any way respond to, or assess the effects of, "pollutants"; or

(2)   Claim or suit by or on behalf of a governmental authority for damages because of testing for, monitoring, cleaning up, removing, containing, treating, detoxifying or neutralizing, or in any way responding to, or assessing the effects of, "pollutants".

In combination, these two exclusions are intended to eliminate coverage for any pollution claim made under Coverage B. The Coverage B pollution exclusions do not contain any of the exceptions that allow limited coverage under the pollution exclusion that applies under Coverage A.

Exclusion O—"War"

In the 2004 revision, ISO added to Coverage B the same war exclusion that appears under Coverage A. This action reflects the concern of insurers that plaintiffs could make allegations for injury resulting from war in terms that might trigger a duty to defend, or even pay damages under Coverage B of the CGL policy.

Exclusion P—Distribution of Material in Violation of Statutes

This exclusion, originally conceived as an endorsement (CG 00 67), has an exact counterpart with the Coverage A exclusions. It was introduced in 2005 by ISO to exclude personal and advertising injury arising out of any action or omission that violates or is alleged to violate the TCPA, the CAN-SPAM Act of 2003, or any other similar statute, ordinance, or regulation that prohibits or limits the sending, transmitting, communicating, or distribution of material or information. The December 2007 revision of the

CGL form has now incorporated the endorsement wording into the CGL form itself. Endorsement CG 00 67 has been withdrawn from use by ISO. And, the April 2013 revision incorporates the wording of endorsement CG 00 68, which has now been withdrawn from use by ISO.

The wording of the exclusion is as follows:

"Personal and advertising injury" arising directly or indirectly out of any action or omission that violates or is alleged to violate:

(1) The Telephone Consumer Protection Act (TCPA), including any amendment of or addition to such law; or

(2) The CAN-SPAM Act of 2003, including any amendment of or addition to such law; or

(3) The Fair Credit Reporting Act (FCRA), and any amendment of or addition to such law, including the Fair and Accurate Credit Transactions Act (FACTA; or

(4) Any federal, state or local statute, ordinance or regulation, other than the TCPA, CAN-SPAM Act of 2003 or FCRA and their amendments and additions, that addresses, prohibits, or limits the printing, dissemination, disposal, collecting, recording, sending, transmitting, communicating or distribution of materials or information.

Endnotes

1. Insurance Services Office, Inc., ISO Circular LI-GL-98-3, 1998 General Liability Multistate Forms Revision To Be Submitted, January 6, 1998, pp. 17-18.

2. ISO Circular LI-GL-98-3, p. 18.

3. ISO Circular LI-GL-98-3, p. 20.

4. This interpretation is supported by the CGL condition titled Separation of Insureds, which states that "this insurance applies ... separately to each insured against whom claim is made or 'suit' is brought." If the insurance applies separately to the insured against whom claim is being made, "the insured" can properly be interpreted to mean that insured and no other.

Chapter 3

Coverage C—Medical Payments

Before the simplified CGL coverage forms were introduced in 1986, medical payments coverage was available by endorsement to general liability policies. Provisions for medical payments coverage are now included as Coverage C in the CGL coverage forms. Medical payments coverage provides a limited amount of insurance to pay medical and funeral expenses of persons (other than insureds) injured in accidents that occur on or next to the named insured's premises or as a result of the named insured's operations. This coverage is payable regardless of whether the insured is legally liable, and so medical payments coverage can be viewed as a way of making prompt payment to accident victims and thereby possibly avoiding a costlier liability claim against the insured.

Coverage C—Medical Payments of the CGL coverage forms is uncomplicated and is expressed with a minimal number of provisions. Most of the provisions are straightforward and do not require much explanation. Moreover, because the stated policy limit applicable to medical payments insurance is usually quite low (such as $5,000 per person), litigation over medical payments coverage is rare. (Note that the med pay coverage is also subject to the general aggregate limit of the policy. This means that if the general aggregate limit is exhausted by claims under coverages A or B of the policy, the insurer has no further obligations under coverage C, even if no other medical payments claims have been presented during the policy period.)

This chapter is brief, providing a cursory description of the Coverage C— Medical Payments provisions. The provisions are divided into two parts titled Insuring Agreement and Exclusions. These provisions have received only very minor modification since they were introduced in 1986.

Insuring Agreement

The insuring agreement for Coverage C-Medical Payments reads as follows:

1. Insuring Agreement

    a. We will pay medical expenses as described below for "bodily injury" caused by an accident:

(1)   On premises you own or rent;

(2)   On ways next to premises you own or rent; or

(3)   Because of your operations;

Provided that:

(1)   The accident takes place in the "coverage territory" and during the policy period;

(2)   The expenses are incurred and reported to us within one year of the date of the accident; and

(3)   The injured person submits to examination, at our expense, by physicians of our choice as often as we reasonably require.

b.   We will make these payments regardless of fault. These payments will not exceed the applicable limit of insurance. We will pay reasonable expenses for:

(1)   First aid administered at the time of an accident;

(2)   Necessary medical, surgical, x-ray and dental services, including prosthetic devices; and

(3)   Necessary ambulance, hospital, professional nursing and funeral services.

Covered accidents can occur anywhere within the coverage territory. However, if an accident does not occur on premises owned or rented by the insured, or on ways (i.e., a road, passage, or channel) next to such premises, the accident must have occurred because of the named insured's operations in order to be covered.

Another requirement is that the accident must take place during the policy period. This is the coverage trigger for Coverage C in both form CG 00 01 and form CG 00 02. The Coverage C trigger is basically the same as the Coverage A occurrence trigger in form CG 00 01.

Note that the expenses must be incurred and reported to the insurer within one year of the date of the accident. Also, the insuring agreement requires the injured person to submit to examination by physicians of the insurer's choice, as often as the insurer reasonably requires; of course, the insurer will pay for the expense of the exams.

Exclusions

Coverage C contains only seven exclusions. This small number of exclusions is facilitated by exclusion (g), which applies to any bodily injury claim excluded under coverage A. Another exclusion having broad application is exclusion (f), which eliminates coverage for BI included within the products-completed operations hazard (a defined term). The seven exclusions are quoted in turn below with brief commentary on each.

2. Exclusions

We will not pay expenses for "bodily injury":

a. Any Insured

To any insured, except "volunteer workers."

A person who qualifies as an insured under the CGL coverage forms cannot collect medical payments. The exception relating to volunteer workers was added in the 2001 CGL revision, the same revision in which the CGL coverage forms were modified to include the named insured's volunteers as insureds. In the absence of this exception to the exclusion, volunteer workers would be excluded from medical payments coverage now that they are insureds. Before the CGL forms were modified to include volunteer workers as insureds, they were not excluded from medical payments coverage, so it was necessary to exempt them from the exclusion of medical payments coverage to any insured in order to maintain their eligibility for medical payments.

b. Hired Person

To a person hired to do work for or on behalf of any insured or a tenant of any insured.

The person hired to do work could be either an employee or an independent contractor. Note that the exclusion applies also not only to persons hired to do work for any insured, but also to persons hired to do work for a tenant of any insured. For example, a painter hired by the named insured's tenant would not be able to collect medical payments if he or she were injured on premises owned by the insured.

c. Injury on Normally Occupied Premises

To a person injured on that part of premises you own or rent that the person normally occupies.

To illustrate, this exclusion would eliminate medical payments coverage for a tenant of the named insured's apartment building if the tenant was injured in his own apartment. If, instead, the tenant was injured while walking down a flight of stairs in a common area of the apartment building, his injury would not be excluded.

d. Workers Compensation and Similar Laws

To a person, whether or not an "employee" of any insured, if benefits for the "bodily injury" are payable or must be

> provided under a workers compensation or disability benefits law or a similar law.

This workers compensation exclusion differs from the Coverage A workers compensation exclusion in that the Coverage C exclusion applies to anyone whose injuries are covered under a workers compensation or disability benefits or a similar law; the injured person does not have to be an employee of any insured. To illustrate, say that an employee of a tree-trimming contractor working for a cable television company is injured while working on the insured's premises. Even though the injured worker is not an employee of the named insured, his injuries would still be excluded because they are compensable under workers compensation.

    e.   Athletics Activities

> To a person injured while practicing, instructing or participating in any physical exercises or games, sports, or athletic contests.

Prior to the 2004 edition of the CGL policy, this exclusion was worded as follows: "To a person injured while taking part in athletics." A question that could come up with this prior wording was whether casual sporting events, such as a softball game at a company picnic or a game of horseshoes at a church picnic, qualified as athletics. *Webster's Third New International Dictionary* defines athletics as "the physical exercise, sports, or games engaged in by athletes." An athlete, in turn, is defined as "one who is trained to compete … in exercises, sports, or games requiring physical strength, agility, or stamina." Thus, unless the injury occurs in a true athletic event—that is, one whose participants are trained to compete in that event as athletes—the prior exclusion should not bar coverage.

Because of questions over the meaning of the word *athletics*, ISO decided that this exclusion required modification so as to more clearly express the underwriting intent. Stating that it received requests from insurance agents and insurers for a more precise definition of athletics, ISO, as part of its 2004 revisions, amended the exclusion to read as reflected above. The ISO Circular announcing this change provided an explanation that the term *athletics* is intended to apply to those participating in any kind of athletics, whether they are organized or not, because they have accepted a greater risk of being injured. The purpose of medical payments is to assist those injured in accidents. It is not intended to be a substitute for a person's own health insurance.

    f.   Products-Completed Operations Hazard

> Included within the "products-completed operations hazard."

Although Coverage A covers the insured's liability for bodily injury or property damage within the products-completed operations hazard, Coverage C excludes expenses for bodily injury included within that hazard. The definition of products-completed operations hazard was discussed in Chapter 1.

g.   Coverage A Exclusions

Excluded under Coverage A.

This exclusion eliminates the need for repeating any of the Coverage A exclusions that are pertinent to medical payments coverage. Thus, for example, expenses for injuries resulting from the use of automobiles are excluded because of the Coverage A auto exclusion.

Chapter 4

Managing the Claims-Made Trigger

As discussed briefly in earlier chapters, the 1990 and later editions of form CG 00 02 have a claims-made trigger for Coverage A and Coverage B. The 1986 edition of form CG 00 02 has a claims-made trigger for Coverage A only and an offense committed trigger for Coverage B. This chapter describes the rationale for, and mechanics of, claims-made coverage in more detail. In order to handle claims-made coverage properly, it is essential to understand the effect of retroactive dates, the need for extended reporting periods, and the consequences of various endorsements for modifying claims-made coverage.

In the interest of not complicating the presentation, only the 1990 and later claims-made policy provisions are quoted in this chapter. Apart from the switch to a claims-made trigger for Coverage B in the 1990 CGL changes, any differences between the 1986 and the later provisions respecting coverage triggers are principally editorial and not substantive.

Reasons for Claims-Made Trigger

As noted in Chapter 1, the coverage trigger of form CG 00 01 is bodily injury or property damage that occurs during the policy period. If someone is injured by the named insured's product today, the occurrence policy in effect today will apply to the loss whether a claim is made against the insured this year or some later year.

The claims-made trigger of form CG 00 02, on the other hand, is the first making of a claim against the insured during the policy period for injury or damage that occurred after the policy's retroactive date. Using the previous example, if someone is injured by the named insured today, the claim against the insured must be made during the policy period (or an extended reporting period, which will be discussed later) of the current claims-made policy in order for that policy to apply to the loss. A claim cannot be made at some later year and still be covered by the claims-made policy of today.

A natural question is why two such opposing coverage triggers are available for the same type of policy. Consider first the occurrence trigger, the traditional coverage trigger for general liability insurance. Ordinarily, the occurrence trigger presents no problem to the insurer. A customer slips and falls in a store, he or she makes a claim against the insured storekeeper, the claim is paid by the storekeeper's insurer, and the file is closed a few months after the accident happened.

But not all claims are so straightforward. Take, for example, an insulation worker who was exposed to asbestos dust from 1950 to 1960. If the worker is diagnosed as having asbestosis thirty years later, he or she may, despite the passing of so many years, be able to recover damages under the occurrence-type liability policies of the asbestos manufacturer that were in effect from 1950 to 1960, if the insurance policies are interpreted according to the exposure theory that has been adopted by some courts. The exposure theory, if applied to this claim, would hold that bodily injury occurred during the entire period in which the worker was exposed to the asbestos dust. See, for example, *Insurance Company of North America v. Forty-Eight Insulations, Inc.*, 633 F.2d 1212 (1980), decided by the United States court of appeals for the sixth circuit.

If the claim were considered in light of yet another interpretation, sometimes called the *triple-trigger theory*, every liability policy that the manufacturer had in effect between the time of the first exposure and the time of the manifestation of the disease could be applicable, not merely the policies in effect during the time of exposure. The triple-trigger theory says that bodily injury occurs while a person is exposed to a hazardous substance, while the substance is "in residence" in the person following exposure, and when the resulting disease manifests itself. See *Keene Corp. v. Insurance Company of North America*, 667 F.2d 1034 (1981), decided by the United States court of appeals for the District of Columbia circuit.

The problems resulting from occurrence-type coverage are thus quite obvious in latent injury cases. The rate that the insurer charges for the coverage, and the loss reserves that the insurer sets aside to pay future claims may both prove to be grossly inadequate, depending in part on unpredictable factors such as the following:

1.   Whether a substance considered to be relatively safe at the time the insurance was issued proves many years later to be hazardous;

2.   The extent of economic inflation and "social" inflation (for example, the tendency of juries to award greater damages than in the past) between the time of exposure and when a claim is made; and

3.   Liberalizations in the law, such as the exposure and triple-trigger theories.

In short, insurers have come to feel that the uncertainties involved in writing occurrence-type coverage for some insureds subject them to an unacceptable risk.

The claims-made trigger provides a possible solution to such problems. In contrast to the occurrence trigger, the claims-made trigger allows coverage to apply under a particular policy only if a claim is made during the term of that policy. The insurer will know, by the end of the policy period, of all claims that may be payable under that policy. It will not have to reserve for unreported claims, as it would have to do under an occurrence policy. Thus, the insurer will be better able to predict an adequate rate for the next policy period. If, five years later, a claim is made against the insured for bodily injury resulting from exposure during the earlier policy periods, the claim will not be covered under any policy other than the one, if any, in effect at the time claim is made.

The foregoing description, however, is somewhat oversimplified. It ignores two claims-made features that can reintroduce some or all of the uncertainty associated with the occurrence trigger. These features are (1) the retroactive date, mentioned earlier, and (2) extended reporting periods. Both features are discussed in detail later in this chapter, along with the other specific provisions of the claims-made trigger. For now, it will suffice to say that because of the options that these features allow—both for insureds and insurers—anyone dealing with the claims-made form must acquire proficiency in arranging claims-made coverage. Failure to do so can result in uninsured losses for the insured, errors and omissions claims against producers, and the insurer's failure to collect an adequate premium.

Occurrence Trigger Provisions

The provision expressing the occurrence trigger is contained in the Coverage A insuring agreement of form CG 00 01. It states that:

This insurance applies to "bodily injury" and "property damage" only if... the "bodily injury" or "property damage" occurs during the policy period.

Essentially the same requirement is expressed in the 1973 comprehensive general liability policy in the definitions of bodily injury and property damage. So, as respects the trigger of coverage, the current form CG 00 01 is virtually identical to the 1973 liability policy.

Another trigger-related provision, also found in the Coverage A insuring agreement of form CG 00 01, is as follows:

Damages because of "bodily injury" include damages claimed by any person or organization for care, loss of services or death resulting at any time from the "bodily injury."

This provision, like a comparable statement in the 1973 definition of bodily injury, makes it clear that if death results from bodily injury at any time—for example, in the following policy period—damages for the resulting death will be considered to be payable under the policy in effect at the time the bodily injury occurred. The definition of property damage makes a similar statement regarding loss of use of tangible property. If, for example, a covered occurrence during the policy period results in loss of use of portions of a building that are not physically injured, the resulting loss of use will be covered under the policy in effect at the time of the occurrence regardless of whether the loss of use extends beyond the policy period.

Montrose Provision

Another provision that affects the CGL occurrence trigger is the so-called *Montrose* or continuous injury provision that appears in the insuring agreement of form CG 00 01. This provision was first added to the occurrence CGL coverage form by endorsement in 1999 and was added to the occurrence form's insuring agreement in the 2001 CGL revision. The *Montrose* provision is so named because it was developed in response to the 1995 California court case of *Montrose Chemical Corp. v. Admiral Insurance Company, et al.*, 10 Cal. 4th 645.

The court decided to adopt the continuous injury trigger which holds that injury or damage is deemed to occur continuously over time (often years) as long as injury continues. As a result, all policies in effect during the period during which injury or damage occurs are potentially triggered.

The Montrose provision, quoted below, attempts to limit application of the continuous (or progressive) injury concept. In a nutshell, if any insured is aware of any injury or damage prior to the policy's inception (new or renewal), any continuation, resumption of, or change in the injury or damage known prior to policy inception will be deemed to have occurred prior to the policy period. On the other hand, injury or damage occurring during the policy period that is not a continuation, resumption or change in injury or damage known to an insured prior to the policy inception date, will include injury or damage that continues, resumes or changes after the policy ends.

   b.   This insurance applies to "bodily injury" and "property damage" only if: ...

      (3)   Prior to the policy period, no insured listed under Paragraph 1. of Section II—Who Is an Insured and no

"employee" authorized by you to give or receive notice of an "occurrence" or claim knew that the "bodily injury" or "property damage" had occurred in whole or in part if such a listed insured or authorized "employee" knew, prior to the policy period, that the "bodily injury" or "property damage" occurred, then any continuation, change or resumption of such "bodily injury" or "property damage" during or after the policy period will be deemed to have been known prior to the policy period.

c.   "Bodily injury" or "property damage" which occurs during the policy period and was not, prior to the policy period, known to have occurred by any insured listed under Paragraph 1. of Section II—Who Is an Insured or any "employee" authorized by you to give or receive notice of an "occurrence" or claim, includes any continuation, change or resumption of that "bodily injury" or "property damage" after the end of the policy period.

d.   "Bodily injury" or "property damage" will be deemed to have been known to have occurred at the earliest time when any Insured listed under Paragraph 1. of Section II—Who Is an Insured or any "employee" authorized by you to give or receive notice of "occurrence" or claim:

(1)   Reports all, or any part, of the "bodily injury" or "property damage" to us or any other insurer;

(2)   Receives a written or verbal demand or claim for damages because of the "bodily injury" or "property damage"; or

(3)   Becomes aware by any other means that "bodily injury" or "property damage" has occurred or has begun to occur.

The *Montrose* provision has been court tested but time will tell whether it will be upheld according to the insurers' intent. Some insurers are not utilizing this provision at all, while other insurers are using their own versions. As discussed in Chapter 1, the definition of property damage attempts to apply the same concept where it reads: "all such loss of use shall be deemed to occur at the time of the physical injury that caused it."

In general, insureds have preferred occurrence-type coverage over claims-made coverage, due to its straightforward approach. Still, it can present some pitfalls. If an insured goes out of business but still has products or work in existence, injuries resulting from those products or work that occur after policy expiration will not be insured under the previous policies. If the insured wants insurance for that exposure, the insured must purchase a separate policy or policies to extend protection past expiration of the last policy in effect while the business was still a going concern.

Another pitfall of occurrence coverage is that the limits of liability for a previous policy may prove to be inadequate for paying claims made many years after the injury occurred. If a product of the insured's is found to have caused bodily injury many years earlier, the resulting claims will be covered by the policy in effect at the time of the injury. Limits that seemed adequate many years ago could be grossly inadequate by contemporary, inflated standards. Moreover, any aggregate limits of liability under the policy may have been reduced by other claims filed in the intervening years.

Despite these pitfalls, occurrence-type coverage is relatively uncomplicated and foolproof from the insured's point of view. As long as the insured keeps occurrence-type coverage in effect at all times, bodily injury or property damage that occurred during that time will potentially be within coverage under one or more of the past policies. Keeping coverage continuous and avoiding coverage gaps does not require a great deal of expertise.

Claims-Made Provisions

The claims-made trigger applicable to Coverage A of form CG 00 02 is expressed in the following statement:

> This insurance applies to "bodily injury" and "property damage" only if...a claim for damages because of the "bodily injury" or "property damage" is first made against any insured...during the policy period or any Section **V**—Extended Reporting Period we provide under Extended Reporting Periods.

An almost identical provision, applying to claims for personal and advertising injury, is used to state the claims-made trigger that applies to Coverage B of the 1990 and later CGL forms.

There are some important points to consider here. The trigger, first of all, is the making of a claim for damages. Although the named insured is required, by another provision in the policy, to notify the insurer as soon as practicable of any occurrence that may result in a claim, notification of an occurrence alone does not trigger coverage. There must be an actual claim for damages by a third party. And, it is the *first* making of a claim for damages that activates coverage. Another provision states that the claim will be considered to have been made once notice of claim has been received and recorded by any insured or the insurer, or when the insurer makes a settlement with the claimant.

The claims-made trigger language originally proposed by ISO required that the notice of claim be in writing. The current language does not require that. However, when it deleted the requirement of written notice of a claim,

ISO added the requirement that notice of claim must be received and recorded. Consequently, the provision in the claims-made form respecting duties of the insured in the event of a claim was also amended to require the insured to "immediately record the specifics of the claim and the date received" and provide written notice of the claim to the insurer as soon as practicable.

Comparable to a provision of the occurrence form discussed earlier is the following provision from the claims-made form:

> All claims for damages because of "bodily injury" to the same person, including damages claimed by any person or organization for care, loss of services, or death resulting at any time from the "bodily injury", will be deemed to have been made at the time the first of these claims is made against any insured.

To illustrate how this provision might apply, say that someone injured by the insured's product first makes a claim for resulting medical expenses a few months after the injury occurs, and those expenses are payable under the policy in effect at the time the claim for damages is made. If, in a later policy period, the claimant dies from her earlier injuries and her estate makes a claim against the insured for loss of services and funeral expenses, that claim will be deemed to have been made at the time the first claim was made. So, the second claim will be payable under the policy in effect at the time the first claim was made. It will not be payable under the policy in effect at the time the second claim was made. Consequently, the additional claim will be subject to the limits of insurance of the *previous* policy. A comparable provision has the same effect for property damage liability claims.

Retroactive Date

The claims-made coverage form also has a provision for imposing a retroactive date. If a retroactive date is shown in the declarations of a claims-made policy, the insurer will not cover any claim for injury or damage that occurred before the retroactive date, even though all other requirements of the claims-made trigger have been met.

The retroactive date provision of Coverage A reads as follows:

> This insurance applies to "bodily injury" and "property damage" only if... the "bodily injury" or "property damage" did not occur before the Retroactive Date, if any, shown in the Declarations or after the end of the policy period.

In the case of Coverage B (in the 1990 and later versions of the CGL form), the retroactive date provision is expressed as follows:

This insurance applies ... only if ... the offense was not committed before the Retroactive Date, if any, shown in the Declarations or after the end of the policy period.

When issuing a claims-made policy to an insured for the first time, the insurer is free to impose whatever retroactive date it deems appropriate, just as the insured may request (though not necessarily receive) whatever retroactive date it deems is in its best interest. Once a retroactive date has been established in a policy, however, ISO rules permit the date to be advanced only with the written consent of the first named insured and then only:

1. If there is a change in carrier;

2. If there is a substantial change in the insured's operations which results in an increased exposure to loss;

3. If the insured fails to provide the company with information the insured knew or should have known about the nature of the risk insured that would have been material to the insurer's acceptance of the risk, or fails to provide information requested by the insurer; or

4. At the request of the insured.

The considerations involved in selecting retroactive dates are discussed later in this chapter. Those considerations are best made after gaining an understanding of the extended reporting periods provision.

Extended Reporting Periods

To summarize, the claims-made trigger has two major requirements: (1) the claim must be first made during the policy period; and (2) the bodily injury or property damage for which the claim is being made must have occurred after the retroactive date, if any, shown in the policy. In the case of Coverage B, the personal and advertising injury offense must have been committed after the retroactive date. If a claim is made after the policy period ends, the expired policy will provide no coverage for the claim, even if requirement (2), above, is met. Accordingly, the purpose of the extended reporting periods, set forth under Section V of the claims-made form, is to provide coverage for such claims under an expired claims-made policy.

Extended reporting periods may be needed in a number of situations. Consider the following examples:

1. An insured goes out of business and cancels its claims-made policy.

2.   An insured's claims-made policy is cancelled by the insurer and the insured is unable to obtain new insurance.

3.   An insured's claims-made policy is replaced with an occurrence policy.

4.   An insured's claims-made policy is replaced with a claims-made policy; however, the new claims-made policy's retroactive date is set at a date later than the retroactive date in the previous policy.

Now, say that a claim is made against each of these insureds, after expiration of the previous policy, for injury that occurred after the retroactive date of the previous policy and before its expiration. Assuming that no extended reporting period applies to the previous policy, the claim will not be covered under the previous policy in any of these examples because the claim was not first made during the previous policy period.

Moreover, the insureds in the first and second examples, because they have not obtained new insurance policies, will have no other insurance. The insured in the third example, even though it has an occurrence policy in effect at the time of the claim, will also be without coverage because the occurrence policy only covers bodily injury and property damage that occur during the policy period. In this example, the injury occurred before the new policy's inception.

The insured in the last example may or may not have coverage for the later claim. Although the claim is made during the policy period of the new claims-made policy, it will not be covered unless the injury or damage occurred after the new retroactive date. If, for example, the new retroactive date is the same as the inception date of the new policy, the insured will not have coverage under the new policy for any claims resulting from injury or damage before that date.

The extended reporting periods provision in Section V of the CGL coverage forms provides, for no additional premium charge, a *basic* extended reporting period of limited duration for claims made after the policy period. The provision also enables the named insured to obtain, for an additional premium, a *supplemental* extended reporting period of unlimited duration for such claims. These extended reporting periods are also referred to as the basic tail and the supplemental tail.

The basic tail and the option to purchase the supplemental tail are provided if the policy is cancelled or not renewed for any reason by either the insured or the insurer. The tails are also available if the insurer renews or replaces the policy with one that either has a later retroactive date or applies on an occurrence basis.

Basic Tail

The basic tail covers claims made up to five years after the end of the policy period, provided the claim results from an occurrence (or, in the case of Coverage B, from an offense) reported to the insurer not later than sixty days after the end of the policy period. Also, of course, the bodily injury or property damage must have occurred (or the personal or advertising injury offense must have been committed) before the end of the policy period and after the applicable retroactive date.

To illustrate, say that a customer is injured on the insured's premises at some time during the policy period. The insured reports the details of the occurrence to the insurer as soon as practicable and before the end of the policy period, but the injured person has not yet made a claim against the insured by the end of the policy period. Because of the basic extended reporting period, any resulting claim will be covered under the expired policy (subject to policy limits and conditions) if the claim is made before the end of the five-year period.

The basic tail also contains a statement that the basic extended reporting period is limited to sixty days for "all other claims." Presumably, "all other claims" refers to any injury or offense that is not reported to the insurer within the initial sixty days after the end of the policy period. Say, for example, that the same occurrence described above happened without the insured's knowledge, and so the insured did not notify the insurer. The unknown and unreported occurrence will be automatically covered under the expired policy only if a claim is first made within sixty days after the end of the policy period. If the insured wants a discovery period of any longer duration, the supplemental tail will need to be purchased.

The basic tail does not apply to claims covered under subsequent insurance purchased by the named insured. To illustrate, say that the insured obtains a new claims-made policy with the same retroactive date as the previous policy, which had been cancelled. A claim is first made during the policy period of the new policy for an accident that occurred during the previous policy period and was reported to the insurer before the end of that period. Although the claim would otherwise qualify for coverage under the five-year tail, the existence of the subsequent insurance for the accident voids any coverage under the previous policy. The policy states that this is true even if the subsequent policy's aggregate limits have been exhausted by previous claims.

Another important feature of the basic tail is that it is subject to aggregate policy limits. If those limits have been reduced by previous claims, those reduced limits will be applicable to any claim made within the basic tail period.

Although the basic tail provides potentially valuable coverage, it does not meet all insureds' needs in all cases. The insured needs only to consider the possibility that a reported occurrence might not result in a claim until five years and one day after policy expiration, or an unknown and unreported occurrence might result in a claim sixty-one days after policy expiration. In either case, the basic tail will provide no coverage whatsoever. Unless the insured's current policy is a claims-made policy with a retroactive date going back to the retroactive date of the expired policy, there will be the possibility of uninsured claims unless the insured purchases the supplemental tail, which provides for an extended reporting period of unlimited duration.

Supplemental Tail

While the basic tail is provided automatically and for no additional premium, the supplemental tail is provided by endorsement, for an additional premium, and only if requested by the insured in writing within sixty days after the end of the policy period. If the insured does not exercise its option within sixty days after the end of the policy period, the insurer will have no obligation to sell the insured the supplemental tail endorsement. Thus, any insured that might need the supplemental tail should make a final determination before the sixty-day period expires. To summarize what was said earlier, the need for the supplemental tail exists when (1) the insured switches from claims-made to occurrence coverage; (2) the insured no longer carries liability insurance; or (3) the previous policy is renewed or replaced with claims-made coverage subject to an advanced retroactive date.

Supplemental tail coverage is activated by adding endorsement CG 27 10, Supplemental Extended Reporting Period Endorsement, to the expired or cancelled policy. (Until revised in 1997, this endorsement was designated CG 27 01.) A notable feature of the endorsement is that it automatically provides separate aggregate limits equaling the policy's original aggregate limits. (The basic tail is subject to the regular policy aggregate limits, even if reduced by previous claims.) Both the endorsement and its separate limits apply only to claims first received and recorded during the supplemental extended reporting period. The supplemental extended reporting period begins when the basic tail ends. Once it takes effect, the supplemental extended reporting period continues forever.

The extended reporting periods provision allows the insurer to determine the premium for the supplemental tail endorsement in accordance with the insurer's rules and rates. The insurer may take into account:

a.   The exposure insured;

b.   Previous types and amounts of insurance;

c.   Limits of insurance available under this Coverage Part for future payment of damages; and

d.   Other related factors.

However, the premium for the endorsement may not exceed 200 percent of the annual premium for the coverage part to which the endorsement would be attached. (The coverage part is the combination of CGL coverage forms and allied endorsements, whether they constitute a monoline policy or merely part of a commercial package policy.) The premium for the extended reporting period endorsement is fully earned upon the endorsement's effective date, and the endorsement cannot be cancelled if the premium is paid promptly when due.

Other Insurance

The supplemental extended reporting period endorsement amends the regular other insurance provisions of the policy so that the coverage of the endorsement is excess over any other valid and collectible insurance available to the insured, whether primary, excess, contingent or on any other basis, "whose policy period begins or continues after the Supplemental Extended Reporting Period begins."

To illustrate, say that an insured's claims-made policy is cancelled and the insured, unable to find replacement coverage within sixty days after cancellation, purchases the supplemental tail to protect against claims for earlier occurrences. Some time later the insured succeeds in obtaining claims-made coverage with a retroactive date that encompasses the earlier policy period. After the new policy takes effect, a claim is made against the insured for injury that occurred during the previous policy period. The claim is covered under both the supplemental tail endorsement and the new claims-made policy. Because of the other insurance provision under discussion, the new policy will be primary insurance and the supplemental tail coverage will be excess. Recall that if a claim is covered under the insured's later policy and the basic tail, the insured cannot collect anything—not even excess cover—under the basic tail coverage.

Considerations in Issuing Claims-Made Policies

Now that the claims-made trigger provisions, including the retroactive date and extended reporting periods, have been described, it is possible to consider the various choices that can be made in arranging claims-made coverage, as well as the consequences of those choices.

For every claims-made policy issued, the insurance company and the insured must negotiate a retroactive date, subject to the ISO rule imposing limitations on when the insurer can advance the retroactive date. There are three possible outcomes:

- The retroactive date may be the same as the policy's inception date;

- The retroactive date may be some date earlier than the policy's inception date; or

- No retroactive date may be imposed.

When the retroactive date indicated is the same as the policy's inception date, Coverage A under that policy will not cover injury or damage that occurred before the policy period. If a claim made during the policy period is to be covered, the bodily injury or property damage from which the claim arose must also have occurred during the policy period. Similarly, Coverage B (when the 1990 or later form is used) will not cover personal and advertising injury caused by an offense committed before the policy period has begun.

Setting the retroactive date as the policy inception date should be acceptable to most insureds if they had been insured exclusively under occurrence liability policies prior to the inception of the claims-made policy. Prior occurrences, in that case, are potentially within the coverage of the occurrence policy or policies in effect at the time the injury or damage occurred.

If, however, the insured had been previously insured under the ISO claims-made form, a retroactive date concurrent with the inception date of the new policy will leave a coverage gap. The new claims-made policy will not cover any claims, even if made during the new policy period, for bodily injury or property damage occurring before that policy's inception date. Nor will Coverage B (1990 and later versions) insure any personal and advertising injury caused by an offense committed before the new policy's inception date. The insured's only automatic coverage for such claims will come by way of the basic tail in the expired policy. Thus, if the insured is unable to obtain a retroactive date that goes back to the inception of the insured's first claims-made policy, the insured should purchase the supplemental tail endorsement under the expiring claims-made policy, unless it wishes to self-insure the exposure that lies beyond the basic tail coverage.

Likewise, the insurer too should consider all the consequences of advancing a retroactive date. If the new policy is a renewal of a claims-made policy issued by the same insurer, the insured will likely request a supplemental extended reporting period endorsement from the insurer. The insurer will be obliged to issue the endorsement, which will, in effect, turn the last claims-made policy into an occurrence liability policy, recreating the uncertainty about future claims that led ISO to introduce claims-made insurance in the first place.

Moreover, the rate for the new claims-made policy will be less than what it would have been had the insurer extended the same retroactive date that applied to the expiring policy. This is because claims-made rates are modified by factors that increase with the number of years (up to five) the insured has been in the claims-made program. The number of years in the claims-made program is measured from the applicable retroactive date. So, when the insurer moves the retroactive date up to the inception date of a renewal, it starts over with the first-year claims-made multiplier and receives less premium than if it could apply the higher claims-made modifier that would otherwise apply. (Of course, the insurer also avoids claims for prior occurrences under the new policy.)

When an insurer is issuing a claims-made policy to an insured for the first time—that is, the policy is not a renewal—the insurer should still consider the possibility of using a retroactive date earlier than the new policy's inception date. Say, for example, the insured had four years of claims-made coverage before making application to the new insurer. If the new insurer proposes a retroactive date concurrent with the new policy's inception date, it will be able to quote a first-year claims-made premium as well as avoid liability for earlier occurrences. However, the insured will for all practical purposes be forced to purchase an extended reporting period endorsement from the previous insurer. If the premium for that endorsement plus the premium for the new policy is considerably more than the premium for renewing the existing policy, the insured may decide not to switch insurers after all.

If the retroactive date on the new policy is set as the inception date of the insured's first claims-made policy, the retroactive date should not create any coverage gaps or require the insured to buy extended reporting period coverage (assuming the new policy has coverage terms as broad as those of the prior policy). In some cases the insurer may be willing to set a retroactive date earlier than the inception date of the new policy but not all the way back to the inception of the insured's first claims-made policy. That could be the case if the insurer felt that reported or unreported occurrences from that prior period could pose an unacceptable risk. Here again, because the new retroactive date does not extend all the way back to the retroactive date of the first claims-made policy, the insured will need to buy the supplemental tail endorsement under the expiring policy in order to avoid a coverage gap.

The third possibility for retroactive dates—not imposing any retroactive date whatsoever—has the effect of providing coverage for claims first made during the current policy period, regardless of when the injury or damage occurred. Although attractive to insureds, this option sees limited use, particularly for insureds whose products or work have been on the market for some time or whose products or work have a potential for causing latent injury.

If, however, the insured had continuous occurrence type coverage in effect for all years leading up to the claims-made policy being issued, the insurer may be amenable to imposing no retroactive date, in view of the fact that earlier occurrences would be covered on a primary basis under the earlier occurrence-type policies and only on an excess basis under the claims-made policy in effect at the time claim was made. (The other insurance provision will be described in more detail in Chapter 5.) The adequacy of the limits of insurance under the earlier policies and the insured's claim history are important factors in the underwriter's decision.

Exclusion of Specific Accidents, Etc.

As said earlier, when a claims-made policy is being issued, injury and damage that occurred before the inception of the new policy can be excluded simply by imposing a retroactive date that is concurrent with the inception date of the new policy. When that is done, all injury or damage that occurred before the new inception date will be excluded, even if claim is first made during the new policy period. The preceding discussion also pointed out why such a retroactive date is not desirable for the insured and in some cases may be undesirable for the insurer. Moreover, there may be situations when ISO rules do not permit the insurer to advance the retroactive date, as discussed earlier.

As an alternative to excluding all prior occurrences through the retroactive date, an ISO endorsement (CG 27 02) is available for excluding specific accidents. An insurer might use this endorsement if it were willing to extend an earlier retroactive date but did not want to be liable for certain injuries known to have occurred before policy inception. The endorsement allows the insurer to exclude the known accident(s) without having to impose a retroactive date that excludes all prior occurrences, known or unknown.

The endorsement, which is entitled Exclusion of Specific Accidents, Products, Work or Locations, can also be used, as its name implies, to exclude specific products, work, or locations. As is the case with specific accidents, the insurer must describe the specific products, work, or locations in the endorsement. When that is done, coverage for the products, work, or locations specified is excluded whether the injury or damage occurred before or after inception of the new policy. Thus, apart from excluding specific accidents known to have happened, the exclusion might be used in the following situations:

- The insured has sold, and continues to sell, a certain product that the insurer does not want to insure for any price. Apart from the particular product, the insurer is willing to insure the rest of the insured's products liability exposure, including claims made during the new policy period for prior accidents involving products other than those for which the insurer wishes to avoid liability. To accomplish these aims, the insurer could provide an earlier retroactive date but attach the exclusionary endorsement with a description of the particular product to be excluded.

- The insured wishes to self-insure certain products or work without excluding the products-completed operations hazard entirely. The insured could ask the insurance company to exclude the particular products or work in consideration of a reduced premium.

- The insurer does not want to assume liability for a particular location of the insured's; or, the insured wants to self-insure the liability exposure arising from a particular location. In either case, excluding the location allows the insurer to provide coverage for the insured's other CGL exposures.

Note that the exclusion must be attached to all subsequent claims-made policies if the insurer wants the effect of the endorsement to continue. To illustrate, say that an insurer is renewing a claims-made policy that excluded a particular accident. If the accident has not resulted in a claim against the insured by renewal time and the insurer is still unwilling to insure the potential claim, the insurer should exclude the accident from the renewal policy as well.

When the exclusion of specific accidents, products, work, or locations is first added to a renewal policy, the insurer must also amend the expiring policy with another endorsement, CG 27 03, entitled Amendment of Section V—Extended Reporting Periods for Specific Accidents, Products, Work or Locations. This endorsement extends the expiring policy's basic tail coverage to apply to the excluded accidents, products, work, or locations. It also gives the insured the option to purchase supplemental tail coverage with respect to those items. Supplemental extended reporting period endorsement CG 27 11 is available for providing that coverage under the expiring policy if the insured elects it. Like the supplemental tail endorsement CG 27 10, endorsement CG 27 11 provides separate aggregate limits equal to the aggregate limits in the policy to which the endorsement is attached. (Until revised in 1997, this endorsement was designated CG 27 04.)

Special Products Problem

When a particular accident has been excluded under a renewal policy as described above, endorsement CG 27 11 provides the means of extending the renewal policy to cover any claims later arising out of that accident. Such is not necessarily the case with products, however. For example, say that the named insured manufactures a batch of 100,000 jars of a contaminated foodstuff, and the jars are widely distributed before the defect is discovered. Upon policy renewal the insurer excludes the entire batch, via endorsement CG 27 02, in the renewal policy.

Besides adding the exclusion to the renewal policy, the insurer will be obliged to amend the expiring policy with endorsement CG 27 03. That will extend the basic tail coverage of the expiring policy to the excluded batch and allow the insured to purchase supplemental tail coverage for the excluded batch. If the insured purchases the supplemental tail, the expired policy will cover, for a period of unlimited duration, any claim first made after the end of the policy period, but only if the claim arises out of an injury that occurred before the expiration date. There is still the possibility, even if the insured has recalled the defective batch, that someone will consume the contaminated product and sustain injury after the renewal policy has gone into effect. Because the injury occurred after the inception of the renewal policy, a resulting claim will be excluded by both the renewal policy and the expired policy, despite the existence of supplemental tail coverage under the expired policy. Note that a similar problem could arise with respect to excluded work or locations.

Consequently, insureds should, if possible, avoid imposition of the exclusion of specified products, work, or locations, unless the insured consciously chooses to self-insure the exposure to loss from injury occurring after the effective date of the exclusion. If the insured wishes to maintain insurance for the exposure despite the insurer's intention to exclude the product, work, or location, the insured must either (1) negotiate with the insurer to have the insurer refrain from adding the exclusion or (2) find another insurer that is willing to insure the exposure.

If the replacement policy is claims-made, it obviously must not contain the exclusion that the previous insurer wanted to use. Beyond that is the matter of retroactive date. If the new policy's retroactive date is later than the expiring policy's, the insured will need to buy supplemental tail coverage under the expiring policy if it wishes to insure, without time limit, its exposure to claims first made after termination of the expiring policy that result from injuries occurring before the termination. In the unlikely event that the retroactive date on the new policy is the same as that on the expiring policy, supplemental tail coverage will be unnecessary, assuming the new insurer has not excluded any prior accidents, products, work, or locations.

If the new policy is on an occurrence basis, it will cover claims, whenever they are first made, that result from injury that occurs during its policy period. However, the insured will need to buy supplemental tail coverage under the expiring policy if the insured wants an extended reporting period of unlimited duration for claims based on injuries that occurred before the inception date of the new occurrence policy.

Chapter 5

General Provisions

This chapter describes three sections of the CGL forms that apply generally to all coverages under the forms. These sections are as follows:

Section II — Who Is an Insured

Section III — Limits of Insurance

Section IV — Commercial General Liability Conditions

Who Is an Insured

Section II of the CGL coverage forms entitled "Who Is an Insured," was modified in 1993, 1996, 2001, and 2004; the current version of the CGL forms (12 07) contains the same wording as the 2004 edition. The commentary in this section does the following:

1. Presents the 2001 and 2004/2007 "Who Is an Insured" provisions.

2. Compares the 1986 and later provisions to the corresponding provisions of the 1973 comprehensive general liability policy and the broad form general liability endorsement (hereinafter referred to as the "old" provisions).

3. Describes the modifications to the "Who Is an Insured" where applicable.

"Who Is an Insured" consists of four parts in the 2001 edition of the CGL policy; part 3 was omitted from the 2004 edition. Each part is discussed in turn below.

Part 1—"You" and Other Designated Persons

Part 1 of Who Is an Insured reads as follows:

1. If you are designated in the Declarations as:

    a. An individual, you and your spouse are insureds, but only with respect to the conduct of a business of which you are the sole owner.

135

b.   A partnership or joint venture, you are an insured. Your members, your partners, and their spouses are also insureds, but only with respect to the conduct of your business.

c.   A limited liability company, you are an insured. Your members also are insureds, but only with respect to the conduct of your business. Your managers are insureds, but only respect to their duties as your managers.

d.   An organization other than a partnership, joint venture or limited liability company, you are an insured. Your "executive officers" and directors are insureds, but only with respect to their duties as your officers or directors. Your stockholders are also insureds, but only with respect to their liability as stockholders.

e.   A trust, you are an insured. Your trustees are also insureds, but only with respect to their duties as trustees.

It is important to understand that if an individual has many business interests and desires protection for his or her individual business liability, being designated as an individual in the liability policy will not fulfill that purpose. The reason is that the individual's coverage is strictly limited to one or more businesses in which the individual is the sole owner or proprietor. Some insurers will cover individuals for their business liability unrelated to sole proprietorships, but it takes a different designation than simply designating that the policy is issued to an individual. One such approach is to state the person's name on the list of named insureds followed by the descriptive, individually; as an example: John Doe, Individually.

A partnership is a business consisting of two or more individuals (partners) who share in losses and profits and have unlimited liability. The formation of a partnership does not require any state filings, unlike a limited liability company or corporation. A joint venture is a partnership for a limited purpose. Once that purpose has been met, the joint venture commonly is dissolved. A limited partnership is an entity comprised of at least one general partner and one or more limited partners. The general partner, which may consist of one or more individuals or corporations, actually manages the entity. The general partner also commonly has the same rights and unlimited liability that confront the partners of a partnership.

In 1996, Who Is an Insured was modified to include various references to limited liability companies, which are an increasingly common alternative to individual proprietorships, partnerships, joint ventures, and corporations. Although this phenomenon was in use in other parts of the world as early as the 1930s, it was first introduced to the U.S. business community in 1977.

Members of a limited liability company are typically the owners, whereas the managers are those elected by the members to manage the entity. The potential liability for the wrongful conduct of the LLC members, in a large part, is analogous to the liability faced by officers and directors of a corporation.

If the named insured is a limited liability company, the company is an insured. The members (essentially, owners) of the company are also insureds, but only with respect to the conduct of the company's business. The company's managers are also insureds, but only with respect to their duties as the company's managers.

Trustees were able to be added to the pre-2001 CGL forms as additional insureds by endorsement. With the introduction of the 2001 CGL forms, trustees of trusts that are named insureds are included as insureds, thus eliminating the need for the additional insured endorsement.

Apart from the additions to limited liability companies and trusts, the above provisions are virtually identical in effect to the parallel portions of the old provisions. An improvement over the old coverage for spouses is the current statement that the spouses of members of a joint venture are insured persons, provided the named insured is a joint venture. Under the old language, spouses are insured persons only if the named insured is a sole proprietor or partnership.

Since at least 1941 and until the 1973 general liability provisions were replaced, stockholders have been considered as insureds *but only while acting within the scope of their duties as such*. However, the italicized wording was replaced in the 1986 and later CGL forms with a provision that reads: "your stockholders are also insureds, but only with respect to their liability as stockholders."

One reason for the amendment might have been cases such as *Turner & Newall v. American Mutual Liability Insurance Company*, 1985 WL 8056 (DDC 1985 applying Pa. law)., in which an insurer was obligated to defend and provide coverage to an English corporation that held stock, through a wholly owned Canadian subsidiary corporation, in an American corporation named as an insured under liability policies. The U.S. District Court for the District of Columbia ruled that the English corporation was covered under the liability policies as a stockholder of the named insured "while acting within the scope of his duties as such" because, in part, of the ambiguity conveyed by the phrase in quotes. As a result, the insurer of the liability policies written for the American corporation was required to pay the English corporation the costs of defending asbestos-related bodily injury suits arising out of the conduct of both the English corporation and the American corporation.

Part 2—Volunteer Workers and Employees

The second part of Who Is an Insured (2001 and 2004/2007 versions) reads as follows:

2.   Each of the following is also an insured:

   a.   Your "volunteer workers" only while performing duties related to the conduct of your business, or your "employees", other than either your "executive officers" (if you are an organization other than a partnership, joint venture or limited liability company) or your managers (if you are a limited liability company), but only for acts within the scope of their employment by you or while performing duties related to the conduct of your business. However, none of these "employees" or "volunteer workers" are insureds for:

      (1)   "Bodily injury" or "personal and advertising injury":

         (a)   To you, to your partners or members (if you are a partnership or joint venture), to your members (if you are a limited liability company), a co-"employee" while in the course of his or her employment or performing duties related to the conduct of your business, or to your other "volunteer workers" while performing duties related to the conduct of your business;

         (b)   To the spouse, child, parent, brother or sister of that co-"employee" as a consequence of Paragraph (1)(a) above;

         (c)   For which there is any obligation to share damages with or repay someone else who must pay damages because of the injury described in Paragraphs (1)(a) or (b) above; or

         (d)   Arising out of his or her providing or failing to provide professional health care services.

      (2)   "Property damage" to property:

         (a)   Owned, occupied or used by,

         (b)   Rented to, in the care, custody or control of, or over which physical control is being exercised for any purpose by

         you, any of your "employees," "volunteer workers," any partner or member (if you are a partnership or joint venture), or any member (if you are a limited liability company).

b.   Any person (other than your "employee" or "volunteer worker"), or any organization while acting as your real estate manager.

c.   Any person or organization having proper temporary custody of your property if you die, but only:

(1)   With respect to liability arising out of the maintenance or use of that property; and

(2)   Until your legal representative has been appointed.

d.   Your legal representative if you die, but only with respect to duties as such. That representative will have all your rights and duties under this Coverage Part.

Volunteers as Insureds

The portions of Section 2.a. regarding volunteer workers have no counterparts in earlier editions of the CGL forms. Newly added in the 2001 edition as an automatic insured is a volunteer worker, a term defined to mean "a person who is not your 'employee', and who donates his or her work and acts at the direction of and within the scope of duties determined by you, and is not paid a fee, salary or other compensation by you or anyone else for their work performed for you."

Definitions

Reference to the quoted term "employee" was an addition to CGL forms in 1993 in order to better facilitate coverage for employee leasing exposures that have grown immensely over recent years. To clarify matters, the term "employee" also needed to be defined. The definition section now defines employee to mean:

"Employee" includes a "leased worker." "Employee" does not include a "temporary worker."

The fact that the word "includes" is used in the above definition instead of "means" avoids limiting the definition of employee solely to a leased worker. The term employee, therefore, can also be taken to mean any employed person, other than an excluded person such as a temporary worker.

And to make it clear that a temporary worker is not given the same status and protection as other employees, including leased workers, the definitions section contains two additional defined terms that were added with the 1993 amendments:

"Leased worker" means a person leased to you by a labor leasing firm under an agreement between you and the labor leasing firm, to perform duties related to the conduct of your business. "Leased worker" does not include a "temporary worker."

"Temporary worker" means a person who is furnished to you to substitute for a permanent "employee" on leave to meet seasonal or short-term workload conditions.

Incidentally, the definition of temporary worker is identical to that definition appearing in the labor contractor endorsement for use with the standard workers compensation policy as issued to the entity that desires to obtain the services of a labor contractor (lessor). Even though defined, this term presents many problems leading to litigation over the meaning of the words "furnished to." The reason for these arguments is that if a worker is considered not to be a temporary one, that worker cannot sue the named insured (employer) and collect damages for any injuries. The defined term "leased worker", on the other hand, is referred to, but undefined, under the workers compensation policy.

Another term now defined is "executive officer," meaning a person holding any of the officer positions created by your charter, constitution, by-laws, or any other similar governing document. One of the primary reasons executive officer is a defined term is to avoid the argument raised by some employees confronted with a fellow employee suit (currently also referred to as a co-employee suit) to maintain that they were acting in the capacity of an executive officer at the time their negligent conduct injured another employee in order to overcome the CGL policy's co-employee exclusion. With this definition of executive officer within the policy, an alleged tortfeasor/co-employee will be unlikely to obtain coverage unless he is in fact an executive officer as defined in the policy.

One can conclude, based on section 2.(a), that those who are automatically included as insureds under CGL forms are volunteer workers, employees, and leased workers. Those who are not insureds under this section are temporary workers and executives, the latter because they are automatically included as an insured in the first section of Who Is an Insured.

Co-Employee Exclusion

Paragraph 2.a.(1)(a), as it now reads above, was introduced with the 1993 edition and is referred to as the co-employee exclusion. It contains language to make it clear that no employee is an insured for bodily injury or personal injury to the named insured's partners or members if the named insured is a partnership or joint venture. Although earlier editions applied only to injury to "you or to a co-employee," ISO has maintained that the revised language is merely a clarification.

Because most states do not permit co-employee suits, many underwriters will delete reference to co-employee suits by endorsement.[1] When such an endorsement is issued, it still leaves intact such exclusions as paragraph 2.a.(1)(a) involving injuries, at the hands of an employee, upon the named insured's partners, members of joint venture, limited liability companies, and sole owners.

It was with the 1990 revision that paragraph 2.a.(1)(b) was introduced. It broadened the co-employee exclusion to preclude coverage for suits made by relatives of an employee against a co-employee. As a result, this wording has the same effect with respect to relatives' suits against co-employees as the employee injury exclusion (exclusion e. of Coverage A) has on relatives' suits against the named insured.

Third Party Actions

Paragraph 2.a.(1)(c) was introduced in 1990 to make clear that coverage is precluded even in such instances as a third party (or third party over) action (discussed in Chapter 1).

Professional Liability Exclusions

The exclusion of injuries arising out of an employee's providing or failing to provide professional health care services [2.a.(1)(d) above] has no counterpart in the old provisions. Ordinarily, a professional liability exclusion endorsement is attached to a CGL policy whenever the insured's classification—for example, physician or hospital—calls for it. Such an exclusion differs from section 2.a.(1)(d) above in that the endorsement excludes professional liability of any insured under the policy, including the named insured. Section 2.a.(1)(d), in contrast, excludes professional liability of the insured employee only; it does not, for example, apply to vicarious liability that the named insured might have for the employee's providing or failing to provide professional health care services.

Therefore, section 2.a.(1)(d) should not be viewed as a substitute for the professional liability exclusions that may be attached to a CGL policy for certain classifications. The intent behind 2.a.(1)(d) seems to be to exclude coverage for professional liability that might fall upon incidental medical personnel of the insured organization, particularly an organization that does not otherwise provide medical services.

So, for example, a nurse employed by a manufacturer to administer first aid to other employees would not be covered for liability arising out of her providing of health care services. As long as the policy is not amended with a professional liability exclusion that applies to the named insured, the named insured would be covered for liability arising out of the employed professional's providing of health care services, assuming no other exclusion applied, such as (in the case of an employee's claim) those relating to injury to employees of the named insured and to workers compensation obligations. If, for example, an employed nurse injured a visitor to the premises in administering first aid to the visitor, the policy would not cover a claim against the nurse but presumably would cover a claim against the employer.

Section 2.a.(1)(d) may be intended, at least partially, as a counterpart to an exclusion under the incidental malpractice liability provisions of the broad form CGL endorsement that commonly was attached to the 1973 CGL policy. The old exclusion applied to any insured engaged in the business or occupation of providing any of a variety of medical services listed under the incidental malpractice coverage. Since an employed medical professional can be viewed as an insured engaged in the occupation of providing medical services, he or she would not have been covered under the old broad form endorsement either. However, the old exclusion applied to any insured in that business or occupation, whereas section 2.a.(1)(d) applies only to employees.

Property Damage Exclusion

Exclusion j of the 1986 CGL coverage forms excluded (among other things) damage to "personal property in your care, custody or control." In the 1990 CGL changes, ISO changed this part of the exclusion j. to apply to "personal property in the care, custody or control of the insured." After making this change, ISO became concerned that the change would be interpreted to mean that the CGL forms would cover damage to employees' property in the care, custody or control of the named insured.

To preclude this interpretation, the 1993 modifications added language to the "Who Is an Insured" property damage exclusion making it clear that no employee is an insured for damage to property in the care, custody, or control of the named insured or over which the insured is exercising physical control for any reason. [See section 2.a.(2).] In ISO's opinion, this change does not involve any change in coverage.

Real Estate Managers, Custodians, and Legal Representatives

Subpart 2.b., respecting real estate managers, is virtually identical to a similar clause under the 1973 general liability coverage part. As a matter of history, this provision, worded a little differently, was first added to general liability policy provisions in 1955. Today, more so than ever, the question of who a real estate manager can encompass is highly litigated because it is a term that is not defined in CGL forms. For example, a court-appointed receiver who managed the real property of creditors was held to be a real estate manager in one case, as was a mortgagee in another case. Subparts 2.c. and 2.d. express the same extent of insured status for custodians and legal representatives following the named insured's death as is provided under the assignment provision in the old general liability policy jacket.

Part 3—Operators of Mobile Equipment

As is noted elsewhere in this book, one of the more significant 2004 revisions has to do with the elimination of coverage for mobile equipment subject to a compulsory or financial responsibility law or other motor vehicle insurance law in the state where the equipment is licensed or principally garaged. Now considered as autos, these land vehicles are subject to coverage by business auto, truckers, or motor carrier coverage forms.

In light of this revision, coverage will no longer apply to operators of mobile equipment registered under any of the applicable laws. In fact, this part of the Who Is an Insured provision was deleted with the 2004 revisions. However, not all insurers will necessarily use the 2004 or the 2007 ISO edition, particularly those insurers who continue to maintain such risks on a CGL policy basis, rather than a commercial auto form. For this reason, the discussion of this part remains intact so as to continue giving readers the valuable background information about the rationale for this provision.

The third part of Who Is an Insured (2001 version only) reads as follows:

3. With respect to "mobile equipment" registered in your name under any motor vehicle registration law, any person is an insured while driving such equipment along a public highway with your permission. Any other person or organization responsible for the conduct of such person is also an insured, but only with respect to liability arising out of the operation of the equipment, and only if no other insurance of any kind is available to that person or organization for this liability. However, no person or organization is an insured with respect to:

   a. "Bodily injury" to a co-"employee" of the person driving the equipment; or

   b. "Property damage" to property owned by, rented to, in the charge of or occupied by you or the employer of any person who is an insured under this provision.

The above provisions respecting insured status for persons operating mobile equipment on public roads have essentially the same effect as similar provisions under the persons insured section of the 1973 general liability form.

An apparent, though not real, difference between the two versions is that the above version applies only to mobile equipment registered in the name of the named insured, while the 1973 version requires that the mobile equipment be registered in the name of the named insured only when the operator is someone other than an employee of the named insured. That is, the 1973 general liability form provided insured status to employees while operating registered equipment on public highways, regardless of whether the equipment was registered in the name of the named insured or another entity. The above provision, viewed by itself, seems to say that registration in the name of the named insured is required in all cases.

However, it must be remembered that, under the current CGL forms, employees are insured persons, apart from this provision, by virtue of part 2.a. of Who Is an Insured, discussed earlier. Therefore, as long as use of mobile equipment is not excluded by some other provision in the policy, employees are covered while driving it on public highways within the scope of their employment by the named insured—regardless of whether it is registered in the name of the named insured or another entity, and, presumably, regardless of whether it is registered. The same is true of any other person or organization that qualifies as an insured apart from the mobile equipment provision—say, the spouse of the named insured.

The problem is that no one knows for sure whether mobile equipment being used on a public highway at the time of an accident is registered in the named insured's name under any motor vehicle registration law, or even needs to be registered. Some owners of mobile equipment required to be registered under a motor vehicle registration law may intentionally forgo such a requirement under the belief that such equipment will never be used on public roads. At the other extreme are owners of mobile equipment who are ignorant of the law concerning registration of mobile equipment. There are also circumstances when certain mobile equipment does not have to be registered.

For any person other than those who otherwise qualify as insureds, the requirement that the equipment must be registered in the name of the named insured is applicable. For example, an independent contractor doing work for the named insured could not qualify as an insured under the named insured's policy while driving mobile equipment registered in his own name. If, instead, the contractor drove mobile equipment registered in the name of the named insured, the contractor would be covered, provided the independent contractor met all other conditions of coverage.

Also covered is any other person or organization responsible for the conduct of persons covered for the operation of the equipment, provided the person or organization has no other available insurance for the accident.

The above provision excludes bodily injury to a co-employee of the person driving the equipment. In the 1973 form, a similar exclusion applies to bodily injury to any fellow employee of such person injured in the course of his or her employment.

Another exclusion applicable to the provision under discussion eliminates coverage for property damage to "property owned by, rented to, in the charge of or occupied by you or the other employer of any person who is an insured under this provision." The 1973 form has a similar exclusion, to the same effect.

Part 4—Newly Acquired Organizations

Part 4 of Who Is an Insured in the 2001 version (part 3 in the 2004 and 2007 version) reads as follows:

4. Any organization you newly acquire or form, other than a partnership, joint venture or limited liability company, and over which you maintain ownership or majority interest, will qualify as a Named Insured if there is no other similar insurance available to that organization. However:

   a. Coverage under this provision is afforded only until the 90th day after you acquire or form the organization or the end of the policy period, whichever is earlier;

   b. Coverage A does not apply to "bodily injury" or "property damage" that occurred before you acquired or formed the organization; and

   c. Coverage B does not apply to "personal and advertising injury" arising out of an offense committed before you acquired or formed the organization.

This category provides essentially the same coverage as the provision titled "automatic coverage—newly acquired organizations" in the broad form comprehensive general liability endorsement. However, in the current forms, reference to limited liability companies has been added, the new term "personal and advertising injury" is substituted for "personal injury" or "advertising injury," and a number of qualifications have been added, which are probably best viewed as clarifications of the coverage previously intended. Among these qualifications are a statement that the coverage does not apply to newly acquired or formed partnerships, joint ventures, or limited liability companies; that the coverage expires at the end of the policy period if that is less than ninety days after the acquisition or formation date; and that Coverages A and B do not apply to incidents that took place prior to the acquisition or formation of the new organization.

Apart from these qualifications, there appears to be an actual difference between the old and current provisions in the matter of other insurance that the organization might have. The current forms refer to "other similar insurance available to that organization." The old language is more stringent, referring to any other insurance under which the new organization is an insured or under which it "would be an insured...but for exhaustion of its limits of liability."

Undeclared Partnerships and Joint Ventures

The final clause under Who Is an Insured states that:

> No person or organization is an insured with respect to the conduct of any current or past partnership or joint venture or limited liability company that is not shown as a Named Insured in the Declarations.

This clause differs from a similar one under the 1973 general liability form in that it includes reference to a limited liability company, and it applies to "any current or *past* partnership or joint venture" (emphasis added), whereas the old wording applies only to "any partnership or joint venture of which the insured is a partner or member." Thus, while the old wording might be interpreted not to exclude partnerships or joint ventures of which the insured was previously, but not at the time of claim, a partner or member, the new language is quite clear in excluding undeclared partnerships or joint ventures regardless of when they existed.

The current wording does not address a problem in interpretation of the earlier joint venture exclusion, which arose in a 1982 case decided by the Minnesota Supreme Court. That court held that the old exclusion did not relieve an insurer of the duty to defend its insured against an allegation of bodily injury arising out of the operation of an undeclared "joint venture or joint enterprise" of which the insured was a member. The decision rested on the fact that the exclusion does not specifically refer to joint enterprises. The case is *Grain Dealers Mutual Ins. Co. v. Cady*, 318 N.W.2d 247 (Minn. 1982).

The exclusion of partnerships or joint ventures that are not named in the policy declarations also has been expanded to exclude unnamed limited liability companies. If coverage is wanted for a present or past limited liability company, it must be shown as a named insured in the policy declarations.

The purpose for this provision is to keep the insurer from encountering any surprises about such business relationships a named insured might have currently, or has had in the past, that can raise the demand for coverage in the future. So, if a CGL policy of a named insured also lists a current or past partnership or joint venture, the foregoing provision confirms that the entity, as named insured, is covered along with its partners or joint venturers, as insureds.

Limits of Insurance

Section III of the CGL coverage forms defines the various limits of insurance and their applicability. This section of the policy differs from pre-1986 forms in a number of ways, particularly with respect to the general aggregate limit under the CGL coverage forms. The Limits of Insurance section is quoted in part below.

1. The Limits of Insurance shown in the Declarations and the rules below fix the most we will pay regardless of the number of:

   a. Insureds;

   b. Claims made or "suits" brought; or

   c. Persons or organizations making claims or bringing "suits".

2. The General Aggregate Limit is the most we will pay for the sum of:

   a. Medical expenses under Coverage C; and

   b. Damages under Coverage A, except damages because of "bodily injury" and "property damage" included in the "products-completed operations hazard"; and

   c. Damages under Coverage B.

3. The Products-Completed Operations Aggregate Limit is the most we will pay under Coverage A for damages because of "bodily injury" and "property damage" included in the "products-completed operations hazard".

4. Subject to Paragraph 2. above, the Personal and Advertising Injury Limit is the most we will pay under Coverage B for the sum of all damages because of all "personal injury" and all "advertising injury" sustained by any one person or organization.

5. Subject to Paragraph 2. or 3. above, whichever applies, the Each Occurrence Limit is the most we will pay for the sum of:

   a. Damages under Coverage A; and

   b. Medical expenses under Coverage C

   because of all "bodily injury" and "property damage" arising out of any one "occurrence".

6.   Subject to Paragraph 5. above, the Damage To Premises Rented To You Limit is the most we will pay under Coverage A for damages because of "property damage" to any one premises, while rented to you, or in the case of damage by fire, while rented to you or temporarily occupied by you with permission of the owner.

7.   Subject to Paragraph 5. above, the Medical Expense Limit is the most we will pay under Coverage C for all medical expenses because of "bodily injury" sustained by any one person.

The wording of clause 6. above was changed in 1998 to show that the term is now the "damage to premises rented to you" limit instead of the "fire damage" limit. This complements the coverage afforded the insured as discussed previously in connection with exclusion j under Coverage A. Note that this clause pertains to damage to premises; fire damage is no longer the only covered cause of loss to property rented to the named insured.

Aggregate Limits

The most important difference between the current and the 1973 limits of liability provisions is that the current forms are subject to a general aggregate limit that limits the total amount payable during the policy period for Coverages A, B, and C, except for products-completed operations claims, which are subject to a separate aggregate limit. Under the 1973 liability policy, there is an aggregate limit applicable to bodily injury resulting from products or completed operations claims, and another aggregate limit applicable to property damage resulting from 1) risks rated on a remuneration basis or contractors equipment rated on a receipts basis; 2) operations performed for the named insured by independent contractors; and 3) the products and completed operations hazards. However, all other claims are subject only to a per occurrence, and not an aggregate, limit.

Consequently, the general aggregate limit can eliminate coverage under the current forms that would exist under the 1973 policy. To illustrate, say that the insured has an each occurrence limit of $500,000 for Coverage A and a general aggregate limit of $1 million. If during the policy period the insurer pays two Coverage A claims (neither involving products or completed operations) worth $500,000 each, the policy will provide no more coverage—under any of the policy's insuring agreements, including A, B, and C—for subsequent claims during the policy period, assuming the claims do not involve products or completed operations. If the coverage were under the 1973 liability policy, the each occurrence limit would still be available for any further claims during the policy period, assuming the claims did not fall under products-completed operations or any of the other categories that are subject to an aggregate limit under the 1973 provisions.

Reduction of the general aggregate limit does not affect the products-completed operations aggregate limit. Each aggregate limit represents a separate amount of insurance. Thus, an insured with a general aggregate limit of $1 million and a products-completed operations aggregate limit of $1 million could conceivably collect up to a total of $2 million under that policy.

Impact on Excess or Umbrella

What the difference described above means, in many cases, is that the insured's umbrella or excess liability insurer, if any, is more likely to become involved in claims that would, under the 1973 policy, be handled only by the primary insurer. Excess and umbrella liability insurers that provide insurance over the current CGL forms are likely to address the increased exposure through appropriate policy provisions. For example, an excess insurer might require the insured 1) to notify the excess insurer if the primary aggregate limits are exhausted, and 2) make a reasonable effort to have the exhausted limits reinstated promptly. Once aware of the exhausted limit, the excess insurer could consider the eventual need for demanding a higher premium or perhaps even canceling the policy.

Another concern with respect to excess or umbrella liability coverage and the claims-made CGL coverage form is the language ordinarily found in umbrella policies that states when the umbrella will drop down and pay claims that would have been covered by the underlying policy except for the reduction or exhaustion of its aggregate limit(s). The usual stipulation is that the umbrella will pay such claims only if the reduction of underlying limits was due to payment of damages for injury that occurred during the policy period of the umbrella policy.

The problem here is that a primary claims-made CGL policy with a retroactive date earlier than the policy's inception date will cover claims first made during that policy period for injury that occurred before the policy period of both the current primary policy and the umbrella policy. Moreover, payment of such claims will reduce or exhaust the aggregate limits of the primary insurance. However, because the injury did not occur during the policy period of the umbrella policy, the umbrella insurer will not be required to provide drop down coverage if the aggregate limit in the primary policy is reduced or exhausted.

One might think that the best course for an insured with claims-made primary coverage is to obtain an umbrella policy that is also on a claims-made basis with a policy period and retroactive date concurrent with those of the primary policy, as well as extended reporting period options that parallel those of the underlying policy. Unfortunately, however, most claims-made excess policies do not offer tail options as broad as those of the ISO form. And, there may be other instances in which an umbrella policy is actually narrower in coverage than the underlying CGL policy. If such is the case, insureds may be faced with some losses that, although covered by their underlying insurance, are not covered by their excess form.

Insureds and their advisers should carefully inspect their excess liability policies for any restrictions along these lines. Agents and brokers should be especially certain that they explain the ramifications of the aggregate limit to their clients. Failure to do so could result in an errors and omissions claim against the agent or broker.

Applicable Endorsements

The general aggregate limit can be modified by endorsement CG 25 03, to apply separately to each of the named insured's projects away from premises owned by or rented to the named insured. Another endorsement, designated CG 25 04, can be used to make the general aggregate limit apply separately to each location owned by or rented to the named insured.

Other Limits

In addition to the two aggregate limits, the CGL coverage form contains an each occurrence limit, a personal and advertising injury limit, a fire damage limit, and a medical expense limit.

The *each occurrence* limit is the most that the insurer will pay, subject to the aggregate limits, for all damages under Coverage A and all medical expenses under Coverage C arising out of one occurrence. In other words, expenses paid under Coverage C reduce the amount payable per occurrence under Coverage A. For example, if one occurrence gives rise to claims under both Coverage A and Coverage C, the total recovery for all claims could not exceed the each occurrence limit. In the 1973 policy, if medical payments coverage was added to the policy, it was subject to a separate limit that did not affect the each occurrence limit applicable to bodily injury and property damage liability.

The *personal and advertising injury* limit is the most that the insurer will pay under Coverage B for all damages because of personal injury or advertising injury sustained by any one person or organization. The personal and advertising injury coverage of the broad form general liability endorsement used with the 1973 policy is subject only to the aggregate limit stated in the endorsement; there is no per person limit in the standard endorsement. Coverage B of the current CGL coverage forms is, as said earlier, subject also to the general aggregate limit.

Thus, it is possible that a Coverage B claim would not be payable, despite a sufficient per person limit for the claim, in the event that a number of Coverage A claims had extinguished the general aggregate limit. This could be true even if there had been no prior Coverage B claims. Under the broad form liability endorsement, the aggregate limit applicable to personal and advertising injury coverage is a separate amount of insurance that cannot be extinguished by prior bodily injury and property damage liability claims under the same policy.

It should also be noted that the per person limit applicable to Coverage B does not appear to apply separately for later offenses against the same person. If, for example, a person was slandered by the named insured on one occasion and awarded the full per person limit in damages, a second instance of slander against the same person during the policy period would not be covered under that policy. This would be the case even if the aggregate limit had not been exhausted.

The *medical expense* limit is the maximum amount payable per person under Coverage C. Under the previous forms, medical payments coverage is ordinarily written with a per person limit and an aggregate limit but is not applied to reduce the each occurrence limit governing bodily injury and property damage liability recoveries.

The *damage to premises rented to you* limit is the most the insurer will pay for property damage to any one premises while rented to the named insured or, in the case of fire, while rented to the named insured or temporarily occupied by the named insured with the permission of the owner. Any payment under this limit reduces the general aggregate limit.

Application of Limits

The final portion of the limits of insurance section is as follows:

> The limits of this Coverage Part apply separately to each consecutive annual period, and to any remaining period of less than 12 months, starting with the beginning of the policy period shown in the Declarations, unless the policy period is extended after issuance for an additional period of less than 12 months. In that case, the additional period will be deemed part of the last preceding period for purposes of determining the Limits of Insurance.

Although this section is largely self-explanatory, an example may be useful. Say that an insured purchases a policy with a three-year policy period beginning July 1, 2009, and ending July 1, 2012. The above provision makes it clear that even if the stated policy limits are depleted by claims during the first year of the policy period, the full stated limits will again be applicable beginning on July 1, 2010 (and again on July 1, 2011).

The provision also addresses situations when an annual policy period is shortened, as might be the case if a policy with an inception date of July 1, 2009 was cancelled on January 1, 2010, instead of expiring on July 1, 2010. Despite the shortening of the last annual period, the full stated limits would apply to claims covered under that period.

If, however, a policy is extended for a period of less than one year—say the insured requests a one-month extension of the policy, after the regular policy term has expired—the limits will not be renewed for that additional period. That is, if the policy limits had been reduced by claims paid during the preceding annual policy period, the reduced amounts of insurance would apply to the extension period, and not the full limits stated in the policy.

Conditions

The CGL coverage forms are subject to conditions contained in Section IV (titled Commercial General Liability Conditions) of the coverage forms; and are also subject to the ISO common policy conditions, a separate form that must be attached to every commercial package or monoline policy issued under current ISO policywriting procedures.

The Section IV conditions concern: (1) bankruptcy, (2) duties in the event of occurrence, claim, or suit, (3) legal action against the insurer, (4) other insurance, (5) premium audit, (6) representations, (7) separation of insureds, and (8) transfer of rights of recovery against others to the insurer (subrogation), and (9) nonrenewal. In addition, the claims-made form contains a tenth condition, concerning the named insured's right to obtain claim information from the insurance company.

The common policy conditions form contains six additional conditions, concerning (1) cancellation, (2) changes, (3) examination of the named insured's books and records, (4) inspections and surveys, (5) premiums, and (6) transfer of the named insured's rights and duties under the policy (assignment).

In most respects, the Section IV conditions correspond closely to previous general liability conditions. Accordingly, they are only summarized here. See the appendices to this book for the full text of the conditions.

The Section IV conditions are as follows:

Bankruptcy

The bankruptcy condition states that neither bankruptcy nor insolvency of the insured or the insured's estate will relieve the insurance company of its obligation under the forms. An equivalent condition appears within the action against company condition of the 1973 policy jacket.

Duties in the Event of Occurrence, Claim, or Suit

The purpose of this condition is to specify what the insured's obligations are as conditions precedent to the insurer's obligation of investigating, defending, or paying damages because of a claim or suit. Due to a 1990 amendment, the named insured must notify the insurer not only of an occurrence but also of an offense. The latter is a necessary addition because Coverage B, dealing with personal injury and advertising injury, applies to offenses, rather than occurrences. Thus, the duties of the named insured are the same whether there is an occurrence or an offense.

Although both the occurrence and claims-made forms stipulate that the named insured must notify the insurer as soon as practicable of an occurrence or offense that may result in a claim, the claims-made form, unlike the occurrence form, states that "notice of an occurrence is not notice of a claim." So, coverage under the claims-made form is not triggered by the named insured's notification that an occurrence may give rise to a claim. It is only when the injured party actually makes a claim that coverage is triggered. In the 1993 and 1996 forms, the provision quoted above has been modified to state that "notice of an occurrence *or offense* is not notice of a claim" (emphasis added). This change is appropriate because Coverage B, which has been on a claims-made basis since the 1990 changes went into effect, responds to offenses, not occurrences. In the absence of the 1993/96 change concerning offenses, an insured with the claims-made form might maintain that, although notice of an occurrence may not be notice of a claim, such is not the case with notice of an offense for purposes of Coverage B.

Prior to introduction of the 1986 CGL forms, the distinction between notifying the insurer of an occurrence and the actual making of claim concerned some insurance agents, brokers, risk managers, regulators, and others, in that they felt it would often allow insurers to avoid liability for claims resulting from occurrences of which the insurer had been notified but for which claim had not yet been made. The insurer, once notified of an occurrence, could either cancel the policy or, upon renewing the policy, exclude the particular accident by endorsement, leaving the insured no option for insuring the accident but to purchase supplemental tail coverage for up to 200 percent of the policy premium.

In response to this concern, ISO amended the extended reporting period provisions in the claims-made policy to provide (in the event of cancellation, nonrenewal, etc.) for an automatic five-year tail for claims resulting from occurrences that the insured reports to the insurer no later than sixty days after policy expiration. So, although notice of an occurrence still does not trigger coverage under the claims-made policy, any resulting claim first made within five years of policy expiration will be covered under the policy in effect at the time of the occurrence, subject, of course, to whatever aggregate limits remain under that policy at the time of claim. This tail coverage applies only if there is no later policy purchased by the named insured that applies to the same loss or would apply but for the exhaustion of its limits of insurance.

Notice of the occurrence must be given to the insurer "as soon as practicable." The notice should include, to the extent possible, how, when, and where the occurrence took place, the names and addresses of any injured persons or witnesses, and the nature and location of any injury or damage arising out of the occurrence.

Moreover, if the insured receives an actual claim, there is now a requirement that the insured must "immediately record the specifics of the claim or suit and the date received," notify the insurer as soon as practicable, and see to it that the insurer receives written notice of the claim as soon as practicable.

Legal Action against Insurer

The legal action against us condition of the current CGL forms has the same purpose as the "action against company" condition of the 1973 policy. Its purpose is to make clear the conditions that must be met before anyone can bring an action against the insurer, including an insured. Until the 2001 CGL policy amendment, this condition stated that a person or organization could sue the insurer to recover on an agreed settlement or on a final judgment against an insured *obtained after an actual trial*. However, because the policy defines suit to allow damages to be awarded through an arbitration or other alternative dispute resolution, judgment can be obtained without first having an actual trial. In light of this fact, the italicized wording above was eliminated in the 2001 revision of CGL forms.

Other Insurance

The other insurance condition specifies how both damages and defense costs under Coverages A and B are to be shared when a loss is covered by two or more insurers. Coverage C, medical payments, is not affected by other insurance and therefore always applies on a primary basis irrespective of other insurance.

When there is other valid and collectible insurance, how loss is apportioned depends on whether the other insurance is primary or excess. If a CGL policy is primary and the other insurance is excess, the CGL policy applies first. If, instead, both policies are considered to be primary, the loss is apportioned by contribution by equal shares if the other insurance permits this method of sharing. If the other insurance does not permit contribution by equal shares, the loss is apportioned by contribution by limits, that is, each insurer's share is based on the ratio of its applicable limit of insurance to the total applicable limits of insurance of all insurers. Both methods of apportionment are identical to the procedures prescribed by the 1973 general liability policy.

Both the occurrence and claims-made CGL coverage forms are stated to be excess over any other insurance under certain conditions.

Part 4.(b)(1) of the other insurance provision reads as follows:

This insurance is excess over:

(a)   Any of the other insurance, whether primary, excess, contingent or on any other basis:

    (i)   That is Fire, Extended Coverage, Builder's Risk, Installation Risk or similar coverage for "your work";

    (ii)   That is Fire insurance for premises rented to you *or temporarily occupied by you with permission of the owner;*

    (iii)   That is insurance purchased by you to cover your liability as a tenant for "property damage" to premises rented to you *or temporarily occupied by you with permission of the owner;* or

    (iv)   If the loss arises out of the maintenance or use of aircraft, "autos" or watercraft to the extent no subject to Exclusion g. of Section I—Coverage A—Bodily Injury and Property Damage Liability.

The italicized portions of the above provisions were added in the 1996 revision. The added language corresponds to the fact that fire legal liability coverage under the 1993 and 1996 editions applies not only to premises rented to the named insured, but also to premises that the named insured temporarily occupies with the owner's permission.

The insurance under the CGL forms is now excess to insurance purchased by the named insured to cover liability as a tenant for property damage to premises rented to or temporarily occupied by the named insured. So, for example, if the named insured rents a building for his business and buys a property insurance policy that gives the named insured coverage for damage to the rented premises for which he is liable, the named insured's CGL form will provide excess insurance to this other policy. That other insurance has to be valid, collectible, and available to the insured for this excess insurance clause to apply.

The next part of the excess insurance paragraphs of the other insurance provision, prior to the 2004 revision, read as follows:

> (b) Any other primary insurance available to you covering liability for damages arising out of the premises or operations for which you have been added as an additional insured by attachment of an endorsement.

This second part was previously contained in two separate endorsements, introduced with the 1996 CGL revision. The endorsements were CG 00 55, Amendment of Other Insurance Condition (CGL Occurrence Version), and CG 00 56 (CGL Claims-Made Version). The endorsements were withdrawn from use in 1998 when the above wording was added to the CGL forms in 1998.

The effect of this provision is to make a person's or organization's own CGL policy excess over the policy modified by endorsement to include that person or organization as an additional insured. Thus, the additional insured is covered on a primary basis on the policy to which the additional insured endorsement is attached and on an excess basis on its own policy. This was heralded as a welcomed addition because a growing number of indemnitees (those who seek to transfer the financial consequences of their liability to indemnitors) also requested additional insured status on an indemnitor's CGL policy on a primary basis. Unless an additional insured endorsement was issued by the insurer that also reflected that the additional insured is to be covered on a primary basis, a dispute by the insurer was almost guaranteed. In fact, in the absence of some acknowledgement that the additional insured was to be protected on a primary basis, the insurer on whose policy the additional insured endorsement was issued often would maintain that the additional insured had its own policy that should also be taken into account in paying damages. The matter of how insurance coverage was to be resolved, according to these insurers, was on a pro rata basis, that is, taking into account the policy of the additional insured and the policy to which the additional insured endorsement was attached. However, this pro rata adjustment defeated one of the purposes of additional insured status, and that was to obtain coverage on a primary basis under the policy to which the additional insured endorsement was attached.

As an aside, this primary/excess insurance application is meant to apply only when the additional insured is added by endorsement.

What is commonly overlooked is that a real estate manager or property management company is automatically included as an additional insured on the CGL policy. Technically then, this means that the CGL policy to which such entity is considered an automatic additional insured, should not apply as primary over the CGL policy issued to that real estate management or property management company as the named insured. What needs to be done, as explained in Chapter 6, is to add the endorsement titled, "Real Estate Property Managed CG 22 70."

One of the problems with part (2) of the above provision is that it applies solely to premises or operations, presumably because ISO had revised some of its more commonly used additional insured endorsements to apply solely to on-going operations. When it introduced the endorsement entitled "Additional Insureds, Owners, Lessees, or Contractors—Completed Operations," CG 20 37, in 2001, a potential problem arose since there was no reference to products and completed operations. Arguably, the undefined word "operations", unless used specifically in the context of the premises and operations hazard, is broad enough to encompass both ongoing and completed operations. To avoid such arguments, however, ISO as part of its 2004 revisions, amended this part of the other insurance provision to read as follows:

(b)   Any other primary insurance available to you covering liability for damages arising out of the premises or operations, or the products and completed operations, for which you have been added as an insured by attachment of an endorsement.

As this provision reads, if the named insured (not its officers, directors, partners, employees, or agents) is added to another policy as an additional insured for products and completed operations, then the named insured's policy will apply as excess for both premises and/or operations, and products and completed operations.

It has been said that there are at least two potential problems with this provision.

First, there is no reference to personal and advertising injury (coverage B), which automatically forms a part of the standard ISO CGL coverage parts and of many independently filed policies. Arguably, liability emanating from premises or operations could encompass various personal and advertising injury offenses. On the other hand, it could mean that the named insured's CGL policy will apply as excess for bodily injury and property damage, but on a primary basis for personal and advertising injury. The question is, how many insurers covering a named insured who is covered as an additional insured by endorsement will take the position that coverage for personal and advertising injury applies on a primary basis, since doing so may come back to haunt them when they are providing coverage to additional insureds.

Second, this primary/excess application is meant to apply only when the additional insured is added by endorsement. What is commonly overlooked, however, is that real estate managers and property management companies are automatically included as additional insureds on the CGL policy. In addition, some independently filed policies incorporating ISO wording include additional insureds without endorsements.

In light of the foregoing, one of the April 2013 revisions with regard to the "other insurance" condition is to delete the phrase "by attachment of an endorsement". Thus, the impact is that insurance provided to a named insured will be excess over any other primary insurance available to the named insured as an additional insured, whether by endorsement or by other means. (Note that this 2013 revision affects both the occurrence form and the claims-made form, as well as the supplemental extended reporting period endorsement (CG 27 10) and the supplemental extended reporting period endorsement for specific accidents, products, work or locations (CG 27 11).

It is also important to keep in mind that the other insurance provision will not work with anything other than other ISO primary policies, or independently filed policies following ISO wording. Some insurers, for example, will attempt to nullify such attempts to give additional insureds coverage on a primary basis by stating that their liability policies apply as excess to anyone, including additional insureds.

To the extent that umbrella/excess liability policies have built-in additional insured provisions (rather than having to be modified by endorsements, which is probably the more common approach), the above other insurance provision of standard liability policies will not work. The probable rationale for the provision is so that coverage will apply on a horizontal, as opposed to a vertical, basis. In other words, the primary policy limits to which an additional insured endorsement is attached are to be exhausted first, followed by the additional insured's own liability policy. If the limits are still not met, then the umbrella/excess policy applicable to the additional insured applies next, followed by the additional insured's own umbrella/excess policy.

In an attempt to avoid this horizontal settlement, those who desire to be additional insureds on the policies of others not only will require coverage on a primary basis, but also on a non-contributing basis. The problem is that some insurers balk at references to non-contributing. To reduce the chances of these types of objections, the term "non-contributing" needs to be defined. One way, for example, is to say that it means that all liability coverage available to the additional insured on a primary and umbrella/excess basis is to apply first, followed by the additional insured's own primary and umbrella/excess policies, to the extent of any required excess coverage. This is another way of explaining the vertical settlement approach.

Whether this will work or not still is open to question because some courts are adamant about exhausting limits horizontally no matter what the policy says. This is why some entities will not accept a combination of primary and excess coverage limits to satisfy the limits they require. In other words, should an entity requiring a minimum of $1 million in limits accept proof of commercial general liability and/or automobile liability limits of $500,000 per occurrence with the difference ($500,000 per occurrence or more) being provided by an umbrella liability policy? Some people would not give this a second thought and would accept such a combination. A closer look, however, reveals that this is not as good a deal as when the primary policies are written for a minimum of $1 million dollars.

The other insurance provision also declares that if the named insured's insurance is excess, the insurer has no duty to defend if any other insurer has such a duty. If no other insured defends, the named insured's insurer will undertake that role.

In addition to being excess to the types of insurance listed above, the claims-made CGL form is also excess over other insurance:

> that is effective prior to the beginning of the policy period shown in the Declarations of this insurance and applies to "bodily injury" or "property damage" on other than a claims-made basis, if:
>
> (a) No Retroactive Date is shown in the Declarations of this insurance; or
>
> (b) The other insurance has a policy period which continues after the Retroactive Date shown in the Declarations of this insurance.

The effect of the above condition is that a claims-made policy provides excess insurance for any loss that is also covered under a prior occurrence liability policy. This situation can arise under two circumstances.

The first such circumstance is when the claims-made policy has no retroactive date. It stands to reason that there is likely to be some overlap between an earlier occurrence policy and a claims-made policy that covers bodily injury or property damage retrospectively without limit as to time. Should this overlap occur, the claims-made policy is to be treated as excess insurance.

The second circumstance is when the policy period of an earlier occurrence policy extends beyond the retroactive date shown in the claims-made policy. To illustrate, assume that the claims-made policy has a retroactive date three years prior to its inception date. An earlier occurrence policy was in force for the same three-year period but was replaced with the present claims-made policy. A claim for bodily injury or property damage is first made following inception of the claims-made policy for injury or damage that occurred after the retroactive date.

In an event such as this, the occurrence policy applies because the trigger of coverage is bodily injury or property damage that occurs during the policy period. The claims-made policy also applies because the claim was first made during its policy period for bodily injury or property damage that occurred after the retroactive date. According to the provision shown above, the occurrence policy is primary and the claims-made policy is excess.

The other insurance clause does not state how coverage provided by the policy's extended reporting periods will coordinate with other available insurance. This matter is governed by a separate provision that is included in the extended reporting periods section of the policy (see Chapter 4).

From the standpoint of defense cost coverage, the CGL coverage forms will not respond for the payment of such costs when they are considered to be excess to another insurer's duty to defend the insured. If no other insurer has the duty to defend the insured, however, the coverage forms contain an affirmative statement that the insurer will undertake the defense refused by another insurer, but will then have all the insured's rights against the insurer that refused to defend.

When insurance under the CGL coverage forms is excess over other insurance, the insurer agrees to pay its share of the amount that exceeds the sum of (1) the total that the other insurance would pay in absence of the excess insurance and (2) the total of all deductible and self-insured amounts under that other insurance. The insurer, when excess, will share this remaining portion of the loss with other applicable excess insurance that is not intended to apply in excess of the insurance limits shown in the declarations.

Premium Audit

The premium audit condition of the current CGL forms is virtually identical to the premium condition of the 1973 liability policy. Its purpose is to make clear that all premiums for coverage are computed with the insurer's rates and rules; that the advance premium is only a deposit premium and that final premium will be based on an audit at the end of the policy period; and that the insured must maintain such records as are deemed necessary by the insurer to compute the premium.

Representations

The representations condition of the current CGL forms is identical to the declarations condition of the 1973 policy. As a result of this condition, the named insured agrees that (1) all statements made in the declarations are accurate and complete, (2) those statements are based on representations made by the named insured to the insurer, and (3) the insurer has issued the policy based on such representations.

Separation of Insureds

The separation of insureds condition of the current CGL forms is also known as the severability of interests clause. As a matter of interest and historical significance, this provision was first introduced with the commercial auto policies in 1955, and with CGL policy provisions in 1966. While there is no condition by the same name in the 1973 policy, the content of this provision appears within the definition of insured in the 1973 policy jacket. So, with the exception of the limits of insurance and the duties specifically assigned to the first named insured, the insurance of both the old and the current forms applies as if each named insured were the only named insured and separately to each insured against whom claim or suit is brought.

Transfer of Rights of Recovery

This condition is the counterpart of the 1973 policy's subrogation clause. Apart from its longer title, the current provision expresses the same content as the previous clause. This condition states that the insurer has rights to recover all or part of any payment the insurer makes, and the insured must do nothing after a loss to impair those rights.

Even though the CGL policy automatically gives a waiver prior to any loss, an endorsement also is available for use with the CGL (and Owners and Contractors Protective Liability, OCP) forms to waive subrogation. The endorsement for use with the CGL coverage form is CG 20 24 and titled "Waiver of Transfer of Rights of Recovery against Others to Us." Given the fact that the condition of the CGL form that is amended by this endorsement already permits a waiver before a loss, what often begs a question is why this endorsement is necessary.

According to ISO's written explanation of this endorsement, it is prescribed for use, before a loss occurs, to waive subrogation rights against the person or organization scheduled in the endorsement. The only possible explanations for this endorsement's use are the following:[3]

First, it could be an underwriting tool when an underwriter want to control to whom waivers will be given for a particular insured.

Second, it could be used in those minority of states, such as California and Washington, where a waiver of subrogation is not recognized prior to a loss, regardless of what the policy says.

Third, the endorsement could be issued to satisfy those who request a policy waiver even though the policy provides that pre-loss waivers are permitted.

The problem with the second reason is that, because of equitable considerations given weight by the courts, it is not known for sure all of the states are in the category that refuse to recognize a waiver prior to a loss. To avoid problems, therefore, it might be a good idea to have the endorsement issued to every CGL policy. Given the fact that many insurers use their own independently filed CGL forms, perhaps an insurer could issue a blanket waiver of subrogation, rather than on a piecemeal basis.

Nonrenewal

Both versions of the CGL coverage form are subject to a nonrenewal provision stating that if the insurer decides not to renew the policy, it must mail or deliver to the first named insured written notice of the nonrenewal not less than thirty days before the expiration date. This provision, which was included in the 1986 claims-made coverage form itself, was added to the 1986 edition of the occurrence form by means of endorsement CG 00 04. Since this condition is now included in the 1990 and later editions of the occurrence form, the endorsement is no longer needed. The policy provision relating to cancellation—see below—is contained in the common policy conditions form

Right to Claim Information

Under the claims-made coverage form only, there is a condition titled "your right to claim and occurrence information", This condition states that the first named insured has the right to obtain insurance company records of reported occurrences and claim payments and reserves relating to any claims-made policy that the insurer has issued to the first named insured in the previous three years. If the insurance company cancels or elects not to renew the policy, it must provide the information no later than thirty days before the date of policy termination. Otherwise, the insurer must only provide the information if it receives a written request from the first named insured within sixty days after the end of the policy period. In that case, the insurer must provide the information within forty-five days after receiving the request.

The common policy conditions are as follows:

Cancellation

The cancellation condition of the common policy conditions expresses the same substance as that of the 1973 general liability policy and enumerates the duties and obligations of the insured and insurer in the event of cancellation. This condition states that the policy can be cancelled by the insurer for nonpayment of premium by giving the insured not less than ten days' notice, whereas thirty days' notice is required for any other reason.

Changes

The changes condition explains that the first named insured shown in the policy declarations is authorized to make changes with the insurer's consent and that the policy's terms can be amended or waived only by endorsement issued by the insurer. The counterpart of this condition under the 1973 liability policy states that notice to any agent or knowledge possessed by any agent shall not affect a waiver or estop the company from asserting any right under the policy. This statement, which is sometimes a source of problems, does not appear in the current condition.

Examination of Books and Records

The examination condition of the current forms is comparable to the "inspection and audit" condition of the 1973 policy. Its purpose under both the current and the old contract is the same. It reserves the insurer's rights to examine the named insured's books and records at any time up to three years after the policy period.

Inspections and Surveys

The current inspections and surveys condition is considerably longer than its counterpart under the 1973 policy. Its purpose is to disclaim any implication that an inspection or survey by the insurer constitutes an undertaking for the benefit of the insured or others concerning the safety of any premises and operations.

The potential liability of insurers for engineering and safety inspection services first became a real concern in 1964, following the Illinois Supreme Court decision in *Nelson v. Union Wire Rope Corp.*, 199 N.E.2d 769. The court in this case held that an insurer of workers compensation insurance was liable in tort for having failed to detect a dangerous condition in the course of its inspection of a material hoist. The court did not maintain that the insurer had a duty to perform an inspection. Rather, the court held that after having done so, the insurer was liable for its negligence in that regard.

As a matter of interest, the first standard general liability policy provisions contained an Inspection and Audit Condition which read: "The company shall be permitted to inspect the insured premises, operations and elevators ...." The same wording of this condition remained unchanged through the 1943, 1947 and 1955 policy changes. After the Nelson case, however, this condition was amended in 1966 (and has remained unchanged to date) with the explanation by the National Bureau of Casualty Underwriters (NBCU) that a modification was necessary in light of recent court decisions. In its written memorandum of changes, the NBCU stated that the modified condition indicates that "the company has the right but no obligation to inspect the insured's property and operations and that neither the existence nor the exercise of the right to inspect shall constitute an undertaking to determine or warrant that the property or operations are safe.

Premiums

The premiums condition of the current CGL forms does not appear to have a counterpart in the 1973 policy. It states that the first named insured is responsible for the payment of premium and will be the payee of any returned premiums by the insurer. If nothing else, this condition does make clear who has the responsibility for paying premiums in cases where there may be more than one named insured in the policy.

Transfer of Rights and Duties

The transfer condition of the current forms is identical in effect to the assignment clause of the 1973 policy. It is a stipulation of the condition that no assignment of interest is binding without the insurer's consent. However, in the event of the named insured's death, all rights and duties will be transferred to the named insured's legal representative and until such representative is appointed, anyone having proper temporary custody of the named insured's property will have the named insured's rights and duties, but only with respect to that property.

This is a very problematic provision that is litigated frequently because mergers and acquisitions have become so prevalent. The problem is that insurers, as a general rule, are adamant that except in the case of death of an individual insured, the named insured's rights and duties under the policy may not be transferred without the insurer's consent. What often happens is that because of a merger or acquisition, the surviving company becomes embroiled in litigation that had it genesis with the company that was purchased and sometimes dissolved and the surviving company now seeks coverage under its liability policy for those damages. With the stakes usually high, these issues, as one might expect, lead to litigation where the results are mixed. However, the consensus appears to be that this condition having to do with transfer of rights holds that an assignment after a loss cannot retroactively make the surviving entity an insured. The assignment only entitles the surviving entity to the proceeds provided, of course, that the purchased company is not still liable for any of the damages.

If the purchased entity still has liability (as is often the case with asset-only acquisitions), the surviving company cannot access coverage of the purchased entity for losses that are still the responsibility of the purchased entity.

The rationale is that the insurer may be adversely affected if the surviving entity became an insured on the policy of the purchased entity, but the insurer should not be adversely affected when a claim or claims for the proceeds have been assigned, since the risk remains the same before and after assignment.

Endnotes

1. The following are the states that permit suits against co-employees: Alaska, Delaware, Illinois, Indiana, Michigan, New York, North Carolina, Ohio, Oklahoma, South Carolina, Tennessee, Utah and Washington. (Source: Larson's Workers' Compensation Desk Edition, (New York: Matthew Bender & Co., Inc.) However, according to this same source, the following states have statutory provisions permitting intentional tort actions against co-employees: Alabama, Arizona, Arkansas, California, Connecticut, Florida, Hawaii, Idaho, Iowa, Kentucky, Louisiana, Maine, Minnesota, Mississippi, Montana, Nebraska, New Hampshire, New Jersey, Oregon, Pennsylvania, South Dakota, West Virginia, Wisconsin, and Wyoming.

2. Donald S. Malecki, "Joint Venture Provision: Its Purpose and Scope," *National Underwriter, Property and Casualty ed.*, June 17, 1977, p. 45.

3. "Subrogation: To Waive Or Not To Waive," *Malecki on Insurance*, Oct. 1994, p. 5, Fort Thomas, KY: Malecki Communications Company.

Chapter 6

CGL Endorsements and Miscellaneous Coverage Forms

ISO maintains a large portfolio of endorsements for amending the CGL coverage forms to suit the needs of the insured or the insurer or to satisfy particular state requirements. These endorsements are summarized below, presented in order of their form numbers as assigned by ISO. The first two digits of the form number indicate the category to which the endorsement belongs; for example, all endorsements designated CG 21 are exclusion endorsements. Endorsements described here are limited to nationwide endorsements; special state endorsements are not described. This chapter also does not describe the following: pollution-related endorsements because they are discussed in Chapter 1 as part of the discussion of pollution exclusion f.; endorsements designed only for use with the claims-made CGL form because these endorsements are discussed in Chapter 4; or endorsements designed only for use with general liability forms other than the CGL coverage forms (such as the separate coverage form for products and completed operations).

This chapter also describes two miscellaneous general liability coverage forms that were introduced as part of the 2004 CGL changes: the electronic data liability coverage form and the product withdrawal coverage form.

The descriptions that follow are merely summaries, intended for quick reference purposes. For complete coverage details, the reader is urged to review the actual ISO endorsements.

Deductible Endorsements

Currently, there is only one endorsement in this category, as described below.

CG 03 00 Deductible Liability Insurance

The CGL coverage forms do not contain a deductible provision. Endorsement CG 03 00 can be used to apply either a per claim deductible or a per occurrence deductible to bodily injury liability, property damage liability, or both coverages combined.

A per claim deductible, under this endorsement, applies to all damages sustained by any one person or organization as a result of any one occurrence. If, for example, a policy is subject to a per person bodily injury deductible and four persons make claim for injuries resulting from one occurrence, the deductible will apply separately to each of the four claims. In contrast, a per occurrence deductible applies to one occurrence only once, regardless of the number of persons injured. It should be pointed out here that the per claim deductible often is selected by named insureds based on price, which is less expensive than the per occurrence deductible. What named insureds do not realize, however, is that if a claim involves more than one person or entity, when a per claim deductible is in effect, the deductible applies separately to each claimant and that amount can add up fairly quickly.

Under the pre-1993 version of this endorsement, both (1) damages payable on behalf of the insured and (2) limits are reduced by the deductible amount. However, the 1993 revision of this endorsement applies on a damages-reduction basis only, in order to maintain consistency with other liability lines

Additional Coverage Endorsements

This category includes endorsements for various coverage extensions.

CG 04 24 Coverage for Injury to Leased Workers

The employers liability exclusion e. excludes bodily injury to an employee of the insured. Since the term "employee" is defined in CGL forms to include leased workers, it is necessary that this endorsement be issued in those cases where the employers liability exclusion is not to encompass leased workers. The defined term "employee" does not include temporary workers, but this endorsement needs to mention that so as to make it clear that temporary workers still remain outside of the employers liability exclusion.

CG 04 31 Year 2000 Computer-Related and Other Electronic Problems—Limited Coverage Options

An endorsement was introduced in 1998 for use with CGL forms titled "Exclusion—Year 2000 Computer-Related and Other Electronic Problems" in anticipation of massive computer-generated problems on January 1, 2000, which actually did not happen, at least not in the numbers that were estimated. When this endorsement was attached and the underwriter was willing to modify the exclusion, some limited coverage was available with CG 04 31. This endorsement provided bodily injury, property damage, or personal and advertising injury (or any combination) at the described location(s), operation(s) or for the described product(s) or service(s).

CG 04 35 Employee Benefits Liability Coverage

ISO introduced its Employee Benefits Liability Coverage Endorsement with its 2001 amendments. The ISO endorsement has many of same features as the employee benefits liability endorsements that insurers have offered since the mid-1960s following the landmark case of *Gediman v. Anheuser Busch*, 193 F.Supp. 72 (E.D.N.Y. 1961), rvs'd by 299 F.2d 537. In the ISO endorsement, coverage is on a claims-made basis and applies to the negligent acts, errors, or omissions committed by insureds in the administration of the named insured's employee benefit program, defined to encompass group life insurance, group accident and health programs, profit-sharing plans, pension plans, unemployment insurance, workers compensation, disability benefits insurance, and kindred plans. However, the endorsement does not cover fiduciary liability of plans within the scope of the Employee Retirement Income Security Act of 1974.

CG 04 36 Limited Product Withdrawal Expense

ISO introduced this endorsement with its 2001 amendments. As its title connotes, the endorsement is intended to provide reimbursement for certain expenses incurred because of a product withdrawal due to a recall or tampering. Product withdrawal coverage was first introduced by domestic insurers in the mid-1960s following the enactment of the Consumer Product Safety Act. Coverage did not sell well because by the time a prospective insured met the underwriting requirements to purchase coverage, the limited coverage was hardly worth the premium, or in some cases smaller businesses could not afford to purchase it. Larger businesses, on the other hand, that could afford to purchase this insurance, implemented recall procedures but decided to expense recall costs if they arose rather than to purchase this coverage. Most insurers therefore withdrew their forms. The one advantage that the ISO endorsement offers is some limited coverage for product tampering.

This is an endorsement that, when introduced in 2001, was limited in scope, just as its title connotes. Understandably, it is subject to a cut-off date, meaning that the product subject to withdrawal, in order to be covered, must have been produced after the date shown in the endorsement schedule. Although the 2001 version of the endorsement applied to the product withdrawal expenses incurred by the named insured or by others who seek reimbursement, the kinds of expenses covered and the extent of coverage were very limited.

This endorsement was amended in 2004 to further restrict coverage, not only by adding more exclusions, but also by limiting coverage solely to expenses incurred by the named insured. Any expenses incurred by vendors in withdrawing the named insured's product and then seeking reimbursement under this endorsement would not be covered. With this change, this endorsement's use will likely be very limited. (In fact, the sales history of products recall coverage in general has not been overwhelming.)

The 2013 revisions produced by ISO do affect CG 04 36. Paragraph **B.3.a.** of CG 04 36 provides, in part, that the insurer may pay all or part of any deductible amount to effect settlement of any claim or suit. Paragraph B.3.b. makes reference to the Participation Percentage indicated in the Declarations. Since this endorsement does not provide liability coverage or coverage for the cost or expense of defending any suit brought against the insured, both of the foregoing provisions are being amended. The reference in paragraph **B.3.a.** "to effect settlement of any claim or suit" is being deleted, since the insuring agreement of the endorsement applies to coverage for product withdrawal expense and not for claims or suits. Likewise, paragraph **B.3.b** is being revised to reinforce that the Participation Percentage is indicated in the schedule of the endorsement, rather than the Declarations. Also, reference to the word "loss" is revised to explicitly refer to each "product withdrawal".

CG 04 37 Electronic Data Liability

In 2002, ISO introduced what was referred as the Electronic Data Liability Endorsement. It was revised two years later, in part, with the deletion of reference in its title to "Endorsement." Subject to an additional premium, this endorsement permits a buy-back of coverage for loss to electronic data. The idea of this endorsement is to not make it subject to exclusion p. of Coverage A in the CGL coverage form, but rather to limit coverage solely to when there is physical injury to tangible property. This endorsement provides coverage by exception, using language that states coverage is excluded for:[1]

Damages arising out of the loss of, loss of use of, damage to, corruption of, inability to access, or inability to manipulate "electronic data" that does not result in physical injury to tangible property.

Under this wording, no coverage applies in the absence of physical injury to tangible property. Thus, if what happens results in loss of use of tangible property not physically injured, no coverage applies.

The above exclusion applies to "damages arising out of ... electronic data that does not result in physical injury to tangible property."

Conversely, if damages arising out of electronic data results in physical injury to tangible property, damages are covered; for example, damages emanating from a plane crash caused by the corruption of electronic data. (Note, however, the 2013 revisions now provide coverage for damages because of bodily injury.)

It is important to note that the loss of electronic data limit of this endorsement (actually a sublimit) is the most the insurer is required to pay for property damage because of all loss of "electronic data" arising out of one occurrence. Any covered other property damage (physical injury to tangible property), on the other hand, would be subject to the policy's per occurrence limit.

Additional Insured Endorsements

There are numerous situations in which the named insured of a CGL policy is asked, or required by contract, to add another person or organization as an additional insured under the named insured's policy. An array of endorsements is available for this purpose.

ISO introduced two revisions of additional insured endorsements that became effective in 2004. The first revision dealt with certain additional insured endorsements with an effective date of July, 2004. The other revision dealt with changes of other endorsements and forms with an effective date of December, 2004. Of the 33 additional insured endorsements, 10 of them were revised extensively in an attempt to eliminate coverage for the additional insured's sole negligence. One endorsement, CG 20 09 Additional Insured—Owners, Lessees, or Contractors—Scheduled Persons or Organizations (For Use When Contractual Liability Coverage Is Not Provided to You Under This policy), was withdrawn from use in 2004. To the extent similar coverage is desired or needs to be issued, the owners and contractors protective liability coverage part is available for this purpose. Although endorsement CG 20 09 has been withdrawn, its description in these pages will remain intact because of the valuable background information it provides.

In 2013, ISO again revised additional insured endorsements. The changes dealing with additional insured endorsements vary.

Issuing separate endorsements for each of the jurisdictions where a named insured operates and is required to provide additional insured endorsements can be cumbersome. So, instead of issuing separate endorsements, as has been the case with some states, the 2013 revision attempts to make the applicable additional insured endorsements flexible enough so that only one endorsement is necessary.

Taking Additional Insured – Owners, Lessees Or Contractors—Scheduled Person Or Organization CG 20 10, for example, the coverage grant is the same as it was with the 2007 edition of this endorsement. In other words, coverage applies to an additional insured for bodily injury, property damage and personal and advertising injury liability caused in whole or in part by (1) the named insured's acts or omissions; or (2) the acts or omissions of those acting on the named insured's behalf, but only for ongoing operations at the locations designated in the endorsement schedule.

Newly added to the above wording by the 2013 revision, however, are two additional provisions. The first provision states that the insurance afforded to such additional insured only applies to the extent permitted by law. The second provision, tied to the first one with the conjunction "and" states that if coverage provided to the additional insured is required by contract or agreement, the insurance provided to the additional insured will not be broader than that which the named insured is otherwise required by contract or agreement to provide to the additional insured.

For purposes of illustration, assume that the person or organization requiring additional insured coverage and the location of the operations is New Jersey. Also, the anti-indemnification statute (see more information on anti-indemnification laws below) requires the named insured (indemnitor) to assume the partial fault of the additional insured (indemnitee).

The state of New Jersey holds void sole fault, unless insurance is available from an authorized insurer. This means sole fault coverage is permitted. What was requested, however, was partial fault, which also is permitted, but it does not have to be from an authorized insurer. This means that this endorsement, as issued granting partial fault, would apply.

(In some cases, however, the endorsement grant of coverage may be more than is sought by an additional insured who desires, knowingly or not, strictly vicarious liability coverage or, at the other extreme, sole fault coverage if written by an authorized insurer.)

Consider as another illustration, Alabama, where hold harmless provisions are not void. If a contract were to require the assumption of sole fault, the most that would be covered is the grant in CG 20 10; that is, partial fault. The reason is that this endorsement, CG 20 10, (as well as other additional insured endorsements incorporating the same provision with the "however" clause) gives partial fault coverage and then states, in effect, that such partial fault only applies to the extent permitted by law, but hinges on what the contract provides and is otherwise permitted by law. This provision could be clearer. Whether a layperson would understand it remains to be seen.

(Note: To the extent that hold harmless agreements are held void and unenforceable, additional insured status may likewise be void and unenforceable. This revolves around anti-indemnification laws and where these laws exist, they can vary by state. If one were to categorize these laws into common groups, the result would be the following:

- Jurisdictions where both sole and partial fault agreements are void and unenforceable, unless certain valid insurance applies

- Jurisdictions where sole fault agreements are void and no insurance exceptions are permitted

- Jurisdictions where sole fault agreements are void, unless certain valid insurance applies

- Jurisdictions where sole and partial fault are void and no insurance exceptions are permitted

- Jurisdictions that do not hold void hold harmless provisions)

It is important to note that, despite the jurisdictions that permit sole fault coverage, many contracts prepared by or on behalf of indemnitees only see vicarious liability. The thinking is that the indemnitee is willing to be accountable for its sole fault and only wants protection from the indemnitor for its sole fault. In other words, it turns out to be a mutual or reciprocal contract that does not involve the assumption of tort liability and, therefore, is not an insured contract.

Another change affecting the additional insured endorsements, within this category, deals with limits of insurance. This states that if coverage provided to an additional insured is required by contract or agreement, the most the insurer will pay on behalf of the additional insured is (1) the amount of insurance required by the contract or agreement, or (2) the amount available under the applicable limits of insurance shown in the Declarations, whichever is less. This endorsement also does not increase the applicable limits of insurance shown in the Declarations.

This revision affects the following additional insured endorsements:

- Additional Insured—Concessionaires Trading Under Your Name, CG 20 03;

- Additional Insured—Controlling Interest, CG 20 05;

- Additional Insured—Engineers, Architects, or Surveyors, CG 20 07;

- Additional Insured—Owners, Lessees Or Contractors—Scheduled Person or Organization, CG 20 10;

- Additional Insured—Managers Or Lessors of Premises, CG 20 11;

- Additional Insured—State Or Government Agency Or Subdivision Or Political Subdivision—Permits Or Authorizations, CG 20 12;

- Additional Insured—State Or Governmental Agency Or Subdivision Or Political Subdivision—Permits Or Authorizations Relating To Premises, CG 20 13;

- Additional Insured—Vendors, CG 20 15;

- Additional Insured—Mortgagee, Assignee Or Receiver, CG 20 18;

- Additional Insured—Executors, Administrators, Trustees Or Beneficiaries, CG 20 33;

- Additional Insured—Owners Or Other Interest From Whom Land Has Been Leased, CG 20 24;

- Additional Insured—Designated Person Or Organization, CG 20 26;

- Additional Insured—Co-Owner Of Insured Premises; Additional Insured—Lessor Of Leased Premises, CG 20 27;

- Additional Insured—Lessor Of Leased Equipment, CG 20 28;

- Additional Insured—Grantor Of Franchise, CG 20 29;

- Additional Insured--Oil Or Gas Operations—Nonoperating, Working Interests, CG 20 30;

- Additional Insured—Engineers, Architects Or Surveyors, CG 20 31;

- Additional Insured—Engineers, Architects Or Surveyors—Not Engaged By The Named Insured, CG 20 32;

- Additional Insured—Owners, Lessees Or Contractors—Automatic Status When Required In Construction, CG 20 33;

- Additional Insured—Lessor Of Leased Equipment—Automatic Status When Required In Lease Agreement With You, CG 20 34;

- Additional Insured—Grantor Of Licenses—Automatic Status When Required By Licensor, CG 20 35;

- Additional Insured—Grantor Of Licenses, CG 20 36;

- Additional Insured—Owners, Lessees Or Contractors— Completed Operations, CG 20 37;

- Additional Insured—State Or Governmental Agency Or Subdivision Or Political Subdivision—Permits Or Authorizations, CG 29 35.

CG 20 01—Primary and Noncontributory – Other Insurance Condition

The Primary and Noncontributory—Other Insurance Condition Endorsement, CG 20 01, is new under the 2013 revision. Its purpose is to provide additional insureds with coverage on a primary and noncontributory basis when it is required by a written contract or agreement. The reason for this endorsement is to appease those who not only demand confirmation on insurance certificates that their additional insured coverage applies on a primary and noncontributory basis, but also are in the position to require coverage on that basis.

This new optional endorsement, however, is subject to two conditions. The first condition is that the additional insured must be a named insured on other insurance available to it. This is not likely to be a problem, since it would be inadvisable for an indemnitee, for example, not to maintain its own liability insurance as a backup. Second, the named insured, on the policy to which this new optional endorsement is attached, must have agreed in a written contract or agreement that its insurance applies on a primary and noncontributory basis; that is, the insurer issuing this endorsement will not seek contribution from any other insurance available to the additional insured. Whether that agreement will be delivered, as promised, hinges on the facts of the matter and whether the insurer desires to provide coverage.

It is important to keep in mind that this optional other insurance endorsement will not work with anything other than ISO primary policies, or independently filed policies using this ISO language. A question that might arise is whether it actually is necessary to mention that additional insured status applies not only on a primary but also a noncontributory basis. In other words, what does the word "noncontributory" add to the equation? Probably nothing.

An explanation of what contribution means is actually what reference to insurance on a primary basis means. In effect, reference to primary and noncontributory is mutually exclusive. Whether this is what a person or organization seeking additional insured status thinks it means is open to question. CG 20 01, in any event, explains "noncontributory" in the same way as this example: This insurance provided to the person or organization shown in the schedule is primary insurance and we will not seek contribution from any other insurance available to that additional insured.

Thus, nothing is changed with this new optional endorsement but it nonetheless will likely be welcomed so long as it appeases those persons or organizations seeking additional insured coverage, and they receive some confirmation that their coverage applies on a primary and noncontributory basis.

When this new optional endorsement is issued, note that it states that it is "added to the Other Insurance Condition and supersedes any provision to the contrary." Part (2) of this optional endorsement also states that the named insured has "agreed in writing ... that this insurance would be primary and would not seek contribution from *any other insurance* available to the additional insured." Instead of saying "any other insurance", it might have been clearer to say "any other primary insurance". The reason for saying this is that some insureds (and their insurers) typically look for a way to tap another insured's excess liability limits; that is, by exhausting limits vertically, rather than horizontally. Some people may say that this opinion is making a mountain out of a mole hill. Perhaps it is, but if an insurer were to attempt to seek contribution from an additional insured's excess insurance for some reason, there is a potential argument that might have been avoided by inserting the word "primary" in the second provision of this new optional endorsement.

CG 20 02 Additional Insured—Club Members

This endorsement includes any members of the named insured club but only with respect to their liability for activities of the club or activities they perform on behalf of the club. It is common today for employers to add employee-related clubs to their liability policies, such as those relating to golf, gun and rifle, health and sports, social and stock investments. This is an employee benefit, particularly since the insurance is a business expense. What must be considered carefully, however, is how the club is listed in the entity's CGL policy; that is, as a named insured or an additional insured. The answer here is that the club should be shown as a named insured because the club's members are not likely to be covered otherwise.

Here is why. If the club is treated as a named insured, the club will likely be rated as such with the automatic attachment of Additional Insured – Club Members CG 20 02, as suggested in the classification tables of the Commercial Lines Manual. This endorsement reads: "WHO IS AN INSURED (Section II) is amended to include any of your members, but only with respect to their liability for your activities or activities on your behalf." The words "your" and "your" refer to the named insured. With more than one named insured applying to the policy, those words should apply to the appropriate named insured; the club in this instance as a named insured.

If the club were to be added as an additional insured, the above endorsement would be of no significance, since the club members would not be covered. The reason is that the words "you" or "your" refer only to the named insured which, in this case, would be the employer and not the club. With the club not being a named insured, club members would not be considered additional insureds despite the attachment of this endorsement.

CG 20 03 Additional Insured—Concessionaires Trading under Your Name

CG 20 03 includes any concessionaire whose name is shown in the endorsement (or in the policy declarations) but only with respect to its liability as a concessionaire trading under the name of the named insured.

CG 20 04 Additional Insured—Condominium Unit Owners

CG 20 04 includes each individual unit owner of the insured condominium but only with respect to liability arising out of the ownership, maintenance, or repair of that portion of the condominium premises that is not reserved for that unit owner's exclusive use or occupancy.

CG 20 05 Additional Insured—Controlling Interest

This endorsement includes any persons or organizations named in the endorsement (or policy declarations) but only with respect to their liability arising out of (1) their financial control of the named insured, or (2) premises they own, maintain, or control while the named insured leases or occupies those premises. However, the additional insured is not covered with respect to structural alterations, new construction, or demolition operations performed by or for the additional insured.

CG 20 07 Additional Insured—Engineers, Architects, or Surveyors

This endorsement includes any architect, engineer, or surveyor engaged by the named insured but only with respect to liability arising out of the named insured's premises or "your work" (as defined in the policy). (When the professional is not engaged by the named insured, it is necessary to use CG 20 32.) The additional insured is not covered for bodily injury, property damage, personal injury, or advertising injury arising out of the rendering of or the failure to render any professional services.

Until the 1993 policy revisions, this endorsement was available for use with both the CGL and OCP coverage forms; under the revision, this endorsement for engineers, architects, and surveyors became available only with the CGL coverage forms. In addition, the coverage of this endorsement became limited solely to operations in progress. To make this change, the term "your work" was deleted because, according to ISO, this term is used in a completed operations context. Substituted in the place of the term "your work" was the phrase "ongoing operations performed by you or on your behalf."

It is important for additional insureds in this category to understand that they will have no protection under this endorsement if they request coverage for a certain period after operations have been completed.

This endorsement was extensively revised in 2004 in an attempt to eliminate coverage for the sole negligence of the additional insured. For a more complete discussion of the rationale for this change and what coverage is intended to be provided, refer to the discussion of endorsement CG 20 10.

The 2013 revision affects endorsement CG 20 07 (as well as CG 20 31 and CG 20 32, which also deal with engineers, architects or surveyors as additional insureds). CG 20 07 falls into the category of endorsements subject to coverage required by contract and meeting the parameters of existing law. So, CG 20 07 is now also subject to one additional revision that is said to be consistent with those applied to the Professional Services Exclusion Endorsements.

CG 20 07 excludes professional services by or for the named insured. Newly being added is another provision stating that no coverage applies even if the claims against any insured "allege negligence or other wrongdoing in the supervision, hiring, employment, training or monitoring of others by that insured", if the occurrence causing bodily injury or property damage, or the offense causing personal and advertising injury involved the rendering of or the failure to render any professional services by or for the named insured. Given that the endorsement deals with additional insureds who are professionals, this additional provision appears to make sense.

CG 20 08 Additional Insured—Users of Golfmobiles

CG 20 08 includes any persons using or legally responsible for golfmobiles loaned or rented to others by the named insured or the named insured's concessionaire but only for their liability arising out of the use of the golfmobiles.

The current endorsement to cover users of golfmobiles as additional insureds, while not defining golfmobiles, provides coverage to any person using or legally responsible for the use golfmobiles; it does not limit additional insured status to persons using golfmobiles for playing golf. The 2013 revision of CG 20 08 does define golfmobile. The definition reads: For purposes of this endorsement, golfmobile means a motorized conveyance that is designed to carry up to four persons on a golf course for the purpose of playing golf; and that is not built or modified after manufacture to exceed a speed of 25 miles per hour on level ground.

Considering that golfmobiles are often used as transportation for other than golfing purposes, the definition added to this endorsement should be considered as a restriction of coverage.

CG 20 09 Additional Insured—Owners, Lessees, or Contractors—Scheduled Persons or Organizations (For Use When Contractual Liability Coverage Is Not Provided to You under This Policy)

This endorsement was withdrawn from use in 2004 because of its limited use, and the fact that the owners and contractors protective liability (OCP) coverage part provides identical coverage, except that the OCP policy is a separate policy, unaffected by the purchaser's own CGL form. If endorsement CG 20 09 were to have been issued instead, it would have applied on a primary basis, but only to the extent that the CGL policy applied to the claim or lawsuit. The description of this endorsement remains intact because of the background information it provides.

CG 20 09 includes the person or organization named in the endorsement (or policy declarations) but only with respect to liability arising out of (1) "your work" performed for the additional insured at the location designated in the endorsement, or (2) acts or omissions of the additional insured(s) in connection with their general supervision of "your work" at the designated location.

The person named as additional insured in this endorsement is ordinarily a property owner or lessee for whom the named insured is performing work under contract. The additional insured could also be a general contractor for whom the named insured is working as a subcontractor. The scope of coverage provided for the additional insured is comparable to that provided for the named insured of the ISO owners and contractors protective (OCP) liability coverage form. The endorsement and the OCP coverage form are alternative ways for a contractor to provide limited insurance for a property owner during the course of the contractor's work. When the endorsement is used, the contractor shares its policy limits with the owner; when the contractor obtains the separate OCP policy, the payment of claims against the owner does not affect the contractor's insurance.

The endorsement is subject to the following exclusions of the CGL coverage form: a. (expected or intended injury), d. (workers compensation and similar laws), e. (employer's liability), f. (pollution), h.2 (using mobile equipment for racing), i. (war), and m. (damage to impaired property or property not physically injured). In addition, the endorsement contains these exclusions:

1. Bodily injury or property damage for which the additional insured is liable solely by contract. There is no coverage for liability assumed under "insured contracts."

2. Bodily injury or property damage occurring after all work on the project is completed or that portion of the work out of which the injury or damage arises has been put to its intended use. The endorsement, like the OCP coverage form, does not provide completed operations liability coverage.

3. Property damage to: property owned or used by, or in the care, custody, or control of the additional insured; or "your work" for the additional insured.

Significantly, endorsement CG 20 09 also contains an exclusion of bodily injury or property damage arising out of any act or omission of the additional insured(s) or any of their employees, other than general supervision of work performed for the additional insured(s) by the named insured.

In the absence of this exclusion, the endorsement might be interpreted to cover acts or omissions of the additional insured as long as they result in the additional insured incurring "liability arising out of ...'your work' for the additional insured(s)." Some courts have interpreted the phrase "liability arising out of" liberally in favor of the insured to mean "originating from," "growing out of," or "flowing from," without a requirement of proximate causation. See, for example, *Merchants Insurance Company of New Hampshire, Inc. v. United States Fidelity & Guaranty Co.*, 143 F.3d 5 (1st Cir. 1998).

However, because of the exclusion quoted above, endorsement CG 20 09 covers acts or omissions of the additional insured only if they are in connection with the additional insured's general supervision of "your work." Endorsement CG 20 10, discussed below, does not contain the exclusion in question.

Because of the limited scope of this endorsement, some property owners prefer to have the contractor indemnify and hold the owner harmless for all liability arising out of the project and back the hold harmless agreement with contractual liability insurance as evidenced by a certificate of insurance.

This endorsement should see limited use because it is to be used only when contractual liability coverage is not provided, that is, the CGL policy is modified with contractual liability limitation endorsement CG 21 39. This endorsement has the same effect as the 1973 CGL policy without modification of the broad form CGL endorsement. The result is contractual liability coverage limited solely to incidental contracts.

As noted above, this endorsement's coverage is limited solely to operations while in progress. But because this endorsement referred to the term "your work," which is used in a completed operations context, this endorsement was revised in 1993 to replace the term "your work" with the phrase "your ongoing operations". Another revision to this endorsement was in 1997 when reference to Form A was deleted and it was retitled to make clear that it is intended to cover the additional insured(s) scheduled on the endorsement.

CG 20 10 Additional Insured—Owners, Lessees, or Contractors—Scheduled Persons or Organizations

This endorsement, relied upon almost exclusively in connection with construction-related work, was revised extensively in 2004. It applies solely to ongoing operations and limits coverage for the additional insured to bodily injury, property damage, personal and advertising injury caused in whole or in part by (1) the named insured's acts or omissions, or (2) the acts or omissions of those acting on the named insured's behalf, in the performance of the named insured's ongoing operations for the additional insured at the locations designated in the schedule.

What the first part of this coverage condition means is that, unless the named insured is responsible *in whole or in part* for resulting injury or damage, the additional insured has no coverage. Sole negligence of the additional insured, in other words, is not covered. If, on the other hand, the additional insured can demonstrate that the named insured is at least one percent at fault, as much as 99% of fault attributable to the additional insured should be covered—on a primary basis—provided ISO forms are used.

If the additional insured is not considered to be covered because of coverage condition (1) above, there still may be an opportunity for full or partial coverage under coverage condition (2). It all depends on whether it can be shown that the additional insured was acting on behalf of the named insured. These situations can include, for example, where a general contractor is an additional insured, a subcontractor is the named insured, and a claim or lawsuit is brought against the general contractor for failing to properly provide a safe place to work. There is a possibility for the general contractor to maintain it was acting on the subcontractor's behalf because, inherent in that allegation of the general contractor's failure to provide a safe place to work, was the general contractor's duty to do so on behalf of the subcontractor. If that liability can be shown, the general contractor, as an additional insured, could be covered to the same extent as if it were a named insured. Only time will tell whether ISO's intent to seriously restrict additional insured coverage under this endorsement will prevail.

Traditionally, this endorsement provided broad coverage to additional insureds. In fact, it was the most commonly requested and sought after endorsement for construction-related work, particularly the November, 1985 edition of the endorsement. The reason was that it included coverage for the additional insured's sole negligence and for both ongoing as well as completed operations. All of this officially ended with the July, 2004 revisions from ISO, as explained previously.

One of the more controversial parts of the pre-2004 edition of this endorsement was the phrase *arising out of*. The reason was that it did not require a direct causal relationship between the named insured's work or operations and the additional insured's liability. Coverage under this endorsement, instead, applied to an additional insured even when the named insured was without fault, due to the additional insured's relationship with the named insured's work.

The 1985 edition of this endorsement was amended in 1993 to remove completed operations coverage. According to ISO, the intent of this endorsement was to limit the additional insured's coverage only while operations were in progress; but the endorsement was not clear on this point, because it referred to the term *your work* which, according to ISO, did not make a distinction between ongoing and completed operations. This endorsement was again amended in 1997 when reference to Form B was deleted and the endorsement was retitled to make clear that it was intended to be used solely to schedule additional insureds, and not to be used as though it were a blanket endorsement.

Although the intent may have been to restrict coverage of this endorsement to ongoing operations, it was possible in some fact patterns to argue that coverage still applied after work had been completed. The reason was that coverage applied to liability arising out of the named insured's ongoing operations. The trigger, in other words, was at the time of liability (negligent act, error or omission) and not at the time of injury or damage. To fix this potential problem, ISO again revised this endorsement in 2001 by adding an exclusion of when injury or damage does not apply. Because this endorsement requires the scheduling of the additional insured's name, it is likely to see limited use. In fact, the trend for several years now has been for insurers to issue blanket additional insured endorsements.

It is important to note that this endorsement cannot be used in a state that has an anti-indemnity statute that holds void and unenforceable sole and/or partial negligence of an indemnitee (one who attempts to transfer the financial consequences of its acts or omissions to the indemnitor) and does not make exception for the validity of any insurance. States in this category include Colorado, New Mexico, North Dakota and Oregon.[2]

CG 20 11 Additional Insured—Managers or Lessors of Premises

A lease of real property may require the lessee to add the lessor or property manager as an additional insured under the lessee's CGL policy. Designed to meet this type of requirement, endorsement CG 20 11 covers the person or organization named in the endorsement for liability arising out of the ownership, maintenance, or use of the premises leased to the named insured and scheduled in the endorsement.

It may be a good idea to have this endorsement issued to a real estate manager, even though the manager is already automatically covered as an additional insured, in order to overcome the primary/excess other insurance issue explained in Chapter 5.

The coverage for the additional insured is subject to all the exclusions of the policy and also does not apply to (1) any occurrence that takes place after the named insured ceases to be a tenant at the scheduled location, or (2) structural alterations, new construction, or demolition operations performed by or on behalf of the additional insured.

CG 20 12 Additional Insured—State or Political Subdivisions

A named insured who obtains a permit from a state or political subdivision to engage in certain activities may be required to name the entity as an additional insured. The state or political subdivision named in the endorsement is covered for operations performed by or on behalf of the named insured for which the permit was issued. The coverage for the additional insured is subject to all the exclusions of the policy plus two exclusions stated in the endorsement. These exclusions eliminate coverage for (1) operations performed for the additional insured, and (2) products and completed operations.

CG 20 13 Additional Insured—State or Political Subdivisions—Permits Relating to Premises

This endorsement insures a state or political subdivision that has issued a permit in connection with premises owned, rented, or controlled by the named insured. The state or political subdivision is covered for the following:

1. The existence, maintenance, repair, construction, erection, or removal of advertising signs, awnings, canopies, cellar entrances, coal holes, driveways, manholes, marquees, hoistaway openings, sidewalk vaults, street banners, or decorations and similar exposures; or

2. The construction, erection, or removal of elevators; or

3. The ownership, maintenance, or use of any elevators covered by this insurance.

CG 20 14 Additional Insured—Users of Teams, Draft, or Saddle Animals

This endorsement insures any person or organization using or legally responsible for the use of draft or saddle animals or vehicles for use with them, provided the use is by the named insured or by others with permission of the named insured.

CG 20 15 Additional Insured—Vendors

CG 20 15 enables a manufacturer or distributor to add a retailer or other vendor of its products to its own CGL or products liability policy. The vendor named in the endorsement is covered for bodily injury or property damage arising out of the products described in the endorsement that are sold or distributed in the vendor's business.

This endorsement was revised in 2004. Although this endorsement's coverage was thought to be limited to the vendor's (1) vicarious liability (that is, to liability imputed to the vendor because of the acts or omissions of the named insured), or (2) partial and independent fault, broader coverage apparently has been possible. For this reason, and to make sure coverage does not apply for the vendor's sole fault, ISO has added an exclusion to its latest endorsement that specifically precludes bodily injury and property damage arising out of the sole negligence of the vendor or its employees or anyone else acting on its behalf, subject to three exceptions.

The first exception applies to inspections, adjustments, tests, or servicing that the vendor has agreed to make or normally undertakes to make in its usual course of business in the distribution or sale of products.

The second exception applies to exclusion A.1.d. dealing with repackaging, other than when unpacked solely for the purpose of inspection, demonstration, testing, or the substitution of parts under instructions from the manufacturer, and then repackaged in the original container.

The third exception applies to exclusion A.1.f. which deals with demonstration, installation, servicing, or repair operations, other than those operations performed at the vendor's premises in connection with the sale of the product.

Because of the above exceptions to the vendor's sole negligence, the coverage of this endorsement is broader than that of other endorsements that may be available from some insurers. The best way to describe the ISO version is that it not only covers the vendor's liability as the conduit, but also as an instrumentality, of products or services.

The vendor is a conduit because of its role in the stream of commerce between it and the distributor or manufacturer. If a defective product causes injury, for example, the vendor may be named in a lawsuit simply because it was the conduit, i.e. the seller, of the manufacturer's product.

The vendor also could serve as an instrumentality. This means doing something more than simply serving as a conduit, i.e., physically handling the product. For example, the additional insured—vendors endorsement, CG 20 15 07 04, states that insurance afforded to the vendor does not apply to any physical or chemical change in the product made intentionally by the vendor. If any such change were to be made negligently (unintentionally), coverage would apply. Likewise, this endorsement does not apply to the vendor's liability stemming from repackaging a product, except when unpacked solely for purposes of demonstrating, testing, or the substituting of parts under instructions from the manufacturer, and then repackaged in the original container. If the vendor inadvertently changes the product which ultimately causes injury or damage, the vendor, serving as an instrumentality of the product, should be covered.

Other, more limited endorsements restrict coverage solely to liability of the vendor as the conduit and not for its own acts or omissions, unlike the ISO endorsement. This is an important distinction commonly overlooked by the legal community when a claim arises. In fact, it is not uncommon for insurers to deny coverage under an ISO-type vendor's endorsement, citing the case of *American White Cross Laboratories v. Continental Insurance Company*, 495 A.2d 152 (N.J. App. Div. 1985), which dealt with an endorsement much more restrictive than the ISO version and limiting coverage to the vendor's role as a conduit, rather than also including its role as an instrumentality.

CG 20 17 Additional Insured—Townhouse Associations

A townhouse association, like a condominium association, requires at least two forms of liability insurance. The first is a non-profit directors and officers liability policy to cover the economic damages that could result from their decisions. The other is a CGL policy to protect them against their liability for injury or damage sustained by others. When a CGL policy is issued to a townhouse association, the above endorsement is appropriate to clarify that townhouse owners who serve as members of the association are protected as additional insureds.

This endorsement has been amended with the 1993 changes to clarify that the endorsement does not cover any liability arising out of the ownership, maintenance, use, or repair of the real property to which the owner has a fee simple title.

CG 20 18 Additional Insured—Mortgagee, Assignee, or Receiver

Paragraph F of the common policy conditions to the CGL policy clarifies that in the event of the named insured's death, all rights and duties are automatically transferred to the named insured's legal representative. The representative therefore is protected as an insured without having to request an endorsement. However, other legal representatives, such as a mortgagee of real property or an assignee or receiver in bankruptcy proceedings, may also desire such protection. If the insurer agrees, these persons or organizations likewise can be protected with the issuance of the above endorsement.

CG 20 20 Additional Insured—Charitable Institutions

The purpose of this endorsement is to amend the "Who Is an Insured" provision of the CGL policy to more closely correspond to the nomenclature of a charitable institution. When attached to the policy, the endorsement includes as insureds the institution's members with respect to their activities on behalf of the institution, including trustees and members who serve on the board of governors.

CG 20 21 Additional Insured—Volunteer Workers

Until revised in 1993, this endorsement was titled "Additional Insured—Volunteers." The purpose of the endorsement is to clarify that the CGL policy will protect authorized volunteers to the same extent as coverage is provided to employees. This means, for example, that the so-called "fellow employee" exclusion that commonly applies to employees will likewise apply to volunteers. ISO withdrew this endorsement with the 2001 policy amendments, which incorporated its provisions into the CGL coverage part.

CG 20 22 Additional Insured—Church Members and Officers

The purpose of this endorsement is to amend the "Who Is an Insured" provision of the CGL policy of a church to include the following persons as insureds with regard to their church-related activities or duties:

- Church members

- Trustees, officials, or members of the board of governors of the church

- Members of the clergy

The title of this endorsement was revised with the 2001 amendments with the deletion of reference to volunteer workers, since the provisions relating to volunteer workers are incorporated into the CGL policy.

CG 20 23 Additional Insured—Executors, Administrators, Trustees, or Beneficiaries

As noted under endorsement CG 20 18, the common policy conditions of the CGL policy recognize that the named insured's rights and duties under the policy will be transferred to a legal representative in the event of the named insured's death. There are occasions, however, when legal representation becomes necessary prior to the named insured's death, such as when the insured is incompetent or when there is a living trust. In any such event, the issuance of this endorsement signifies that such person or organization is an additional insured but only while acting within the scope of his duties.

The 1993 revision of this endorsement expanded the category of an insured to include any executor, administrator, trustee, or beneficiary of the named insured's living trust.

CG 20 24 Additional Insured—Owners or Other Interests from Whom Land Has Been Leased

This endorsement is virtually identical to CG 20 11—Additional Insured—Managers or Lessors of Premises. The only apparent difference between the two is that one applies specifically to land and the other applies to the more general term "premises."

CG 20 25 Additional Insured—Elective, Appointive Executive Officers—Public or Municipal Corporations

The purpose of this endorsement is to amend the "Who Is an Insured" provision to correspond more closely to the nomenclature of public and municipal corporations.

CG 20 26 Additional Insured—Designated Person or Organization

The endorsement is designed to provide protection to a person or organization, as an additional insured, whose status may not otherwise qualify for one of the other additional insured endorsements. This endorsement was commonly requested as an alternative to additional insured endorsement CG 20 10 carrying the 1985 edition date. It is still commonly relied on as a substitute for endorsement CG 20 10.

This is also one of the endorsements that was amended in 2004 with the restriction that the bodily injury, property damage, and personal and advertising injury be caused in whole or in part by the named insured's acts or omissions or the acts or omissions of those acting on the named insured's behalf.

One of the problems with this endorsement, insofar as insurers are concerned, is that coverage may not necessarily be limited solely to ongoing operations. Under some circumstances, coverage could apply even after operations are completed. The reason is that coverage is not limited to bodily injury or property damage arising out of ongoing operations, but instead to liability in the performance of the named insured's ongoing operations. There can be instances, therefore, when negligence occurs during the performance of ongoing operations, but injury or damage does not occur until after operations are completed. Also, there is no wording in this endorsement stating that insurance does not apply to injury or damage occurring after all work to be performed has been completed, or at least that portion of the named insured's work that has been put to its intended use by someone other than another contractor or subcontractor engaged in performing operations on the same project.

CG 20 27 Additional Insured—Co-owner of Premises

The named insured who owns several properties, some of which are co-owned, may require this endorsement to protect the interests of those with whom property is co-owned. Both the name of the person or organization and the location of premises must be described on the endorsement.

CG 20 28 Additional Insured—Lessor of Leased Equipment

When a person or organization leases equipment, it may be required to add the lessor as an additional insured on the lessee's CGL policy. This is the endorsement earmarked for that purpose. It should be noted, however, that it will not protect the lessor against its sole negligence. Coverage instead is limited to liability caused in whole or in part by the named insured's maintenance, operations, or use of equipment leased to the named insured by the person or organization identified in the endorsement.

This endorsement is intended to be used only to schedule (name) the additional insured. A blanket endorsement (CG 20 34) also is available for those common situations when lessors need to be given additional insured status.

CG 20 29 Additional Insured—Grantor of Franchise

When the grantor of a franchise requires protection as an additional insured on the CGL policy of the grantee, this is the endorsement designed for that purpose.

CG 20 30 Oil or Gas Operations—Nonoperating, Working Interests

This endorsement is designed to add as insureds those persons or entities that have a nonoperating, working interest in any oil or gas lease, such as investors. When this endorsement is attached it amends the "Who Is An Insured" provision by providing such insureds with protection in the event claim or suit is brought against them because of their nonoperating or working interest.

CG 20 31 Additional Insured—Engineers, Architects, or Surveyors

This endorsement was introduced for use with the 1993 policy amendments. It is designed for use solely with the OCP policy. However, its scope is identical to its counterpart endorsement, CG 20 07, which is used when the professional is engaged by the named insured.

CG 20 32 Additional Insured—Engineers, Architects, or Surveyors Not Engaged by the Named Insured

Endorsement CG 20 07, discussed earlier in this chapter, is available for naming as an additional insured an engineer, architect, or surveyor hired by the named insured. The purpose of endorsement CG 20 32, in contrast, is to provide additional insured status to an engineer, architect, or surveyor that has *not* been hired by the named insured. This situation might arise, for example, if the named insured is a construction company that has been hired by a property owner to work on a project with an engineer, architect, or surveyor that has also been hired by the property owner, and the contract requires the named insured to name the engineer, architect, or surveyor as an additional insured under the named insured's CGL policy.

This is another one of the endorsements that limits coverage to liability caused in whole or in part by the named insured's acts or omissions, or the acts or omissions of those acting on the named insured's behalf in the performance of the named insured's ongoing operations performed by the named insured or on the named insured's behalf.

The endorsement also adds to the policy a professional services exclusion with respect to the engineers, architects, or surveyors named in the endorsement's schedule.

CG 20 33 Additional Insured—Owners, Lessees or Contractors—Automatic Status When Required in Construction Agreement with You

With the growing demand for additional insured status under endorsement CG 20 10 dealing with owners, lessees, or contractors, and the inability of underwriters to issue a blanket endorsement without first amending endorsement CG 20 10 to apply on that basis, ISO decided to issue a blanket, automatic endorsement in 1997, CA 20 33. As its title connotes, the endorsement's use is limited to instances where additional insured status is required in a construction agreement with the named insured that is in writing. Other than that requirement, the coverage is identical to the additional insured endorsement CG 20 10.

Because underwriters will not be able to review additional insured requests on an individual basis to determine what other endorsements might be required, such as exclusionary endorsements relating to professional liability exposures, this endorsement automatically includes a professional services exclusion. The problem with this exclusion is that it applies to all insureds. Thus, the fact that the policy contains a separation of insureds condition is likely to have no effect, because the exclusion applies to injury or damage arising out of the rendering or failure to render professional services, regardless of who performed or failed to perform them.

Another problem with CG 20 33 are the words "with you". One should not, of course, rely on the title of endorsements, but those two words limit the persons or organizations desiring additional insured status to only those involved in the contract; in other words, only those in privity. This endorsement, for example, will not cover so-called "upstream" persons or organizations desiring additional insured status, such as projects owners when the contract is between a general contractor and subcontractor, or when a general contractor (and project owner) desires additional insured status when the contract is between a subcontractor and sub-subcontractor.

Since this endorsement excludes the professional services exposure, it is being revised in the 2013 edition to include the following additional exclusion: no coverage applies even if the claims against any insured allege negligence or other wrongdoing in the supervision, hiring, employment, training or monitoring of others by that insured.

(CG 20 33, by the way, is likely to see limited use in the future because of the introduction of endorsement CG 20 38, Additional Insured—Owners, lessees, Or Contractors—Automatic Status For Other Parties When required In Written Construction Agreement. See the discussion on CG 20 38).

CG 20 34 Additional Insured—Lessor of Leased Equipment—Automatic Status When Required in Lease Agreement with You

ISO introduced this endorsement in 1997 to accommodate lessees who are required to provide additional insured status to lessors of leased equipment without being required to name such persons or organizations in the endorsement.

In order for a party to qualify for the issuance of this endorsement, there must be a written contract or agreement requiring such additional insured status. The coverage that applies is limited to liability for bodily injury, property damage, and personal and advertising injury caused in whole or in part by the named insured's maintenance, operation, or use of equipment leased to it by such person or organization. Any injury or damage caused by faulty maintenance on the part of the additional insured would not be covered. The additional insured's status as such also ends when the contract or agreement with the named insured for the leased equipment ends. This coverage also does not apply to any occurrence that takes place after the equipment lease expires.

CG 20 35 Additional Insured—Grantor of Licenses—Automatic Status When Required by Licensor

This endorsement was introduced by ISO with the 2001 amendments to facilitate the requests of persons or organizations who desire additional insured status for grantors of licenses. This endorsement will cover such grantors of licenses who make and distribute products. An example given by ISO is a sweatshirt manufacturer who imprints the logo of universities or professional sports teams. In order for manufacturers to use the logo and sell the products, they must first obtain a license from the institution. To that end, licensors may contractually require that they be named as additional insureds on the licensees' liability policies. The automatic status ends when the licensing agreement is no longer in existence between the two parties.

CG 20 36 Additional Insured—Grantor of Licenses

This endorsement, like the preceding one, was introduced for use in 2001. It is used when requests are infrequent and the grantor of the license therefore can be scheduled on the endorsement.

CG 20 37 Additional Insured—Owners, Lessees, or Contractors—Completed Operations

Currently the requests for additional insured status on a sole fault basis including completed operations coverage in the construction setting are frequent and only one current ISO additional insured endorsement (CG 20 26) can accommodate those requests. However, that endorsement applies on a scheduled basis. Some insurers are using the 1985 edition of CG 20 10 and charging an additional premium.

To meet the growing requests of additional insureds who prescribe completed operations coverage in their written contracts, ISO introduced, with its 2001 amendments, the above titled endorsement to be issued for an additional premium on a scheduled basis, that is, naming the person or organization and describing the location and description of the completed operations. However, it cannot be written alone, since coverage is limited to completed operations. What also is required is either the blanket additional insured endorsement CG 20 33 or the scheduled one, CG 20 10, since both grant additional insured coverage limited to ongoing operations and, as of the 2001 edition, specifically exclude the completed operations hazard.

CG 20 38 Additional Insured—Owners, Lessees or Contractors—Automatic Status for Other Parties When Required In Written Construction Agreement

As mentioned with reference to Additional Insured—Owners, Lessees Or Contractors—Automatic Status When Required In Construction Agreement With You CG 20 33, the words "With You" in this title and in the context of this endorsement will not apply to a person or organization desiring additional insured status if it is not a party to the contract or agreement. In other words, there is no privity. Examples are project owners who want additional insured status when the contract is between the general contractor and subcontractor, and when a general contractor (and project owner) request additional insured status when the contract is between a subcontractor and sub-subcontractor. These persons or organizations not in privity with the parties involved in the contract are referred to as "upstream" insureds. It would be possible to automatically provide these upstream persons or organizations with additional insured coverage under this endorsement with the elimination of the words "With You". Instead, however, ISO is introducing another blanket automatic endorsement titled, Additional Insured—Owners, Lessees Or Contractors—Automatic Status For Other Parties When Required In Written Construction Agreement, CG 20 38.

(Obtaining upstream status is a problem. Two court cases, of undoubtedly many, that exemplify that problem are *AB Green Gansevoort, LLC v. Peter Scalamandre & Sons, Inc., et al.* 102 A.D.3d 425 (2013), and *Westfield Insurance Co. v. FCL Builders, Inc.*, 948 N.E.2d 115 (2011).)

Although this new automatic additional insured endorsement CG 20 38 is an optional one, it should be recommended in every instance, since it can avoid some problems for producers. Without this new endorsement, producers would have to read every contract to determine whether any upstream persons or organizations were involved and then be careful how the certificate of insurance is prepared. Confirming that additional insured status exists but that it does not apply to upstream insureds could present problems to producers, such as accusations of failure to procure coverage. With this new optional endorsement, producers do not have to read contracts (many do not anyway) and can feel somewhat more secure in listing additional insured status on the certificate.

It is important to note, however, the maximum coverage that would apply is the additional insured's partial fault and that is subject to what is required in the contract and whether that requirement is otherwise permitted by law. It is also important to keep in mind that new automatic endorsement is a standard ISO issue; whether other insurers will follow suit is open to question. Finally, caution should be exercised that some disingenuous insurer does not issue an endorsement with the same title but preclude coverage for upstream insureds in the body of the copy. In other words, one should not rely fully on the title of endorsements; the endorsements need to be read fully.

Exclusion Endorsements

There are many situations when either an insured or an insurer will desire to exclude certain coverages that may otherwise be provided by or potentially within the coverage of the policy. ISO has prepared the following endorsements to be used for the purposes as noted.

CG 21 00 Exclusion—All Hazards in Connection with Designated Premises

This endorsement is designed for at least three purposes. The first is to convert the CGL form to a more limited form of protection comparable to the owners, landlords, and tenants (OL&T) policy that was replaced by ISO when the current CGL forms were introduced in 1986. This endorsement also can be used to exclude a given location that presents an exposure that the underwriter does not wish to undertake, or to exclude a location that may be specifically covered under a separate policy. Whatever the reason, both Coverages A and B are eliminated with respect to the premises designated in the endorsement, along with operations emanating from those premises, including goods or products manufactured or distributed from those premises.

Except for some isolated situations, this endorsement is not suited for use with the CGL policy provisions. In fact, this endorsement may nullify two major advantages of the CGL policy: 1) automatic coverage for new insurable exposures related to existing ones, and 2) those new exposures not related in any way to existing covered ones.

CG 21 01 Exclusion—Athletic or Sports Participants

The purpose of this endorsement is to make clear that the named insured who is a sponsor of any sport or athletic contest, event, or exhibition, as described therein, will not have any insurance under its policy for bodily injury sustained by a person while he or she is a participant in such an event; there is accident insurance available for this kind of an exposure. However, this endorsement would not preclude coverage if a third party were to be allegedly injured by such a participant.

Many businesses engage in either paying for specified equipment or writing a check to a little league or other athletic contest, event or exhibition. A question here is at what point is an event or sport considered to be sponsored as opposed to one involving a donation? The distinction between sponsoring or simply donating money or material things is usually not an issue in relation to liability so long as there is no exercise of control, which, if present, can create a liability exposure. If a business provides nothing more than a donation, whether to purchase equipment or to obtain some form of advertising, such as sponsorships of a bowling team, a little league baseball or soccer team, it may be difficult to place responsibility on the sponsor or donor for resulting injuries or damage. Some of the important considerations for avoiding accountability (liability), following a monetary donation or purchase of equipment for the event are to (1) not control the event; (2) not hold the event on the sponsor's or donor's business property; or (3) not conduct itself so as to give the impression a joint venture exists between itself and the entity actually conducting the event.

When all of the foregoing are avoided, and there is no other activity that would indicate or imply a strict business relationship, businesses might enjoy the benefits of being a sponsor without the accompanying liability that may result in an obligation of pay damages. Much will depend on the laws of various jurisdictions and the specific activity.

CG 21 04 Exclusion—Products/Completed Operations Hazard

This endorsement is designed to exclude both bodily injury and property damage arising from the products-completed operations hazard, as that term is defined in the CGL forms. The endorsement can be used when an insured does not desire products-completed operations liability insurance for some reason, or the underwriter is not willing to provide that coverage. However, this endorsement should not be used when, for example, a classification automatically includes products liability coverage as part of the premises-operations exposure. The reason is that if an additional products exposure arises during the policy period, it will be excluded if this endorsement has been issued.

CG 21 16 Exclusion—Designated Professional Services

The apparent purpose for this endorsement is to exclude those professional liability exposures that are best covered by other specialty policies. It can be a troublesome exclusion for both the insured and the insurer.

Insureds must be especially careful to see that the exposure to be excluded can be covered under a professional liability policy. If, for example, this endorsement were to be attached to the CGL policy of an insurance agency, the insured could be without vital insurance coverage.

The reason is that an agent's errors and omissions policy generally excludes liability because of bodily injury, property damage, personal injury, and advertising injury. If the insured were a physician instead, this exclusion would be more acceptable because medical malpractice liability policies commonly include coverage against all injury without definition.

This endorsement also can be a problem to insurers because the term "professional services" is not defined. Its meaning therefore may be a question that only a court can answer.

CG 21 17 Exclusion—Movement of Buildings or Structures

This endorsement is designed to make clear that no coverage will apply to an organization whose business may involve the movement of buildings or structures. This is an exposure that requires a special rate. The reason for excluding liability because of personal injury and advertising injury is not readily apparent, since neither is likely to be the result of such an exposure.

CG 21 31 Limited Exclusion – Designated Operations Covered By a Consolidated (Wrap-Up) Insurance Program

This endorsement is similar to endorsement 21 54, except that coverage under the CGL policy remains intact for the work that was performed by the named insured under a wrap-up when the wrap-up has been cancelled, has expired, or is no longer available to the named insured contractor for reasons other than the exhaustion of the wrap-up policy's limits.

Stating that the exclusion for projects covered by a wrap-up program does not apply if the wrap-up no longer applies for any reason other than exhaustion of limits means that the exception can apply in a variety of ways. However, since the last sentence of the last paragraph of this endorsement states that the named insured must advise the insurer of any cancellation, nonrenewal or termination, some insurers are likely to argue that the exception to this exclusion applies only when the policy has been cancelled, nonrenewed or terminated and nothing more.

CG 21 32 Communicable Disease Exclusion

In the wake of diseases that can be transmitted from one person to another, ISO, on behalf of its insurers felt the time was ripe to make available an endorsement to exclude bodily injury, property damage, personal injury and advertising injury arising out of the actual or alleged transmission of a communicable disease. Although communicable disease is undefined in this endorsement, the ISO explanatory memorandum accompanying the introduction of this exclusionary endorsement mentions the following three kinds of diseases that apparently are of concern to underwriters: (1) avian flu, (2) severe acute respiratory syndrome (SARS), and (3) rotaviruses (an infection that affects children and involves diarrhea).

CG 21 33 Exclusion—Designated Product

This endorsement is designed to exclude coverage for bodily injury and property damage arising from the product designated in the endorsement. Such an endorsement can be attached to either the CGL or products/ completed operations liability coverage parts. This endorsement may be used by an underwriter who does not wish to cover a particular exposure, or it can be used at the insured's discretion when a given products exposure is being covered by another liability policy or being handled under a captive or self-insurance program.

CG 21 34 Exclusion—Designated Work

The reasons for using this endorsement correspond to those dealing with designated products. However, the exposure excluded here concerns the named insured's work, that is, work performed by or on its behalf and including materials, parts, or equipment furnished in connection therewith. This is an ideal exclusion when a construction contractor is performing certain work under a wrap-up program being handled on an "ex-insurance" basis; that is, where the project owner or general contractor is providing all the insurance.

CG 21 35 Exclusion—Coverage C—Medical Payments

Medical payments coverage was originally designed to reduce the chances of a subsequent bodily injury lawsuit and to enhance a business's goodwill; whether those purposes are served by this coverage is uncertain. However, sometimes underwriters are not interested in providing this coverage — which is payable without having to show fault — for businesses where there is high potential for bodily injury claims, such as restaurants, bowling alleys, and schools. In addition, those businesses that are not overly concerned about this kind of goodwill and are more interested in cutting insurance costs may exercise their right to use this exclusion.

If medical payments coverage is excluded by this endorsement, the supplementary payments provision is modified by this endorsement with some additional, limited protection for expenses incurred by the insured for first aid as may be administered to others at the time of an accident involving bodily injury. While there is no limit on the amount payable, coverage is contingent on bodily injury that would otherwise be covered by the policy. This limited protection also is referred to as "immediate medical payments coverage."

The 1993 amendment to this endorsement clarified that coverage is limited to the payment of first aid expenses *administered* to others at the time of the accident. Some cosmetic changes were made to this endorsement with the 2001 edition, but without change in the scope of coverage.

CG 21 36 Exclusion—New Entities

The CGL policy automatically includes under the "Who Is an Insured" provision any organization the named insured acquires or forms, other than a partnership or joint venture, and over which the named insured maintains ownership or majority interest. However, such automatic coverage is limited to ninety days or the end of the policy, whichever is earlier. This endorsement eliminates all automatic protection for new entities that would otherwise apply in the endorsement's absence. The endorsement may be required for underwriting reasons or by an insured who desires to maintain a policy for one entity.

This endorsement was revised editorially effective in March, 2005, with no impact on coverage. However, a possible complication here is that if products and completed operations coverage is not otherwise excluded, coverage still applies for any goods or products manufactured, sold, handled, distributed, or disposed by a person or organization whose business or assets the named insured has acquired. The entity itself may not be covered, but liability emanating from its goods or services apparently would.

CG 21 37 Exclusion—Employees and Volunteer Workers as Insureds

Since the introduction of the 1986 CGL policy provisions, employees have been automatically included as additional insureds. Prior to that time, employees had to be added by endorsement, either with an employees as insured endorsement or as part of the broad form CGL endorsement. The addition of coverage for employees is viewed by some as a perk or one of the many other benefits employees receive from their employers. Employers also could be confronted with a problem if an insurer were to defend and pay damages on behalf of the employer and then file a subrogation action against a negligent employee who is also not an insured. Employees may also be more readily helpful to employers in the event of litigation confronting both.

However, there may be instances when an employer does not want its employees covered as insureds, or an underwriter may not desire to cover employees, particularly following a frequency of claims. Whatever the reason, an exclusion is available to exclude employees. Now that volunteers are automatically included within the CGL policy provisions as of the 2001 amendments, this endorsement also takes care of deleting volunteers as additional insureds when necessary.

When this endorsement was attached to CGL policy provisions, some insurers apparently found out that even though employees were not considered to be insureds, coverage remained intact for an employer's vicarious liability arising out of employees' employment-related acts or omissions involving aircraft, autos, and watercraft. The reason coverage applied to the employer was that the aircraft, autos, and watercraft exclusion did not apply when these vehicles were operated by someone other than an insured, such as employees excluded by endorsement.

So with the 1997 revisions involving primarily endorsements, ISO closed that gap. The result is that exclusion g. directed at bodily injury or property damage arising out of the ownership, maintenance, use, or entrustment to others of any aircraft, auto, or watercraft, not only applies to those vehicles owned, operated by, rented or loaned to any insured, but also to any employee or volunteer (now defined terms) while in the course of his or her employment. The impact of this part of the exclusion is that coverage for employer's nonownership liability, stemming from the acts of its excluded employees and volunteers, should be the subject of commercial auto, aircraft, or watercraft insurance. However, nonownership coverage remains intact for liability emanating from the acts or omissions of, for example, any independent contractor who is not also an insured. This latter exception in all likelihood applies for purposes of any gray area gaps that are possible between the CGL and other policies mentioned, but on an excess basis.

The other provision of CGL policy exclusion g. modified by this endorsement in 1997 deals with the subparagraph (3) exception of the parking of nonowned autos on or on the ways next to the premises owned or rented to the named insured. By exception to the current policy exclusion, coverage does apply as long as the auto is not owned by or rented or loaned to the named insured or any insured. Were it not for the endorsement's change in 1997, coverage would have applied to the employer's vicarious liability in this instance, too. However, the endorsement precludes coverage even here for the employer's vicarious liability when employees are excluded as insureds.

As noted above, this endorsement was modified with the 2001 amendments to include volunteers because they are automatically covered by CGL policy provisions.

CG 21 38 Exclusion—Personal and Advertising Injury

The purpose of this endorsement is to exclude both the personal injury and advertising injury coverages automatically included in the CGL forms. It is more likely to be used as an underwriter's tool to preclude coverage, than an endorsement that a business may desire to be issued for purposes of cutting costs. If personal injury coverage is desired and advertising injury is not, the appropriate endorsement is CG 21 40 Exclusion—Advertising Injury.

CG 21 39 Contractual Liability Limitation

When this endorsement, which was introduced in 1988, is issued, it eliminates the blanket contractual liability coverage that automatically applies under the CGL form and replaces it with protection that is limited to the insured contract as defined: L-lease of premises; E-easement agreements; A-agreements required by municipalities other than for work to be performed for municipalities; S-side track (railroad) agreements; and E-elevator maintenance agreements. The effect of this endorsement is to limit the coverage to the equivalent of what is known as incidental contracts coverage under the 1973 comprehensive general liability policy provisions. This endorsement can only serve to the detriment of indemnitors (those who assume the financial consequences of tort liability of others) where (1) anti-indemnity statutes exist that preclude sole or partial negligence but remain unaffected by the validity of contractual liability or additional insured status,[3] or where (2) no hold harmless provisions prohibitions exist and indemnitors assume the sole or partial fault of indemnitees.[4]

The 1993 revision to this endorsement made four changes: (1) substituted letters for the numbered contracts comprising the defined term "insured contracts"; (2) changed the definition of insured contract to track with the language used in paragraphs a. through e. of the definition of insured contract in the CGL and products coverage forms; (3) deleted the requirement that the insured contract be in writing; (4) deleted the exception at the end of the endorsement and added language to paragraph a. of the definition to indicate that a contract for a lease of premises does not include that portion of such contract that indemnifies any person or organization for damage by fire to premises rented to the named insured or temporarily occupied by the named insured with permission of the owner.

CG 21 40 Coverage B—Personal Injury Liability Only (Advertising Injury Liability Not Included) (Occurrence Version)

Until retitled as noted above in the 1992 and 1996 CGL revisions, this endorsement was titled "Exclusion—Advertising Injury." The purpose of the endorsement remains the same: to limit Coverage B of the CGL coverage form (occurrence version only) to personal injury liability coverage. Endorsement CG 21 48 can be used for the same purpose with the claims-made version of the CGL coverage form.

ISO withdrew both of these endorsements in the 1998 CGL revisions because the personal injury and advertising injury definitions were combined into one definition of personal and advertising injury in the 1998 CGL forms.

CG 21 41 Exclusion—Intercompany Products Suits

The manufacturer and its subsidiaries that process components of a product or distribute them may be charged more than once for their products liability coverage. This so-called double dipping is viewed as being warranted among insurers because the liability policy will provide coverage and defense if one insured sues another insured. This is known as *cross liability coverage*. If such suit is remote, it might be to the manufacturer's advantage to delete these intercompany sales in calculating products liability insurance premiums. But to compensate for that cut in costs, the insurer may insist on this intercompany products suits exclusionary endorsement. Note that the exclusion is limited solely to the named insured's products hazard. Thus, all other cross liability exposures are covered, unless specifically excluded.

CG 21 42 Exclusion—Explosion, Collapse, and Underground Property Damage (Specified Operations)

This is one of two exclusionary endorsements that are available to modify the coverage that is otherwise available automatically under the CGL form against damage caused by the explosion, collapse, and underground hazards. This endorsement is designed to exclude coverage at the described location against the designated hazard: explosion, collapse, underground property damage, or any combination thereof.

Note that this endorsement has been shown incorrectly to also be applicable to the products and completed operations liability coverage part. Reference to that coverage part was eliminated in the 2004 revisions of the CGL program.

CG 21 43 Exclusion—Explosion, Collapse, and Underground Property Damage Hazard (Specified Operations Excepted)

When this endorsement is attached to the policy, all coverage against the X, C, and U hazards, as automatically provided by the policy, is excluded, except as designated in the exclusion. This endorsement has been shown incorrectly to also be applicable to the products and completed operations liability coverage part. This reference has been eliminated with the 2004 revisions.

Both of the above endorsements commonly are used by underwriters who do not wish to provide X, C, and U coverage on a blanket and automatic basis. They prefer to underwrite the exposure first before providing the coverage.

CG 21 44 Limitation of Coverage to Designated Premises or Projects

This endorsement's purpose is to limit coverage to the premises or project(s) specifically designated in the endorsement. A property syndicate that purchases real estate or constructs condominium projects may desire to cover each such location separately, particularly if the membership varies by project. It is common, for example, for a general partnership to have different limited partnership participation. Note that coverage under this endorsement is limited to the premises as described and operations necessary or incidental to those premises. While this limitation is similar to the coverage that once was offered by the owners, landlords, and tenants (OL&T) policy, as well as manufacturers and contractors (M&C) policy, the coverage of this endorsement is broader, since it does not exclude the products-completed operations hazard, unlike the OL&T and M&C policies.

Nonetheless, this endorsement still is undesirable for the same reasons as noted with respect to endorsement CG 21 00, Exclusion—All Hazards in Connection with Designated Premises. In other words, if an individual or business qualifies for the basic provisions of the CGL policy, this protection of the policy should be provided. On the other hand, if the risk does not qualify for anything other than a stripped down version of the CGL policy or a policy with this limitation attached, it would be in the insurer's best interest to decline the risk altogether rather than being faced with a possible costly argument later. Given the number of arguments generated by this endorsement, the trade-off of premium versus potential argument is simply not worth it. The excess and surplus lines market approach of using an OL&T policy is a much better way to handle the situation. This latter method at least serves as a "red flag" that unless precautions are taken in light of coverage limitations, problems can be expected—as attested to by many cases that have sought resolution from the courts over the years.

CG 21 45 Exclusion—Damage to Premises Rented to You

Prior to the 1998 CGL policy revisions, this endorsement was titled Exclusion—Fire Damage Legal Liability. It was designed to eliminate the fire legal liability coverage that is automatically provided under the policy, subject to a basic limit of $100,000. The endorsement's name was changed with the 1998 amendments to reflect the title of coverage being provided within the basic policy provisions. Specifically, an exception to exclusion j., Damage to Property, was made to provide additional coverage for damage to premises rented to the named insured on a short-term basis. The particulars concerning this change were explained in more depth in Chapter 1 in relation to exclusion j.

The prior exclusionary endorsement was sufficient to exclude fire damage legal liability coverage. But with the additional coverage for damage to premises rented to the named insured on a short-term basis, the endorsement had to be revised in 1998 so as to encompass the additional coverage when this exclusion is issued.

CG 21 46 Exclusion—Abuse or Molestation Exclusion

This endorsement is utilized by underwriters in those instances where the possibility of abuse and molestation is relatively high, such as day care centers, pre-school institutions, juvenile centers, and municipalities. When attached to the CGL policy, coverage is excluded for bodily injury, property damage, personal injury, and advertising injury arising out of the two exposures as noted in the endorsement. Sometimes a lawsuit will be filed against an employer because of its negligent investigation, employment, and/or supervision of an alleged offender. If this should occur, it is the endorsement's purpose to exclude any protection that may be sought here as well.

This endorsement was amended in 1993 by numbering and lettering the endorsement to make it consistent with other CGL forms. Also, the endorsement now has lead-in language to clarify which section of the CGL form is modified by this wording.

CG 21 47 Employment Related Practices Exclusion

In 1988, Insurance Services Office proposed a new exclusion in CGL coverage forms relating to employment discrimination and similar offenses. While ISO described the new exclusion as a clarification, the Risk and Insurance Management Society and other parties opposed the change. Following public hearings by the NAIC and meetings between ISO and NAIC, ISO agreed not to add this exclusion to the coverage forms but, instead, to make the exclusion available by endorsement.

This exclusion can be viewed as an extension of employer's liability exclusion e. because it appears to be an insurer defense against attempts by insureds to secure coverage under their CGL policies for damages arising from wrongful terminations and other employment-related practices that have proliferated over the past several years. Before the exclusionary endorsement is discussed, it is worthwhile to explain its probable rationale.

Those who maintain that damages against employers because of wrongful termination and related practices are covered by CGL insurance depend mainly on three arguments: (1) emotional distress, which is the commonly alleged result, is deemed to be bodily injury or sickness; (2) the alleged offense is not subject to employer's liability exclusion e. because emotional distress or other resulting injury manifests after employment has been terminated, rather than during the course of employment; and, (3) although the policy excludes intentional injury, it does not exclude injury resulting from an intentional act if the insured did not intend to cause injury. Thus, unless the insurer can prove without a doubt that the employer had the conscious intention to cause the injury that resulted, the employer's CGL policy should cover such claim or suit.

In certain jurisdictions, insurers have been successful in denying coverage despite the absence of any employment related exclusion for the following reasons. First, emotional distress is not considered to be bodily injury, as that term is defined in the policy. To constitute bodily injury, there must be some injury to the human body of a physical nature. See, for example, *St. Paul Fire & Marine Insurance Company v. Campbell County School District No. 1*, 612 F. Supp. 285 (D.Wyo.1985) and *Rolette County v. Western Casualty & Surety Co.*, 452 F. Supp. 125 (D.N.D. 1978). Second, the alleged emotional distress is not deemed to be caused by an occurrence because the result is not an accident. See *E-Z Loader Boat Trailers, Inc. v. Travelers Indemnity Co.*, 726 P.2d 439 (Wash. 1986).

The weakness in the defense of the insurers is that employer's liability exclusion e. confines itself to bodily injury that arises "out of and during the course of employment." Endorsement CG 21 47 apparently is designed to combat that weakness. It eliminates coverage for:

"Bodily injury" arising out of any:

(1)   Refusal to employ;

(2)   Termination of employment;

(3)   Coercion, demotion, evaluation, reassignment, discipline, defamation, harassment, humiliation, discrimination or other employment-related practices, policies, acts or omissions; or

(4)   Consequential "bodily injury" as a result of (1) through (3) above.

This exclusion applies whether the insured may be held liable as an employer or in any other capacity and to any other obligation to share damages with or to repay someone else who must pay damages because of the injury. Also, if attached to the occurrence or claims-made forms, this exclusion affects both Coverages A and B. While use of this exclusionary endorsement will depend on underwriting discretion, its probable use is in those jurisdictions where the courts have ruled for coverage.

The 1993 edition of this endorsement has been numbered and lettered to track with other CGL forms; also, both the bodily injury (Coverage A) and personal injury (Coverage B) paragraphs have been amended to state that the injury excluded is to the person who has been wronged, or to that person's spouse, child, parent, brother, or sister. Finally, the consequential injury language of this endorsement was revised to be consistent with the language in the employer's liability exclusion of the CGL forms.

Both this endorsement and CG 29 51 (for use with the Owners and Contractors Protective Liability and Pollution Liability coverage parts) were revised in 2007 in light of two court cases that, according to ISO, required it to reinforce what is intended to be excluded.

The first case is *Peterborough Oil Company v. Great American Insurance Co., 397 F. Supp. 2d 230 (D. Mass. 2005)*. This case dealt with the malicious prosecution of a former employee. The significance of this case was that coverage was held to apply despite an employment-related practices exclusion, because the phrase "employment-related act or omission," as used in the exclusion, did not mention malicious prosecution, which was a covered offense under personal and advertising injury coverage. In light of this case, both of the aforementioned endorsements now specifically refer to malicious prosecution as another one of the listed employment-related practices, policies, acts or omissions considered to be excluded.

The second case is *Owners Insurance Co. v. Clayton, 614 S.E. 2d 611 (S.C. 2005)*. This case held that an exclusion for employment-related practices was not applicable to post-employment situations where the alleged injury did not arise out of an employment-related scenario, but instead out of defamatory comments made after the employee was terminated. As a result of this case, both of the above endorsements have been changed to state that the exclusion applies whether the injury-causing event takes place before, during, or after employment of that person.

CG 21 48 Coverage B—Personal Injury Liability Only (Advertising Injury Liability Not Included) (Claims-Made Version)

Formerly titled "Exclusion—Advertising Injury," this endorsement is the claims-made counterpart to endorsement CG 21 40, which is used with the occurrence form. Both endorsements were withdrawn by ISO as part of the 1998 CGL revision.

CG 21 50 Amendment of Liquor Liability Exclusion

This endorsement is an alternative to the liquor liability exclusion contained in the CGL coverage forms. The endorsement is described in Chapter 1 in connection with exclusion c under coverage A of the CGL form.

The built-in liquor exclusions of the two CGL Coverage Forms are as broad as they can be, but the issuance of standard endorsements is also available. Currently Amendment Of Liquor Liability Exclusion Endorsement CG 21 50, when issued, modifies the coverage part's liquor exclusion by extending the exclusion to apply to businesses which regularly serve alcoholic beverages, whether or not a profit is derived. (For informational purposes, Amendment Of Liquor Liability CG 29 52 is similar to the preceding endorsement CG 21 50, except that it applies to the Products/Completed Operations Liability Coverage Part.)

Two other optional exclusionary endorsements are Amendment Of Liquor Liability—Exception For Scheduled Activities CG 21 51 and CG 29 53. (The latter is similar to the CG 21 51, except that it applies to the Products/ Completed Operations Liability Coverage Part.) When these endorsements are issued, the exclusion for liquor makes an exception for the scheduled premises or activities. The word "premises" in the endorsement titles is newly added with the 2013 revisions.

All four endorsements are also amended by all of the exclusionary additions introduced with the 2013 revision. Thus, added to these endorsements are the following changes: (1) The exclusion will also apply if one of the reasons for which any insured may be liable for bodily injury or property damage is causing or contributing to the intoxication of any person, including causing or contributing to the intoxication of any person because alcoholic beverages were permitted to be brought on the named insured's premises for consumption thereon; (2) The exclusion applies even if the claims against any insured allege the negligence or wrongdoing in the supervision, hiring, employment, training or monitoring of others; and providing or failing to provide transportation with respect to any person that may be under the influence of alcohol—if the occurrence which caused the bodily injury or property damage involved that which is involved in Paragraphs (1), (2), (3) of exclusion c (i.e., selling to a minor or in violation of a Dram Shop Act); and (3) All four of the above endorsements also are amended to read as precluding the BYOB exposure (that is, the exclusion will apply if an insured permits any person to bring any alcoholic beverages on the named insured's premises for consumption thereon).

From ISO's perspective, the first change is considered a restriction, the second one a clarification, and the third one a restriction.

CG 21 51 Amendment of Liquor Liability Exclusion— Exception for Scheduled Activities

This endorsement contains the exclusion expressed in endorsement CG 21 50 but states that the exclusion does not apply to any event specified in the endorsement.

CG 21 52 Exclusion—Financial Services

This endorsement, intended for use with CGL insurance for financial institutions, was introduced with the 1996 CGL revisions. Its purpose is to exclude coverage (under Coverage A or Coverage B) for bodily injury, property damage, personal injury, or advertising injury resulting from the insured's rendering of or failure to render any of a long list of financial services.

CG 21 53 Exclusion—Designated Ongoing Operations

This endorsement was introduced with the 1996 CGL revisions. Its purpose is to exclude bodily injury or property damage arising out of ongoing operations described in the endorsement schedule. A situation when this endorsement might be appropriate is when a particular work project is being covered under a separate CGL policy.

CG 21 54 Exclusion—Designated Operations Covered by a Consolidated (Wrap-Up) Insurance Program

Introduced in the 1996 CGL revisions, this endorsement excludes liability for bodily injury and property damage arising out of either ongoing operations or products and completed operations at a specified project location when coverage for the project is being provided under a consolidated or "wrap-up" program. (Even though there may be some potential problems with it, it might be advisable for an insured to seek the issuance of endorsement CG 21 31 Limited Exclusion—Designated Operations Covered by a Consolidated (Wrap-Up) Insurance Program.)

CG 21 56 Exclusion—Funeral Services

ISO introduced this endorsement with the 1997 CGL changes. The exclusion contained in the current endorsement was formerly a part of endorsement CG 21 16, Exclusion—Designated Professional Services. However, this endorsement and the three separate exclusionary endorsements mentioned next were developed to clarify specifically the type of professional services being excluded.

When issued, endorsement CG 21 56 excludes liability arising out of errors or omissions arising out of the handling, embalming, disposal, burial, cremation, or disinterment of dead bodies. The endorsement is mandatory for cemeteries, crematories, funeral homes, chapels, and mausoleums. A potential problem for insurers here is that the endorsement does not specifically mention that liability arising out of negligent acts also is not covered,

CG 21 57 Exclusion—Counseling Services

This is another one of the exclusions that formed a part of endorsement CG 21 16, and as of 1997 is a separate endorsement. It excludes liability arising out of advisory services or counseling with respect to such things as mental health, crisis prevention, social services, and kindred subjects. This endorsement is mandatory for mission, settlement or halfway house risks.

CG 21 58 Exclusion—Professional Veterinarian Services

The third endorsement that formerly was included within CG 21 16 is endorsement CG 21 58, mandatory for veterinarian or veterinary hospital risks. It excludes three categories of risks:

- Diagnostic testing, surgical or dental procedures used for the prevention, detection or treatment of any sickness, disease, condition or injury in animals, including the furnishing or prescription of drugs or medical, dental or surgical supplies;

- The rendering or failure to render any advice or instruction on health maintenance; and

- Errors or omissions in the handling or treatment of dead animals.

CG 21 59 Exclusion—Diagnostic Testing Laboratories

Under ISO rules, this endorsement is mandatory for medical or X-ray laboratories. It excludes bodily injury, property damage, or personal and advertising injury arising out of medical or diagnostic testing and procedures used for the detection, diagnosis, or treatment of any sickness, disease, or injury; or for the evaluation of a patient's response to treatment. The endorsement also excludes injury or damage arising out of the reporting of or reliance upon the results of the services described above.

CG 21 60 Exclusion—Year 2000 Computer-Related and Other Electronic Problems

CG 21 61 Exclusion—Year 2000 Computer-Related and Other Electronic Problems—Products/Completed Operations

CG 21 62 Exclusion—Year 2000 Computer-Related and Other Electronic Problems—With Exception for Bodily Injury on Your Premises

CG 21 63 Year 2000 Computer-Related and Other Electronic Problems—Exclusion of Specified Coverages for Designated Locations, Operations, Products, or Services

CG 21 64 Year 2000 Computer-Related and Other Electronic Problems—Exclusion of Specified Coverages for Designated Products or Completed Operations

ISO developed the above five exclusionary endorsements in anticipation of possibly catastrophic losses that could have occurred on January 1, 2000 if computers had failed to recognize the year 2000. Although catastrophic losses did not occur, ISO had not withdrawn the endorsements as of its recent CGL revision.

CG 21 66 Exclusion—Volunteer Workers

This endorsement was introduced by ISO with its 2001 revisions in order to provide a means by which to remove volunteer workers as insureds from the CGL policy now that volunteer workers are automatically included in the basic provisions as of the 2001 revisions.

When the 2001 version of this endorsement is issued, however, the employer still may have nonownership liability coverage under the CGL policy for aircraft, auto, and watercraft operated by volunteer workers. The reason is that the aircraft, auto, or watercraft exclusion is applicable to insureds. But when volunteers are excluded, they are no longer insureds, meaning that the foregoing exclusion would not apply to the extent any of those vehicles were to be operated by a volunteer. To overcome this problem, the 2004 revision of CG 21 66 adds new language to the exclusion to indicate that liability arising out of the ownership, maintenance, or entrustment to others of any aircraft, auto, or watercraft operated by volunteer workers of the named insured is excluded.

This endorsement has been shown incorrectly to also be applicable to the products and completed operations liability coverage part. Reference to that coverage part was eliminated as part of the 2004 revisions.

CG 21 67 Fungi or Bacteria Exclusion

This endorsement, introduced in 2002, eliminates coverage for bodily injury, property damage, and personal and advertising injury that would not have occurred, in whole or in part, but for the actual, alleged, or threatened inhalation of, ingestion of, contact with, exposure to, existence of, or presence of any fungi or bacteria on or within a building or structure. Also not covered is any loss, cost, or expenses in having to abate, test, monitor, etc., the effects of fungi or bacteria by any insured or by any other person or entity. Thus, the costs incurred by the insured are excluded, as are the costs incurred by others who then seek reimbursement from the insured.

This exclusion, however, is stated not to apply to any fungi or bacteria on or contained in a good or product intended for consumption. The 2004 revision of CG 21 67 added the word *bodily* to precede the word *consumption*. As a result of this amendment, the exclusion does not apply to any fungi or bacteria on or contained in a good or product intended for bodily consumption.

Terrorism Endorsement Options

The Terrorism Risk Insurance Act (TRIA) is a program within the Department of the Treasury in which the Federal Government will share losses with the insurance industry from terrorists' attacks. Participation of the Federal Government is activated when the Secretary of the Treasury certifies an act of terrorism committed by individuals acting on behalf of any foreign interest, provided the TRIA results in aggregate losses in excess of the amount stated in the Act. Insofar as insured losses from a certified act of terrorism, the Federal Government will reimburse insurers for a percentage of losses, stated in the Act, in excess of the insurer's retention, based on a specified percentage of the insurer's earned premium for the year preceding the loss. Insured losses covered by the program are capped at $100 billion per year, unless action of Congress changes that amount. All insurers providing general liability insurance are required to participate in this program. For all new and renewal business, insurers must make available to insureds coverage for losses caused by certified acts of terrorism. The insurer also must disclose to the policyholder the premium for loses covered and the Federal share of compensation for such losses at the time of offer, purchase and renewal of the policy.

The following consists of a brief description of the available endorsements. Readers are urged to refer to the endorsements to determine the entire agreement.

CG 21 70 CAP On Losses from Certified Acts of Terrorism

This endorsement was introduced in 2002 and modified in 2008. When coverage for certified acts of terrorism is to be provided, this endorsement provides coverage for both certified acts of terrorism and other acts of terrorism, provided that the insurer will not pay any amount for injury or damage for any certified act of terrorism after the amounts of all such events in a statutory period exceed the cap provided by the Act.

CG 21 71 Exclusion of Other Acts of Terrorism Committed Outside the United States; CAP On Losses from Certified Acts of Terrorism

This endorsement was introduced in 2002 and modified in 2008. When coverage for certified acts of terrorism is to be provided, this endorsement provides coverage for certified acts of terrorism, subject to the cap on liability and the underlying policy provisions, and excludes other acts of terrorism, subject to a $25 million threshold, with no dollar threshold on nuclear, biological or chemical events.

CG 21 73 Exclusion of Certified Acts of Terrorism

This endorsement was introduced in 2002 and modified in 2008. It is available when coverage is not to be provided or provided subject to a specific limitation. When issued, it excludes coverage for certified acts of terrorism but provides coverage for other acts, subject to underlying policy provisions.

CG 21 75 Exclusion of Certified Acts of Terrorism and Exclusion of Other Acts of Terrorism Committed Outside the United States

This endorsement was introduced in 2002 and modified in 2008. It is available when coverage for certified acts of terrorism is not to be provided. When issued, it excludes all losses arising out of certified acts of terrorism and other acts of terrorism, subject to a $25 million threshold and with no dollar threshold on nuclear, biological or chemical events.

CG 21 76 Exclusion of Punitive Damages Related to a Certified Act of Terrorism

This endorsement was modified in 2008. When this endorsement is issued, the policy does not apply to terrorism punitive damages; that is, damages arising directly or indirectly, out of a "certified act of terrorism," as defined in the endorsement, that are awarded as punitive damages.

CG 21 77 Exception to Terrorism Exclusion For Certified Acts of Terrorism; CAP On Losses From Certified Acts of Terrorism

This endorsement was introduced in 2002. When TRIA was introduced, it voided all exclusions of terrorism that might have been in effect that were required to be offered by TRIA. If an insured decides to purchase insurance, this endorsement when attached to the CGL coverage form restored terrorism coverage, as prescribed by TRIA but leaves undisturbed any terrorism exclusion relating to noncertified acts of terrorism.

CG 21 78 Removal of Terrorism Exclusion; CAP On Losses From Certified Acts of Terrorism

This endorsement was introduced in 2002. It is used when an insured chooses to purchase terrorism insurance but whose CGL policy currently is subject to a terrorism exclusion. When this endorsement is issued, it makes clear that any existing terrorism exclusion does not apply. This endorsement also includes a provision stating that an insurer may be relieved of its obligation to pay covered losses once the $100 billion aggregate for a calendar year has been exceeded.

CG 21 80 Certified Acts of Terrorism Aggregate Limit: CAP On Losses From Certified Acts of Terrorism

This endorsement was introduced in 2002 and modified in 2008. This endorsement is to be issued when coverage is to be provided for certified acts of terrorism, subject to the aggregate limit and coverage for other acts of terrorism, subject to full policy limits. Coverage, however, is subject to the cap on liability for losses and subject to underlying policy provisions.

CG 21 84 Exclusion of Certified Nuclear, Biological, Chemical or Radiological Acts of Terrorism; CAP On Losses From Certified Acts of Terrorism

This endorsement was introduced in 2002 and modified in 2008. It is issued to exclude coverage for losses arising out of a certified act of terrorism that involves nuclear, biological or chemical materials but provides coverage for other acts of terrorism, subject to underlying policy provisions.

CG 21 86 Exclusion—Exterior Insulation Finish Systems

This optional endorsement introduced with the 2004 revisions will likely be attached to every CGL policy issued to a contractor. Commonly referred to in short as EIFS, this finish is an exterior building finish composed of layers of plywood, insulation board, reinforcing mesh, base, and finish coats. Its end product has the appearance of stucco or stone in any number of colors, and is intended to make the building or structure more energy efficient. It is a system developed in Europe in the 1950s and was first introduced for use in the United States in the mid-1970s.

The installation requires experienced, manufacturer-trained specialists, but this apparently has not been the case in all instances. Or, contractors have not necessarily been properly trained to perform quality work on the remaining portions of projects. Whatever the situation, water intrusion into these systems has resulted in many claims for construction defects as well as damage to other property.

(For purposes of this 2004 filing, endorsements also will be available for use with the products and completed operations liability coverage form, and the owners and contractors protective liability coverage form.)

CG 21 87 Conditional Exclusion of Terrorism (Relating To Disposition of Federal Terrorism Risk Insurance Act

This endorsement was introduced in 2007. Contemplating that TRIA might not be extended or be substantially changed, this is one of several endorsements insurers could use during the policy period to define the extent to which terrorism insurance would otherwise apply. This particular endorsement introduces a terrorism exclusion that overrides all other coverage provisions relating to terrorism.

CG 21 88 Conditional Exclusion of Terrorism (Relating To Disposition of Federal Terrorism Risk Insurance Act)

This conditional endorsement introduced in 2007 is issued to exclude coverage for terrorism that involved nuclear, biological or chemical materials. This would then leave intact any underlying terrorism coverage not involving nuclear, biological or chemical materials.

CG 21 89 Conditional Limitation of Coverage For Terrorism On An Annual Aggregate Basis (Relating To Disposition Of Federal Terrorism Risk Insurance Act

The last of the conditional endorsements, also introduced in 2007, this endorsement provides terrorism coverage, subject to an aggregate limit and any underlying policy provisions.

The following three endorsement options are to be used when policies become effective on or after the date when TRIA coverage has terminated, or have become effective on or after the date when an extension of TRIA has gone into effect, if the program was extended with certain changes in terrorism coverage or increases in insurer retention or participation in losses.

CG 21 90 Exclusion of Terrorism

Modified in 2006, this endorsement when issued excludes terrorism coverage.

CG 21 91 Exclusion of Terrorism Involving Nuclear, Biological Or Chemical Terrorism

This endorsement was modified in 2006. It is issued to exclude terrorism coverage involving nuclear, biological or chemical materials, thereby leaving intact any terrorism coverage that does not affect nuclear, biological or chemical materials.

CG 21 92 Limitation of Coverage For Terrorism On An Annual Aggregate Basis

Modified in 2006, this endorsement is issued to provide terrorism coverage, subject to an aggregate limit and any underlying policy provisions.

CG 21 93 Extended Reporting Period for Terrorism Coverage

This endorsement was introduced in 2004. When condition exclusion endorsement CG 21 87 or 21 88 is issued to a CGL policy written on a claims-made basis, it is necessary to also attach this endorsement CG 21 93. In doing so, the endorsement provides an extended reporting period of five years from the date the conditional exclusion goes into effect, for claims arising out of a terrorism incident occurring prior to the date the conditional exclusion became effective. This endorsement is not to be issued if the policy is subject to endorsement CG 21 75.

CG 21 96 Exclusion—Silica or Silica-Related Dust

This endorsement was introduced by ISO in 2004 to be effective in March, 2005 on a voluntary basis to exclude bodily injury, property damage, and personal and advertising injury arising out of silica or silica-related dust. Also excluded are the losses, costs, and expenses arising in whole or in part out of the abating, testing for, monitoring, cleaning up, removing, containing, treating, etc., of silica or silica-related dust. Although once viewed solely as an occupational hazard, silica-related lawsuits are now said to be filed against manufacturers, distributors, and vendors of products containing silica.

CG 21 97 Abuse or Molestation Exclusion – Specified Professional Services

Prior to 2007, the one endorsement available to exclude abuse or molestation of a person while in the care, custody or control of any insured was Abuse or Molestation Exclusion CG 21 46. This endorsement, CG 21 97, was introduced in 2007 in order to give underwriters another tool in which to handle the exclusion for abuse or molestation by certain specified professionals. An example could be a hotel's spa that offers body massages and other services for a charge. For a spa, however, it would also be necessary to issue the Professional Liability Exclusion—Spas or Personal Enhancement Facilities, CG 22 90. This endorsement (22 90) alone would not be sufficient because abuse or molestation would not likely be considered a professional service, unless specifically addressed as it is with endorsement CG 21 97.

According to ISO, this new endorsement CG 21 97 is less restrictive than the previous endorsement CG 21 97 because when CG 21 97 is issued, it would permit coverage for professional services not specifically described.

Endorsements for Certain Types of Risks

Many insureds are confronted with certain types of risks that may require special treatment. The following endorsements were developed by ISO to be used with policies covering these risks.

CG 22 24 Exclusion—Inspection, Appraisal, and Survey Companies

This endorsement is designed to preclude coverage against claims or suits that allege bodily injury, property damage, personal injury, or advertising injury arising from the rendering of or failure to render professional services of the type of service-related companies described above. The rationale is that these exposures should be covered by professional liability policies. Unfortunately, the E&O-type policies that are available for these types of businesses are limited to liability coverage for errors or omissions that result in economic damages that are not based on injury or damage. In fact, bodily injury, property damage, personal injury, and advertising injury usually are excluded from these E&O policies. Therefore, when this endorsement is attached, it can create a gap for which protection may not otherwise be available.

CG 22 27 Exclusion—Bodily Injury to Railroad Passengers

This exclusionary endorsement is intended to preclude all coverage because of bodily injury to a person while on, entering into, or alighting from, a passenger train.

CG 22 28 Exclusion—Travel Agency Tours (Limitation of Coverage)

This endorsement is intended for travel agencies whose services extend beyond the United States, its territories and possessions, Puerto Rico, and Canada. The endorsement was revised in 2004 to correctly refer to the appropriate coverage territory definition that does not apply. The effect is to bar coverage if the injury or damage arises out of the activities of a person while outside the United States, its territories, possessions, Puerto Rico, or Canada.

CG 22 29 Exclusion—Property Entrusted

This endorsement is designed for security and patrol agencies and warehouses, which commonly are entrusted with property of others. The exclusion, which supplements the care, custody, or control exclusion, eliminates coverage to property of others that is entrusted to the named insured for safekeeping or to property on premises owned or rented to the named insured. The exclusion does not apply when property of others is located on premises of others.

CG 22 30 Exclusion—Corporal Punishment

This endorsement, frequently added to policies covering schools, excludes coverage for bodily injury, property damage, personal injury, or advertising injury to any student or pupil arising out of any corporal punishment administered by or at the direction of any insured. If the insurer is willing to cover corporal punishment, coverage can be provided by attaching endorsement CG 22 67, Corporal Punishment.

The 1993 amendment to this endorsement changed reference in the exclusionary language from "any student or pupil" to "your student" to better express that the exclusion is intended to apply to the named insured's students.

CG 22 31 Exclusion—Riot, Civil Commotion, or Mob Action (Governmental Subdivisions)

This endorsement is designed to exclude injury and damage arising from riots and civil commotion that may take place from time to time within the municipalities or other governmental subdivisions throughout the United States. In some cases, depending on the law of the jurisdiction, the governmental subdivision is not liable for resulting injury or damage that occurs during riots or during periods when preventative measures are taken. However, most insurers automatically attach this endorsement whenever they provide liability insurance for governmental subdivisions.

CG 22 32 Exclusion—Professional Services—Blood Banks

The purpose of this exclusionary endorsement is to prevent the granting of liability coverage for claims or suits that should be covered by medical professional policies. When this endorsement is attached to the CGL policy, it excludes bodily injury and property damage arising out of the rendering of or failure to render professional services in connection with the making of a blood donation, or in the handling or distributing of the blood product by the named insured. This endorsement also excludes the liability of any insured for acts or omissions as a doctor of medicine.

This endorsement was amended in 1998 to be more consistent with the coverage provided by the Blood Banks Professional Liability Coverage Form (PR 00 07) introduced by ISO in 1997. This endorsement is said to more closely mirror the language of the professional liability trigger of a "medical incident" as defined in the coverage form.

CG 22 33 Exclusion—Testing or Consulting Errors and Omissions

This is an optional endorsement that is intended to exclude liability arising out of an error, omission, defect, or deficiency of any test, evaluation, consultation or advice performed or given by or on behalf of any insured, including the reporting of or reliance upon any such test or evaluation.

An important point to note here is that the terms "error" and "omission" have been held not to encompass "negligence." See for example *Aitchinson v. Founders Ins. Co.*, 333 P.2d 178 (Cal. App. 1958). Thus, an allegation of injury or damage because of negligence might be covered despite this endorsement.

CG 22 34 Exclusion—Construction Management Errors and Omissions

A general contractor can be defined as the person or entity with responsibility and control over the means, methods, sequences and techniques of the work in general, including the coordination and supervision of the work of subcontractors. Some general contractors also may perform some of the work. Although a general contractor does not have to be a professional or to perform work considered to be of a professional nature, it is common to find general contractors with professionals on staff, or who are qualified to, and in fact, function as construction managers.

The term "construction management" is generally taken to encompass the activities undertaken by a construction manager whose professional services are engaged by the project owner to coordinate and manage the entire project from start to finish. The activities of a construction manager can vary widely, depending on the nature of the project and the owner's needs. The American Institute of Architects' agreement between the project owner and construction manager describes the scope of the construction manager's work to include (1) basic services, (2) construction phase administrative services, (3) additional services, (4) contingent additional services, (5) optional additional services. With knowledge and expertise in the means, and methods of construction, labor, materials and the ability to direct, work with, and make decisions over the entire project, including design, the general objective of the construction manager is to help produce a quality project, with as little delay as possible, and at the least possible cost.

The endorsement is designed for contractors who are involved in construction management such as design-build projects. The fact that a contractor's professional liability policy is likely to be written by a different insurer than the one that writes the contractor's general liability policy means there may be a gray area between the two policies. In fact, this problem confronts most businesses that offer professional services.

Despite its title, this endorsement does not limit the exclusion of bodily injury, property damage, personal injury, or advertising injury to errors and omissions. Coverage is flatly excluded if such injury or damage arises from any of the various activities noted in the endorsement. However, excepted from this exclusion, and therefore covered, is bodily injury and property damage due to construction or demolition work done by the named insured or its employees or subcontractors, subject to other policy exclusions.

The 1993 version of this endorsement includes reference to "employee," as a defined term. This change also was made because the exclusion does not apply to bodily injury or property damage due to construction or demolition work by the named insured or its employees.

In light of the 2001 CGL policy amendment that expands the definition of employee to include volunteers, what applies here to employees also applies to volunteers.

CG 22 36 Exclusion—Products and Professional Services (Druggists)

This endorsement is intended to exclude the kind of coverage that normally is provided by a druggists liability policy. In fact, coverage for this excluded exposure can be brought back into the CGL form through the attachment of endorsement CG 22 69, if the insurer is willing to do so and is not otherwise precluded from offering such insurance. There is, of course, a distinct advantage to obtaining both professional and general liability insurance from the same insurer.

The 1993 change to this endorsement changed the phrase "professional services" to "professional health care services" in order to emphasize the nature of services intended to be excluded.

CG 22 37 Exclusion—Products and Professional Services (Optical and Hearing Aid Establishments)

This endorsement is comparable in purpose to the previous one dealing with druggists. If coverage is desired for this exposure in conjunction with the CGL policy, it is necessary to attach CG 22 65, Optical and Hearing Aid Establishments.

The 1993 change to this endorsement is identical to the change noted in the discussion of endorsement CG 22 36.

Following the introduction by ISO of the Optometrists Professional Liability Coverage Form in 1997, it became necessary, with the 1998 CGL policy revisions, to amend this endorsement, CG 22 37, so that it would more closely correspond to the products liability exclusion of the Optometrists coverage form.

CG 22 38 Exclusion—Fiduciary or Representative Liability of Financial Institutions

Until revised in 1996, this endorsement was titled "Exclusion—Financial Institutions." The exclusion may be attached when a bank or other financial institution is covered by the CGL policy. The exclusion is designed to avoid covering liability in connection with property in which the named insured is acting in a fiduciary or representative capacity. According to *Black's Law Dictionary*, 5th edition, a fiduciary is a person or entity who handles money or property which is not his or her own for the benefit of others. If coverage is desired for this exposure under the CGL policy, it is necessary to add endorsement CG 24 11, Fiduciaries—Fiduciary Interest.

CG 22 39 Exclusion—Camp or Campground

This endorsement is designed to exclude the medical professional liability exposure of any camp or campground that owns or operates an infirmary with facilities for lodging and treatment. If the camp or campground does not maintain such a medical facility, the named insured should at least have protection under its CGL policy against its vicarious liability that could be imputed because of the acts of medical professionals in administering aid at the time of injury. The specific provision which should provide this protection to the named insured is under paragraph 2.a. (1) (d) of the "Who Is an Insured" provision of the CGL policy. This provision is commonly referred to as incidental medical malpractice coverage.

Note also that this endorsement specifically excludes the payment of medical expenses under Coverage C for bodily injury to any camper. Accident insurance is a better alternative.

In addition to numbering and lettering this endorsement to make it more consistent with other CGL forms, the 1993 revision made two additional changes. First, the meaning of "health service or treatment" coverage has been expanded to include therapeutic service, and advice and instruction. Second, reference to "cosmetic or tonsorial service or treatment" has been replaced with the following: "service, treatment, advice, or instruction for the purpose of appearance or skin enhancement, hair removal or replacement, or personal grooming."

CG 22 40 Exclusion—Medical Payments to Children (Day Care Centers)

Since the activities of children at day care centers commonly can result in bodily injury, this endorsement is designed to exclude the payment of such expenses under Coverage C. Accident insurance is a better alternative. However, if bodily injury is serious enough to prompt a claim or lawsuit for damages, Coverage A should apply subject to any exclusions or limitations of the CGL policy as issued.

CG 22 41 Exclusion—Housing Projects Sites

This endorsement excludes buildings that exist on the site of a proposed housing authority at the time of their acquisition by a housing authority or that are to be demolished. A 1993 revision modified the exclusion to apply solely to bodily injury and property damage because neither personal injury nor advertising injury is of any concern with regard to vacant buildings or buildings in the course of demolition.

With the 2001 amendments, this endorsement was further amended to make the exclusion contingent on the condition that bodily injury or property damage occur during the period of vacancy preceding demolition of the building or during that demolition.

CG 22 42 Exclusion—Existence or Maintenance of Streets, Roads, Highways, or Bridges

This exclusion commonly is added to the CGL policy of a municipality or other governmental subdivision unless coverage is desired. In fact, the insurance rating basis of total operating expenditures does not take into consideration this exposure dealing with the existence hazards of streets, roads and bridges, as well as their maintenance. When coverage is desired, this exclusion is not added and the classification is designated in the policy schedule. The exposure unit is per mile.

CG 22 43 Exclusion—Engineers, Architects, or Surveyors Professional Liability

The basic CGL policy provisions exclude, by exception to the definition of insured contract, any liability under contract or agreement that indemnifies an architect, engineer, or surveyor, or under which the insured, if such a professional, assumes liability arising from its rendering or failure to render professional services. When this endorsement is attached, the policy also excludes all other professional liability which could otherwise attach in the absence of assumption of liability under contract or agreement. The purpose of this endorsement, therefore, is to keep the insurer from paying a loss that can be covered under a professional liability policy.

Since this is a kind of "clean sweep" of an exclusion, it should not be combined when the CGL policy is modified with the exclusions of the following two types of endorsements discussed later: CG 22 79 Exclusion – Contractors – Professional Liability, or CG 22 80 Limited Exclusion – Contractors – Professional Liability. If combined, the result can be an ambiguity and an argument with a result that is likely to be unpredictable. (Unfortunately, while this caveat can be largely avoided with the CGL policy, such is not commonly the case with umbrella liability policies, which commonly are modified with endorsement CG 22 43 when written for construction work.)

CG 22 44 Exclusion—Health or Cosmetic Services

The purpose of this endorsement is to prevent the insurer from having to respond to damages for an exposure that is better covered under some kind of professional liability policy. It is a general endorsement and is earmarked for use when the CG 22 45 noted below is not otherwise applicable.

With the 1993 revisions, the title of this endorsement was changed to read: "Exclusion—Services Furnished by Health Care Providers." Other changes made were: (1) the words "advice or instruction" were added to exclusion a.; (2) exclusion b., dealing with "health service or treatment", replaced such words with "health or therapeutic service, treatment, advice, or instruction"; (3) reference in exclusion c. to the phrase "cosmetic or tonsorial service or treatment" was replaced with the phrase "service, treatment, advice, or instruction for the purpose of appearance or skin enhancement, hair removal or replacement, or personal grooming."

CG 22 45 Exclusion—Specified Health or Cosmetic Services

The purpose of this endorsement, like the one above, is to preclude coverage against an exposure that requires special insurance. However, this form is designed for operations as itemized: cosmetic, ear piercing, tonsorial, massage, physiotherapy, chiropody, hearing aid, optical, or optometrical service or treatment.

The title of this endorsement was changed in 1993 to read: "Exclusion—Specified Therapeutic or Cosmetic Services." Also, the phrase "cosmetic, ear piercing, tonsorial, massage, physiotherapy, chiropody, hearing aid, optical or optometrical service or treatment" was replaced with the phrase "service, treatment, advice, or instruction for the purpose of appearance or skin enhancement, hair removal or replacement, personal grooming or therapy."

CG 22 46 Exclusion—Rolling Stock—Railroad Construction

The liability of railroads stemming from rolling stock (e.g., box cars, tank cars, and flat bed cars) is specifically excluded by this endorsement. However, by exception, coverage does apply for bodily injury or property damage claims arising out of the movement of such rolling stock while at a job site for purposes of construction or maintenance operations performed by the railroad. The kind of coverage that should be considered to cover damage to the rolling stock itself stemming from work for railroads is a railroad protective liability policy.

CG 22 47 Exclusion—Saline Substances Contamination

This endorsement generally is added to the CGL policy of an oil or gas lease operator to exclude property damage resulting from the "saline substance contamination hazard," as defined in the endorsement.

CG 22 48 Exclusion—Insurance and Related Operations

The intent behind this exclusionary endorsement is not readily apparent. It excludes bodily injury, property damage, personal injury, and advertising injury because of the activities as noted. However, the natural result of such activities is economic damages that are not based on such injury or damage. Thus, the apparent rationale for this exclusion is to require the insurance company or related institution to obtain an errors and omissions policy or a directors and officers liability policy. Unfortunately, the latter two policies commonly exclude liability because of bodily injury, property damage, personal injury, and advertising injury. The result is a potential gap in protection whenever this endorsement is attached to a CGL policy of an insurance company.

CG 22 50 Exclusion—Public Utilities—Failure to Supply

Water districts, water companies, gas dealers or distributors, electric light companies or power cooperatives, municipalities that provide utility services and other entities that supply similar services to the public and business sector may have something in common. If they purchase commercial general liability insurance, they are likely to find their liability policies subject to this exclusion. When this endorsement is attached to a CGL coverage form, this exclusion attempts to serve at least two purposes:

The first purpose is to exclude damages and costs arising out of an entity's business decision to intentionally withhold (in whole or in part) an adequate quantity of its product for use or consumption by others. An example is when a utility voluntarily cuts back the amount of power generated in order to conserve usage because of a prolonged heat wave and drought. As a result, a manufacturer, for example, may be unable to utilize all of its production facilities resulting in loss of use of machinery.

The second purpose is to assure coverage, by exception to the exclusions, for failure to supply, stemming from sudden and accidental injury to tangible property owned or used by the entity (supplier). For example, if the reason a water company must reduce the supply of its product to users is because of the destruction of one of its pumps by fire, resulting liability should be covered by the policy. (As an aside, there apparently have been no problems over the meaning of "sudden and accidental," as used in this endorsement, unlike the problems having to do with the pollution exclusion where there are two schools of thought and argument: The first school of thought is that reference to "sudden and accidental" conveys a temporal meaning and the second school of thought is that it conveys a non-temporal meaning, i.e., unexpected and unintended without limitation as to time.

This endorsement is somewhat more liberal than many others used by insurers. A more restrictive endorsement will not grant any exception. All injury or damage arising out of complete or partial failure to supply various utilities is flatly excluded.

CG 22 50 is being revised under the 2013 revisions to apply to the failure to adequately supply biofuels. The reason for this change is because one of the new manual classifications applies to Biofuels Distributor Risks.

CG 22 51 Exclusion—Law Enforcement Activities

This endorsement excludes those kinds of claims or suits involving bodily injury, property damage, or personal injury that can result from law enforcement activities and are commonly covered by law enforcement liability policies. However, this endorsement does not exclude liability arising out of the ownership, maintenance, or use of the named insured's premises that are not ordinarily incidental to law enforcement activities.

This is an important exception because law enforcement liability policies limit their protection to liability arising from the rendering of or failure to render law enforcement activities. Without this exception, law enforcement officers could be without insurance protection for an act or omission that is not deemed to be law enforcement related.

The 1993 amendment to the 1985 version of this endorsement removed the paragraph that clarified that this exclusion did not apply to liability arising out of the ownership, maintenance, or use of the named insured's premises that are not ordinarily incidental to law enforcement activities. However, this intent can still be inferred because the 1993 version (and the current version) of the endorsement excludes bodily injury, property damage, personal injury and advertising injury arising out of any act or omission *resulting from law enforcement activities*. A potential problem with this version is that unnecessary time and expense may be required in order to infer the coverage intent.

CG 22 52 Exclusion—Medical Payments Coverage (Inmates, Patients, or Prisoners)

This exclusionary endorsement is required whenever a CGL policy covers a health care facility, mission, settlement, halfway house, or penal institution. When attached, the endorsement precludes under Coverage C any expenses for bodily injury to any inmate, patient, or prisoner who is being treated, cared for, detained, or imprisoned by the facility designated in the endorsement. Also, this endorsement precludes any medical payments for services performed by the insured, its employees, or any person or organization under contract to the named insured to provide such services.

The 1993 change to this endorsement placed quotes around the word "employee," in order to track with the definition of "employee" in the 1993 CGL forms.

CG 22 53 Exclusion—Laundry and Dry Cleaning Damage

This exclusion, which can be added to the CGL policy of a laundromat, eliminates coverage for property damage to property being laundered or dry cleaned arising out of the operation of any self-service or coin-operated machine. Such losses might be considered a predictable business expense that is more economical for the laundromat to retain.

CG 22 54 Exclusion—Logging and Lumbering Operations

When the named insured is in the business of logging or lumbering, its CGL policy, with this endorsement attached, is intended to exclude property damage due to fire, or to property damage, however caused, to any vehicle while being loaded or unloaded. The fact that the term "vehicle" is not defined could conceivably mean that it encompasses autos, mobile equipment, aircraft, and watercraft.

What a logger should seriously consider is a Loggers Property Damage Liability policy. While these policies differ, some will cover precisely what is excluded by this endorsement, along with a variety of other coverages geared for the logger whose logging or sawmill operations may damage the property of others.

CG 22 56 Exclusion—Injury to Volunteer Firefighters

Volunteer firefighters generally are either subject to state workers compensation laws or are protected under special accident and health plans against injury while performing their duties. When a CGL policy is issued to a governmental subdivision or to a self-supporting and independent fire fighting unit, this exclusion is designed to preclude the payment of damages for bodily injury or personal injury sustained by these volunteers. (As of the 2001 CGL policy amendments, volunteers are automatically included as insureds. Prior to this change, it was said to be advisable to add the Additional Insured—Volunteers Endorsement, CG 20 21. However, CG 20 21 no longer is necessary, and was therefore withdrawn as of the 2001 amendments.)

CG 22 57 Exclusion—Underground Resources and Equipment

This is a mandatory endorsement for certain oil and gas producing or servicing risks for liability arising out of property damage included with the "underground resources and equipment hazard," a term defined as property damage to:

- Oil, gas, water or other mineral substances which have not been reduced to physical possession above the surface of the earth or above the surface of any body of water;

- Any well, hole, formation, strata or area in or through which exploration for or production of any substance is carried on;

- Any casing, pipe, bit, tool, pump or drilling or well servicing machinery or equipment located beneath the surface of the earth in any such well or hole or beneath the surface of any body of water.

Endorsement CG 22 62 is required to obtain coverage for what is excluded here.

CG 22 58 Exclusion—Described Hazards (Carnivals, Circuses, and Fairs)

Whether it is a governmental entity or a nonprofit organization that is hosting a carnival, circus, or fair, its CGL policy generally will contain this exclusion. Coverage may be available from the insurer for excess over the liability insurance provided by the owner-operator of the amusement devices. Otherwise, protection may be required from the excess and surplus lines market.

CG 22 59 Exclusion—Medical Payments to Members (Horseback Riding Clubs)

This endorsement was in use for a number of years to preclude medical payments for any member of a horseback riding club who sustained injury arising out of any activities in connection with the operations of the insured horseback riding club. Endorsement CG 20 02, Additional Insured—Club Members also has been used to add members of a horseback riding club as insureds. Since there is an exclusion under Coverage C in the CGL policy precluding medical payments to insureds, ISO withdrew endorsement CG 22 59 with its 2001 amendments, since it would be redundant to continue the use of this endorsement.

CG 22 60 Limitation of Coverage—Real Estate Operations

This endorsement is designed to tailor CGL coverage to a smaller type of real estate operation, such as one whose sole operations are limited to the sale or rental of property and not to property management. When this endorsement is attached to the CGL policy, coverage is limited to the premises used by the named insured for general office purposes. Coverage also is extended to activities involved with premises listed for sale or rental, as long as (1) the property is not managed by or in the care, custody, or control of the named insured; or (2) the named insured does not act as an agent for the collection of rents.

Prior to an amendment in 2007, coverage was limited solely to injury or damage arising out of the ownership, operation, maintenance of use of the premises listed with the named insured for sale or rental, subject to certain conditions. Since, in custom and practice, real estate agents also sell properties not listed by them, the restriction as to listings has been eliminated. As this endorsement currently reads, it applies to injury or damage arising out of the ownership, operation, maintenance or use of premises listed or shown by the insured.

CG 22 62 Underground Resources and Equipment Coverage

This endorsement can be used to cover certain oil and gas producing exposures that are excluded by mandatory endorsement CG 22 57, Exclusion—Underground Resources and Equipment, subject to a separate aggregate limit and other specific exclusions and conditions contained in endorsement CG 22 62.

This coverage endorsement was revised with the 2001 CGL policy amendments by the addition of an exception to exclusion j.(4) in the CGL form, to state that the exclusion:

... does not apply to any "property damage" included within the "underground resources hazard" other than "property damage" to that particular part of any real property on which operations are being performed by you or on your behalf if the "property damage" arises out of those operations.

This change was prompted by various insurance agents groups. Specifically, it has been questioned whether this endorsement overrides certain CGL policy provisions. The questioners have pointed to paragraph E.2(b.) of the definitions section of endorsement CG 22 62, which reads: "any well, hole, formation, strata or area in or through which exploration for or production of any substance is carried on." Some people have maintained that the foregoing sentence implies that property damage to the listed items caused by a servicing contractor is to be covered under the contractor's endorsed policy, regardless of exclusions, such as the care, custody, or control exclusion, j.(4) of CGL forms. It has been explained that coverage remains subject to the CGL policy exclusions.

Also, paragraph D of endorsement CG 22 62 imposes duties upon the insured, so it has been moved to the conditions section of the CGL forms effective with the 2001 amendments.

CG 22 63 Stevedoring Operations (Limited Completed Operations Coverage)

This endorsement modifies the definition of "products-completed operations hazard" so that it does *not* include bodily injury or property damage arising out of occurrences *not* on board vessels at the site of operations after the operations have been completed or abandoned. Thus, such occurrences would be subject to the general aggregate limit rather than the products-completed operations aggregate limit.

CG 22 64 Pesticide or Herbicide Applicator Coverage

Were it not for this endorsement, one of the primary exposures of an applicator's business would be excluded because of the almost absolute pollution or contamination exclusion of the CGL policy. The Commercial Lines Manual of ISO requires the use of this endorsement with classifications representing crop spraying by contractors, fumigating, orchards and vineyards by contractors, pest control services, and tree pruning, dusting, spraying, repairing, trimming or fumigating.

So when this endorsement is issued to the above businesses, paragraph (1.)(d.) of pollution exclusion f. of Section I – Coverage A – bodily injury and property damage does not apply to an off-site premises in connection with the named insured's operations, provided it meets and complies with all standards of any statute, ordinance, regulation, or license requirement of federal, state, or local governments.

It is important to note that this endorsement will not fulfill the coverage desired when employees or independent contractors of the named insured are applying chemicals to the named insured's own property, such as country clubs or garden nurseries. The only alternative short of having to purchase a special environmental liability policy would be to add CG 24 15, limited pollution liability extension endorsement to the CGL policy, limited solely to the application of pesticides and herbicides and subject to the added proviso that coverage also is contingent on meeting all the standards that are listed in endorsement CG 24 15.

Note that with the 2013 revisions, the title of this endorsement is changed. The revised title is Pesticide or Herbicide Applicator Limited Pollution Coverage.

CG 22 65 Optical and Hearing Aid Establishments

This endorsement is necessary for an optical or hearing aid establishment that requires coverage for its professional liability loss exposure. The endorsement, in effect, offsets CG 22 37 Exclusion—Products and Professional Services Optical and Hearing Aid Establishments.

Paragraph 2.a.(1)(d) of the "Who Is an Insured" provision of the CGL forms indicates that the named insured's employees are not insureds for bodily injury or property damage arising out of their providing or failure to provide professional health care services. In order to ensure that the named insured's employees in an optical or hearing aid establishment are protected, the 1993 amendment to this endorsement modified the above section of the "Who Is an Insured" provision to effect coverage for such employees. This endorsement also changed the phrase "professional services" to the phrase "professional health care services."

Following the introduction by ISO of the Optometrists Professional Liability Coverage Form in 1997, it became necessary, with the 1998 CGL policy revisions, to amend this endorsement, CG 22 65, so that it would more closely correspond to the products liability exclusion of the professional coverage form.

CG 22 66 Misdelivery of Liquid Products Coverage

This endorsement is necessary for any entity whose business involves the delivery of liquid products because it clarifies a gray area that otherwise applies between the CGL and business auto coverage forms. The nature of the businesses, according to the ISO Commercial Lines Manual that require this endorsement are: anhydrous ammonia dealers and distributors, chemical distributors, fertilizer dealers and distributors, fuel oil or kerosene dealers and distributors, gas dealers or distributors, gasoline distributors, and milk depots and dealers.

When attached, this endorsement modifies exclusion g. of the CGL policy by specifically excepting, and therefore covering, bodily injury or property damage arising out of (1) the delivery of any liquid product into a wrong receptacle or to a wrong address, or (2) the erroneous delivery of one liquid product for another by an auto—if the injury or damage occurs after such operations have been completed or abandoned at the site of the delivery. If injury or damage should occur during the unloading process, coverage might apply under the business auto or truckers policy, depending on the circumstances. The fact that this endorsement does not address pollution losses means that the pollution exclusion still applies. For fuel oil distributors and other businesses involved in pollutants, this endorsement does not hold much promise of coverage.

CG 22 67 Corporal Punishment

When corporal punishment coverage is purchased, it is necessary to clarify that the intentional injury exclusion of the CGL policy does not apply; otherwise, coverage could be denied. Thus, when this endorsement is attached, it states that the intentional injury exclusion does not apply to bodily injury resulting from the use of reasonable force to protect persons or property, and to any corporal punishment to any student or pupil by or at the direction of any insured.

The 1993 amendment to this endorsement clarified that the coverage for bodily injury resulting from corporal punishment is intended to apply solely to the named insured's students.

CG 22 68 Operation of Customers Autos on Particular Premises

By exception to exclusion g. of the CGL policy, coverage does apply for bodily injury or property damage arising out of the valet parking of an auto that is not owned by or rented or loaned to the named insured. This endorsement provides similar, though broader, coverage for liability arising out of customers' autos on the premises (and adjoining ways) of auto repair or service shops, car washes, gasoline stations, and tire dealers. While the regular exception to exclusion g. applies only to parking of customers' autos, this endorsement does not limit the covered activity to parking. The chief requirement is that the auto be on (or on ways next to) the insured premises.

To answer a question that occasionally arises, this endorsement would be necessary for a car wash operation where employees actually take possession of the vehicles and maneuver them through the wash system. The reason is that this kind of service exceeds the mere parking of autos not owned, rented or loaned to the named insured.

It is important to note that this coverage does not apply to physical damage to a customer's auto. The named insured would require garagekeepers insurance for this exposure.

This endorsement was amended in 1993 to clarify what provisions of the CGL forms are affected by this endorsement. Also, lead-in language was added to make clear that the term "customer's auto" is defined in the definitions section of the CGL forms.

CG 22 69 Druggists

This endorsement is necessary when a druggist desires to add professional and products liability insurance to an existing CGL policy. If this endorsement is not purchased, the CGL coverage form is issued with CG 22 36 Exclusion—Products and Professional Services (Druggists).

The 1993 amendment to this endorsement corresponds to the same change that affects endorsement CG 22 65. Thus, this endorsement makes clear that employees of druggists will be covered for their liability arising out of the rendering of or failure to render professional health care services as pharmacists.

With an increasing number of state laws permitting the expansion of the duties and responsibilities of pharmacists, the professional liability exposure has expanded beyond what ISO has intended to cover. For example, many of the statutes permit pharmacists to prescribe and administer drugs and vaccinations and perform specific duties such as blood tests. This endorsement, therefore, was changed with the 2001 CGL policy amendments to exclude certain types of pharmacists that are more of a professional nature and do not fall within the traditional duties of pharmacists. In light of this change, ISO has also introduced a new endorsement, CG 22 97, Druggists—Broadened Coverage, to be used in those states where broader duties of pharmacists are permitted.

Note that the 2001 exclusion might now be in violation of certain state or federal law. Therefore, the endorsement was changed under the 2013 revisions to include an exception to the exclusion with respect to the administering of vaccinations in accordance with any applicable state or federal law.

CG 22 70 Real Estate Property Managed

According to the ISO Commercial Lines Manual, this endorsement is mandatory whenever real estate agents or property managers are classified under code 47052 ("Real Estate Property Managed") because they manage properties of others. This classification is used to determine the rate to be applied against estimated receipts (from managed properties) in calculating the premium. It is not used to calculate premiums for property used for offices in conducting the real estate agents' or property managers' business.

That particular exposure is classified and rated under code 47050 ("Real Estate Agents").

When this endorsement is issued, it is intended to serve two purposes.

The first purpose is to preclude coverage for the real estate agent or property manager for any liability having to do with property damage to the property it manages or operates, or for which the real estate agent or property manager acts as an agent for the collection of rents. Unfortunately, leaving the real estate agent or property manager (named insured) with no coverage under its CGL policy for damage or destruction of the real estate that it manages or operates means there are only three options to secure protection: (1) purchase insurance on the property; (2) be named as an additional insured on the owner's property insurance; or (3) obtain a waiver of subrogation and indemnity rights from the property owner.

The second purpose of this endorsement is to clarify that, with respect to liability arising out of the real estate agent's or property manager's management of the property, the policy issued to that person or entity (to which this endorsement is attached) is considered to be excess insurance over any other valid and collectible insurance available to it. The reason this endorsement provides coverage and applies on an excess basis is because the standard CGL policy (and most independently filed policies) automatically include as an insured (on a primary basis) any person or organization while acting as the property owner's real estate manager.

So, the real estate manager should have primary coverage, as an additional insured under the owner's CGL policy for liability because of bodily injury, property damage or for offenses dealing with personal and advertising injury sustained by third parties. If excess coverage is necessary, it would come from the real estate agent's or property manager's own CGL policy to which endorsement CG 22 70 is attached. (Note that CG 22 70 is revised now to reinforce the point that the insurance provided is excess over any other insurance available, whether such insurance is primary or excess.)

An important point to consider here is this: suppose the real estate agent or property manager (1) does not purchase insurance on the actual property being managed, (2) is not listed as an additional insured under the property owner's insurance, and (3) does not obtain a waiver of subrogation and indemnity rights from the property owner. Assume further that the real estate agent or property manager negligently causes extensive damage to the managed property. Based on the Real Estate Property Managed Endorsement (CG 22 70) being attached to the real estate manager's own CGL policy, there would be no coverage for that liability, according to the first part of this endorsement which reads: this insurance does not apply to property damage to property you operate or manage or as to which you act as agent for the collection of rents or in any other supervisory capacity.

The question then arises: if, as a real estate manager, the named insured is not covered under his own CGL form, will the liability policy of the entity for whom the named insured is employed to render services as a real estate manager cover the manager for damage to real property that he or she has been employed to operate or manage? The answer is no. The reason is because of the damage to property exclusion in the CGL form. Subsection j(1) excludes property damage to property that the named insured owns, rents, or occupies. Thus, even if the real estate manager is liable for damaging the owner's property, the policy of the owner will not pay the owner on behalf of the real estate manager for damage to such property.

In summary, no coverage applies to property damage to property a real estate manager operates or manages under the real estate manager's own liability policy because of endorsement CG 22 70. And, coverage is not applicable under the liability policy of the owner who employs the services of the real estate manager because of the damage to property exclusion.

What about the second part of CG 22 70 that says that coverage applies on an excess basis for liability arising out of the property being managed? While that is not the intent of the endorsement (unless damage to a third party arises out of the property manager's management of the property), it may seem reasonable to some people (and the courts) to conclude that coverage does apply for that liability, at least on an excess basis.

A dispute between two insurers that bore out the ambiguity of this endorsement is *Allstate Insurance Company v. The West American Insurance Company*, No. 09-CV-00967-RBJMJW (U.S. D.C., CO. 2011). The underlying case (i.e., the case preceding this one between two insurers), was between a homeowners association and the developer-builder involving a variety of construction and maintenance problems. Allstate provided liability insurance to both the developer and property manager during the periods 1997-2003. West American then provided coverage for the periods 2003-2005.

When the underlying case was settled, Allstate paid most of the settlement amount and then sought contribution from West American, which maintained that it had no contractual liability to its named insureds (developer and property manager) because of the Real Estate Property Managed Endorsement. This endorsement, with the exception of two words, is virtually identical to the one of ISO. It read: this insurance does not apply to property damage to property you operate or manage as to which you act as agent for the collection of rents or in any other supervisory capacity. With respect to your liability arising out of your management of property for which you are acting as real estate manager this insurance is excess over any other valid and collective insurance available to you.

West American, citing the first paragraph of the endorsement, argued that because the alleged property damage was caused by the property manager, there was no coverage. According to the court, the first paragraph of that endorsement could rationally be interpreted in that manner. However, the second paragraph indicated that liability arising from the property manager's management of the property applied excess to other applicable coverage. From the court's perspective, this created an ambiguity, because the two paragraphs of the endorsement could be read as inconsistent; that is, damage to property managed by the manager is not covered, but damage caused by the manager is covered. Either way, said the court, as a matter of law, the endorsement did not exclude coverage in this case.

Based on the fact that the second part of the endorsement can thus be argued to be read in two reasonable ways, it is likely that insurers will have to amend this endorsement if they want to eliminate having to pay for what they think should not be covered. The question is whether the second part of the endorsement is even necessary, given that property managers are viewed as additional insureds on a primary basis of the liability policies issued to property owners. In light of the possibility of other insurance disputes, perhaps the second part of the endorsement could be moved to the other insurance provision. Whatever the solution, trying to accomplish two purposes with one endorsement does not seem to work here.

In the final analysis, endorsement CG 22 70 can be problematic and invalidate more coverage than a real estate manager would ever expect. However, much depends on the facts of each case.

CG 22 71 Colleges or Schools (Limited Form)

Either this endorsement or endorsement CG 22 72 must be attached to a CGL policy when a college or school is operated by the named insured or on its behalf. (The only difference between the two endorsements is that the latter one includes Coverage C for medical payments.) These endorsements have the following effects on CGL coverage:

1. They exclude coverage for:

   - bodily injury or property damage arising out of the transportation of students to and from schools; and

- liability arising out of the rendering of or failure to render professional health care services if the college or school owns or operates either an infirmary with facilities for lodging and treatment or a public clinic or hospital.

2. They add the following parties as additional insureds:

- the trustees or members of the Board of Governors, if the college or school is a private charitable or educational institution;

- any board member or commissioners, if the college or school is a public board or commission; and

- any student teachers teaching as part of their educational requirements.

These two endorsements were amended in 1997 with the addition of an exclusion of injury to athletic or sports participants instead of requiring the issuance of endorsement CG 21 01, Exclusion—Athletic or Sports Participants, when called for in the CLM footnote relating to the "Stadiums" classification. This exclusion reads as follows:

"Bodily injury" to any person while practicing for or participating in any sports or athletic contest or exhibition if there is no direct management, organization or supervision of such sports or athletic contest by any insured.

While this exclusion will apply regardless of whether the insured school has a stadium, its application will be restricted to situations in which the qualifications listed in the exclusion are met.

When the college or school owns or operates an infirmary with facilities for lodging and treatment or a public clinic or hospital, professional services are specifically excluded. A new exclusion being added in the recent revisions states that the professional services are excluded even if claims against any insured allege negligence or other wrongdoing in the supervision, hiring, employment, training, or monitoring of others by that insured—provided the occurrence which caused the bodily injury or property damage or the offense which caused the personal and advertising injury involved the provisions as stated with regard to the professional services exclusion.

Another revision to CG 22 71 deals with exclusion g. on the CGL form that pertains to aircraft, auto, or watercraft. This exclusion on CG 22 71 consists of two paragraphs. The first paragraph (which has not been revised) precludes coverage for injury or damage arising out of the ownership, maintenance, operation, use, loading or unloading or entrustment to others of any aircraft, auto or watercraft that is owned, operated or hired by any insured; this provision also defines the word "hired" to include any contract to furnish transportation of students to and from schools. The second paragraph precludes coverage even if claims against any insured (changed from the insured) allege negligence or other wrongdoing in the supervision, hiring, employment, training, or monitoring of others by the insured—provided the occurrence which caused the bodily injury or property damage involved the ownership, maintenance, use, loading or unloading or entrustment to others of any aircraft, auto or watercraft that is owned, operated or hired by any insured.

(New to this exclusion is the preceding phrase that is underlined for emphasis. It formerly read: that is owned, operated or rented or loaned to any insured.)

CG 22 72 Colleges or Schools

This endorsement is the same as CG 22 71, discussed above, except that CG 22 72 includes coverage for medical expenses.

CG 22 73 Exclusion—Oil or Gas Producing Operations

There are exceptions to the pollution exclusion of the CGL coverage forms under paragraph (1)(d) of that exclusion. However, when the business of the named insured concerns oil or gas producing operations, this endorsement eliminates the exceptions. This exclusion applies to locations on which the named insured is performing operations.

CG 22 74 Amendment of Contractual Liability Exclusion for Personal Injury Limited to False Arrest, Detention, or Imprisonment for Designated Contracts or Agreements

Until revised in 1996, this endorsement was titled "Amendment of Contractual Liability Exclusion for Personal Injury." The endorsement modifies the Coverage B exclusion of liability assumed under contract. The result is that Coverage B applies to liability for false arrest, detention, or imprisonment that the insured assumes under a contract designated in the endorsement schedule.

The 1992 and 1996 versions of the endorsement also provide for the payment of related defense costs assumed under a designated contract, subject to provisions similar to those contained in the 1992 and 1996 CGL forms relating to coverage of defense costs assumed under an "insured contract" under Coverage A.

The endorsement was amended again in 1997 to more specifically state that the payment of defense expenses and/or the providing of a defense to an indemnitee applies only to personal injury arising out of the offenses of false arrest, detention, or imprisonment.

The current version of CG 22 74 (10 01) is titled "Limited Contractual Liability Coverage for Personal and Advertising Injury". This version of the endorsement clearly states that the contractual liability exclusion does not apply to liability for personal and advertising injury if the personal and advertising injury arises out of the offenses of false arrest, detention or imprisonment.

CG 22 75 Professional Liability Exclusion—Computer Software

This endorsement, introduced in 1998, states that it excludes bodily injury, property damage, personal and advertising injury arising out of the rendering of, or failure to render any service by or on behalf of the named insured in connection with the selling, licensing, franchising or furnishing of computer software, including EDP processing programs, designs, manuals and instructions. Use of the phraseology "rendering of, or failure to render" is common to professional liability exclusions and is intended to serve as a "clean sweep."

An important question here, however, is why this exclusion is labeled as a professional liability one when, in fact, it does not even mention the word professional within the contents of the exclusion. Are the words "any service" meant to exclude all services or only those of a professional nature, as the title of this endorsement suggests? The problem for any business looking for liability insurance to cover what is being excluded may have difficulty, not in finding the coverage, but in obtaining coverage that will apply to any act, error or omission. If it turns out that the best a business can obtain is coverage for negligent acts, errors or omissions, there may be a gap, because there is a difference between any act, which includes an intentional and unintentional act, and a negligent act, which is limited to an unintentional act.

The 1993 amendment to this endorsement introduced the entire text of the CGL contractual liability exclusion but without the usual exception relating to "insured contracts." In the previous edition, the endorsement simply stated that the exception to exclusion b. (contractual liability) did not apply.

CG 22 76 Professional Liability Exclusion— Health or Exercise Clubs

This endorsement excludes the professional liability exposure of persons who render services or advice relating to health and exercise clubs.

Care must be exercised by such businesses that the person who provides such services otherwise qualifies for professional liability insurance that will at least encompass the liability that is excluded by this endorsement.

CG 22 77 Professional Liability Exclusion— Electronic Data Processing

This endorsement excludes the professional liability exposures that arise out of electronic data processing services, whether performed by or on behalf of the named insured. Consequently, if the named insured is subject to this endorsement and performs such services it should ascertain that its professional liability policy encompasses what is excluded by this endorsement. If the services are to be performed by others, the named insured should obtain proper proof that the firm performing the services has adequate professional liability insurance, since this endorsement also excludes the vicarious liability of the insured when work is performed by others.

CG 22 78 Hazardous Material Contractors

When this endorsement is attached to the CGL coverage form of a contractor who handles hazardous materials, it modifies exclusion f. (pollution) to allow coverage for bodily injury or property damage resulting from the removal, replacement, repair, enclosure, or encapsulation of any hazardous material.

CG 22 79 Exclusion—Contractors—Professional Liability

This endorsement is intended to be added to policies covering construction firms that also provide professional engineering, architectural, or surveying services to others. The endorsement excludes liability for professional engineering, architectural, or surveying services (1) that the named insured provides to others in the capacity of an engineer, architect, or surveyor; and (2) that the named insured provides, or hires independent professionals to provide, in connection with construction performed by the named insured.

However, the endorsement specifically preserves coverage for "services within construction means, methods, techniques, sequences, and procedures employed by you in connection with your operations in your capacity as a construction contractor." This language is intended to clarify that such services that are part of construction operations will not be excluded by the professional services exclusion.

This endorsement was introduced as part of the 1996 CGL policy revisions because of the case of *Harbor Insurance Company v. OMNI*

Construction, Inc., 912 F.2d 1520 (D.C. Cir. 1990). This case held that liability coverage for a general contractor was excluded when an endorsement similar to CG 22 43, Exclusion—Engineers, Architects, or Surveyors Professional Liability (prior to the current edition), was attached to the contractor's umbrella liability policy. After shoring designed by a subcontractor on the project caused the partial collapse of an adjacent building, the general contractor, who also maintained a professional liability policy, sought coverage under his umbrella policy. In doing so, the contractor maintained that the design work of sheeting and shoring, which allegedly caused the damage, was not a "professional service" but rather the "means and methods of construction," or an operation "incidental" to the construction work.

The crux of the general contractor's claim was that in the custom and practice of the construction business, professional services performed by a subcontractor incidental to the contractor's construction work are referred to as "means and methods of construction," rather than "professional services." Under the general contractor's interpretation, a loss caused by defective engineering work (a professional service) where both the engineering work and its implementation are done by a single contractor, would be considered incidental to the construction and therefore covered.

The court nonetheless held that the exclusionary endorsement was clear and unambiguous. As such, the court agreed with the insurer, which maintained that (1) damage to the adjacent building was caused by an error in design of the shoring system of a subcontractor, (2) such design work constituted a professional service, and (3) the resulting loss therefore was excluded.

Thus, when the classification "Engineers or Architects—consulting—not engaged in actual construction" is applicable, the ISO manual rules recommend that endorsement CG 22 43 be used. ISO warns, however, that when applied to a construction contracting risk, this endorsement may exclude some of the basic contracting functions performed by the risk based on blueprints or plans by others or by themselves in their capacity as an engineer, architect or surveyor. Therefore, endorsement CG 22 79 was introduced. It applies to the professional liability of contractors (1) who provide architectural, engineering, or surveying services to others; (2) who subcontract the design portion of a job; and (3) who are involved in design and build work. However, this exclusion does not apply to an insured contractor's liability arising out of services within construction means, methods, techniques, sequences, or procedures employed by the named insured in connection with its operations as a construction contractor, whether or not such services are considered to be professional services.

CG 22 80 Limited Exclusion—Contractors—Professional Liability

This endorsement was introduced at the same time as the above endorsement, CG 22 79, for purposes of addressing professional services rendered by or for a named insured construction firm. This endorsement is intended for policies covering construction contractors who may also provide professional services to others. The endorsement is similar to endorsement CG 22 79 in that both exclude professional errors or omissions in connection with engineering, architectural, or surveying services that the named insured provides in its capacity as an engineer, architect, or surveyor. However, unlike endorsement CG 22 79, CG 22 80 does *not* exclude coverage for the liability of a contractor who designs and builds a project for others, whether the design work is performed by the named insured or a subcontractor.

It may be interesting to note that underwriters are reluctant to issue this endorsement despite the fact it is an exclusion. What appears to worry underwriters is the exception to the exclusion of this endorsement which states that the professional services excluded do not apply to the named insured's operations in connection with construction work performed by the named insured or on its behalf. Based on the arrangement in the above OMNI Construction case, it would have been necessary to have this endorsement and not endorsement CG 22 79 to cover the claim in question. Prospects cannot simply accept endorsement 22 79 because it is more readily available without first identifying the nature of the exposure. Above all, when either of these endorsements is issued, insureds must see to it that the policy also is not amended with CG 22 43 Exclusion – Engineers, Architects, or Surveyors Professional Liability (the "clean sweep" exclusion).

CG 22 81 Exclusion—Erroneous Delivery or Mixture and Resulting Failure of Seed to Germinate—Seed Merchants

This endorsement, introduced in 1996, was designed to be attached to policies whose named insured takes the following rating classification: "Seed Merchants—excluding misdelivery, error in mixture, and germination failure" (class code 16890). Accordingly, the endorsement excludes a seed merchant's liability for property damage arising out of (1) the erroneous delivery of seed, (2) an error in mechanical mixture of seed, and (3) the failure of seed to germinate.

For less extensive seed merchant exclusions, see endorsements CG 24 18 and CG 24 19.

CG 22 87 Exclusion—Adult Day Care Centers

This endorsement affects bodily injury, property damage, personal and advertising injury, and medical payments coverages under the CGL forms. It excludes coverage arising out of the rendering of or failure to render medical or nursing service, treatment, advice, or instructions by any insured. Also excluded are health or therapeutic services, any service for the purpose of appearance or skin enhancement, and medical payments expenses for bodily injury to any person in the care of the insured.

CG 22 88 Professional Liability Exclusion— Electronic Data Processing Services and Computer Consulting or Programming Services

This endorsement excludes coverage for bodily injury, property damage, or personal and advertising injury arising out of the rendering of or failure to render electronic data processing, computer consulting, or computer programming services, advice, or instruction by the insured. The endorsement also excludes these services if they are provided by any person or organization for whose acts or omissions the insured is legally responsible.

CG 22 89 Exclusion—Property Damage to Electronic Data (Computer Software Manufacturer)

This endorsement's intended purpose is to exclude property damage to electronic data arising out of computer software programs (1) developed and manufactured by the named insured, (2) developed by the named insured and made by others under a contract, or (3) developed by others and manufactured by the named insured.

As part of the 1998 policy revisions, this endorsement was amended to redefine paragraph f. of the definition of insured contract so as not to include any licensing, franchising, or similar agreement with respect to the manufacturing and/or development of computer software programs.

This endorsement was withdrawn with the 2001 revisions because those revisions included new endorsements that exclude professional liability for Internet-related professions.

CG 22 90 Professional Liability Exclusion—Spas or Personal Enhancement Facilities

This endorsement excludes coverage for injury or damage arising out of any professional services performed by the insured in conjunction with any spa or personal enhancement facility described in the endorsement's schedule. Such services include acts of the insured in connection with professional services or advice that may directly impact the health or physical appearance of the insured's clients.

CG 22 91 Exclusion—Telecommunication Equipment or Service Providers Errors and Omissions

This endorsement excludes bodily injury, property damage, or personal and advertising injury arising out of any error, omission, defect, or deficiency in any evaluation, consultation, or advice given by the insured in this particular business.

The problem with this endorsement is that insureds subject to it will likely be unable to obtain an errors or omissions policy that will include coverage for bodily injury, property damage, and personal and advertising injury. What an errors or omissions policy generally covers is the economic damages that result from a negligent act, error, or omission. That is what should be excluded by this endorsement instead of bodily injury, property damage, and personal and advertising injury. As a result, there is likely to be a gap in coverage between the CGL and E&O policies.

CG 22 92 Snowplowing Operations Coverage

Until 2007, there was an obstacle in obtaining coverage for snowplowing after the work has been completed. Let's take the individuals, for example, who on a part time basis to earn extra money use their ubiquitous pick up trucks with snow plow attachments. The ISO personal auto policy would cover such business use of pick up trucks during the snowplowing process by exception to exclusion 7. The question is, however, whether that policy would cover the insured's liability after the snowplowing is completed. A great deal here hinges on the meaning of how far "use" of a covered auto can be stretched. It is an argument that individuals can ill afford to encounter. It also is doubtful that an insurer will permit the issuance of an insurance certificate to a business, such as Wal-Mart confirming that the appropriate coverage is being provided.

Those individuals who maintain a business auto policy (BAP) should have no problem having a certificate of insurance issued. The problem is that the BAP excludes bodily injury or property damage arising out of the named insured's work after that work has been completed or abandoned. On the other hand, the CGL coverage form—to the extent these individuals even maintain one—excludes claims arising out of the ownership, maintenance, use or entrustment to others of any auto owned or operated by or rented or loaned to any insured.

The questions then are how to protect (1) these individuals who offer their snowplowing services to others, (2) property owners for work performed by others, and (3) property owners who perform their own snowplowing work.

It may be easier to fill the coverage gap now with the introduction by ISO in 2007 of its Snowplowing Operations Coverage endorsement CG 22 92, applicable in most jurisdictions. When issued, this endorsement amends the aircraft, auto or watercraft exclusion g. of the CGL coverage form, and states concisely that with the "products-completed operations hazard," this exclusion does not apply to any auto used for snowplowing operations. With this new endorsement, the independent contractor's BAP will apply to bodily injury or property damage happening during snowplowing work, while its CGL policy will apply for injury or damage taking place after the work has been completed.

Property owners and those responsible for maintaining business real property, including parking lots, still need to be concerned about adequate coverage, given that they, too, are likely to be named in any legal action. Fortunately, no additional coverage for the property owner or other entity maintaining such property is necessary in order to obtain completed operations coverage for snowplowing operations performed by others, other than an existing CGL policy. The reason is that, while the CGL policy excludes bodily injury or property damage arising out of the ownership, maintenance, use or entrustment to another of an auto owned or operated by or rented or loaned to any insured, this exclusion does not apply when the auto is owned or operated by an independent contractor. The CGL policy, therefore, should provide coverage to the property owner or entity that has responsibility for maintaining the premises both during snowplowing work and after the work has been completed.

If the property owner or entity responsible for the property conducts its own snow removal operations, it will require a BAP for coverage for injury or damage during the removal process, and endorsement CG 22 92 attached to its CGL policy for coverage after the work has been completed. The ISO Commercial General Liability Rules filing shows with reference to "Snow and Ice Removal Contractor" to refer to the "Street Cleaning Classification," which includes snow removal. That classification in the Commercial Lines Manual Classification Table, however, excludes the drivers' payroll when snow plow operations are performed by auto. To accommodate the use of autos in snow removal under the CGL policy, ISO has introduced a new classification code for snowplow operations, with the coverage cost basis being the drivers' payroll.

CG 22 93 Lawn Care Services Coverage

This endorsement was introduced for use with the 1998 revisions for purposes of narrowing the pollution exclusion f. of CGL forms by stating that paragraph (1)(d) of that exclusion does not apply to the application of herbicides or pesticides by an insured on lawns under the named insured's regular care, for which the insured is not required to obtain a license or permit to apply herbicides or pesticides. The kind of chemicals for which this endorsement has applied are those obtained over-the-counter.

In 2007, the class code for lawn care services was revised so as to encompass the use of chemicals requiring a license or permit. In light of this change, this CG 22 93 endorsement was modified with the deletion of the phrase "for which the insured is not required to obtain a license or permit to apply." With this revision, coverage applies to insureds required to obtain a license or permit to apply herbicides and pesticides on lawns where they regularly work.

Note that under the 2013 revisions, the title of this endorsement is changed. The revised title is Lawn Care Services Limited Pollution Coverage. The reason put forth for this change is said to better reflect the purpose of CG 22 93.

CG 22 94 Exclusion—Damage to Work Performed by Subcontractors on Your Behalf

This is one of two endorsements newly introduced with the 2001 CGL policy revisions to combat coverage for construction defects. The other exclusion is CG 22 95. Even though construction defects are considered business risks and not covered under the liability policy of the contractor who performed the work, coverage still can apply whenever an insured (a general contractor, for example) uses subcontractors. The reason is that by exception to exclusion l. (Damage to Your Work), coverage may apply, for example, to: (1) damage to the general contractor's work arising out of a subcontractor's work, (2) damage to a subcontractor's work, or (3) if the insured is a subcontractor, damage to a general contractor's work or another subcontractor's work.

This is a blanket-type endorsement that amends exclusion l. by deleting the subcontractor exception for all exposures. The impact, therefore, is to virtually eliminate broad form property damage coverage for the completed operations hazard.

As a matter of interest and perhaps of historical significance, broad form property damage coverage was first introduced in 1955 and affected exposures relating solely to work while in progress. It was not until 1969 that broad form property damage became available for completed operations. During both decades, the coverage was available solely on an advisory basis on behalf of the ISO predecessors. Broad form property damage was available by endorsement either with or without completed operations until the introduction of the broad form CGL endorsement in 1976. At that time, broad form property damage automatically included coverage for completed operations. In fact, it was a requirement of eligibility for the broad form CGL endorsement that the insured maintain both products and completed operations coverage. When the simplified CGL forms were introduced in 1986, the tradition of automatically including completed operations by exception to exclusion l. was continued. So the offer of broad form property damage including completed operations coverage lasted approximately thirty-six years.

With this endorsement being available as an underwriting tool, insurers may add the endorsement to some CGL policies of general contractors. Producers and risk managers should try to avoid this endorsement being imposed on their contractor insureds. If they cannot avoid the endorsement, they should explain its full impact to insureds that are affected.

Unfortunately for insureds, as discussed in Chapter 1, some insurers have been successful in maintaining that defective work is neither an occurrence nor property damage. When a court is convinced of this argument, it is unnecessary for such an insurer to rely on any exclusion, including this endorsement. Some insurers in this category, in successfully denying coverage, also offer special insurance to compensate for their action but most of such coverage is inferior and not recommended for purchase.

CG 22 95 Exclusion—Damage to Work Performed by Subcontractors on Your Behalf—Designated Sites or Operations

This endorsement was introduced at the same time as CG 22 94 and for the same reasons. Its purpose is to delete coverage for designated sites or operations, rather than on a blanket basis as is the function of endorsement CG 22 94.

CG 22 96 Limited Exclusion—Personal and Advertising Injury—Lawyers

This endorsement was new to the 2001 CGL policy revisions and is intended to close a potential gap in coverage that currently exists with CGL forms. Currently, endorsement CG 21 38, Exclusion—Personal and Advertising Injury, is attached to all CGL policies covering lawyers' offices. The reason for this mandatory endorsement is that personal and advertising injury coverage often can be provided by a lawyers professional liability policy. The endorsement can apply even when a lawyer engages in some services that are not considered to be professional in nature, such as acting as a landlord. These types of activities may also be excluded by the lawyers professional liability policy in some instances.

Thus, to fill a potential coverage gap, this endorsement, CG 22 96, which is optional, may be used when the lawyer's professional liability policy provides personal and advertising injury coverage for professional services only.

CG 22 97 Druggists—Broadened Coverage

For the purpose of this endorsement, which was revised with the 2001 amendments, refer to the explanation under endorsement CG 22 69—Druggists. This broadened coverage endorsement applies in those states that permit pharmacists to perform broader duties.

CG 22 98 Exclusion—Internet Service Providers and Internet Access Providers Errors and Omissions

This endorsement was introduced with the 2001 CGL policy revisions to exclude coverage for bodily injury or property damage arising out of the rendering of or failure to render Internet service or Internet access that is provided by or on behalf of any insured. ISO made an editorial revision to this endorsement in 2004 by removing references to personal and advertising injury, since personal and advertising injury arising from these exposures is already precluded by exclusion j. of coverage B.

This endorsement is comprised of two parts: The first part excludes an error, omission, defect or deficiency in any evaluation, consultation or advice concerning Internet services, and the second part excludes the failure to adequately provide any such services or access.

A possible problem with this exclusion for the insurer is the omission of the term "negligent act," since there are differences between negligent act, error or omission. For example, the court in the case of *First Newton National Bank v. General Casualty Co.,426 N.W.2d 618 (1988),* held that an exclusion for claims arising out of error or omission or mistake committed by the insured did not include negligence. The policy, therefore, covered the negligent claims. In fact, even if this exclusion were to include negligent acts, there still would be room for arguing that an intentional act remains covered, because the term "any act" is broader than negligent act and does not encompass error or omission. A case in point is *Continental Cas. Co. v. Cole, 809 F.2d 891 (D.C.Cir. 1987)*, where the policy language "error, negligent omission or negligent act of the insured" was held to cover all errors, not only negligent ones, and included intentional acts.

The problem with this endorsement confronting insureds is that they will likely be unable to obtain an errors or omissions policy that will include coverage for bodily injury, property damage, and personal and advertising injury. What an errors or omissions policy generally covers is the economic damages that result from a negligent act, error, or omission. That is what should be excluded by this endorsement instead of bodily injury, property damage, and personal and advertising injury. As a result, there will likely be a gap in coverage between the CGL and E&O policies.

CG 22 99 Professional Liability Exclusion— Web-Site Designers

This endorsement was introduced with the 2001 CGL policy revisions to exclude coverage for injury or damage arising out of the rendering of or failure to render Web site designer or consultant services by the insured or anyone for whom the insured has a legal responsibility. ISO made an editorial revision to this endorsement in 2004 by removing references to personal and advertising injury, since personal and advertising injury arising from these exposures are already precluded by exclusion j. of coverage B.

Why this endorsement is titled a professional liability exclusion rather than an errors or omissions exclusion is unclear, considering that young people today can do wonders in design work without having to attend any special schooling. Perhaps it is because of the term *designers*. A larger question is whether policies for Web site designers will be true professional liability policies, or only errors and omissions policies. The difference is significant because errors and omissions policies do not commonly cover bodily injury or property damage.

CG 23 01 Exclusion—Real Estate Agents or Brokers Errors or Omissions

This endorsement, newly introduced with the 2004 revisions, is mandatory for all policies covering real estate agents or brokers. By excluding bodily injury, property damage, and personal and advertising injury arising out of any misrepresentation, error, or omission by an insured real estate agent or broker, CG 23 01 automatically creates a gap in coverage. The reason is that a real estate agent's or broker's errors or omissions policy will not likely include coverage for bodily injury, property damage, or personal and advertising injury. What should have been excluded here are damages because of misrepresentation, error, or omission, other than bodily injury, property damage, or personal and advertising injury damages.

Coverage Amendment Endorsements

CG 24 01 Nonbinding Arbitration

This endorsement is designed for use with CGL, liquor, OCP, pollution, products/completed operations, and railroad protective coverage parts.

It gives both the insured and insurer the right to submit their differences to arbitration proceedings, but the decision is not binding. This means the party dissatisfied with the decision can appeal it to a court of competent jurisdiction. The nature of an insured's business may prompt the use of this endorsement at the time the coverage part is issued.

CG 24 02 Binding Arbitration

The only difference between this endorsement and the preceding one is that the decision agreed to by two of the three arbitrators is binding on the insured and insurer.

CG 24 03 Waiver of Charitable Immunity

This endorsement usually is added automatically to CGL policies of charitable institutions. It clarifies that the insurer will waive any immunity in the event of any claim against the institution (insured), unless the institution requests in writing that the insurer not do so. The endorsement therefore is more for the protection of the insurer than the institution. This endorsement also clarifies that waiver of immunity as a defense will not subject the insurer to liability in excess of the policy's limit.

CG 24 04 Waiver of Transfer of Rights of Recovery against Others to Us

The subrogation condition of CGL forms states in effect that if the insured has rights to recover from a third party all or part of any payment the insurer has made, those rights are transferred to the insurer. Also, the insured must do nothing *after* loss to impair those rights.

The inference, therefore, is that the insured can waive the insurer's rights of subrogation *before* a loss. However, not all courts (those of California and Washington are examples) agree with that premise. In states such as these, it is advisable to add this waiver of subrogation endorsement. A potential problem with the endorsement is that it applies only to the party scheduled. It seems logical to assume that if a corporation is scheduled, the waiver also applies to any officer, director, or stockholder. Likewise, if a partnership is scheduled, it would appear that the waiver also applies to the partners. Unfortunately, the endorsement is not clear on this point and could therefore lead to problems. It is also incumbent upon those who service clients to check contracts for waivers of subrogation so that this endorsement can be issued. A better alternative would be to issue this on a blanket basis thereby avoiding the chances that the issuance of this endorsement may be overlooked.

This endorsement was originally designed for use with the CGL and OCP coverage parts. However, the 1993 amendment removed reference to the OCP coverage part in this endorsement because a separate endorsement, CG 29 88, is designed for use with the OCP coverage part.

CG 24 05 Financial Institutions (Reporting Provision and Limitation to Fiduciary or Representative Interest)

This is a reporting form that would commonly be added to the policy of a bank or other financial institution to make clear the obligations of the trust department when it acquires and relinquishes properties of others. To this end, the named insured must report to the insurer every sixty days the properties acquired and relinquished. However, the insurer must be notified immediately whenever the named insured acquires control of a business and assumes its active management or control. While the reporting results may be used for premium determination, failure of the insured to report as required will not invalidate the insurance.

This endorsement was revised in 2004 to include the provisions extending the CGL policy to cover fiduciary interests as contained in CG 24 11 Fiduciaries—Fiduciary Interest. By doing so, it is no longer necessary to attach both endorsements to limit coverage under the CGL policy for damages solely arising out of the insured's trust operations.

CG 24 06 Liquor Liability—Bring Your Own Alcohol Establishments

A new optional endorsement with reference to the liquor liability exclusions of the CGL Coverage Part, is CG 24 06 for use with the Liquor Liability Coverage Form CG 00 33 (Occurrence) or CG 00 34 (Claims-Made) that provides coverage to insureds who permit any person to bring their own beverages on the premises for consumption.

With this new endorsement, both liquor endorsements CG 21 50 and CG 21 51 also are revised to indicate that the liquor liability exclusion in the CGL Coverage Form will apply to BYOB exposures.

CG 24 07 Products/Completed Operations Hazard Redefined

This endorsement is designed primarily for establishments that serve food and beverages for consumption on their business premises. When attached to the CGL policy, the endorsement redefines the "products-completed operations hazard" to include products consumed on the premises where they are sold. Consequently, claims arising out of food and beverages consumed on the named insured's premises are subject to the products-completed operations aggregate limit, rather than the general aggregate limit. Or, if the policy *excludes* the products-completed operations hazard, such claims are excluded.

CG 24 08 Liquor Liability

When attached to the CGL policy, this endorsement deletes the liquor liability exclusion. The other method of providing coverage is to purchase the separate liquor liability coverage part CG 00 33 (occurrence) or CG 00 34 (claims-made), if available from the insurer. Otherwise, such insurance may be available from a specialty lines insurer.

This endorsement was revised in 1993 to reflect the title of the deleted exclusion. Thus, the endorsement now reads: "Exclusion c.—Liquor Liability of COVERAGE A—Bodily Injury and Property Damage Liability (Section I—Coverages) does not apply."

CG 24 09 Governmental Subdivisions

This endorsement is automatically added to the CGL policy whenever a municipality or other political subdivision is the named insured. It has two purposes. The first is to change the nomenclature of the "Who Is an Insured" provision to conform more closely to governmental entities. This amendment apparently was prompted by a number of court decisions that held the persons insured provisions of earlier liability policies to be inappropriate to governmental entities.

This endorsement also clarifies that land motor vehicles designed for travel on public roads and owned or leased by the governmental subdivision are to be considered as autos, rather than mobile equipment, if the only reason for considering such vehicles as mobile equipment is that they are maintained for use exclusively on streets and highways that such entity owns. If it were not for this endorsement, a governmental subdivision could dispense with automobile liability insurance by maintaining that all of its vehicles are mobile equipment and, hence, covered automatically under the CGL policy.

The 1993 change to this endorsement amended the text of the definition of mobile equipment so as to make it easier to read.

CG 24 10 Excess Provision—Vendors

Vendors who desire protection as additional insureds on CGL policies of manufacturers can be added under endorsement CG 20 15 Additional Insured—Vendors. Whenever such vendor also maintains its own CGL policy, the insurer may amend the policy with the addition of this endorsement. The effect is to make the vendor's own CGL policy excess over the manufacturer's CGL policy to which endorsement CG 20 15 is attached.

This endorsement was revised with the 1993 changes to also make it applicable to the separate Products/Completed Operations Coverage Part. In addition, language was added to this latest version of the endorsement to clarify that it amends the "Other Insurance" condition of the CGL forms.

This endorsement was withdrawn from use by ISO in 1997. It is no longer needed because the other insurance conditions of CGL forms make an insured's own CGL policy excess over insurance provided by any other liability policy when that insured is covered by that other policy as an additional insured. It is important to note that if an insurer does not incorporate the other insurance provisions of the current CGL policy into its own policy, then this endorsement obviously would still be necessary. This caveat is being mentioned because some insurers use some ISO policy provisions but not necessarily all of them. A tell-tale sign is when the coverage form contains a copyright notice stating that it includes copyrighted material of ISO.

CG 24 11 Fiduciaries—Fiduciary Interest

The purpose of this endorsement is to tailor protection of the CGL coverage form to an entity that has a fiduciary interest in the property of others. For example, the endorsement redefines the "Who Is an Insured" provision to include certain persons and organizations commonly associated with trusts and guardianships of real and personal property, such as a ward, a life tenant, and an heir.

In addition to restructuring the endorsement's format and making some editorial changes in 1998, ISO amended the lead-in language of

CG 24 11 to indicate that the coverage provided applies to injury or damage "... arising out of the ownership, maintenance or use, including all related operations, of property...."

CG 24 12 Boats

The basic CGL policy provisions limit liability coverage of watercraft to those less than twenty-six feet long, not owned by the named insured, and not being used to carry persons or property for a charge. These limitations can be amended with the attachment of endorsement CG 24 12. When the endorsement is attached for an additional premium as designated, exclusion g. of the CGL coverage form is amended so that liability coverage does apply to any watercraft owned, used by, or rented to the insured and described in the schedule. Also protected as an insured is any person or organization legally responsible for the use of a covered watercraft owned by the named insured, provided that actual use is with the named insured's permission.

CG 24 13 Amendment of Personal and Advertising Injury Definition

CG 24 13 is a new exclusionary endorsement.

Currently, Coverage B., Personal and Advertising Injury Liability covers the "oral or written publication, in any manner, of material that violates a person's right of privacy". CG 24 13 eliminates that coverage. This, according to ISO, is a restriction. Given the fact that this coverage has taken on importance with the Internet, the issuance of this endorsement can result in a serious restriction of coverage.

CG 24 14 Waiver of Governmental Immunity

This endorsement is comparable in purpose and scope to endorsement CG 24 03, Waiver of Charitable Immunity. Waiver of Governmental Immunity Endorsement, CG 24 14, for use with the CGL, provides an option to an insured that has immunity but is willing to waive such an immunity as a defense otherwise applicable. This endorsement is now revised so that it can also apply in connection with the Owners and Contractors Protective Liability Coverage Part and the Railroad Protective Liability Coverage Part.

CG 24 16 Canoes or Rowboats

This endorsement was introduced in 2007 to better accommodate the hotels/motels classifications regarding watercraft. Prior to this change, the classifications for hotels/motels with pools or beaches contained a footnote to the effect that coverage was included for the operation of owned watercraft of the kind described by using the endorsement CG 24 12 for boats. Hotels/motels without pools or beaches, on the other hand, included coverage for the operation of owned canoes and rowboats by attaching the same endorsement CG 24 12.

Under this current change, the hotels/motels classifications having pools or beaches have been revised to reflect that owned watercraft, other than owned canoes and rowboats, need to be separately classified, rated and covered under endorsement CG 24 12. The hotels/motels classifications where there are no pools or beaches are covered with the attachment of a new endorsement, Canoes or Rowboats CG 24 16, which has been introduced in 2007 for that use.

When CG 24 16 is attached to a CGL coverage form issued to a hotel or motel that has no pools or beaches, exclusion g. under Coverage A is amended so as to not apply to bodily injury or property damage arising out of any canoe or rowboat owned, or used by, or rented to the insured. Section II – Who Is An Insured also is amended to include as an insured any person or organization legally responsible for the use of any canoe or rowboat the named insured owns, provided the actual use by that person or organization is with the named insured's permission.

CG 24 17 Contractual Liability—Railroads

As explained in Chapter 1, the CGL definition of "insured contract" does not include a contract or agreement that indemnifies a railroad for bodily injury or property damage resulting from construction or demolition operations on or within fifty feet of railroad property. However, this limitation can be deleted by attaching endorsement CG 24 17.

The purpose of the endorsement is to provide contractual liability coverage, under a contractor's CGL policy, for liability that the contractor assumes under a contract in which the contractor agrees to hold harmless or indemnify a railroad. Whether this endorsement, which can provide sole or partial fault coverage of the railroad, is permissible, however, will hinge on the applicability of any anti-indemnity statute. The usual steps having to do with contractual liability (and additional insured coverage) is to (1) read the contract specifications, (2) determine the nature of the contractual assumption, (3) determine whether an anti-indemnity statute applies and its restrictions, and (4) the kind of coverage required. If sole or partial fault is void and unenforceable but the statute does not affect the validity of insurance, this is the endorsement that should be issued. Otherwise, the more limited endorsement CG 24 27 will have to suffice.

CG 24 18 Seed Merchants—Coverage for Erroneous Delivery or Mixture and Resulting Failure of Seed to Germinate

This endorsement, introduced with the 1996 CGL revision, is designed to be added to a CGL policy covering a seed merchant classified for rating purposes as "Seed Merchants—NOC" (class code 16891). The endorsement makes it clear that the policy will cover erroneous delivery of seed, errors in mechanical mixture of seeds, and failure of seed to germinate if the failure to germinate results from 1) delivery of wrong seed, 2) delivery of seed at the wrong time or season, or 3) an error in mechanical mixture of seed.

Liability coverage for Seed Merchants is a specialized form of protection that is available by endorsement to the CGL policy. Actually, three different endorsements are available and they need to be issued in conjunction with the products/completed operations coverage part. Two of these endorsements CG 24 18 and CG 24 19 are available by attachment to the CGL coverage part, whereas the third endorsement CG 24 20 is issued when products/completed operations coverage is written under a separate coverage part. Both endorsements CG 24 18 and CG 24 20 offer the same coverage, which is for loss from erroneous delivery or mixture and resulting failure of seed to germinate, whereas endorsement CG 24 19 does not provide coverage for loss from failure of seed to germinate.

Considering the nature of coverages offered by these endorsements, their intent needs to be fully understood or disputes can develop. A lawsuit wherein the insured was provided coverage similar to the ISO standard endorsements covering failure to germinate is *Delta & Pine Land Company v. Nationwide Agribusiness Company, Nationwide Mutual Insurance Company*, 530 F.3d 395 (2008).

Delta & Pine Land Company (DPL) developed, marketed, and sold cotton seed to farmers to be used for the purpose of raising and selling cotton. In 2002, fifty-six individual farmers filed suit against DPL alleging that they had suffered substantial losses in crop yields because DPL sold them a mixture of old NuCotn 33 B cotton seed negligently blended with new seed. DPL maintained both CGL and umbrella liability policies issued by Nationwide.

When served with the farmers' complaint, DPL filed a declaratory judgment action against its insurer for both defense and indemnification. The district court ultimately granted summary judgment in favor of the insurer on the ground that the claims asserted by the farmers were not covered either under the CGL policy or the umbrella liability policy. An appeal was made to the United States Fifth Circuit Court of Appeals.

Peering into the coverage itself, the court noted that the CGL policy was amended by a Seed Merchants endorsement, which stated in part that damages because of property damage also included "loss resulting from … an error in mechanical mixture of seed". The way DPL viewed this endorsement, it enlarged coverage of the policy by expanding covered property damage to include losses resulting from an error in mechanical mixture of seed. The insurer, on the other hand, read the endorsement to still mandate that a claim must be for property damage as originally defined by the unendorsed CGL policy.

The appeals court, however, stated that the insurer's view did not logically follow and, in fact, would make the endorsement a meaningless and ineffectual provision. The court went on to say that, since DPL presented a reasonable reading of the endorsement, that reading would have to be adopted so as to resolve any ambiguity or doubt in favor of the insured. Since the farmers alleged a loss caused by a negligent, and therefore erroneous, mixing of seed, the court said it read the endorsement as providing coverage, thereby triggering the insurer's duty to defend DPL against the farmers' suit.

Turning to the umbrella policy, the court held that coverage likewise applied for the same reasons the CGL policy was held to be applicable for the defense of the insured, notwithstanding the policy's more limited definition of property damage.

The insurer, however, also felt that two exclusions applied but could not convince the court of their application. These involved the (1) Expected or Intended Injury Exclusion; and the (2) Your Product Exclusion.

The reason the first exclusion was held to be inapplicable by the court was that the exclusion applied to property damage expected or intended from the standpoint of the insured. The farmers, however, primarily asserted damages resulting from the negligent or grossly negligent mixing of seed and not damages resulting from intentional injury. Turning to the second exclusion, the insurer argued that a decreased crop yield was damage to DPL's own product, the cotton seed, and, therefore, was excluded. The court, however, disagreed, explaining that it read the exclusion as not applying to the situation. The farmers, the court explained, did not complain of damage to DPL's seed but, instead, for damage to the farmers' crop land use, i.e., their crop yield. While the seed was DPL's product, the court said, the resulting crop and its use of the crop land were the farmers' separate property.

The court's conclusion was that the endorsements to the CGL and umbrella liability policies provided coverage to the extent of imposing a duty to defend against the farmers' claims and that none of the exclusions applied. The court did, however, state that whether the insurer had an obligation to indemnify was premature.

CG 24 19 Seed Merchants—Coverage for Erroneous Delivery or Mixture (Resulting Failure of Seed to Germinate Not Included)

This endorsement, like CG 24 18, was introduced with the 1996 CGL revision. Endorsement CG 24 19 is used with CGL policies covering seed merchants classified as "Seed Merchants—excluding germination failure" (class code 16892). The endorsement provides the same coverage as CG 24 18, minus coverage for resulting failure of seed to germinate.

CG 24 22 Amendment of Coverage Territory— Worldwide Coverage

CG 24 23 Amendment of Coverage Territory— Additional Scheduled Countries

CG 24 24 Amendment of Coverage Territory— Worldwide Coverage with Specified Exceptions

These three endorsements for broadening the regular CGL coverage territory (discussed in Chapter 1) were introduced with the 2001 CGL revision. All three endorsements contain several boilerplate conditions concerning suits outside the United States, Puerto Rico, or Canada, which will not be described here. Apart from these conditions, each endorsement takes a different approach to expanding the coverage territory, as described below.

Endorsement CG 24 22 defines the coverage territory as "anywhere in the world with the exception of any country or jurisdiction which is subject to trade or other economic sanction or embargo by the United States of America." This is the broadest coverage territory of the three.

Endorsement CG 24 23 defines the coverage territory in the same way as in the CGL coverage forms plus "any other country specified in the Schedule of this endorsement."

Endorsement CG 24 24 defines the coverage territory as anywhere in the world except (1) the countries specifically listed in the endorsement's schedule, and (2) any country subject to trade or other economic sanction or embargo by the United States. However, the worldwide coverage extensions provided by the coverage territory definition in the CGL coverage forms still apply under this modified definition. (The worldwide coverage extensions relate to products, persons temporarily away from the United States or Canada, and personal and advertising injury offenses committed through the Internet.)

As discussed in Chapter 1, products made in foreign countries and imported for use or sale in the United States or other countries can present a problem, unless one of these endorsements is issued or a foreign products liability policy is issued. The reason is that the CGL coverage form requires not only injury or damage during the policy period, but also an occurrence within the coverage territory. An important question that is sometimes difficult to answer is: Where did the occurrence of a defective product take place? In the United States or in some other country? If the latter, does the named insured have some kind of worldwide coverage?

Note that the three coverage territories endorsements—CG 24 22, CG 24 23, and CG 24 24—have been revised. The revision affects the so-called alpha numeric paragraph designators of the Other Insurance Condition in the CGL coverage forms. These endorsements are being revised to maintain consistency with the changes made in the Other Insurance Condition noted in multistate filing GL-2006-OCTFR. There is no impact on coverage according to ISO.

CG 24 25 Limited Fungi or Bacteria Coverage

As the title of this endorsement (which was introduced in 2002) connotes, coverage on a limited basis is offered, but solely for bodily injury and property damage; personal and advertising injury is specifically excluded to the same extent as in endorsement CG 21 67. This limited coverage endorsement is subject to a separate aggregate limit.

CG 24 25 was revised in 2004 to make an editorial revision concerning the limits of insurance section of the CGL form. Thus, coverage is available in light of this endorsement but only if, and to the extent that, limits are available under the aggregate limit. As a result of this amendment, it should be clearer that the policy's limits applicable to other coverages would continue to apply to losses arising out of fungi or bacteria incidents, but only when the fungi and bacteria liability aggregate has not been exhausted.

CG 24 26 Amendment of Insured Contract Definition

This endorsement was introduced as part of a July, 2004 filing by ISO along with revisions involving additional insured endorsements. It is a tool for underwriters who want to exclude coverage for tort liability assumed under a contract (other than those types of contracts specifically listed under paragraphs a. through e. of the policy definition of insured contract) when the indemnitor (the one who agrees to hold the indemnitee harmless) or anyone acting on the indemnitor's behalf does not cause, in whole or in part, the injury or damage involved. According to Commercial Lines Manual Rule 36.C.22, this endorsement may be issued in conjunction with an additional insured endorsement when applicable. This means that CG 24 26 could be issued whether or not an additional insured endorsement also is to be issued.

Some people may view this rule permitting the issuance of a more limiting contractual coverage endorsement as being unfair until they realize how often some underwriters have been issuing CG 21 39, contractual liability limitation endorsement, which completely eliminates coverage for tort liability assumptions under any contract other than the specific types of contracts listed in paragraphs a. through e. of the policy definition of insured contract.

Actually, either one of these limiting endorsements may generate problems in those 7 states that have no anti-indemnity statutes, and in an additional 27 states that hold sole fault or sole/partial assumptions of liability to be unenforceable, unless insurance is in place to cover them. Most of these statutes also prescribe the type of acceptable insurer covering the hold harmless agreement. Some of these statutes refer to an admitted insurer, others to an authorized insurer, and still others to a licensed insurer. Insurance, furthermore, does not mean self-insurance. A hold harmless agreement by a self-insurer, therefore, will be void and unenforceable in any one of the 27 states having an insurance exception, recognizing that self-insurance is not considered to be insurance.

A case in point is *USX Corporation v. Liberty Mutual Insurance Company and Turner Construction Company*, 645 N.E.2d 396 (App. Ct. Ill., 1994). The general contractor here asked to be an additional insured and to be covered for its hold harmless agreement with the subcontractor who was a qualified self-insurer. Upon being sued by the subcontractor's employee, the general contractor sought coverage from the subcontractor. While the state's anti-indemnity statute held sole fault assumptions of liability to be void and unenforceable, it at the time made an exception for insurance by an admitted insurer. The problem was that because the subcontractor was self-insured, no insurance was in place to meet that state statute's exception.

Currently, CG 24 26 and CG 24 27 (discussed next) are issued when the intent is to reduce the degree of coverage having to do with contractual liability. Without these endorsements, the contractual liability coverage of the CGL coverage form could provide coverage for the sole fault of an indemnitee, if sole fault were required in a contract or agreement and not held to be void and unenforceable under an anti-indemnification statute. So when these endorsements are issued, coverage for sole fault is reduced to partial fault of the indemnitee. In other words, the bodily injury or property damage must be caused in whole or in part by the named insured or by those acting on behalf of the named insured. This coverage has been in existence for several years.

ISO has stated, with reference to the current revision, that over the past few years, several states have enacted anti-indemnification laws, with exceptions, having to do with construction contracts dealing with sole fault assumptions. In response to these changes, CG 24 26 and CG 24 27 are revised with an additional provision. The additional provision states that the partial fault coverage is considered an insured contract only if such assumption is prescribed by contract or agreement and is otherwise permitted by law. In other words, it could turn out where the most coverage provided is for the vicarious liability of the indemnitee. This could occur if the contract does not require the assumption of the indemnitee's tort liability by the indemnitor.

A number of states have anti-indemnity statutes that hold sole and/or partial fault assumptions to be void and unenforceable, unless insurance is written with an admitted or authorized insurer. Also, some states do not have anti-indemnity statutes. Admittedly, many entities do not ask for sole fault assumptions. But those who do, and where this is otherwise permitted by law, would not receive that broad coverage in light of endorsements CG 24 26 and CG 24 27. What happens then is that the indemnitors (named insured) could be confronted with an allegation of failure to procure or breach of contract.

Note that another change that affects endorsement CG 24 26 is that it now also applies to the Products/Completed Operations Coverage Parts, in addition to the CGL Coverage Parts.

CG 24 27 Limited Contractual Liability—Railroads

This endorsement, effective in many states in March 2005, provides coverage similar to that provided by endorsement CG 24 17, except that as this endorsement's title connotes, it is limited in scope. Specifically, coverage will be limited to injury or damage that is caused in whole or in part by the named insured or those acting on behalf of the named insured. Especially important is that coverage will not be provided for injury or damage arising out of the sole negligence of the railroad.

Considering how demanding some railroads are when work is being performed on or near their property, care must be exercised that this endorsement is not issued when endorsement CG 24 17 should apply instead. It probably would behoove railroads to specify what they want in contracts, and confirm the coverages requested instead of simply accepting a certificate of insurance without some warning.

As noted previously, the same revision that changed CG 24 26 also applies to CG 24 27. However, CG 24 27 does not apply to the Products/Completed Operations coverage forms.

Amendment of Limits Endorsements

Four endorsements are available for amending the limits of insurance in various ways.

CG 25 01 Amendment of Limits of Insurance (Designated Projects or Premises)

Endorsement CG 25 01 modifies a CGL coverage form or an OCP coverage form to provide amended limits at any project or premises designated in the endorsement. This endorsement was withdrawn from use with the 2004 CGL policy revisions, along with endorsement CG 25 11, Amendment of Limits of Insurance (Designated Projects or Premises) for use with the Owners and Contractors Protective Liability policy. Both were withdrawn because it was said by ISO that these endorsements were rarely used, since it is an uncommon occurrence for a specific project to have a separate limit of insurance.

CG 25 02 Amendment of Limits of Insurance

This endorsement replaces the limits shown in the policy declarations with the limits shown in the endorsement.

CG 25 03 Designated Construction Project(s) General Aggregate Limit

This endorsement was originally developed in connection with the CGL policy simplification program under which a general aggregate limit was introduced. The purpose of this endorsement was to enable insured contractors in the construction business to meet their contractual obligations to maintain separate amounts of liability insurance for specific construction projects performed. This avoids a situation where the general aggregate limit applicable to one construction project could be eroded by claims at or from other construction projects where the insured contractor might also be engaged at the same time.

The endorsement was revised in 1997 to specifically set forth in the language of the endorsement how the various aggregate limits apply, with respect to each construction project of the insured, whether or not the specific loss can be pinpointed to a specific construction project. With this amendment, an insured will have available for a premises-operations loss either the Designated Construction Project Aggregate Limit, if the loss can be attributed solely to a specific construction project, or the policy General Aggregate Limit, if the loss cannot be attributed to a single construction project. Thus, with this latest endorsement, a given premises-operations claim will reduce only one General Aggregate Limit; either the Designated Construction Project General Aggregate Limit or the policy General Aggregate Limit, but not both.

CG 25 04 Designated Location(s) General Aggregate Limit

ISO introduced this endorsement in connection with the CGL policy simplification program, under which a general aggregate limit was first introduced in 1986. This endorsement enabled insureds with multiple locations to maintain separate amounts of liability insurance for each such location. This avoided a situation where the general aggregate limit applicable to one location could be eroded by losses at or from other locations connected with the insured's operations.

With the 1997 CGL policy amendments, this endorsement was revised to set forth how the various aggregate limits are to apply with respect to each location of the insured, whether or not the specific claim can be attributed to a specific location. With this latest endorsement, an insured will have available for a premises-operations claim either the Designated Location General Aggregate Limit, if the claim can be attributed solely to a specific location, or the policy General Aggregate Limit, if the claim cannot be attributed to a single location. Thus, with this revised endorsement, a given premises-operations claim will reduce only one General Aggregate Limit; either the Designated Location General Aggregate Limit or the policy General Aggregate Limit, but not both.

CG 25 14 Designated Location(s) Aggregate Limit

This is a new endorsement intended to provide an additional underwriting tool for insurers according to ISO. This endorsement is for use with the Liquor Liability coverage forms. It makes a separate designated location aggregate limit available for each location of the insured listed in the schedule of the endorsement. CG 25 14 applies with respect to losses that can be attributed only to the selling, serving, or furnishing of alcoholic beverages from a single designated location, while such losses that cannot be attributed to a single location are subject to the policy aggregate limit instead.

Claims-Made Endorsements

The first four endorsements listed here and designed for use with the claims-made CGL form only are the subject of extended treatment in Chapter 4; only their form numbers and names are shown below.

CG 27 02 Exclusion of Specific Accidents, Products, Work, or Locations

CG 27 03 Amendment of Section V— Extended Reporting Periods for Specific Accidents, Products, Work, or Locations

CG 27 10 Supplemental Extended Reporting Period

CG 27 11 Supplemental Extended Reporting Period Endorsement for Specific Accidents, Products, Work, or Locations

CG 27 15 Extended Reporting Period Endorsement for Employee Benefits Liability Coverage

With the 2001 CGL policy amendments, ISO introduced an Employee Benefits Liability Coverage endorsement for use with the CGL forms. This endorsement provides that an insured may purchase an extended reporting period of five years for an additional premium. Endorsement CG 27 15 is what provides that so-called tail coverage.

CG 31 73 Extended Reporting Period Endorsement for Electronic Data Liability Coverage

This endorsement was introduced with the electronic data liability coverage form in 2004. The endorsement can be used to add an extended reporting period to this coverage form, which applies on a claims-made basis. The extended reporting period covers claims first made within three years after the policy expires. The claim must be for electronic data loss that occurred before the end of the policy period and on or after any applicable retroactive date applicable to the policy. The endorsement does not increase or reinstate the limits of insurance.

Other Endorsements

Various other endorsements are available for modifying the CGL coverage forms. Examples of these endorsements are described below.

CG 31 15 Construction Project Management Protective Liability Coverage Endorsement

In 1997, the American Institute of Architects revised its General Conditions of the Contract for Construction A 201 to add a provision permitting the use of Project Management Protective Liability (PMPL) Coverage in lieu of additional insured endorsements. There has been only one insurer providing this coverage and its policy is not approved in all states. However, if one were to compare this Project Management Protective Liability Coverage with an Owners and Contractors Protective Liability (OCP) policy, one would see a marked similarity. The PMPL policy has since been withdrawn from use, and its reference has also been removed from the American Institute of Architects General Conditions Contract Form A 201.

When it comes to construction work, owners and contractors are not keen on accepting an OCP policy even though it is a separate policy for separate limits listing owners and contractors as the named insureds. The problem is that coverage is limited to ongoing operations, and sole fault coverage of the named insureds is limited to their general supervision of the work. This is a problem when an owner or general contractor is confronted with a third party action and an allegation for failing to provide a safe place to work. The question is whether such allegation can be equated with liability emanating from general supervision.

It is doubtful that this endorsement is being requested, given its few differences with the OCP policy. What is now problematic is what coverage should be obtained, given that additional insured endorsements covering sole fault are few in number. It could turn out where contractual liability coverage offers the best protection. Much will depend on the nature of the contractual assumption, the applicability of any anti-indemnity statute and whether the CGL policy is modified with one of the limiting endorsements, CG 21 39 or 24 26. If neither of these is issued and sole or partial fault assumptions of liability are permitted, contractual liability coverage may be the best alternative, despite the problems over the way defense coverage is handled, as mentioned in Chapter 1.

CG 31 74 Exclusion of Newly Acquired Organizations as Insureds

This endorsement was introduced with the 2004 revisions to be used optionally in conjunction with the new product withdrawal coverage form. When issued, this endorsement removes newly acquired organizations from the Who is an Insured section of the product withdrawal coverage form. However, even if this endorsement were to be issued, some coverage for the exposures of newly acquired organizations would still remain because the form's definition of "your product" includes products manufactured, sold, handled, distributed, or disposed of by a person or organization whose business or assets the named insured has acquired.

CG 99 01 Motor Vehicle Laws

This endorsement was withdrawn with the 2004 CGL policy revisions because mobile equipment subject to financial responsibility laws, motor vehicle insurance laws, and similar laws will be considered as autos instead of mobile equipment. Because not all insurers will utilize the 2004/2007 CGL policy edition, particularly those that write large fleets of mobile equipment, CG 99 01 will likely still be used. The explanation of the withdrawn endorsement therefore remains intact here for reference purposes.

This endorsement is added to CGL policies that have been certified as proof of financial responsibility as required under the provisions of a motor vehicle financial responsibility law. Although the CGL coverage forms do not cover "autos," they do cover "mobile equipment" that in some cases may be subject to a state financial responsibility law.

The endorsement states that bodily injury and property damage liability insurance will comply with the provisions of the law to the extent of the coverage and limits the law requires. In addition, the insurer promises to provide, with respect to mobile equipment to which the policy applies, any liability, uninsured motorists, underinsured motorists, no-fault, or other coverages required by any motor vehicle insurance law, up to the limits required by the law.

Miscellaneous Coverage Forms

ISO offers miscellaneous general liability coverage forms. Because many insurance and risk management professionals may not yet be completely familiar with these forms, the forms are briefly described here.

CG 00 30 and CG 00 40

In the 2000 filing, ISO revised the Aircraft, Auto Or Watercraft exclusion, along with the definitions of auto and mobile equipment to exclude coverage for bodily injury and property damage arising out of the ownership, maintenance or use of land vehicles that are subject to a compulsory or financial responsibility law or other motor vehicle law, since such coverage is a better fit with the commercial auto policy. According to

ISO, although the changes made to the definition of auto and mobile equipment would consider mobile equipment subject to motor vehicle statutory requirements an auto, the operation of certain mobile equipment would still be covered by the CGL policy. The exception to the exclusion was revised to maintain coverage for the operation of some mobile equipment, such as cherry pickers, under the CGL. This revision, it was said, was incorporated into the Pollution Liability Limited Coverage Form Designated Sites CG 00 40, but not incorporated into the Pollution Liability Coverage Form Designated Sites CG 00 39.

The purpose of the April 2013 revision is to change the Aircraft, Auto, Rolling Stock, Or Watercraft exclusion in the pollution liability coverage forms to address claims for negligence in the supervision, hiring, employment, training or monitoring of others when such claims involve injury or damage arising out of automobile use.

CG 00 35 Railroad Protective Liability Coverage Form

Briefly, the purpose for this coverage form is to protect the railroad when work is being performed on railroad property by contractors. The railroad can obtain this insurance and charge it to the contractor or the contractor can obtain it for the railroad. It is similar in concept to the Owners and Contractors Protective Liability Coverage Form, which means that coverage is on a primary basis but is limited to operations in progress. Once the work is completed, coverage ends.

The revisions of this coverage form center on the pollution liability.

When the revision of 2000 was introduced, the Railroad Insurance Management Association requested that the same level of coverage found under Pollution Exclusion Amendment endorsement CG 28 31 be provided. ISO therefore revised the exception to the pollution exclusion of CG 00 35 to provide coverage for bodily injury or property damage arising out of the escape of fuels or lubricants from equipment used at the job location. CG 28 31 was said to generally provide coverage for bodily injury or property damage arising out of pollutants at or from the job location on which the insured or contractors working for the insured were performing operations, if the pollutants, other than fuels or lubricants for equipment used at the job location, were brought onto the location in connection with the insured operations. The April 2013 revision involves changing the pollution exclusion again to expand the exception to the exclusion with respect to bodily injury or property damage arising out of fuel or lubricants for equipment used at the job location. The current edition of the form reads as follows: Bodily injury or property damage arising out of fuels or lubricants for equipment used at the job location.

One of the problems that still remains intact with this coverage form concerns Coverage B—Physical Damage to Property. This form defines "physical damage to property" to mean "direct and accidental loss of or damage to ... buildings". While a contractor was working on an old railroad tunnel, it collapsed causing extensive delay in train service not to speak of direct physical damage to the tunnel itself. The insurer denied coverage because it maintained that a tunnel was a structure, rather than a building. The court agreed. Since railroads use many tunnels, this is an important exposure that needs to be fixed. The case is *Montana Rail Link, Inc. v. The Travelers Indemnity Company*, 2011 WL 578690.

CG 00 65 Electronic Data Liability Coverage Form

The CGL policy definition of property damage specifically precludes electronic data as tangible property, and CGL exclusion p. specifically precludes damages arising out of the loss of use of, damage to, corruption of, inability to access, or inability to manipulate electronic data. Accordingly, consideration should be given to obtaining some coverage for the numerous electronic data exposures that exist and that can result in serious losses.

As noted earlier, ISO has made available an electronic data liability endorsement (CG 04 37), but it only applies to loss emanating from physical injury to tangible property. This endorsement, for example, might be suitable for an excavation contractor that severs a fiber optic cable that causes loss of electronic data. It is not adequate in a case, for example, where furniture movers drop a heavy object going down stairs that, in a chain of events, causes disruption of the business's computer system. Unlike the electronic data liability endorsement, the electronic data liability coverage form covers both physical damage to tangible property and loss of use of tangible property that is not physically damaged.

The coverage form's insuring agreement resembles the Coverage A insuring agreement of the CGL form, which (apart from applicable exclusions) is broad enough to encompass liability for any act, error, or omission. Closer scrutiny of the electronic data liability coverage form reveals that the insurance applies to loss of electronic data only if caused by accident, negligent act, error, or omission.

CG 00 65 has 10 exclusions. Among them is liability assumed under any contract or agreement, other than liability the insured would have in the absence of the contract or agreement; loss of electronic data by the named insured or anyone acting on its behalf in providing computer products or services (as defined in CG 00 65); damages that are bodily injury, property damage, or personal and advertising injury; a delay or failure to perform a contract or agreement; any infringement of intellectual property rights; criminal or fraudulent acts; and violation of an anti-trust law.

The electronic data liability coverage form is written on a claims-made basis. To extend the reporting period for three years, it is necessary to attach CG 31 73, extended reporting period endorsement for electronic data liability coverage, at a cost of 100% of the expiring coverage's premium.

Note that there may be some problems with this form.

First, the term "electronic data incident" is defined to mean "an accident, or a negligent act, error or omission ... which results in a loss of electronic data." The CGL policy, on the other hand, covers any act (intentional or unintentional), error or omission so long as the resulting injury or damage is not intentional. CG 00 65, therefore, limits coverage solely to unintentional acts.

A second problem is that this coverage form does not cover damages that are bodily injury, property damage, or personal and advertising injury. CG 00 65 coverage is limited to damages because of loss of electronic data (a defined term). What is not encompassed by this coverage form, therefore, are damages other than to electronic data arising out of an electronic incident (a defined term).

Another point to note is that, under the CGL forms filing of 2006, ISO revised exclusion i. dealing with Infringement of Copyright, Patent, Trademark or Trade Secret in CGL Coverage Forms CG 00 01 (occurrence) and CG 00 02 (claims-made). This change was said to be introduced to reinforce the fact that the exclusion did not apply to personal and advertising injury arising out the use of another's advertising idea in the named insured's advertisement. At that time, a similar revision was added to exclusion g., Infringement Of Intellectual Property Rights in the Electronic Data Liability Coverage Form, CG 00 65; however, the revisions for 2013 delete this 2006 revision.

According to ISO, the Electronic Data Liability Coverage Form CG 00 65 generally provides coverage against damages because of loss of electronic data that is caused by an electronic data incident. Since the exception that was added to exclusion g. is said to have no application to the coverage provided by this coverage form, the exception is being deleted. The following phrase is being deleted: "Under this exclusion, such other intellectual property rights do not include the use of another's advertising idea in your advertisement."

CG 00 66 Product Withdrawal Coverage Form

The product withdrawal coverage form, introduced by ISO in 2004, consists of two primary coverage sections. The first is Coverage A—product withdrawal expense, which is virtually identical to the limited product withdrawal expense endorsement (CG 04 36), discussed previously. The second section is Coverage B—product withdrawal. This pays sums the insured is legally obligated to pay and, therefore, will not only include the costs incurred by the insured to withdraw or recall a product from the market or from use, but will also pay others who have incurred those costs and seek reimbursement from the insured.

Both coverage sections of this form include tampering coverage, which is considered to be a definite plus. Both also have a cut-off date that serves almost like a retroactive date. In other words, coverage is only going to apply to the sale of products produced after the cut-off date designated in the declarations.

If Coverage B—product withdrawal is desired, an endorsement is available to exclude the more limited Coverage A; the endorsement is CG 31 68, exclusion—Coverage A—product withdrawal expense. If, on the other hand, it is Coverage A that is desired, CG 31 69, exclusion—Coverage B—product withdrawal liability needs to be attached.

Coverage B, which also includes product replacement, repair, or repurchase, is subject to 15 exclusions: breach of warranty and failure to conform to intended purpose; infringement of copyright, patent, trade secret, trade dress, or trademark; deterioration, decomposition, or chemical transformation; loss of goodwill, market share, revenue, profit, or due to redesigning the product; expiration of shelf life; known defect; governmental ban; fines and penalties; intercompany lawsuits; contractual liability; pollution; pollution-related (i.e., clean up) costs; war; loss of use of property; and bodily injury or property damage.

One of the problems with this coverage form that could serve to the detriment of insurers is that product withdrawal is a defined term that includes recall. However, the governmental ban exclusion applies to recalls, a term that is not separately defined. To correct this, the insurer needs to substitute the defined term *product withdrawal* for the term *recall*. A similar problem applies to Coverage B.

Two other endorsements are available for use with CG 00 66. One is coverage extension—Coverage A—product restoration expense, CG 31 72. If this endorsement is purchased, the insurer agrees to reimburse the insured for the reasonable and necessary costs directly related to withdrawal in order for the insured to regain goodwill, market share, or profit, and for costs to redesign the named insured's product. This coverage, however, is subject to a sub-limit.

The other endorsement is CG 31 74, exclusion of newly acquired organizations as insureds. Interestingly, the definition of "your product" on CG 00 66 means under clause 14.a.(3), a person or organization whose business or assets the named insured has acquired. So, if this exclusionary endorsement were to be issued, it would appear that some coverage still remains intact.

Professional Services Exclusion Endorsements

Currently, a number of endorsements are available to exclude liability emanating from the rendering of, or failure to, professional services. Despite these exclusions, it is sometimes possible to still obtain coverage depending on the fact pattern and the exclusionary wording. An example is the unpublished opinion in the case of *Liberty Life Ins. Co. v. Travelers Indemnity Co. of IL, 181 F.3d 88 (4th Cir. 1999)*, which ISO cites as the basis for another revision dealing with the professional services exclusion.

In this case, the Court of Appeals considered whether a negligent supervision claim was covered even though the act of the person being supervised was found to be excluded. The underlying suit, in part, was said to have sought damages from the insurer based on its alleged negligence in the hiring, supervising and retaining of an employee. The court held that the exclusions that barred coverage for the claim against the employee, did not apply to this insurer in its oversight role as the agent's principal.

In a 2001 revision of CGL provisions, ISO introduced language to the exclusion applying to aircraft, auto or watercraft for claims alleging negligence or other wrongdoing in the supervision, hiring, employment, training or monitoring of others by an insured, if the occurrence that caused the bodily injury or property damage involved the ownership, maintenance, use, loading or unloading or entrustment of any aircraft, auto or watercraft owned or operated by or rented or loaned to any insured. To reinforce the professional services exclusion, this same exclusionary wording is being added to the following endorsements:

- Exclusion—Designated Professional Services CG 21 16

- Exclusion—Financial Services CG 21 52

- Exclusion—Funeral Services CG 21 56

- Exclusion—Counseling Services CG 21 57

- Exclusion—Professional Veterinarian Services CG 21 58

- Exclusion—Diagnostic Testing Laboratories CG 21 59

- Exclusion—Inspection, Appraisal and Survey Companies CG 22 24

- Exclusion—Professional Services Banks CG 22 32

- Exclusion—Construction Management Errors And Omissions CG 22 34

- Exclusion—Products And Professional Services (Druggists)

- Exclusion—Products And Professional Services (Optical And Hearing Aid Establishments

- Exclusion—Camps Or Playgrounds CG 22 39

- Exclusion—Engineers, Architects Or Surveyors Professional Liability CG 22 43

- Exclusion—Services Furnished By Health Care Providers CG 22 44

- Exclusion—Specified Therapeutic Or Cosmetic Services

- Exclusion—Insurance And Related Operations CG 22 48

- Exclusion—Druggists CG 22 69

- Exclusion—Colleges Or Schools (Limited Form) CG22 71

- Exclusion—Colleges Or Schools CG 22 72

- Professional Liability Exclusion—Computer Software CG 22 75

- Professional Liability Exclusion—Health Or Exercise Clubs Or Commercially Operated Health Or Exercise Facilities CG 22 76

- Professional Liability Exclusion—Computer Data Processing CG 22 77

- Exclusion—Contractors—Professional Liability CG 22 79

- Limited Exclusion—Contractors—Professional Liability CG 22 80

- Exclusion—Adult Day Care Centers CG 22 87

- Professional Liability Exclusion—Electronic Data Processing Services And Computer Consulting Or Programming Services CG 22 88

- Professional Liability Exclusion—Spas Or Personal Enhancement Facilities CG 22 90

- Exclusion—Telecommunication Equipment Or Service Providers Errors And Omissions CG 22 91

- Limited Exclusion—Personal And Advertising Injury—Lawyers CG 22 96

- Exclusion—Internet Services Providers And Internet Access Providers CG 22 98

- Professional Liability Exclusion—Website Designers CG 22 99

- Exclusion—Real Estate Agents Or Brokers Errors Or Omissions CG 23 01

- Construction Projection Management Protective Liability Coverage CG 31 15

Endnotes

1. Copyright, ISO Properties, Inc., 2003.
2. While the anti-indemnity statutes of many states hold void and unenforceable both sole and partial fault assumptions, they remain unaffected by the validity of insurance from, for example, an admitted insurer or authorized insurer or licensed insurer. When a named insured (indemnitor) assumes the sole fault of an additional insured (indemnitee), there may be a problem with the failure to procure proper coverage (breach of contract) when this ISO endorsement is issued because it attempts to preclude sole fault coverage.
3. States in this category are: Alaska, Arkansas, California, Connecticut, Delaware, Georgia, Hawaii, Illinois, Kansas, Kentucky, Louisiana, Maryland, Minnesota, Mississippi, Montana, Nebraska, New Jersey, New York, North Carolina, Ohio, Oklahoma, Rhode Island, South Carolina, Texas, Virginia, West Virginia
4. States in this category are Alabama, Maine, Nevada, Pennsylvania, Vermont, Wisconsin and Wyoming.

Chapter 7

Commercial Umbrella Liability Insurance

An umbrella liability policy has a net effect of providing the insured with an "umbrella" of liability protection over the insured's primary liability insurance. This approach to liability risk management has attracted many insureds and insurers, and is now quite commonly written for both large and small risks. These pages offer an introduction to commercial umbrella liability insurance.

General Features

An umbrella liability policy can accomplish the following purposes: providing coverage over the primary liability insurance carried by the insured in the event that the primary insurance is exhausted by a loss; providing coverage of liability exposures for which there is no primary insurance or where the primary policy contains an exclusion which is not similarly excluded under the umbrella policy. (More generally, the umbrella policy is to protect the insured in the event of a catastrophic loss wherein the loss exceeds the limits of liability in the primary liability policy.) And in keeping with these purposes, most umbrella insurers generally require the insureds to purchase primary insurance coverage: general liability insurance, auto liability insurance, and sometimes workers compensation and employers liability insurance.

Umbrella liability insurance policies are mostly not prescribed by any rating or advisory organization. Umbrella underwriting rules are largely a matter of the judgment of the insurer; and rating is almost entirely a matter of individual judgment, not only from insurer to insurer, but also varying with the individual risk.

While most umbrella policies do resemble one another in a broad, general way, significant individual differences will be found from one umbrella policy to the next. In fact, many of the umbrella provisions are negotiable with most underwriters. Umbrella underwriting is highly individualistic, and is quite responsive to individual risk differences and to changing conditions. This is true as to specific risks or classes of insureds as well as to general trends in underwriting profitability. Consequently, significant differences will often be found even in the provisions of the umbrella policies of the same insurer for different insureds or classes or the same insured at different times. So it is important that each umbrella policy be examined for its particular provisions.

Among the many differences commonly encountered among umbrella policies are the following:

- definition of who is insured

- coverage territory

- limitations or restrictions on coverage, which may appear in the coverage description, the definitions, the exclusions, or the policy conditions

- sublimits and use of aggregate limits

- "pay on behalf" versus "reimbursement" insuring agreements

- definition of bodily injury or personal injury, with some policies including mental injury coverage

In general, an umbrella liability policy is written only for a risk that has a broad and substantial program of underlying coverage—insurers usually require commercial general liability and automobile liability insurance with substantial bodily injury and property damage limits. A requirement of underlying liability limits of $1,000,000 is not uncommon. For insureds with severe advertising or other personal injury, or other special liability exposures, underlying coverage with high limits in these areas may also be required if these exposures are to be included in the umbrella coverage.

Umbrella policy conditions usually call for maintenance of the underlying coverage, with the umbrella insurer's part in a loss being determined as if the underlying contract were in force, even if it is not. The exception—an important one—is where an underlying policy is totally exhausted by payment of loss, in which case the umbrella policy drops down to replace the exhausted underlying protection. Note that drop down provisions usually exclude carrier bankruptcy and the failure of the insured to maintain insurance as reasons for a drop down.

Likewise, though there have been some fluctuations on this point, insurers require that the amount of loss absorbed by the insured as respects uninsured or self-insured exposures be a certain amount. When the umbrella policy was first introduced, most umbrella contracts were written with this amount—the "retention" or "drop down" limit—at $25,000; however, the amount can now range from zero dollars on up. Such flexibility in choice of retention limits no doubt has had much to do with the increased activity in this field.

A significant point of variation has to do with defense coverage. Practically all umbrella liability contracts have provisions that, in effect, protect the right of the umbrella insurer to take over or participate in the defense of a claim that may involve it. Most of the original umbrella contracts did not provide any defense coverage with respect to claims which appeared likely to stay within the retention. The tendency now, however, is to include defense coverage for uninsured exposures even when loss does not appear likely to involve the umbrella contract. Also, some contracts include defense coverage of losses where, because the underlying insurance is exhausted by loss payments, the umbrella policy comes in as primary coverage. Another important difference is the inclusion of defense and appeal costs within the limits of coverage in some umbrella policies, while others provide them as supplementary payments outside the limits of coverage.

Specific Features

An umbrella policy may have some specific features to contrast its nature with primary insurance policies. (Note: the ISO commercial liability umbrella policy, CU 00 01, is used here as an example of specific umbrella features.)

The duty of the umbrella insurer to defend the insured has been mentioned. There is a clause in the ISO commercial liability insurance policy pertaining to the transfer of defense from the primary insurer to the umbrella insurer when the underlying limits of insurance have been used up in the payment of judgments or settlements.

ERISA claims and employment-related practices claims are usually excluded from coverage under the umbrella policy.

Coverage for claims arising out of the ownership, maintenance, or use of covered autos is included in the umbrella policy along with the general liability coverage.

Any additional insured under any policy of underlying insurance will automatically be an insured under the umbrella policy. Such coverage is not broader than coverage provided by the underlying insurance.

If the underlying insurer or the insured elects not to appeal a judgment in excess of the retained limit, the umbrella insurer reserves the right to do so at its own expense. The umbrella insurer will also pay for taxable court costs, pre- and post-judgment interest and disbursements associated with the appeal.

The umbrella policy requires the insured to maintain underlying insurance in full effect without reduction of coverage or limits (except for the reduction of the aggregate limits that results from payment of claims, settlements, or judgments). The failure to maintain underlying insurance will not invalidate insurance provided by the umbrella policy, but the umbrella coverage applies as if the underlying insurance were in full effect.

Retained limit, self-insured retention, ultimate net loss, and underlying insurance are all terms that are defined in the umbrella policy since these terms are pertinent to the insuring agreements, exclusions, and conditions in the umbrella policy.

Umbrella Coverage Issues

Among the coverage disputes that can be peculiar to umbrella policies (and excess policies) are questions about "indemnity versus pay-on-behalf of" language in the insuring agreements and "drop down" coverage.

Policies that indemnify the insured do not require the insurer to make payment to the insured until the insured has first made payment for covered damages or expenses. In other words, the language requires the insured to use his own funds to pay for damages and defense and then seek reimbursement from the insurer. Under the pay-on-behalf-of language, the insurer promises to pay damages on behalf of the insured. This means that the insured does not have to first make payment and then seek reimbursement from the insurer. Expenses for defense are normally paid by the insurer as they are incurred if the umbrella insurer has taken over the defense role.

Note that some umbrella policies do not contain language such as "indemnify" or "pay-on-behalf-of". Instead, such policies provide that the insurer will "pay the loss" or will "pay those sums the insured is legally obligated to pay". This means that the umbrella insurer will pay the amounts owed by the insured, or basically, will pay on behalf of the insured. In the actual payment practices of umbrella insurers, there may be little difference between "indemnify", "pay-on-behalf-of", or "pay the loss" policies. However, an insured clearly would be better off with the other-than-indemnify language.

As for drop down coverage, this usually comes into play when the primary carrier becomes insolvent and this affects excess coverage.

By definition and longstanding principles, excess liability insurance comes into play not until all other valid insurance has been exhausted in paying a loss. However, if the primary limits have not been exhausted due to payment of claims, but rather, are not available to apply to existing claims due to the insolvency of the primary carrier, is the excess insurer required to fill the void and drop down to pay the sums that the insured has become legally obligated to pay? Legal opinion is split rather simply into those that favor drop down and those that do not. The overwhelming majority opinion is that the insolvency of the primary carrier does not mean that the insured's excess carrier has to drop down to primary coverage. (Note that the ISO commercial liability umbrella policy specifically states that its insurance will not replace the underlying insurance in the event of bankruptcy or insolvency of the underlying insurer. The umbrella insurance applies as if the underlying insurance were in full effect.)

As an example of judicial opinion, the Supreme Court of Louisiana held that the umbrella policy did not drop down to provide dollar one coverage after the insolvency of the primary insurer. This case is *Huggins v. Gerry Lane Enterprises, Inc.*, 957 So.2d 127 (2007). The Court said that the umbrella insurer was liable only for the ultimate net loss in excess of applicable limits of scheduled underlying insurance. Another example is *Highlands Insurance Company v. Gerber Products Company*, 702 F.Supp. 109 (1988) wherein the United States District Court in Maryland said that "excess carriers ordinarily are not required to provide drop down coverage in the event of the insolvency of an underlying insurer. An exception to this general rule exists only where an insurer has used language in its policy that creates a genuine ambiguity as to the scope of coverage". This thinking was reiterated in another case from a U.S. District Court, *McGirt v. Royal Insurance Company of America*, 399 F.Supp.2d 655 (2005).

Of course, there are judicial decisions that favor drop down coverage but those are usually based on the ambiguity of the policy language. The policies in those cases contained terms like "amount recoverable" or "amount collectible" and the courts construed the terms as ambiguous, resulting in decisions favorable to the insured. So, conversely, where policy terms refer to a fixed amount of primary coverage or declare that exhaustion of underlying limits of insurance is only payment of claims, courts will limit the liability of excess insurers to the amount in excess of the specified underlying limit; in other words, no drop down. As an example of the need for insurers to insert explicit language into umbrella liability policies, see *Domingue v. Legion Indemnity Company*, 918 So.2d 1213 (2006). In that case, the policy required the underlying insurance to be available "regardless of the bankruptcy or insolvency of the underlying insurer". Based on that language, the Louisiana court of appeals said "there is clearly no drop down under this policy provision since the collectability of the underlying insurance was not available due to Legion's insolvency".

Chapter 8

Commercial Liability Umbrella Policy

Insurance Services Office (ISO) has developed a commercial liability umbrella form. The coverage is excess over commercial general liability and automobile liability coverages. The Commercial Liability Umbrella Form, CU 00 01 04 13, provides coverage when aggregate limits of underlying insurance—that is, any policies of insurance listed in the declarations under the schedule of underlying insurance—are exhausted. A self-insured retention applies to exposures not covered by underlying insurance.

This chapter presents a general overview and analysis of CU 00 01. The sections of the form are reproduced here, followed by an analysis of that section. The form itself is reproduced in the appendix of this coverage guide.

Coverage A – Bodily Injury and Property Damage Liability

1. Insuring Agreement

    a. We will pay on behalf of the insured the "ultimate net loss" in excess of the "retained limit" because of "bodily injury" or "property damage" to which this insurance applies. We will have the right and duty to defend the insured against any "suit" seeking damages for such "bodily injury" or "property damage" when the "underlying insurance" does not provide coverage or the limits of "underlying insurance" have been exhausted. When we have no duty to defend, we will have the right to defend, or to participate in the defense of, the insured against any other "suit" seeking damages to which this insurance may apply. However, we will have no duty to defend the insured against any "suit" seeking damages for "bodily injury" or "property damage" to which this insurance does not apply. At our discretion, we may investigate any "occurrence" that may involve this insurance and settle any resultant claim or "suit", for which we have the duty to defend. But:

(1) The amount we will pay for the "ultimate net loss" is limited as described in Section III – Limits Of Insurance; and

(2) Our right and duty to defend ends when we have used up the applicable limit of insurance in the payment of judgments or settlements under Coverages A or B.

No other obligation or liability to pay sums or perform acts or services is covered unless explicitly provided for under Supplementary Payments – Coverages A or B.

b. This insurance applies to "bodily injury" or "property damage" that is subject to an applicable "retained limit". If any other limit, such as a sublimit, is specified in the "underlying insurance", this insurance does not apply to "bodily injury" or "property damage" arising out of that exposure unless that limit is specified in the Declarations under the Schedule of "underlying insurance".

c. This insurance applies to "bodily injury" and "property damage" only if:

(1) The "bodily injury" or "property damage" is caused by an "occurrence" that takes place in the "coverage territory";

(2) The "bodily injury" or "property damage" occurs during the policy period; and

(3) Prior to the policy period, no insured listed under Paragraph 1 of Section II—Who Is An Insured and no "employee" authorized by you to give or receive notice of an "occurrence" or claim, knew that the "bodily injury" or "property damage" had occurred, in whole or in part. If such a listed insured or authorized "employee" knew, prior to the policy period, that the "bodily injury" or "property damage" occurred, then any continuation, change or resumption of such "bodily injury" or "property damage" during or after the policy period will be deemed to have been known prior to the policy period.

d. "Bodily injury" or "property damage" which occurs during the policy period and was not, prior to the policy period, known to have occurred by any insured listed under Paragraph 1. of Section II – Who Is An Insured or any "employee" authorized by you to give or receive notice of an "occurrence" or claim, includes any continuation, change or resumption of that "bodily injury" or "property damage" after the end of the policy period.

e.   "Bodily injury" or "property damage" will be deemed to have been known to have occurred at the earliest time when any insured listed under Paragraph 1. of Section II—Who Is An Insured or any "employee" authorized by you to give or receive notice of an "occurrence" or claim:

(1)   Reports all, or any part, of the "bodily injury" or "property damage" to us or any other insurer;

(2)   Receives a written or verbal demand or claim for damages because of the "bodily injury" or "property damage"; or

(3)   Becomes aware by any other means that "bodily injury" or "property damage" has occurred or has begun to occur.

f.   Damages because of "bodily injury" include damages claimed by any person or organization for care, loss of services or death resulting at any time from the "bodily injury".

Analysis

The language of this insuring agreement is essentially the same as that of the standard Commercial General Liability (CGL) coverage form, with a few exceptions in terms.

As an example, under the terms of the umbrella policy, the insurer agrees to pay the ultimate net loss in excess of the retained limit because of bodily injury or property damage to which the insurance applies. "Ultimate net loss" is a defined term on the policy, as is "retained limit," and both terms are unique to an umbrella policy. The ultimate net loss is the total sum, after reduction for recoveries or salvages collectible, that the insured becomes legally obligated to pay by reason of settlement or judgments or any arbitration or other alternate dispute method entered into with the consent of the umbrella insurer or the underlying insurer. The retained limit is the available limits of underlying insurance scheduled in the declarations or the self-insured retention, whichever applies.

In other words, the ultimate net loss is the amount the insured, and hence, the umbrella insurer, has to pay for the claim(s) successfully made against the insured. The retained limit is the limit of insurance that the underlying insurance policy provides to the insured for coverage of the claim(s) made against him. Note that under the terms of the umbrella policy, the self-insured retention is the dollar amount that will be paid by the insured before the umbrella insurance becomes applicable only with respect to occurrences or offenses that are not covered by the underlying insurance. This is logical because if the underlying insurance policies offer coverage for a liability exposure facing the insured, having a Self-Insured Retention (SIR) also apply to the exposure would give the umbrella insurer a double layer of protection. (The SIR does not apply to occurrences or offenses that would have been covered by the underlying insurance but for the exhaustion of applicable limits.)

The umbrella policy insuring agreement also stipulates that the insurer has the right and duty to defend when the underlying insurance is exhausted or not applicable. In other words, the duty to defend is primarily on the shoulders of the underlying primary carrier. However, the umbrella insurer will step in to defend the insured when the underlying coverage limits of insurance have been used up in the payment of judgments or settlements, or when the underlying insurance simply does not apply to the claim or lawsuit. And, the liability umbrella insuring agreement does declare that when the insurer has no duty to defend, it does have the right to defend or to participate in the defense of the insured. This is to make sure that the interests of the umbrella insurer are not ignored or compromised when the underlying insurance carrier assumes the defense of the insured and the settlement of the lawsuit.

Note that the umbrella policy also states, like the CGL form, that it will not provide coverage for bodily injury or property damage that was known by an insured to have occurred prior to the policy period. This is a reaction to the Montrose Chemical Corporation decision from California. The follow-up clauses in this insuring agreement make it clear that the insurer wants to clarify when bodily injury or property damage is deemed to have been known by an insured. The first two paragraphs in clause are self-explanatory and could easily be proven. However, the third paragraph is rather broad in scope and could be problematic should an insurer try to prove when and if an insured somehow "becomes aware" of bodily injury or property damage.

Coverage A Exclusions

Exclusions

This insurance does not apply to:

a. Expected or Intended Injury

"Bodily injury" or "property damage" expected or intended from the standpoint of the insured. This exclusion does not apply to "bodily injury" resulting from the use of reasonable force to protect persons or property.

b. Contractual Liability

"Bodily injury" or "property damage" for which the insured is obligated to pay damages by reason of the assumption of liability in a contract or agreement. This exclusion does not apply to liability for damages:

(1) That the insured would have in the absence of the contract or agreement; or

(2) Assumed in a contract or agreement that is an "insured contract", provided the "bodily injury" or "property damage" occurs subsequent to the execution of the contract or agreement. Solely for the purposes of liability assumed in an "insured contract", reasonable attorney fees and necessary litigation expenses incurred by or for a party other than an insured are deemed to be damages because of "bodily injury" or "property damage", provided:

(a) Liability to such party, for, or for the cost of, that party's defense has also been assumed in the same "insured contract"; and

(b) Such attorney fees and litigation expenses are for defense of that party against a civil or alternative dispute resolution proceeding in which damages to which this insurance applies are alleged.

c. Liquor Liability

"Bodily injury" or "property damage" for which any insured may be held liable by reason of:

(1) Causing or contributing to the intoxication of any person;

(2) The furnishing of alcoholic beverages to a person under the legal drinking age or under the influence of alcohol; or

(3) Any statute, ordinance or regulation relating to the sale, gift, distribution or use of alcoholic beverages.

This exclusion applies even if the claims against any insured allege negligence or other wrongdoing in:

(a) The supervision, hiring, employment, training or monitoring of others by that insured; or

(b) Providing or failing to provide transportation with respect to any person that may be under the influence of alcohol;

if the "occurrence" which caused the "bodily injury" or "property damage" involved that which is described in Paragraph (1), (2) or (3) above.

However, this exclusion applies only if you are in the business of manufacturing, distributing, selling, serving or furnishing alcoholic beverages. For the purposes of this exclusion, permitting a person to bring alcoholic beverages on your premises, for consumption on your premises, whether or not a fee is charged or a license is required for such activity, is not by itself considered the business of selling, serving or furnishing alcoholic beverages.

This exclusion does not apply to the extent that valid "underlying insurance" for the liquor liability risks described above exists or would have existed but for the exhaustion of underlying limits for "bodily injury" and "property damage". To the extent this exclusion does not apply, the insurance provided under this Coverage Part for the liquor liability risks described above will follow the same provisions, exclusions and limitations that are contained in the applicable "underlying insurance" unless otherwise directed by this insurance.

Analysis

These exclusions are the same as exclusions a, b, and c of the CGL coverage form.

However, note that the liquor liability exclusion in this umbrella policy does not apply if liquor liability is covered in an underlying policy, that is, the exclusion does not apply to the extent that valid underlying insurance for the liquor liability risks exists or would have existed but for the exhaustion of underlying limits. If that is the case, the umbrella coverage will follow the provisions, exclusions, and limitations of the underlying insurance.

This liquor liability exclusion was revised by ISO in 2013 to address Bring Your Own (BYO) establishments. Some restaurants allow customers to bring their own bottles of alcohol into the premises and then charge a corkage fee and require that the beverages be poured and served by restaurant employees. This raised the question as to whether such practices are subject to the liquor liability exclusion. To address this issue, ISO added the following language to the exclusion: "permitting a person to bring alcoholic beverages on your premises, for consumption on your premises, whether or not a fee is charged or a license is required for such activity, is not by itself considered the business of selling, serving or furnishing alcoholic beverages." Thus, since the liquor liability exclusion applies only if the insured is in the business of manufacturing, distributing, selling, serving, or furnishing alcoholic beverages, this language allows coverage for a BYO situation.

ISO also reviewed the following court decisions regarding liquor liability in liability policies for the 2013 revision:

Penn-America Ins. Co. v. Peccadillos, 27 A.3d 259 (Pa. Super. 2011): the court in this case found that a CGL policy's duty to defend is triggered when an insured allegedly continued to sell alcohol to visibly intoxicated customers, who the insured then ejected from its premises. The customers drove away from the establishment and caused an accident that resulted in deaths drivers and passengers in other vehicles.

McGuire v. Curry, 766 N.W.2d 501 (S.D. 2009): In this case, the court ruled that an employer can be held liable for actions of underage employees if the employer allowed them unsupervised and unrestricted access to alcoholic beverages. The court found that the employer had a duty to supervise the underage employee.

Essex Ins. Co. v. Cafe Dupont, LLC, 674 F.Supp. 2d 166 (D.D.C. 2009): The court found that a provision in a CGL policy that excluded damages or injuries arising out of any act or omission by the insured or the insured's employees regarding failure to provide transportation or detaining or failing to detain any person or assuming or not assuming responsibility for the well-being, care, or supervision of a person under the influence of alcohol applied to any intoxicated person, not just those who became intoxicated in the insured's establishment.

As a result of ISO's review of these court decisions, the liquor liability exclusion was revised to state that the exclusion applies even if claims against the insured allege negligence in the supervision, hiring, employment, training, or monitoring of others. The exclusion also applies if negligence or wrongdoing in providing or failing to provide transportation for any person under the influence of alcohol is alleged.

    d.   Workers' Compensation and Similar Laws

        Any obligation of the insured under a workers' compensation, disability benefits or unemployment compensation law or any similar law.

    e.   ERISA

        Any obligation of the insured under the Employees' Retirement Income Security Act of 1974 (ERISA), and any amendments thereto or any similar federal, state or local statute.

    f.   Auto Coverages

        (1)   "Bodily Injury" or "property damage" arising out of the ownership, maintenance or use of any "auto" which is not a "covered auto"; or

        (2)   Any loss, cost, or expense payable under or resulting from any first party physical damage coverage; no-fault law; personal injury protection or auto medical payments coverage; or uninsured or underinsured motorist law.

    g.   Employers Liability

        "Bodily injury" to:

        (1)   An "employee" of the insured arising out of and in the course of:

            (a)   Employment by the insured; or

            (b)   Performing duties related to the conduct of the insured's business; or

        (2)   The spouse, child, parent, brother or sister of that "employee" as a consequence of Paragraph (1) above.

This exclusion applies whether the insured may be liable as an employer or in any other capacity, and to any obligation to share damages with or repay someone else who must pay damages because of the injury.

This exclusion does not apply to liability assumed by the insured under an "insured contract".

With respect to injury arising out of a "covered auto", this exclusion does not apply to "bodily injury" to domestic "employees" not entitled to workers' compensation benefits. For the purposes of this insurance, a domestic "employee" is a person engaged in household or domestic work performed principally in connection with a residence premises.

This exclusion does not apply to the extent that valid "underlying insurance" for the employer's liability risks described above exists or would have existed but for the exhaustion of underlying limits for "bodily injury". To the extent this exclusion does not apply, the insurance provided under this Coverage Part for the employer's liability risks described above will follow the same provisions, exclusions and limitations that are contained in the applicable "underlying insurance" unless otherwise directed by this insurance.

h. Employment-related Practices

"Bodily injury" to:

(1) A person arising out of any:

(a) Refusal to employ that person;

(b) Termination of that person's employment; or

(c) Employment-related practices, policies, acts or omissions, such as coercion, demotion, evaluation, reassignment, discipline, defamation, harassment, humiliation or discrimination directed at that person; or

(2) The spouse, child, parent, brother or sister of that person as a consequence of "bodily injury" to that person at whom any of the employment-related practices described in Paragraphs (a), (b), or (c) above is directed.

This exclusion applies whether the injury-causing event described in Paragraphs (a), (b), or (c) above occurs before employment, during employment, or after employment of that person.

This exclusion applies whether the insured may be liable as an employer or in any other capacity, and to any obligation to share damages with or repay someone else who must pay damages because of the injury.

Analysis

This set of exclusions is not out of the ordinary. Workers compensation, ERISA obligations, auto coverages, employers' liability, and employment-related practices are all areas typically not covered by a general liability policy. What stands out here are the exceptions that the umbrella policy makes.

For example, the auto exclusion applies to autos that are not covered autos; that is, autos to which underlying insurance does not apply. The umbrella policy does provide coverage for covered autos, which is defined in CU 00 01 as only those autos to which underlying insurance applies.

Also, domestic employees who do not qualify for workers compensation insurance are not included in the exclusion with respect to bodily injuries arising out of a covered auto. A domestic employee is a person engaged in household or domestic work performed principally in connection with a residence premises. For example, a maid is injured in an auto accident due to the negligence of the insured. The maid is not entitled to workers compensation based on state law. This umbrella policy would not exclude coverage for the insured if the insured became legally obligated to pay for the damages suffered by the maid. The underlying auto policy of the insured should, of course, act as the primary insurance, but if need be, this umbrella policy would also apply to the claim.

As another example of an exception, the umbrella policy provides coverage for employers liability risks on a follow-form basis if coverage exists in an underlying policy.

    i.   Pollution

        (1)   "Bodily injury" or "property damage" which would not have occurred in whole or part but for the actual, alleged or threatened discharge, dispersal, seepage, migration, release or escape of "pollutants" at any time; or

(2)   "Pollution cost or expense".

This exclusion does not apply if valid "underlying insurance" for the pollution liability risks described above exists or would have existed but for the exhaustion of underlying limits for "bodily injury" and "property damage". To the extent this exclusion does not apply, the insurance provided under this Coverage Part for the pollution risks described above will follow the same provisions, exclusions and limitations that are contained in the "underlying insurance", unless otherwise directed by this insurance.

Analysis

The umbrella contains an absolute pollution exclusion. There are no stated exceptions as can be found on the CGL form. However, if underlying coverage exists for pollution liability, the exclusion does not apply.

j.   Aircraft or Watercraft

"Bodily injury" or "property damage" arising out of the ownership, maintenance, use or entrustment to others of any aircraft or watercraft owned or operated by or rented or loaned to any insured. Use includes operation and "loading or unloading".

This exclusion applies even if the claims against any insured allege negligence or other wrongdoing in the supervision, hiring, employment, training or monitoring of others by that insured, if the "occurrence" which caused the "bodily injury" or "property damage" involved the ownership, maintenance, use or entrustment to others of any aircraft or watercraft that is owned or operated by or rented or loaned to any insured.

This exclusion does not apply to:

(1)   A watercraft while ashore on premises you own or rent;

(2)   A watercraft you do not own that is:

(a)   Less than fifty feet long; and

(b)   Not being used to carry persons or property for a charge;

(3) Liability assumed under any "insured contract" for the ownership, maintenance or use of aircraft or watercraft.

(4) The extent that valid "underlying insurance" for the aircraft or watercraft liability risks described above exists or would have existed but for the exhaustion of underlying limits for "bodily injury" or "property damage". To the extent this exclusion does not apply, the insurance provided under this Coverage Part for the aircraft or watercraft risks described above will follow the same provisions, exclusions and limitations that are contained in the "underlying insurance" unless otherwise directed by this insurance; or

(5) Aircraft that is:

    (a) Chartered by, loaned to, or hired by you with a paid crew; and

    (b) Not owned by any insured.

k. Racing Activities

"Bodily injury" or "property damage" arising out of the use of "mobile equipment" or "autos" in, or while in practice for, or while being prepared for, any prearranged professional or organized racing, speed, demolition, or stunting activity or contest.

l. War

"Bodily injury" or "property damage", however caused, arising, directly or indirectly, out of:

(1) War, including undeclared or civil war;

(2) Warlike action by a military force, including action in hindering or defending against an actual or expected attack, by any government, sovereign or other authority using military personnel or other agents; or

(3) Insurrection, rebellion, revolution, usurped power, or action taken by governmental authority in hindering or defending against any of these.

Analysis

The aircraft or watercraft exclusion does not mention autos because, unlike the CGL policy, the umbrella policy does not exclude bodily injury or property damage arising out of the ownership, maintenance, use, or entrustment of an auto owned or operated by, rented, or loaned to any insured. As long as the underlying insurance provides coverage for covered autos, the umbrella policy follows form. For that matter, the umbrella policy does extend coverage to aircraft and watercraft liability risks that underlying insurance covers, or would cover but for the exhaustion of underlying limits for bodily injury or property damage.

The umbrella also broadens watercraft coverage by increasing the specified size limitation found in the CGL form from less than twenty-six to less than fifty feet long; of course, the watercraft is not covered under either the CGL form or the umbrella policy if it is used to carry persons or property for a charge or owned by the named insured. As for aircraft coverage, the umbrella policy does apply to nonowned aircraft that is chartered by, loaned to, or hired by the named insured with a paid crew.

The war exclusion reflects the major rewording of that exclusion after the attack on the World Trade Center. The war exclusion reflects the thinking that has arisen since the attack on the World Trade Center that standard liability policies are not meant to insure against such catastrophic losses as can be caused by terrorist militant groups.

 m. Damage to Property

   "Property damage" to:

  (1) Property:

    (a) You own, rent, or occupy including any costs or expenses incurred by you, or any other person, organization, or entity, for repair, replacement, enhancement, restoration, or maintenance of such property for any reason, including prevention of injury to a person or damage to another's property; or

    (b) Owned or transported by the insured and arising out of the ownership, maintenance or use of a "covered auto".

  (2) Premises you sell, give away or abandon, if the "property damage" arises out of any part of those premises;

(3) Property loaned to you;

(4) Personal property in the care, custody or control of the insured;

(5) That particular part of real property on which you or any contractors or subcontractors working directly or indirectly on your behalf are performing operations, if the "property damage" arises out of those operations; or

(6) That particular part of any property that must be restored, repaired or replaced because "your work" was incorrectly performed on it.

Paragraph (2) of this exclusion does not apply if the premises are "your work" and were never occupied, rented or held for rental by you.

Paragraphs (1)(b), (3), (4), (5) and (6) of this exclusion do not apply to liability assumed under a sidetrack agreement.

Paragraphs (3) and (4) of this exclusion do not apply to liability assumed under a written Trailer Interchange agreement.

Paragraph (6) of this exclusion does not apply to "property damage" included in the "products-completed operations hazard".

n. Damage to Your Product

"Property damage" to "your product" arising out of it or any part of it.

o. Damage to Your Work

"Property damage" to "your work" arising out of it or any part of it and included in the "products-completed operations hazard". This exclusion does not apply if the damaged work or the work out of which the damage arises was performed on your behalf by a subcontractor.

p. Damage to Impaired Property Or Property Not Physically Injured

"Property damage" to "impaired property" or property that has not been physically injured, arising out of:

(1) A defect, deficiency, inadequacy or dangerous condition in "your product" or "your work"; or

(2) A delay or failure by you or anyone acting on your behalf to perform a contract or agreement in accordance with its terms.

This exclusion does not apply to the loss of use of other property arising out of sudden and accidental physical injury to "your product" or "your work" after it has been put to its intended use.

q. Recall of Products, Work, or Impaired Property

Damages claimed for any loss, cost or expense incurred by you or others for the loss of use, withdrawal, recall, inspection, repair, replacement, adjustment, removal or disposal of:

(1) "Your product";

(2) "Your work"; or

(3) "Impaired property";

if such product, work, or property is withdrawn or recalled from the market or from use by any person or organization because of a known or suspected defect, deficiency, inadequacy or dangerous condition in it.

Analysis

The exclusions are basically the same as those found on the CGL policy, with one addition. The umbrella policy excludes damage to property the insured owns or transports and that arises out of the ownership, maintenance, or use of a covered auto. This is in keeping with the fact that CU 00 01 is a liability policy, and a liability policy is not written to provide coverage for first party physical damage claims.

r. Personal and Advertising Injury

"Bodily injury" arising out of "personal and advertising injury".

s.   Professional Services

"Bodily injury" or "property damage" due to rendering of or failure to render any professional service. This includes but is not limited to:

(1)   Legal, accounting or advertising services;

(2)   Preparing, approving, or failing to prepare or approve maps, shop drawings, opinions, reports, surveys, field orders, change orders or drawings or specifications;

(3)   Inspection, supervision, quality control, architectural or engineering activities done by or for you on a project on which you serve as construction manager;

(4)   Engineering services, including related supervisory or inspection services;

(5)   Medical, surgical, dental, X-ray or nursing services treatment, advice or instruction;

(6)   Any health or therapeutic service treatment, advice or instruction;

(7)   Any service, treatment, advice or instruction for the purpose of appearance or skin enhancement, hair removal or replacement or personal grooming or therapy;

(8)   Any service, treatment, advice or instruction relating to physical fitness, including service, treatment, advice or instruction in connection with diet, cardio-vascular fitness, body building or physical training programs;

(9)   Optometry or optical or hearing aid services including the prescribing, preparation, fitting, demonstration or distribution of ophthalmic lenses and similar products or hearing aid devices;

(10) Body piercing services;

(11) Services in the practice of pharmacy;

(12) Law enforcement or firefighting services; and

(13) Handling, embalming, disposal, burial, cremation or disinterment of dead bodies.

This exclusion applies even if the claims against any insured allege negligence or other wrongdoing in the supervision, hiring, employment, training or monitoring of others by that insured, if the "occurrence" which caused the "bodily injury" or "property damage", involved the rendering of or failure to render any professional service.

t.   Electronic Data

Damages arising out of the loss of, loss of use of, damage to, corruption of, inability to access or inability to manipulate electronic data.

However, this exclusion does not apply to liability for damages because of "bodily injury".

As used in this exclusion, electronic data means information, facts or programs stored as or on, created or used on, or transmitted to or from computer software, including systems and applications software, hard or floppy disks, CD-ROMS, tapes, drives, cells, data processing devices or any other media which are used with electronically controlled equipment.

This exclusion does not apply if valid "underlying insurance" for the electronic data risks described above exists or would have existed but for the exhaustion of underlying limits for "bodily injury" and "property damage". The insurance provided under this Coverage Part will follow the same provisions, exclusions and limitations that are contained in the applicable "underlying insurance", unless otherwise directed by this insurance.

u.   Recording and Distribution of Material or Information In Violation of Law

"Bodily injury" or "property damage" arising directly or indirectly out of any action or omission that violates or is alleged to violate:

(1)   The Telephone Consumer Protection Act (TCPA), including any amendment of or addition to such law;

    (2)   The CAN-SPAM Act of 2003, including any amendment of or addition to such law;

    (3)   The Fair Credit Reporting Act (FCRA), and any amendment of or addition to such law, including the Fair and Accurate Credit Transactions Act (FACTA); or

    (4)   Any federal, state or local statute, ordinance or regulation, other than the TCPA, CAN-SPAM Act of 2003 or FCRA and their amendments and additions, that addresses, prohibits, or limits the printing, dissemination, disposal, collecting, recording, sending, transmitting, communicating or distribution of material or information.

Analysis

Bodily injury arising out of personal and advertising injury is covered by coverage B under the terms of the umbrella policy, so such injury is specifically excluded under coverage A. This is to prevent double liability coverage under the one umbrella policy.

The umbrella policy has a professional services exclusion that is not found on the CGL form (although the CGL form does usually exclude professional services liability through the use of an endorsement). Such an exposure is a specialized risk and should be insured under a professional liability policy. In 2013, ISO added language to address liability for negligent supervision claims caused by rendering or failure to render professional services, which is a reinforcement of coverage intent.

Another exclusion on the current umbrella coverage form pertains to damages arising out of loss of, loss of use of, or damage to electronic data. It is meant to strengthen the point that the umbrella form does not cover damages revolving around electronic data—an item that is not tangible property. Coverage A under the umbrella policy applies to damage to and to loss of use of tangible property. While some court decisions have blurred the distinction between tangible property and intangible property (for example, computer hardware and computer software respectively), the fact remains that the umbrella policy was not meant to apply to damage to other than tangible property. The definition of "property damage" has been revised to note that electronic data is not tangible property for the purposes of umbrella liability insurance; this exclusion will complement that definition.

Note that in the 2013 revision of CU 00 01, ISO broadened coverage under the electronic data exclusion by providing an exception for liability for damages because of bodily injury. The change was made due to requests to ISO that this exception be added. ISO also incorporated the recording and distribution of material or information in violation of law exclusion in the 2013 revision. The exclusion was previously found on mandatory endorsement CU 00 04, which was withdrawn from use.

Coverage B – Personal and Advertising Injury Liability

1. Insuring Agreement

    a. We will pay on behalf of the insured the "ultimate net loss" in excess of the "retained limit" because of "personal and advertising injury" to which this insurance applies. We will have the right and duty to defend the insured against any "suit" seeking damages for such "personal and advertising injury" when the "underlying insurance" does not provide coverage or the limits of "underlying insurance" have been exhausted. When we have no duty to defend, we will have the right to defend, or to participate in the defense of, the insured against any other "suit" seeking damages to which this insurance may apply. However, we will have no duty to defend the insured against any "suit" seeking damages for "personal and advertising injury" to which this insurance does not apply. At our discretion, we may investigate any offense that may involve this insurance and settle any resultant claim or "suit", for which we have the duty to defend. But:

        (1) The amount we will pay for the "ultimate net loss" is limited as described in Section III – Limits Of Insurance; and

        (2) Our right and duty to defend end when we have used up the applicable limit of insurance in the payment of judgments or settlements under Coverages A or B.

             No other obligation or liability to pay sums or perform acts or services is covered unless explicitly provided for under Supplementary Payments — Coverages A and B.

    b. This insurance applies to "personal and advertising injury" that is subject to an applicable "retained limit". If any other limit, such as a sublimit, is specified in the "underlying insurance", this insurance does not apply to "personal and advertising injury" arising out of that exposure unless that limit is specified in the Declarations under the Schedule of "underlying insurance".

c. This insurance applies to "personal and advertising injury" caused by an offense arising out of your business but only if the offense was committed in the "coverage territory" during the policy period.

Analysis

The coverage B insuring agreement has basically the same promises as the coverage A agreement, except that it applies to personal and advertising injury instead of bodily injury and property damage. Of course, coverage B applies to offenses arising out of the named insured's business, as opposed to occurrences, but this is in keeping with the fact that coverage B deals with intentional acts and not accidents.

Note that, unlike the coverage A insuring agreement, the coverage B insuring agreement does not have clauses pertaining to prior knowledge (the so-called Montrose provisions). Presumably, these provisions, which attempt to limit application of the continuous injury concept, are not pertinent to personal and advertising injuries as defined in the umbrella policy. Can something like false arrest, wrongful eviction, libel or slander, or infringement of another's copyright or slogan be injuries that occur continuously over time? Since the Montrose provisions are still being tested in court, any need for the provisions to be attached to the coverage B insuring agreement cannot be definitively answered.

Coverage B Exclusions

2. Exclusions

This insurance does not apply to:

a. "Personal and advertising injury":

(1) Knowing Violation of Rights of Another

Caused by or at the direction of the insured with the knowledge that the act would violate the rights of another and would inflict "personal and advertising injury";

(2) Material Published With Knowledge of Falsity

Arising out of oral or written publication, in any manner, of material, if done by or at the direction of the insured with knowledge of its falsity;

(3) Material Published Prior to Policy Period

Arising out of oral or written publication, in any manner, of material whose first publication took place before the beginning of the policy period;

(4) Criminal Acts

Arising out of a criminal act committed by or at the direction of the insured;

(5) Contractual Liability

For which the insured has assumed liability in a contract or agreement. This exclusion does not apply to:

(a) Liability for damages that the insured would have in the absence of the contract or agreement.

(b) Liability for false arrest, detention or imprisonment assumed in a contract or agreement.

Analysis

The exclusions are similar in wording and effect to those found in the coverage B section of the commercial general liability policy, but some observations can still be made.

Exclusions 1 and 2 seem to contradict the fact that coverage B covers the insured against certain described offenses that result from intentional acts. After all, knowingly violating the rights of another and knowingly publishing false material certainly are intentional acts. However, the aim of the exclusions is to eliminate coverage only in situations when the insured commits a personal and advertising injury knowing that the act will injure another. If the insured did not know that the act would violate the rights of another or that the material was false, the exclusions are not applicable.

Exclusions 3 and 4 are obvious in their intent. CU 00 01, like other liability policies, is not meant to cover acts that happen before the policy period begins or acts that are criminal.

Notice that the umbrella policy in exclusion (5), contractual liability, explicitly exempts liability for false arrest, detention, or imprisonment assumed in a contract or agreement.

(6) Breach of Contract

Arising out of a breach of contract, except an implied contract to use another's advertising idea in your "advertisement";

(7) Quality or Performance of Goods – Failure to Conform to Statements

Arising out of the failure of goods, products or services to conform with any statement of quality or performance made in your "advertisement";

(8) Wrong Description of Prices

Arising out of the wrong description of the price of goods, products or services stated in your "advertisement";

(9) Infringement of Copyright, Patent, Trademark or Trade Secret

Arising out of the infringement of copyright, patent, trademark, trade secret or other intellectual property rights. Under this exclusion, such other intellectual property rights do not include the use of another's advertising idea in your "advertisement". However, this exclusion does not apply to infringement, in your "advertisement", of copyright, trade dress or slogan.

(10) Insureds in Media and Internet Type Businesses

Committed by an insured whose business is:

(a) Advertising, broadcasting, publishing or telecasting;

(b) Designing or determining content of web-sites for others; or

(c) An Internet search, access, content or service provider.

However, this exclusion does not apply to Paragraphs 14.a, b. and c. of "personal and advertising injury" under the Definitions Section.

For the purposes of this exclusion, the placing of frames, borders or links, or advertising, for you or others anywhere on the Internet, is not by itself, considered the business of advertising, broadcasting, publishing or telecasting.

(11) Electronic Chatrooms or Bulletin Boards

Arising out of an electronic chatroom or bulletin board the insured hosts, owns, or over which the insured exercises control.

(12) Unauthorized Use of Another's Name or Product

Arising out of the unauthorized use of another's name or product in your e-mail address, domain name or metatag, or any other similar tactics to mislead another's potential customers.

(13) Pollution

Arising out of the actual, alleged or threatened discharge, dispersal, seepage, migration, release or escape of "pollutants" at any time.

(14) Employment-related Practices.

To:

(a)   A person arising out of any:

    i.   Refusal to employ that person;

    ii.   Termination of that person's employment; or

    iii.   Employment-related practices, policies, acts or omissions, such as coercion, demotion, evaluation, reassignment, discipline, defamation, harassment, humiliation or discrimination directed at that person; or

(b) The spouse, child, parent, brother or sister of that person as a consequence of "personal and advertising injury" to that person at whom any of the employment-related practices described in Paragraphs (i), (ii), or (iii) above is directed.

This exclusion applies whether the injury-causing event described in Paragraphs (i), (ii), or (iii) above occurs before employment, during employment, or after employment of that person.

This exclusion applies whether the insured may be liable as an employer or in any other capacity, and to any obligation to share damages with or repay someone else who must pay damages because of the injury.

(15) Professional Services

Arising out of the rendering of or failure to render any professional service. This includes but is not limited to:

(a) Legal, accounting or advertising services;

(b) Preparing, approving, or failing to prepare or approve maps, shop drawings, opinions, reports, surveys, field orders, change orders or drawings or specifications;

(c) Inspection, supervision, quality control, architectural or engineering activities done by or for you on a project on which you serve as construction manager;

(d) Engineering services, including related supervisory or inspection services;

(e) Medical, surgical, dental, x-ray or nursing services treatment, advice or instruction;

(f) Any health or therapeutic service treatment, advice or instruction;

(g) Any service, treatment, advice, or instruction for the purpose of appearance or skin enhancement, hair removal or replacement or personal grooming or therapy;

(h) Any service, treatment, advice or instruction relating to physical fitness, including service, treatment, advice or instruction in connection with diet, cardio-vascular fitness, body building or physical training programs;

(i) Optometry or optical or hearing aid services including the prescribing, preparation, fitting, demonstration or distribution of ophthalmic lenses and similar products or hearing aid devices;

(j) Body piercing services;

(k) Services in the practice of pharmacy;

(l) Law enforcement or firefighting services; and

(m) Handling, embalming, disposal, burial, cremation or disinterment of dead bodies.

This exclusion applies even if the claims against any insured allege negligence or other wrongdoing in the supervision, hiring, employment, training or monitoring of others by that insured, if the offense which caused the "personal and advertising injury", involved the rendering of or failure to render any professional service.

(16) War

However caused, arising, directly or indirectly, out of:

(a) War, including undeclared or civil war;

(b) Warlike action by a military force, including action in hindering or defending against an actual or expected attack, by any government, sovereign or other authority using military personnel or other agents; or

(c) Insurrection, rebellion, revolution, usurped power, or action taken by governmental authority in hindering or defending against any of these.

(17) Recording and Distribution of Material or Information In Violation of Law

Arising directly or indirectly out of any action or omission that violates or is alleged to violate:

(a) The Telephone Consumer Protection Act (TCPA), including any amendment of or addition to such law;

(b) The CAN-SPAM Act of 2003, including any amendment of or addition to such law;

(c) The Fair Credit Reporting Act (FCRA), and any amendment of or addition to such law, including the Fair and Accurate Credit Transactions Act (FACTA); or

(d) Any federal, state or local statute, ordinance or regulation, other than the TCPA, CAN-SPAM Act of 2003 or FCRA and their amendments and additions, that addresses, prohibits, or limits the printing, dissemination, disposal, collecting, recording, sending, transmitting, communicating or distribution of material or information

b.   "Pollution cost or expense".

Analysis

Exclusions (6), (7), (8), (9), (10), (11), and (12) are similar to commercial general liability policy exclusions pertaining to coverage B, personal and advertising injury liability. (Note that an implied contract, as worded in an exception to exclusion 6, is an agreement that is legitimately inferred from the conduct of the parties or by the law as a matter of reason and justice.) Exclusion 7 pertaining to the quality or performance of goods is aimed at preventing the umbrella insurer from having to pay claims made by consumers that are disappointed with the quality or performance of the insured's goods, products, or services. As for exclusion 9, note that the exception to the exclusion is important because it restores coverage for infringement of copyright, trade dress, or slogan that occurs in the named insured's advertisement.

Exclusions (10), (11), and (12) are a reflection of the response to the liability exposures created by the Internet and websites. Note the exception in exclusion 10 for certain personal injuries; these are false arrest, detention, or imprisonment, malicious prosecution, and the wrongful eviction or invasion of the right of private occupancy of a room or premises that a person occupies.

The pollution exclusion is present to prevent coverage B from applying to a pollution spill that a claimant may allege is a wrongful entry into or invasion of the right of private occupancy. Coverage B also does not apply to pollution cost or expense, that is, cleanup costs associated with any pollution spill or release. Note that there are no exceptions to this exclusion.

Coverage B also has exclusions for employment-related practices liability and the rendering of or failure to render professional services. Employment-related practices in exclusion 14 refers to things like refusal to employ, termination of employment, coercion, defamation, harassment, and discrimination. In exclusion 15, the umbrella policy contains a list of professional services; this list is not all-inclusive. The exposures noted in exclusions 14 and 15 are meant to be covered by other liability forms or specialty type policies.

The war exclusion precludes any coverage under the personal and advertising injury liability section of the umbrella form that does not exist under the bodily injury and property damage liability section pertaining to war or warlike actions. Someone could claim a personal injury (for example, false arrest, slander, or libel) arising out of a warlike action, such as a terrorist attack, and then the insured would seek coverage under the umbrella form. This exclusion prevents insurance coverage under the insured's umbrella policy.

In the 2013 revision of the umbrella policy, the same change was made to the recording and distribution of material or information in violation of the law exclusion (17) as was made in the coverage A exclusions in CU 00 01.

Supplementary Payments – Coverages A and B

1. We will pay, with respect to any claim we investigate or settle, or any "suit" against an insured we defend, when the duty to defend exists:

   a. All expenses we incur.

   b. Up to $2,000 for cost of bail bonds (including bonds for related traffic law violations) required because of an "occurrence" we cover. We do not have to furnish these bonds.

    c.   The cost of bonds to release attachments, but only for bond amounts within the applicable limit of insurance. We do not have to furnish these bonds.

    d.   All reasonable expenses incurred by the insured at our request to assist us in the investigation or defense of the claim or "suit", including actual loss of earnings up to $250 a day because of time off from work.

    e.   All court costs taxed against the insured in the "suit". However, these payments do not include attorneys' fees or attorneys' expenses taxed against the insured.

    f.   Prejudgment interest awarded against the insured on that part of the judgment we pay. If we make an offer to pay the applicable limit of insurance, we will not pay any prejudgment interest based on that period of time after the offer.

    g.   All interest on the full amount of any judgment that accrues after entry of the judgment and before we have paid, offered to pay, or deposited in court the part of the judgment that is within the applicable limit of insurance.

    These payments will not reduce the limits of insurance.

Analysis

This section is identical to the commercial general liability policy, except that the umbrella policy allows up to $2,000 for the cost of bail bonds as opposed to the $250 limit under the CGL form. And, the umbrella policy will pay for the bail bonds required because of an occurrence covered by the policy, while the CGL form pays for bail bonds required because of accidents or traffic law violations arising out of the use of any vehicle to which the bodily injury liability coverage applies. So, in keeping with the scope of the umbrella policy, it provides broader supplementary payments.

    2.   When we have the right but not the duty to defend the insured and elect to participate in the defense, we will pay our own expenses but will not contribute to the expenses of the insured or the "underlying insurer".

    3.   If we defend an insured against a "suit" and an indemnitee of the insured is also named as a party to the "suit", we will defend that indemnitee if all of the following conditions are met:

a.   The "suit" against the indemnitee seeks damages for which the insured has assumed the liability of the indemnitee in a contract or agreement that is an "insured contract";

b.   This insurance applies to such liability assumed by the insured;

c.   The obligation to defend, or the cost of the defense of, that indemnitee, has also been assumed by the insured in the same "insured contract";

d.   The allegations in the "suit" and the information we know about the "occurrence" are such that no conflict appears to exist between the interests of the insured and the interests of the indemnitee;

e.   The indemnitee and the insured ask us to conduct and control the defense of that indemnitee against such "suit" and agree that we can assign the same counsel to defend the insured and the indemnitee; and

f.   The indemnitee:

   (1)   Agrees in writing to:

      (a)   Cooperate with us in the investigation, settlement or defense of the "suit";

      (b)   Immediately send us copies of any demands, notices, summonses or legal papers received in connection with the "suit";

      (c)   Notify any other insurer whose coverage is available to the indemnitee; and

      (d)   Cooperate with us with respect to coordinating other applicable insurance available to the indemnitee; and

   (2)   Provides us with written authorization to:

      (a)   Obtain records and other information related to the "suit"; and

      (b)   Conduct and control the defense of the indemnitee in such "suit".

So long as the above conditions are met, attorneys' fees incurred by us in the defense of that indemnitee, necessary litigation expenses incurred by us and necessary litigation expenses incurred by the indemnitee at our request will be paid as Supplementary Payments. Notwithstanding the provisions of Paragraph 2.b.(2) of Section I— Coverage A—Bodily Injury And Property Damage Liability, such payments will not be deemed to be damages for "bodily injury" and "property damage" and will not reduce the limits of insurance.

Our obligation to defend an insured's indemnitee and to pay for attorneys' fees and necessary litigation expenses as Supplementary Payments ends when we have used up the applicable limit of insurance in the payment of judgments, or settlements, or the conditions set forth above, or the terms of the agreement described in Paragraph f. above, are no longer met.

Analysis

The umbrella states that where the insurer has the right to defend but not the duty, it is only responsible for its own expenses if it chooses to participate in the defense. The umbrella insurer will not contribute to defense costs expended by either the insured or the primary insurer, even if it benefits from that defense. This reinforces the idea that the primary insurer is the main party responsible for defending the insured against a lawsuit and thus, is usually the party that pays defense costs.

While the umbrella policy will defend an indemnitee of the insured if that person is named as a party in a lawsuit against the insured, all the conditions listed in this part of the umbrella policy must be met before that defense will take place. The umbrella policy, like the CGL form, lists several explicit conditions that must be met, and these should be known by the insured since the insured is the party that has agreed (in an insured contract) to assume the liability of the indemnitee, and thus, to bear the ultimate responsibility for the indemnification and defense of the indemnitee.

Section II – Who Is an Insured

1. Except for liability arising out of the ownership, maintenance, or use of "covered autos":

    a. If you are designated in the Declarations as:

        (1) An individual, you and your spouse are insureds, but only with respect to the conduct of a business of which you are the sole owner.

(2) A partnership or joint venture, you are an insured. Your members, your partners, and their spouses are also insureds, but only with respect to the conduct of your business.

(3) A limited liability company, you are an insured. Your members are also insureds, but only with respect to the conduct of your business. Your managers are insureds, but only with respect to their duties as your managers.

(4) An organization other than a partnership, joint venture or limited liability company, you are an insured. Your "executive officers" and directors are insureds, but only with respect to their duties as your officers or directors. Your stockholders are also insureds, but only with respect to their liability as stockholders.

(5) A trust, you are insured. Your trustees are also insureds, but only with respect to their duties as trustees.

b. Each of the following is also an insured:

(1) Your "volunteer workers" only while performing duties related to the conduct of your business, your "employees", other than either your "executive officers" (if you are an organization other than a partnership, joint venture or limited liability company) or your managers (if you are a limited liability company), but only for acts within the scope of their employment by you or while performing duties related to the conduct of your business. However, none of these "employees" or "volunteer workers" are insureds for:

(a) "Bodily injury" or "personal and advertising injury":

(i) To you, to your partners or members (if you are a partnership or joint venture), to your members (if you are a limited liability company), to a co-"employee" in the course of his or her employment or performing duties related to the conduct of your business, or to your other "volunteer workers" while performing duties related to the conduct of your business:

          (ii) To the spouse, child, parent, brother or sister of that co-"employee" or "volunteer worker" as a consequence of Paragraph (a)(i) above; or

          (iii) For which there is any obligation to share damages with or repay someone else who must pay damages because of the injury described in Paragraphs (a)(i) or (ii) above.

     (b) "Property damage" to property:

          (i) Owned, occupied or used by;

          (ii) Rented to, in the care, custody or control of, or over which physical control is being exercised for any purpose by:

              you, any of your "employees", "volunteer workers", any partner or member (if you are a partnership or joint venture), or any member (if you are a limited liability company).

   (2) Any person (other than your "employee" or "volunteer worker"), or any organization while acting as your real estate manager.

   (3) Any person or organization having proper temporary custody of your property if you die, but only:

     (a) With respect to liability arising out of the maintenance or use of that property; and

     (b) Until your legal representative has been appointed.

   (4) Your legal representative if you die, but only with respect to duties as such. That representative will have all your rights and duties under this Coverage Part.

  c. Any organization you newly acquire or form, other than a partnership, joint venture or limited liability company, and over which you maintain ownership or majority interest, will qualify as a Named Insured if there is no other similar insurance available to that organization. However:

(1) Coverage under this provision is afforded only until the 90th day after you acquire or form the organization or the end of the policy period, whichever is earlier;

(2) Coverage A does not apply to "bodily injury" or "property damage" that occurred before you acquired or formed the organization; and

(3) Coverage B does not apply to "personal and advertising injury" arising out of an offense committed before you acquired or formed the organization.

Analysis

In the first sentence note that the umbrella policy excludes from the who is an insured category, those entities that may have liability arising out of the ownership, maintenance, or use of covered autos; liability arising from covered autos is addressed in Paragraph 2 of this section, as shown next.

The remainder of paragraph 1 in the who is an insured section of CU 00 01 mirrors the wording in the commercial general liability policy.

2. Only with respect to liability arising out of the ownership, maintenance, or use of "covered autos":

a. You are an insured.

b. Anyone else while using with your permission a "covered auto" you own, hire, or borrow is also an insured except:

(1) The owner or anyone else from whom you hire or borrow a "covered auto". This exception does not apply if the "covered auto" is a trailer or semi-trailer connected to a "covered auto" you own.

(2) Your "employee" if the "covered auto" is owned by that "employee" or a member of his or her household.

(3) Someone using a "covered auto" while he or she is working in a business of selling, servicing, repairing, parking or storing "autos" unless that business is yours.

(4) Anyone other than your "employees", partners (if you are a partnership), members (if you are a

limited liability company), or a lessee or borrower or any of their "employees", while moving property to or from a "covered auto".

(5) A partner (if you are a partnership), or a member (if you are a limited liability company) for a "covered auto" owned by him or her or a member of his or her household.

(6) Employees" with respect to "bodily injury" to:

(a) Any fellow "employee" of the insured arising out of and in the course of the fellow "employee's" employment or while performing duties related to the conduct of your business; or

(b) The spouse, child, parent, brother or sister of that fellow "employee" as a consequence of Paragraph (a) above.

c.   Anyone liable for the conduct of an insured described above is also an insured, but only to the extent of that liability.

3.   Any additional insured under any policy of "underlying insurance" will automatically be an insured under this insurance.

Subject to Section III – Limits Of Insurance, if coverage provided to the additional insured is required by a contract or agreement, the most we will pay on behalf of the additional insured is the amount of insurance:

a.   Required by the contract or agreement, less any amounts payable by any "underlying insurance"; or

b.   Available under the applicable Limits of Insurance shown in the Declarations; whichever is less.

Additional insured coverage provided by this insurance will not be broader than coverage provided by the "underlying insurance".

No person or organization is an insured with respect to the conduct of any current or past partnership, joint venture or limited liability company that is not shown as a Named Insured in the Declarations.

Analysis

Paragraph 2 lists separate qualifications for who is an insured with respect to the ownership, maintenance, or use of covered autos. It is similar to the who is an insured provision of the Business Auto Coverage form (BAP).

Owners of covered autos that the named insured hires or borrows are not insureds. Employees who injure fellow employees in the course of employment are also not considered insureds under the umbrella policy. (In the 2013 revision, ISO added that employees who cause bodily injury to the spouse, child, parent, brother, or sister of a fellow employee are also excluded from being considered an insured.) If an employee of the named insured is driving a company car on business with a fellow employee as a passenger and has an at-fault accident, the umbrella policy will not provide coverage for the driving employee because he is not considered an insured should the fellow employee file a lawsuit against the driver. The named insured is still considered an insured for coverage purposes, but of course, the workers comp and employers' liability exclusions would normally prevent insurance under the umbrella policy from applying to a claim by the injured employee against the named insured employer.

Since the "who is an insured" provisions closely follow underlying general liability and auto policies provisions on the subject, it then naturally follows that additional insureds under any policy of underlying insurance are automatically considered insureds under CU 00 01. But, there are limitations to note.

For example, the additional insured coverage provided by the umbrella policy is only as broad as the coverage provided by the underlying insurance; in other words, the additional insured has no insurance coverages that the insured under the underlying insurance policies does not have. Also, if coverage provided to the additional insured is required by a contract, the most the umbrella insurer will pay on behalf of the additional insured is the amount required by the contract, less any amount payable by underlying insurance. This allows the umbrella insurer to have a definite contractually required amount that it can set aside for payment on behalf of an additional insured.

Section III – Limits of Insurance

1.   The Limits of Insurance shown in the Declarations and the rules below fix the most we will pay regardless of the number of:

   a.   Insureds;

b. Claims made, "suits" brought, or number of vehicles involved; or

c. Persons or organizations making claims or bringing "suits".

2. The Aggregate Limit is the most we will pay for the sum of all "ultimate net loss" under:

a. Coverage A, except "ultimate net loss" because of "bodily injury" or "property damage" arising out of the ownership, maintenance or use of a "covered auto"; and

b. Coverage B.

3. Subject to 2. above, the Each Occurrence Limit is the most we will pay for the sum of all "ultimate net loss" under Coverage A because of all "bodily injury" and "property damage" arising out of one "occurrence".

4. Subject to 2. above, the Personal and Advertising Injury Limit is the most we will pay under Coverage B for the sum of all "ultimate net loss" because of all "personal and advertising injury" sustained by any one person or organization.

5. If there is "underlying insurance" with a policy period that is non-concurrent with the policy period of this Commercial Liability Umbrella Coverage Part, the "retained limit(s)" will only be reduced or exhausted by payments for:

a. "Bodily injury" or "property damage" which occurs during the policy period of this Coverage Part; or

b. "Personal and advertising injury" for offenses that are committed during the policy period of this Coverage Part.

However, if any "underlying insurance" is written on a claims-made basis, the "retained limit(s)" will only be reduced or exhausted by claims for that insurance that are made during the policy period, or any Extended Reporting Period, of this Coverage Part.

The Aggregate Limit, as described in Paragraph 2. above, applies separately to each consecutive annual period and to any remaining period and to any remaining period of less than twelve months, starting with the beginning of the policy period shown in the Declarations, unless the policy period is extended after issuance for an additional period of less than twelve months. In that case, the additional period will be deemed part of the last preceding period for purposes of determining the Limits of Insurance.

Analysis

This section of the umbrella policy establishes the most that the insurer will pay for a claim or lawsuit against the insured. The limits that are set on the declarations page will not be exceeded regardless of the number of insureds, claims, or number of vehicles involved. The limits of insurance section notes that the policy has an aggregate limit, an each occurrence limit, and an any one person or organization limit.

The aggregate limit is the sum of all ultimate net loss under coverage A and B of the policy, except for auto claims; auto claims, for some reason, are not counted against the aggregate limit of the umbrella policy. Of course, bodily injury or property damage arising out of the use or ownership of a covered auto is subject to the each occurrence limit.

Coverage A has the each occurrence limit. As an example of these limits, say the insured's policy has a $2,000,000 aggregate limit, a $1,000,000 each occurrence limit. If the insured is liable for bodily injuries to another person arising out of one occurrence, and the ultimate net loss reaches the $1,000,000 mark, the insured has that amount available for the claim. Once that claim is paid, the insured has $1,000,000 of the aggregate limit left for other claims that may arise during the policy period. If the ultimate net loss from that one occurrence is $1,500,000, the insured still has only the $1,000,000 limit available for payment because of the each occurrence limit.

Coverage B has the any one person or organization limit. For example, if the insured has a total of $2,000,000 available as the aggregate limit during the policy period, but only a $500,000 per person limit on coverage B claims, the most the insurer will pay for personal and advertising injury to any one person or organization is $500,000. If more than one person suffers such injuries, each can collect up to $500,000, but if the aggregate limit of $2,000,000 is reached during the policy period, the insured has no more limits of insurance available under the umbrella policy for payments to claimants.

Section IV – Conditions

1. Appeals

    If the "underlying insurer" or insured elects not to appeal a judgment in excess of the "retained limit", we may do so at our own expense. We will also pay for taxable court costs, pre- and post-judgment interest and disbursements associated with such appeal. In no event will this provision increase our liability beyond the applicable Limits of Insurance described in Section III – Limits Of Insurance.

2. Bankruptcy

   a. Bankruptcy of Insured

   Bankruptcy or insolvency of the insured or of the insured's estate will not relieve us of our obligations under this Coverage Part.

   b. Bankruptcy of Underlying Insurer

   Bankruptcy or insolvency of the "underlying insurer" will not relieve us of our obligations under this Coverage Part.

   However, this insurance will not replace the "underlying insurance" in the event of bankruptcy or insolvency of the "underlying insurer". This insurance will apply as if the "underlying insurance" were in full effect.

3. Duties in the Event of Occurrence, Offense, Claim or Suit

   a. You must see to it that we are notified as soon as practicable of an "occurrence" or an offense, regardless of the amount, which may result in a claim. To the extent possible, notice should include:

      (1) How, when and where the "occurrence" or offense took place;

      (2) The names and addresses of any injured persons and witnesses; and

      (3) The nature and location of any injury or damage arising out of the "occurrence" or offense.

   b. If a claim is made or "suit" is brought against any insured, you must:

      (1) Immediately record the specifics of the claim or "suit" and the date received; and

(2) Notify us as soon as practicable.

You must see to it that we receive written notice of the claim or "suit" as soon as practicable.

c. You and any other involved insured must:

(1) Immediately send us copies of any demands, notices, summonses or legal papers received in connection with the claim or "suit";

(2) Authorize us to obtain records and other information;

(3) Cooperate with us in the investigation or settlement of the claim or defense against the "suit"; and

(4) Assist us, upon our request, in the enforcement of any right against any person or organization which may be liable to the insured because of injury or damage to which this insurance may also apply.

d. No insured will, except at that insured's own cost, voluntarily make a payment, assume any obligation, or incur any expense, other than for first aid, without our consent.

Analysis

The umbrella coverage form basically offers the same conditions as the CGL policy.

While CU 00 01 does not relieve the insurer of its duty in the event the underlying insurer becomes insolvent or goes bankrupt, the umbrella policy does not replace the underlying insurance. As an example: damages to the claimant total $2,000,000; the underlying limits are $1,500,000 and the umbrella policy has a limit of insurance of $2,000,000; the underlying insurer becomes insolvent; the umbrella policy will only cover damages beyond the underlying limits, or $500,000.

The umbrella policy affords the insurer the right to appeal judgments, in excess of the limits of underlying insurance, even if the underlying insurer or the insured chooses not to appeal. The umbrella insurer agrees to pay for the expenses of such an appeal, along with taxable costs, prejudgment and post judgment interest, and disbursements.

4. Legal Action against Us

No person or organization has a right under this Coverage Part:

a.   To join us as a party or otherwise bring us into a "suit" asking for damages from an insured; or

b.   To sue us on this Coverage Part unless all of its terms have been fully complied with.

A person or organization may sue us to recover on an agreed settlement or on a final judgment against an insured; but we will not be liable for damages that are not payable under the terms of this Coverage Part or that are in excess of the applicable limit of insurance. An agreed settlement means a settlement and release of liability signed by us, the insured and the claimant or the claimant's legal representative.

5.   Other Insurance

a.   This insurance is excess over, and shall not contribute with any other insurance, whether primary, excess, contingent or on any other basis. This condition will not apply to insurance specifically written as excess over this Coverage Part.

When this insurance is excess, we will have no duty under Coverage A or B to defend the insured against any "suit" if any other insurer has a duty to defend the insured against that "suit". If no other insurer defends, we will undertake to do so, but we will be entitled to the insured's rights against all those other insurers.

b.   When this insurance is excess over other insurance, we will pay only our share of the "ultimate net loss" that exceeds the sum of:

(1)   The total amount that all such other insurance would pay for the loss in the absence of the insurance provided under this Coverage Part; and

(2)   The total of all deductibles and self-insured amounts under all that other insurance.

6.   Premium Audit

a.   We will compute all premiums for this Coverage Part in accordance with our rules and rates.

b.   Premium shown in this Coverage Part as advance premium is a deposit premium only. At the close of each audit period we will compute the earned premium for that period and send notice to the first Named Insured. The due date for audit and retrospective premiums is the date shown as the due date on the bill. If the sum of the advance and audit premiums paid for the policy period is greater than the earned premium, we will return the excess to the first Named Insured.

c.   The first Named Insured must keep records of the information we need for premium computation, and send us copies at such times as we may request.

7.   Representations or Fraud

By accepting this policy, you agree:

a.   The statements in the Declarations are accurate and complete;

b.   Those statements are based upon representations you made to us;

c.   We have issued this policy in reliance upon your representations; and

d.   This policy is void in any case of fraud by you as it relates to this policy or any claim under this policy.

8.   Separation of Insureds

Except with respect to the Limits of Insurance, and any rights or duties specifically assigned in this Coverage Part to the Named Insured, this insurance applies:

a.   As if each Named Insured were the only Named Insured; and

b.   Separately to each insured against whom claim is made or "suit" is brought.

9.   Transfer of Rights of Recovery against Others to Us

If the insured has rights to recover all or part of any payment we have made under this Coverage Part, those rights are transferred to us. The insured must do nothing after loss to impair them. At our request, the insured will bring "suit" or transfer those rights to us and help us enforce them.

10. When We Do Not Renew

If we decide not to renew this Coverage Part, we will mail or deliver to the first Named Insured shown in the Declarations written notice of the nonrenewal not less than 30 days before the expiration date.

If notice is mailed, proof of mailing will be sufficient proof of notice.

Analysis

Again, most of the conditions listed here are standard general liability provisions. The umbrella policy does add a disclaimer that specifically voids the policy for fraud by the named insured relating to the policy or claims under the policy. Of course, if the insurer wants to void a policy due to fraud on the part of the insured, the insurer has the responsibility to prove that fraud has been committed by the insured; a mere allegation of fraud will not be sufficient to void the policy coverages.

11. Loss Payable

Liability under this Coverage Part does not apply to a given claim unless and until:

a. The insured or insured's "underlying insurer" has become obligated to pay the "retained limit"; and

b. The obligation of the insured to pay the "ultimate net loss" in excess of the "retained limit" has been determined by a final settlement or judgment or written agreement among the insured, claimant and us.

12. Transfer of Defense

When the underlying limits of insurance have been used up in the payment of judgments or settlements, the duty to defend will be transferred to us. We will cooperate in the transfer of control to us of any outstanding claims or "suits" seeking damages to which this insurance applies which would have been covered by the "underlying insurance" had the applicable limit not been used up.

13. Maintenance of Underlying Insurance

Any "underlying insurance" must be maintained in full effect without reduction of coverage or limits except for the reduction of the aggregate limit in accordance with the provisions of such "underlying insurance" that results from payment of claims, settlement, or judgments to which this insurance applies.

Such exhaustion or reduction is not a failure to maintain "underlying insurance". Failure to maintain "underlying insurance" will not invalidate insurance provided under this Coverage Part, but insurance provided under this Coverage Part will apply as if the "underlying insurance" were in full effect.

If there is an increase in the scope of coverage of any "underlying insurance" during the term of this policy, our liability will be no more than it would have been if there had been no such increase.

You must notify us in writing as soon as practicable if any "underlying insurance" is cancelled, not renewed, replaced or otherwise terminated, or if the limits or scope of coverage of any "underlying insurance" is changed.

14. Expanded Coverage Territory

a.   If a "suit" is brought in a part of the "coverage territory" that is outside of the United States of America (including its territories and possessions), Puerto Rico or Canada, and we are prevented by law, or otherwise, from defending the insured, the insured will initiate a defense of the "suit". We will reimburse the insured, under Supplementary Payments, for any reasonable and necessary expenses incurred for the defense of a "suit" seeking damages to which this insurance applies, that we would have paid had we been able to exercise our right and duty to defend.

If the insured becomes legally obligated to pay sums because of damages to which this insurance applies in a part of the "coverage territory" that is outside of the United States of America (including its territories and possessions), Puerto Rico or Canada, and we are prevented by law, or otherwise, from paying such sums on the insured's behalf, we will reimburse the insured for such sums.

b.   All payments or reimbursements we make for damages because of judgments or settlements will be made in U.S.

currency at the prevailing exchange rate at the time the insured became legally obligated to pay such sums. All payments or reimbursements we make for expenses under Supplementary Payments will be made in U.S. currency at the prevailing exchange rate at the time the expenses were incurred.

c.   Any disputes between you and us as to whether there is coverage under this policy must be filed in the courts of the United States of America (including its territories and possessions), Canada or Puerto Rico.

d.   The insured must fully maintain any coverage required by law, regulation or other governmental authority during the policy period, except for reduction of the aggregate limits due to payments of claims, judgments or settlements.

Failure to maintain such coverage required by law, regulation or other governmental authority will not invalidate this insurance. However, this insurance will apply as if the required coverage by law, regulation or other governmental authority was in full effect.

Analysis

This set of conditions helps describe the nature of the umbrella policy.

One of the provisions declares that liability under the umbrella policy will not apply unless and until the insured or the underlying insurer become obligated to pay the available limits of the scheduled underlying insurance. In other words, if the limits of insurance on the underlying policy or the self-insured retention of the insured are not breached, the umbrella policy will not come into play.

Another provision states that when the underlying limits of insurance have been used up in the payment of judgments or settlements, the umbrella insurer will take over the duty to defend the insured. The underlying insurance policy has a declaration that its duty to defend ends when the applicable limit of insurance is used up, so this particular provision tells the insured that his defense is still being handled by an insurer.

Another provision requires the maintenance of underlying insurance. Failure to maintain underlying insurance will not invalidate the umbrella policy coverage, but the umbrella insurer will apply the insurance of the umbrella policy as if the underlying insurance were in full effect.

As an example: the underlying insurance has policy limits of $1,000,000, and the umbrella policy applies to the ultimate net loss in excess of this amount; the insured cancels the underlying insurance policy in the middle of the policy period; if a loss then occurs, the umbrella policy will not pay the claim unless the amount of the claim is more than the $1,000,000 limit of the underlying policy.

Since the umbrella policy has an expansive coverage territory by definition, the last of the policy's conditions recognizes this expansion by describing what will happen if a lawsuit against the insured is brought in an area outside the United States, Puerto Rico, or Canada. Should that happen, the umbrella insurer declares that, if it is prevented by law or otherwise from defending the insured, the insured should defend itself and the insurer will then reimburse the insured. The insurer will pay any reasonable and necessary expenses incurred by the insured for the defense against the lawsuit. And, should the insured lose the lawsuit and become obligated to pay the plaintiff, this last condition on the umbrella policy acts to reassure the insured. The umbrella insurer promises that if it is prevented by law or otherwise from paying the amount due, the insured should pay it and the insurer will reimburse the insured for the amount paid.

This final condition on CU 00 01 says that all payments or reimbursements made for such damages as described in the previous paragraph will be made in U.S. currency at the prevailing exchange rate at the time the insured became legally obligated to pay. And, any disputes between the insured and the named insured as to whether there is coverage under the umbrella form have to be settled in a court of the U.S., Canada, or Puerto Rico; the insured is not free to pick just any jurisdiction around the world in which to file a coverage dispute lawsuit.

Section V – Definitions

1. "Advertisement" means a notice that is broadcast or published to the general public or specific market segments about your goods, products or services for the purpose of attracting customers or supporters. For the purposes of this definition:

    a. Notices that are published include material placed on the Internet or on similar electronic means of communication; and

    b. Regarding web sites, only that part of a website that is about your goods, products or services for the purpose of attracting customers or supporters is considered an advertisement.

2. "Auto" means:

    a. A land motor vehicle, trailer or semi-trailer designed for travel on public roads, including any attached machinery or equipment; or

    b. Any other land vehicle that is subject to a compulsory or financial responsibility law or other motor vehicle insurance law where it is licensed or principally garaged.

    However, "auto" does not include "mobile equipment".

3. "Bodily injury" means bodily injury, disability, sickness or disease sustained by a person, including death resulting from any of these at any time. "Bodily injury" includes mental anguish or other mental injury resulting from "bodily injury".

4. "Coverage territory" means anywhere in the world with the exception of any country or jurisdiction which is subject to trade or other economic sanctions or embargo by the United States of America.

5. "Covered auto" means only those "autos" to which "underlying insurance" applies.

6. "Employee" includes a "leased worker". "Employee" does not include a "temporary worker".

7. "Executive officer" means a person holding any of the officer positions created by your charter, constitution, by-laws or any other similar governing document.

8. "Impaired property" means tangible property, other than "your product" or "your work", that cannot be used or is less useful because:

    a. It incorporates "your product" or "your work" that is known or thought to be defective, deficient, inadequate or dangerous; or

    b. You have failed to fulfill the terms of a contract or agreement;

        if such property can be restored to use by the repair, replacement, adjustment or removal of "your product" or "your work", or your fulfilling the terms of the contract or agreement.

Analysis

Definitions 1, 2, 6, 7, and 8 are taken from the definitions section of the CGL policy. Note that the auto definition in CU 00 01, as in CG 00 01, attempts to draw a clear line between an auto and mobile equipment for purposes of liability coverage placement.

CU 00 01 does expand the bodily injury definition to include mental anguish or other mental injury resulting from bodily injury. This is not to say that the umbrella policy would apply to mental injury resulting from mental stress. An actual bodily injury is required before any mental stress or anguish claims are accepted as covered by the umbrella policy.

Coverage territory encompasses a broader reach in the umbrella than in the CGL policy. In the umbrella policy, the coverage territory is mostly worldwide and applies to operations of the insured, products and completed operations of the insured, and other liability exposures. And, the coverage territory (in connection with the expanded coverage territory condition in CU 00 01) for the umbrella policy does not require a lawsuit against the insured to be brought in the U.S., Puerto Rico, or Canada. The suit can be brought just about anywhere in the world and the umbrella insurer will honor its duty to defend.

9. "Insured contract" means:

  a. A contract for a lease of premises. However, that portion of the contract for a lease of premises that indemnifies any person or organization for damage by fire to premises while rented to you or temporarily occupied by you with permission of the owner is not an "insured contract";

  b. A sidetrack agreement;

  c. Any easement or license agreement, except in connection with construction or demolition operations on or within 50 feet of a railroad;

  d. An obligation, as required by ordinance, to indemnify a municipality, except in connection with work for a municipality;

  e. An elevator maintenance agreement;

  f. That part of any contract or agreement entered into, as part of your business, pertaining to the rental or lease, by you or any of your "employees", of any "auto". However, such contract or agreement shall not be considered an "insured contract" to the extent that it obligates you or any of your "employees" to pay for "property damage" to any "auto" rented or leased by you or any of your "employees".

g. That part of any other contract or agreement pertaining to your business (including an indemnification of a municipality in connection with work performed for a municipality) under which you assume the tort liability of another party to pay for "bodily injury" or "property damage" to a third person or organization. Tort liability means a liability that would be imposed by law in the absence of any contract or agreement.

Paragraphs f. and g. do not include that part of any contract or agreement:

(1) That indemnifies a railroad for "bodily injury" or "property damage" arising out of construction or demolition operations, within 50 feet of any railroad property and affecting any railroad bridge or trestle, tracks, roadbeds, tunnel, underpass or crossing;

(2) That pertains to the loan, lease or rental of an "auto" to you or any of your "employees", if the "auto" is loaned, leased or rented with a driver; and

(3) That holds a person or organization engaged in the business of transporting property by "auto" for hire harmless for your use of a "covered auto" over a route or territory that person or organization is authorized to serve by public authority.

Analysis

The umbrella policy differs from the CGL policy definition of "insured contract" by adding provisions for auto rental or lease contracts. This is merely a reproduction of the definition of insured contract that appears in the business auto coverage form and reinforces the fact that the umbrella policy does apply to auto liability exposures. And note that—pertaining to an auto rental or lease contract—the definition of an insured contract also states that the auto contract is not considered an insured contract to the extent that it obligates the named insured or any employee to pay for property damage to any auto rented or leased by the named insured or any employee. This is in keeping with the fact that CU 00 01 does not extend coverage to any loss, cost, or expense payable under or resulting from any auto first-party physical damage coverage, and the fact that property damage to personal property in the care, custody, or control of the insured is excluded.

10. "Leased worker" means a person leased to you by a labor leasing firm under an agreement between you and the labor leasing firm, to perform duties related to the conduct of your business. "Leased worker" does not include a "temporary worker".

11. "Loading or unloading" means the handling of property:

    a.   After it is moved from the place where it is accepted for movement into or onto an aircraft or watercraft or "auto";

    b.   While it is in or on an aircraft or watercraft or "auto"; or

    c.   While it is being moved from an aircraft or watercraft or "auto" to the place where it is finally delivered;

       but "loading or unloading" does not include the movement of property by means of a mechanical device, other than a hand truck, that is not attached to the aircraft or watercraft or "auto".

12. "Mobile equipment" means any of the following types of land vehicles, including any attached machinery or equipment:

    a.   Bulldozers, farm machinery, forklifts and other vehicles designed for use principally off public roads;

    b.   Vehicles maintained for use solely on or next to premises you own or rent;

    c.   Vehicles that travel on crawler treads;

    d.   Vehicles, whether self-propelled or not, maintained primarily to provide mobility to permanently mounted:

       (1)   Power cranes, shovels, loaders, diggers or drills; or

       (2)   Road construction or resurfacing equipment such as graders, scrapers or rollers;

e. Vehicles not described in a., b., c. or d. above that are not self-propelled and are maintained primarily to provide mobility to permanently attached equipment of the following types:

(1) Air compressors, pumps and generators, including spraying, welding, building cleaning, geophysical exploration, lighting and well servicing equipment; or

(2) Cherry pickers and similar devices used to raise or lower workers;

f. Vehicles not described in a., b., c. or d. above maintained primarily for purposes other than the transportation of persons or cargo. However, self-propelled vehicles with the following types of permanently attached equipment are not "mobile equipment" but will be considered "autos":

(1) Equipment designed primarily for:

(a) Snow removal;

(b) Road maintenance, but not construction or resurfacing; or

(c) Street cleaning;

(2) Cherry pickers and similar devices mounted on automobile or truck chassis and used to raise or lower workers; and

(3) Air compressors, pumps and generators, including spraying, welding, building cleaning, geophysical exploration, lighting and well servicing equipment.

However, "mobile equipment" does not include land vehicles that are subject to a compulsory or financial responsibility law or other motor vehicle insurance law where it is licensed or principally garaged. Land vehicles subject to a compulsory or financial responsibility law or other motor vehicle insurance law are considered "autos".

"Occurrence" means an accident, including continuous or repeated exposure to substantially the same general harmful conditions.

Analysis

Definitions 10, 11, 12, and 13 mirror the definitions in the CGL policy. The definition of "mobile equipment" complements the definition of "auto" pertaining to land vehicles that are subject to financial responsibility laws or other motor vehicle insurance laws; such vehicles are considered autos and claims involving such vehicles are handled as auto claims, not general liability claims.

14. "Personal and advertising injury" means injury, including consequential "bodily injury", arising out of one or more of the following offenses:

   a. False arrest, detention or imprisonment;

   b. Malicious prosecution;

   c. The wrongful eviction from, wrongful entry into, or invasion of the right of private occupancy of a room, dwelling or premises that a person occupies, committed by or on behalf of its owner, landlord or lessor;

   d. Oral or written publication of material that slanders or libels a person or organization or disparages a person's or organization's goods, products or services;

   e. Oral or written publication, in any manner, of material that violates a person's right to privacy;

   f. The use of another's advertising idea in your "advertisement"; or

   g. Infringing upon another's copyright, trade dress or slogan in your "advertisement".

15. "Pollutants" mean any solid, liquid, gaseous or thermal irritant or contaminant, including smoke, vapor, soot, fumes, acid, alkalis, chemicals and waste. Waste includes materials to be recycled, reconditioned or reclaimed.

16. "Pollution cost or expense" means any loss, cost or expense arising out of any:

   a. Request, demand, order or statutory or regulatory requirement that any insured or others test for, monitor, clean up, remove, contain, treat, detoxify or neutralize, or in any way respond to, or assess the effects of "pollutants"; or

b.   Claim or suit by or on behalf of a governmental authority for damages because of testing for, monitoring, cleaning up, removing, containing, treating, detoxifying or neutralizing, or in any way responding to, or assessing the effects of, "pollutants".

17.   "Products-completed operations hazard":

a.   Includes all "bodily injury" and "property damage" occurring away from premises you own or rent and arising out of "your product" or "your work" except:

(1)   Products that are still in your physical possession; or

(2)   Work that has not yet been completed or abandoned. However, "your work" will be deemed completed at the earliest of the following times:

(a)   When all of the work called for in your contract has been completed.

(b)   When all of the work to be done at the job site has been completed if your contract calls for work at more than one job site.

(c)   When that part of the work done at a job site has been put to its intended use by any person or organization other than another contractor or subcontractor working on the same project.

Work that may need service, maintenance, correction, repair or replacement, but which is otherwise complete, will be treated as completed.

b.   Does not include "bodily injury" or "property damage" arising out of:

(1)   The transportation of property, unless the injury or damage arises out of a condition in or on a vehicle not owned or operated by you, and that condition was created by the "loading or unloading" of that vehicle by any insured; or

(2) The existence of tools, uninstalled equipment or abandoned or unused materials

Analysis

This set of definitions mirrors those on the CGL form and the BAP. CU 00 01 contains the definition of pollution cost or expense just like the BAP.

18. "Property damage" means:

a. Physical injury to tangible property, including all resulting loss of use of that property. All such loss of use shall be deemed to occur at the time of the physical injury that caused it; or

b. Loss of use of tangible property that is not physically injured. All such loss of use shall be deemed to occur at the time of the "occurrence" that caused it.

With respect to the ownership, maintenance, or use of "covered autos", property damage also includes "pollution cost and expense", but only to the extent that coverage exists under the "underlying insurance" or would have existed but for the exhaustion of the underlying limits.

For the purposes of this insurance, with respect to other than the ownership, maintenance, or use of "covered autos", electronic data is not tangible property. As used in this definition, electronic data means information, facts or programs stored as or on, created or used on, or transmitted to or from computer software(including systems and applications software), hard or floppy disks, CD-ROMs, tapes, drives, cells, data processing devices or any other media which are used with electronically controlled equipment.

19. "Retained limit" means the available limits of "underlying insurance" scheduled in the declarations or the "self-insured retention", whichever applies.

20. "Self-insured retention" means the dollar amount listed in the declarations that will be paid by the insured before this insurance becomes applicable only with respect to "occurrences" or offenses not covered by the "underlying insurance". The "self-insurance retention" does not apply to "occurrences" or offenses which would have been covered by "underlying insurance" but for the exhaustion of applicable limits.

21. "Suit" means a civil proceeding in which damages because of "bodily injury", "property damage" or "personal and advertising injury" to which this insurance applies are alleged. "Suit" includes:

    a.   An arbitration proceeding in which such damages are claimed and to which the insured must submit or does submit with our consent; or

    b.   Any other alternative dispute resolution proceeding in which such damages are claimed and to which the insured submits with our consent or the "underlying insurer's" consent.

22. "Temporary worker" means a person who is furnished to you to substitute for a permanent "employee" on leave or to meet seasonal or short-term workload conditions.

Analysis

Definition 18 expands the general liability definition of "property damage" to include pollution cost or expense for covered autos, provided that the same coverage exists in the underlying insurance. This enables the umbrella policy to back up an underlying auto insurance policy since a standard business auto policy does cover, to a degree, pollution cost or expense. The coverage A insuring agreement of CU 00 01 refers to bodily injury and property damage, and if pollution cost or expense were not included in the definition of property damage, the coverage that does exist for this particular exposure under an underlying auto insurance policy would not extend into the umbrella scope of coverage.

The definition of "property damage" also makes the point that electronic data is not tangible property so that there can be no inference that damage to things like computer disks or other electronic data is to be covered under the terms of this policy.

"Retained limits" and "self-insured retentions" are defined here because the umbrella policy comes into play when these limits are exceeded in a claim against the insured. The retained limits are the limits of insurance for the respective underlying insurance policies and are scheduled on the declarations page of the umbrella policy. The self-insured retention is the amount that the insured will pay up front for a claim before the umbrella policy applies. This self-insured retention becomes applicable only with respect to occurrences or offenses that are not covered by the underlying insurance. This is logical because if the underlying insurance policies offer coverage for a liability exposure facing the insured, having a self-insured retention also apply to the exposure would give the umbrella insurer a double layer of protection.

23. "Ultimate net loss" means the total sum, after reduction for recoveries or salvages collectible, that the insured becomes legally obligated to pay as damages by reason of settlement or judgments or any arbitration or other alternate dispute method entered into with our consent or the "underlying insurer's" consent.

24. "Underlying insurance" means any policies of insurance listed in the declarations under the schedule of "underlying insurance".

25. "Underlying insurer" means any insurer who provides any policy of insurance listed in the schedule of "underlying insurance".

26. "Volunteer worker" means a person who is not your "employee", and who donates his or her work and acts at the direction of and within the scope of duties determined by you, and is not paid a fee, salary or other compensation by you or anyone else for their work performed for you.

27. "Your product":

 a. Means:

 (1) Any goods or products, other than real property, manufactured, sold, handled, distributed or disposed of by:

 (a) You;

 (b) Others trading under your name; or

 (c) A person or organization whose business or assets you have acquired; and

 (2) Containers (other than vehicles), materials, parts or equipment furnished in connection with such goods or products.

 b. Includes:

 (1) Warranties or representations made at any time with respect to the fitness, quality, durability, performance or use of "your product"; and

        (2)   The providing of or failure to provide warnings or instructions.

    c.   Does not include vending machines or other property rented to or located for the use of others but not sold.

28. "Your work":

    a.   Means:

        (1)   Work or operations performed by you or on your behalf; and

        (2)   Materials, parts or equipment furnished in connection with such work or operations.

    b.   Includes:

        (1)   Warranties or representations made at any time with respect to the fitness, quality, durability, performance or use of "your work", and

        (2)   The providing of or failure to provide warnings or instructions.

Analysis

Definitions 24 and 25 simply reflect the nature of the umbrella coverage. The umbrella policy comes into play when the underlying insurance is used up: That is the rationale behind umbrella policies. It then makes sense to define exactly what "underlying insurance" and "underlying insurers" are so that all parties to the umbrella insurance contract understand the lines of coverage that exist for the insured.

"Ultimate net loss", definition 23, is an important term to define since the insuring agreements of CU 00 01 pertain to paying such a loss on behalf of the insured. The ultimate net loss amount tells the insured and the insurers exactly how much the claim against the insured costs.

The other definitions listed here mirror those found on the standard underlying CGL coverage form.

Endorsements

There are several endorsements that can be used to modify the coverage provided by CU 00 01. The following information is a brief discussion of some of these endorsements.

CU 04 03 12 07, Employee Benefits Liability Coverage, is a claims-made endorsement. Under the provisions of CU 04 03, the insurer agrees to pay on behalf of the insured the ultimate net loss in excess of the retained limit because of any negligent act, error, or omission of the insured committed in the administration of the employee benefit program.

"Administration" means providing information to employees with respect to eligibility for or scope of employee benefit programs. It also includes handling records in connection with the program, and effecting, continuing, or terminating the participation of any employee in the program.

An employee benefit program provides some or all of the following benefits to employees: group life insurance; group accident or health insurance; dental, vision, and hearing plans; flexible spending accounts; profit sharing plans; employee savings plans; pension plans; unemployment insurance; social security benefits; workers compensation benefits; vacation plans; leave of absence programs; and any other similar benefits designated in the schedule.

The endorsement does not apply to: dishonest, fraudulent, or criminal acts; bodily injury; property damage; personal and advertising liability; failure to perform a contract; insufficiency of funds; ERISA; taxes or fines; employment-related practices; inadequacy of performance of investments or of advice to any person with respect to participation in the employee benefit program; or failure of the insured to comply with any mandatory workers compensation, unemployment compensation insurance, social security, or disability benefits laws or any similar law.

CU 04 12 04 13, Condominiums, Co-Ops, Associations – Directors and Officers Liability Coverage Endorsement, was introduced with the 2013 revision of the umbrella policy. Three coverages are available under the endorsement: management liability, association reimbursement, and association liability. Coverage is provided on a claims-made basis. When attached to the CU 00 01, this endorsement provides a broadening of coverage.

CU 21 00 09 00, Exclusion – All Hazards in Connection with Designated Premises, is an exclusionary endorsement pertaining to liability arising out of any specific premises. This endorsement excludes coverage for all hazards in connection with a designated premises.

CU 21 02 09 00, Exclusion – Products-Completed Operations Hazard, excludes coverage for liability arising out of the products/completed operations hazard.

CU 21 03 09 00, Exclusion – Designated Work, excludes bodily injury or property damage included in the products-completed operations hazard and arising out of the work of the named insured. The description of the work is listed in the schedule of the endorsement.

CU 21 07 12 05, Contractual Liability Limitation, is an optional endorsement pertaining to contractual liability. This endorsement replaces the definition of "insured contract" that is on CU 00 01. Paragraph g. of the definition is dropped; this pertains to a contract by which the insured assumes the tort liability of another.

CU 21 09 09 00, Exclusion – Explosion, Collapse and Underground Property Damage Hazard (Specified Operations), applies to liability coverage for property damage included within the explosion, the collapse, or the underground property damage hazards, and limits the coverage to specified operations.

CU 21 11 09 00, Limitation of Coverage to Designated Premises or Project, states that the insurance applies only to bodily injury, property damage, or personal and advertising injury arising out of the ownership, maintenance, or use of the premises shown in the schedule and operations necessary or incidental to those premises.

CU 21 12 09 00, Abuse or Molestation Exclusion, excludes coverage for liability for abuse or molestation of a person in the care, custody, or control of an insured.

CU 21 15 04 13, Exclusion – Financial Services, is an exclusion for bodily injury, property damage, or personal and advertising injury resulting from the rendering of or the failure to render financial services by any insured to others. The endorsement could be used to modify exposures presented by accountants, banks, securities, and brokers in conjunction with CU 22 04 when fiduciary coverage is being excluded.

CU 21 16 09 00, Exclusion – Designated Ongoing Operations, excludes bodily injury or property damage arising out of the ongoing operations described in the schedule of the endorsement.

CU 21 25 12 01, Total Pollution Exclusion Endorsement, totally eliminates coverage for pollution liability that is not already precluded by the exclusionary language of the umbrella policy.

CU 21 27 12 04, Fungi or Bacteria Exclusion, excludes bodily injury or property damage that would not have occurred but for the inhalation of, ingestion of, contact with, or the presence of any fungi or bacteria on or within a building or structure.

CU 21 42 12 04, Exclusion – Exterior Insulation and Finish Systems, excludes coverage for injuries or damages arising out of or caused by exterior insulation and finish systems (EIFS).

CU 21 43 12 04, Exclusion – Designated Products, excludes coverage for injury or damage included in the products-completed operations hazard and arising out of any of the named insured's products shown in the schedule.

CU 21 50 03 05, Silica or Silica-Related Dust Exclusion, excludes coverage for injury or damage arising out of the inhalation of, ingestion of, exposure to, or presence of silica or silica-related dust.

CU 21 51 12 05, Total Pollution Exclusion with a Hostile Fire Exception, is an optional endorsement that totally excludes bodily injury or property damage that would not have occurred in whole or in part but for the release or discharge of pollutants at any time; in other words, a total pollution exclusion. This endorsement does allow one exception however; the pollution exclusion does not apply to bodily injury or property damage arising out of the heat, smoke, or fumes from a hostile fire under most circumstances.

CU 21 52 12 05, Total Pollution Exclusion with a Building Heating, Cooling and Dehumidifying Equipment Exception and a Hostile Fire Exception, is a similar endorsement except that it adds another exception to the absolute pollution exclusion. This endorsement adds an exception for bodily injury caused by smoke, fumes, vapor, or soot produced by or originating from building heating, cooling, and dehumidifying equipment.

CU 21 58 05 09, Communicable Disease Exclusion, is the communicable disease exclusion.

CU 21 70 12 07, Abuse or Molestation Exclusion – Specified Professional Services, prevents coverage for abuse or molestation by anyone of any person while in the care, custody, or control of any insured.

CU 22 03 09 00, Exclusion – Riot, Civil Commotion or Mob Action – Governmental Subdivisions, eliminates coverage for liability arising out of riot, civil commotion, or mob action, or any act or omission in connection with the prevention of or suppression of mob action, riot, or civil commotion.

CU 22 06 09 00, Exclusion – Existence or Maintenance of Streets, Roads, Highways or Bridges, eliminates coverage for liability of a government entity arising out of its ownership of, control of, or maintenance of streets, roads, highways, or bridges.

CU 22 32 09 00, Agricultural Produce Trailers – Seasonal, is the agricultural produce trailers seasonal endorsement which provides coverage for farm trailers and semitrailers with a load capacity exceeding 2,000 pounds. This is not used when the load is livestock.

CU 22 35 09 00, Truckers – Insurance for Non-Trucking Use, can be used when autos are neither rented nor used for business purposes or to haul someone else's trailers, in other words, nontrucking activities (bobtailing or deadheading).

CU 22 36 12 05, Truckers – Uniform Intermodal Interchange Endorsement Form UIIE – 1, was revised in order to correspond with the amendments to the Uniform Intermodal Interchange and Facilities Access Agreement. A new paragraph has been added to the endorsement with respect to the motor carrier indemnifying indemnitees without regard to whether their liability is vicarious, implied by law, or as the result of the fault or negligence of the indemnitees. And, a new paragraph has been added to exclude indemnity for damages that occur during the presence of the motor carrier on the premises of the facility operator and that are caused by the negligence or intentional acts or omissions of the indemnitees.

CU 22 38 12 01, Truckers – Named Lessee as Insured – Notice of Cancellation, provides that the named lessee will be given thirty days advance notice if the policy is cancelled or liability coverage limits are reduced.

CU 24 04 12 05, Financial Institutions – Fiduciary Interest Only, is an optional endorsement. It pertains to coverage for bodily injury, property damage, and personal and advertising injury arising out of the ownership, maintenance, or use of property in trust for which the named insured is acting in a fiduciary or representative capacity.

CU 24 06 12 04, Fiduciaries – Fiduciary Interest, adds fiduciary coverage for banks or other financial institutions. This endorsement also adds, as additional insureds, any cofiduciary or corepresentative of the named insured with respect to acts or omissions as such; any person or organization responsible for acts or omissions of the named insured in a fiduciary or representative capacity; and any beneficiary, devisee, ward, legatee, heir, or distributor of the trust, guardianship or estate, and any coowner or life tenant of the property, with respect to acts or omissions as such.

CU 24 09 03 05, Contractual Liability – Railroads, pertains to coverage for liability of a railroad assumed by the insured. If the insured has not purchased a railroad protective liability policy, or if the railroad has not requested that one be in place, this endorsement provides coverage.

CU 24 14 09 00, Fellow Employee Auto Coverage, adds fellow employee coverage for all of the named insured's employees. Fellow employee auto coverage for designated employees/positions can be added by using CU 24 15 09 00, Fellow Employee Auto Coverage for Designated Employees/Positions.

CU 24 16 09 00, Broad Form Products Coverage, eliminates the exclusion for property damage to the named insured's products.

CU 24 17 02 02, Individual Named Insured – Auto Coverage, provides coverage for a private passenger type auto that is not used for public transportation or rented to others, or a pickup or van not used in the business of the named insured.

CU 24 18 12 01, Repossessed Autos, applies to auto finance companies and banks that, in the course of business, repossess and resell financed autos.

CU 24 19 12 01, Lessor – Additional Insured and Loss Payee, pertains to additional insured status for a lessor of leased autos. The lessor is listed on the schedule of the endorsement and, the insurer promises, if the policy is cancelled by the insurer, to mail notice to the lessor in accordance with the cancellation common policy conditions. And, if the named insured cancels the policy, the insurer will mail notice to the lessor.

CU 24 20 09 00, Broadened Bodily Injury Definition, is an endorsement that broadens the definition of bodily injury by removing the "resulting from bodily injury" language in the umbrella policy definition. Mental anguish or other mental injury standing alone is considered bodily injury through the use of this endorsement.

CU 24 23 12 07, Coverage for Professional Services, eliminates the exclusion relating to professional services.

CU 24 31 04 13, Limited Contractual Liability – Railroads, is an optional endorsement that replaces the definition of "insured contract" on the umbrella policy. The part of the standard definition of "insured contract" pertaining to any easement or license agreement contains an exception in connection with construction or demolition operations on or within fifty feet or a railroad. This endorsement deletes that exception so that any easement or license agreement is now considered to be an insured contract. This endorsement applies only with respect to operations performed for or affecting a scheduled railroad at a designated job site shown in the schedule on the endorsement.

CU 24 32 04 13, Limited Coverage Territory, is an optional endorsement that replaces the definition of "coverage territory." The Commercial Liability Umbrella Policy provides worldwide coverage for bodily injury or property damage caused by an occurrence. This endorsement limits the coverage territory to that as defined on the CGL form, CG 00 01. There are two other endorsements in this vein: CU 24 33 04 13, Limited Coverage Territory – Additional Scheduled Countries, and CU 24 35 04 13, Amendment of Coverage Territory – Worldwide Coverage with Specified Exceptions. CU 24 33 defines "coverage territory" the same as CU 24 32, but then allows the insured to add specified additional countries; so, the coverage territory is basically extended to include any countries listed in the schedule of the endorsement. CU 24 35 amends the worldwide coverage provided in the umbrella policy to preclude specific countries listed in the schedule; in other words, the coverage territory is worldwide except for those countries specified in the schedule on the endorsement.

CU 24 36 12 05, Products-Completed Operations Aggregate Limit of Insurance, is an optional endorsement that provides a separate aggregate limit for the products-completed operations hazard. The umbrella policy contains a single aggregate limit that applies to all ultimate net loss under coverage A (bodily injury and property damage liability), and coverage B (personal and advertising injury liability). CU 24 36 12 05 provides a separate aggregate limit that will apply to all ultimate net loss under coverage A for damages because of bodily injury or property damage included in the products-completed operations hazard.

CU 24 37 12 05, Non-Concurrency of Policy Periods – Retained Limit, is a mandatory endorsement that revises the limits of insurance clause in the umbrella policy. This clause does not address how the retained limit is impacted when underlying insurance is reduced or exhausted by occurrences that occur prior to the policy period of CU 00 01. CU 24 37 revises the clause to indicate that if there is underlying insurance with a policy period that is not concurrent with the policy period of the umbrella policy, then the retained limit will only be reduced or exhausted if the injury or damage occurred or was committed during the policy period of the umbrella policy. If the policy period of the underlying insurance is not concurrent with the policy period of the umbrella policy, this may mean a reduction in coverage.

CU 27 10 04 13, Extended Reporting Period Endorsement for Employee Benefits Liability Coverage, applies to the employee benefits liability coverage endorsement, noted previously. CU 27 10 simply provides an extended period during which a claim may be made under the employee benefits endorsement. CU 27 10 will not take effect unless the additional premium for it is paid when due.

Chapter 9

Commercial Excess Liability Coverage Form

Insurance Services Office (ISO) has developed the Commercial Excess Liability Coverage Form, CX 00 01 04 13, which was introduced as a part of the commercial umbrella liability program. The form was designed to sit atop various ISO and independent company policies, including general liability, commercial auto, employers liability, and businessowners. CX 00 01 declares that coverage will follow the same provisions, exclusions, and limitations that are contained in the applicable "controlling underlying insurance" (a defined term), unless otherwise directed by the excess coverage form. Moreover, the coverage provided by CX 00 01 will not be broader than that provided by the applicable controlling underlying insurance.

This chapter offers a general overview of CX 00 01. The coverages, exclusions, conditions, and definitions of the form are noted and analyzed.

Section I—Coverages

1. Insuring Agreement

   a. We will pay on behalf of the insured the "ultimate net loss" in excess of the "retained limit" because of "injury or damage" to which insurance provided under this Coverage Part applies.

      We will have the right and duty to defend the insured against any suit seeking damages for such "injury or damage" when the applicable limits of "controlling underlying insurance" have been exhausted in accordance with the provisions of such "controlling underlying insurance".

      When we have no duty to defend, we will have the right to defend, or to participate in the defense of, the insured against any other suit seeking damages for "injury or damage". However, we will have no duty to defend the insured against any suit seeking damages for which insurance under this policy does not apply.

343

At our discretion, we may investigate any "event" that may involve this insurance and settle any resultant claim or suit, for which we have the duty to defend.

But:

(1) The amount we will pay for "ultimate net loss" is limited as described in Section II – Limits Of Insurance; and

(2) Our right and duty to defend ends when we have used up the applicable limit of insurance in the payment of judgments or settlements under this Coverage Part. However, if the policy of "controlling underlying insurance" specifies that limits are reduced by defense expenses, our right and duty to defend ends when we have used up the applicable limit of insurance in the payment of defense expenses, judgments or settlements under this Coverage Part.

b. This insurance applies to "injury or damage" that is subject to an applicable "retained limit". If any other limit, such as a sublimit, is specified in the "controlling underlying insurance", this insurance does not apply to "injury or damage" arising out of that exposure unless that limit is specified in the Declarations under the Schedule of "controlling underlying insurance".

c. If the "controlling underlying insurance" requires, for a particular claim, that the "injury or damage" occur during its policy period in order for that coverage to apply, then this insurance will only apply to that "injury or damage" if it occurs during the policy period of this Coverage Part. If the "controlling underlying insurance" requires that the "event" causing the particular "injury or damage" takes place during its policy period in order for that coverage to apply, then this insurance will apply to the claim only if the "event" causing that "injury or damage" takes place during the policy period of this Coverage Part.

d. Any additional insured under any policy of "controlling underlying insurance" will automatically be an additional insured under this insurance. If coverage provided to the additional insured is required by a contract or agreement, the most we will pay on behalf of the additional insured is the amount of insurance required by the contract, less any amounts payable by any "controlling underlying insurance".

Additional insured coverage provided by this insurance will not be broader than coverage provided by the "controlling underlying insurance".

Analysis

The insuring agreement explains that the insured agrees to pay on behalf of the insured the ultimate net loss (that is, the total sum, after reduction for recoveries, or salvages collectible, that the insured becomes legally obligated to pay as damages by reason of settlements, judgments, binding arbitration, or any other binding alternate dispute resolution proceeding entered into with the insurer's consent). The ultimate net loss includes defense expenses if the underlying insurance specifies that limits are reduced by defense expenses.

This portion of the policy also describes when the insured has a right and duty to defend the insured. The insurer has a right to defend against any suit seeking damages for injury or damage when the applicable limits of the controlling underlying insurance have been exhausted. When the insurer has no duty to defend, it will still have the right to defend, or to participate in the defense of, the insured against any other suit seeking damages. The insurer, of course, has no duty to defend the insured against any suit seeking damages for which insurance under excess liability coverage does not apply. The policy also gives the insurer the right to investigate any occurrence, offense, accident, act, or other event, to which the applicable controlling underlying insurance applies.

Section I also explains that the insurance applies to injury or damage subject to an applicable retained limit (the available limits of controlling underlying insurance applicable to the claim).

The insuring agreement refers to both when "injury or damage" occur, and when the "event causing the particular injury or damage" takes place; both, of course are required to happen during the policy period of both the underlying insurance and the excess liability coverage form. In other words, if the underlying insurance requires that the injury occur during the policy period in order for its coverage to apply, the excess policy does likewise and will only apply to the injury that occurs during the excess policy period. If the underlying insurance will apply if the event causing the injury occurs during its policy period, and not the actual injury itself, the excess policy coverage will apply to the claim only if the event takes place during its policy period.

CX 00 01 also provides that additional insureds listed on the controlling underlying insurance are automatically considered additional insureds under the excess policy. The excess coverage will not be any broader than it is under the controlling underlying insurance. Note that if coverage provided to the additional insured is required by a contract or agreement, the most the excess insurer will pay on behalf of the additional insured is the amount required by the contract (less any amounts payable by a controlling underlying insurance). In other words, the excess insurer is making its coverage amount for additional insureds contingent on what is being required in a contract or agreement, so the coverage amount should be clearly listed and understood by the parties involved in the agreement.

2.   Exclusions

The following exclusions, and any other exclusions added by endorsement, apply to this Coverage Part. In addition, the exclusions applicable to any "controlling underlying insurance" apply to this insurance unless superseded by the following exclusions, or superseded by any other exclusions added by endorsement to this Coverage Part.

Insurance provided under this Coverage Part does not apply to:

a.   Medical Payments

Medical payments coverage or expenses that are provided without regard to fault, whether or not provided by the applicable "controlling underlying insurance".

b.   Auto

Any loss, cost or expense payable under or resulting from any of the following auto coverages:

(1) First-party physical damage coverage;

(2) No-fault coverage;

(3) Personal injury protection or auto medical payments coverage; or

(4) Uninsured or underinsured motorists coverage.

c.   Pollution

(1) "Injury or damage" which would not have occurred, in whole or in part, but for the actual, alleged or

threatened discharge, dispersal, seepage, migration, release or escape of pollutants at any time.

(2) Any loss, cost or expense arising out of any:

(a) Request, demand, order or statutory or regulatory requirement that any insured or others test for, monitor, clean up, remove, contain, treat, detoxify or neutralize, or in any way respond to, or assess the effects of, pollutants; or

(b) Claim or suit by or on behalf of a governmental authority for damages because of testing for, monitoring, cleaning up, removing, containing, treating, detoxifying or neutralizing, or in any way responding to, or assessing the effects of, pollutants.

This exclusion does not apply to the extent that valid "controlling underlying insurance" for the pollution liability risks described above exists or would have existed but for the exhaustion of underlying limits for "injury or damage". Medical payments coverage or expenses that are provided without regard to fault, whether or not provided by the applicable "controlling underlying insurance".

d. Workers' Compensation and Similar Laws

Any obligation of the insured under a workers' compensation, disability benefits or unemployment compensation law or any similar law.

Analysis

The exclusions section of CX 00 01 notes that the exclusions applicable to any controlling underlying insurance also apply to the excess coverage; in other words, the excess liability policy can be said to "follow form". This is so, unless the exclusions listed in CX 00 01 supersede those in the underlying insurance.

Note that CX 00 01 does not provide medical payments regardless of whether the underlying insurance does so.

The auto exclusion in CX 00 01 precludes coverage for auto physical damage coverage, no-fault coverage, personal injury protection coverage, and uninsured/underinsured motorists coverage, just like the commercial liability umbrella coverage form, CU 00 01.

The pollution exclusion is an absolute pollution exclusion with no stated exceptions. The exclusion uses the "would not have occurred but for ..." language to reinforce its total nature. And yet, CX 00 01 then declares that, if controlling underlying coverage exists for pollution liability, its pollution exclusion does not apply to that extent.

Section II—Limits of Insurance

1. The Limits of Insurance shown in the Declarations, and the rules below fix the most we will pay regardless of the number of:

   a. Insureds;

   b. Claims made or suits brought, or number of vehicles involved;

   c. Persons or organizations making claims or bringing suits; or

   d. Limits available under any "controlling underlying insurance".

2. The Limits of Insurance of this Coverage Part will apply as follows:

   a. This insurance only applies in excess of the "retained limit".

   b. The Aggregate Limit is the most we will pay for the sum of all "ultimate net loss", for all "injury or damage" covered under this Coverage Part.

      However, this Aggregate Limit only applies to "injury or damage" that is subject to an aggregate limit of insurance under the "controlling underlying insurance".

   c. Subject to Paragraph 2.b. above, the Each Occurrence Limit is the most we will pay for the sum of all "ultimate net loss" under this insurance because of all "injury or damage: arising out of any one "event".

   d. If the Limits of Insurance of the "controlling underlying insurance" are reduced by defense expenses by the terms of that policy, any payments for defense expenses we will make will reduce our applicable Limits of Insurance in the same manner.

3. If any "controlling underlying insurance" has a policy period that is different from the policy period of this Coverage Part then, for

the purposes of this insurance, the "retained limit" will only be reduced or exhausted by payments made for "injury or damage" covered under this insurance.

The Aggregate Limit of this Coverage Part applies separately to each consecutive annual period of this Coverage Part and to any remaining period of this Coverage Part of less than twelve months, starting with the beginning of the policy period shown in the Declarations, unless the policy period is extended after issuance for an additional period of less than twelve months. In that case, the additional period will be deemed part of the last preceding period for purposes of determining the Limits of Insurance.

Analysis

This section of the policy establishes the most that the insurer will pay for a claim or lawsuit against the insured; and, in keeping with the excess coverage afforded by CX 00 01, the insurance only applies in excess of the retained limit (the available limits of controlling underlying insurance applicable to the claim). The limits that are set on the declarations page of the excess liability policy will not be exceeded regardless of the number of insureds, claims, or number of vehicles involved.

The limits of insurance section notes that the policy has an aggregate limit and an each occurrence limit. The aggregate limit is the sum of all ultimate net loss covered under the policy. Note that this limit only applies to injury or damage that is subject to an aggregate limit of insurance under the controlling underlying insurance. In other words, the injury or damage has to be subject to an aggregate limit in the underlying insurance policy before the aggregate limit in CX 00 01 comes into play.

The each occurrence limit simply points out that that is the most the excess insurer will pay because of all injury or damage arising out of any one event. In other words, if the excess policy has an aggregate limit of $2 million and an each occurrence limit of $500,000, the $500,000 is the most the policy will pay for all injuries and damages arising out of one event. Then, if three more, separate occurrences happen, the most that would be paid for those separate occurrences would be $500,000 each. If those separate occurrences eventually add up to the $2 million aggregate, the insured will be on his own when it comes to paying the claims.

As for defense expenses, if the underlying insurance policy states that defense costs reduce the stated limits of insurance on that policy, the excess policy will follow suit.

Section III—Conditions

The following conditions apply. In addition, the conditions applicable to any "controlling underlying insurance" are also applicable to the coverage provided under this insurance unless superseded by the following conditions.

1.   Appeals

If the "controlling underlying insurer" or insured elects not to appeal a judgment in excess of the "retained limit", we may do so at our own expense. We will also pay for taxable court costs, pre- and post- judgment interest and disbursements associated with such appeal. In no event will this provision increase our liability beyond the applicable Limits of Insurance described in Section II-Limits of Insurance.

2.   Bankruptcy

a.   Bankruptcy of Insured

Bankruptcy or insolvency of the insured or of the insured's estate will not relieve us of our obligations under this Coverage Part.

b.   Bankruptcy of Controlling Underlying Insurer

Bankruptcy or insolvency of the "controlling underlying insurer" will not relieve us of our obligations under this Coverage Part.

However, insurance provided under this Coverage Part will not replace any "controlling underlying insurance" in the event of bankruptcy or insolvency of the "controlling under-lying insurer". This insurance provided under this Coverage Part will apply as if the "controlling underlying insurance" were in full effect and recoverable.

3.   Duties In the Event of an Event, Claim or Suit

a.   You must see to it that we are notified as soon as practicable of an "event", regardless of the amount, which may result in a claim under this insurance. To the extent possible, notice should include:

(1)   How, when and where the "event" took place;

(2) The names and addresses of any injured persons and witnesses; and

(3) The nature and location of any "injury or damage" arising out of the "event".

b. If a claim is made or suit is brought against any insured, you must:

(1) Immediately record the specifics of the claim or suit and the date received; and

(2) Notify us as soon as practicable.

You must see to it that we receive written notice of the claim or suit as soon as practicable.

c. You and any other insured involved must:

(1) Immediately send us copies of any demands, notices, summonses or legal papers received in connection with the claim or suit;

(2) Authorize us to obtain records and other information;

(3) Cooperate with us in the investigation or settlement of the claim or defense against the suit; and

(4) Assist us, upon our request, in the enforcement of any right against any person or organization which may be liable to the insured because of "injury or damage" to which this insurance may also apply.

d. No insured will, except at that insured's own cost, voluntarily make a payment, assume any obligation, or incur any expense, other than for first aid, without our consent.

Analysis

CX 00 01 offers many of the same conditions as the CGL policy and the commercial umbrella policy.

Among the conditions listed is the bankruptcy provision, which explains that the policy will not relieve the insurer of its obligations under the excess policy in the event the controlling underlying insurer (or the insured) becomes insolvent or goes bankrupt. This clause also declares that the bankruptcy of the underlying insurer does not mean that the excess insurer will replace the controlling underlying insurance; the excess insurance will apply as if the controlling underlying insurance were in full effect and recoverable. In other words, the excess insurer is saying that its policy is not intended to drop down and take the place of the underlying insurer in case the underlying insurer files for bankruptcy or becomes insolvent.

The policy also affords the insurer the right to appeal judgments, in excess of the limits of underlying insurance, even if the controlling underlying insurer or the insured chooses not to appeal. The excess insurer agrees to pay for the expenses of such an appeal, along with taxable costs, prejudgment and post judgment interest, and disbursements associated with the appeal; these agreed-upon payments will not increase the excess insurer's liability beyond the applicable limits stated in the limits of insurance section of the policy.

Another provision here explains the specific duties of the insured in case of an event (an occurrence, offense, accident, or act to which the applicable controlling underlying insurance applies) that may result in a claim under CX 00 01. These include the duty to notify the insurer of an event as soon as practicable (a term that usually has to be determined by a court based on the facts of the situation), and the duty to refrain from making voluntary payments without the insurer's consent.

4. First Named Insured Duties

The first Named Insured is the person or organization first named in the Declarations and is responsible for the payment of all premiums. The first Named Insured will act on behalf of all other Named Insureds for giving and receiving of notice of cancellation or the receipt of any return premium that may become payable.

At our request, the first Named Insured will furnish us, as soon as practicable, with a complete copy of any "controlling underlying insurance" and any subsequently issued endorsements or policies which may in any way affect the insurance provided under this Coverage Part.

5. Cancellation

a. The first Named Insured shown in the Declarations may cancel this policy by mailing or delivering to us advance written notice of cancellation.

b.   We may cancel this policy by mailing or delivering to the first Named Insured written notice of cancellation at least:

(1)   10 days before the effective date of cancellation if we cancel for nonpayment of premium; or

(2)   30 days before the effective date of cancellation if we cancel for any other reason.

c.   We will mail or deliver our notice to the first Named Insured's last mailing address known to us.

d.   Notice of cancellation will state the effective date of cancellation. The policy period will end on that date.

e.   If this policy is cancelled, we will send the first Named Insured any premium refund due. If we cancel, the refund will be pro rata. If the first Named Insured cancels, the refund may be less than pro rata. The cancellation will be effective even if we have not made or offered a refund.

f.   If notice is mailed, proof of mailing will be sufficient proof of notice.

6.   Changes

This Coverage Part contains all the agreements between you and us concerning the insurance afforded. The first Named Insured is authorized by all other insureds to make changes in the terms of this Coverage Part with our consent. This Coverage Part's terms can be amended or waived only by endorsement.

7.   Maintenance of/Changes to Controlling Underlying Insurance

Any "controlling underlying insurance" must be maintained in full effect without reduction of coverage or limits except for the reduction of aggregate limits in accordance with the provisions of such "controlling underlying insurance" that results from "injury or damage" to which this insurance applies.

Such exhaustion or reduction is not a failure to maintain "controlling underlying insurance". Failure to maintain "controlling underlying insurance" will not invalidate insurance provided under this coverage Part, but insurance provided under this Coverage Part will apply as if the "controlling underlying insurance" were in full effect.

The first Named Insured must notify us in writing, as soon as practicable, if any "controlling underlying insurance" is cancelled, not renewed, replaced or otherwise terminated, or if the limits or scope of coverage of any "controlling underlying insurance" is changed.

8. Other Insurance

a. This insurance is excess over, and shall not contribute with any other insurance, whether primary, excess, contingent or on any other basis. This condition will not apply to insurance specifically written as excess over this Coverage Part.

When this insurance is excess, if no other insurer defends, we may undertake to do so, but we will be entitled to the insured's rights against all those other insurers.

b. When this insurance is excess over other insurance, we will pay only our share of the "ultimate net loss" that exceeds the sum of:

(1) The total amount that all such other insurance would pay for the loss in the absence of the insurance provided under this Coverage Part; and

(2) The total of all deductibles and self-insured amounts under all that other insurance.

Analysis

Note that CX 00 01 specifically sets out duties for the first named insured. The excess policy has already listed other duties for "you", a term that CX 00 01 has already identified as the named insured shown in the declarations; however, for whatever reasons, CX 00 01 goes on to specify duties for the first named insured. These duties include being responsible for the payment of all premiums and the giving and receiving of notice of cancellation. (These duties for the first named insured are usually found in the common policy conditions form, IL 00 17.) The first named insured also has the duty, upon a request from the excess insurer, to furnish to the excess insurer a complete copy of any controlling underlying insurance and any subsequently issued endorsements that may affect the coverage provided by CX 00 01. (There is no provision here that spells out the consequences for coverage if the first named insured does not have a complete copy of the underlying insurance policy.)

Note that the cancellation and changes conditions single out the actions that the first named insured may take under the terms of this excess policy; again, the actions usually listed in IL 00 17.

Another provision requires the maintenance of underlying insurance. Failure to maintain controlling underlying insurance will not invalidate the excess policy coverage, but the excess insurer will apply the insurance of the excess policy as if the controlling underlying insurance were in full effect (in other words, no drop down). The first named insured has the duty to notify the excess insurer in writing, as soon as practicable, if any controlling underlying insurance is cancelled, not renewed, or terminated, or if the limits or scope of coverage of any controlling underlying insurance is changed.

The other insurance clause makes the points that CX 00 01 is excess over any other insurance, but if no other insurer defends the insured, the excess insurer may undertake that duty. In such an instance, the insured's rights against the other insurer(s) pass on to the excess insurer.

9.   Premium Audit.

    a.   We will compute all premiums for this Coverage Part in accordance with our rules and rates.

    b.   If this policy is auditable, the premium shown in this Coverage Part as advance premium is a deposit premium only. At the close of each audit period, we will compute the earned premium for that period and send notice to the first Named Insured. The due date for audit premium is the date shown as the due date on the bill. If the sum of the advance and audit premiums paid for the policy period is greater than the earned premium, we will return the excess to the first Named Insured.

    c.   The first Named Insured must keep records of the information we need for premium computation, and send us copies at such times as we may request.

10. Loss Payable

Liability under this Coverage Part does not apply to a given claim unless and until:

    a.   The insured or insured's "controlling underlying insurer" has become obligated to pay the "retained limit"; and

b.   The obligation of the insured to pay the "ultimate net loss" in excess of the retained limit" has been determined by a final settlement or judgment or written agreement among the insured, claimant, "controlling underlying insurer" (or a representative of one or more of these) and us.

11. Legal Action against Us

No person or organization has a right under this Coverage Part:

a.   To join us as a party or otherwise bring us into a suit asking for damages from an insured; or

b.   To sue us on this Coverage Part unless all of its terms have been fully complied with.

A person or organization may sue us to recover on an agreed settlement or on a final judgment against an insured; but we will not be liable for damages that are not payable under the terms of this Coverage Part or that are in excess of the applicable limit of insurance. An agreed settlement means a settlement and release of liability signed by us, the insured, "controlling underlying insurer" and the claimant or the claimant's legal representative.

12. Transfer of Defense

a.   Defense Transferred to Us

When the limits of "controlling underlying insurance" have been exhausted, in accordance with the provisions of "controlling underlying insurance", we may elect to have the defense transferred to us. We will cooperate in the transfer of control to us of any outstanding claims or suits seeking damages to which this insurance applies which would have been covered by the "controlling underlying insurance" had the applicable limit not been exhausted.

b.   Defense Transferred by Us

When our limits of insurance have been exhausted our duty to provide a defense will cease.

We will cooperate in the transfer of control of defense to any insurer specifically written as excess over this Coverage Part of any outstanding claims or suits seeking damages to which this insurance applies and which would have been covered by the "controlling underlying insurance" had the applicable limit not been exhausted.

In the event that there is no insurance written as excess over this Coverage Part, we will cooperate in the transfer of control to the insured and its designated representative.

13. When We Do Not Renew

If we decide not to renew this Coverage Part, we will mail or deliver to the first Named Insured shown in the Declarations written notice of the nonrenewal not less than thirty days before the expiration date.

If notice is mailed, proof of mailing will be sufficient proof of notice.

Analysis

The premium audit condition is standard wording.

The loss payable condition declares that CX 00 01 is not going to apply to a given claim unless and until the insured or the insured's controlling underlying insurer has become obligated to pay the retained limit (the available limits of controlling underlying insurance applicable to the claim). Furthermore, the obligation of the insured to pay the ultimate net loss in excess of the retained limit has to be determined by a final judgment (after any appeal has been answered) or written agreement among the parties to the event, that is, the insured, the claimant, the controlling underlying insurer, and the excess insurer.

Of note is the provision stating that when the controlling underlying limits of insurance have been exhausted in the payment of judgments or settlements, the excess insurer may elect to have the defense transferred to it. The controlling underlying insurance policy has a declaration that its duty to defend ends when the applicable limit of insurance is used up, so this particular provision tells the insured that his defense is still being handled by an insurer.

The transfer of defense condition also states that when the excess insurer's limits of insurance have been exhausted, its duty to provide a defense ends. The excess insurer does promise to cooperate in the transfer of control of defense to any insurer specifically written as excess over CX 00 01.

If there is no insurance written as excess, the insurer agrees to cooperate in the transfer of control to the insured and its designated representative.

Section IV—Definitions

The definitions applicable to any "controlling underlying insurance" also apply to this insurance. In addition, the following definitions apply.

1. "Controlling underlying insurance" means any policy of insurance or self-insurance listed in the Declarations under the Schedule of "controlling underlying insurance".

2. "Controlling underlying insurer" means any insurer who provides any policy of insurance listed in the Declarations under the Schedule of "controlling underlying insurance".

3. "Event" means an occurrence, offense, accident, act, or other event, to which the applicable "controlling underlying insurance" applies.

4. "Injury or Damage" means any injury or damage covered in the applicable "controlling underlying insurance" arising from an "event".

5. "Retained limit" means the available limits of "controlling underlying insurance" applicable to the claim.

6. "Ultimate net loss" means the total sum, after reduction for recoveries, or salvages collectible, that the insured becomes legally obligated to pay as damages by reason of:

    a. Settlements, judgments, binding arbitration; or

    b. Other binding alternate dispute resolution proceeding entered into with our consent.

        "Ultimate net loss" includes defense expenses if the "controlling underlying insurance" specifies that limits are reduced by defense expenses.

Analysis

CX 00 01 notes at the beginning of its definitions section that the definitions applicable to any controlling underlying insurance also apply to CX 00 01. So, terms like "bodily injury", "employee", "property damage", "pollutants", and "your product" have the same meaning in the excess policy as they do in the underlying insurance policy.

The controlling underlying insurance is any policy of insurance or self-insurance listed in the declarations of CX 00 01. This would include policies like the general liability policy and the auto policy.

Note that the 2013 edition of CX 00 01 revised the definition of "event" to remove the word "occurrence" from quotation marks. The word "occurrence" is not a defined term on CX 00 01.

CX 00 01 applies to the ultimate net loss. As noted previously, the ultimate net loss means the total sum, after reduction for recoveries, or salvages collectible, that the insured becomes legally obligated to pay as damages by reason of settlements, judgments, binding arbitration, or other binding alternate dispute resolution proceeding entered into with the consent of the excess insurer. So, CX 00 01 will pay the amount that the insured owes for a claim in excess of the amount retained by the insured, either through an underlying insurance policy or through self-insurance.

Appendices

A: CG Policy Jacket Provisions

   1973 Comprehensive General Liability Form

   Broad Form endorsement

B: 1986 Occurrence Coverage Form

   1986 Claims-Made Coverage Form

C: 1990 Occurrence Coverage Form

   1990 Claims-Made Coverage Form

D: 1992 Changes in Commercial General Liability Coverage Form Endorsement

E: 1993 Occurrence Coverage Form

   1993 Claims-Made Coverage Form

F: 1996 Occurrence Coverage Form

   1996 Claims-Made Coverage Form

G: 1998 Occurrence Coverage Form

   1998 Claims-Made Coverage Form

H: 2001 Occurrence Coverage Form

   2001 Claims-Made Coverage Form

I: 2004 Occurrence Coverage Form

   2004 Claims-Made Coverage Form

J: 2007 Occurrence Coverage Form

   2007 Claims-Made Coverage Form

K: 2013 Occurrence Coverage Form

   2013 Claims-Made Coverage Form

L: CGL Declarations

M: Common Policy Conditions

N: Commercial Liability Umbrella Coverage Form

O: Commercial Excess Liability Coverage Form

GENERAL INSURING AGREEMENT

In consideration of the payment of the premium, in reliance upon the statements in the declarations made a part hereof and subject to all of the terms of this policy, the company agrees with the named insured as follows:

1. This policy is composed of this jacket, the declarations page with the applicable Coverage Parts, and any supplementary declarations or schedule pages and endorsements made a part hereof;
2. The provisions of one Coverage Part do not apply to the insurance afforded under any other Coverage Part.

SUPPLEMENTARY PAYMENTS

The company will pay, in addition to the applicable limit of liability:

(a) all expenses incurred by the company, all costs taxed against the insured in any suit defended by the company and all interest on the entire amount of any judgment therein which accrues after entry of the judgment and before the company has paid or tendered or deposited in court that part of the judgment which does not exceed the limit of the company's liability thereon;

(b) premiums on appeal bonds required in any such suit, premiums on bonds to release attachments in any such suit for an amount not in excess of the applicable limit of liability of this policy, and the cost of bail bonds required of the insured because of accident or traffic law violation arising out of the use of any vehicle to which this policy applies, not to exceed $250 per bail bond, but the company shall have no obligation to apply for or furnish any such bonds;

(c) expenses incurred by the insured for first aid to others, at the time of an accident, for bodily injury to which this policy applies;

(d) reasonable expenses incurred by the insured at the company's request in assisting the company in the investigation or defense of any claim or suit, including actual loss of earnings not to exceed $25 per day.

DEFINITIONS

When used in this policy:

"**automobile**" means a land motor vehicle, trailer or semi-trailer designed for travel on public roads (including any machinery or apparatus attached thereto), but does not include mobile equipment;

"**bodily injury**" means bodily injury, sickness or disease sustained by any person which occurs during the policy period, including death at any time resulting therefrom;

"**completed operations hazard**" includes bodily injury and property damage arising out of operations or reliance upon a representation or warranty made at any time with respect thereto, but only if the bodily injury or property damage occurs after such operations have been completed or abandoned and occurs away from premises owned by or rented to the named insured. "Operations" include materials, parts or equipment furnished in connection therewith. Operations shall be deemed completed at the earliest of the following times:

(1) when all operations to be performed by or on behalf of the named insured under the contract have been completed,

(2) when all operations to be performed by or on behalf of the named insured at the site of the operations have been completed, or

(3) when the portion of the work out of which the injury or damage arises has been put to its intended use by any person or organization other than another contractor or subcontractor engaged in performing operations for a principal as a part of the same project.

Operations which may require further service or maintenance work, or correction, repair or replacement because of any defect or deficiency, but which are otherwise complete, shall be deemed completed.

The completed operations hazard does not include bodily injury or property damage arising out of

(a) operations in connection with the transportation of property, unless the bodily injury or property damage arises out of a condition in or on a vehicle created by the loading or unloading thereof,

(b) the existence of tools, uninstalled equipment or abandoned or unused materials, or

(c) operations for which the classification stated in the policy or in the company's manual specifies "including completed operations";

"**elevator**" means any hoisting or lowering device to connect floors or landings, whether or not in service, and all appliances thereof including any car, platform, shaft, hoistway, stairway, runway, power equipment and machinery; but does not include an automobile servicing hoist, or a hoist without a platform outside a building if without mechanical power or if not attached to building walls, or a hod or material hoist used in alteration, construction or demolition operations, or an inclined conveyor used exclusively for carrying property or a dumbwaiter used exclusively for carrying property and having a compartment height not exceeding four feet;

"**incidental contract**" means any written

(1) lease of premises,

(2) easement agreement, except in connection with construction or demolition operations on or adjacent to a railroad,

(3) undertaking to indemnify a municipality required by municipal ordinance, except in connection with work for the municipality,

(4) sidetrack agreement, or

(5) elevator maintenance agreement;

"**insured**" means any person or organization qualifying as an insured in the "Persons Insured" provision of the applicable insurance coverage. The insurance afforded applies separately to each insured against whom claim is made or suit is brought, except with respect to the limits of the company's liability;

"**mobile equipment**" means a land vehicle (including any machinery or apparatus attached thereto), whether or not self-propelled,

(1) not subject to motor vehicle registration, or

(2) maintained for use exclusively on premises owned by or rented to the named insured, including the ways immediately adjoining, or

(3) designed for use principally off public roads, or

(4) designed or maintained for the sole purpose of affording mobility to equipment of the following types forming an integral part of or permanently attached to such vehicle: power cranes, shovels, loaders, diggers and drills; concrete mixers (other than the mix-in-transit type); graders, scrapers, rollers and other road construction or repair equipment; air-compressors, pumps and generators, including spraying, welding and building cleaning equipment; and geophysical exploration and well servicing equipment;

"**named insured**" means the person or organization named in Item 1 of the declarations of this policy;

"**named insured's products**" means goods or products manufactured, sold, handled or distributed by the named insured or by others trading under his name, including any container thereof (other than a vehicle), but "named insured's products" shall not include a vending machine or any property other than such container, rented to or located for use of others but not sold;

"**occurrence**" means an accident, including continuous or repeated exposure to conditions, which results in bodily injury or property damage neither expected nor intended from the standpoint of the insured;

"**policy territory**" means,

(1) the United States of America, its territories or possessions, or Canada, or

(2) international waters or air space, provided the bodily injury or property damage does not occur in the course of travel or transportation to or from any other country, state or nation, or

(3) anywhere in the world with respect to damages because of bodily injury or property damage arising out of a product which was sold for use or consumption within the territory described in paragraph (1) above, provided the original suit for such damages is brought within such territory;

"**products hazard**" includes bodily injury and property damage arising out of the named insured's products or reliance upon a representation or warranty made at any time with respect thereto, but only if the bodily injury or property damage occurs away from premises owned by or rented to the named insured and after physical possession of such products has been relinquished to others;

"**property damage**" means (1) physical injury to or destruction of tangible property which occurs during the policy period, including the loss of use thereof at any time resulting therefrom, or (2) loss of use of tangible property which has not been physically injured or destroyed provided such loss of use is caused by an occurrence during the policy period;

CONDITIONS

1. Premium. All premiums for this policy shall be computed in accordance with the company's rules, rates, rating plans, premiums and minimum premiums applicable to the insurance afforded herein.

Premium designated in this policy as "advance premium" is a deposit premium only which shall be credited to the amount of the earned premium due at the end of the policy period. At the close of each period (or part thereof terminating with the end of the policy period) designated in the declarations as the audit period the earned premium shall be computed for such period and, upon notice thereof to the named insured, shall become due and payable. If the total earned premium for the policy period is less than the premium previously paid, the company shall return to the named insured the unearned portion paid by the named insured.

The named insured shall maintain records of such information as is necessary for premium computation, and shall send copies of such records to the company at the end of the policy period and at such times during the policy period as the company may direct.

2. Inspection and Audit. The company shall be permitted but not obligated to inspect the named insured's property and operations at any time. Neither the company's right to make inspections nor the making thereof nor any report thereon shall constitute an undertaking, on behalf of or for the benefit of the named insured or others, to determine or warrant that such property or operations are safe or healthful, or are in compliance with any law, rule or regulation.

The company may examine and audit the named insured's books and records at any time during the policy period and extensions thereof and within three years after the final termination of this policy, as far as they relate to the subject matter of this insurance.

(Conditions are continued on Jacket Page 2)

JACKET PAGE 2

CONDITIONS (Continued)

3. Financial Responsibility Laws. When this policy is certified as proof of financial responsibility for the future under the provisions of any motor vehicle financial responsibility law, such insurance as is afforded by this policy for bodily injury liability or for property damage liability shall comply with the provisions of such law to the extent of the coverage and limits of liability required by such law. The insured agrees to reimburse the company for any payment made by the company which it would not have been obligated to make under the terms of this policy except for the agreement contained in this paragraph.

4. Insured's Duties in the Event of Occurrence, Claim or Suit. (a) In the event of an occurrence, written notice containing particulars sufficient to identify the insured and also reasonably obtainable information with respect to the time, place and circumstances thereof, and the names and addresses of the injured and of available witnesses, shall be given by or for the insured to the company or any of its authorized agents as soon as practicable.

(b) If claim is made or suit is brought against the insured, the insured shall immediately forward to the company every demand, notice, summons or other process received by him or his representative.

(c) The insured shall cooperate with the company and, upon the company's request, assist in making settlements, in the conduct of suits and in enforcing any right of contribution or indemnity against any person or organization who may be liable to the insured because of injury or damage with respect to which insurance is afforded under this policy; and the insured shall attend hearings and trials and assist in securing and giving evidence and obtaining the attendance of witnesses. The insured shall not, except at his own cost, voluntarily make any payment, assume any obligation or incur any expense other than for first aid to others at the time of accident.

5. Action Against Company. No action shall lie against the company unless, as a condition precedent thereto, there shall have been full compliance with all of the terms of this policy, nor until the amount of the insured's obligation to pay shall have been finally determined either by judgment against the insured after actual trial or by written agreement of the insured, the claimant and the company.

Any person or organization or the legal representative thereof who has secured such judgment or written agreement shall thereafter be entitled to recover under this policy to the extent of the insurance afforded by this policy. No person or organization shall have any right under this policy to join the company as a party to any action against the insured to determine the insured's liability, nor shall the company be impleaded by the insured or his legal representative. Bankruptcy or insolvency of the insured or of the insured's estate shall not relieve the company of any of its obligations hereunder.

6. Other Insurance. The insurance afforded by this policy is primary insurance, except when stated to apply in excess of or contingent upon the absence of other insurance. When this insurance is primary and the insured has other insurance which is stated to be applicable to the loss on an excess or contingent basis, the amount of the company's liability under this policy shall not be reduced by the existence of such other insurance.

When both this insurance and other insurance apply to the loss on the same basis, whether primary, excess or contingent, the company shall not be liable under this policy for a greater proportion of the loss than that stated in the applicable contribution provision below:

(a) **Contribution by Equal Shares.** If all of such other valid and collectible insurance provides for contribution by equal shares, the company shall not be liable for a greater proportion of such loss than would be payable if each insurer contributes an equal share until the share of each insurer equals the lowest applicable limit of liability under any one policy or the full amount of the loss is paid, and with respect to any amount of loss not so paid the remaining insurers then continue to contribute equal shares of the remaining amount of the loss until each such insurer has paid its limit in full or the full amount of the loss is paid.

(b) **Contribution by Limits.** If any of such other insurance does not provide for contribution by equal shares, the company shall not be liable for a greater proportion of such loss than the applicable limit of liability under this policy for such loss bears to the total applicable limit of liability of all valid and collectible insurance against such loss.

7. Subrogation. In the event of any payment under this policy, the company shall be subrogated to all the insured's rights of recovery therefor against any person or organization and the insured shall execute and deliver instruments and papers and do whatever else is necessary to secure such rights. The insured shall do nothing after loss to prejudice such rights.

8. Changes. Notice to any agent or knowledge possessed by any agent or by any other person shall not effect a waiver or a change in any part of this policy or estop the company from asserting any right under the terms of this policy; nor shall the terms of this policy be waived or changed, except by endorsement issued to form a part of this policy, signed by a duly authorized officer or representative of the company.

9. Assignment. Assignment of interest under this policy shall not bind the company until its consent is endorsed hereon; if, however, the named insured shall die, such insurance as is afforded by this policy shall apply (1) to the named insured's legal representative, as the named insured, but only while acting within the scope of his duties as such, and (2) with respect to the property of the named insured, to the person having proper temporary custody thereof, as insured, but only until the appointment and qualification of the legal representative.

10. Three Year Policy. If this policy is issued for a period of three years any limit of the company's liability stated in this policy as "aggregate" shall apply separately to each consecutive annual period thereof.

11. Cancelation. This policy may be canceled by the named insured by surrender thereof to the company or any of its authorized agents or by mailing to the company written notice stating when thereafter the cancelation shall be effective. This policy may be canceled by the company by mailing to the named insured at the address shown in this policy written notice stating when not less than ten days thereafter such cancelation shall be effective. The mailing of notice as aforesaid shall be sufficient proof of notice. The time of the surrender or the effective date and hour of cancelation stated in the notice shall become the end of the policy period. Delivery of such written notice either by the named insured or by the company shall be equivalent to mailing.

If the named insured cancels, earned premium shall be computed in accordance with the customary short rate table and procedure. If the company cancels, earned premium shall be computed pro-rata. Premium adjustment may be made either at the time cancelation is effected or as soon as practicable after cancelation becomes effective, but payment or tender of unearned premium is not a condition of cancelation.

12. Declarations. By acceptance of this policy, the named insured agrees that the statements in the declarations are his agreements and representations, that this policy is issued in reliance upon the truth of such representations and that this policy embodies all agreements existing between himself and the company or any of its agents relating to this insurance.

As respects the company previously designated, the following correlative provision forms a part of this policy:

This is a perpetual mutual corporation owned by and operated for the benefit of its members. This is a non-assessable, participating policy under which the Board of Directors in its discretion may determine and pay unabsorbed premium deposit refunds (dividends) to the insured.

IN WITNESS WHEREOF, the company designated on the Declarations Page has caused this policy to be signed by its President and Secretary, but this policy shall not be valid unless countersigned on the Declarations Page by a duly authorized representative of the company.

GL 00 02
(Ed. 01-73)

STANDARD COVERAGE PART
COMPREHENSIVE GENERAL LIABILITY INSURANCE

These provisions must be printed or assembled together with the Standard Provisions for General-Automobile Liability Policies to form a complete policy and are subject to the general instructions applicable thereto.

REFERENCE NOTES

1—Matter in brackets may be omitted.

2—The word "policy" may be substituted for the matter in brackets when no other Coverage Part is assembled herewith.

3—Matter in brackets may be omitted from the policy provided the substance is included in an endorsement to be attached to the policy when coverage for the hazard is to be excluded.

4—The word "schedule" should be substituted if the company elects to state limits of liability in the Coverage Part.

5—Matter in brackets may be included, omitted or amended at the option of the company. Such matter may be printed as a separate schedule and made part of the policy by adding the following item to the declarations:

"The declarations are completed on an accompanying schedule designated 'General Liability Hazards'."

GL 00 02
(Ed. 01-73)

[Part 1 _____] ¹
COMPREHENSIVE GENERAL LIABILITY INSURANCE

I. COVERAGE A—BODILY INJURY LIABILITY

COVERAGE B—PROPERTY DAMAGE LIABILITY

The company will pay on behalf of the **insured** all sums which the **insured** shall become legally obligated to pay as damages because of

[Coverage] ¹ A. **bodily injury** or

[Coverage] ¹ B. **property damage**

to which this [insurance] ² applies, caused by an **occurrence**, and the company shall have the right and duty to defend any suit against the **insured** seeking damages on account of such **bodily injury** or **property damage**, even if any of the allegations of the suit are groundless, false or fraudulent, and may make such investigation and settlement of any claim or suit as it deems expedient, but the company shall not be obligated to pay any claim or judgment or to defend any suit after the applicable limit of the company's liability has been exhausted by payment of judgments or settlements.

Exclusions

This [insurance] ² does not apply [under Part _____] ¹:

(a) to liability assumed by the **insured** under any contract or agreement except an **incidental contract**; but this exclusion does not apply to a warranty of fitness or quality of the **named insured's products** or a warranty that work performed by or on behalf of the **named insured** will be done in a workmanlike manner;

(b) to **bodily injury** or **property damage** arising out of the ownership, maintenance, operation, use, loading or unloading of

(1) any **automobile** or aircraft owned or operated by or rented or loaned to any **insured**, or

(2) any other **automobile** or aircraft operated by any person in the course of his employment by any **insured**;

but this exclusion does not apply to the parking of an **automobile** on premises owned by, rented to or controlled by the **named insured** or the ways immediately adjoining, if such **automobile** is not owned by or rented or loaned to any **insured**;

(c) to **bodily injury** or **property damage** arising out of (1) the ownership, maintenance, operation, use, loading or unloading of any **mobile equipment** while being used in any prearranged or organized racing, speed or demolition contest or in any stunting activity or in practice or preparation for any such contest or activity or (2) the operation or use of any snowmobile or trailer designed for use therewith;

(d) to **bodily injury** or **property damage** arising out of and in the course of the transportation of **mobile equipment** by an **automobile** owned or operated by or rented or loaned to any **insured**;

(e) to **bodily injury** or **property damage** arising out of the ownership, maintenance, operation, use, loading or unloading of

(1) any watercraft owned or operated by or rented or loaned to any **insured**, or

(2) any other watercraft operated by any person in the course of his employment by any **insured**;

but this exclusion does not apply to watercraft while ashore on premises owned by, rented to or controlled by the **named insured**;

(f) to **bodily injury** or **property damage** arising out of the discharge, dispersal, release or escape of smoke, vapors, soot, fumes, acids, alkalis, toxic chemicals, liquids or gases, waste materials or other irritants, contaminants or pollutants into or upon land, the atmosphere or any water course or body of water; but this exclusion does not apply if such discharge, dispersal, release or escape is sudden and accidental;

(g) to **bodily injury** or **property damage** due to war, whether or not declared, civil war, insurrection, rebellion or revolution or to any act or condition incident to any of the foregoing, with respect to

(1) liability assumed by the **insured** under an **incidental contract**, or

(2) expenses for first aid under the Supplementary Payments provision;

(h) to **bodily injury** or **property damage** for which the **insured** or his indemnitee may be held liable

(1) as a person or organization engaged in the business of manufacturing, distributing, selling or serving alcoholic beverages, or

(2) if not so engaged, as an owner or lessor of premises used for such purposes,

if such liability is imposed

(i) by, or because of the violation of, any statute, ordinance or regulation pertaining to the sale, gift, distribution or use of any alcoholic beverage, or

(ii) by reason of the selling, serving or giving of any alcoholic beverage to a minor or to a person under the influence of alcohol or which causes or contributes to the intoxication of any person;

but part (ii) of this exclusion does not apply with respect to liability of the **insured** or his indemnitee as an owner or lessor described in (2) above;

(i) to any obligation for which the **insured** or any carrier as his insurer may be held liable under any workmen's compensation, unemployment compensation or disability benefits law, or under any similar law;

(j) to **bodily injury** to any employee of the **insured** arising out of and in the course of his employment by the **insured** or to any obligation of the **insured** to indemnify another because of damages arising out of such injury; but this exclusion does not apply to liability assumed by the **insured** under an **incidental contract**;

(k) to **property damage** to

(1) property owned or occupied by or rented to the **insured**,

(2) property used by the **insured**, or

(3) property in the care, custody or control of the **insured** or as to which the **insured** is for any purpose exercising physical control;

but parts (2) and (3) of this exclusion do not apply with respect to liability under a written sidetrack agreement and part (3) of this exclusion does not apply with respect to **property damage** (other than to **elevators**) arising out of the use of an **elevator** at premises owned by, rented to or controlled by the **named insured**;

(l) to **property damage** to premises alienated by the **named insured** arising out of such premises or any part thereof;

(m) to loss of use of tangible property which has not been physically injured or destroyed resulting from

(1) a delay in or lack of performance by or on behalf of the **named insured** of any contract or agreement, or

(2) the failure of the **named insured's products** or work performed by or on behalf of the **named insured** to meet the level of performance, quality, fitness or durability warranted or represented by the **named insured**;

but this exclusion does not apply to loss of use of other tangible property resulting from the sudden and accidental physical injury to or destruction of the **named insured's products** or work performed by or on behalf of the **named insured** after such products or work have been put to use by any person or organization other than an **insured**;

(n) to **property damage** to the **named insured's products** arising out of such products or any part of such products;

(o) to **property damage** to work performed by or on behalf of the **named insured** arising out of the work or any portion thereof, or out of materials, parts or equipment furnished in connection therewith;

(p) to damages claimed for the withdrawal, inspection, repair, replacement, or loss of use of the **named insured's products** or work completed by or for the **named insured** or of any property of which such products or work form a part, if such products, work or property are withdrawn from the market or from use because of any known or suspected defect or deficiency therein;

[(q) to **property damage** included within:

(1) the **explosion hazard** in connection with operations identified in this policy by a classification code number which includes the symbol "x",

(2) the **collapse hazard** in connection with operations identified in this policy by a classification code number which includes the symbol "c",

GL 00 02
(Ed. 01-73)

(3) the underground property damage hazard in connection with operations identified in this policy by a classification code number which includes the symbol "u".]

II.   PERSONS INSURED

Each of the following is an insured under this [insurance] to the extent set forth below:

(a) if the named insured is designated in the declarations as an individual, the person so designated but only with respect to the conduct of a business of which he is the sole proprietor, and the spouse of the named insured with respect to the conduct of such a business;

(b) if the named insured is designated in the declarations as a partnership or joint venture, the partnership or joint venture so designated and any partner or member thereof but only with respect to his liability as such;

(c) if the named insured is designated in the declarations as other than an individual, partnership or joint venture, the organization so designated and any executive officer, director or stockholder thereof while acting within the scope of his duties as such;

(d) any person (other than an employee of the named insured) or organization while acting as real estate manager for the named insured; and

(e) with respect to the operation, for the purpose of locomotion upon a public highway, of mobile equipment registered under any motor vehicle registration law,

(i) an employee of the named insured while operating any such equipment in the course of his employment, and

(ii) any other person while operating with the permission of the named insured any such equipment registered in the name of the named insured and any person or organization legally responsible for such operation, but only if there is no other valid and collectible insurance available, either on a primary or excess basis, to such person or organization;

provided that no person or organization shall be an insured under this paragraph (e) with respect to:

(1) bodily injury to any fellow employee of such person injured in the course of his employment, or

(2) property damage to property owned by, rented to, in charge of or occupied by the named insured or the employer of any person described in subparagraph (ii).

This insurance does not apply to bodily injury or property damage arising out of the conduct of any partnership or joint venture of which the insured is a partner or member and which is not designated in this policy as a named insured.

III.   LIMITS OF LIABILITY

Regardless of the number of (1) insureds under this policy, (2) persons or organizations who sustain bodily injury or property damage, or (3) claims made or suits brought on account of bodily injury or property damage, the company's liability [under Part ____] is limited as follows:

Coverage A—The total liability of the company for all damages, including damages for care and loss of services, because of bodily injury sustained by one or more persons as the result of any one occurrence shall not exceed the limit of bodily injury liability stated in the [declarations] as applicable to "each occurrence."

Subject to the above provision respecting "each occurrence", the total liability of the company for all damages because of (1) all bodily injury included within the completed operations hazard and (2) all bodily injury included within the products hazard shall not exceed the limit of bodily injury liability stated in the [declarations] as "aggregate".

Coverage B—The total liability of the company for all damages because of all property damage sustained by one or more persons or organizations as the result of any one occurrence shall not exceed the limit of property damage liability stated in the [declarations] as applicable to "each occurrence".

Subject to the above provision respecting "each occurrence", the total liability of the company for all damages because of all property damage to which this coverage applies and described in any of the numbered subparagraphs below shall not exceed the limit of property damage liability stated in the [declarations] as "aggregate":

(1) all property damage arising out of premises or operations rated on a remuneration basis or contractor's equipment rated on a receipts basis, including property damage for which liability is assumed under any incidental contract relating to such premises or operations, but excluding property damage included in subparagraph (2) below;

(2) all property damage arising out of and occurring in the course of operations performed for the named insured by independent contractors and general supervision thereof by the named insured, including any such property damage for which liability is assumed under any incidental contract relating to such operations, but this subparagraph (2) does not include property damage arising out of maintenance or repairs at premises owned by or rented to the named insured or structural alterations at such premises which do not involve changing the size of or moving buildings or other structures;

(3) all property damage included within the products hazard and all property damage included within the completed operations hazard.

Such aggregate limit shall apply separately to the property damage described in subparagraphs (1), (2) and (3) above, and under subparagraphs (1) and (2), separately with respect to each project away from premises owned by or rented to the named insured.

Coverages A and B—For the purpose of determining the limit of the company's liability, all bodily injury and property damage arising out of continuous or repeated exposure to substantially the same general conditions shall be considered as arising out of one occurrence.

IV.   POLICY TERRITORY

This [insurance] applies only to bodily injury or property damage which occurs within the policy territory.

GL 00 02
(Ed. 01-73)

[Schedule]

Coverages	Limits of Liability		Advance Premium
A. Bodily Injury Liability	$ $	each occurrence aggregate	$
B. Property Damage Liability	$ $	each occurrence aggregate	$
	Total Advance Premium		$

General Liability Hazards

Description of Hazards	Code No.	Premium Bases	Rates		Advance Premium	
			BI	PD	BI	PD
Premises—Operations		(a) Area (sq. ft.) (b) Frontage (c) Remuneration	(a) Per 100 sq. ft. of Area (b) Per linear ft. (c) Per $100 of Remuneration			
Escalators (Number at Premises)		Number Insured	Per Landing			
Independent Contractors		Cost	Per $100 of Cost			
Completed Operations		(a) Receipts	(a) Per $1,000 of Receipts			
Products		(b) Sales	(b) Per $1,000 of Sales			

Location of all premises owned by, rented to or controlled by the **named insured**

(Enter "same" if same location as address shown in Item 1. of declarations)

Interest of **named insured** in such premises _____

(Describe interest, such as "owner", "general lessee" or "tenant")

Part occupied by **named insured** _____

The foregoing discloses all hazards insured hereunder known to exist at the effective date of this policy, unless otherwise stated herein.

GL 00 02 01 73   Page 4 of 4

GL 04 04
(Ed. 5-81)

This endorsement forms a part of the policy to which attached, effective on the inception date of the policy unless otherwise stated herein.

(The following information is required only when this endorsement is issued subsequent to preparation of policy.)

Endorsement effective   Policy No.   Endorsement No.

Named Insured

Countersigned by _____

(Authorized Representative)

This endorsement modifies such insurance as is afforded by the provisions of the policy relating to the following:

COMPREHENSIVE GENERAL LIABILITY INSURANCE

BROAD FORM COMPREHENSIVE GENERAL LIABILITY ENDORSEMENT

Schedule

Personal Injury and Advertising Injury Liability
Aggregate Limit shall be the per occurrence bodily injury liability limit unless otherwise indicated herein:
Limit of Liability $_____ Aggregate.

Limit of Liability—Premises Medical Payments Coverage: $1,000 each person unless otherwise indicated herein:
$_____each person.

Limit of Liability—Fire Legal Liability Coverage: $50,000 per occurrence unless otherwise indicated herein:
$_____per occurrence.

Premium Basis	Advance Premium
_____% of the Total Comprehensive General Liability Bodily Injury and Property Damage Premium as Otherwise Determined.	$

MINIMUM PREMIUM $

I. CONTRACTUAL LIABILITY COVERAGE

(A) The definition of **incidental contract** is extended to include any oral or written contract or agreement relating to the conduct of the **named insured's** business.

(B) The insurance afforded with respect to liability assumed under an incidental contract is subject to the following additional exclusions:

(1) to **bodily injury** or **property damage** for which the **insured** has assumed liability under any **incidental contract**, if such injury or damage occurred prior to the execution of the **incidental contract**;

(2) if the **insured** is an architect, engineer or surveyor, to **bodily injury** or **property damage** arising out of the rendering of or the failure to render professional services by such **insured**, including

(a) the preparation or approval of maps, drawings, opinions, reports, surveys, change orders, designs or specifications, and

(b) supervisory, inspection or engineering services;

(3) if the indemnitee of the **insured** is an architect, engineer or surveyor, to the liability of the indemnitee, his agents or employees, arising out of

(a) the preparation or approval of or the failure to prepare or approve maps, drawings, opinions, reports, surveys, change orders, designs or specifications, or

(b) the giving of or the failure to give directions or instructions by the indemnitee, his agents or employees, provided such giving or failure to give is the primary cause of the **bodily injury** or **property damage**;

(4) to any obligation for which the **insured** may be held liable in an action on a contract by a third party beneficiary for **bodily injury** or **property damage** arising out of a project for a public authority; but this exclusion does not apply to an action by the public authority or any other person or organization engaged in the project;

(5) to **bodily injury** or **property damage** arising out of construction or demolition operations, within 50 feet of any railroad property, and **affecting any railroad bridge or trestle, tracks, road** beds, tunnel, underpass or crossing; but this exclusion does not apply to sidetrack agreements.

(C) The following exclusions applicable to Coverages A (Bodily Injury) and B (Property Damage) do not apply to this Contractual Liability Coverage: (b), (c) (2), (d) and (e).

(D) The following additional condition applies:

Arbitration
The company shall be entitled to exercise all of the **insured's** rights in the choice of arbitrators and in the conduct of any arbitration proceeding.

II. PERSONAL INJURY AND ADVERTISING INJURY LIABILITY COVERAGE

(A) The company will pay on behalf of the insured all sums which the insured shall become legally obligated to pay as damages because of personal injury or advertising injury to which this insurance applies, sustained by any person or organization and arising out of the conduct of the named insured's business, within the policy territory, and the company shall have the right and duty to defend any suit against the insured seeking damages on account of such injury, even if any of the allegations of the suit are groundless, false or fraudulent, and may make such investigation and settlement of any claim or suit as it deems expedient, but the company shall not be obligated to pay any claim or judgment or to defend any suit after the applicable limit of the company's liability has been exhausted by payment of judgments or settlements.

(B) This insurance does not apply:

(1) to liability assumed by the insured under any contract or agreement;

(2) to personal injury or advertising injury arising out of the wilful violation of a penal statute or ordinance committed by or with the knowledge or consent of the insured;

(3) to personal injury or advertising injury arising out of a publication or utterance of a libel or slander, or a publication or utterance in violation of an individual's right of privacy, if the first injurious publication or utterance of the same or similar material by or on behalf of the named insured was made prior to the effective date of this insurance;

(4) to personal injury or advertising injury arising out of libel or slander or the publication or utterance of defamatory or disparaging material concerning any person or organization or goods, products or services, or in violation of an individual's right of privacy, made by or at the direction of the insured with knowledge of the falsity thereof;

(5) to personal injury or advertising injury arising out of the conduct of any partnership or joint venture of which the insured is a partner or member and which is not designated in the declarations of the policy as a named insured;

(6) to advertising injury arising out of

(a) failure of performance of contract, but this exclusion does not apply to the unauthorized appropriation of ideas based upon alleged breach of implied contract, or

(b) infringement of trademark, service mark or trade name, other than titles or slogans, by use thereof on or in connection with goods, products or services sold, offered for sale or advertised, or

(c) incorrect description or mistake in advertised price of goods, products or services sold, offered for sale or advertised;

(7) with respect to advertising injury

(a) to any insured in the business of advertising, broadcasting, publishing or telecasting, or

(b) to any injury arising out of any act committed by the insured with actual malice.

(C) Limits of Liability

Regardless of the number of (1) insureds hereunder, (2) persons or organizations who sustain injury or damage, or (3) claims made or suits brought on account of personal injury or advertising injury, the total limit of the company's liability under this coverage for all damages shall not exceed the limit of liability stated in this endorsement as "aggregate".

(D) Additional Definitions

"Advertising Injury" means injury arising out of an offense committed during the policy period occurring in the course of the named insured's advertising activities, if such injury arises out of libel, slander, defamation, violation of right of privacy, piracy, unfair competition, or infringement of copyright, title or slogan.

"Personal Injury" means injury arising out of one or more of the following offenses committed during the policy period:

(1) false arrest, detention, imprisonment, or malicious prosecution;

(2) wrongful entry or eviction or other invasion of the right of private occupancy;

(3) a publication or utterance

(a) of a libel or slander or other defamatory or disparaging material, or

(b) in violation of an individual's right of privacy;

except publications or utterances in the course of or related to advertising, broadcasting, publishing or telecasting activities conducted by or on behalf of the named insured shall not be deemed personal injury.

III. PREMISES MEDICAL PAYMENTS COVERAGE

The company will pay to or for each person who sustains bodily injury caused by accident all reasonable medical expense incurred within one year from the date of the accident on account of such bodily injury, provided such bodily injury arises out of (a) a condition in the insured premises, or (b) operations with respect to which the named insured is afforded coverage for bodily injury liability under the policy.

This insurance does not apply:

(A) to bodily injury

(1) arising out of the ownership, maintenance, operation, use, loading or unloading of

(a) any automobile or aircraft owned or operated by or rented or loaned to any insured, or

(b) any other automobile or aircraft operated by any person in the course of his employment by any insured;

but this exclusion does not apply to the parking of an automobile on the insured premises, if such automobile is not owned by or rented or loaned to any insured;

(2) arising out of

(a) the ownership, maintenance, operation, use, loading or unloading of any mobile equipment while being used in any prearranged or organized racing, speed or demolition contest or in any stunting activity or in practice or preparation for any such contest or activity, or

(b) the operation or use of any snowmobile or trailer designed for use therewith;

(i) owned or operated by or rented or loaned to any insured, or

(ii) operated by any person in the course of his employment by any insured;

(3) arising out of the ownership, maintenance, operation, use, loading or unloading of

(a) any watercraft owned or operated by or rented or loaned to any insured, or

(b) any other watercraft operated by any person in the course of his employment by any insured;

but this exclusion does not apply to watercraft while ashore on the insured premises;

(4) arising out of and in the course of the transportation of mobile equipment by an automobile owned or operated by or rented or loaned to the named insured;

(B) to bodily injury

(1) included within the completed operations hazard or the products hazard;

(2) arising out of operations performed for the named insured by independent contractors other than

(a) maintenance and repair of the insured premises, or

(b) structural alterations at such premises which do not involve changing the size of or moving buildings or other structures;

(3) resulting from the selling, serving or giving of any alcoholic beverage

(a) in violation of any statute, ordinance or regulation,

(b) to a minor,

(c) to a person under the influence of alcohol, or

(d) which causes or contributes to the intoxication of any person,

if the named insured is a person or organization engaged in the business of manufacturing, distributing, selling or serving alcoholic beverages, or if not so engaged, is an owner or lessor of premises used for such purposes, but only part (a) of this exclusion (B) (3) applies when the named insured is such an owner or lessor;

(4) due to war, whether or not declared, civil war, insurrection, rebellion or revolution, or to any act or condition incident to any of the foregoing;

(C) to bodily injury

(1) to the named insured, any partner thereof, any tenant or other person regularly residing on the insured premises or any employee of any of the foregoing if the bodily injury arises out of and in the course of his employment therewith;

(2) to any other tenant if the bodily injury occurs on that part of the insured premises rented from the named insured or to any employee of such a tenant if the bodily injury occurs on the tenant's part of the insured premises and arises out of and in the course of his employment for the tenant;

(3) to any person while engaged in maintenance and repair of the insured premises or alteration, demolition or new construction at such premises;

(4) to any person if any benefits for such bodily injury are payable or required to be provided under any workmen's compensation, unemployment compensation or disability benefits law, or under any similar law;

(5) to any person practicing, instructing or participating in any physical training, sport, athletic activity or contest whether on a formal or informal basis;

(6) if the named insured is a club, to any member of the named insured;

(7) if the named insured is a hotel, motel, or tourist court, to any guest of the named insured;

(D) to any medical expense for services by the named insured, any employee thereof or any person or organization under contract to the named insured to provide such services.

LIMITS OF LIABILITY

The limit of liability for Premises Medical Payments Coverage is $1,000 each person unless otherwise stated in the schedule of this endorsement. The limit of liability applicable to "each person" is the limit of the company's liability for all medical expense for bodily injury to any one person as the result of any one accident; but subject to the above provision respecting "each person", the total liability of the company under Premises Medical Payments Coverage for all medical expense for bodily injury to two or more persons as the result of any one accident shall not exceed the limit of bodily injury liability stated in the policy as applicable to "each occurrence".

When more than one medical payments coverage afforded by the policy applies to the loss, the company shall not be liable for more than the amount of the highest applicable limit of liability.

ADDITIONAL DEFINITIONS

When used herein:

"insured premises" means all premises owned by or rented to the named insured with respect to which the named insured is afforded coverage for bodily injury liability under this policy, and includes the ways immediately adjoining on land;

"medical expense" means expenses for necessary medical, surgical, x-ray and dental services, including prosthetic devices, and necessary ambulance, hospital, professional nursing and funeral services.

ADDITIONAL CONDITION

Medical Reports; Proof and Payment of Claim

As soon as practicable the injured person or someone on his behalf shall give to the company written proof of claim, under oath if required, and shall, after each request from the company, execute authorization to enable the company to obtain medical reports and copies of records. The injured person shall submit to physical examination by physicians selected by the company when and as often as the company may reasonably require. The company may pay the injured person or any person or organization rendering the services and the payment shall reduce the amount payable hereunder for such injury. Payment hereunder shall not constitute an admission of liability of any person or, except hereunder, of the company.

IV. HOST LIQUOR LAW LIABILITY COVERAGE

Exclusion (h) does not apply with respect to liability of the insured or his indemnitee arising out of the giving or serving of alcoholic beverages at functions incidental to the named insured's business, provided the named insured is not engaged in the business of manufacturing, distributing, selling or serving of alcoholic beverages.

V. FIRE LEGAL LIABILITY COVERAGE—REAL PROPERTY

With respect to property damage to structures or portions thereof rented to or leased to the named insured, including fixtures permanently attached thereto, if such property damage arises out of fire

(A) All of the exclusions of the policy, other than the Nuclear Energy Liability Exclusion (Broad Form), are deleted and replaced by the following:

This insurance does not apply to liability assumed by the insured under any contract or agreement.

(B) The limit of property damage liability as respects this Fire Legal Liability Coverage—Real Property is $50,000 each occurrence unless otherwise stated in the schedule of this endorsement.

(C) The Fire Legal Liability Coverage—Real Property shall be excess insurance over any valid and collectible property insurance (including any deductible portion thereof), available to the insured, such as, but not limited to, Fire, Extended Coverage, Builder's Risk Coverage or Installation Risk Coverage, and the Other Insurance Condition of the policy is amended accordingly.

VI. BROAD FORM PROPERTY DAMAGE LIABILITY COVERAGE (Including Completed Operations)

The insurance for property damage liability applies, subject to the following additional provisions:

(A) Exclusions (k) and (o) are replaced by the following:

(1) to property owned or occupied by or rented to the insured, or, except with respect to the use of elevators, to property held by the insured for sale or entrusted to the insured for storage or safekeeping;

(2) except with respect to liability under a written sidetrack agreement or the use of elevators

(a) to property while on premises owned by or rented to the insured for the purpose of having operations performed on such property by or on behalf of the insured,

(b) to tools or equipment while being used by the insured in performing his operations,

(c) to property in the custody of the insured which is to be installed, erected or used in construction by the insured,

(d) to that particular part of any property, not on premises owned by or rented to the insured,

(i) upon which operations are being performed by or on behalf of the insured at the time of the property damage arising out of such operations, or

(ii) out of which any property damage arises, or

(iii) the restoration, repair or replacement of which has been made or is necessary by reason of faulty workmanship thereon by or on behalf of the insured;

(3) with respect to the completed operations hazard and with respect to any classification stated in the policy or in the company's manual as "including completed operations", to property damage to work performed by the named insured arising out of such work or any portion thereof, or out of such materials, parts or equipment furnished in connection therewith.

(B) The Broad Form Property Damage Liability Coverage shall be excess insurance over any valid and collectible property insurance (including any deductible portion thereof) available to the **insured**, such as, but not limited to, Fire, Extended Coverage, Builder's Risk Coverage or Installation Risk Coverage, and the Other Insurance Condition of the policy is amended accordingly.

VII. INCIDENTAL MEDICAL MALPRACTICE LIABILITY COVERAGE

The definition of **bodily injury** is amended to include Incidental Medical Malpractice Injury.

Incidental Medical Malpractice Injury means injury arising out of the rendering of or failure to render, during the policy period, the following services:

(A) medical, surgical, dental, x-ray or nursing service or treatment or the furnishing of food or beverages in connection therewith; or

(B) the furnishing or dispensing of drugs or medical, dental or surgical supplies or appliances.

This coverage does not apply to:

(1) expenses incurred by the **insured** for first-aid to others at the time of an accident and the "Supplementary Payments" provision and the "Insured's Duties in the Event of Occurrence, Claim or Suit" Condition are amended accordingly;

(2) any **insured** engaged in the business or occupation of providing any of the services described under VII (A) and (B) above;

(3) injury caused by any indemnitee if such indemnitee is engaged in the business or occupation of providing any of the services described under VII (A) and (B) above.

VIII. NON-OWNED WATERCRAFT LIABILITY COVERAGE (under 26 feet in length)

Exclusion (e) does not apply to any watercraft under 26 feet in length provided such watercraft is neither owned by the **named insured** nor being used to carry persons or property for a charge.

Where the **insured** is, irrespective of this coverage, covered or protected against any loss or claim which would otherwise have been paid by the company under this endorsement, there shall be no contribution or participation by this company on the basis of excess, contributing, deficiency, concurrent, or double insurance or otherwise.

IX. LIMITED WORLDWIDE LIABILITY COVERAGE

The definition of **policy territory** is amended to include the following:

(4) Anywhere in the world with respect to **bodily injury**, **property damage**, **personal injury** or **advertising injury** arising out of the activities of any **insured** permanently domiciled in the United States of America though temporarily outside the United States of America, its territories and possessions or Canada, provided the original suit for damages because of any such injury or damage is brought within the United States of America, its territories or possessions or Canada.

Such insurance as is afforded by paragraph (4) above shall not apply:

(a) to **bodily injury** or **property damage** included within the **completed operations hazard** or the **products hazard**;

(b) to Premises Medical Payments Coverage.

X. ADDITIONAL PERSONS INSURED

As respects **bodily injury**, **property damage** and **personal injury** and **advertising injury** coverages, under the provision "Persons Insured", the following are added as insureds:

(A) Spouse—Partnership—If the **named insured** is a partnership, the spouse of a partner but only with respect to the conduct of the business of the **named insured**;

(B) Employee—Any employee (other than executive officers) of the **named insured** while acting within the scope of his duties as such, but the insurance afforded to such employee does not apply:

(1) to **bodily injury** or **personal injury** to another employee of the **named insured** arising out of or in the course of his employment;

(2) to **personal injury** or **advertising injury** to the **named insured** or, if the **named insured** is a partnership or joint venture, any partner or member thereof, or the spouse of any of the foregoing;

(3) to **property damage** to property owned, occupied or used by, rented to, in the care, custody or control of or over which physical control is being exercised for any purpose by another employee of the **named insured**, or by the **named insured** or, if the **named insured** is a partnership or joint venture, by any partner or member thereof or by the spouse of any of the foregoing.

XI. EXTENDED BODILY INJURY COVERAGE

The definition of **occurrence** includes any intentional act by or at the direction of the **insured** which results in **bodily injury**, if such injury arises solely from the use of reasonable force for the purpose of protecting persons or property.

XII. AUTOMATIC COVERAGE—NEWLY ACQUIRED ORGANIZATIONS (90 DAYS)

The word **insured** shall include as **named insured** any organization which is acquired or formed by the **named insured** and over which the **named insured** maintains ownership or majority interest, other than a joint venture, provided this insurance does not apply to **bodily injury**, **property damage**, **personal injury** or **advertising injury** with respect to which such new organization under this policy is also an **insured** under any other similar liability or indemnity policy or would be an **insured** under any such policy but for exhaustion of its limits of liability. The insurance afforded hereby shall terminate 90 days from the date any such organization is acquired or formed by the **named insured**.

COMMERCIAL GENERAL LIABILITY COVERAGE FORM

Various provisions in this policy restrict coverage. Read the entire policy carefully to determine rights, duties and what is and is not covered.

Throughout this policy the words "you" and "your" refer to Named Insured shown in the Declarations. The words "we," "us" and "our" refer to the Company providing this insurance.

The word "insured" means any person or organization qualifying as such under SECTION II – WHO IS AN INSURED.

Other words and phrases that appear in quotation marks have special meaning. Refer to SECTION V – DEFINITIONS.

SECTION I - COVERAGES

COVERAGE A. BODILY INJURY AND PROPERTY DAMAGE LIABILITY

1. Insuring Agreement.

a. We will pay those sums that the insured becomes legally obligated to pay as damages because of "bodily injury" or "property damage" to which this insurance applies. No other obligation or liability to pay sums or perform acts or services is covered unless explicitly provided for under SUPPLEMENTARY PAYMENTS – COVERAGES A AND B. This insurance applies only to "bodily injury" and "property damage" which occurs during the policy period. The "bodily injury" or "property damage" must be caused by an "occurrence." The "occurrence" must take place in the "coverage territory." We will have the right and duty to defend any "suit" seeking those damages. But:

(1) The amount we will pay for damages is limited as described in SECTION III – LIMITS OF INSURANCE;

(2) We may investigate and settle any claim or "suit" at our discretion; and

(3) Our right and duty to defend end when we have used up the applicable limit of insurance in the payment of judgments or settlements under Coverages A or B or medical expenses under Coverage C.

b. Damages because of "bodily injury" include damages claimed by any person or organization for care, loss of services or death resulting at any time from the "bodily injury."

c. "Property damage" that is loss of use of tangible property that is not physically injured shall be deemed to occur at the time of the "occurrence" that caused it.

2. Exclusions.

This insurance does not apply to:

a. "Bodily injury" or "property damage" expected or intended from the standpoint of the insured. This exclusion does not apply to "bodily injury" resulting from the use of reasonable force to protect persons or property.

b. "Bodily injury" or "property damage" for which the insured is obligated to pay damages by reason of the assumption of liability in a contract or agreement. This exclusion does not apply to liability for damages:

(1) Assumed in a contract or agreement that is an "insured contract;" or

(2) That the insured would have in the absence of the contract or agreement.

c. "Bodily injury" or "property damage" for which any insured may be held liable by reason of:

(1) Causing or contributing to the intoxication of any person;

(2) The furnishing of alcoholic beverages to a person under the legal drinking age or under the influence of alcohol; or

(3) Any statute, ordinance or regulation relating to the sale, gift, distribution or use of alcoholic beverages.

This exclusion applies only if you are in the business of manufacturing, distributing, selling, serving or furnishing alcoholic beverages.

d. Any obligation of the insured under a workers compensation, disability benefits or unemployment compensation law or any similar law.

e. "Bodily injury" to:

(1) An employee of the insured arising out of and in the course of employment by the insured; or

(2) The spouse, child, parent, brother or sister of that employee as a consequence of (1) above.

This exclusion applies:

(1) Whether the insured may be liable as an employer or in any other capacity; and

(2) To any obligation to share damages with or repay someone else who must pay damages because of the injury.

This exclusion does not apply to liability assumed by the insured under an "insured contract."

COMMERCIAL GENERAL LIABILITY
COVERAGE FORM

f.(1) "Bodily injury" or "property damage" arising out of the actual, alleged or threatened discharge, dispersal, release or escape of pollutants:

(a) At or from premises you own, rent or occupy;

(b) At or from any site or location used by or for you or others for the handling, storage, disposal, processing or treatment of waste;

(c) Which are at any time transported, handled, stored, treated, disposed of, or processed as waste by or for you or any person or organization for whom you may be legally responsible; or

(d) At or from any site or location on which you or any contractors or subcontractors working directly or indirectly on your behalf are performing operations:

(i) if the pollutants are brought on or to the site or location in connection with such operations; or

(ii) if the operations are to test for, monitor, clean up, remove, contain, treat, detoxify or neutralize the pollutants.

(2) Any loss, cost, or expense arising out of any governmental direction or request that you test for, monitor, clean up, remove, contain, treat, detoxify or neutralize pollutants.

Pollutants means any solid, liquid, gaseous or thermal irritant or contaminant, including smoke, vapor, soot, fumes, acids, alkalis, chemicals and waste. Waste includes materials to be recycled, reconditioned or reclaimed.

g. "Bodily injury" or "property damage" arising out of the ownership, maintenance, use or entrustment to others of any aircraft, "auto" or watercraft owned or operated by or rented or loaned to any insured. Use includes operation and "loading or unloading."

This exclusion does not apply to:

(1) A watercraft while ashore on premises you own or rent.

(2) A watercraft you do not own that is:

(a) Less than 26 feet long; and

(b) Not being used to carry persons or property for a charge;

(3) Parking an "auto" on, or on the ways next to, premises you own or rent, provided the "auto" is not owned by or rented or loaned to you or the insured;

(4) Liability assumed under any "insured contract" for the ownership, maintenance or use of aircraft or watercraft; or

(5) "Bodily injury" or "property damage" arising out of the operation of any of the equipment listed in paragraph f.(2) or f.(3) of the definition of "mobile equipment" (Section V.8).

h. "Bodily injury" or "property damage" arising out of:

(1) The transportation of "mobile equipment" by an "auto" owned or operated by or rented or loaned to any insured; or

(2) The use of "mobile equipment" in, or while in practice or preparation for, a prearranged racing, speed or demolition contest or in any stunting activity.

I. "Bodily injury" or "property damage" due to war, whether or not declared, or any act or condition incident to war. War includes civil war, insurrection, rebellion or revolution. This exclusion applies only to liability assumed under a contract or agreement.

j. "Property damage" to:

(1) Property you own, rent, or occupy;

(2) Premises you sell, give away or abandon, if the "property damage" arises out of any part of those premises;

(3) Property loaned to you;

(4) Personal property in your care, custody or control;

(5) That particular part of real property on which you or any contractors or subcontractors working directly or indirectly on your behalf are performing operations, if the "property damage" arises out of those operations; or

(6) That particular part of any property that must be restored, repaired or replaced because "your work" was incorrectly performed on it.

Paragraph (2) of this exclusion does not apply if the premises are "your work" and were never occupied, rented or held for rental by you.

Paragraphs (3), (4), (5) and (6) of this exclusion do not apply to liability assumed under a sidetrack agreement.

Paragraph (6) of this exclusion does not apply to "property damage" included in the "products-completed operations hazard."

k. "Property damage" to "your product" arising out of it or any part of it.

l. "Property damage" to "your work" arising out of it or any part of it and included in the "products–completed operations hazard."

This exclusion does not apply if the damaged work or the work out of which the damage arises was performed on your behalf by a subcontractor

m. "Property damage" to "impaired property" or property that has not been physically injured, arising out of:

(1) A defect, deficiency, inadequacy or dangerous condition in "your product" or "your work;" or

(2) A delay or failure by you or anyone acting on your behalf to perform a contract or agreement in accordance with its terms.

This exclusion does not apply to the loss of use of other property arising out of sudden and accidental physical injury to "your product" or "your work" after it has been put to its intended use.

n. Damages claimed for any loss, cost or expense incurred by you or others for the loss of use, withdrawal, recall, inspection, repair, replacement, adjustment, removal or disposal of:

(1) "Your product;"

(2) "Your work;" or

(3) "Impaired property;"

if such product, work, or property is withdrawn or recalled from the market or from use by any person or organization because of a known or suspected defect, deficiency, inadequacy or dangerous condition in it.

Exclusions c. through n. do not apply to damage by fire to premises rented to you. A separate limit of insurance applies to this coverage as described in SECTION III – LIMITS OF INSURANCE.

COVERAGE B. PERSONAL AND ADVERTISING INJURY LIABILITY

1. Insuring Agreement

a. We will pay those sums that the insured becomes legally obligated to pay as damages because of "personal injury" or "advertising injury" to which this insurance applies. No other obligation or liability to pay sums or perform acts or services is covered unless explicitly provided for under SUPPLEMENTARY PAYMENTS – COVERAGES A AND B. We will have the right and duty to defend any "suit" seeking those damages. But:

(1) The amount we will pay for damages is limited as described in SECTION III – LIMITS OF INSURANCE;

(2) We may investigate and settle any claim or "suit" at our discretion; and

(3) Our right and duty to defend end when we have used up the applicable limit of insurance in the payment of judgments or settlement under Coverages A or B or medical expenses under Coverage C.

b. This insurance applies to "personal injury" only if caused by an offense:

(1) Committed in the "coverage territory" during the policy period; and

(2) Arising out of the conduct of your business excluding advertising, publishing, broadcasting or telecasting done by or for you.

c. This insurance applies to "advertising injury" only if caused by an offense committed:

(1) In the "coverage territory" during the policy period; and

(2) In the course of advertising your goods, products or services.

2. Exclusions.

This insurance does not apply to:

a. "Personal injury" or "advertising injury:"

(1) Arising out of oral or written publication of material, if done by or at the direction of the insured with knowledge of its falsity;

(2) Arising out of oral or written publication of material whose first publication took place before the beginning of the policy period;

(3) Arising out of the willful violation of a penal statute or ordinance committed by or with the consent of the insured; or

(4) For which the insured has assumed liability in a contract or agreement. This exclusion does not apply to liability for damages that the insured would have in the absence of the contract or agreement.

b. "Advertising injury" arising out of:

(1) Breach of contract, other than misappropriation of advertising ideas under an implied contract;

(2) The failure of goods, products or services to conform with advertised quality or performance;

(3) The wrong description of the price of goods, products or services; or

COMMERCIAL GENERAL LIABILITY
COVERAGE FORM

(4) An offense committed by an insured whose business is advertising, broadcasting, publishing or telecasting.

COVERAGE C. MEDICAL PAYMENTS

1. Insuring Agreement.

a. We will pay medical expenses as described below for "bodily injury" caused by an accident:

(1) On premises you own or rent;

(2) On ways next to premises you own or rent; or

(3) Because of your operations;

provided that:

(1) The accident takes place in the "coverage territory" and during the policy period;

(2) The expenses are incurred and reported to us within one year of the date of the accident; and

(3) The injured person submits to examination, at our expense, by physicians of our choice as often as we reasonably require.

b. We will make these payments regardless of fault. These payments will not exceed the applicable limit of insurance. We will pay reasonable expenses for:

(1) First aid at the time of an accident;

(2) Necessary medical, surgical, x-ray and dental services, including prosthetic devices; and

(3) Necessary ambulance, hospital, professional nursing and funeral services.

2. Exclusions.

We will not pay expenses for "bodily injury:"

a. To any insured.

b. To a person hired to do work for or on behalf of any insured or a tenant of any insured.

c. To a person injured on that part of premises you own or rent that the person normally occupies.

d. To a person, whether or not an employee of any insured, if benefits for the "bodily injury" are payable or must be provided under a workers compensation or disability benefits law or a similar law.

e. To a person injured while taking part in athletics.

f. Included within the "products-completed operations hazard."

g. Excluded under Coverage A.

h. Due to war, whether or not declared, or any act or condition incident to war. War includes civil war, insurrection, rebellion or revolution.

SUPPLEMENTARY PAYMENTS - COVERAGES A AND B

We will pay, with respect to any claim or "suit" we defend:

1. All expenses we incur.

2. Up to $250 for cost of bail bonds required because of accidents or traffic law violations arising out of the use of any vehicle to which the Bodily Injury Liability Coverage applies. We do not have to furnish these bonds.

3. The cost of bonds to release attachments, but only for bond amounts within the applicable limit of insurance. We do not have to furnish these bonds.

4. All reasonable expenses incurred by the insured at our request to assist us in the investigation or defense of the claim or "suit," including actual loss of earnings up to $100 a day because of time off from work.

5. All costs taxed against the insured in the "suit."

6. Pre-judgment interest awarded against the insured on that part of the judgment we pay. If we make an offer to pay the applicable limit of insurance, we will not pay any pre-judgment interest based on that period of time after the offer.

7. All interest on the full amount of any judgment that accrues after entry of the judgment and before we have paid, offered to pay, or deposited in court the part of the judgment that is within the applicable limit of insurance.

These payments will not reduce the limits of insurance.

SECTION II - WHO IS AN INSURED

1. If you are designated in the Declarations as:

a. An individual, you and your spouse are insureds, but only with respect to the conduct of a business of which you are the sole owner.

b. A partnership or joint venture, you are an insured. Your members, your partners, and their spouses are also insureds, but only with respect to the conduct of your business.

 CG 00 01 11 85 ☐

COMMERCIAL GENERAL LIABILITY
COVERAGE FORM

c. An organization other than a partnership or joint venture, you are an insured. Your executive officers and directors are insureds, but only with respect to their duties as your officers or directors. Your stockholders are also insureds, but only with respect to their liability as stockholders.

2. Each of the following is also an insured:

a. Your employees, other than your executive officers, but only for acts within the scope of their employment by you. However, none of these employees is an insured for:

(1) "Bodily injury" or "personal injury" to you or to a co-employee while in the course of his or her employment; or

(2) "Bodily injury" or "personal injury" arising out of his or her providing or failing to provide professional health care services; or

(3) "Property damage" to property owned or occupied by or rented or loaned to that employee, any of your other employees, or any of your partners or members (if you are a partnership or joint venture).

b. Any person (other than your employee), or any organization while acting as your real estate manager.

c. Any person or organization having proper temporary custody of your property if you die, but only:

(1) With respect to liability arising out of the maintenance or use of that property; and

(2) Until your legal representative has been appointed.

d. Your legal representative if you die, but only with respect to duties as such. That representative will have all your rights and duties under this Coverage Part.

3. With respect to "mobile equipment" registered in your name under any motor vehicle registration law, any person is an insured while driving such equipment along a public highway with your permission. Any other person or organization responsible for the conduct of such person is also an insured, but only with respect to liability arising out of the operation of the equipment, and only if no other insurance of any kind is available to that person or organization for this liability. However, no person or organization is an insured with respect to:

a. "Bodily injury" to a co-employee of the person driving the equipment; or

b. "Property damage" to property owned by, rented to, in the charge of or occupied by you or the employer of any person who is an insured under this provision.

4. Any organization you newly acquire or form, other than a partnership or joint venture, and over which you maintain ownership or majority interest, will be deemed to be a Named Insured if there is no other similar insurance available to that organization. However:

a. Coverage under this provision is afforded only until the 90th day after you acquire or form the organization or the end of the policy period, whichever is earlier;

b. Coverage A does not apply to "bodily injury" or "property damage" that occurred before you acquired or formed the organization; and

c. Coverage B does not apply to "personal injury" or "advertising injury" arising out of an offense committed before you acquired or formed the organization.

No person or organization is an insured with respect to the conduct of any current or past partnership or joint venture that is not shown as a Named Insured in the Declarations.

SECTION III - LIMITS OF INSURANCE

1. The Limits of Insurance shown in the Declarations and the rules below fix the most we will pay regardless of the number of:

a. Insureds;

b. Claims made or "suits" brought; or

c. Persons or organizations making claims or bringing "suits."

2. The General Aggregate Limit is the most we will pay for the sum of:

a. Medical expenses under Coverage C; and

b. Damages under Coverage A and Coverage B, except damages because of injury and damage included in the "products-completed operations hazard."

3. The Products-Completed Operations Aggregate Limit is the most we will pay under Coverage A for damages because of injury and damage included in the "products-completed operations hazard."

4. Subject to 2. above, the Personal and Advertising Injury Limit is the most we will pay under Coverage B for the sum of all damages because of all "personal injury" and all "advertising injury" sustained by any one person or organization.

COMMERCIAL GENERAL LIABILITY
COVERAGE FORM

5. Subject to 2. or 3. above, whichever applies, the Each Occurrence Limit is the most we will pay for the sum of:

   a. Damages under Coverage A; and

   b. Medical expenses under Coverage C because of all "bodily injury" and "property damage" arising out of any one "occurrence."

6. Subject to 5. above, the Fire Damage Limit is the most we will pay under Coverage A for damages because of "property damage" to premises rented to you arising out of any one fire.

7. Subject to 5. above, the Medical Expense Limit is the most we will pay under Coverage C for all medical expenses because of "bodily injury" sustained by any one person.

The limits of this Coverage Part apply separately to each consecutive annual period and to any remaining period of less than 12 months, starting with the beginning of the policy period shown in the Declarations, unless the policy period is extended after issuance for an additional period of less than 12 months. In that case, the additional period will be deemed part of the last preceding period for purposes of determining the Limits of Insurance.

SECTION IV - COMMERCIAL GENERAL LIABILITY CONDITIONS

1. Bankruptcy.

   Bankruptcy or insolvency of the insured or of the insured's estate will not relieve us of our obligations under this Coverage Part.

2. Duties In The Event Of Occurrence, Claim or Suit.

   a. You must see to it that we are notified promptly of an "occurrence" which may result in a claim. Notice should include:

      (1) How, when and where the "occurrence" took place; and

      (2) The names and addresses of any injured persons and witnesses.

   b. If a claim is made or "suit" is brought against any insured, you must see to it that we receive prompt written notice of the claim or "suit."

   c. You and any other involved insured must:

      (1) Immediately send us copies of any demands, notices, summonses or legal papers received in connection with the claim or "suit;"

      (2) Authorize us to obtain records and other information;

      (3) Cooperate with us in the investigation, settlement or defense of the claim or "suit;" and

   (4) Assist us, upon our request, in the enforcement of any right against any person or organization which may be liable to the insured because of injury or damage to which this insurance may also apply.

   d. No insureds will, except at their own cost, voluntarily make a payment, assume any obligation, or incur any expense, other than for first aid, without our consent.

3. Legal Action Against Us.

   No person or organization has a right under this Coverage Part:

   a. To join us as a party or otherwise bring us into a "suit" asking for damages from an insured; or

   b. To sue us on this Coverage Part unless all of its terms have been fully complied with.

   A person or organization may sue us to recover on an agreed settlement or on a final judgment against an insured obtained after an actual trial; but we will not be liable for damages that are not payable under the terms of this Coverage Part or that are in excess of the applicable limit of insurance. An agreed settlement means a settlement and release of liability signed by us, the insured and the claimant or the claimant's legal representative.

4. Other Insurance.

   If other valid and collectible insurance is available to the insured for a loss we cover under Coverages A or B of this Coverage Part, our obligations are limited as follows:

   a. Primary Insurance

   This insurance is primary except when b. below applies. If this insurance is primary, our obligations are not affected unless any of the other insurance is also primary. Then, we will share with all that other insurance by the method described in c. below.

   b. Excess Insurance

   This insurance is excess over any of the other insurance, whether primary, excess, contingent or on any other basis:

      (1) That is Fire, Extended Coverage, Builder's Risk, Installation Risk or similar coverage for "your work;"

      (2) That is Fire insurance for premises rented to you; or

      (3) If the loss arises out of the maintenance or use of aircraft, "autos" or watercraft to the extent not subject to Exclusion g. of Coverage A (Section I).

COMMERCIAL GENERAL LIABILITY
COVERAGE FORM

When this insurance is excess, we will have no duty under Coverage A or B to defend any claim or "suit" that any other insurer has a duty to defend. If no other insurer defends, we will undertake to do so, but we will be entitled to the insured's rights against all those other insurers.

When this insurance is excess over other insurance, we will pay only our share of the amount of the loss, if any, that exceeds the sum of:

(1) The total amount that all such other insurance would pay for the loss in the absence of this insurance; and

(2) The total of all deductible and self-insured amounts under all that other insurance.

We will share the remaining loss, if any, with any other insurance that is not described in this Excess Insurance provision and was not bought specifically to apply in excess of the Limits of Insurance shown in the Declarations of this Coverage Part.

c. Method of Sharing

If all of the other insurance permits contribution by equal shares, we will follow this method also. Under this approach each insurer contributes equal amounts until it has paid its applicable limit of insurance or none of the loss remains, whichever comes first.

If any of the other insurance does not permit contribution by equal shares, we will contribute by limits. Under this method, each insurer's share is based on the ratio of its applicable limit of insurance to the total applicable limits of insurance of all insurers.

5. Premium Audit.

a. We will compute all premiums for this Coverage Part in accordance with our rules and rates.

b. Premium shown in this Coverage Part as advance premium is a deposit premium only. At the close of each audit period we will compute the earned premium for that period. Audit premiums are due and payable on notice to the first Named Insured. If the sum of the advance and audit premiums paid for the policy term is greater than the earned premium, we will return the excess to the first Named Insured.

c. The first Named Insured must keep records of the information we need for premium computation, and send us copies at such times as we may request.

6. Representations.

By accepting this policy, you agree:

a. The statements in the Declarations are accurate and complete;

b. Those statements are based upon representations you made to us; and

c. We have issued this policy in reliance upon your representations.

7. Separation Of Insureds.

Except with respect to the Limits of Insurance, and any rights or duties specifically assigned in this Coverage Part to the first Named Insured, this insurance applies:

a. As if each Named Insured were the only Named Insured; and

b. Separately to each insured against whom claim is made or "suit" is brought.

8. Transfer Of Rights Of Recovery Against Others To Us.

If the insured has rights to recover all or part of any payment we have made under this Coverage Part, those rights are transferred to us. The insured must do nothing after loss to impair them. At our request, the insured will bring "suit" or transfer those rights to us and help us enforce them.

SECTION V - DEFINITIONS

1. "Advertising injury" means injury arising out of one or more of the following offenses:

a. Oral or written publication of material that slanders or libels a person or organization or disparages a person's or organization's goods, products or services;

b. Oral or written publication of material that violates a person's right of privacy;

c. Misappropriation of advertising ideas or style of doing business; or

d. Infringement of copyright, title or slogan.

2. "Auto" means a land motor vehicle, trailer or semitrailer designed for travel on public roads, including any attached machinery or equipment. But "auto" does not include "mobile equipment."

3. "Bodily injury" means bodily injury, sickness or disease sustained by a person, including death resulting from any of these at any time.

4. "Coverage territory" means:

a. The United States of America (including its territories and possessions), Puerto Rico and Canada.

COMMERCIAL GENERAL LIABILITY
COVERAGE FORM

b. International waters or airspace, provided the injury or damage does not occur in the course of travel or transportation to or from any place not included in a. above; or

c. All parts of the world if:

(1) The injury or damage arises out of:

(a) Goods or products made or sold by you in the territory described in a. above; or

(b) The activities of a person whose home is in the territory described in a. above, but is away for a short time on your business; and

(2) The insured's responsibility to pay damages is determined in a "suit" on the merits, in the territory described in a. above or in a settlement we agree to.

5. "Impaired property" means tangible property, other than "your product" or "your work," that cannot be used or is less useful because:

a. It incorporates "your product" or "your work" that is known or thought to be defective, deficient, inadequate or dangerous; or

b. You have failed to fulfill the terms of a contract or agreement;

if such property can be restored to use by:

a. The repair, replacement, adjustment or removal of "your product" or "your work;" or

b. Your fulfilling the terms of the contract or agreement.

6. "Insured contract" means:

a. A lease of premises;

b. A sidetrack agreement;

c. An easement or license agreement in connection with vehicle or pedestrian private railroad crossings at grade;

d. Any other easement agreement, except in connection with construction or demolition operations on or within 50 feet of a railroad;

e. An indemnification of a municipality as required by ordinance, except in connection with work for a municipality;

f. An elevator maintenance agreement; or

g. That part of any other contract or agreement pertaining to your business under which you assume the tort liability of another to pay damages because of "bodily injury" or "property damage" to a third person or organization, if the contract or agreement is made prior to the "bodily injury" or "property damage". Tort liability

means a liability that would be imposed by law in the absence of any contract or agreement.

An "insured contract" does not include that part of any contract or agreement:

a. That indemnifies an architect, engineer or surveyor for injury or damage arising out of:

(1) Preparing, approving or failing to prepare or approve maps, drawings, opinions, reports, surveys, change orders, designs or specifications; or

(2) Giving directions or instructions, or failing to give them, if that is the primary cause of the injury or damage.

b. Under which the insured, if an architect, engineer or surveyor, assumes liability for injury or damage arising out of the insured's rendering or failing to render professional services, including those listed in a. above and supervisory, inspection or engineering services; or

c. That indemnifies any person or organization for damage by fire to premises rented or loaned to you.

7. "Loading or unloading" means the handling of property:

a. After it is moved from the place where it is accepted for movement into or onto an aircraft, watercraft or "auto;"

b. While it is in or on an aircraft, watercraft or "auto;" or

c. While it is being moved from an aircraft, watercraft or "auto" to the place where it is finally delivered;

but "loading or unloading" does not include the movement of property by means of a mechanical device, other than a hand truck, that is not attached to the aircraft, watercraft or "auto."

8. "Mobile equipment" means any of the following types of land vehicles, including any attached machinery or equipment:

a. Bulldozers, farm machinery, forklifts and other vehicles designed for use principally off public roads;

b. Vehicles maintained for use solely on or next to premises you own or rent.

c. Vehicles that travel on crawler treads;

d. Vehicles, whether self-propelled or not, maintained primarily to provide mobility to permanently mounted:

(1) Power cranes, shovels, loaders, diggers or drills; or

COMMERCIAL GENERAL LIABILITY
COVERAGE FORM

(2) Road construction or resurfacing equipment such as graders, scrapers or rollers;

e. Vehicles not described in a., b., c. or d. above that are not self-propelled and are maintained primarily to provide mobility to permanently attached equipment of the following types:

(1) Air compressors, pumps and generators, including spraying, welding, building cleaning, geophysical exploration, lighting and well servicing equipment; or

(2) Cherry pickers and similar devices used to raise or lower workers;

f. Vehicles not described in a., b., c. or d. above maintained primarily for purposes other than the transportation of persons or cargo.

However, self-propelled vehicles with the following types of permanently attached equipment are not "mobile equipment" but will be considered "autos."

(1) Equipment designed primarily for:

(a) Snow removal;

(b) Road maintenance, but not construction or resurfacing;

(c) Street cleaning.

(2) Cherry pickers and similar devices mounted on automobile or truck chassis and used to raise or lower workers; and

(3) Air compressors, pumps and generators, including spraying, welding, building cleaning, geophysical exploration, lighting and well servicing equipment.

9. "Occurrence" means an accident, including continuous or repeated exposure to substantially the same general harmful conditions.

10. "Personal injury" means injury, other than "bodily injury," arising out of one or more of the following offenses:

a. False arrest, detention or imprisonment;

b. Malicious prosecution.

c. Wrongful entry into, or eviction of a person from, a room, dwelling or premises that the person occupies;

d. Oral or written publication of material that slanders or libels a person or organization or disparages a person's or organization's goods, products or services; or

e. Oral or written publication of material that violates a person's right of privacy.

11. a. "Products-completed operations hazard" includes all "bodily injury" and "property damage" occurring away from premises you own or rent and arising out of "your product" or "your work" except:

(1) Products that are still in your physical possession; or

(2) Work that has not yet been completed or abandoned.

b. "Your work" will be deemed completed at the earliest of the following times:

(1) When all of the work called for in your contract has been completed.

(2) When all of the work to be done at the site has been completed if your contract calls for work at more than one site.

(3) When that part of the work done at a job site has been put to its intended use by any person or organization other than another contractor or subcontractor working on the same project.

Work that may need service, maintenance, correction, repair or replacement, but which is otherwise complete, will be treated as completed.

c. This hazard does not include "bodily injury" or "property damage" arising out of:

(1) The transportation of property, unless the injury or damage arises out of a condition in or on a vehicle created by the "loading or unloading" of it;

(2) The existence of tools, uninstalled equipment or abandoned or unused materials;

(3) Products or operations for which the classification in this Coverage Part or in our manual of rules includes products or completed operations.

12. "Property damage" means:

a. Physical injury to tangible property, including all resulting loss of use of that property; or

b. Loss of use of tangible property that is not physically injured.

13. "Suit" means a civil proceeding in which damages because of "bodily injury," "property damage," "personal injury" or "advertising injury" to which this insurance applies are alleged. "Suit" includes an arbitration proceeding alleging such damages to which you must submit or submit with our consent.

COMMERCIAL GENERAL LIABILITY
COVERAGE FORM

14. "Your product" means.

a. Any goods or products, other than real property, manufactured, sold, handled, distributed or disposed of by:

(1) You;

(2) Others trading under your name; or

(3) A person or organization whose business or assets you have acquired; and

b. Containers (other than vehicles), materials, parts or equipment furnished in connection with such goods or products.

"Your product" includes warranties or representations made at any time with respect to the fitness, quality, durability or performance of any of the items included in a. and b. above.

"Your product" does not include vending machines or other property rented to or located for the use of others but not sold.

15. "Your work" means:

a. Work or operations performed by you or on your behalf; and

b. Materials, parts or equipment furnished in connection with such work or operations.

"Your work" includes warranties or representations made at any time with respect to the fitness, quality, durability or performance of any of the items included in a. or b. above.

COMMERCIAL GENERAL LIABILITY COVERAGE FORM

COVERAGE A. PROVIDES CLAIMS MADE COVERAGE. PLEASE READ THE ENTIRE FORM CAREFULLY.

Various provisions in this policy restrict coverage. Read the entire policy carefully to determine rights, duties and what is and is not covered.

Throughout this policy the words "you" and "your" refer to the Named Insured shown in the Declarations. The words "we," "us" and "our" refer to the Company providing this insurance.

The word "insured" means any person or organization qualifying as such under SECTION II – WHO IS AN INSURED.

Other words and phrases that appear in quotation marks have special meaning. Refer to SECTION VI – DEFINITIONS.

SECTION 1 - COVERAGES

COVERAGE A. BODILY INJURY AND PROPERTY DAMAGE LIABILITY

1. Insuring Agreement.

  a. We will pay those sums that the insured becomes legally obligated to pay as damages because of "bodily injury" or "property damage" to which this insurance applies. No other obligation or liability to pay sums or perform acts or services is covered unless explicitly provided for under SUPPLEMENTARY PAYMENTS – COVERAGES A AND B. This insurance does not apply to "bodily injury" or "property damage" which occurred before the Retroactive Date, if any, shown in the Declarations or which occurs after the policy period. The "bodily injury" or "property damage" must be caused by an "occurrence." The "occurrence" must take place in the "coverage territory." We will have the right and duty to defend any "suit" seeking those damages. But:

    (1) The amount we will pay for damages is limited as described in SECTION III – LIMITS OF INSURANCE;

    (2) We may, at our discretion, investigate any "occurrence" and settle any claim or "suit" that may result; and

    (3) Our right and duty to defend end when we have used up the applicable limit of insurance in the payment of judgments or settlements under Coverages A or B or medical expenses under Coverage C.

  b. This insurance applies to "bodily injury" and "property damage" only if a claim for damages because of the "bodily injury" or "property damage" is first made against any insured during the policy period.

    (1) A claim by a person or organization seeking damages will be deemed to have been made when notice of such claim is received and recorded by any insured or by us, whichever comes first.

    (2) All claims for damages because of "bodily injury" to the same person, including damages claimed by any person or organization for care, loss of services, or death resulting at any time from the "bodily injury," will be deemed to have been made at the time the first of those claims is made against any insured.

    (3) All claims for damages because of "property damage" causing loss to the same person or organization as a result of an "occurrence" will be deemed to have been made at the time the first of those claims is made against any insured.

2. Exclusions.

This insurance does not apply to:

  a. "Bodily injury" or "property damage" expected or intended from the standpoint of the insured. This exclusion does not apply to "bodily injury" resulting from the use of reasonable force to protect persons or property.

  b. "Bodily injury" or "property damage" for which the insured is obligated to pay damages by reason of the assumption of liability in a contract or agreement. This exclusion does not apply to liability for damages:

    (1) Assumed in a contract or agreement that is an "insured contract;" or

    (2) That the insured would have in the absence of the contract or agreement.

  c. "Bodily injury" or "property damage" for which any insured may be held liable by reason of:

    (1) Causing or contributing to the intoxication of any person;

    (2) The furnishing of alcoholic beverages to a person under the legal drinking age or under the influence of alcohol, or

    (3) Any statute, ordinance or regulation relating to the sale, gift, distribution or use of alcoholic beverages.

This exclusion applies only if you are in the business of manufacturing, distributing, selling, serving or furnishing alcoholic beverages.

COMMERCIAL GENERAL LIABILITY
COVERAGE FORM

d. Any obligation of the insured under a workers compensation, disability benefits or unemployment compensation law or any similar law.

e. "Bodily injury" to:

(1) An employee of the insured arising out of and in the course of employment by the insured; or

(2) The spouse, child, parent, brother or sister of that employee as a consequence of (1) above.

This exclusion applies:

(1) Whether the insured may be liable as an employer or in any other capacity; and

(2) To any obligation to share damages with or repay someone else who must pay damages because of the injury.

This exclusion does not apply to liability assumed by the insured under an "insured contract."

f. (1) "Bodily injury" or "property damage" arising out of the actual, alleged or threatened discharge, dispersal, release or escape of pollutants:

(a) At or from premises you own, rent or occupy;

(b) At or from any site or location used by or for you or others for the handling, storage, disposal, processing or treatment of waste;

(c) Which are at any time transported, handled, stored, treated, disposed of, or processed as waste by or for you or any person or organization for whom you may be legally responsible; or

(d) At or from any site or location on which you or any contractors or subcontractors working directly or indirectly on your behalf are performing operations:

(i) if the pollutants are brought on or to the site or location in connection with such operations; or

(ii) if the operations are to test for, monitor, clean up, remove, contain, treat, detoxify or neutralize the pollutants.

(2) Any loss, cost, or expense arising out of any governmental direction or request that you test for, monitor, clean up, remove, contain, treat, detoxify or neutralize pollutants.

Pollutants means any solid, liquid, gaseous or thermal irritant or contaminant, including smoke, vapor, soot, fumes, acids, alkalis, chemicals and waste. Waste includes materials to be recycled, reconditioned or reclaimed.

g. "Bodily injury" or "property damage" arising out of the ownership, maintenance, use or entrustment to others of any aircraft, "auto" or watercraft owned or operated by or rented or loaned to any insured. Use includes operation and "loading or unloading."

This exclusion does not apply to:

(1) A watercraft while ashore on premises you own or rent;

(2) A watercraft you do not own that is:

(a) Less than 26 feet long; and

(b) Not being used to carry persons or property for a charge;

(3) Parking an "auto" on, or on the ways next to, premises you own or rent, provided the "auto" is not owned by or rented or loaned to you or the insured;

(4) Liability assumed under any "insured contract" for the ownership, maintenance or use of aircraft or watercraft; or

(5) "Bodily injury" or "property damage" arising out of the operation of any of the equipment listed in paragraph f.(2) or f.(3) of the definition of "mobile equipment" (Section VI.8).

h. "Bodily injury" or "property damage" arising out of:

(1) The transportation of "mobile equipment" by an "auto" owned or operated by or rented or loaned to any insured; or

(2) The use of "mobile equipment" in, or while in practice or preparation for a prearranged racing, speed or demolition contest or in any stunting activity.

i. "Bodily injury" or "property damage" due to war, whether or not declared, or any act or condition incident to war. War includes civil war, insurrection, rebellion or revolution. This exclusion applies only to liability assumed under a contract or agreement.

j. "Property damage" to:

(1) Property you own, rent, or occupy;

(2) Premises you sell, give away or abandon, if the "property damage" arises out of any part of those premises;

(3) Property loaned to you;

(4) Personal property in your care, custody or control;

(5) That particular part of real property on which you or any contractors or subcontractors working directly or indirectly on your behalf are performing operations, if the "property damage" arises out of those operations; or

(6) That particular part of any property that must be restored, repaired or replaced because "your work" was incorrectly performed on it.

Paragraph (2) of this exclusion does not apply if the premises are "your work" and were never occupied, rented or held for rental by you.

Paragraphs (3), (4), (5) and (6) of this exclusion do not apply to liability assumed under a sidetrack agreement.

Paragraph (6) of this exclusion does not apply to "property damage" included in the "products-completed operations hazard."

k. "Property damage" to "your product" arising out of it or any part of it.

l. "Property damage" to "your work" arising out of it or any part of it and included in the "products-completed operations hazard."

This exclusion does not apply if the damaged work or the work out of which the damage arises was performed on your behalf by a subcontractor.

m. "Property damage" to "impaired property" or property that has not been physically injured, arising out of:

(1) A defect, deficiency, inadequacy or dangerous condition in "your product" or "your work;" or

(2) A delay or failure by you or anyone acting on your behalf to perform a contract or agreement in accordance with its terms.

This exclusion does not apply to the loss of use of other property arising out of sudden and accidental physical injury to "your product" or "your work" after it has been put to its intended use.

n. Damages claimed for any loss, cost or expense incurred by you or others for the loss of use, withdrawal, recall, inspection, repair, replacement, adjustment, removal or disposal of:

(1) "Your product,"

(2) "Your work;" or

(3) "Impaired property;"

if such product, work, or property is withdrawn or recalled from the market or from use by any person or organization because of a known or suspected defect,

COMMERCIAL GENERAL LIABILITY
COVERAGE FORM

deficiency, inadequacy or dangerous condition in it.

Exclusions c. through n. do not apply to damage by fire to premises rented to you. A separate limit of insurance applies to this coverage as described in SECTION III – LIMITS OF INSURANCE.

COVERAGE B. PERSONAL AND ADVERTISING INJURY LIABILITY

1. Insuring Agreement.

a. We will pay those sums that the insured becomes legally obligated to pay as damages because of "personal injury" or "advertising injury" to which this insurance applies. No other obligation or liability to pay sums or perform acts or services is covered unless explicitly provided for under SUPPLEMENTARY PAYMENTS – COVERAGES A AND B. We will have the right and duty to defend any "suit" seeking those damages. But;

(1) The amount we will pay for damages is limited as described in SECTION III – LIMITS OF INSURANCE;

(2) We may investigate and settle any claim or "suit" at our discretion; and

(3) Our right and duty to defend end when we have used up the applicable limit of insurance in the payment of judgments or settlements under Coverages A or B or medical expenses under Coverage C.

b. This insurance applies to "personal injury" only if caused by an offense:

(1) Committed in the "coverage territory" during the policy period; and

(2) Arising out of the conduct of your business, excluding advertising, publishing, broadcasting or telecasting done by or for you.

c. This insurance applies to "advertising injury" only if caused by an offense committed:

(1) In the "coverage territory" during the policy period; and

(2) In the course of advertising your goods, products or services.

2. Exclusions.

This insurance does not apply to:

a. "Personal injury" or "advertising injury:"

(1) Arising out of oral or written publication of material, if done by or at the direction of the insured with knowledge of its falsity;

COMMERCIAL GENERAL LIABILITY
COVERAGE FORM

(2) Arising out of oral or written publication of material whose first publication took place before the beginning of the policy period;

(3) Arising out of the willful violation of a penal statute or ordinance committed by or with the consent of the insured; or

(4) For which the insured has assumed liability in a contract or agreement. This exclusion does not apply to liability for damages that the insured would have in the absence of the contract or agreement.

b. "Advertising injury" arising out of:

(1) Breach of contract, other than misappropriation of advertising ideas under an implied contract;

(2) The failure of goods, products or services to conform with advertised quality or performance;

(3) The wrong description of the price of goods, products or services; or

(4) An offense committed by an insured whose business is advertising, broadcasting, publishing or telecasting.

COVERAGE C. MEDICAL PAYMENTS

1. Insuring Agreement.

a. We will pay medical expenses as described below for "bodily injury" caused by an accident:

(1) On premises you own or rent;

(2) On ways next to premises you own or rent; or

(3) Because of your operations;

provided that:

(1) The accident takes place in the "coverage territory" and during the policy period;

(2) The expenses are incurred and reported to us within one year of the date of the accident; and

(3) The injured person submits to examination, at our expense, by physicians of our choice as often as we reasonably require.

b. We will make these payments regardless of fault. These payments will not exceed the applicable limit of insurance. We will pay reasonable expenses for:

(1) First aid at the time of an accident;

(2) Necessary medical, surgical, x-ray and dental services, including, prosthetic devices; and

(3) Necessary ambulance, hospital, professional nursing and funeral services.

2. Exclusions.

We will not pay expenses for "bodily injury:"

a. To any insured.

b. To a person hired to do work for or on behalf of any insured or a tenant of any insured.

c. To a person injured on that part of premises you own or rent that the person normally occupies.

d. To a person, whether or not an employee of any insured, if benefits for the "bodily injury" are payable or must be provided under a workers compensation or disability benefits law or a similar law.

e. To a person injured while taking part in athletics.

f. Included within the "products-completed operations hazard."

g. Excluded under Coverage A.

h. Due to war, whether or not declared, or any act or condition incident to war. War includes civil war, insurrection, rebellion or revolution.

SUPLEMENTARY PAYMENTS - COVERAGES A AND B

We will pay, with respect to any claim or "suit" we defend:

1. All expenses we incur.

2. Up to $250 for cost of bail bonds required because of accidents or traffic law violations arising out of the use of any vehicle to which the Bodily Injury Liability Coverage applies. We do not have to furnish these bonds.

3. The cost of bonds to release attachments, but only for bond amounts within the applicable limit of insurance. We do not have to furnish these bonds.

4. All reasonable expenses incurred by the insured at our request to assist us in the investigation or defense of the claim or "suit," including actual loss of earnings up to $100 a day because of time off from work.

5. All costs taxed against the insured in the "suit."

6. Pre-judgment interest awarded against the insured on that part of the judgment we pay. If we make an offer to pay the applicable limit of insurance, we will not pay any pre-judgment interest based on that period of time after the offer.

COMMERCIAL GENERAL LIABILITY
COVERAGE FORM

7. All interest on the full amount of any judgment that accrues after entry of the judgment and before we have paid, offered to pay, or deposited in court the part of the judgment that is within the applicable limit of insurance.

These payments will not reduce the limits of insurance.

SECTION II - WHO IS AN INSURED

1. If you are designated in the Declarations as:

a. An individual, you and your spouse are insureds, but only with respect to the conduct of a business of which you are the sole owner.

b. A partnership or joint venture, you are an insured. Your members, your partners, and their spouses are also insureds, but only with respect to the conduct of your business.

c. An organization other than a partnership or joint venture, you are an insured. Your executive officers and directors are insureds, but only with respect to their duties as your officers or directors. Your stockholders are also insureds, but only with respect to their liability as stockholders.

2. Each of the following is also an insured:

a. Your employees, other than your executive officers, but only for acts within the scope of their employment by you. However, none of these employees is an insured for:

(1) "Bodily injury" or "personal injury" to you or to a co-employee while in the course of his or her employment; or

(2) "Bodily injury" or "personal injury" arising out of his or her providing or failing to provide professional health care services; or

(3) "Property damage" to property owned or occupied by or rented or loaned to that employee, any of your other employees, or any of your partners or members (if you are a partnership or joint venture).

b. Any person (other than your employee) or any organization while acting as your real estate manager.

c. Any person or organization having proper temporary custody of your property if you die, but only:

(1) With respect to liability arising out of the maintenance or use of that property; and

(2) Until your legal representative has been appointed.

d. Your legal representative if you die, but only with respect to duties as such. That representative will have all your rights and duties under this Coverage Part.

3. With respect to "mobile equipment" registered in your name under any motor vehicle registration law, any person is an insured while driving such equipment along a public highway with your permission. Any other person or organization responsible for the conduct of such person is also an insured, but only with respect to liability arising out of the operation of the equipment, and only if no other insurance of any kind is available to that person or organization for this liability. However no person or organization is an insured with respect to:

a. "Bodily injury" to a co-employee of the person driving the equipment; or

b. "Property damage" to property owned by, rented to, in the charge of or occupied by you or the employer of any person who is an insured under this provision.

4. Any organization you newly acquire or form, other than a partnership or joint venture, and over which you maintain ownership or majority interest, will be deemed to be a Named Insured if there is no other similar insurance available to that organization. However:

a. Coverage under the provision is afforded only until the 90th day after you acquire or form the organization or the end of the policy period, whichever is earlier;

b. Coverage A does not apply to "bodily injury" or "property damage" that occurred before you acquired or formed the organization; and

c. Coverage B does not apply to "personal injury" or "advertising injury" arising out of an offense committed before you acquired or formed the organization.

No person or organization is an insured with respect to the conduct of any current or past partnership or joint venture that is not shown as a Named Insured in the Declarations.

SECTION III - LIMITS OF INSURANCE

1. The Limits of Insurance shown in the Declarations and the rules below fix the most we will pay regardless of the number of:

a. Insureds;

b. Claims made or "suits" brought; or

c. Persons or organizations making claims or bringing "suits."

2. The General Aggregate Limit is the most we will pay for the sum of:

a. Medical expenses under Coverage C; and

COMMERCIAL GENERAL LIABILITY
COVERAGE FORM

b. Damages under Coverage A and Coverage B, except damages because of injury and damage included in the "products-completed operations hazard."

3. The Products-Completed Operations Aggregate Limit is the most we will pay under Coverage A for damages because of injury and damage included in the "products-completed operations hazard."

4. Subject to 2. above, the Personal and Advertising Injury Limit is the most we will pay under Coverage B for the sum of all damages because of all "personal injury" and all "advertising injury" sustained by any one person or organization.

5. Subject to 2. or 3. above, whichever applies, the Each Occurrence Limit is the most we will pay for the sum of:

   a. Damages under Coverage A; and

   b. Medical expenses under Coverage C

   because of all "bodily injury" and "property damage" arising out of any one "occurrence."

6. Subject to 5. above, the Fire Damage Limit is the most we will pay under Coverage A for damages because of "property damage" to premises rented to you arising out of any one fire.

7. Subject to 5. above, the Medical Expense Limit is the most we will pay under Coverage C for all medical expenses because of "bodily injury" sustained by any one person.

The limits of this Coverage Part apply separately to each consecutive annual period and to any remaining period of less than 12 months, starting with the beginning of the policy period shown in the Declarations, unless the policy period is extended after issuance for an additional period of less than 12 months. In that case, the additional period will be deemed part of the last preceding period for purposes of determining the Limits of Insurance.

SECTION IV - COMMERCIAL GENERAL LIABILITY CONDITIONS

1. Bankruptcy.

Bankruptcy or insolvency of the insured or of the insured's estate will not relieve us of our obligations under this Coverage Part.

2. Duties In The Event Of Occurrence, Claim Or Suit.

a. You must see to it that we are notified as soon as practicable of an "occurrence" which may result in a claim. To the extent possible, notice should include:

   (1) How, when and where the "occurrence" took place;

   (2) The names and addresses of any injured persons and witnesses; and

   (3) The nature and location of any injury or damage arising out of the "occurrence."

   Notice of an "occurrence" is not notice of a claim.

b. If a claim is received by any insured you must:

   (1) Immediately record the specifics of the claim and the date received; and

   (2) Notify us as soon as practicable.

   You must see to it that we receive written notice of the claim as soon as practicable.

c. You and any other involved insured must:

   (1) Immediately send us copies of any demands, notices, summonses or legal papers received in connection with the claim or a "suit;"

   (2) Authorize us to obtain records and other information;

   (3) Cooperate with us in the investigation, settlement or defense of the claim or "suit;" and

   (4) Assist us, upon our request, in the enforcement of any right against any person or organization which may be liable to the insured because of injury or damage to which this insurance may also apply.

d. No insureds will, except at their own cost, voluntarily make a payment, assume any obligation, or incur any expense, other than for first aid, without our consent.

3. Legal Action Against Us.

No person or organization has a right under this Coverage Part:

a. To join us as a party or otherwise bring us into a "suit" asking for damages from an insured; or

b. To sue us on this Coverage Part unless all of its terms have been fully complied with.

A person or organization may sue us to recover on an agreed settlement or on a final judgment against an insured obtained after an actual trial; but we will not be liable for damages that are not payable under the terms of this Coverage Part or that are in excess of the applicable limit of insurance. An agreed settlement means a settlement and release of liability signed by us, the insured and the claimant or the claimant's legal representative.

COMMERCIAL GENERAL LIABILITY
COVERAGE FORM

4. Other Insurance.

If other valid and collectible insurance is available to the insured for a loss we cover under Coverages A or B of this Coverage Part, our obligations are limited as follows:

a. Primary Insurance

This insurance is primary except when b. below applies. If this insurance is primary, our obligations are not affected unless any of the other insurance is also primary. Then, we will share with all that other insurance by the method described in c. below.

b. Excess Insurance

This insurance is excess over any of the other insurance, whether primary, excess, contingent or on any other basis:

(1) That is effective prior to the beginning of the policy period shown in the Declarations of this insurance and applies to "bodily injury" or "property damage" on other than a claims-made basis if:

   (a) No Retroactive Date is shown in the Declarations of this insurance; or

   (b) The other insurance has a policy period which continues after the Retroactive Date shown in the Declarations of this insurance;

(2) That is Fire, Extended Coverage, Builders' Risk, Installation Risk or similar coverage for "your work."

(3) That is Fire insurance for premises rented to you; or

(4) If the loss arises out of the maintenance or use of aircraft, "autos" or watercraft to the extent not subject to Exclusion g. of Coverage A (Section 1).

When this insurance is excess, we will have no duty under Coverages A or B to defend any claim or "suit" that any other insurer has a duty to defend. If no other insurer defends, we will undertake to do so, but we will be entitled to the insured's rights against all those other insurers.

When this insurance is excess over other insurance, we will pay only our share of the amount of the loss, if any, that exceeds the sum of:

(1) The total amount that all such other insurance would pay for the loss in the absence of this insurance; and

(2) The total of all deductible and self-insured amounts under all that other insurance.

We will share the remaining loss, if any, with any other insurance that is not described in this Excess Insurance provision

and was not brought specifically to apply in excess of the Limits of Insurance shown in the Declarations of this Coverage Part.

c. Method of Sharing

If all of the other insurance permits contribution by equal shares, we will follow this method also. Under this approach each insurer contributes equal amounts until it has paid its applicable limit of insurance or none of the loss remains, whichever comes first.

If any of the other insurance does not permit contribution by equal shares, we will contribute by limits. Under this method, each insurer's share is based on the ratio of its applicable limit of insurance to the total applicable limits of insurance of all insurers.

5. Premium Audit.

a. We will compute all premiums for this Coverage Part in accordance with our rules and rates.

b. Premium shown in this Coverage Part as advance premium is a deposit premium only. At the close of each audit period we will compute the earned premium for that period. Audit premiums are due and payable on notice to the first Named Insured. If the sum of the advance and audit premiums paid for the policy term is greater than the earned premium, we will return the excess to the first Named Insured.

c. The first Named Insured must keep records of the information we need for premium computation, and send us copies at such times as we may request.

6. Representations.

By accepting this policy, you agree:

a. The statements in the Declarations are accurate and complete;

b. Those statements are based upon representations you made to us; and

c. We have issued this policy in reliance upon your representations.

7. Separation Of Insureds.

Except with respect to the Limits of Insurance, and any rights or duties specifically assigned to the first Named Insured, this insurance applies;

a. As if each Named Insured were the only Named Insured; and

b. Separately to each insured against whom claim is made or "suit" is brought.

COMMERCIAL GENERAL LIABILITY
COVERAGE FORM

8. Transfer Of Rights Of Recovery Against Others To Us.

If the insured has rights to recover all or part of any payment we have made under this Coverage Part, those rights are transferred to us. The insured must do nothing after loss to impair them. At our request, the insured will bring "suit" or transfer those rights to us and help us enforce them.

9. When We Do Not Renew.

If we decide not to renew this Coverage Part, we will mail or deliver to the first Named Insured shown in the Declarations written notice of the nonrenewal not less than 30 days before the expiration date.

If notice is mailed, proof of mailing will be sufficient proof of notice.

10. Your Right to Claim and "Occurrence" Information.

We will provide the first Named Insured shown in the Declarations the following information relating to this and any preceding general liability claims made Coverage Part we have issued to you during the previous three years:

a. A list or other record of each "occurrence," not previously reported to any other insurer, of which we were notified in accordance with paragraph 2.a. of this Section. We will include the date and brief description of the "occurrence" if that information was in the notice we received.

b. A summary by policy year, of payments made and amounts reserved, stated separately, under any applicable General Aggregate Limit and Products-Completed Operations Aggregate Limit.

Amounts reserved are based on our judgment. They are subject to change and should not be regarded as ultimate settlement values.

If we cancel or elect not to renew this Coverage Part, we will provide such information no later than 30 days before the date of policy termination. In other circumstances, we will provide this information only if we receive a written request from the first Named Insured within 60 days after the end of the policy period. In this case, we will provide this information within 45 days of receipt of the request.

We compile claim and "occurrence" information for our own business purposes and exercise reasonable care in doing so. In providing this information to the first Named Insured, we make no representations or warranties to insureds, insurers, or others to whom this information is furnished by or

on behalf of any insured. Cancellation or non-renewal will be effective even if we inadvertently provide inaccurate information.

SECTION V - EXTENDED REPORTING PERIODS

1. We will provide one or more Extended Reporting Periods, as described below, if:

a. This Coverage Part is cancelled or not renewed; or

b. We renew or replace this Coverage Part with insurance that:

(1) Has a Retroactive Date later than the date shown in the Declarations of this Coverage Part; or

(2) Does not apply to "bodily injury" or "property damage" on a claims-made basis.

2. A Basic Extended Reporting Period is automatically provided without additional charge. This period starts with the end of the policy period and lasts for:

a. Five years for claims arising out of an "occurrence" reported to us, not later than 60 days after the end of the policy period, in accordance with paragraph 2.a. of SECTION IV - COMMERCIAL GENERAL LIABILITY CONDITIONS; or

b. Sixty days for all other claims.

The Basic Extended Reporting Period does not apply to claims that are covered under any subsequent insurance you purchase, or that would be covered but for exhaustion of the amount of insurance applicable to such claims.

3. A Supplemental Extended Reporting Period of unlimited duration is available, but only by an endorsement and for an extra charge. This supplemental period starts:

a. Five years after the end of the policy period for claims arising out of an "occurrence" reported to us, not later than 60 days after the end of the policy period, in accordance with paragraph 2.a. of SECTION IV - COMMERCIAL GENERAL LIABILITY CONDITIONS; or

b. Sixty days after the end of the policy period for all other claims.

You must give us a written request for the endorsement within 60 days after the end of the policy period. The Supplemental Extended Reporting Period will not go into effect unless you pay the additional premium promptly when due.

We will determine the additional premium in accordance with our rules and rates. In doing so, we may take into account the following:

a. The exposures insured;

b. Previous types and amounts of insurance;

c. Limits of Insurance available under this Coverage Part for future payment of damages; and

d. Other related factors.

The additional premium will not exceed 200% of the annual premium for this Coverage Part.

This endorsement shall set forth the terms, not inconsistent with this Section, applicable to the Supplemental Extended Reporting Period, including a provision to the effect that the insurance afforded for claims first received during such period is excess over any other valid and collectible insurance available under policies in force after the Supplemental Extended Reporting Period starts.

4. Extended Reporting Periods do not extend the policy period or change the scope of coverage provided. They apply only to claims for "bodily injury" or "property damage" that occurs before the end of the policy period (but not before the Retroactive Date, if any, shown in the Declarations).

Claims for such injury or damage which are first received and recorded during the Basic Extended Reporting Period (or during the Supplemental Extended Reporting Period, if it is in effect) will be deemed to have been made on the last day of the policy period.

Once in effect, Extended Reporting Periods may not be cancelled.

5. Extended Reporting Periods do not reinstate or increase the Limits of Insurance applicable to any claim to which this Coverage Part applies, except to the extent described in paragraph 6. of this Section.

6. If the Supplemental Extended Reporting Period is in effect, we will provide the separate aggregate limits of insurance described below, but only for claims first received and recorded during the Supplemental Extended Reporting Period.

The separate aggregate limits of insurance will be equal to the dollar amount shown in the Declarations in effect at the end of the policy period for such of the following limits of insurance for which a dollar amount has been entered:

General Aggregate Limit
Products–Completed Operations Aggregate Limit

Paragraphs 2. and 3. of SECTION III – LIMITS OF INSURANCE will be amended accordingly. The Each Occurrence Limit and the Fire Damage Limit shown in the Declarations will then continue to apply, as set forth in paragraphs 5. and 6. of that Section.

SECTION VI - DEFINITIONS

1. "Advertising injury" means injury arising out of one or more of the following offenses:

   a. Oral or written publication of material that slanders or libels a person or organization or disparages a person's or organization's goods, products or services;

   b. Oral or written publication of material that violates a person's right of privacy;

   c. Misappropriation of advertising ideas or style of doing business; or

   d. Infringement of copyright, title or slogan.

2. "Auto" means a land motor vehicle, trailer or semitrailer designed for travel on public roads, including any attached machinery or equipment. But "auto" does not include "mobile equipment."

3. "Bodily Injury" means bodily injury, sickness or disease sustained by a person, including death resulting from any of these at any time.

4. "Coverage territory" means:

   a. The United States of America (including its territories and possessions), Puerto Rico and Canada;

   b. International waters or airspace, provided the injury or damage does not occur in the course of travel or transportation to or from any place not included in a. above; or

   c. All parts of the world if:

      (1) The injury or damages arises out of:

         (a) Goods or products made or sold by you in the territory described in a. above; or

         (b) The activities of a person whose home is in the territory described in a. above, but is away for a short time on your business; and

      (2) The insured's responsibility to pay damages is determined in a "suit" on the merits, in the territory described in a. above or in a settlement we agree to.

5. "Impaired property" means tangible property, other than "your product" or "your work," that cannot be used or is less useful because;

   a. It incorporates "your product" or "your work" that is known or thought to be defective, deficient, inadequate or dangerous; or

   b. You have failed to fulfill the terms of a contract or agreement;

   if such property can be restored to use by:

COMMERCIAL GENERAL LIABILITY
COVERAGE FORM

a. The repair, replacement, adjustment or removal of "your product" or "your work;" or

b. Your fulfilling the terms of the contract or agreement.

6. "Insured contract" means:

a. A lease of premises;

b. A sidetrack agreement;

c. An easement or license agreement in connection with vehicle or pedestrian private railroad crossing at grade;

d. Any other easement agreement, except in connection with construction or demolition operations on or within 50 feet of a railroad;

e. An indemnification of a municipality as required by ordinance, except in connection with work for a municipality;

f. An elevator maintenance agreement; or

g. That part of any other contract or agreement pertaining to your business under which you assume the tort liability of another to pay damages because of "bodily injury" or "property damage" to a third person or organization, if the contract or agreement is made prior to the "bodily injury" or "property damage." Tort liability means a liability that would be imposed by law in the absence of any contract or agreement.

An "insured contract" does not include that part of any contract or agreement:

a. That indemnifies an architect, engineer or surveyor for injury or damage arising out of:

(1) Preparing, approving or failing to prepare or approve maps, drawings, opinions, reports, surveys, change orders, designs or specifications; or

(2) Giving directions or instructions, or failing to give them, if that is the primary cause of the injury or damage;

b. Under which the insured, if an architect, engineer or surveyor, assumes liability for injury or damage arising out of the insured's rendering or failing to render professional services, including those listed in a. above and supervisory, inspection or engineering services; or

c. That indemnifies any person or organization for damage by fire to premises rented or loaned to you.

7. "Loading or unloading" means the handling of property:

a. After it is moved from the place where it is accepted for movement into or onto an aircraft, watercraft or "auto;"

b. While it is in or on an aircraft, watercraft or "auto;" or

c. While it is being moved from an aircraft, watercraft or "auto" to the place where it is finally delivered;

but "loading or unloading" does not include the movement of property by means of a mechanical device, other than a hand truck, that is not attached to the aircraft, watercraft or "auto."

8. "Mobile equipment" means any of the following types of land vehicles, including any attached machinery or equipment:

a. Bulldozers, farm machinery, forklifts and other vehicles designed for use principally off public roads;

b. Vehicles maintained for use solely on or next to premises you own or rent;

c. Vehicles that travel on crawler treads;

d. Vehicles, whether self-propelled or not, maintained primarily to provide mobility to permanently mounted:

(1) Power cranes, shovels, loaders, diggers or drills; or

(2) Road construction or resurfacing equipment such as graders, scrapers or rollers;

e. Vehicles not described in a., b., c. or d. above that are not self-propelled and are maintained primarily to provide mobility to permanently attached equipment of the following types:

(1) Air compressors, pumps and generators, including spraying, welding, building cleaning, geophysical exploration, lighting and well servicing equipment; or

(2) Cherry pickers and similar devices used to raise or lower workers;

f. Vehicles not described in a., b., c. or d. above maintained primarily for purposes other than the transportation of persons or cargo.

However, self-propelled vehicles with the following types of permanently attached equipment are not "mobile equipment" but will be considered "autos:"

(1) Equipment designed primarily for:

(a) Snow removal;

(b) Road maintenance, but not construction or resurfacing;

(c) Street cleaning;

(2) Cherry pickers and similar devices mounted on automobile or truck chassis and used to raise or lower workers; and

(3) Air compressors, pumps and generators, including spraying, welding, building cleaning, geophysical exploration, lighting and well servicing equipment.

9. "Occurrence" means an accident, including continuous or repeated exposure to substantially the same general harmful conditions.

10. "Personal injury" means injury, other than "bodily injury," arising out of one or more of the following offenses:

a. False arrest, detention or imprisonment;

b. Malicious prosecution;

c. Wrongful entry into, or eviction of a person from, a room, dwelling or premises that the person occupies;

d. Oral or written publication of material that slanders or libels a person or organization or disparges a person's or organization's goods, products or services; or

e. Oral or written publication of material that violates a person's right of privacy.

11. a. "Products–completed operations hazard" includes all "bodily injury" and "property damage" occurring away from premises you own or rent and arising out of "your product" or "your work" except:

(1) Products that are still in your physical possession; or

(2) Work that has not yet been completed or abandoned.

b. "Your work" will be deemed completed at the earliest of the following times:

(1) When all of the work called for in your contract has been completed.

(2) When all of the work to be done at the site has been completed if your contract calls for work at more than one site.

(3) When that part of the work done at a job site had been put to its intended use by any person or organization other than another contractor or subcontractor working on the same project.

Work that may need service, maintenance, correction, repair or replacement, but which is otherwise complete, will be treated as completed.

c. This hazard does not include "bodily injury" or "property damage" arising out of:

(1) The transportation of property, unless the injury or damage arises out of a condition in or on a vehicle created by the "loading or unloading" of it:

(2) The existence of tools, uninstalled equipment or abandoned or unused materials;

(3) Products or operations for which the classification in this Coverage Part or in our manual of rules includes products or completed operations.

12. "Property damage" means:

a. Physical injury to tangible property, including all resulting loss of use of that property; or

b. Loss of use of tangible property that is not physically injured.

13. "Suit" means a civil proceeding in which damages because of "bodily injury," "property damage," "personal injury" or "advertising injury" to which this insurance applies are alleged. "Suit" includes an arbitration proceeding alleging such damages to which you must submit or submit with our consent.

14. "Your product" means:

a. Any goods or products, other than real property, manufactured, sold, handled, distributed or disposed of by:

(1) You;

(2) Others trading under your name; or

(3) A person or organization whose business or assets you have acquired; and

b. Containers (other than vehicles), materials, parts or equipment furnished in connection with such goods or products.

"Your product" includes warranties or representations made at any time with respect to the fitness, quality, durability or performance of any of the items included in a. and b. above.

"Your product" does not include vending machines or other property rented to or located for the use of others but not sold.

15. "Your work" means:

a. Work or operations performed by you or on your behalf; and

b. Materials, parts or equipment furnished in connection with such work or operations.

"Your work" includes warranties or representations made at any time with respect to the fitness, quality, durability or performance of any of the items included in a. or b. above.

COMMERCIAL GENERAL LIABILITY COVERAGE FORM

Various provisions in this policy restrict coverage. Read the entire policy carefully to determine rights, duties and what is and is not covered.

Throughout this policy the words "you" and "your" refer to the Named Insured shown in the Declarations, and any other person or organization qualifying as a Named Insured under this policy. The words "we," "us" and "our" refer to the company providing this insurance.

The word "insured" means any person or organization qualifying as such under WHO IS AN INSURED (SECTION II).

Other words and phrases that appear in quotation marks have special meaning. Refer to DEFINITIONS (SECTION V).

SECTION I - COVERAGES

COVERAGE A. BODILY INJURY AND PROPERTY DAMAGE LIABILITY

1. Insuring Agreement.

a. We will pay those sums that the insured becomes legally obligated to pay as damages because of "bodily injury" or "property damage" to which this insurance applies. We will have the right and duty to defend any "suit" seeking those damages. We may at our discretion investigate any "occurrence" and settle any claim or "suit" that may result. But:

(1) The amount we will pay for damages is limited as described in LIMITS OF INSURANCE (SECTION III); and

(2) Our right and duty to defend end when we have used up the applicable limit of insurance in the payment of judgments or settlements under Coverages A or B or medical expenses under Coverage C.

No other obligation or liability to pay sums or perform acts or services is covered unless explicitly provided for under SUPPLEMENTARY PAYMENTS - COVERAGES A AND B.

b. This insurance applies to "bodily injury" and "property damage" only if:

(1) The "bodily injury" or "property damage" is caused by an "occurrence" that takes place in the "coverage territory;" and

(2) The "bodily injury" or "property damage" occurs during the policy period.

c. Damages because of "bodily injury" include damages claimed by any person or organization for care, loss of services or death resulting at any time from the "bodily injury."

2. Exclusions.

This insurance does not apply to:

a. "Bodily injury" or "property damage" expected or intended from the standpoint of the insured. This exclusion does not apply to "bodily injury" resulting from the use of reasonable force to protect persons or property.

b. "Bodily injury" or "property damage" for which the insured is obligated to pay damages by reason of the assumption of liability in a contract or agreement. This exclusion does not apply to liability for damages:

(1) Assumed in a contract or agreement that is an "insured contract," provided the "bodily injury" or "property damage" occurs subsequent to the execution of the contract or agreement; or

(2) That the insured would have in the absence of the contract or agreement.

c. "Bodily injury" or "property damage" for which any insured may be held liable by reason of:

(1) Causing or contributing to the intoxication of any person;

(2) The furnishing of alcoholic beverages to a person under the legal drinking age or under the influence of alcohol; or

(3) Any statute, ordinance or regulation relating to the sale, gift, distribution or use of alcoholic beverages.

This exclusion applies only if you are in the business of manufacturing, distributing, selling, serving or furnishing alcoholic beverages.

COMMERCIAL GENERAL LIABILITY
COVERAGE FORM

d. Any obligation of the insured under a workers' compensation, disability benefits or unemployment compensation law or any similar law.

e. "Bodily injury" to:

(1) An employee of the insured arising out of and in the course of employment by the insured; or

(2) The spouse, child, parent, brother or sister of that employee as a consequence of (1) above.

This exclusion applies:

(1) Whether the insured may be liable as an employer or in any other capacity; and

(2) To any obligation to share damages with or repay someone else who must pay damages because of the injury.

This exclusion does not apply to liability assumed by the insured under an "insured contract."

f. (1) "Bodily injury" or "property damage" arising out of the actual, alleged or threatened discharge, dispersal, seepage, migration, release or escape of pollutants:

(a) At or from any premises, site or location which is or was at any time owned or occupied by, or rented or loaned to, any insured;

(b) At or from any premises, site or location which is or was at any time used by or for any insured or others for the handling, storage, disposal, processing or treatment of waste;

(c) Which are or were at any time transported, handled, stored, treated, disposed of, or processed as waste by or for any insured or any person or organization for whom you may be legally responsible; or

(d) At or from any premises, site or location on which any insured or any contractors or subcontractors working directly or indirectly on any insured's behalf are performing operations:

(i) if the pollutants are brought on or to the premises, site or location in connection with such operations by such insured, contractor or subcontractor; or

(ii) if the operations are to test for, monitor, clean up, remove, contain, treat, detoxify or neutralize, or in any way respond to, or assess the effects of pollutants.

Subparagraphs (a) and (d)(i) do not apply to "bodily injury" or "property damage" arising out of heat, smoke or fumes from a hostile fire.

As used in this exclusion, a hostile fire means one which becomes uncontrollable or breaks out from where it was intended to be.

(2) Any loss, cost or expense arising out of any:

(a) Request, demand or order that any insured or others test for, monitor, clean up, remove, contain, treat, detoxify or neutralize, or in any way respond to, or assess the effects of pollutants; or

(b) Claim or suit by or on behalf of a governmental authority for damages because of testing for, monitoring, cleaning up, removing, containing, treating, detoxifying or neutralizing, or in any way responding to, or assessing the effects of pollutants.

Pollutants means any solid, liquid, gaseous or thermal irritant or contaminant, including smoke, vapor, soot, fumes, acids, alkalis, chemicals and waste. Waste includes materials to be recycled, reconditioned or reclaimed.

g. "Bodily injury" or "property damage" arising out of the ownership, maintenance, use or entrustment to others of any aircraft, "auto" or watercraft owned or operated by or rented or loaned to any insured. Use includes operation and "loading or unloading."

This exclusion does not apply to:

(1) A watercraft while ashore on premises you own or rent;

(2) A watercraft you do not own that is:

    (a) Less than 26 feet long; and

    (b) Not being used to carry persons or property for a charge;

(3) Parking an "auto" on, or on the ways next to, premises you own or rent, provided the "auto" is not owned by or rented or loaned to you or the insured;

(4) Liability assumed under any "insured contract" for the ownership, maintenance or use of aircraft or watercraft; or

(5) "Bodily injury" or "property damage" arising out of the operation of any of the equipment listed in paragraph f.(2) or f.(3) of the definition of "mobile equipment" (Section V.8.).

h. "Bodily injury" or "property damage" arising out of:

(1) The transportation of "mobile equipment" by an "auto" owned or operated by or rented or loaned to any insured; or

(2) The use of "mobile equipment" in, or while in practice or preparation for, a prearranged racing, speed or demolition contest or in any stunting activity.

i. "Bodily injury" or "property damage" due to war, whether or not declared, or any act or condition incident to war. War includes civil war, insurrection, rebellion or revolution. This exclusion applies only to liability assumed under a contract or agreement.

j. "Property damage" to:

(1) Property you own, rent, or occupy;

(2) Premises you sell, give away or abandon, if the "property damage" arises out of any part of those premises;

(3) Property loaned to you;

(4) Personal property in the care, custody or control of the insured;

(5) That particular part of real property on which you or any contractors or subcontractors working directly or indirectly on your behalf are performing operations, if the "property damage" arises out of those operations; or

(6) That particular part of any property that must be restored, repaired or replaced because "your work" was incorrectly performed on it.

Paragraph (2) of this exclusion does not apply if the premises are "your work" and were never occupied, rented or held for rental by you.

Paragraphs (3), (4), (5) and (6) of this exclusion do not apply to liability assumed under a sidetrack agreement.

Paragraph (6) of this exclusion does not apply to "property damage" included in the "products-completed operations hazard."

k. "Property damage" to "your product" arising out of it or any part of it.

l. "Property damage" to "your work" arising out of it or any part of it and included in the "products-completed operations hazard."

This exclusion does not apply if the damaged work or the work out of which the damage arises was performed on your behalf by a subcontractor.

m. "Property damage" to "impaired property" or property that has not been physically injured, arising out of:

(1) A defect, deficiency, inadequacy or dangerous condition in "your product" or "your work;" or

(2) A delay or failure by you or anyone acting on your behalf to perform a contract or agreement in accordance with its terms.

This exclusion does not apply to the loss of use of other property arising out of sudden and accidental physical injury to "your product" or "your work" after it has been put to its intended use.

n. Damages claimed for any loss, cost or expense incurred by you or others for the loss of use, withdrawal, recall, inspection, repair, replacement, adjustment, removal or disposal of:

COMMERCIAL GENERAL LIABILITY
COVERAGE FORM

(1) "Your product;"

(2) "Your work;" or

(3) "Impaired property;"

if such product, work, or property is withdrawn or recalled from the market or from use
by any person or organization because of a
known or suspected defect, deficiency, inadequacy or dangerous condition in it.

Exclusions c. through n. do not apply to damage
by fire to premises rented to you. A separate limit
of insurance applies to this coverage as described
in LIMITS OF INSURANCE (SECTION III).

COVERAGE B. PERSONAL AND ADVERTIS-ING INJURY LIABILITY

1. Insuring Agreement.

a. We will pay those sums that the insured becomes legally obligated to pay as damages
because of "personal injury" or "advertising
injury" to which this coverage part applies.
We will have the right and duty to defend any
"suit" seeking those damages. We may at our
discretion investigate any "occurrence" or offense and settle any claim or "suit" that may
result. But:

(1) The amount we will pay for damages is
limited as described in LIMITS OF IN-
SURANCE (SECTION III); and

(2) Our right and duty to defend end when
we have used up the applicable limit of
insurance in the payment of judgments or
settlements under Coverage A or B or
medical expenses under Coverage C.

No other obligation or liability to pay sums or
perform acts or services is covered unless explicitly provided for under SUPPLEMENTARY
PAYMENTS - COVERAGES A AND B.

b. This insurance applies to:

(1) "Personal injury" caused by an offense
arising out of your business, excluding
advertising, publishing, broadcasting or
telecasting done by or for you;

(2) "Advertising injury" caused by an offense
committed in the course of advertising
your goods, products or services;

but only if the offense was committed in the
"coverage territory" during the policy period.

2. Exclusions.

This insurance does not apply to:

a. "Personal injury" or "advertising injury:"

(1) Arising out of oral or written publication
of material, if done by or at the direction
of the insured with knowledge of its falsity;

(2) Arising out of oral or written publication
of material whose first publication took
place before the beginning of the policy
period;

(3) Arising out of the willful violation of a
penal statute or ordinance committed by
or with the consent of the insured; or

(4) For which the insured has assumed liability
in a contract or agreement. This exclusion
does not apply to liability for damages that
the insured would have in the absence of
the contract or agreement.

b. "Advertising injury" arising out of:

(1) Breach of contract, other than misappropriation of advertising ideas under an implied contract;

(2) The failure of goods, products or services to conform with advertised quality or performance;

(3) The wrong description of the price of goods, products or services; or

(4) An offense committed by an insured whose business is advertising, broadcasting, publishing or telecasting.

COVERAGE C. MEDICAL PAYMENTS

1. Insuring Agreement.

a. We will pay medical expenses as described below for "bodily injury" caused by an accident:

(1) On premises you own or rent;

(2) On ways next to premises you own or rent; or

(3) Because of your operations;

provided that:

(1) The accident takes place in the "coverage territory" and during the policy period;

(2) The expenses are incurred and reported to us within one year of the date of the accident; and

(3) The injured person submits to examination, at our expense, by physicians of our choice as often as we reasonably require.

b. We will make these payments regardless of fault. These payments will not exceed the applicable limit of insurance. We will pay reasonable expenses for:

(1) First aid at the time of an accident;

(2) Necessary medical, surgical, x-ray and dental services, including prosthetic devices; and

COMMERCIAL GENERAL LIABILITY
COVERAGE FORM

(3) Necessary ambulance, hospital, professional nursing and funeral services.

2. Exclusions.

We will not pay expenses for "bodily injury:"

a. To any insured.

b. To a person hired to do work for or on behalf of any insured or a tenant of any insured.

c. To a person injured on that part of premises you own or rent that the person normally occupies.

d. To a person, whether or not an employee of any insured, if benefits for the "bodily injury" are payable or must be provided under a workers' compensation or disability benefits law or a similar law.

e. To a person injured while taking part in athletics.

f. Included within the "products-completed operations hazard."

g. Excluded under Coverage A.

h. Due to war, whether or not declared, or any act or condition incident to war. War includes civil war, insurrection, rebellion or revolution.

SUPPLEMENTARY PAYMENTS - COVERAGES A AND B

We will pay, with respect to any claim or "suit" we defend:

1. All expenses we incur.

2. Up to $250 for cost of bail bonds required because of accidents or traffic law violations arising out of the use of any vehicle to which the Bodily Injury Liability Coverage applies. We do not have to furnish these bonds.

3. The cost of bonds to release attachments, but only for bond amounts within the applicable limit of insurance. We do not have to furnish these bonds.

COMMERCIAL GENERAL LIABILITY
COVERAGE FORM

4. All reasonable expenses incurred by the insured at our request to assist us in the investigation or defense of the claim or "suit," including actual loss of earnings up to $100 a day because of time off from work.

5. All costs taxed against the insured in the "suit."

6. Prejudgment interest awarded against the insured on that part of the judgment we pay. If we make an offer to pay the applicable limit of insurance, we will not pay any prejudgment interest based on that period of time after the offer.

7. All interest on the full amount of any judgment that accrues after entry of the judgment and before we have paid, offered to pay, or deposited in court the part of the judgment that is within the applicable limit of insurance.

These payments will not reduce the limits of insurance.

SECTION II - WHO IS AN INSURED

1. If you are designated in the Declarations as:

   a. An individual, you and your spouse are insureds, but only with respect to the conduct of a business of which you are the sole owner.

   b. A partnership or joint venture, you are an insured. Your members, your partners, and their spouses are also insureds, but only with respect to the conduct of your business.

   c. An organization other than a partnership or joint venture, you are an insured. Your executive officers and directors are insureds, but only with respect to their duties as your officers or directors. Your stockholders are also insureds, but only with respect to their liability as stockholders.

2. Each of the following is also an insured:

   a. Your employees, other than your executive officers, but only for acts within the scope of their employment by you. However, no employee is an insured for:

      (1) "Bodily injury" or "personal injury" to you or to a co-employee while in the course of his or her employment, or the spouse, child, parent, brother or sister of that co-employee as a consequence of such "bodily injury" or "personal injury," or for any obligation to share damages with or repay someone else who must pay damages because of the injury; or

      (2) "Bodily injury" or "personal injury" arising out of his or her providing or failing to provide professional health care services; or

      (3) "Property damage" to property owned or occupied by or rented or loaned to that employee, any of your other employees, or any of your partners or members (if you are a partnership or joint venture).

   b. Any person (other than your employee), or any organization while acting as your real estate manager.

   c. Any person or organization having proper temporary custody of your property if you die, but only:

      (1) With respect to liability arising out of the maintenance or use of that property; and

      (2) Until your legal representative has been appointed.

   d. Your legal representative if you die, but only with respect to duties as such. That representative will have all your rights and duties under this Coverage Part.

3. With respect to "mobile equipment" registered in your name under any motor vehicle registration law, any person is an insured while driving such equipment along a public highway with your permission. Any other person or organization responsible for the conduct of such person is also an insured, but only with respect to liability arising out of the operation of the equipment, and only if no other insurance of any kind is available to that person or organization for this liability. However, no person or organization is an insured with respect to:

   a. "Bodily injury" to a co-employee of the person driving the equipment; or

   b. "Property damage" to property owned by, rented to, in the charge of or occupied by you or the employer of any person who is an insured under this provision.

4. Any organization you newly acquire or form, other than a partnership or joint venture, and over which you maintain ownership or majority interest, will qualify as a Named Insured if there is no other similar insurance available to that organization. However:

   a. Coverage under this provision is afforded only until the 90th day after you acquire or form the organization or the end of the policy period, whichever is earlier;

b. Coverage A does not apply to "bodily injury" or "property damage" that occurred before you acquired or formed the organization; and

c. Coverage B does not apply to "personal injury" or "advertising injury" arising out of an offense committed before you acquired or formed the organization.

No person or organization is an insured with respect to the conduct of any current or past partnership or joint venture that is not shown as a Named Insured in the Declarations.

SECTION III - LIMITS OF INSURANCE

1. The Limits of Insurance shown in the Declarations and the rules below fix the most we will pay regardless of the number of:

   a. Insureds;

   b. Claims made or "suits" brought; or

   c. Persons or organizations making claims or bringing "suits."

2. The General Aggregate Limit is the most we will pay for the sum of:

   a. Medical expenses under Coverage C;

   b. Damages under Coverage A, except damages because of "bodily injury" or "property damage" included in the "products-completed operations hazard;" and

   c. Damages under Coverage B.

3. The Products-Completed Operations Aggregate Limit is the most we will pay under Coverage A for damages because of "bodily injury" and "property damage" included in the "products-completed operations hazard."

4. Subject to 2. above, the Personal and Advertising Injury Limit is the most we will pay under Coverage B for the sum of all damages because of all "personal injury" and all "advertising injury" sustained by any one person or organization.

5. Subject to 2. or 3. above, whichever applies, the Each Occurrence Limit is the most we will pay for the sum of:

   a. Damages under Coverage A; and

   b. Medical expenses under Coverage C

   because of all "bodily injury" and "property damage" arising out of any one "occurrence."

6. Subject to 5. above, the Fire Damage Limit is the most we will pay under Coverage A for damages because of "property damage" to premises rented to you arising out of any one fire.

7. Subject to 5. above, the Medical Expense Limit is the most we will pay under Coverage C for all medical expenses because of "bodily injury" sustained by any one person.

The limits of this Coverage Part apply separately to each consecutive annual period and to any remaining period of less than 12 months, starting with the beginning of the policy period shown in the Declarations, unless the policy period is extended after issuance for an additional period of less than 12 months. In that case, the additional period will be deemed part of the last preceding period for purposes of determining the Limits of Insurance.

SECTION IV - COMMERCIAL GENERAL LIABILITY CONDITIONS

1. Bankruptcy.

   Bankruptcy or insolvency of the insured or of the insured's estate will not relieve us of our obligations under this Coverage Part.

2. Duties In The Event Of Occurrence, Claim Or Suit.

   a. You must see to it that we are notified as soon as practicable of an "occurrence" or an offense which may result in a claim. To the extent possible, notice should include:

      (1) How, when and where the "occurrence" or offense took place;

      (2) The names and addresses of any injured persons and witnesses; and

      (3) The nature and location of any injury or damage arising out of the "occurrence" or offense.

   b. If a claim is made or "suit" is brought against any insured, you must:

      (1) Immediately record the specifics of the claim or "suit" and the date received; and

      (2) Notify us as soon as practicable.

      You must see to it that we receive written notice of the claim or "suit" as soon as practicable.

COMMERCIAL GENERAL LIABILITY
COVERAGE FORM

c. You and any other involved insured must:

(1) Immediately send us copies of any demands, notices, summonses or legal papers received in connection with the claim or "suit;"

(2) Authorize us to obtain records and other information;

(3) Cooperate with us in the investigation, settlement or defense of the claim or "suit;" and

(4) Assist us, upon our request, in the enforcement of any right against any person or organization which may be liable to the insured because of injury or damage to which this insurance may also apply.

d. No insureds will, except at their own cost, voluntarily make a payment, assume any obligation, or incur any expense, other than for first aid, without our consent.

3. **Legal Action Against Us.**

No person or organization has a right under this Coverage Part:

a. To join us as a party or otherwise bring us into a "suit" asking for damages from an insured; or

b. To sue us on this Coverage Part unless all of its terms have been fully complied with.

A person or organization may sue us to recover on an agreed settlement or on a final judgment against an insured obtained after an actual trial; but we will not be liable for damages that are not payable under the terms of this Coverage Part or that are in excess of the applicable limit of insurance. An agreed settlement means a settlement and release of liability signed by us, the insured and the claimant or the claimant's legal representative.

4. **Other Insurance.**

If other valid and collectible insurance is available to the insured for a loss we cover under Coverages A or B of this Coverage Part, our obligations are limited as follows:

a. Primary Insurance

This insurance is primary except when b. below applies. If this insurance is primary, our obligations are not affected

unless any of the other insurance is also primary. Then, we will share with all that other insurance by the method described in c. below.

b. Excess Insurance

This insurance is excess over any of the other insurance, whether primary, excess, contingent or on any other basis:

(1) That is Fire, Extended Coverage, Builder's Risk, Installation Risk or similar coverage for "your work;"

(2) That is Fire insurance for premises rented to you; or

(3) If the loss arises out of the maintenance or use of aircraft, "autos" or watercraft to the extent not subject to Exclusion g. of Coverage A (Section I).

When this insurance is excess, we will have no duty under Coverage A or B to defend any claim or "suit" that any other insurer has a duty to defend. If no other insurer defends, we will undertake to do so, but we will be entitled to the insured's rights against all those other insurers.

When this insurance is excess over other insurance, we will pay only our share of the amount of the loss, if any, that exceeds the sum of:

(1) The total amount that all such other insurance would pay for the loss in the absence of this insurance; and

(2) The total of all deductible and self-insured amounts under all that other insurance.

We will share the remaining loss, if any, with any other insurance that is not described in this Excess Insurance provision and was not bought specifically to apply in excess of the Limits of Insurance shown in the Declarations of this Coverage Part.

c. Method of Sharing

If all of the other insurance permits contribution by equal shares, we will follow this method also. Under this approach each insurer contributes equal amounts until it has paid its applicable limit of insurance or none of the loss remains, whichever comes first.

      CG 00 01 11 88   □

If any of the other insurance does not permit contribution by equal shares, we will contribute by limits. Under this method, each insurer's share is based on the ratio of its applicable limit of insurance to the total applicable limits of insurance of all insurers.

5. Premium Audit.

a. We will compute all premiums for this Coverage Part in accordance with our rules and rates.

b. Premium shown in this Coverage Part as advance premium is a deposit premium only. At the close of each audit period we will compute the earned premium for that period. Audit premiums are due and payable on notice to the first Named Insured. If the sum of the advance and audit premiums paid for the policy term is greater than the earned premium, we will return the excess to the first Named Insured.

c. The first Named Insured must keep records of the information we need for premium computation, and send us copies at such times as we may request.

6. Representations.

By accepting this policy, you agree:

a. The statements in the Declarations are accurate and complete;

b. Those statements are based upon representations you made to us; and

c. We have issued this policy in reliance upon your representations.

7. Separation Of Insureds.

Except with respect to the Limits of Insurance, and any rights or duties specifically assigned in this Coverage Part to the first Named Insured, this insurance applies:

a. As if each Named Insured were the only Named Insured; and

b. Separately to each insured against whom claim is made or "suit" is brought.

8. Transfer Of Rights Of Recovery Against Others To Us.

If the insured has rights to recover all or part of any payment we have made under this Coverage

COMMERCIAL GENERAL LIABILITY
COVERAGE FORM

Part, those rights are transferred to us. The insured must do nothing after loss to impair them. At our request, the insured will bring "suit" or transfer those rights to us and help us enforce them.

9. When We Do Not Renew.

If we decide not to renew this Coverage Part, we will mail or deliver to the first Named Insured shown in the Declarations written notice of the nonrenewal not less than 30 days before the expiration date.

If notice is mailed, proof of mailing will be sufficient proof of notice.

SECTION V - DEFINITIONS

1. "Advertising injury" means injury arising out of one or more of the following offenses:

a. Oral or written publication of material that slanders or libels a person or organization or disparages a person's or organization's goods, products or services;

b. Oral or written publication of material that violates a person's right of privacy;

c. Misappropriation of advertising ideas or style of doing business; or

d. Infringement of copyright, title or slogan.

2. "Auto" means a land motor vehicle, trailer or semitrailer designed for travel on public roads, including any attached machinery or equipment. But "auto" does not include "mobile equipment."

3. "Bodily injury" means bodily injury, sickness or disease sustained by a person, including death resulting from any of these at any time.

4. "Coverage territory" means:

a. The United States of America (including its territories and possessions), Puerto Rico and Canada;

b. International waters or airspace, provided the injury or damage does not occur in the course of travel or transportation to or from any place not included in a. above; or

c. All parts of the world if:

(1) The injury or damage arises out of:

(a) Goods or products made or sold by you in the territory described in a. above; or

COMMERCIAL GENERAL LIABILITY
COVERAGE FORM

      (b) The activities of a person whose home is in the territory described in a. above, but is away for a short time on your business; and

    (2) The insured's responsibility to pay damages is determined in a "suit" on the merits, in the territory described in a. above or in a settlement we agree to.

5. "Impaired property" means tangible property, other than "your product" or "your work," that cannot be used or is less useful because:

  a. It incorporates "your product" or "your work" that is known or thought to be defective, deficient, inadequate or dangerous; or

  b. You have failed to fulfill the terms of a contract or agreement;

if such property can be restored to use by:

  a. The repair, replacement, adjustment or removal of "your product" or "your work;" or

  b. Your fulfilling the terms of the contract or agreement.

6. "Insured contract" means:

  a. A lease of premises;

  b. A sidetrack agreement;

  c. Any easement or license agreement, except in connection with construction or demolition operations on or within 50 feet of a railroad;

  d. An obligation, as required by ordinance, to indemnify a municipality, except in connection with work for a municipality;

  e. An elevator maintenance agreement;

  f. That part of any other contract or agreement pertaining to your business (including an indemnification of a municipality in connection with work performed for a municipality) under which you assume the tort liability of another party to pay for "bodily injury" or "property damage" to a third person or organization. Tort liability means a liability that would be imposed by law in the absence of any contract or agreement.

An "insured contract" does not include that part of any contract or agreement:

  a. That indemnifies any person or organization for "bodily injury" or "property damage" arising out of construction or demolition operations, within 50 feet of any railroad property and affecting any railroad bridge or trestle, tracks, road-beds, tunnel, underpass or crossing;

  b. That indemnifies an architect, engineer or surveyor for injury or damage arising out of:

    (1) Preparing, approving or failing to prepare or approve maps, drawings, opinions, reports, surveys, change orders, designs or specifications; or

    (2) Giving directions or instructions, or failing to give them, if that is the primary cause of the injury or damage;

  c. Under which the insured, if an architect, engineer or surveyor, assumes liability for an injury or damage arising out of the insured's rendering or failure to render professional services, including those listed in b. above and supervisory, inspection or engineering services; or

  d. That indemnifies any person or organization for damage by fire to premises rented or loaned to you.

7. "Loading or unloading" means the handling of property:

  a. After it is moved from the place where it is accepted for movement into or onto an aircraft, watercraft or "auto;"

  b. While it is in or on an aircraft, watercraft or "auto;" or

  c. While it is being moved from an aircraft, watercraft or "auto" to the place where it is finally delivered;

but "loading or unloading" does not include the movement of property by means of a mechanical device, other than a hand truck, that is not attached to the aircraft, watercraft or "auto."

8. "Mobile equipment" means any of the following types of land vehicles, including any attached machinery or equipment:

    Copyright, Insurance Services Office, Inc., 1982, 1988   CG 00 01 11 88   ☐

a. Bulldozers, farm machinery, forklifts and other vehicles designed for use principally off public roads;

b. Vehicles maintained for use solely on or next to premises you own or rent;

c. Vehicles that travel on crawler treads;

d. Vehicles, whether self-propelled or not, maintained primarily to provide mobility to permanently mounted:

(1) Power cranes, shovels, loaders, diggers or drills; or

(2) Road construction or resurfacing equipment such as graders, scrapers or rollers;

e. Vehicles not described in a., b., c. or d. above that are not self-propelled and are maintained primarily to provide mobility to permanently attached equipment of the following types:

(1) Air compressors, pumps and generators, including spraying, welding, building cleaning, geophysical exploration, lighting and well servicing equipment; or

(2) Cherry pickers and similar devices used to raise or lower workers;

f. Vehicles not described in a., b., c. or d. above maintained primarily for purposes other than the transportation of persons or cargo.

However, self-propelled vehicles with the following types of permanently attached equipment are not "mobile equipment" but will be considered "autos:"

(1) Equipment designed primarily for:

(a) Snow removal;

(b) Road maintenance, but not construction or resurfacing;

(c) Street cleaning;

(2) Cherry pickers and similar devices mounted on automobile or truck chassis and used to raise or lower workers; and

(3) Air compressors, pumps and generators, including spraying, welding, building cleaning, geophysical exploration, lighting and well servicing equipment.

9. "Occurrence" means an accident, including continuous or repeated exposure to substantially the same general harmful conditions.

10. "Personal injury" means injury, other than "bodily injury," arising out of one or more of the following offenses:

a. False arrest, detention or imprisonment;

b. Malicious prosecution;

c. The wrongful eviction from, wrongful entry into, or invasion of the right of private occupancy of a room, dwelling or premises that a person occupies by or on behalf of its owner, landlord or lessor;

d. Oral or written publication of material that slanders or libels a person or organization or disparages a person's or organization's goods, products or services; or

e. Oral or written publication of material that violates a person's right of privacy.

11.a. "Products-completed operations hazard" includes all "bodily injury" and "property damage" occurring away from premises you own or rent and arising out of "your product" or "your work" except:

(1) Products that are still in your physical possession; or

(2) Work that has not yet been completed or abandoned.

b. "Your work" will be deemed completed at the earliest of the following times:

(1) When all of the work called for in your contract has been completed.

(2) When all of the work to be done at the site has been completed if your contract calls for work at more than one site.

(3) When that part of the work done at a job site has been put to its intended use by any person or organization other than another contractor or subcontractor working on the same project.

Work that may need service, maintenance, correction, repair or replacement, but which is otherwise complete, will be treated as completed.

c. This hazard does not include "bodily injury" or "property damage" arising out of:

COMMERCIAL GENERAL LIABILITY
COVERAGE FORM

(1) The transportation of property, unless the injury or damage arises out of a condition in or on a vehicle created by the "loading or unloading" of it;

(2) The existence of tools, uninstalled equipment or abandoned or unused materials;

(3) Products or operations for which the classification in this Coverage Part or in our manual of rules includes products or completed operations.

12. "Property damage" means:

a. Physical injury to tangible property, including all resulting loss of use of that property. All such loss of use shall be deemed to occur at the time of the physical injury that caused it; or

b. Loss of use of tangible property that is not physically injured. All such loss shall be deemed to occur at the time of the "occurrence" that caused it.

13. "Suit" means a civil proceeding in which damages because of "bodily injury," "property damage," "personal injury" or "advertising injury" to which this insurance applies are alleged. "Suit" includes:

a. An arbitration proceeding in which such damages are claimed and to which you must submit or do submit with our consent; or

b. Any other alternative dispute resolution proceeding in which such damages are claimed and to which you submit with our consent.

14. "Your product" means:

a. Any goods or products, other than real property, manufactured, sold, handled, distributed or disposed of by:

(1) You;

(2) Others trading under your name; or

(3) A person or organization whose business or assets you have acquired; and

b. Containers (other than vehicles), materials, parts or equipment furnished in connection with such goods or products.

"Your product" includes:

a. Warranties or representations made at any time with respect to the fitness, quality, durability, performance or use of "your product;" and

b. The providing of or failure to provide warnings or instructions.

"Your product" does not include vending machines or other property rented to or located for the use of others but not sold.

15. "Your work" means:

a. Work or operations performed by you or on your behalf; and

b. Materials, parts or equipment furnished in connection with such work or operations.

"Your work" includes:

a. Warranties or representations made at any time with respect to the fitness, quality, durability, performance or use of "your work;" and

b. The providing of or failure to provide warnings or instructions.

COMMERCIAL GENERAL LIABILITY COVERAGE FORM

COVERAGES A. AND B. PROVIDE CLAIMS-MADE COVERAGE. PLEASE READ THE ENTIRE FORM CAREFULLY.

Various provisions in this policy restrict coverage. Read the entire policy carefully to determine rights, duties and what is and is not covered.

Throughout this policy the words "you" and "your" refer to the Named Insured shown in the Declarations, and any other person or organization qualifying as a Named Insured under this policy. The words "we," "us" and "our" refer to the Company providing this insurance.

The word "insured" means any person or organization qualifying as such under WHO IS AN INSURED (Section II).

Other words and phrases that appear in quotation marks have special meaning. Refer to DEFINITIONS (Section VI).

SECTION I - COVERAGES

COVERAGE A. BODILY INJURY AND PROPERTY DAMAGE LIABILITY

1. **Insuring Agreement.**

   a. We will pay those sums that the insured becomes legally obligated to pay as damages because of "bodily injury" or "property damage" to which this insurance applies. We will have the right and duty to defend any "suit" seeking those damages. We may at our discretion investigate any "occurrence" and settle any claim or "suit" that may result. But:

      (1) The amount we will pay for damages is limited as described in LIMITS OF INSURANCE (Section III); and

      (2) Our right and duty to defend end when we have used up the applicable limit of insurance in the payment of judgments or settlements under Coverages A or B or medical expenses under Coverage C.

      No other obligation or liability to pay sums or perform acts or services is covered unless explicitly provided for under SUPPLEMENTARY PAYMENTS - COVERAGES A AND B.

   b. This insurance applies to "bodily injury" and "property damage" only if:

   (1) The "bodily injury" or "property damage" is caused by an "occurrence" that takes place in the "coverage territory;"

   (2) The "bodily injury" or "property damage" did not occur before the Retroactive Date, if any, shown in the Declarations or after the end of the policy period; and

   (3) A claim for damages because of the "bodily injury" or "property damage" is first made against any insured, in accordance with paragraph c. below, during the policy period or any Extended Reporting Period we provide under EXTENDED REPORTING PERIODS (Section V).

   c. A claim by a person or organization seeking damages will be deemed to have been made at the earlier of the following times:

   (1) When notice of such claim is received and recorded by any insured or by us, whichever comes first; or

   (2) When we make settlement in accordance with paragraph 1.a. above.

   All claims for damages because of "bodily injury" to the same person, including damages claimed by any person or organization for care, loss of services, or death resulting at any time from the "bodily injury" will be deemed to have been made at the time the first of these claims is made against any insured.

2. **Exclusions.**

   This insurance does not apply to:

   a. "Bodily injury" or "property damage" expected or intended from the standpoint of the insured. This exclusion does not apply to "bodily injury" resulting from the use of reasonable force to protect persons or property.

   b. "Bodily injury" or "property damage" for which the insured is obligated to pay damages by reason of the assumption of liability in a contract or agreement. This exclusion does not apply to liability for damages:

**COMMERCIAL GENERAL LIABILITY
COVERAGE FORM**

(1) Assumed in a contract or agreement that is an "insured contract" provided the "bodily injury" or "property damage" occurs subsequent to the execution of the contract or agreement; or

(2) That the insured would have in the absence of the contract or agreement.

c. "Bodily injury" or "property damage" for which any insured may be held liable by reason of:

(1) Causing or contributing to the intoxication of any person;

(2) The furnishing of alcoholic beverages to a person under the legal drinking age or under the influence of alcohol; or

(3) Any statute, ordinance or regulation relating to the sale, gift, distribution or use of alcoholic beverages.

This exclusion applies only if you are in the business of manufacturing, distributing, selling, serving or furnishing alcoholic beverages.

d. Any obligation of the insured under a workers compensation, disability benefits or unemployment compensation law or any similar law.

e. "Bodily injury" to:

(1) An employee of the insured arising out of and in the course of employment by the insured; or

(2) The spouse, child, parent, brother or sister of that employee as a consequence of (1) above.

This exclusion applies:

(1) Whether the insured may be liable as an employer or in any other capacity; and

(2) To any obligation to share damages with or repay someone else who must pay damages because of the injury.

This exclusion does not apply to liability assumed by the insured under an "insured contract."

f. (1) "Bodily injury" of "property damage" arising out of the actual, alleged or threatened discharge, dispersal, see page, migration, release or escape of pollutants:

(a) At or from any premises, site or location which is or was at any time owned or occupied by, or rented or loaned to, any insured;

(b) At or from any premises, site or location which is or was at any time used by or for any insured or others for the handling, storage, disposal, processing or treatment of waste;

(c) Which are or were at any time transported, handled, stored, treated, disposed of, or processed as waste by or for any insured or any person or organization for whom you may be legally responsible; or

(d) At or from any premises, site or location on which any insured or any contractors or subcontractors working directly or indirectly on any insured's behalf are performing operations:

(i) If the pollutants are brought on or to the premises, site or location in connection with such operations by such insured, contractor or subcontractor; or

(ii) If the operations are to test for, monitor, clean up, remove, contain, treat, detoxify or neutralize, or in any way respond to, or assess the effects of pollutants.

Subparagraphs (a) and (d)(i) do not apply to "bodily injury" or "property damage" arising out of heat, smoke or fumes from a hostile fire.

As used in this exclusion, a hostile fire means one which becomes uncontrollable or breaks out from where it was intended to be.

(2) Any loss, cost or expense arising out of any:

(a) request, demand or order that any insured or others test for, monitor, clean up, remove, contain, treat, detoxify or neutralize, or in any way respond to, or assess the effects of pollutants; or

(b) claim or suit by or on behalf of a governmental authority for damages because of testing for, monitoring, cleaning up, removing, containing, treating, detoxifying or neutralizing or in any way responding to or assessing the effects of pollutants.

Pollutants means any solid, liquid, gaseous or thermal irritant or contaminant, including smoke, vapor, soot, fumes, acids, alkalis, chemicals and waste. Waste includes materials to be recycled, reconditioned or reclaimed.

g. "Bodily injury" or "property damage" arising out of the ownership, maintenance, use or entrustment to others of any aircraft, "auto" or watercraft owned or operated by or rented or loaned to any insured. Use includes operation and "loading or unloading."

This exclusion does not apply to:

(1) A watercraft while ashore on premises you own or rent;

(2) A watercraft you do not own that is:

(a) Less than 26 feet long; and

(b) Not being used to carry persons or property for a charge;

(3) Parking an "auto" on, or on the ways next to, premises you own or rent, provided the "auto" is not owned by or rented or loaned to you or the insured;

(4) Liability assumed under any "insured contract" for the ownership, maintenance or use of aircraft or watercraft; or

(5) "Bodily injury" or "property damage" arising out of the operation of any of the equipment listed in paragraph f.(2) or f.(3) of the definition of "mobile equipment" (Section VI.8).

h. "Bodily injury" or "property damage" arising out of:

(1) The transportation of "mobile equipment" by an "auto" owned or operated by or rented or loaned to any insured; or

(2) The use of "mobile equipment" in, or while in practice or preparation for, a prearranged racing, speed or demolition contest or in any stunting activity.

i. "Bodily injury" or "property damage" due to war, whether or not declared, or any act or condition incident to war. War includes civil war, insurrection, rebellion or revolution. This exclusion applies only to liability assumed under a contract or agreement.

j. "Property damage" to:

(1) Property you own, rent, or occupy;

(2) Premises you sell, give away or abandon, if the "property damage" arises out of any part of those premises;

(3) Property loaned to you;

(4) Personal property in the care, custody or control of the insured;

(5) That particular part of real property on which you or any contractors or subcontractors working directly or indirectly on your behalf are performing operations, if the "property damage" arises out of those operations; or

(6) That particular part of any property that must be restored, repaired or replaced because "your work" was incorrectly performed on it.

Paragraph (2) of this exclusion does not apply if the premises are "your work" and were never occupied, rented or held for rental by you.

Paragraphs (3), (4), (5) and (6) of this exclusion do not apply to liability assumed under a sidetrack agreement.

Paragraph (6) of this exclusion does not apply to "property damage" included in the "products-completed operations hazard."

k. "Property damage" to "your product" arising out of it or any part of it.

COMMERCIAL GENERAL LIABILITY
COVERAGE FORM

l. "Property damage" to "your work" arising out of it or any part of it and included in the "products-completed operations hazard."

This exclusion does not apply if the damaged work or the work out of which the damage arises was performed on your behalf by a subcontractor.

m. "Property damage" to "impaired property" or property that has not been physically injured, arising out of:

(1) A defect, deficiency, inadequacy or dangerous condition in "your product" or "your work;" or

(2) A delay or failure by you or anyone acting on your behalf to perform a contract or agreement in accordance with its terms.

This exclusion does not apply to the loss of use of other property arising out of sudden and accidental physical injury to "your product" or "your work" after it has been put to its intended use.

n. Damages claimed for any loss, cost or expense incurred by you or others for the loss of use, withdrawal, recall, inspection, repair, replacement, adjustment, removal or disposal of:

(1) "Your product;"

(2) "Your work;" or

(3) "Impaired property;"

if such product, work, or property is withdrawn or recalled from the market or from use by any person or organization because of a known or suspected defect, deficiency, inadequacy or dangerous condition in it.

Exclusions c. through n. do not apply to damage by fire to premises rented to you. A separate limit of insurance applies to this coverage as described in LIMITS OF INSURANCE (Section III).

COVERAGE B. PERSONAL AND ADVERTISING INJURY LIABILITY

1. Insuring Agreement.

a. We will pay those sums that the insured becomes legally obligated to pay as damages because of "personal injury" or "advertising injury" to which this coverage part applies. We will have the right and duty to defend any "suit" seeking those damages. We may at our discretion investigate any "occurrence" or offense and settle any claim or "suit" that may result. But:

(1) The amount we will pay for damages is limited as described in LIMITS OF INSURANCE (Section III); and

(2) Our right and duty to defend end when we have used up the applicable limit of insurance in the payment of judgments or settlements under Coverage A or B or medical expenses under Coverage C.

No other obligation or liability to pay sums or perform acts or services is covered unless explicitly provided for under SUPPLEMENTARY PAYMENTS - COVERAGES A AND B.

b. This insurance applies to:

(1) "Personal injury" caused by an offense arising out of your business, excluding advertising, publishing, broadcasting or telecasting done by or for you;

(2) "Advertising injury" caused by an offense committed in the course of advertising your goods, products or services;

but only if:

(1) The offense was committed in the "coverage territory;"

(2) The offense was not committed before the Retroactive Date, if any, shown in the Declarations or after the end of the policy period; and

(3) A claim for damages because of the "personal injury" or "advertising injury" is first made against any insured, in accordance with paragraph c. below, during the policy period or any Extended Reporting Period we provide under EXTENDED REPORTING PERIODS (Section V).

c. A claim made by a person or organization seeking damages will be deemed to have been made at the earlier of the following times:

(1) When notice of such claim is received and recorded by any insured or by us, whichever comes first; or

(2) When we make settlement in accordance with paragraph 1.a. above.

All claims for damages because of "personal injury" or "advertising injury" to the same person or organization as a result of an offense will be deemed to have been made at the time the first of those claims is made against any insured.

2. Exclusions.

This insurance does not apply to:

a. "Personal injury" or "advertising injury:"

(1) Arising out of oral or written publication of material, if done by or at the direction of the insured with knowledge of its falsity;

(2) Arising out of oral or written publication of material whose first publication took place before the Retroactive Date, if any shown in the Declarations;

(3) Arising out of the willful violation of a penal statute or ordinance committed by or with the consent of the insured; or

(4) For which the insured has assumed liability in a contract or agreement. This exclusion does not apply to liability for damages that the insured would have in the absence of the contract or agreement.

b. "Advertising injury" arising out of:

(1) Breach of contract, other than misappropriation of advertising ideas under an implied contract;

(2) The failure of goods, products or services to conform with advertised quality or performance;

(3) The wrong description of the price of goods, products or services; or

(4) An offense committed by an insured whose business is advertising, broadcasting, publishing or telecasting.

COVERAGE C. MEDICAL PAYMENTS

1. Insuring Agreement.

a. We will pay medical expenses as described below for "bodily injury" caused by an accident:

(1) On premises you own or rent;

(2) On ways next to premises you own or rent; or

(3) Because of your operations;

provided that:

(1) The accident takes place in the "coverage territory" and during the policy period;

COMMERCIAL GENERAL LIABILITY
COVERAGE FORM

(2) The expenses are incurred and reported to us within one year of the date of the accident; and

(3) The injured person submits to examination, at our expense, by physicians of our choice as often as we reasonably require.

b. We will make these payments regardless of fault. These payments will not exceed the applicable limit of insurance. We will pay reasonable expenses for:

(1) First aid at the time of an accident;

(2) Necessary medical, surgical, x-ray and dental services, including prosthetic devices; and

(3) Necessary ambulance, hospital, professional nursing and funeral services.

2. Exclusions.

We will not pay expenses for "bodily injury:"

a. To any insured.

b. To a person hired to do work for or on behalf of any insured or a tenant of any insured.

c. To a person injured on that part of premises you own or rent that the person normally occupies.

d. To a person, whether or not an employee of any insured, if benefits for the "bodily injury" are payable or must be provided under a workers compensation or disability benefits law or a similar law.

e. To a person injured while taking part in athletics.

f. Included within the "products-completed operations hazard."

g. Excluded under Coverage A.

h. Due to war, whether or not declared, or any act or condition incident to war. War includes civil war, insurrection, rebellion or revolution.

SUPPLEMENTARY PAYMENTS - COVERAGES A AND B

We will pay, with respect to any claim or "suit" we defend:

1. All expenses we incur.

2. Up to $250 for cost of bail bonds required because of accidents or traffic law violations arising out of the use of any vehicle to which the Bodily Injury Liability Coverage applies. We do not have to furnish these bonds.

3. The cost of bonds to release attachments, but only for bond amounts within the applicable limit of insurance. We do not have to furnish these bonds.

4. All reasonable expenses incurred by the insured at our request to assist us in the investigation or defense of the claim or "suit," including actual loss of earnings up to $100 a day because of time off from work.

5. All costs taxed against the insured in the "suit."

6. Prejudgment interest awarded against the insured on that part of the judgment we pay. If we make an offer to pay the applicable limit of insurance, we will not pay any prejudgment interest based on that period of time after the offer.

7. All interest on the full amount of any judgment that accrues after entry of the judgment and before we have paid, offered to pay, or deposited in court the part of the judgment that is within the applicable limit of insurance.

These payments will not reduce the limits of insurance.

SECTION II - WHO IS AN INSURED

1. If you are designated in the Declarations as:

a. An individual, you and your spouse are insureds, but only with respect to the conduct of a business of which you are the sole owner.

b. A partnership or joint venture, you are an insured. Your members, your partners, and their spouses are also insureds, but only with respect to the conduct of your business.

c. An organization other than a partnership or joint venture, you are an insured. Your executive officers and directors are insureds, but only with respect to their duties as your officers or directors. Your stockholders are also insureds, but only with respect to their liability as stockholders.

2. Each of the following is also an insured:

       CG 00 02 11 88   ☐

a. Your employees, other than your executive officers, but only for acts within the scope of their employment by you. However, no employee is an insured for:

   (1) "Bodily injury" or "personal injury" to you or to a co-employee while in the course of his or her employment, or the spouse, child, parent, brother or sister of that co-employee as a consequence of such "bodily injury" or "personal injury," or for any obligation to share damages with or repay someone else who must pay damages because of the injury; or

   (2) "Bodily injury" or "personal injury" arising out of his or her providing or failing to provide professional health care services; or

   (3) "Property damage" to property owned or occupied by or rented or loaned to that employee, any of your other employees, or any of your partners or members (if you are a partnership or joint venture).

b. Any person (other than your employee) or any organization while acting as your real estate manager.

c. Any person or organization having proper temporary custody of your property if you die, but only:

   (1) With respect to liability arising out of the maintenance or use of that property; and

   (2) Until your legal representative has been appointed.

d. Your legal representative if you die, but only with respect to duties as such. That representative will have all your rights and duties under this Coverage Part.

3. With respect to "mobile equipment" registered in your name under any motor vehicle registration law, any person is an insured while driving such equipment along a public highway with your permission. Any other person or organization responsible for the conduct of such person is also an insured, but only with respect to liability arising out of the operation of the equipment, and only if no other insurance of any kind is available to that person or organization for this liability. However, no person or organization is an insured with respect to:

a. "Bodily injury" to a co-employee of the person driving the equipment; or

b. "Property damage" to property owned by, rented to, in the charge of or occupied by you or the employer of any person who is an insured under this provision.

4. Any organization you newly acquire or form, other than a partnership or joint venture, and over which you maintain ownership or majority interest, will qualify as a Named Insured if there is no other similar insurance available to that organization. However:

a. Coverage under this provision is afforded only until the 90th day after you acquire or form the organization or the end of the policy period, whichever is earlier;

b. Coverage A does not apply to "bodily injury" or "property damage" that occurred before you acquired or formed the organization; and

c. Coverage B does not apply to "personal injury" or "advertising injury" arising out of an offense committed before you acquired or formed the organization.

No person or organization is an insured with respect to the conduct of any current or past partnership or joint venture that is not shown as a Named Insured in the Declarations.

SECTION III - LIMITS OF INSURANCE

1. The Limits of Insurance shown in the Declarations and the rules below fix the most we will pay regardless of the number of:

a. Insureds;

b. Claims made or "suits" brought; or

c. Persons or organizations making claims or bringing "suits."

2. The General Aggregate Limit is the most we will pay for the sum of:

a. Medical expenses under Coverage C;

b. Damages under Coverage A, except damages because of "bodily injury" or "property damage" included in the "products-completed operations hazard;" and

c. Damages under Coverage B.

COMMERCIAL GENERAL LIABILITY
COVERAGE FORM

3. The Products-Completed Operations Aggregate Limit is the most we will pay under Coverage A for damages because of "bodily injury" and "property damage" included in the "products-completed operations hazard."

4. Subject to 2. above, the Personal and Advertising Injury Limit is the most we will pay under Coverage B for the sum of all damages because of all "personal injury" and all "advertising injury" sustained by any one person or organization.

5. Subject to 2. or 3. above, whichever applies, the Each Occurrence Limit is the most we will pay for the sum of:

a. Damages under Coverage A; and

b. Medical expenses under Coverage C

because of all "bodily injury" and "property damage" arising out of any one "occurrence."

6. Subject to 5. above, the Fire Damage Limit is the most we will pay under Coverage A for damages because of "property damage" to premises rented to you arising out of any one fire.

7. Subject to 5. above, the Medical Expense Limit is the most we will pay under Coverage C for all medical expenses because of "bodily injury" sustained by any one person.

The limits of this Coverage Part apply separately to each consecutive annual period and to any remaining period of less than 12 months, starting with the beginning of the policy period shown in the Declarations, unless the policy period is extended after issuance for an additional period of less than 12 months. In that case, the additional period will be deemed part of the last preceding period for purposes of determining the Limits of Insurance.

SECTION IV - COMMERCIAL GENERAL LIABILITY CONDITIONS

1. Bankruptcy.

Bankruptcy or insolvency of the insured or of the insured's estate will not relieve us of our obligations under this Coverage Part.

2. Duties In The Event Of Occurrence, Claim Or Suit.

a. You must see to it that we are notified as soon as practicable of an "occurrence" or offense which may result in a claim. To the extent possible, notice should include:

(1) How, when and where the "occurrence" or offense took place;

(2) The names and addresses of any injured persons and witnesses; and

(3) The nature and location of any injury or damage arising out of the "occurrence" or offense.

Notice of an "occurrence" is not notice of a claim.

b. If a claim is received by any insured you must:

(1) Immediately record the specifics of the claim and the date received; and

(2) Notify us as soon as practicable.

You must see to it that we receive written notice of the claim as soon as practicable.

c. You and any other involved insured must:

(1) Immediately send us copies of any demands, notices, summonses or legal papers received in connection with the claim or a "suit;"

(2) Authorize us to obtain records and other information;

(3) Cooperate with us in the investigation, settlement or defense of the claim or "suit;" and

(4) Assist us, upon our request, in the enforcement of any right against any person or organization which may be liable to the insured because of injury or damage to which this insurance may also apply.

d. No insureds will, except at their own cost, voluntarily make a payment, assume any obligation, or incur any expense, other than for first aid, without our consent.

3. Legal Action Against Us.

No person or organization has a right under this Coverage Part:

a. To join us as a party or otherwise bring us into a "suit" asking for damages from an insured; or

b. To sue us on this Coverage Part unless all of its terms have been fully complied with.

A person or organization may sue us to recover on an agreed settlement or on a final judgment against an insured obtained after an actual trial; but we will not be liable for damages that are not payable under the terms of this Coverage Part or that are in excess of the applicable limit of insurance. An agreed settlement means a settlement and release of liability signed by us, the insured and the claimant or the claimant's legal representative.

4. Other Insurance.

If other valid and collectible insurance is available to the insured for a loss we cover under Coverages A or B of this Coverage Part, our obligations are limited as follows:

a. Primary Insurance

This insurance is primary except when b. below applies. If this insurance is primary, our obligations are not affected unless any of the other insurance is also primary. Then, we will share with all that other insurance by the method described in c. below.

b. Excess Insurance

This insurance is excess over any of the other insurance, whether primary, excess, contingent or on any other basis:

(1) That is effective prior to the beginning of the policy period shown in the Declarations of this insurance and applies to "bodily injury" or "property damage" on other than a claims-made basis, if:

(a) No Retroactive Date is shown in the Declarations of this insurance; or

(b) The other insurance has a policy period which continues after the Retroactive Date shown in the Declarations of this insurance;

(2) That is Fire, Extended Coverage, Builders' Risk, Installation Risk or similar coverage for "your work;"

(3) That is Fire insurance for premises rented to you; or

(4) If the loss arises out of the maintenance or use of aircraft, "autos" or watercraft to the extent not subject to Exclusion g. of Coverage A (Section I).

When this insurance is excess, we will have no duty under Coverages A or B to defend any claim or "suit" that any other insurer has a duty to defend. If no other insurer defends, we will undertake to do so, but we will be entitled to the insured's rights against all those other insurers.

When this insurance is excess over other insurance, we will pay only our share of the amount of the loss, if any, that exceeds the sum of:

(1) The total amount that all such other insurance would pay for the loss in the absence of this insurance; and

(2) The total of all deductible and self-insured amounts under all that other insurance.

We will share the remaining loss, if any, with any other insurance that is not described in this Excess Insurance provision and was not bought specifically to apply in excess of the Limits of Insurance shown in the Declarations of this Coverage Part.

c. Method of Sharing

If all of the other insurance permits contribution by equal shares, we will follow this method also. Under this approach each insurer contributes equal amounts until it has paid its applicable limit of insurance or none of the loss remains, whichever comes first.

COMMERCIAL GENERAL LIABILITY
COVERAGE FORM

If any of the other insurance does not permit contribution by equal shares, we will contribute by limits. Under this method, each insurer's share is based on the ratio of its applicable limit of insurance to the total applicable limits of insurance of all insurers.

5. Premium Audit.

a. We will compute all premiums for this Coverage Part in accordance with our rules and rates.

b. Premium shown in this Coverage Part as advance premium is a deposit premium only. At the close of each audit period we will compute the earned premium for that period.

Audit premiums are due and payable on notice to the first Named Insured. If the sum of the advance and audit premiums paid for the policy term is greater than the earned premium, we will return the excess to the first Named Insured.

c. The first Named Insured must keep records of the information we need for premium computation, and send us copies at such times as we may request.

6. Representations.

By accepting this policy, you agree:

a. The statements in the Declarations are accurate and complete;

b. Those statements are based upon representations you made to us; and

c. We have issued this policy in reliance upon your representations.

7. Separation Of Insureds.

Except with respect to the Limits of Insurance, and any rights or duties specifically assigned to the first Named Insured, this insurance applies:

a. As if each Named Insured were the only Named Insured; and

b. Separately to each insured against whom claim is made or "suit" is brought.

8. Transfer Of Rights Of Recovery Against Others To Us.

If the insured has rights to recover all or

part of any payment we have made under this Coverage Part, those rights are transferred to us. The insured must do nothing after loss to impair them. At our request, the insured will bring "suit" or transfer those rights to us and help us enforce them.

9. When We Do Not Renew.

If we decide not to renew this Coverage Part, we will mail or deliver to the first Named Insured shown in the Declarations written notice of the nonrenewal not less than 30 days before the expiration date.

If notice is mailed, proof of mailing will be sufficient proof of notice.

10. Your Right to Claim and "Occurrence" Information.

We will provide the first Named Insured shown in the Declarations the following information relating to this and any preceding general liability claims-made Coverage Part we have issued to you during the previous three years:

a. A list or other record of each "occurrence," not previously reported to any other insurer, of which we were notified in accordance with paragraph 2.a. of this Section. We will include the date and brief description of the "occurrence" if that information was in the notice we received.

b. A summary by policy year, of payments made and amounts reserved, stated separately, under any applicable General Aggregate Limit and Products-Completed Operations Aggregate Limit.

Amounts reserved are based on our judgment. They are subject to change and should not be regarded as ultimate settlement values.

You must not disclose this information to any claimant or any claimant's representative without our consent.

If we cancel or elect not to renew this Coverage Part, we will provide such information no later than 30 days before the date of policy termination. In other circumstances, we will provide this information only if we receive a written request from the first Named Insured within 60 days after the end of the policy period. In this case, we will provide this information within 45 days of receipt of the request.

We compile claim and "occurrence" information for our own business purposes and exercise reasonable care in doing so. In providing this information to the first Named Insured, we make no representations or warranties to insureds, insurers, or others to whom this information is furnished by or on behalf of any insured. Cancellation or non-renewal will be effective even if we inadvertently provide inaccurate information.

SECTION V - EXTENDED REPORTING PERIODS

1. We will provide one or more Extended Reporting Periods, as described below, if:

   a. This Coverage Part is cancelled or not renewed; or

   b. We renew or replace this Coverage Part with insurance that:

      (1) Has a Retroactive Date later than the date shown in the Declarations of this Coverage Part; or

      (2) Does not apply to "bodily injury," "property damage," "personal injury" or "advertising injury" on a claims-made basis.

2. Extended Reporting Periods do not extend the policy period or change the scope of coverage provided. They apply only to claims for:

   a. "Bodily injury" or "property damage" that occurs before the end of the policy period but not before the Retroactive Date, if any, shown in the Declarations; or

   b. "Personal injury" or "advertising injury" caused by an offense committed before the end of the policy period but not before the Retroactive Date, if any, shown in the Declarations.

   Once in effect, Extended Reporting Periods may not be cancelled.

3. A Basic Extended Reporting Period is automatically provided without additional charge. This period starts with the end of the policy period and lasts for:

   a. Five years for claims because of "bodily injury" and "property damage" arising out of an "occurrence" reported to us, not

      later than 60 days after the end of the policy period, in accordance with paragraph 2.a. of COMMERCIAL GENERAL LIABILITY CONDITIONS (Section IV);

   b. Five years because of claims for "personal injury" and "advertising injury" arising out of an offense reported to us, not later than 60 days after the end of the policy period, in accordance with paragraph 2.a. of COMMERCIAL GENERAL LIABILITY CONDITIONS (Section IV); or

   c. Sixty days for all other claims.

   The Basic Extended Reporting Period does not apply to claims that are covered under any subsequent insurance you purchase, or that would be covered but for exhaustion of the amount of insurance applicable to such claims.

4. A Supplemental Extended Reporting Period of unlimited duration is available, but only by an endorsement and for an extra charge. This supplemental period starts when the Basic Extended Reporting Period, set forth in paragraph 3. above, ends.

   You must give us a written request for the endorsement within 60 days after the end of the policy period. The Supplemental Extended Reporting Period will not go into effect unless you pay the additional premium promptly when due.

   We will determine the additional premium in accordance with our rules and rates. In doing so, we may take into account the following:

   a. The exposures insured;

   b. Previous types and amounts of insurance;

   c. Limits of Insurance available under this Coverage Part for future payment of damages; and

   d. Other related factors.

COMMERCIAL GENERAL LIABILITY
COVERAGE FORM

The additional premium will not exceed 200% of the annual premium for this Coverage Part.

This endorsement shall set forth the terms, not inconsistent with this Section, applicable to the Supplemental Extended Reporting Period, including a provision to the effect that the insurance afforded for claims first received during such period is excess over any other valid and collectible insurance available under policies in force after the Supplemental Extended Reporting Period starts.

5. The Basic Extended Reporting Period does not reinstate or increase the Limits of Insurance.

6. If the Supplemental Extended Reporting Period is in effect, we will provide the separate aggregate limits of insurance described below, but only for claims first received and recorded during the Supplemental Extended Reporting Period.

The separate aggregate limits of insurance will be equal to the dollar amount shown in the Declarations in effect at the end of the policy period for such of the following limits of insurance for which a dollar amount has been entered:

General Aggregate Limit
Products-Completed Operations Aggregate Limit

Paragraphs 2. and 3. of LIMITS OF INSURANCE (Section III) will be amended accordingly. The Personal and Advertising Injury Limit, the Each Occurrence Limit and the Fire Damage Limit shown in the Declarations will then continue to apply, as set forth in paragraphs 4., 5. and 6. of that Section.

SECTION VI - DEFINITIONS

1. "Advertising injury" means injury arising out of one or more of the following offenses:

   a. Oral or written publication of material that slanders or libels a person or organization or disparages a person's or organization's goods, products or services;

   b. Oral or written publication of material that violates a person's right of privacy;

   c. Misappropriation of advertising ideas or style of doing business; or

   d. Infringement of copyright, title or slogan.

2. "Auto" means a land motor vehicle, trailer or semitrailer designed for travel on public roads, including any attached machinery or equipment. But "auto" does not include "mobile equipment."

3. "Bodily injury" means bodily injury, sickness or disease sustained by a person, including death resulting from any of these at any time.

4. "Coverage territory" means:

   a. The United States of America (including its territories and possessions), Puerto Rico and Canada;

   b. International waters or airspace, provided the injury or damage does not occur in the course of travel or transportation to or from any place not included in a. above; or

   c. All parts of the world if:

      (1) The injury or damage arises out of:

         (a) Goods or products made or sold by you in the territory described in a. above; or

         (b) The activities of a person whose home is in the territory described in a. above, but is away for a short time on your business; and

      (2) The insured's responsibility to pay damages is determined in a "suit" on the merits, in the territory described in a. above or in a settlement we agree to.

5. "Impaired property" means tangible property, other than "your product" or "your work," that cannot be used or is less useful because:

   a. It incorporates "your product" or "your work" that is known or thought to be defective, deficient, inadequate or dangerous; or

   b. You have failed to fulfill the terms of a contract or agreement;

   if such property can be restored to use by:

   a. The repair, replacement, adjustment or removal of "your product" or "your work;" or

   b. Your fulfilling the terms of the contract or agreement.

6. "Insured contract" means:

   a. A lease of premises;

   b. A sidetrack agreement;

c. Any easement or license agreement, except in connection with construction or demolition operations on or within 50 feet of a railroad;

d. An obligation, as required by ordinance, to indemnify a municipality, except in connection with work for a municipality;

e. An elevator maintenance agreement;

f. That part of any other contract or agreement pertaining to your business (including an indemnification of a municipality in connection with work performed for a municipality) under which you assume the tort liability of another party to pay for "bodily injury" or "property damage" to a third person or organization. Tort liability means a liability that would be imposed by law in the absence of any contract or agreement.

An "insured contract" does not include that part of any contract or agreement:

a. That indemnifies any person or organization for "bodily injury" or "property damage" arising out of construction or demolition operations, within 50 feet of any railroad property and affecting any railroad bridge or trestle, tracks, road beds, tunnel, underpass or crossing;

b. That indemnifies an architect, engineer or surveyor for injury or damage arising out of:

(1) Preparing, approving or failing to prepare or approve maps, drawings, opinions, reports, surveys, change orders, designs or specifications; or

(2) Giving directions or instructions, or failing to give them, if that is the primary cause of the injury or damage;

c. Under which the insured, if an architect, engineer or surveyor, assumes liability for an injury or damage arising out of the insured's rendering or failure to render professional services, including those listed in b. above and supervisory, inspection or engineering services; or

d. That indemnifies any person or organization for damage by fire to premises rented or loaned to you.

7. "Loading or unloading" means the handling of property:

a. After it is moved from the place where it is accepted for movement into or onto an aircraft, watercraft or "auto;"

b. While it is in or on an aircraft, watercraft or "auto;" or

c. While it is being moved from an aircraft, watercraft or "auto" to the place where it is finally delivered;

but "loading or unloading" does not include the movement of property by means of a mechanical device, other than a hand truck, that is not attached to the aircraft, watercraft or "auto."

8. "Mobile equipment" means any of the following types of land vehicles, including any attached machinery or equipment:

a. Bulldozers, farm machinery, forklifts and other vehicles designed for use principally off public roads;

b. Vehicles maintained for use solely on or next to premises you own or rent;

c. Vehicles that travel on crawler treads;

d. Vehicles, whether self-propelled or not, maintained primarily to provide mobility to permanently mounted:

(1) Power cranes, shovels, loaders, diggers or drills; or

(2) Road construction or resurfacing equipment such as graders, scrapers or rollers;

e. Vehicles not described in a., b., c. or d. above that are not self-propelled and are maintained primarily to provide mobility to permanently attached equipment of the following types:

(1) Air compressors, pumps and generators, including spraying, welding, building cleaning, geophysical exploration, lighting and well servicing equipment; or

(2) Cherry pickers and similar devices used to raise or lower workers;

f. Vehicles not described in a., b., c. or d. above maintained primarily for purposes other than the transportation of persons or cargo.

COMMERCIAL GENERAL LIABILITY
COVERAGE FORM

However, self-propelled vehicles with the following types of permanently attached equipment are not "mobile equipment" but will be considered "autos:"

(1) Equipment designed primarily for:

   (a) Snow removal;

   (b) Road maintenance, but not construction or resurfacing;

   (c) Street cleaning;

(2) Cherry pickers and similar devices mounted on automobile or truck chassis and used to raise or lower workers; and

(3) Air compressors, pumps and generators, including spraying, welding, building cleaning, geophysical exploration, lighting and well servicing equipment.

9. "Occurrence" means an accident, including continuous or repeated exposure to substantially the same general harmful conditions.

10. "Personal injury" means injury, other than "bodily injury," arising out of one or more of the following offenses:

a. False arrest, detention or imprisonment;

b. Malicious prosecution;

c. The wrongful eviction from, wrongful entry into, or invasion of the right of private occupancy of a room, dwelling or premises that a person occupies by or on behalf of its owner, landlord or lessor.

d. Oral or written publication of material that slanders or libels a person or organization or disparages a person's or organization's goods, products or services; or

e. Oral or written publication of material that violates a person's right of privacy.

11. a. "Products-completed operations hazard" includes all "bodily injury" and "property damage" occurring away from premises you own or rent and arising out of "your product" or "your work" except:

(1) Products that are still in your physical possession; or

(2) Work that has not yet been completed or abandoned.

b. "Your work" will be deemed completed at the earliest of the following times:

(1) When all of the work called for in your contract has been completed.

(2) When all of the work to be done at the site has been completed if your contract calls for work at more than one site.

(3) When that part of the work done at a job site had been put to its intended use by any person or organization other than another contractor or subcontractor working on the same project.

Work that may need service, maintenance, correction, repair or replacement, but which is otherwise complete, will be treated as completed.

c. This hazard does not include "bodily injury" or "property damage" arising out of:

(1) The transportation of property, unless the injury or damage arises out of a condition in or on a vehicle created by the "loading or unloading" of it;

(2) The existence of tools, uninstalled equipment or abandoned or unused materials;

(3) Products or operations for which the classification in this Coverage Part or in our manual of rules includes products or completed operations.

12. "Property damage" means:

a. Physical injury to tangible property, including all resulting loss of use of that property. All such loss of use shall be deemed to occur at the time of the physical injury that caused it; or

b. Loss of use of tangible property that is not physically injured. All such loss of use shall be deemed to occur at the time of the "occurrence" that caused it.

13. "Suit" means a civil proceeding in which damage because of "bodily injury," "property damage," "personal injury" or "advertising injury" to which this insurance applies are alleged. "Suit" includes:

a. An arbitration proceeding in which such damages are claimed and to which you must submit or do submit with our consent; or

b. Any other alternative dispute resolution proceeding in which such damages are claimed and to which you submit with our consent.

14. "Your product" means:

a. Any goods or products, other than real property, manufactured, sold, handled, distributed or disposed of by:

(1) You;

(2) Others trading under your name; or

(3) A person or organization whose business or assets you have acquired; and

b. Containers (other than vehicles), materials, parts or equipment furnished in connection with such goods or products.

"Your product" includes:

a. Warranties or representations made at any time with respect to the fitness, quality, durability, performance or use of "your product;" and

b. The providing of or failure to provide warnings or instructions.

"Your product" does not include vending machines or other property rented to or located for the use of others but not sold.

15. "Your work" means:

a. Work or operations performed by you or on your behalf; and

b. Materials, parts or equipment furnished in connection with such work or operations.

"Your work" includes:

a. Warranties or representations made at any time with respect to the fitness, quality, durability, performance or use of "your work;" and

b. The providing of or failure to provide warnings or instructions.

COMMERCIAL GENERAL LIABILITY
CG 00 43 05 92

THIS ENDORSEMENT CHANGES THE POLICY. PLEASE READ IT CAREFULLY.

CHANGES IN COMMERCIAL GENERAL LIABILITY COVERAGE FORM

This endorsement modifies insurance provided under the following:

COMMERCIAL GENERAL LIABILITY COVERAGE PART

A. Paragraph **1.a.** of COVERAGE A - BODILY IN-JURY AND PROPERTY DAMAGE LIABILITY (Section I - Coverages) is replaced by the following:

1. Insuring Agreement

a. We will pay those sums that the insured becomes legally obligated to pay as dam-ages because of "bodily injury" or "prop-erty damage" to which this insurance applies. We will have the right and duty to defend the insured against any "suit" seeking those damages. However, we will have no duty to defend the insured against any "suit" seeking damages for "bodily in-jury" or "property damage" to which this insurance does not apply. We may, at our discretion, investigate any "occurrence" and settle any claim or "suit" that may re-sult. But:

(1) The amount we will pay for damages is limited as described in LIMITS OF INSURANCE (SECTION III); and

(2) Our right and duty to defend end when we have used up the applicable limit of insurance in the payment of judg-ments or settlements under Coverages A or B or medical expenses under Coverage C.

No other obligation or liability to pay sums or perform acts or services is covered un-less explicitly provided for under SUP-PLEMENTARY PAYMENTS - COVER-AGES A AND B.

B. Paragraph **2.b.** of COVERAGE A - BODILY IN-JURY AND PROPERTY DAMAGE LIABILITY (Section I - Coverages) is replaced by the fol-lowing:

2. Exclusions

This insurance does not apply to:

b. "Bodily injury" or "property damage" for which the insured is obligated to pay damages by reason of the assumption of liability in a contract or agreement. This exclusion does not apply to liability for damages:

(1) That the insured would have in the ab-sence of the contract or agreement; or

(2) Assumed in a contract or agreement that is an "insured contract", provided the "bodily injury" or "property dam-age" occurs subsequent to the exe-cution of the contract or agreement. Solely for the purposes of liability as-sumed in an "insured contract", rea-sonable attorney fees and necessary litigation expenses incurred by or for a party other than an insured are deemed to be damages because of "bodily in-jury" or "property damage", provided:

(a) Liability to such party for, or for the cost of, that party's defense has also been assumed in the same "insured contract"; and

(b) Such attorney fees and litigation expenses are for defense of that party against a civil or alternative dispute resolution proceeding in which damages to which this insur-ance applies are alleged.

C. Paragraph **1.a.** of COVERAGE B - PERSONAL AND ADVERTISING INJURY LIABILITY (Section I - Coverages) is replaced by the following:

1. **Insuring Agreement**

   a. We will pay those sums that the insured becomes legally obligated to pay as damages because of "personal injury" or "advertising injury" to which this insurance applies. We will have the right and duty to defend the insured against any "suit" seeking those damages. However, we will have no duty to defend the insured against any "suit" seeking damages for "personal injury" or "advertising injury" to which this insurance does not apply. We may, at our discretion, investigate any "occurrence" or offense and settle any claim or "suit" that may result. But:

      (1) The amount we will pay for damages is limited as described in LIMITS OF INSURANCE (SECTION III); and

      (2) Our right and duty to defend end when we have used up the applicable limit of insurance in the payment of judgments or settlements under Coverages A or B or medical expenses under Coverage C.

      No other obligation or liability to pay sums or perform acts or services is covered unless explicitly provided for under SUPPLEMENTARY PAYMENTS - COVERAGES A AND B.

D. The first sentence of SUPPLEMENTARY PAYMENTS - COVERAGES A AND B is replaced by the following:

   We will pay, with respect to any claim we investigate or settle, or any "suit" against an insured we defend:

E. Paragraph **2.c.(3)** of the DUTIES IN THE EVENT OF OCCURRENCE, CLAIM OR SUIT Condition (Section IV - Commercial General Liability Conditions) is replaced by the following:

2. **Duties in the Event of Occurrence, Claim or Suit**

   c. You and any other involved insured must:

      (3) Cooperate with us in the investigation or settlement of the claim or defense against the "suit"; and

F. Paragraph **2.d.** of the DUTIES IN THE EVENT OF OCCURRENCE, CLAIM OR SUIT Condition (Section IV - Commercial General Liability Conditions) is replaced by the following:

2. **Duties in the Event of Occurrence, Claim or Suit**

   d. No insured will, except at that insured's own cost, voluntarily make a payment, assume any obligation, or incur any expense, other than for first aid, without our consent.

G. The second paragraph of paragraph **4.b.** of the OTHER INSURANCE Condition (Section IV - Commercial General Liability Conditions) is replaced by the following:

4. **Other Insurance**

   b. **Excess Insurance**

   When this insurance is excess, we will have no duty under Coverages A or B to defend the insured against any "suit" if any other insurer has a duty to defend the insured against that "suit". If no other insurer defends, we will undertake to do so, but we will be entitled to the insured's rights against all those other insurers.

H. The definition of "suit" in DEFINITIONS is replaced by the following:

16. "Suit" means a civil proceeding in which damages because of "bodily injury", "property damage", "personal injury" or "advertising injury" to which this insurance applies are alleged. "Suit" includes:

   a. An arbitration proceeding in which such damages are claimed and to which the insured must submit or does submit with our consent; or

   b. Any other alternative dispute resolution proceeding in which such damages are claimed and to which the insured submits with our consent.

COMMERCIAL GENERAL LIABILITY COVERAGE FORM

Various provisions in this policy restrict coverage. Read the entire policy carefully to determine rights, duties and what is and is not covered.

Throughout this policy the words "you" and "your" refer to the Named Insured shown in the Declarations, and any other person or organization qualifying as a Named Insured under this policy. The words "we", "us" and "our" refer to the company providing this insurance.

The word "insured" means any person or organization qualifying as such under WHO IS AN INSURED (SECTION II).

Other words and phrases that appear in quotation marks have special meaning. Refer to DEFINITIONS (SECTION V).

SECTION I - COVERAGES

COVERAGE A. BODILY INJURY AND PROPERTY DAMAGE LIABILITY

1. **Insuring Agreement.**

   a. We will pay those sums that the insured becomes legally obligated to pay as damages because of "bodily injury" or "property damage" to which this insurance applies. We will have the right and duty to defend any "suit" seeking those damages. We may at our discretion investigate any "occurrence" and settle any claim or "suit" that may result. But:

      (1) The amount we will pay for damages is limited as described in LIMITS OF INSURANCE (SECTION III); and

      (2) Our right and duty to defend end when we have used up the applicable limit of insurance in the payment of judgments or settlements under Coverages A or B or medical expenses under Coverage C.

      No other obligation or liability to pay sums or perform acts or services is covered unless explicitly provided for under SUPPLEMENTARY PAYMENTS - COVERAGES A AND B.

   b. This insurance applies to "bodily injury" and "property damage" only if:

      (1) The "bodily injury" or "property damage" is caused by an "occurrence" that takes place in the "coverage territory"; and

      (2) The "bodily injury" or "property damage" occurs during the policy period.

   c. Damages because of "bodily injury" include damages claimed by any person or organization for care, loss of services or death resulting at any time from the "bodily injury".

2. **Exclusions.**

   This insurance does not apply to:

   a. **Expected or Intended Injury**

      "Bodily injury" or "property damage" expected or intended from the standpoint of the insured. This exclusion does not apply to "bodily injury" resulting from the use of reasonable force to protect persons or property.

   b. **Contractual Liability**

      "Bodily injury" or "property damage" for which the insured is obligated to pay damages by reason of the assumption of liability in a contract or agreement. This exclusion does not apply to liability for damages:

      (1) Assumed in a contract or agreement that is an "insured contract", provided the "bodily injury" or "property damage" occurs subsequent to the execution of the contract or agreement; or

      (2) That the insured would have in the absence of the contract or agreement.

   c. **Liquor Liability**

      "Bodily injury" or "property damage" for which any insured may be held liable by reason of:

      (1) Causing or contributing to the intoxication of any person;

      (2) The furnishing of alcoholic beverages to a person under the legal drinking age or under the influence of alcohol; or

      (3) Any statute, ordinance or regulation relating to the sale, gift, distribution or use of alcoholic beverages.

      This exclusion applies only if you are in the business of manufacturing, distributing, selling, serving or furnishing alcoholic beverages.

d. Workers Compensation and Similar Laws

Any obligation of the insured under a workers compensation, disability benefits or unemployment compensation law or any similar law.

e. Employer's Liability

"Bodily injury" to:

(1) An "employee" of the insured arising out of and in the course of:

    (a) Employment by the insured; or

    (b) Performing duties related to the conduct of the insured's business; or

(2) The spouse, child, parent, brother or sister of that "employee" as a consequence of paragraph (1) above.

This exclusion applies:

(1) Whether the insured may be liable as an employer or in any other capacity; and

(2) To any obligation to share damages with or repay someone else who must pay damages because of the injury.

This exclusion does not apply to liability assumed by the insured under an "insured contract".

f. Pollution

(1) "Bodily injury" or "property damage" arising out of the actual, alleged or threatened discharge, dispersal, seepage, migration, release or escape of pollutants:

    (a) At or from any premises, site or location which is or was at any time owned or occupied by, or rented or loaned to, any insured;

    (b) At or from any premises, site or location which is or was at any time used by or for any insured or others for the handling, storage, disposal, processing or treatment of waste;

    (c) Which are or were at any time transported, handled, stored, treated, disposed of, or processed as waste by or for any insured or any person or organization for whom you may be legally responsible; or

    (d) At or from any premises, site or location on which any insured or any contractors or subcontractors working directly or indirectly on any insured's behalf are performing operations:

        (i) If the pollutants are brought on or to the premises, site or location in connection with such operations by such insured, contractor or subcontractor; or

        (ii) If the operations are to test for, monitor, clean up, remove, contain, treat, detoxify or neutralize, or in any way respond to, or assess the effects of pollutants.

Subparagraphs (a) and (d)(i) do not apply to "bodily injury" or "property damage" arising out of heat, smoke or fumes from a hostile fire.

As used in this exclusion, a hostile fire means one which becomes uncontrollable or breaks out from where it was intended to be.

(2) Any loss, cost or expense arising out of any:

    (a) Request, demand or order that any insured or others test for, monitor, clean up, remove, contain, treat, detoxify or neutralize, or in any way respond to, or assess the effects of pollutants; or

    (b) Claim or suit by or on behalf of a governmental authority for damages because of testing for, monitoring, cleaning up, removing, containing, treating, detoxifying or neutralizing, or in any way responding to, or assessing the effects of pollutants.

Pollutants means any solid, liquid, gaseous or thermal irritant or contaminant, including smoke, vapor, soot, fumes, acids, alkalis, chemicals and waste. Waste includes materials to be recycled, reconditioned or reclaimed.

g. Aircraft, Auto or Watercraft

"Bodily injury" or "property damage" arising out of the ownership, maintenance, use or entrustment to others of any aircraft, "auto" or watercraft owned or operated by or rented or loaned to any insured. Use includes operation and "loading or unloading".

         CG 00 01 10 93   ☐

This exclusion does not apply to:

(1) A watercraft while ashore on premises you own or rent;

(2) A watercraft you do not own that is:

(a) Less than 26 feet long; and

(b) Not being used to carry persons or property for a charge;

(3) Parking an "auto" on, or on the ways next to, premises you own or rent, provided the "auto" is not owned by or rented or loaned to you or the insured;

(4) Liability assumed under any "insured contract" for the ownership, maintenance or use of aircraft or watercraft; or

(5) "Bodily injury" or "property damage" arising out of the operation of any of the equipment listed in paragraph f.(2) or f.(3) of the definition of "mobile equipment".

h. Mobile Equipment

"Bodily injury" or "property damage" arising out of:

(1) The transportation of "mobile equipment" by an "auto" owned or operated by or rented or loaned to any insured; or

(2) The use of "mobile equipment" in, or while in practice for, or while being prepared for, any prearranged racing, speed, demolition, or stunting activity.

i. War

"Bodily injury" or "property damage" due to war, whether or not declared, or any act or condition incident to war. War includes civil war, insurrection, rebellion or revolution. This exclusion applies only to liability assumed under a contract or agreement.

j. Damage to Property

"Property damage" to:

(1) Property you own, rent, or occupy;

(2) Premises you sell, give away or abandon, if the "property damage" arises out of any part of those premises;

(3) Property loaned to you;

(4) Personal property in the care, custody or control of the insured;

(5) That particular part of real property on which you or any contractors or subcontractors working directly or indirectly on your behalf are performing operations, if the "property damage" arises out of those operations; or

(6) That particular part of any property that must be restored, repaired or replaced because "your work" was incorrectly performed on it.

Paragraph (2) of this exclusion does not apply if the premises are "your work" and were never occupied, rented or held for rental by you.

Paragraphs (3), (4), (5) and (6) of this exclusion do not apply to liability assumed under a sidetrack agreement.

Paragraph (6) of this exclusion does not apply to "property damage" included in the "products-completed operations hazard".

k. Damage to Your Product

"Property damage" to "your product" arising out of it or any part of it.

l. Damage to Your Work

"Property damage" to "your work" arising out of it or any part of it and included in the "products-completed operations hazard".

This exclusion does not apply if the damaged work or the work out of which the damage arises was performed on your behalf by a subcontractor.

m. Damage to Impaired Property or Property Not Physically Injured

"Property damage" to "impaired property" or property that has not been physically injured, arising out of:

(1) A defect, deficiency, inadequacy or dangerous condition in "your product" or "your work"; or

(2) A delay or failure by you or anyone acting on your behalf to perform a contract or agreement in accordance with its terms.

This exclusion does not apply to the loss of use of other property arising out of sudden and accidental physical injury to "your product" or "your work" after it has been put to its intended use.

n. **Recall of Products, Work or Impaired Property**

Damages claimed for any loss, cost or expense incurred by you or others for the loss of use, withdrawal, recall, inspection, repair, replacement, adjustment, removal or disposal of:

(1) "Your product";

(2) "Your work"; or

(3) "Impaired property";

if such product, work, or property is withdrawn or recalled from the market or from use by any person or organization because of a known or suspected defect, deficiency, inadequacy or dangerous condition in it.

Exclusions c. through n. do not apply to damage by fire to premises while rented to you or temporarily occupied by you with permission of the owner. A separate limit of insurance applies to this coverage as described in LIMITS OF INSURANCE (Section III).

COVERAGE B. PERSONAL AND ADVERTISING INJURY LIABILITY

1. Insuring Agreement.

a. We will pay those sums that the insured becomes legally obligated to pay as damages because of "personal injury" or "advertising injury" to which this insurance applies. We will have the right and duty to defend any "suit" seeking those damages. We may at our discretion investigate any "occurrence" or offense and settle any claim or "suit" that may result. But:

(1) The amount we will pay for damages is limited as described in LIMITS OF INSURANCE (SECTION III); and

(2) Our right and duty to defend end when we have used up the applicable limit of insurance in the payment of judgments or settlements under Coverage A or B or medical expenses under Coverage C.

No other obligation or liability to pay sums or perform acts or services is covered unless explicitly provided for under SUPPLEMENTARY PAYMENTS - COVERAGES A AND B.

b. This insurance applies to:

(1) "Personal injury" caused by an offense arising out of your business, excluding advertising, publishing, broadcasting or telecasting done by or for you;

(2) "Advertising injury" caused by an offense committed in the course of advertising your goods, products or services;

but only if the offense was committed in the "coverage territory" during the policy period.

2. Exclusions.

This insurance does not apply to:

a. "Personal injury" or "advertising injury":

(1) Arising out of oral or written publication of material, if done by or at the direction of the insured with knowledge of its falsity;

(2) Arising out of oral or written publication of material whose first publication took place before the beginning of the policy period;

(3) Arising out of the willful violation of a penal statute or ordinance committed by or with the consent of the insured; or

(4) For which the insured has assumed liability in a contract or agreement. This exclusion does not apply to liability for damages that the insured would have in the absence of the contract or agreement.

b. "Advertising injury" arising out of:

(1) Breach of contract, other than misappropriation of advertising ideas under an implied contract;

(2) The failure of goods, products or services to conform with advertised quality or performance;

(3) The wrong description of the price of goods, products or services; or

(4) An offense committed by an insured whose business is advertising, broadcasting, publishing or telecasting.

COVERAGE C. MEDICAL PAYMENTS

1. Insuring Agreement.

a. We will pay medical expenses as described below for "bodily injury" caused by an accident:

    (1) On premises you own or rent;

    (2) On ways next to premises you own or rent; or

    (3) Because of your operations;

    provided that:

    (1) The accident takes place in the "coverage territory" and during the policy period;

    (2) The expenses are incurred and reported to us within one year of the date of the accident; and

    (3) The injured person submits to examination, at our expense, by physicians of our choice as often as we reasonably require.

b. We will make these payments regardless of fault. These payments will not exceed the applicable limit of insurance. We will pay reasonable expenses for:

    (1) First aid administered at the time of an accident;

    (2) Necessary medical, surgical, x-ray and dental services, including prosthetic devices; and

    (3) Necessary ambulance, hospital, professional nursing and funeral services.

2. Exclusions.

We will not pay expenses for "bodily injury":

a. To any insured.

b. To a person hired to do work for or on behalf of any insured or a tenant of any insured.

c. To a person injured on that part of premises you own or rent that the person normally occupies.

d. To a person, whether or not an "employee" of any insured, if benefits for the "bodily injury" are payable or must be provided under a workers compensation or disability benefits law or a similar law.

e. To a person injured while taking part in athletics.

f. Included within the "products-completed operations hazard".

g. Excluded under Coverage A.

h. Due to war, whether or not declared, or any act or condition incident to war. War includes civil war, insurrection, rebellion or revolution.

SUPPLEMENTARY PAYMENTS - COVERAGES A AND B

We will pay, with respect to any claim or "suit" we defend:

1. All expenses we incur.

2. Up to $250 for cost of bail bonds required because of accidents or traffic law violations arising out of the use of any vehicle to which the Bodily Injury Liability Coverage applies. We do not have to furnish these bonds.

3. The cost of bonds to release attachments, but only for bond amounts within the applicable limit of insurance. We do not have to furnish these bonds.

4. All reasonable expenses incurred by the insured at our request to assist us in the investigation or defense of the claim or "suit", including actual loss of earnings up to $100 a day because of time off from work.

5. All costs taxed against the insured in the "suit".

6. Prejudgment interest awarded against the insured on that part of the judgment we pay. If we make an offer to pay the applicable limit of insurance, we will not pay any prejudgment interest based on that period of time after the offer.

7. All interest on the full amount of any judgment that accrues after entry of the judgment and before we have paid, offered to pay, or deposited in court the part of the judgment that is within the applicable limit of insurance.

These payments will not reduce the limits of insurance.

SECTION II - WHO IS AN INSURED

1. If you are designated in the Declarations as:

   a. An individual, you and your spouse are insureds, but only with respect to the conduct of a business of which you are the sole owner.

   b. A partnership or joint venture, you are an insured. Your members, your partners, and their spouses are also insureds, but only with respect to the conduct of your business.

   c. An organization other than a partnership or joint venture, you are an insured. Your "executive officers" and directors are insureds, but only with respect to their duties as your officers or directors. Your stockholders are also insureds, but only with respect to their liability as stockholders.

2. Each of the following is also an insured:

   a. Your "employees", other than your "executive officers", but only for acts within the scope of their employment by you or while performing duties related to the conduct of your business. However, no "employee" is an insured for:

   (1) "Bodily injury" or "personal injury":

      (a) To you, to your partners or members (if you are a partnership or joint venture), or to a co-"employee" while in the course of his or her employment or while performing duties related to the conduct of your business;

      (b) To the spouse, child, parent, brother or sister of that co-"employee" as a consequence of paragraph (1)(a) above;

      (c) For which there is any obligation to share damages with or repay someone else who must pay damages because of the injury described in paragraphs (1)(a) or (b) above; or

      (d) Arising out of his or her providing or failing to provide professional health care services.

   (2) "Property damage" to property:

      (a) Owned, occupied or used by,

      (b) Rented to, in the care, custody or control of, or over which physical control is being exercised for any purpose by

      you, any of your "employees" or, if you are a partnership or joint venture, by any partner or member.

   b. Any person (other than your "employee"), or any organization while acting as your real estate manager.

   c. Any person or organization having proper temporary custody of your property if you die, but only:

      (1) With respect to liability arising out of the maintenance or use of that property; and

      (2) Until your legal representative has been appointed.

   d. Your legal representative if you die, but only with respect to duties as such. That representative will have all your rights and duties under this Coverage Part.

3. With respect to "mobile equipment" registered in your name under any motor vehicle registration law, any person is an insured while driving such equipment along a public highway with your permission. Any other person or organization responsible for the conduct of such person is also an insured, but only with respect to liability arising out of the operation of the equipment, and only if no other insurance of any kind is available to that person or organization for this liability. However, no person or organization is an insured with respect to:

   a. "Bodily injury" to a co-"employee" of the person driving the equipment; or

   b. "Property damage" to property owned by, rented to, in the charge of or occupied by you or the employer of any person who is an insured under this provision.

4. Any organization you newly acquire or form, other than a partnership or joint venture, and over which you maintain ownership or majority interest, will qualify as a Named Insured if there is no other similar insurance available to that organization. However:

   a. Coverage under this provision is afforded only until the 90th day after you acquire or form the organization or the end of the policy period, whichever is earlier;

           CG 00 01 10 93   ▢

b. Coverage A does not apply to "bodily injury" or "property damage" that occurred before you acquired or formed the organization; and

c. Coverage B does not apply to "personal injury" or "advertising injury" arising out of an offense committed before you acquired or formed the organization.

No person or organization is an insured with respect to the conduct of any current or past partnership or joint venture that is not shown as a Named Insured in the Declarations.

SECTION III - LIMITS OF INSURANCE

1. The Limits of Insurance shown in the Declarations and the rules below fix the most we will pay regardless of the number of:

   a. Insureds;

   b. Claims made or "suits" brought; or

   c. Persons or organizations making claims or bringing "suits".

2. The General Aggregate Limit is the most we will pay for the sum of:

   a. Medical expenses under Coverage C;

   b. Damages under Coverage A, except damages because of "bodily injury" or "property damage" included in the "products-completed operations hazard"; and

   c. Damages under Coverage B.

3. The Products-Completed Operations Aggregate Limit is the most we will pay under Coverage A for damages because of "bodily injury" and "property damage" included in the "products-completed operations hazard".

4. Subject to 2. above, the Personal and Advertising Injury Limit is the most we will pay under Coverage B for the sum of all damages because of all "personal injury" and all "advertising injury" sustained by any one person or organization.

5. Subject to 2. or 3. above, whichever applies, the Each Occurrence Limit is the most we will pay for the sum of:

   a. Damages under Coverage A; and

   b. Medical expenses under Coverage C

   because of all "bodily injury" and "property damage" arising out of any one "occurrence".

6. Subject to 5. above, the Fire Damage Limit is the most we will pay under Coverage A for damages because of "property damage" to premises, while rented to you or temporarily occupied by you with permission of the owner, arising out of any one fire.

7. Subject to 5. above, the Medical Expense Limit is the most we will pay under Coverage C for all medical expenses because of "bodily injury" sustained by any one person.

The Limits of Insurance of this Coverage Part apply separately to each consecutive annual period and to any remaining period of less than 12 months, starting with the beginning of the policy period shown in the Declarations, unless the policy period is extended after issuance for an additional period of less than 12 months. In that case, the additional period will be deemed part of the last preceding period for purposes of determining the Limits of Insurance.

SECTION IV - COMMERCIAL GENERAL LIABILITY CONDITIONS

1. Bankruptcy.

   Bankruptcy or insolvency of the insured or of the insured's estate will not relieve us of our obligations under this Coverage Part.

2. Duties In The Event Of Occurrence, Offense, Claim Or Suit.

   a. You must see to it that we are notified as soon as practicable of an "occurrence" or an offense which may result in a claim. To the extent possible, notice should include:

      (1) How, when and where the "occurrence" or offense took place;

      (2) The names and addresses of any injured persons and witnesses; and

      (3) The nature and location of any injury or damage arising out of the "occurrence" or offense.

   b. If a claim is made or "suit" is brought against any insured, you must:

      (1) Immediately record the specifics of the claim or "suit" and the date received; and

      (2) Notify us as soon as practicable.

      You must see to it that we receive written notice of the claim or "suit" as soon as practicable.

c. You and any other involved insured must:

(1) Immediately send us copies of any demands, notices, summonses or legal papers received in connection with the claim or "suit";

(2) Authorize us to obtain records and other information;

(3) Cooperate with us in the investigation, settlement or defense of the claim or "suit"; and

(4) Assist us, upon our request, in the enforcement of any right against any person or organization which may be liable to the insured because of injury or damage to which this insurance may also apply.

d. No insureds will, except at their own cost, voluntarily make a payment, assume any obligation, or incur any expense, other than for first aid, without our consent.

3. Legal Action Against Us.

No person or organization has a right under this Coverage Part:

a. To join us as a party or otherwise bring us into a "suit" asking for damages from an insured; or

b. To sue us on this Coverage Part unless all of its terms have been fully complied with.

A person or organization may sue us to recover on an agreed settlement or on a final judgment against an insured obtained after an actual trial; but we will not be liable for damages that are not payable under the terms of this Coverage Part or that are in excess of the applicable limit of insurance. An agreed settlement means a settlement and release of liability signed by us, the insured and the claimant or the claimant's legal representative.

4. Other Insurance.

If other valid and collectible insurance is available to the insured for a loss we cover under Coverages A or B of this Coverage Part, our obligations are limited as follows:

a. **Primary Insurance**

This insurance is primary except when b. below applies. If this insurance is primary, our obligations are not affected unless any of the other insurance is also primary. Then, we will share with all that other insurance by the method described in c. below.

b. **Excess Insurance**

This insurance is excess over any of the other insurance, whether primary, excess, contingent or on any other basis:

(1) That is Fire, Extended Coverage, Builder's Risk, Installation Risk or similar coverage for "your work";

(2) That is Fire insurance for premises rented to you; or

(3) If the loss arises out of the maintenance or use of aircraft, "autos" or watercraft to the extent not subject to Exclusion g. of Coverage A (Section I).

When this insurance is excess, we will have no duty under Coverage A or B to defend any claim or "suit" that any other insurer has a duty to defend. If no other insurer defends, we will undertake to do so, but we will be entitled to the insured's rights against all those other insurers.

When this insurance is excess over other insurance, we will pay only our share of the amount of the loss, if any, that exceeds the sum of:

(1) The total amount that all such other insurance would pay for the loss in the absence of this insurance; and

(2) The total of all deductible and self-insured amounts under all that other insurance.

We will share the remaining loss, if any, with any other insurance that is not described in this Excess Insurance provision and was not bought specifically to apply in excess of the Limits of Insurance shown in the Declarations of this Coverage Part.

c. **Method of Sharing**

If all of the other insurance permits contribution by equal shares, we will follow this method also. Under this approach each insurer contributes equal amounts until it has paid its applicable limit of insurance or none of the loss remains, whichever comes first.

If any of the other insurance does not permit contribution by equal shares, we will contribute by limits. Under this method, each insurer's share is based on the ratio of its applicable limit of insurance to the total applicable limits of insurance of all insurers.

5. Premium Audit.

a. We will compute all premiums for this Coverage Part in accordance with our rules and rates.

b. Premium shown in this Coverage Part as advance premium is a deposit premium only. At the close of each audit period we will compute the earned premium for that period. Audit premiums are due and payable on notice to the first Named Insured. If the sum of the advance and audit premiums paid for the policy period is greater than the earned premium, we will return the excess to the first Named Insured.

c. The first Named Insured must keep records of the information we need for premium computation, and send us copies at such times as we may request.

6. Representations.

By accepting this policy, you agree:

a. The statements in the Declarations are accurate and complete;

b. Those statements are based upon representations you made to us; and

c. We have issued this policy in reliance upon your representations.

7. Separation Of Insureds.

Except with respect to the Limits of Insurance, and any rights or duties specifically assigned in this Coverage Part to the first Named Insured, this insurance applies:

a. As if each Named Insured were the only Named Insured; and

b. Separately to each insured against whom claim is made or "suit" is brought.

8. Transfer Of Rights Of Recovery Against Others To Us.

If the insured has rights to recover all or part of any payment we have made under this Coverage Part, those rights are transferred to us. The insured must do nothing after loss to impair them. At our request, the insured will bring "suit" or transfer those rights to us and help us enforce them.

9. When We Do Not Renew.

If we decide not to renew this Coverage Part, we will mail or deliver to the first Named Insured shown in the Declarations written notice of the nonrenewal not less than 30 days before the expiration date.

If notice is mailed, proof of mailing will be sufficient proof of notice.

SECTION V - DEFINITIONS

1. "Advertising injury" means injury arising out of one or more of the following offenses:

a. Oral or written publication of material that slanders or libels a person or organization or disparages a person's or organization's goods, products or services;

b. Oral or written publication of material that violates a person's right of privacy;

c. Misappropriation of advertising ideas or style of doing business; or

d. Infringement of copyright, title or slogan.

2. "Auto" means a land motor vehicle, trailer or semitrailer designed for travel on public roads, including any attached machinery or equipment. But "auto" does not include "mobile equipment".

3. "Bodily injury" means bodily injury, sickness or disease sustained by a person, including death resulting from any of these at any time.

4. "Coverage territory" means:

a. The United States of America (including its territories and possessions), Puerto Rico and Canada;

b. International waters or airspace, provided the injury or damage does not occur in the course of travel or transportation to or from any place not included in a. above; or

c. All parts of the world if:

(1) The injury or damage arises out of:

(a) Goods or products made or sold by you in the territory described in a. above; or

(b) The activities of a person whose home is in the territory described in a. above, but is away for a short time on your business; and

(2) The insured's responsibility to pay damages is determined in a "suit" on the merits, in the territory described in a. above or in a settlement we agree to.

5. "Employee" includes a "leased worker". "Employee" does not include a "temporary worker".

6. "Executive officer" means a person holding any of the officer positions created by your charter, constitution, by-laws or any other similar governing document.

7. "Impaired property" means tangible property, other than "your product" or "your work", that cannot be used or is less useful because:

a. It incorporates "your product" or "your work" that is known or thought to be defective, deficient, inadequate or dangerous; or

b. You have failed to fulfill the terms of a contract or agreement;

if such property can be restored to use by:

a. The repair, replacement, adjustment or removal of "your product" or "your work"; or

b. Your fulfilling the terms of the contract or agreement.

8. "Insured contract" means:

a. A contract for a lease of premises. However, that portion of the contract for a lease of premises that indemnifies any person or organization for damage by fire to premises while rented to you or temporarily occupied by you with permission of the owner is not an "insured contract";

b. A sidetrack agreement;

c. Any easement or license agreement, except in connection with construction or demolition operations on or within 50 feet of a railroad;

d. An obligation, as required by ordinance, to indemnify a municipality, except in connection with work for a municipality;

e. An elevator maintenance agreement;

f. That part of any other contract or agreement pertaining to your business (including an indemnification of a municipality in connection with work performed for a municipality) under which you assume the tort liability of another party to pay for "bodily injury" or "property damage" to a third person or organization. Tort liability means a liability that would be imposed by law in the absence of any contract or agreement.

Paragraph f. does not include that part of any contract or agreement:

(1) That indemnifies a railroad for "bodily injury" or "property damage" arising out of construction or demolition operations, within 50 feet of any railroad property and affecting any railroad bridge or trestle, tracks, road-beds, tunnel, underpass or crossing;

(2) That indemnifies an architect, engineer or surveyor for injury or damage arising out of:

(a) Preparing, approving or failing to prepare or approve maps, drawings, opinions, reports, surveys, change orders, designs or specifications; or

(b) Giving directions or instructions, or failing to give them, if that is the primary cause of the injury or damage; or

(3) Under which the insured, if an architect, engineer or surveyor, assumes liability for an injury or damage arising out of the insured's rendering or failure to render professional services, including those listed in (2) above and supervisory, inspection or engineering services.

9. "Leased worker" means a person leased to you by a labor leasing firm under an agreement between you and the labor leasing firm, to perform duties related to the conduct of your business. "Leased worker" does not include a "temporary worker".

10. "Loading or unloading" means the handling of property:

a. After it is moved from the place where it is accepted for movement into or onto an aircraft, watercraft or "auto";

b. While it is in or on an aircraft, watercraft or "auto"; or

c. While it is being moved from an aircraft, watercraft or "auto" to the place where it is finally delivered;

but "loading or unloading" does not include the movement of property by means of a mechanical device, other than a hand truck, that is not attached to the aircraft, watercraft or "auto".

11. "Mobile equipment" means any of the following types of land vehicles, including any attached machinery or equipment:

a. Bulldozers, farm machinery, forklifts and other vehicles designed for use principally off public roads;

b. Vehicles maintained for use solely on or next to premises you own or rent;

c. Vehicles that travel on crawler treads;

d. Vehicles, whether self-propelled or not, maintained primarily to provide mobility to permanently mounted:

(1) Power cranes, shovels, loaders, diggers or drills; or

(2) Road construction or resurfacing equipment such as graders, scrapers or rollers;

e. Vehicles not described in a., b., c. or d. above that are not self-propelled and are maintained primarily to provide mobility to permanently attached equipment of the following types:

(1) Air compressors, pumps and generators, including spraying, welding, building cleaning, geophysical exploration, lighting and well servicing equipment; or

(2) Cherry pickers and similar devices used to raise or lower workers;

f. Vehicles not described in a., b., c. or d. above maintained primarily for purposes other than the transportation of persons or cargo.

However, self-propelled vehicles with the following types of permanently attached equipment are not "mobile equipment" but will be considered "autos":

(1) Equipment designed primarily for:

(a) Snow removal;

(b) Road maintenance, but not construction or resurfacing; or

(c) Street cleaning;

(2) Cherry pickers and similar devices mounted on automobile or truck chassis and used to raise or lower workers; and

(3) Air compressors, pumps and generators, including spraying, welding, building cleaning, geophysical exploration, lighting and well servicing equipment.

12. "Occurrence" means an accident, including continuous or repeated exposure to substantially the same general harmful conditions.

13. "Personal injury" means injury, other than "bodily injury", arising out of one or more of the following offenses:

a. False arrest, detention or imprisonment;

b. Malicious prosecution;

c. The wrongful eviction from, wrongful entry into, or invasion of the right of private occupancy of a room, dwelling or premises that a person occupies by or on behalf of its owner, landlord or lessor;

d. Oral or written publication of material that slanders or libels a person or organization or disparages a person's or organization's goods, products or services; or

e. Oral or written publication of material that violates a person's right of privacy.

14. a. "Products-completed operations hazard" includes all "bodily injury" and "property damage" occurring away from premises you own or rent and arising out of "your product" or "your work" except:

(1) Products that are still in your physical possession; or

(2) Work that has not yet been completed or abandoned.

b. "Your work" will be deemed completed at the earliest of the following times:

(1) When all of the work called for in your contract has been completed.

(2) When all of the work to be done at the site has been completed if your contract calls for work at more than one site.

(3) When that part of the work done at a job site has been put to its intended use by any person or organization other than another contractor or subcontractor working on the same project.

Work that may need service, maintenance, correction, repair or replacement, but which is otherwise complete, will be treated as completed.

c. This hazard does not include "bodily injury" or "property damage" arising out of:

(1) The transportation of property, unless the injury or damage arises out of a condition in or on a vehicle created by the "loading or unloading" of it;

(2) The existence of tools, uninstalled equipment or abandoned or unused materials; or

(3) Products or operations for which the classification in this Coverage Part or in our manual of rules includes products or completed operations.

15. "Property damage" means:

a. Physical injury to tangible property, including all resulting loss of use of that property. All such loss of use shall be deemed to occur at the time of the physical injury that caused it; or

b. Loss of use of tangible property that is not physically injured. All such loss of use shall be deemed to occur at the time of the "occurrence" that caused it.

16. "Suit" means a civil proceeding in which damages because of "bodily injury", "property damage", "personal injury" or "advertising injury" to which this insurance applies are alleged. "Suit" includes:

a. An arbitration proceeding in which such damages are claimed and to which you must submit or do submit with our consent; or

b. Any other alternative dispute resolution proceeding in which such damages are claimed and to which you submit with our consent.

17. "Your product" means:

a. Any goods or products, other than real property, manufactured, sold, handled, distributed or disposed of by:

(1) You;

(2) Others trading under your name; or

(3) A person or organization whose business or assets you have acquired; and

b. Containers (other than vehicles), materials, parts or equipment furnished in connection with such goods or products.

"Your product" includes:

a. Warranties or representations made at any time with respect to the fitness, quality, durability, performance or use of "your product"; and

b. The providing of or failure to provide warnings or instructions.

"Your product" does not include vending machines or other property rented to or located for the use of others but not sold.

18. "Temporary worker" means a person who is furnished to you to substitute for a permanent "employee" on leave or to meet seasonal or short-term workload conditions.

19. "Your work" means:

a. Work or operations performed by you or on your behalf; and

b. Materials, parts or equipment furnished in connection with such work or operations.

"Your work" includes:

a. Warranties or representations made at any time with respect to the fitness, quality, durability, performance or use of "your work"; and

b. The providing of or failure to provide warnings or instructions.

       CG 00 01 10 93   □

COMMERCIAL GENERAL LIABILITY COVERAGE FORM

COVERAGES A. AND B. PROVIDE
CLAIMS-MADE COVERAGE.
PLEASE READ THE ENTIRE FORM CAREFULLY.

Various provisions in this policy restrict coverage. Read the entire policy carefully to determine rights, duties and what is and is not covered.

Throughout this policy the words "you" and "your" refer to the Named Insured shown in the Declarations, and any other person or organization qualifying as a Named Insured under this policy. The words "we", "us" and "our" refer to the Company providing this insurance.

The word "insured" means any person or organization qualifying as such under WHO IS AN INSURED (Section II).

Other words and phrases that appear in quotation marks have special meaning. Refer to DEFINITIONS (Section VI).

SECTION I - COVERAGES

COVERAGE A. BODILY INJURY AND PROPERTY DAMAGE LIABILITY

1. Insuring Agreement.

a. We will pay those sums that the insured becomes legally obligated to pay as damages because of "bodily injury" or "property damage" to which this insurance applies. We will have the right and duty to defend any "suit" seeking those damages. We may at our discretion investigate any "occurrence" and settle any claim or "suit" that may result. But:

(1) The amount we will pay for damages is limited as described in LIMITS OF INSURANCE (Section III); and

(2) Our right and duty to defend end when we have used up the applicable limit of insurance in the payment of judgments or settlements under Coverages A or B or medical expenses under Coverage C.

No other obligation or liability to pay sums or perform acts or services is covered unless explicitly provided for under SUPPLEMENTARY PAYMENTS - COVERAGES A AND B.

b. This insurance applies to "bodily injury" and "property damage" only if:

(1) The "bodily injury" or "property damage" is caused by an "occurrence" that takes place in the "coverage territory";

(2) The "bodily injury" or "property damage" did not occur before the Retroactive Date, if any, shown in the Declarations or after the end of the policy period; and

(3) A claim for damages because of the "bodily injury" or "property damage" is first made against any insured, in accordance with paragraph c. below, during the policy period or any Extended Reporting Period we provide under EXTENDED REPORTING PERIODS (Section V).

c. A claim by a person or organization seeking damages will be deemed to have been made at the earlier of the following times:

(1) When notice of such claim is received and recorded by any insured or by us, whichever comes first; or

(2) When we make settlement in accordance with paragraph 1.a. above.

All claims for damages because of "bodily injury" to the same person, including damages claimed by any person or organization for care, loss of services, or death resulting at any time from the "bodily injury", will be deemed to have been made at the time the first of those claims is made against any insured.

All claims for damages because of "property damage" causing loss to the same person or organization will be deemed to have been made at the time the first of those claims is made against any insured.

2. Exclusions.

This insurance does not apply to:

a. **Expected or Intended Injury**

"Bodily injury" or "property damage" expected or intended from the standpoint of the insured. This exclusion does not apply to "bodily injury" resulting from the use of reasonable force to protect persons or property.

b. Contractual Liability

"Bodily injury" or "property damage" for which the insured is obligated to pay damages by reason of the assumption of liability in a contract or agreement. This exclusion does not apply to liability for damages:

(1) Assumed in a contract or agreement that is an "insured contract" provided the "bodily injury" or "property damage" occurs subsequent to the execution of the contract or agreement; or

(2) That the insured would have in the absence of the contract or agreement.

c. Liquor Liability

"Bodily injury" or "property damage" for which any insured may be held liable by reason of:

(1) Causing or contributing to the intoxication of any person;

(2) The furnishing of alcoholic beverages to a person under the legal drinking age or under the influence of alcohol; or

(3) Any statute, ordinance or regulation relating to the sale, gift, distribution or use of alcoholic beverages.

This exclusion applies only if you are in the business of manufacturing, distributing, selling, serving or furnishing alcoholic beverages.

d. Workers Compensation and Similar Laws

Any obligation of the insured under a workers compensation, disability benefits or unemployment compensation law or any similar law.

e. Employer's Liability

"Bodily injury" to:

(1) An "employee" of the insured arising out of and in the course of:

(a) Employment by the insured; or

(b) Performing duties related to the conduct of the insured's business; or

(2) The spouse, child, parent, brother or sister of that "employee" as a consequence of paragraph (1) above.

This exclusion applies:

(1) Whether the insured may be liable as an employer or in any other capacity; and

(2) To any obligation to share damages with or repay someone else who must pay damages because of the injury.

This exclusion does not apply to liability assumed by the insured under an "insured contract".

f. Pollution

(1) "Bodily injury" or "property damage" arising out of the actual, alleged or threatened discharge, dispersal, seepage, migration, release or escape of pollutants:

(a) At or from any premises, site or location which is or was at any time owned or occupied by, or rented or loaned to, any insured;

(b) At or from any premises, site or location which is or was at any time used by or for any insured or others for the handling, storage, disposal, processing or treatment of waste;

(c) Which are or were at any time transported, handled, stored, treated, disposed of, or processed as waste by or for any insured or any person or organization for whom you may be legally responsible; or

(d) At or from any premises, site or location on which any insured or any contractors or subcontractors working directly or indirectly on any insured's behalf are performing operations:

(i) If the pollutants are brought on or to the premises, site or location in connection with such operations by such insured, contractor or subcontractor; or

(ii) If the operations are to test for, monitor, clean up, remove, contain, treat, detoxify or neutralize, or in any way respond to, or assess the effects of pollutants.

Subparagraphs (a) and (d)(i) do not apply to "bodily injury" or "property damage" arising out of heat, smoke or fumes from a hostile fire.

Copyright, Insurance Services Office, Inc., 1992   CG 00 02 10 93   □

As used in this exclusion, a hostile fire means one which becomes uncontrollable or breaks out from where it was intended to be.

(2) Any loss, cost or expense arising out of any:

(a) Request, demand or order that any insured or others test for, monitor, clean up, remove, contain, treat, detoxify or neutralize, or in any way respond to, or assess the effects of pollutants; or

(b) Claim or "suit" by or on behalf of a governmental authority for damages because of testing for, monitoring, cleaning up, removing, containing, treating, detoxifying or neutralizing, or in any way responding to, or assessing the effects of pollutants.

Pollutants means any solid, liquid, gaseous or thermal irritant or contaminant, including smoke, vapor, soot, fumes, acids, alkalis, chemicals and waste. Waste includes materials to be recycled, reconditioned or reclaimed.

g. **Aircraft, Auto or Watercraft**

"Bodily injury" or "property damage" arising out of the ownership, maintenance, use or entrustment to others of any aircraft, "auto" or watercraft owned or operated by or rented or loaned to any insured. Use includes operation and "loading or unloading".

This exclusion does not apply to:

(1) A watercraft while ashore on premises you own or rent;

(2) A watercraft you do not own that is:

(a) Less than 26 feet long; and

(b) Not being used to carry persons or property for a charge;

(3) Parking an "auto" on, or on the ways next to, premises you own or rent, provided the "auto" is not owned by or rented or loaned to you or the insured;

(4) Liability assumed under any "insured contract" for the ownership, maintenance or use of aircraft or watercraft; or

(5) "Bodily injury" or "property damage" arising out of the operation of any of the equipment listed in paragraph f.(2) or f.(3) of the definition of "mobile equipment".

h. **Mobile Equipment**

"Bodily injury" or "property damage" arising out of:

(1) The transportation of "mobile equipment" by an "auto" owned or operated by or rented or loaned to any insured; or

(2) The use of "mobile equipment" in, or while in practice for, or while being prepared for, any prearranged racing, speed, demolition, or stunting activity.

i. **War**

"Bodily injury" or "property damage" due to war, whether or not declared, or any act or condition incident to war. War includes civil war, insurrection, rebellion or revolution. This exclusion applies only to liability assumed under a contract or agreement.

j. **Damage to Property**

"Property damage" to:

(1) Property you own, rent, or occupy;

(2) Premises you sell, give away or abandon, if the "property damage" arises out of any part of those premises;

(3) Property loaned to you;

(4) Personal property in the care, custody or control of the insured;

(5) That particular part of real property on which you or any contractors or subcontractors working directly or indirectly on your behalf are performing operations, if the "property damage" arises out of those operations; or

(6) That particular part of any property that must be restored, repaired or replaced because "your work" was incorrectly performed on it.

Paragraph (2) of this exclusion does not apply if the premises are "your work" and were never occupied, rented or held for rental by you.

Paragraphs (3), (4), (5) and (6) of this exclusion do not apply to liability assumed under a sidetrack agreement.

Paragraph (6) of this exclusion does not apply to "property damage" included in the "products-completed operations hazard".

k. **Damage to Your Product**

"Property damage" to "your product" arising out of it or any part of it.

l. Damage to Your Work

"Property damage" to "your work" arising out of it or any part of it and included in the "products-completed operations hazard".

This exclusion does not apply if the damaged work or the work out of which the damage arises was performed on your behalf by a subcontractor.

m. Damage to Impaired Property or Property Not Physically Injured

"Property damage" to "impaired property" or property that has not been physically injured, arising out of:

(1) A defect, deficiency, inadequacy or dangerous condition in "your product" or "your work"; or

(2) A delay or failure by you or anyone acting on your behalf to perform a contract or agreement in accordance with its terms.

This exclusion does not apply to the loss of use of other property arising out of sudden and accidental physical injury to "your product" or "your work" after it has been put to its intended use.

n. Recall of Products, Work or Impaired Property

Damages claimed for any loss, cost or expense incurred by you or others for the loss of use, withdrawal, recall, inspection, repair, replacement, adjustment, removal or disposal of:

(1) "Your product";

(2) "Your work"; or

(3) "Impaired property";

if such product, work, or property is withdrawn or recalled from the market or from use by any person or organization because of a known or suspected defect, deficiency, inadequacy or dangerous condition in it.

Exclusions **c.** through **n.** do not apply to damage by fire to premises while rented to you or temporarily occupied by you with permission of the owner. A separate limit of insurance applies to this coverage as described in LIMITS OF INSURANCE (Section III).

COVERAGE B. PERSONAL AND ADVERTISING INJURY LIABILITY

1. Insuring Agreement.

a. We will pay those sums that the insured becomes legally obligated to pay as damages because of "personal injury" or "advertising injury" to which this insurance applies. We will have the right and duty to defend any "suit" seeking those damages. We may at our discretion investigate any "occurrence" or offense and settle any claim or "suit" that may result. But:

(1) The amount we will pay for damages is limited as described in LIMITS OF INSURANCE (Section III); and

(2) Our right and duty to defend end when we have used up the applicable limit of insurance in the payment of judgments or settlements under Coverage A or B or medical expenses under Coverage C.

No other obligation or liability to pay sums or perform acts or services is covered unless explicitly provided for under SUPPLEMENTARY PAYMENTS - COVERAGES A AND B.

b. This insurance applies to:

(1) "Personal injury" caused by an offense arising out of your business, excluding advertising, publishing, broadcasting or telecasting done by or for you;

(2) "Advertising injury" caused by an offense committed in the course of advertising your goods, products or services;

but only if:

(1) The offense was committed in the "coverage territory";

(2) The offense was not committed before the Retroactive Date, if any, shown in the Declarations or after the end of the policy period; and

(3) A claim for damages because of the "personal injury" or "advertising injury" is first made against any insured, in accordance with paragraph c. below, during the policy period or any Extended Reporting Period we provide under EXTENDED REPORTING PERIODS (Section V).

c. A claim made by a person or organization seeking damages will be deemed to have been made at the earlier of the following times:

   (1) When notice of such claim is received and recorded by any insured or by us, whichever comes first; or

   (2) When we make settlement in accordance with paragraph 1.a. above.

   All claims for damages because of "personal injury" or "advertising injury" to the same person or organization as a result of an offense will be deemed to have been made at the time the first of those claims is made against any insured.

2. Exclusions.

This insurance does not apply to:

a. "Personal injury" or "advertising injury":

   (1) Arising out of oral or written publication of material, if done by or at the direction of the insured with knowledge of its falsity;

   (2) Arising out of oral or written publication of material whose first publication took place before the Retroactive Date, if any, shown in the Declarations;

   (3) Arising out of the willful violation of a penal statute or ordinance committed by or with the consent of the insured; or

   (4) For which the insured has assumed liability in a contract or agreement. This exclusion does not apply to liability for damages that the insured would have in the absence of the contract or agreement.

b. "Advertising injury" arising out of:

   (1) Breach of contract, other than misappropriation of advertising ideas under an implied contract;

   (2) The failure of goods, products or services to conform with advertised quality or performance;

   (3) The wrong description of the price of goods, products or services; or

   (4) An offense committed by an insured whose business is advertising, broadcasting, publishing or telecasting.

COVERAGE C. MEDICAL PAYMENTS

1. Insuring Agreement.

a. We will pay medical expenses as described below for "bodily injury" caused by an accident:

   (1) On premises you own or rent;

   (2) On ways next to premises you own or rent; or

   (3) Because of your operations;

   provided that:

   (1) The accident takes place in the "coverage territory" and during the policy period;

   (2) The expenses are incurred and reported to us within one year of the date of the accident; and

   (3) The injured person submits to examination, at our expense, by physicians of our choice as often as we reasonably require.

b. We will make these payments regardless of fault. These payments will not exceed the applicable limit of insurance. We will pay reasonable expenses for:

   (1) First aid administered at the time of an accident;

   (2) Necessary medical, surgical, x-ray and dental services, including prosthetic devices; and

   (3) Necessary ambulance, hospital, professional nursing and funeral services.

2. Exclusions.

We will not pay expenses for "bodily injury":

a. To any insured.

b. To a person hired to do work for or on behalf of any insured or a tenant of any insured.

c. To a person injured on that part of premises you own or rent that the person normally occupies.

d. To a person, whether or not an "employee" of any insured, if benefits for the "bodily injury" are payable or must be provided under a workers compensation or disability benefits law or a similar law.

e. To a person injured while taking part in athletics.

f. Included within the "products-completed operations hazard".

g. Excluded under Coverage A.

h. Due to war, whether or not declared, or any act or condition incident to war. War includes civil war, insurrection, rebellion or revolution.

SUPPLEMENTARY PAYMENTS - COVERAGES A AND B

We will pay, with respect to any claim or "suit" we defend:

1. All expenses we incur.

2. Up to $250 for cost of bail bonds required because of accidents or traffic law violations arising out of the use of any vehicle to which the Bodily Injury Liability Coverage applies. We do not have to furnish these bonds.

3. The cost of bonds to release attachments, but only for bond amounts within the applicable limit of insurance. We do not have to furnish these bonds.

4. All reasonable expenses incurred by the insured at our request to assist us in the investigation or defense of the claim or "suit", including actual loss of earnings up to $100 a day because of time off from work.

5. All costs taxed against the insured in the "suit".

6. Prejudgment interest awarded against the insured on that part of the judgment we pay. If we make an offer to pay the applicable limit of insurance, we will not pay any prejudgment interest based on that period of time after the offer.

7. All interest on the full amount of any judgment that accrues after entry of the judgment and before we have paid, offered to pay, or deposited in court the part of the judgment that is within the applicable limit of insurance.

These payments will not reduce the limits of insurance.

SECTION II - WHO IS AN INSURED

1. If you are designated in the Declarations as:

a. An individual, you and your spouse are insureds, but only with respect to the conduct of a business of which you are the sole owner.

b. A partnership or joint venture, you are an insured. Your members, your partners, and their spouses are also insureds, but only with respect to the conduct of your business.

c. An organization other than a partnership or joint venture, you are an insured. Your "executive officers" and directors are insureds, but only with respect to their duties as your officers or directors. Your stockholders are also insureds, but only with respect to their liability as stockholders.

2. Each of the following is also an insured:

a. Your "employees", other than your "executive officers", but only for acts within the scope of their employment by you or while performing duties related to the conduct of your business. However, no "employee" is an insured for:

(1) "Bodily injury" or "personal injury":

(a) To you, to your partners or members (if you are a partnership or joint venture), or to a co-"employee" while in the course of his or her employment or while performing duties related to the conduct of your business;

(b) To the spouse, child, parent, brother or sister of that co-"employee" as a consequence of paragraph (1)(a) above;

(c) For which there is any obligation to share damages with or repay someone else who must pay damages because of the injury described in paragraphs (1)(a) or (b) above; or

(d) Arising out of his or her providing or failing to provide professional health care services.

(2) "Property damage" to property:

(a) Owned, occupied or used by,

(b) Rented to, in the care, custody or control of, or over which physical control is being exercised for any purpose by

you, any of your "employees" or, if you are a partnership or joint venture, by any partner or member.

b. Any person (other than your "employee") or any organization while acting as your real estate manager.

c. Any person or organization having proper temporary custody of your property if you die, but only:

(1) With respect to liability arising out of the maintenance or use of that property; and

Copyright, Insurance Services Office, Inc., 1992   CG 00 02 10 93   □

(2) Until your legal representative has been appointed.

d. Your legal representative if you die, but only with respect to duties as such. That representative will have all your rights and duties under this Coverage Part.

3. With respect to "mobile equipment" registered in your name under any motor vehicle registration law, any person is an insured while driving such equipment along a public highway with your permission. Any other person or organization responsible for the conduct of such person is also an insured, but only with respect to liability arising out of the operation of the equipment, and only if no other insurance of any kind is available to that person or organization for this liability. However, no person or organization is an insured with respect to:

a. "Bodily injury" to a co-"employee" of the person driving the equipment; or

b. "Property damage" to property owned by, rented to, in the charge of or occupied by you or the employer of any person who is an insured under this provision.

4. Any organization you newly acquire or form, other than a partnership or joint venture, and over which you maintain ownership or majority interest, will qualify as a Named Insured if there is no other similar insurance available to that organization. However:

a. Coverage under this provision is afforded only until the 90th day after you acquire or form the organization or the end of the policy period, whichever is earlier;

b. Coverage A does not apply to "bodily injury" or "property damage" that occurred before you acquired or formed the organization; and

c. Coverage B does not apply to "personal injury" or "advertising injury" arising out of an offense committed before you acquired or formed the organization.

No person or organization is an insured with respect to the conduct of any current or past partnership or joint venture that is not shown as a Named Insured in the Declarations.

SECTION III - LIMITS OF INSURANCE

1. The Limits of Insurance shown in the Declarations and the rules below fix the most we will pay regardless of the number of:

a. Insureds;

b. Claims made or "suits" brought; or

c. Persons or organizations making claims or bringing "suits".

2. The General Aggregate Limit is the most we will pay for the sum of:

a. Medical expenses under Coverage C;

b. Damages under Coverage A, except damages because of "bodily injury" or "property damage" included in the "products-completed operations hazard"; and

c. Damages under Coverage B.

3. The Products-Completed Operations Aggregate Limit is the most we will pay under Coverage A for damages because of "bodily injury" and "property damage" included in the "products-completed operations hazard".

4. Subject to **2.** above, the Personal and Advertising Injury Limit is the most we will pay under Coverage B for the sum of all damages because of all "personal injury" and all "advertising injury" sustained by any one person or organization.

5. Subject to **2.** or **3.** above, whichever applies, the Each Occurrence Limit is the most we will pay for the sum of:

a. Damages under Coverage A; and

b. Medical expenses under Coverage C

because of all "bodily injury" and "property damage" arising out of any one "occurrence".

6. Subject to **5.** above, the Fire Damage Limit is the most we will pay under Coverage A for damages because of "property damage" to premises, while rented to you or temporarily occupied by you with permission of the owner, arising out of any one fire.

7. Subject to **5.** above, the Medical Expense Limit is the most we will pay under Coverage C for all medical expenses because of "bodily injury" sustained by any one person.

The Limits of Insurance of this Coverage Part apply separately to each consecutive annual period and to any remaining period of less than 12 months, starting with the beginning of the policy period shown in the Declarations, unless the policy period is extended after issuance for an additional period of less than 12 months. In that case, the additional period will be deemed part of the last preceding period for purposes of determining the Limits of Insurance.

SECTION IV - COMMERCIAL GENERAL LIABILITY CONDITIONS

1. Bankruptcy.

Bankruptcy or insolvency of the insured or of the insured's estate will not relieve us of our obligations under this Coverage Part.

2. Duties In The Event Of Occurrence, Offense, Claim Or Suit.

a. You must see to it that we are notified as soon as practicable of an "occurrence" or offense which may result in a claim. To the extent possible, notice should include:

(1) How, when and where the "occurrence" or offense took place;

(2) The names and addresses of any injured persons and witnesses; and

(3) The nature and location of any injury or damage arising out of the "occurrence" or offense.

Notice of an "occurrence" or offense is not notice of a claim.

b. If a claim is received by any insured, you must:

(1) Immediately record the specifics of the claim and the date received; and

(2) Notify us as soon as practicable.

You must see to it that we receive written notice of the claim as soon as practicable.

c. You and any other involved insured must:

(1) Immediately send us copies of any demands, notices, summonses or legal papers received in connection with the claim or a "suit";

(2) Authorize us to obtain records and other information;

(3) Cooperate with us in the investigation, settlement or defense of the claim or "suit"; and

(4) Assist us, upon our request, in the enforcement of any right against any person or organization which may be liable to the insured because of injury or damage to which this insurance may also apply.

d. No insureds will, except at their own cost, voluntarily make a payment, assume any obligation, or incur any expense, other than for first aid, without our consent.

3. Legal Action Against Us.

No person or organization has a right under this Coverage Part:

a. To join us as a party or otherwise bring us into a "suit" asking for damages from an insured; or

b. To sue us on this Coverage Part unless all of its terms have been fully complied with.

A person or organization may sue us to recover on an agreed settlement or on a final judgment against an insured obtained after an actual trial; but we will not be liable for damages that are not payable under the terms of this Coverage Part or that are in excess of the applicable limit of insurance. An agreed settlement means a settlement and release of liability signed by us, the insured and the claimant or the claimant's legal representative.

4. Other Insurance.

If other valid and collectible insurance is available to the insured for a loss we cover under Coverages A or B of this Coverage Part, our obligations are limited as follows:

a. **Primary Insurance**

This insurance is primary except when **b.** below applies. If this insurance is primary, our obligations are not affected unless any of the other insurance is also primary. Then, we will share with all that other insurance by the method described in **c.** below.

b. **Excess Insurance**

This insurance is excess over any of the other insurance, whether primary, excess, contingent or on any other basis:

(1) That is effective prior to the beginning of the policy period shown in the Declarations of this insurance and applies to "bodily injury" or "property damage" on other than a claims-made basis, if:

(a) No Retroactive Date is shown in the Declarations of this insurance; or

(b) The other insurance has a policy period which continues after the Retroactive Date shown in the Declarations of this insurance;

(2) That is Fire, Extended Coverage, Builders' Risk, Installation Risk or similar coverage for "your work";

(3) That is Fire insurance for premises rented to you; or

(4) If the loss arises out of the maintenance or use of aircraft, "autos" or watercraft to the extent not subject to Exclusion **g.** of Coverage A (Section I).

When this insurance is excess, we will have no duty under Coverages A or B to defend any claim or "suit" that any other insurer has a duty to defend. If no other insurer defends, we will undertake to do so, but we will be entitled to the insured's rights against all those other insurers.

CG 00 02 10 93 □

When this insurance is excess over other insurance, we will pay only our share of the amount of the loss, if any, that exceeds the sum of:

(1) The total amount that all such other insurance would pay for the loss in the absence of this insurance; and

(2) The total of all deductible and self-insured amounts under all that other insurance.

We will share the remaining loss, if any, with any other insurance that is not described in this Excess Insurance provision and was not bought specifically to apply in excess of the Limits of Insurance shown in the Declarations of this Coverage Part.

c. Method of Sharing

If all of the other insurance permits contribution by equal shares, we will follow this method also. Under this approach each insurer contributes equal amounts until it has paid its applicable limit of insurance or none of the loss remains, whichever comes first.

If any of the other insurance does not permit contribution by equal shares, we will contribute by limits. Under this method, each insurer's share is based on the ratio of its applicable limit of insurance to the total applicable limits of insurance of all insurers.

5. Premium Audit.

a. We will compute all premiums for this Coverage Part in accordance with our rules and rates.

b. Premium shown in this Coverage Part as advance premium is a deposit premium only. At the close of each audit period we will compute the earned premium for that period.

Audit premiums are due and payable on notice to the first Named Insured. If the sum of the advance and audit premiums paid for the policy period is greater than the earned premium, we will return the excess to the first Named Insured.

c. The first Named Insured must keep records of the information we need for premium computation, and send us copies at such times as we may request.

6. Representations.

By accepting this policy, you agree:

a. The statements in the Declarations are accurate and complete;

b. Those statements are based upon representations you made to us; and

c. We have issued this policy in reliance upon your representations.

7. Separation Of Insureds.

Except with respect to the Limits of Insurance, and any rights or duties specifically assigned in this Coverage Part to the first Named Insured, this insurance applies:

a. As if each Named Insured were the only Named Insured; and

b. Separately to each insured against whom claim is made or "suit" is brought.

8. Transfer Of Rights Of Recovery Against Others To Us.

If the insured has rights to recover all or part of any payment we have made under this Coverage Part, those rights are transferred to us. The insured must do nothing after loss to impair them. At our request, the insured will bring "suit" or transfer those rights to us and help us enforce them.

9. When We Do Not Renew.

If we decide not to renew this Coverage Part, we will mail or deliver to the first Named Insured shown in the Declarations written notice of the nonrenewal not less than 30 days before the expiration date.

If notice is mailed, proof of mailing will be sufficient proof of notice.

10.Your Right to Claim and "Occurrence" Information.

We will provide the first Named Insured shown in the Declarations the following information relating to this and any preceding general liability claims-made Coverage Part we have issued to you during the previous three years:

a. A list or other record of each "occurrence", not previously reported to any other insurer, of which we were notified in accordance with paragraph **2.a.** of the DUTIES IN THE EVENT OF OCCURRENCE, OFFENSE, CLAIM OR SUIT Condition in COMMERCIAL GENERAL LIABILITY CONDITIONS (Section IV). We will include the date and brief description of the "occurrence" if that information was in the notice we received.

b. A summary by policy year, of payments made and amounts reserved, stated separately, under any applicable General Aggregate Limit and Products-Completed Operations Aggregate Limit.

Amounts reserved are based on our judgment. They are subject to change and should not be regarded as ultimate settlement values.

You must not disclose this information to any claimant or any claimant's representative without our consent.

If we cancel or elect not to renew this Coverage Part, we will provide such information no later than 30 days before the date of policy termination. In other circumstances, we will provide this information only if we receive a written request from the first Named Insured within 60 days after the end of the policy period. In this case, we will provide this information within 45 days of receipt of the request.

We compile claim and "occurrence" information for our own business purposes and exercise reasonable care in doing so. In providing this information to the first Named Insured, we make no representations or warranties to insureds, insurers, or others to whom this information is furnished by or on behalf of any insured. Cancellation or non-renewal will be effective even if we inadvertently provide inaccurate information.

SECTION V - EXTENDED REPORTING PERIODS

1. We will provide one or more Extended Reporting Periods, as described below, if:

   a. This Coverage Part is cancelled or not renewed; or

   b. We renew or replace this Coverage Part with insurance that:

      (1) Has a Retroactive Date later than the date shown in the Declarations of this Coverage Part; or

      (2) Does not apply to "bodily injury", "property damage", "personal injury" or "advertising injury" on a claims-made basis.

2. Extended Reporting Periods do not extend the policy period or change the scope of coverage provided. They apply only to claims for:

   a. "Bodily injury" or "property damage" that occurs before the end of the policy period but not before the Retroactive Date, if any, shown in the Declarations; or

   b. "Personal injury" or "advertising injury" caused by an offense committed before the end of the policy period but not before the Retroactive Date, if any, shown in the Declarations.

   Once in effect, Extended Reporting Periods may not be cancelled.

3. A Basic Extended Reporting Period is automatically provided without additional charge. This period starts with the end of the policy period and lasts for:

   a. Five years with respect to claims because of "bodily injury" and "property damage" arising out of an "occurrence" reported to us, not later than 60 days after the end of the policy period, in accordance with paragraph 2.a. of the DUTIES IN THE EVENT OF OCCURRENCE, OFFENSE, CLAIM OR SUIT Condition in COMMERCIAL GENERAL LIABILITY CONDITIONS (Section IV);

   b. Five years with respect to claims because of "personal injury" and "advertising injury" arising out of an offense reported to us, not later than 60 days after the end of the policy period, in accordance with paragraph 2.a. of the DUTIES IN THE EVENT OF OCCURRENCE, OFFENSE, CLAIM OR SUIT Condition in COMMERCIAL GENERAL LIABILITY CONDITIONS (Section IV); and

   c. Sixty days with respect to claims arising from "occurrences" or offenses not previously reported to us.

   The Basic Extended Reporting Period does not apply to claims that are covered under any subsequent insurance you purchase, or that would be covered but for exhaustion of the amount of insurance applicable to such claims.

4. The Basic Extended Reporting Period does not reinstate or increase the Limits of Insurance.

5. A Supplemental Extended Reporting Period of unlimited duration is available, but only by an endorsement and for an extra charge. This supplemental period starts when the Basic Extended Reporting Period, set forth in paragraph 3. above, ends.

   You must give us a written request for the endorsement within 60 days after the end of the policy period. The Supplemental Extended Reporting Period will not go into effect unless you pay the additional premium promptly when due.

   We will determine the additional premium in accordance with our rules and rates. In doing so, we may take into account the following:

   a. The exposures insured;

   b. Previous types and amounts of insurance;

   c. Limits of Insurance available under this Coverage Part for future payment of damages; and

   d. Other related factors.

         CG 00 02 10 93   □

The additional premium will not exceed 200% of the annual premium for this Coverage Part.

This endorsement shall set forth the terms, not inconsistent with this Section, applicable to the Supplemental Extended Reporting Period, including a provision to the effect that the insurance afforded for claims first received during such period is excess over any other valid and collectible insurance available under policies in force after the Supplemental Extended Reporting Period starts.

6. If the Supplemental Extended Reporting Period is in effect, we will provide the supplemental aggregate limits of insurance described below, but only for claims first received and recorded during the Supplemental Extended Reporting Period.

The supplemental aggregate limits of insurance will be equal to the dollar amount shown in the Declarations in effect at the end of the policy period for such of the following limits of insurance for which a dollar amount has been entered:

General Aggregate Limit
Products-Completed Operations Aggregate Limit

Paragraphs 2. and 3. of LIMITS OF INSURANCE (Section III) will be amended accordingly. The Personal and Advertising Injury Limit, the Each Occurrence Limit and the Fire Damage Limit shown in the Declarations will then continue to apply, as set forth in paragraphs 4., 5. and 6. of that Section.

SECTION VI - DEFINITIONS

1. "Advertising injury" means injury arising out of one or more of the following offenses:

   a. Oral or written publication of material that slanders or libels a person or organization or disparages a person's or organization's goods, products or services;

   b. Oral or written publication of material that violates a person's right of privacy;

   c. Misappropriation of advertising ideas or style of doing business; or

   d. Infringement of copyright, title or slogan.

2. "Auto" means a land motor vehicle, trailer or semitrailer designed for travel on public roads, including any attached machinery or equipment. But "auto" does not include "mobile equipment".

3. "Bodily injury" means bodily injury, sickness or disease sustained by a person, including death resulting from any of these at any time.

4. "Coverage territory" means:

   a. The United States of America (including its territories and possessions), Puerto Rico and Canada;

   b. International waters or airspace, provided the injury or damage does not occur in the course of travel or transportation to or from any place not included in a. above; or

   c. All parts of the world if:

      (1) The injury or damage arises out of:

         (a) Goods or products made or sold by you in the territory described in a. above; or

         (b) The activities of a person whose home is in the territory described in a. above, but is away for a short time on your business; and

      (2) The insured's responsibility to pay damages is determined in a "suit" on the merits, in the territory described in a. above or in a settlement we agree to.

5. "Employee" includes a "leased worker". "Employee" does not include a "temporary worker".

6. "Executive officer" means a person holding any of the officer positions created by your charter, constitution, by-laws or any other similar governing document.

7. "Impaired property" means tangible property, other than "your product" or "your work", that cannot be used or is less useful because:

   a. It incorporates "your product" or "your work" that is known or thought to be defective, deficient, inadequate or dangerous; or

   b. You have failed to fulfill the terms of a contract or agreement;

   if such property can be restored to use by:

   a. The repair, replacement, adjustment or removal of "your product" or "your work"; or

   b. Your fulfilling the terms of the contract or agreement.

8. "Insured contract" means:

   a. A contract for a lease of premises. However, that portion of the contract for a lease of premises that indemnifies any person or organization for damage by fire to premises while rented to you or temporarily occupied by you with permission of the owner is not an "insured contract";

b. A sidetrack agreement;

c. Any easement or license agreement, except in connection with construction or demolition operations on or within 50 feet of a railroad;

d. An obligation, as required by ordinance, to indemnify a municipality, except in connection with work for a municipality;

e. An elevator maintenance agreement;

f. That part of any other contract or agreement pertaining to your business (including an indemnification of a municipality in connection with work performed for a municipality) under which you assume the tort liability of another party to pay for "bodily injury" or "property damage" to a third person or organization. Tort liability means a liability that would be imposed by law in the absence of any contract or agreement.

Paragraph f. does not include that part of any contract or agreement:

(1) That indemnifies a railroad for "bodily injury" or "property damage" arising out of construction or demolition operations, within 50 feet of any railroad property and affecting any railroad bridge or trestle, tracks, road-beds, tunnel, underpass or crossing;

(2) That indemnifies an architect, engineer or surveyor for injury or damage arising out of:

(a) Preparing, approving or failing to prepare or approve maps, drawings, opinions, reports, surveys, change orders, designs or specifications; or

(b) Giving directions or instructions, or failing to give them, if that is the primary cause of the injury or damage; or

(3) Under which the insured, if an architect, engineer or surveyor, assumes liability for an injury or damage arising out of the insured's rendering or failure to render professional services, including those listed in (2) above and supervisory, inspection or engineering services.

9. "Leased worker" means a person leased to you by a labor leasing firm under an agreement between you and the labor leasing firm, to perform duties related to the conduct of your business. "Leased worker" does not include a "temporary worker".

10. "Loading or unloading" means the handling of property:

a. After it is moved from the place where it is accepted for movement into or onto an aircraft, watercraft or "auto";

b. While it is in or on an aircraft, watercraft or "auto"; or

c. While it is being moved from an aircraft, watercraft or "auto" to the place where it is finally delivered;

but "loading or unloading" does not include the movement of property by means of a mechanical device, other than a hand truck, that is not attached to the aircraft, watercraft or "auto".

11. "Mobile equipment" means any of the following types of land vehicles, including any attached machinery or equipment:

a. Bulldozers, farm machinery, forklifts and other vehicles designed for use principally off public roads;

b. Vehicles maintained for use solely on or next to premises you own or rent;

c. Vehicles that travel on crawler treads;

d. Vehicles, whether self-propelled or not, maintained primarily to provide mobility to permanently mounted:

(1) Power cranes, shovels, loaders, diggers or drills; or

(2) Road construction or resurfacing equipment such as graders, scrapers or rollers;

e. Vehicles not described in a., b., c. or d. above that are not self-propelled and are maintained primarily to provide mobility to permanently attached equipment of the following types:

(1) Air compressors, pumps and generators, including spraying, welding, building cleaning, geophysical exploration, lighting and well servicing equipment; or

(2) Cherry pickers and similar devices used to raise or lower workers;

f. Vehicles not described in a., b., c. or d. above maintained primarily for purposes other than the transportation of persons or cargo.

However, self-propelled vehicles with the following types of permanently attached equipment are not "mobile equipment" but will be considered "autos":

(1) Equipment designed primarily for:

(a) Snow removal;

Copyright, Insurance Services Office, Inc., 1992   CG 00 02 10 93   □

(b) Road maintenance, but not construction or resurfacing; or

(c) Street cleaning;

(2) Cherry pickers and similar devices mounted on automobile or truck chassis and used to raise or lower workers; and

(3) Air compressors, pumps and generators, including spraying, welding, building cleaning, geophysical exploration, lighting and well servicing equipment.

12. "Occurrence" means an accident, including continuous or repeated exposure to substantially the same general harmful conditions.

13. "Personal injury" means injury, other than "bodily injury", arising out of one or more of the following offenses:

a. False arrest, detention or imprisonment;

b. Malicious prosecution;

c. The wrongful eviction from, wrongful entry into, or invasion of the right of private occupancy of a room, dwelling or premises that a person occupies by or on behalf of its owner, landlord or lessor;

d. Oral or written publication of material that slanders or libels a person or organization or disparages a person's or organization's goods, products or services; or

e. Oral or written publication of material that violates a person's right of privacy.

14. a. "Products-completed operations hazard" includes all "bodily injury" and "property damage" occurring away from premises you own or rent and arising out of "your product" or "your work" except:

(1) Products that are still in your physical possession; or

(2) Work that has not yet been completed or abandoned.

b. "Your work" will be deemed completed at the earliest of the following times:

(1) When all of the work called for in your contract has been completed.

(2) When all of the work to be done at the site has been completed if your contract calls for work at more than one site.

(3) When that part of the work done at a job site has been put to its intended use by any person or organization other than another contractor or subcontractor working on the same project.

Work that may need service, maintenance, correction, repair or replacement, but which is otherwise complete, will be treated as completed.

c. This hazard does not include "bodily injury" or "property damage" arising out of:

(1) The transportation of property, unless the injury or damage arises out of a condition in or on a vehicle created by the "loading or unloading" of it;

(2) The existence of tools, uninstalled equipment or abandoned or unused materials; or

(3) Products or operations for which the classification in this Coverage Part or in our manual of rules includes products or completed operations.

15. "Property damage" means:

a. Physical injury to tangible property, including all resulting loss of use of that property. All such loss of use shall be deemed to occur at the time of the physical injury that caused it; or

b. Loss of use of tangible property that is not physically injured. All such loss of use shall be deemed to occur at the time of the "occurrence" that caused it.

16. "Suit" means a civil proceeding in which damages because of "bodily injury", "property damage", "personal injury" or "advertising injury" to which this insurance applies are alleged. "Suit" includes:

a. An arbitration proceeding in which such damages are claimed and to which you must submit or do submit with our consent; or

b. Any other alternative dispute resolution proceeding in which such damages are claimed and to which you submit with our consent.

17. "Your product" means:

a. Any goods or products, other than real property, manufactured, sold, handled, distributed or disposed of by:

(1) You;

(2) Others trading under your name; or

(3) A person or organization whose business or assets you have acquired; and

b. Containers (other than vehicles), materials, parts or equipment furnished in connection with such goods or products.

"Your product" includes:

a. Warranties or representations made at any time with respect to the fitness, quality, durability, performance or use of "your product"; and

b. The providing of or failure to provide warnings or instructions.

"Your product" does not include vending machines or other property rented to or located for the use of others but not sold.

18. "Temporary worker" means a person who is furnished to you to substitute for a permanent "employee" on leave or to meet seasonal or short-term workload conditions.

19. "Your work" means:

a. Work or operations performed by you or on your behalf; and

b. Materials, parts or equipment furnished in connection with such work or operations.

"Your work" includes:

a. Warranties or representations made at any time with respect to the fitness, quality, durability, performance or use of "your work"; and

b. The providing of or failure to provide warnings or instructions.

COMMERCIAL GENERAL LIABILITY
CG 00 01 01 96

COMMERCIAL GENERAL LIABILITY COVERAGE FORM

Various provisions in this policy restrict coverage. Read the entire policy carefully to determine rights, duties and what is and is not covered.

Throughout this policy the words "you" and "your" refer to the Named Insured shown in the Declarations, and any other person or organization qualifying as a Named Insured under this policy. The words "we", "us" and "our" refer to the company providing this insurance.

The word "insured" means any person or organization qualifying as such under WHO IS AN INSURED (SECTION II).

Other words and phrases that appear in quotation marks have special meaning. Refer to DEFINITIONS (SECTION V).

SECTION I - COVERAGES

COVERAGE A. BODILY INJURY AND PROPERTY DAMAGE LIABILITY

1. Insuring Agreement

a. We will pay those sums that the insured becomes legally obligated to pay as damages because of "bodily injury" or "property damage" to which this insurance applies. We will have the right and duty to defend the insured against any "suit" seeking those damages. However, we will have no duty to defend the insured against any "suit" seeking damages for "bodily injury" or "property damage" to which this insurance does not apply. We may, at our discretion, investigate any "occurrence" and settle any claim or "suit" that may result. But:

(1) The amount we will pay for damages is limited as described in LIMITS OF INSURANCE (SECTION III); and

(2) Our right and duty to defend end when we have used up the applicable limit of insurance in the payment of judgments or settlements under Coverages A or B or medical expenses under Coverage C.

No other obligation or liability to pay sums or perform acts or services is covered unless explicitly provided for under SUPPLEMENTARY PAYMENTS - COVERAGES A AND B.

b. This insurance applies to "bodily injury" and "property damage" only if:

(1) The "bodily injury" or "property damage" is caused by an "occurrence" that takes place in the "coverage territory"; and

(2) The "bodily injury" or "property damage" occurs during the policy period.

c. Damages because of "bodily injury" include damages claimed by any person or organization for care, loss of services or death resulting at any time from the "bodily injury".

2. Exclusions

This insurance does not apply to:

a. **Expected or Intended Injury**

"Bodily injury" or "property damage" expected or intended from the standpoint of the insured. This exclusion does not apply to "bodily injury" resulting from the use of reasonable force to protect persons or property.

b. **Contractual Liability**

"Bodily injury" or "property damage" for which the insured is obligated to pay damages by reason of the assumption of liability in a contract or agreement. This exclusion does not apply to liability for damages:

(1) That the insured would have in the absence of the contract or agreement; or

(2) Assumed in a contract or agreement that is an "insured contract", provided the "bodily injury" or "property damage" occurs subsequent to the execution of the contract or agreement. Solely for the purposes of liability assumed in an "insured contract", reasonable attorney fees and necessary litigation expenses incurred by or for a party other than an insured are deemed to be damages because of "bodily injury" or "property damage", provided:

(a) Liability to such party for, or for the cost of, that party's defense has also been assumed in the same "insured contract"; and

(b) Such attorney fees and litigation expenses are for defense of that party against a civil or alternative dispute resolution proceeding in which damages to which this insurance applies are alleged.

c. Liquor Liability

"Bodily injury" or "property damage" for which any insured may be held liable by reason of:

(1) Causing or contributing to the intoxication of any person;

(2) The furnishing of alcoholic beverages to a person under the legal drinking age or under the influence of alcohol; or

(3) Any statute, ordinance or regulation relating to the sale, gift, distribution or use of alcoholic beverages.

This exclusion applies only if you are in the business of manufacturing, distributing, selling, serving or furnishing alcoholic beverages.

d. Workers Compensation and Similar Laws

Any obligation of the insured under a workers compensation, disability benefits or unemployment compensation law or any similar law.

e. Employer's Liability

"Bodily injury" to:

(1) An "employee" of the insured arising out of and in the course of:

(a) Employment by the insured; or

(b) Performing duties related to the conduct of the insured's business; or

(2) The spouse, child, parent, brother or sister of that "employee" as a consequence of paragraph (1) above.

This exclusion applies:

(1) Whether the insured may be liable as an employer or in any other capacity; and

(2) To any obligation to share damages with or repay someone else who must pay damages because of the injury.

This exclusion does not apply to liability assumed by the insured under an "insured contract".

f. Pollution

(1) "Bodily injury" or "property damage" arising out of the actual, alleged or threatened discharge, dispersal, seepage, migration, release or escape of pollutants:

(a) At or from any premises, site or location which is or was at any time owned or occupied by, or rented or loaned to, any insured;

(b) At or from any premises, site or location which is or was at any time used by or for any insured or others for the handling, storage, disposal, processing or treatment of waste;

(c) Which are or were at any time transported, handled, stored, treated, disposed of, or processed as waste by or for any insured or any person or organization for whom you may be legally responsible; or

(d) At or from any premises, site or location on which any insured or any contractors or subcontractors working directly or indirectly on any insured's behalf are performing operations:

(i) If the pollutants are brought on or to the premises, site or location in connection with such operations by such insured, contractor or subcontractor; or

(ii) If the operations are to test for, monitor, clean up, remove, contain, treat, detoxify or neutralize, or in any way respond to, or assess the effects of pollutants.

Subparagraph (d)(i) does not apply to "bodily injury" or "property damage" arising out of the escape of fuels, lubricants or other operating fluids which are needed to perform the normal electrical, hydraulic or mechanical functions necessary for the operation of "mobile equipment" or its parts, if such fuels, lubricants or other operating fluids escape from a vehicle part designed to hold, store or receive them. This exception does not apply if the fuels, lubricants or other operating fluids are intentionally discharged, dispersed or released, or if such fuels, lubricants or other operating fluids are brought on or to the premises, site or location with the intent to be discharged, dispersed or released as part of the operations being performed by such insured, contractor or subcontractor.

Subparagraphs (a) and (d)(I) do not apply to "bodily injury" or "property damage" arising out of heat, smoke or fumes from a hostile fire.

As used in this exclusion, a hostile fire means one which becomes uncontrollable or breaks out from where it was intended to be.

(2) Any loss, cost or expense arising out of any:

(a) Request, demand or order that any insured or others test for, monitor, clean up, remove, contain, treat, detoxify or neutralize, or in any way respond to, or assess the effects of pollutants; or

(b) Claim or suit by or on behalf of a governmental authority for damages because of testing for, monitoring, cleaning up, removing, containing, treating, detoxifying or neutralizing, or in any way responding to, or assessing the effects of pollutants.

Pollutants means any solid, liquid, gaseous or thermal irritant or contaminant, including smoke, vapor, soot, fumes, acids, alkalis, chemicals and waste. Waste includes materials to be recycled, reconditioned or reclaimed.

g. Aircraft, Auto or Watercraft

"Bodily injury" or "property damage" arising out of the ownership, maintenance, use or entrustment to others of any aircraft, "auto" or watercraft owned or operated by or rented or loaned to any insured. Use includes operation and "loading or unloading".

This exclusion does not apply to:

(1) A watercraft while ashore on premises you own or rent;

(2) A watercraft you do not own that is:

(a) Less than 26 feet long; and

(b) Not being used to carry persons or property for a charge;

(3) Parking an "auto" on, or on the ways next to, premises you own or rent, provided the "auto" is not owned by or rented or loaned to you or the insured;

(4) Liability assumed under any "insured contract" for the ownership, maintenance or use of aircraft or watercraft; or

(5) "Bodily injury" or "property damage" arising out of the operation of any of the equipment listed in paragraph f.(2) or f.(3) of the definition of "mobile equipment".

h. Mobile Equipment

"Bodily injury" or "property damage" arising out of:

(1) The transportation of "mobile equipment" by an "auto" owned or operated by or rented or loaned to any insured; or

(2) The use of "mobile equipment" in, or while in practice for, or while being prepared for, any prearranged racing, speed, demolition, or stunting activity.

i. War

"Bodily injury" or "property damage" due to war, whether or not declared, or any act or condition incident to war. War includes civil war, insurrection, rebellion or revolution. This exclusion applies only to liability assumed under a contract or agreement.

j. Damage to Property

"Property damage" to:

(1) Property you own, rent, or occupy;

(2) Premises you sell, give away or abandon, if the "property damage" arises out of any part of those premises;

(3) Property loaned to you;

(4) Personal property in the care, custody or control of the insured;

(5) That particular part of real property on which you or any contractors or subcontractors working directly or indirectly on your behalf are performing operations, if the "property damage" arises out of those operations; or

(6) That particular part of any property that must be restored, repaired or replaced because "your work" was incorrectly performed on it.

Paragraph (2) of this exclusion does not apply if the premises are "your work" and were never occupied, rented or held for rental by you.

Paragraphs **(3)**, **(4)**, **(5)** and **(6)** of this exclusion do not apply to liability assumed under a sidetrack agreement.

Paragraph **(6)** of this exclusion does not apply to "property damage" included in the "products-completed operations hazard".

k. Damage to Your Product

"Property damage" to "your product" arising out of it or any part of it.

l. Damage to Your Work

"Property damage" to "your work" arising out of it or any part of it and included in the "products-completed operations hazard".

This exclusion does not apply if the damaged work or the work out of which the damage arises was performed on your behalf by a subcontractor.

m. Damage to Impaired Property or Property Not Physically Injured

"Property damage" to "impaired property" or property that has not been physically injured, arising out of:

(1) A defect, deficiency, inadequacy or dangerous condition in "your product" or "your work": or

(2) A delay or failure by you or anyone acting on your behalf to perform a contract or agreement in accordance with its terms.

This exclusion does not apply to the loss of use of other property arising out of sudden and accidental physical injury to "your product" or "your work" after it has been put to its intended use.

n. Recall of Products, Work or Impaired Property

Damages claimed for any loss, cost or expense incurred by you or others for the loss of use, withdrawal, recall, inspection, repair, replacement, adjustment, removal or disposal of:

(1) "Your product";

(2) "Your work"; or

(3) "Impaired property";

if such product, work, or property is withdrawn or recalled from the market or from use by any person or organization because of a known or suspected defect, deficiency, inadequacy or dangerous condition in it.

Exclusions **c.** through **n.** do not apply to damage by fire to premises while rented to you or temporarily occupied by you with permission of the owner. A separate limit of insurance applies to this coverage as described in LIMITS OF INSURANCE (Section III).

COVERAGE B. PERSONAL AND ADVERTISING INJURY LIABILITY

1. Insuring Agreement

a. We will pay those sums that the insured becomes legally obligated to pay as damages because of "personal injury" or "advertising injury" to which this insurance applies. We will have the right and duty to defend the insured against any "suit" seeking those damages. However, we will have no duty to defend the insured against any "suit" seeking damages for "personal injury" or "advertising injury" to which this insurance does not apply. We may, at our discretion, investigate any "occurrence" or offense and settle any claim or "suit" that may result. But:

(1) The amount we will pay for damages is limited as described in LIMITS OF INSURANCE (SECTION III); and

(2) Our right and duty to defend end when we have used up the applicable limit of insurance in the payment of judgments or settlements under Coverages A or B or medical expenses under Coverage C.

No other obligation or liability to pay sums or perform acts or services is covered unless explicitly provided for under SUPPLEMENTARY PAYMENTS - COVERAGES A AND B.

b. This insurance applies to:

(1) "Personal injury" caused by an offense arising out of your business, excluding advertising, publishing, broadcasting or telecasting done by or for you;

(2) "Advertising injury" caused by an offense committed in the course of advertising your goods, products or services;

but only if the offense was committed in the "coverage territory" during the policy period.

2. Exclusions

This insurance does not apply to:

a. "Personal injury" or "advertising injury":

(1) Arising out of oral or written publication of material, if done by or at the direction of the insured with knowledge of its falsity;

(2) Arising out of oral or written publication of material whose first publication took place before the beginning of the policy period;

(3) Arising out of the willful violation of a penal statute or ordinance committed by or with the consent of the insured;

(4) For which the insured has assumed liability in a contract or agreement. This exclusion does not apply to liability for damages that the insured would have in the absence of the contract or agreement; or

(5) Arising out of the actual, alleged or threatened discharge, dispersal, seepage, migration, release or escape of pollutants at any time.

b. "Advertising injury" arising out of:

(1) Breach of contract, other than misappropriation of advertising ideas under an implied contract;

(2) The failure of goods, products or services to conform with advertised quality or performance;

(3) The wrong description of the price of goods, products or services; or

(4) An offense committed by an insured whose business is advertising, broadcasting, publishing or telecasting.

c. Any loss, cost or expense arising out of any:

(1) Request, demand or order that any insured or others test for, monitor, clean up, remove, contain, treat, detoxify or neutralize, or in any way respond to, or assess the effects of pollutants; or

(2) Claim or suit by or on behalf of a governmental authority for damages because of testing for, monitoring, cleaning up, removing, containing, treating, detoxifying or neutralizing, or in any way responding to, or assessing the effects of pollutants.

Pollutants means any solid, liquid, gaseous or thermal irritant or contaminant, including smoke, vapor, soot, fumes, acids, alkalis, chemicals and waste. Waste includes materials to be recycled, reconditioned or reclaimed.

COVERAGE C. MEDICAL PAYMENTS

1. Insuring Agreement

a. We will pay medical expenses as described below for "bodily injury" caused by an accident:

(1) On premises you own or rent;

(2) On ways next to premises you own or rent; or

(3) Because of your operations;

provided that:

(1) The accident takes place in the "coverage territory" and during the policy period;

(2) The expenses are incurred and reported to us within one year of the date of the accident; and

(3) The injured person submits to examination, at our expense, by physicians of our choice as often as we reasonably require.

b. We will make these payments regardless of fault. These payments will not exceed the applicable limit of insurance. We will pay reasonable expenses for:

(1) First aid administered at the time of an accident;

(2) Necessary medical, surgical, x-ray and dental services, including prosthetic devices; and

(3) Necessary ambulance, hospital, professional nursing and funeral services.

2. Exclusions

We will not pay expenses for "bodily injury":

a. To any insured.

b. To a person hired to do work for or on behalf of any insured or a tenant of any insured.

c. To a person injured on that part of premises you own or rent that the person normally occupies.

d. To a person, whether or not an "employee" of any insured, if benefits for the "bodily injury" are payable or must be provided under a workers compensation or disability benefits law or a similar law.

e. To a person injured while taking part in athletics.

f. Included within the "products-completed operations hazard".

g. Excluded under Coverage A.

h. Due to war, whether or not declared, or any act or condition incident to war. War includes civil war, insurrection, rebellion or revolution.

SUPPLEMENTARY PAYMENTS - COVERAGES A AND B

We will pay, with respect to any claim we investigate or settle, or any "suit" against an insured we defend:

1. All expenses we incur.

2. Up to $250 for cost of bail bonds required because of accidents or traffic law violations arising out of the use of any vehicle to which the Bodily Injury Liability Coverage applies. We do not have to furnish these bonds.

3. The cost of bonds to release attachments, but only for bond amounts within the applicable limit of insurance. We do not have to furnish these bonds.

4. All reasonable expenses incurred by the insured at our request to assist us in the investigation or defense of the claim or "suit", including actual loss of earnings up to $250 a day because of time off from work.

5. All costs taxed against the insured in the "suit".

6. Prejudgment interest awarded against the insured on that part of the judgment we pay. If we make an offer to pay the applicable limit of insurance, we will not pay any prejudgment interest based on that period of time after the offer.

7. All interest on the full amount of any judgment that accrues after entry of the judgment and before we have paid, offered to pay, or deposited in court the part of the judgment that is within the applicable limit of insurance.

These payments will not reduce the limits of insurance.

If we defend an insured against a "suit" and an indemnitee of the insured is also named as a party to the "suit", we will defend that indemnitee if all of the following conditions are met:

a. The "suit" against the indemnitee seeks damages for which the insured has assumed the liability of the indemnitee in a contract or agreement that is an "insured contract";

b. This insurance applies to such liability assumed by the insured;

c. The obligation to defend, or the cost of the defense of, that indemnitee, has also been assumed by the insured in the same "insured contract";

d. The allegations in the "suit" and the information we know about the "occurrence" are such that no conflict appears to exist between the interests of the insured and the interests of the indemnitee;

e. The indemnitee and the insured ask us to conduct and control the defense of that indemnitee against such "suit" and agree that we can assign the same counsel to defend the insured and the indemnitee; and

f. The indemnitee:

  (1) Agrees in writing to:

    (a) Cooperate with us in the investigation, settlement or defense of the "suit";

    (b) Immediately send us copies of any demands, notices, summonses or legal papers received in connection with the "suit";

    (c) Notify any other insurer whose coverage is available to the indemnitee; and

    (d) Cooperate with us with respect to coordinating other applicable insurance available to the indemnitee; and

  (2) Provides us with written authorization to:

    (a) Obtain records and other information related to the "suit"; and

    (b) Conduct and control the defense of the indemnitee in such "suit".

So long as the above conditions are met, attorneys fees incurred by us in the defense of that indemnitee, necessary litigation expenses incurred by us and necessary litigation expenses incurred by the indemnitee at our request will be paid as Supplementary Payments. Notwithstanding the provisions of paragraph 2.b.(2) of COVERAGE A - BODILY INJURY AND PROPERTY DAMAGE LIABILITY (Section I - Coverages), such payments will not be deemed to be damages for "bodily injury" and "property damage" and will not reduce the limits of insurance.

Our obligation to defend an insured's indemnitee and to pay for attorneys fees and necessary litigation expenses as Supplementary Payments ends when:

a. We have used up the applicable limit of insurance in the payment of judgments or settlements; or

b. The conditions set forth above, or the terms of the agreement described in paragraph f. above, are no longer met.

 CG 00 01 01 96 ☐

SECTION II - WHO IS AN INSURED

1. If you are designated in the Declarations as:

   a. An individual, you and your spouse are insureds, but only with respect to the conduct of a business of which you are the sole owner.

   b. A partnership or joint venture, you are an insured. Your members, your partners, and their spouses are also insureds, but only with respect to the conduct of your business.

   c. A limited liability company, you are an insured. Your members are also insureds, but only with respect to the conduct of your business. Your managers are insureds, but only with respect to their duties as your managers.

   d. An organization other than a partnership, joint venture or limited liability company, you are an insured. Your "executive officers" and directors are insureds, but only with respect to their duties as your officers or directors. Your stockholders are also insureds, but only with respect to their liability as stockholders.

2. Each of the following is also an insured:

   a. Your "employees", other than either your "executive officers" (if you are an organization other than a partnership, joint venture or limited liability company) or your managers (if you are a limited liability company), but only for acts within the scope of their employment by you or while performing duties related to the conduct of your business. However, none of these "employees" is an insured for:

      (1) "Bodily injury" or "personal injury":

         (a) To you, to your partners or members (if you are a partnership or joint venture), to your members (if you are a limited liability company), or to a co-"employee" while that co-"employee" is either in the course of his or her employment or performing duties related to the conduct of your business;

         (b) To the spouse, child, parent, brother or sister of that co-"employee" as a consequence of paragraph **(1)(a)** above;

         (c) For which there is any obligation to share damages with or repay someone else who must pay damages because of the injury described in paragraphs **(1)(a)** or **(b)** above; or

         (d) Arising out of his or her providing or failing to provide professional health care services.

   (2) "Property damage" to property:

      (a) Owned, occupied or used by,

      (b) Rented to, in the care, custody or control of, or over which physical control is being exercised for any purpose by

      you, any of your "employees", any partner or member (if you are a partnership or joint venture), or any member (if you are a limited liability company).

   b. Any person (other than your "employee"), or any organization while acting as your real estate manager.

   c. Any person or organization having proper temporary custody of your property if you die, but only:

      (1) With respect to liability arising out of the maintenance or use of that property; and

      (2) Until your legal representative has been appointed.

   d. Your legal representative if you die, but only with respect to duties as such. That representative will have all your rights and duties under this Coverage Part.

3. With respect to "mobile equipment" registered in your name under any motor vehicle registration law, any person is an insured while driving such equipment along a public highway with your permission. Any other person or organization responsible for the conduct of such person is also an insured, but only with respect to liability arising out of the operation of the equipment, and only if no other insurance of any kind is available to that person or organization for this liability. However, no person or organization is an insured with respect to:

   a. "Bodily injury" to a co-"employee" of the person driving the equipment; or

   b. "Property damage" to property owned by, rented to, in the charge of or occupied by you or the employer of any person who is an insured under this provision.

4. Any organization you newly acquire or form, other than a partnership, joint venture or limited liability company, and over which you maintain ownership or majority interest, will qualify as a Named Insured if there is no other similar insurance available to that organization. However:

   a. Coverage under this provision is afforded only until the 90th day after you acquire or form the organization or the end of the policy period, whichever is earlier;

b. Coverage A does not apply to "bodily injury" or "property damage" that occurred before you acquired or formed the organization; and

c. Coverage B does not apply to "personal injury" or "advertising injury" arising out of an offense committed before you acquired or formed the organization.

No person or organization is an insured with respect to the conduct of any current or past partnership, joint venture or limited liability company that is not shown as a Named Insured in the Declarations.

SECTION III - LIMITS OF INSURANCE

1. The Limits of Insurance shown in the Declarations and the rules below fix the most we will pay regardless of the number of:

   a. Insureds;

   b. Claims made or "suits" brought; or

   c. Persons or organizations making claims or bringing "suits".

2. The General Aggregate Limit is the most we will pay for the sum of:

   a. Medical expenses under Coverage C;

   b. Damages under Coverage A, except damages because of "bodily injury" or "property damage" included in the "products-completed operations hazard"; and

   c. Damages under Coverage B.

3. The Products-Completed Operations Aggregate Limit is the most we will pay under Coverage A for damages because of "bodily injury" and "property damage" included in the "products-completed operations hazard".

4. Subject to 2. above, the Personal and Advertising Injury Limit is the most we will pay under Coverage B for the sum of all damages because of all "personal injury" and all "advertising injury" sustained by any one person or organization.

5. Subject to 2. or 3. above, whichever applies, the Each Occurrence Limit is the most we will pay for the sum of:

   a. Damages under Coverage A; and

   b. Medical expenses under Coverage C

   because of all "bodily injury" and "property damage" arising out of any one "occurrence".

6. Subject to 5. above, the Fire Damage Limit is the most we will pay under Coverage A for damages because of "property damage" to premises, while rented to you or temporarily occupied by you with permission of the owner, arising out of any one fire.

7. Subject to 5. above, the Medical Expense Limit is the most we will pay under Coverage C for all medical expenses because of "bodily injury" sustained by any one person.

The Limits of Insurance of this Coverage Part apply separately to each consecutive annual period and to any remaining period of less than 12 months, starting with the beginning of the policy period shown in the Declarations, unless the policy period is extended after issuance for an additional period of less than 12 months. In that case, the additional period will be deemed part of the last preceding period for purposes of determining the Limits of Insurance.

SECTION IV - COMMERCIAL GENERAL LIABILITY CONDITIONS

1. **Bankruptcy**

   Bankruptcy or insolvency of the insured or of the insured's estate will not relieve us of our obligations under this Coverage Part.

2. **Duties In The Event Of Occurrence, Offense, Claim Or Suit**

   a. You must see to it that we are notified as soon as practicable of an "occurrence" or an offense which may result in a claim. To the extent possible, notice should include:

      (1) How, when and where the "occurrence" or offense took place;

      (2) The names and addresses of any injured persons and witnesses; and

      (3) The nature and location of any injury or damage arising out of the "occurrence" or offense.

   b. If a claim is made or "suit" is brought against any insured, you must:

      (1) Immediately record the specifics of the claim or "suit" and the date received; and

      (2) Notify us as soon as practicable.

      You must see to it that we receive written notice of the claim or "suit" as soon as practicable.

         CG 00 01 01 96   ☐

c. You and any other involved insured must:

(1) Immediately send us copies of any demands, notices, summonses or legal papers received in connection with the claim or "suit";

(2) Authorize us to obtain records and other information;

(3) Cooperate with us in the investigation or settlement of the claim or defense against the "suit"; and

(4) Assist us, upon our request, in the enforcement of any right against any person or organization which may be liable to the insured because of injury or damage to which this insurance may also apply.

d. No insured will, except at that insured's own cost, voluntarily make a payment, assume any obligation, or incur any expense, other than for first aid, without our consent.

3. Legal Action Against Us

No person or organization has a right under this Coverage Part:

a. To join us as a party or otherwise bring us into a "suit" asking for damages from an insured; or

b. To sue us on this Coverage Part unless all of its terms have been fully complied with.

A person or organization may sue us to recover on an agreed settlement or on a final judgment against an insured obtained after an actual trial; but we will not be liable for damages that are not payable under the terms of this Coverage Part or that are in excess of the applicable limit of insurance. An agreed settlement means a settlement and release of liability signed by us, the insured and the claimant or the claimant's legal representative.

4. Other Insurance

If other valid and collectible insurance is available to the insured for a loss we cover under Coverages A or B of this Coverage Part, our obligations are limited as follows:

a. Primary Insurance

This insurance is primary except when b. below applies. If this insurance is primary, our obligations are not affected unless any of the other insurance is also primary. Then, we will share with all that other insurance by the method described in c. below.

b. Excess Insurance

This insurance is excess over any of the other insurance, whether primary, excess, contingent or on any other basis:

(1) That is Fire, Extended Coverage, Builder's Risk, Installation Risk or similar coverage for "your work";

(2) That is Fire insurance for premises rented to you or temporarily occupied by you with permission of the owner; or

(3) If the loss arises out of the maintenance or use of aircraft, "autos" or watercraft to the extent not subject to Exclusion g. of Coverage A (Section I).

When this insurance is excess, we will have no duty under Coverages A or B to defend the insured against any "suit" if any other insurer has a duty to defend the insured against that "suit". If no other insurer defends, we will undertake to do so, but we will be entitled to the insured's rights against all those other insurers.

When this insurance is excess over other insurance, we will pay only our share of the amount of the loss, if any, that exceeds the sum of:

(1) The total amount that all such other insurance would pay for the loss in the absence of this insurance; and

(2) The total of all deductible and self-insured amounts under all that other insurance.

We will share the remaining loss, if any, with any other insurance that is not described in this Excess Insurance provision and was not bought specifically to apply in excess of the Limits of Insurance shown in the Declarations of this Coverage Part.

c. Method of Sharing

If all of the other insurance permits contribution by equal shares, we will follow this method also. Under this approach each insurer contributes equal amounts until it has paid its applicable limit of insurance or none of the loss remains, whichever comes first.

If any of the other insurance does not permit contribution by equal shares, we will contribute by limits. Under this method, each insurer's share is based on the ratio of its applicable limit of insurance to the total applicable limits of insurance of all insurers.

5. Premium Audit

a. We will compute all premiums for this Coverage Part in accordance with our rules and rates.

b. Premium shown in this Coverage Part as advance premium is a deposit premium only. At the close of each audit period we will compute the earned premium for that period. Audit premiums are due and payable on notice to the first Named Insured. If the sum of the advance and audit premiums paid for the policy period is greater than the earned premium, we will return the excess to the first Named Insured.

c. The first Named Insured must keep records of the information we need for premium computation, and send us copies at such times as we may request.

6. Representations

By accepting this policy, you agree:

a. The statements in the Declarations are accurate and complete;

b. Those statements are based upon representations you made to us; and

c. We have issued this policy in reliance upon your representations.

7. Separation Of Insureds

Except with respect to the Limits of Insurance, and any rights or duties specifically assigned in this Coverage Part to the first Named Insured, this insurance applies:

a. As if each Named Insured were the only Named Insured; and

b. Separately to each insured against whom claim is made or "suit" is brought.

8. Transfer Of Rights Of Recovery Against Others To Us

If the insured has rights to recover all or part of any payment we have made under this Coverage Part, those rights are transferred to us. The insured must do nothing after loss to impair them. At our request, the insured will bring "suit" or transfer those rights to us and help us enforce them.

9. When We Do Not Renew

If we decide not to renew this Coverage Part, we will mail or deliver to the first Named Insured shown in the Declarations written notice of the nonrenewal not less than 30 days before the expiration date.

If notice is mailed, proof of mailing will be sufficient proof of notice.

SECTION V - DEFINITIONS

1. "Advertising injury" means injury arising out of one or more of the following offenses:

a. Oral or written publication of material that slanders or libels a person or organization or disparages a person's or organization's goods, products or services;

b. Oral or written publication of material that violates a person's right of privacy;

c. Misappropriation of advertising ideas or style of doing business; or

d. Infringement of copyright, title or slogan.

2. "Auto" means a land motor vehicle, trailer or semitrailer designed for travel on public roads, including any attached machinery or equipment. But "auto" does not include "mobile equipment".

3. "Bodily injury" means bodily injury, sickness or disease sustained by a person, including death resulting from any of these at any time.

4. "Coverage territory" means:

a. The United States of America (including its territories and possessions), Puerto Rico and Canada;

b. International waters or airspace, provided the injury or damage does not occur in the course of travel or transportation to or from any place not included in a. above; or

c. All parts of the world if:

(1) The injury or damage arises out of:

(a) Goods or products made or sold by you in the territory described in a. above; or

(b) The activities of a person whose home is in the territory described in **a.** above, but is away for a short time on your business; and

(2) The insured's responsibility to pay damages is determined in a "suit" on the merits, in the territory described in **a.** above or in a settlement we agree to.

5. "Employee" includes a "leased worker". "Employee" does not include a "temporary worker".

6. "Executive officer" means a person holding any of the officer positions created by your charter, constitution, by-laws or any other similar governing document.

7. "Impaired property" means tangible property, other than "your product" or "your work", that cannot be used or is less useful because:

   a. It incorporates "your product" or "your work" that is known or thought to be defective, deficient, inadequate or dangerous; or

   b. You have failed to fulfill the terms of a contract or agreement;

   if such property can be restored to use by:

   a. The repair, replacement, adjustment or removal of "your product" or "your work"; or

   b. Your fulfilling the terms of the contract or agreement.

8. "Insured contract" means:

   a. A contract for a lease of premises. However, that portion of the contract for a lease of premises that indemnifies any person or organization for damage by fire to premises while rented to you or temporarily occupied by you with permission of the owner is not an "insured contract";

   b. A sidetrack agreement;

   c. Any easement or license agreement, except in connection with construction or demolition operations on or within 50 feet of a railroad;

   d. An obligation, as required by ordinance, to indemnify a municipality, except in connection with work for a municipality;

   e. An elevator maintenance agreement;

   f. That part of any other contract or agreement pertaining to your business (including an indemnification of a municipality in connection with work performed for a municipality) under which you assume the tort liability of another party to pay for "bodily injury" or "property damage" to a third person or organization. Tort liability means a liability that would be imposed by law in the absence of any contract or agreement.

   Paragraph **f.** does not include that part of any contract or agreement:

   (1) That indemnifies a railroad for "bodily injury" or "property damage" arising out of construction or demolition operations, within 50 feet of any railroad property and affecting any railroad bridge or trestle, tracks, road-beds, tunnel, underpass or crossing;

   (2) That indemnifies an architect, engineer or surveyor for injury or damage arising out of:

      (a) Preparing, approving, or failing to prepare or approve, maps, shop drawings, opinions, reports, surveys, field orders, change orders or drawings and specifications; or

      (b) Giving directions or instructions, or failing to give them, if that is the primary cause of the injury or damage; or

   (3) Under which the insured, if an architect, engineer or surveyor, assumes liability for an injury or damage arising out of the insured's rendering or failure to render professional services, including those listed in **(2)** above and supervisory, inspection, architectural or engineering activities.

9. "Leased worker" means a person leased to you by a labor leasing firm under an agreement between you and the labor leasing firm, to perform duties related to the conduct of your business. "Leased worker" does not include a "temporary worker".

10. "Loading or unloading" means the handling of property:

    a. After it is moved from the place where it is accepted for movement into or onto an aircraft, watercraft or "auto";

b. While it is in or on an aircraft, watercraft or "auto"; or

c. While it is being moved from an aircraft, watercraft or "auto" to the place where it is finally delivered;

but "loading or unloading" does not include the movement of property by means of a mechanical device, other than a hand truck, that is not attached to the aircraft, watercraft or "auto".

11. "Mobile equipment" means any of the following types of land vehicles, including any attached machinery or equipment:

a. Bulldozers, farm machinery, forklifts and other vehicles designed for use principally off public roads;

b. Vehicles maintained for use solely on or next to premises you own or rent;

c. Vehicles that travel on crawler treads;

d. Vehicles, whether self-propelled or not, maintained primarily to provide mobility to permanently mounted:

    (1) Power cranes, shovels, loaders, diggers or drills; or

    (2) Road construction or resurfacing equipment such as graders, scrapers or rollers;

e. Vehicles not described in **a.**, **b.**, **c.** or **d.** above that are not self-propelled and are maintained primarily to provide mobility to permanently attached equipment of the following types:

    (1) Air compressors, pumps and generators, including spraying, welding, building cleaning, geophysical exploration, lighting and well servicing equipment; or

    (2) Cherry pickers and similar devices used to raise or lower workers;

f. Vehicles not described in **a.**, **b.**, **c.** or **d.** above maintained primarily for purposes other than the transportation of persons or cargo.

However, self-propelled vehicles with the following types of permanently attached equipment are not "mobile equipment" but will be considered "autos":

    (1) Equipment designed primarily for:

        (a) Snow removal;

        (b) Road maintenance, but not construction or resurfacing; or

        (c) Street cleaning;

    (2) Cherry pickers and similar devices mounted on automobile or truck chassis and used to raise or lower workers; and

    (3) Air compressors, pumps and generators, including spraying, welding, building cleaning, geophysical exploration, lighting and well servicing equipment.

12. "Occurrence" means an accident, including continuous or repeated exposure to substantially the same general harmful conditions.

13. "Personal injury" means injury, other than "bodily injury", arising out of one or more of the following offenses:

a. False arrest, detention or imprisonment;

b. Malicious prosecution;

c. The wrongful eviction from, wrongful entry into, or invasion of the right of private occupancy of a room, dwelling or premises that a person occupies by or on behalf of its owner, landlord or lessor;

d. Oral or written publication of material that slanders or libels a person or organization or disparages a person's or organization's goods, products or services; or

e. Oral or written publication of material that violates a person's right of privacy.

14. "Products-completed operations hazard":

a. Includes all "bodily injury" and "property damage" occurring away from premises you own or rent and arising out of "your product" or "your work" except:

    (1) Products that are still in your physical possession; or

    (2) Work that has not yet been completed or abandoned. However, "your work" will be deemed completed at the earliest of the following times:

        (a) When all of the work called for in your contract has been completed.

        (b) When all of the work to be done at the job site has been completed if your contract calls for work at more than one job site.

        (c) When that part of the work done at a job site has been put to its intended use by any person or organization other than another contractor or subcontractor working on the same project.

Work that may need service, maintenance, correction, repair or replacement, but which is otherwise complete, will be treated as completed.

 CG 00 01 01 96   ☐

b. Does not include "bodily injury" or "property damage" arising out of:

(1) The transportation of property, unless the injury or damage arises out of a condition in or on a vehicle not owned or operated by you, and that condition was created by the "loading or unloading" of that vehicle by any insured;

(2) The existence of tools, uninstalled equipment or abandoned or unused materials; or

(3) Products or operations for which the classification, listed in the Declarations or in a policy schedule, states that products-completed operations are subject to the General Aggregate Limit.

15. "Property damage" means:

a. Physical injury to tangible property, including all resulting loss of use of that property. All such loss of use shall be deemed to occur at the time of the physical injury that caused it; or

b. Loss of use of tangible property that is not physically injured. All such loss of use shall be deemed to occur at the time of the "occurrence" that caused it.

16. "Suit" means a civil proceeding in which damages because of "bodily injury", "property damage", "personal injury" or "advertising injury" to which this insurance applies are alleged. "Suit" includes:

a. An arbitration proceeding in which such damages are claimed and to which the insured must submit or does submit with our consent; or

b. Any other alternative dispute resolution proceeding in which such damages are claimed and to which the insured submits with our consent.

17. "Temporary worker" means a person who is furnished to you to substitute for a permanent "employee" on leave or to meet seasonal or short-term workload conditions.

18. "Your product" means:

a. Any goods or products, other than real property, manufactured, sold, handled, distributed or disposed of by:

(1) You;

(2) Others trading under your name; or

(3) A person or organization whose business or assets you have acquired; and

b. Containers (other than vehicles), materials, parts or equipment furnished in connection with such goods or products.

"Your product" includes:

a. Warranties or representations made at any time with respect to the fitness, quality, durability, performance or use of "your product"; and

b. The providing of or failure to provide warnings or instructions.

"Your product" does not include vending machines or other property rented to or located for the use of others but not sold.

19. "Your work" means:

a. Work or operations performed by you or on your behalf; and

b. Materials, parts or equipment furnished in connection with such work or operations.

"Your work" includes:

a. Warranties or representations made at any time with respect to the fitness, quality, durability, performance or use of "your work"; and

b. The providing of or failure to provide warnings or instructions.

COMMERCIAL GENERAL LIABILITY
CG 00 02 01 96

COMMERCIAL GENERAL LIABILITY COVERAGE FORM

COVERAGES A. AND B. PROVIDE CLAIMS-MADE COVERAGE. PLEASE READ THE ENTIRE FORM CAREFULLY.

Various provisions in this policy restrict coverage. Read the entire policy carefully to determine rights, duties and what is and is not covered.

Throughout this policy the words "you" and "your" refer to the Named Insured shown in the Declarations, and any other person or organization qualifying as a Named Insured under this policy. The words "we", "us" and "our" refer to the Company providing this insurance.

The word "insured" means any person or organization qualifying as such under WHO IS AN INSURED (Section II).

Other words and phrases that appear in quotation marks have special meaning. Refer to DEFINITIONS (Section VI).

SECTION I - COVERAGES
COVERAGE A. BODILY INJURY AND PROPERTY DAMAGE LIABILITY

1. **Insuring Agreement**

   a. We will pay those sums that the insured becomes legally obligated to pay as damages because of "bodily injury" or "property damage" to which this insurance applies. We will have the right and duty to defend the insured against any "suit" seeking those damages. However, we will have no duty to defend the insured against any "suit" seeking damages for "bodily injury" or "property damage" to which this insurance does not apply. We may, at our discretion, investigate any "occurrence" and settle any claim or "suit" that may result. But:

      (1) The amount we will pay for damages is limited as described in LIMITS OF INSURANCE (Section III); and

      (2) Our right and duty to defend end when we have used up the applicable limit of insurance in the payment of judgments or settlements under Coverages A or B or medical expenses under Coverage C.

   No other obligation or liability to pay sums or perform acts or services is covered unless explicitly provided for under SUPPLEMENTARY PAYMENTS - COVERAGES A AND B.

   b. This insurance applies to "bodily injury" and "property damage" only if:

      (1) The "bodily injury" or "property damage" is caused by an "occurrence" that takes place in the "coverage territory";

      (2) The "bodily injury" or "property damage" did not occur before the Retroactive Date, if any, shown in the Declarations or after the end of the policy period; and

      (3) A claim for damages because of the "bodily injury" or "property damage" is first made against any insured, in accordance with paragraph c. below, during the policy period or any Extended Reporting Period we provide under EXTENDED REPORTING PERIODS (Section V).

   c. A claim by a person or organization seeking damages will be deemed to have been made at the earlier of the following times:

      (1) When notice of such claim is received and recorded by any insured or by us, whichever comes first; or

      (2) When we make settlement in accordance with paragraph **1.a.** above.

   All claims for damages because of "bodily injury" to the same person, including damages claimed by any person or organization for care, loss of services, or death resulting at any time from the "bodily injury", will be deemed to have been made at the time the first of those claims is made against any insured.

   All claims for damages because of "property damage" causing loss to the same person or organization will be deemed to have been made at the time the first of those claims is made against any insured.

2. **Exclusions**

This insurance does not apply to:

a. **Expected or Intended Injury**

"Bodily injury" or "property damage" expected or intended from the standpoint of the insured. This exclusion does not apply to "bodily injury" resulting from the use of reasonable force to protect persons or property.

b. **Contractual Liability**

"Bodily injury" or "property damage" for which the insured is obligated to pay damages by reason of the assumption of liability in a contract or agreement. This exclusion does not apply to liability for damages:

(1) That the insured would have in the absence of the contract or agreement; or

(2) Assumed in a contract or agreement that is an "insured contract", provided the "bodily injury" or "property damage" occurs subsequent to the execution of the contract or agreement. Solely for the purposes of liability assumed in an "insured contract", reasonable attorney fees and necessary litigation expenses incurred by or for a party other than an insured are deemed to be damages because of "bodily injury" or "property damage", provided:

(a) Liability to such party for, or for the cost of, that party's defense has also been assumed in the same "insured contract"; and

(b) Such attorney fees and litigation expenses are for defense of that party against a civil or alternative dispute resolution proceeding in which damages to which this insurance applies are alleged.

c. **Liquor Liability**

"Bodily injury" or "property damage" for which any insured may be held liable by reason of:

(1) Causing or contributing to the intoxication of any person;

(2) The furnishing of alcoholic beverages to a person under the legal drinking age or under the influence of alcohol; or

(3) Any statute, ordinance or regulation relating to the sale, gift, distribution or use of alcoholic beverages.

This exclusion applies only if you are in the business of manufacturing, distributing, selling, serving or furnishing alcoholic beverages.

d. **Workers Compensation and Similar Laws**

Any obligation of the insured under a workers compensation, disability benefits or unemployment compensation law or any similar law.

e. **Employer's Liability**

"Bodily injury" to:

(1) An "employee" of the insured arising out of and in the course of:

(a) Employment by the insured; or

(b) Performing duties related to the conduct of the insured's business; or

(2) The spouse, child, parent, brother or sister of that "employee" as a consequence of paragraph (1) above.

This exclusion applies:

(1) Whether the insured may be liable as an employer or in any other capacity; and

(2) To any obligation to share damages with or repay someone else who must pay damages because of the injury.

This exclusion does not apply to liability assumed by the insured under an "insured contract".

f. **Pollution**

(1) "Bodily injury" or "property damage" arising out of the actual, alleged or threatened discharge, dispersal, seepage, migration, release or escape of pollutants:

(a) At or from any premises, site or location which is or was at any time owned or occupied by, or rented or loaned to, any insured;

(b) At or from any premises, site or location which is or was at any time used by or for any insured or others for the handling, storage, disposal, processing or treatment of waste;

         CG 00 02 01 96

(c) Which are or were at any time transported, handled, stored, treated, disposed of, or processed as waste by or for any insured or any person or organization for whom you may be legally responsible; or

(d) At or from any premises, site or location on which any insured or any contractors or subcontractors working directly or indirectly on any insured's behalf are performing operations:

  (i) If the pollutants are brought on or to the premises, site or location in connection with such operations by such insured, contractor or subcontractor; or

  (ii) If the operations are to test for, monitor, clean up, remove, contain, treat, detoxify or neutralize, or in any way respond to, or assess the effects of pollutants.

Subparagraph **(d)(i)** does not apply to "bodily injury" or "property damage" arising out of the escape of fuels, lubricants or other operating fluids which are needed to perform the normal electrical, hydraulic or mechanical functions necessary for the operation of "mobile equipment" or its parts, if such fuels, lubricants or other operating fluids escape from a vehicle part designed to hold, store or receive them. This exception does not apply if the fuels, lubricants or other operating fluids are intentionally discharged, dispersed or released, or if such fuels, lubricants or other operating fluids are brought on or to the premises, site or location with the intent to be discharged, dispersed or released as part of the operations being performed by such insured, contractor or subcontractor.

Subparagraphs **(a)** and **(d)(i)** do not apply to "bodily injury" or "property damage" arising out of heat, smoke or fumes from a hostile fire.

As used in this exclusion, a hostile fire means one which becomes uncontrollable or breaks out from where it was intended to be.

(2) Any loss, cost or expense arising out of any:

  (a) Request, demand or order that any insured or others test for, monitor, clean up, remove, contain, treat, detoxify or neutralize, or in any way respond to, or assess the effects of pollutants; or

  (b) Claim or suit by or on behalf of a governmental authority for damages because of testing for, monitoring, cleaning up, removing, containing, treating, detoxifying or neutralizing, or in any way responding to, or assessing the effects of pollutants.

Pollutants means any solid, liquid, gaseous or thermal irritant or contaminant, including smoke, vapor, soot, fumes, acids, alkalis, chemicals and waste. Waste includes materials to be recycled, reconditioned or reclaimed.

g. Aircraft, Auto or Watercraft

"Bodily injury" or "property damage" arising out of the ownership, maintenance, use or entrustment to others of any aircraft, "auto" or watercraft owned or operated by or rented or loaned to any insured. Use includes operation and "loading or unloading".

This exclusion does not apply to:

(1) A watercraft while ashore on premises you own or rent;

(2) A watercraft you do not own that is:

  (a) Less than 26 feet long; and

  (b) Not being used to carry persons or property for a charge;

(3) Parking an "auto" on, or on the ways next to, premises you own or rent, provided the "auto" is not owned by or rented or loaned to you or the insured;

(4) Liability assumed under any "insured contract" for the ownership, maintenance or use of aircraft or watercraft; or

(5) "Bodily injury" or "property damage" arising out of the operation of any of the equipment listed in paragraph **f.(2)** or **f.(3)** of the definition of "mobile equipment"

h. Mobile Equipment

"Bodily injury" or "property damage" arising out of:

(1) The transportation of "mobile equipment" by an "auto" owned or operated by or rented or loaned to any insured; or

(2) The use of "mobile equipment" in, or while in practice for, or while being prepared for, any prearranged racing, speed, demolition, or stunting activity.

i. War

"Bodily injury" or "property damage" due to war, whether or not declared, or any act or condition incident to war. War includes civil war, insurrection, rebellion or revolution. This exclusion applies only to liability assumed under a contract or agreement.

j. Damage to Property

"Property damage" to:

(1) Property you own, rent, or occupy;

(2) Premises you sell, give away or abandon, if the "property damage" arises out of any part of those premises;

(3) Property loaned to you;

(4) Personal property in the care, custody or control of the insured;

(5) That particular part of real property on which you or any contractors or subcontractors working directly or indirectly on your behalf are performing operations, if the "property damage" arises out of those operations; or

(6) That particular part of any property that must be restored, repaired or replaced because "your work" was incorrectly performed on it.

Paragraph (2) of this exclusion does not apply if the premises are "your work" and were never occupied, rented or held for rental by you.

Paragraphs (3), (4), (5) and (6) of this exclusion do not apply to liability assumed under a sidetrack agreement.

Paragraph (6) of this exclusion does not apply to "property damage" included in the "products-completed operations hazard".

k. Damage to Your Product

"Property damage" to "your product" arising out of it or any part of it.

l. Damage to Your Work

"Property damage" to "your work" arising out of it or any part of it and included in the "products-completed operations hazard".

This exclusion does not apply if the damaged work or the work out of which the damage arises was performed on your behalf by a subcontractor.

m. Damage to Impaired Property or Property Not Physically Injured

"Property damage" to "impaired property" or property that has not been physically injured, arising out of:

(1) A defect, deficiency, inadequacy or dangerous condition in "your product" or "your work"; or

(2) A delay or failure by you or anyone acting on your behalf to perform a contract or agreement in accordance with its terms.

This exclusion does not apply to the loss of use of other property arising out of sudden and accidental physical injury to "your product" or "your work" after it has been put to its intended use.

n. Recall of Products, Work or Impaired Property

Damages claimed for any loss, cost or expense incurred by you or others for the loss of use, withdrawal, recall, inspection, repair, replacement, adjustment, removal or disposal of:

(1) "Your product";

(2) "Your work"; or

(3) "Impaired property";

if such product, work, or property is withdrawn or recalled from the market or from use by any person or organization because of a known or suspected defect, deficiency, inadequacy or dangerous condition in it.

Exclusions c. through n. do not apply to damage by fire to premises while rented to you or temporarily occupied by you with permission of the owner. A separate limit of insurance applies to this coverage as described in LIMITS OF INSURANCE (Section III).

         CG 00 02 01 96

COVERAGE B. PERSONAL AND ADVERTISING INJURY LIABILITY

1. Insuring Agreement

a. We will pay those sums that the insured becomes legally obligated to pay as damages because of "personal injury" or "advertising injury" to which this insurance applies. We will have the right and duty to defend the insured against any "suit" seeking those damages. However, we will have no duty to defend the insured against any "suit" seeking damages for "personal injury" or "advertising injury" to which this insurance does not apply. We may, at our discretion, investigate any "occurrence" or offense and settle any claim or "suit" that may result. But:

(1) The amount we will pay for damages is limited as described in LIMITS OF INSURANCE (Section III); and

(2) Our right and duty to defend end when we have used up the applicable limit of insurance in the payment of judgments or settlements under Coverages A or B or medical expenses under Coverage C.

No other obligation or liability to pay sums or perform acts or services is covered unless explicitly provided for under SUPPLEMENTARY PAYMENTS - COVERAGES A AND B.

b. This insurance applies to:

(1) "Personal injury" caused by an offense arising out of your business, excluding advertising, publishing, broadcasting or telecasting done by or for you;

(2) "Advertising injury" caused by an offense committed in the course of advertising your goods, products or services;

but only if:

(1) The offense was committed in the "coverage territory";

(2) The offense was not committed before the Retroactive Date, if any, shown in the Declarations or after the end of the policy period; and

(3) A claim for damages because of the "personal injury" or "advertising injury" is first made against any insured, in accordance with paragraph c. below, during the policy period or any Extended Reporting Period we provide under EXTENDED REPORTING PERIODS (Section V).

c. A claim made by a person or organization seeking damages will be deemed to have been made at the earlier of the following times:

(1) When notice of such claim is received and recorded by any insured or by us, whichever comes first; or

(2) When we make settlement in accordance with paragraph 1.a. above.

All claims for damages because of "personal injury" or "advertising injury" to the same person or organization as a result of an offense will be deemed to have been made at the time the first of those claims is made against any insured.

2. Exclusions

This insurance does not apply to:

a. "Personal injury" or "advertising injury":

(1) Arising out of oral or written publication of material, if done by or at the direction of the insured with knowledge of its falsity;

(2) Arising out of oral or written publication of material whose first publication took place before the Retroactive Date, if any, shown in the Declarations;

(3) Arising out of the willful violation of a penal statute or ordinance committed by or with the consent of the insured;

(4) For which the insured has assumed liability in a contract or agreement. This exclusion does not apply to liability for damages that the insured would have in the absence of the contract or agreement; or

(5) Arising out of the actual, alleged or threatened discharge, dispersal, seepage, migration, release or escape of pollutants at any time.

b. "Advertising injury" arising out of:

(1) Breach of contract, other than misappropriation of advertising ideas under an implied contract;

(2) The failure of goods, products or services to conform with advertised quality or performance;

(3) The wrong description of the price of goods, products or services; or

(4) An offense committed by an insured whose business is advertising, broadcasting, publishing or telecasting.

c. Any loss, cost or expense arising out of any:

(1) Request, demand or order that any insured or others test for, monitor, clean up, remove, contain, treat, detoxify or neutralize, or in any way respond to, or assess the effects of pollutants; or

(2) Claim or suit by or on behalf of a governmental authority for damages because of testing for, monitoring, cleaning up, removing, containing, treating, detoxifying or neutralizing, or in any way responding to, or assessing the effects of pollutants.

Pollutants means any solid, liquid, gaseous or thermal irritant or contaminant, including smoke, vapor, soot, fumes, acids, alkalis, chemicals and waste. Waste includes materials to be recycled, reconditioned or reclaimed.

COVERAGE C. MEDICAL PAYMENTS

1. Insuring Agreement

a. We will pay medical expenses as described below for "bodily injury" caused by an accident:

(1) On premises you own or rent;

(2) On ways next to premises you own or rent; or

(3) Because of your operations;

provided that:

(1) The accident takes place in the "coverage territory" and during the policy period;

(2) The expenses are incurred and reported to us within one year of the date of the accident; and

(3) The injured person submits to examination, at our expense, by physicians of our choice as often as we reasonably require.

b. We will make these payments regardless of fault. These payments will not exceed the applicable limit of insurance. We will pay reasonable expenses for:

(1) First aid administered at the time of an accident,

(2) Necessary medical, surgical, x-ray and dental services, including prosthetic devices; and

(3) Necessary ambulance, hospital, professional nursing and funeral services.

2. Exclusions

We will not pay expenses for "bodily injury":

a. To any insured.

b. To a person hired to do work for or on behalf of any insured or a tenant of any insured.

c. To a person injured on that part of premises you own or rent that the person normally occupies.

d. To a person, whether or not an "employee" of any insured, if benefits for the "bodily injury" are payable or must be provided under a workers compensation or disability benefits law or a similar law.

e. To a person injured while taking part in athletics.

f. Included within the "products-completed operations hazard".

g. Excluded under Coverage A.

h. Due to war, whether or not declared, or any act or condition incident to war. War includes civil war, insurrection, rebellion or revolution.

SUPPLEMENTARY PAYMENTS - COVERAGES A AND B

We will pay, with respect to any claim we investigate or settle or any "suit" against an insured we defend:

1. All expenses we incur.

2. Up to $250 for cost of bail bonds required because of accidents or traffic law violations arising out of the use of any vehicle to which the Bodily Injury Liability Coverage applies. We do not have to furnish these bonds.

3. The cost of bonds to release attachments, but only for bond amounts within the applicable limit of insurance. We do not have to furnish these bonds.

4. All reasonable expenses incurred by the insured at our request to assist us in the investigation or defense of the claim or "suit", including actual loss of earnings up to $250 a day because of time off from work.

5. All costs taxed against the insured in the "suit".

6. Prejudgment interest awarded against the insured on that part of the judgment we pay. If we make an offer to pay the applicable limit of insurance, we will not pay any prejudgment interest based on that period of time after the offer.

7. All interest on the full amount of any judgment that accrues after entry of the judgment and before we have paid, offered to pay, or deposited in court the part of the judgment that is within the applicable limit of insurance.

These payments will not reduce the limits of insurance.

   CG 00 02 01 96

If we defend an insured against a "suit" and an indemnitee of the insured is also named as a party to the "suit", we will defend that indemnitee if all of the following conditions are met:

a. The "suit" against the indemnitee seeks damages for which the insured has assumed the liability of the indemnitee in a contract or agreement that is an "insured contract";

b. This insurance applies to such liability assumed by the insured;

c. The obligation to defend, or the cost of the defense of, that indemnitee, has also been assumed by the insured in the same "insured contract";

d. The allegations in the "suit" and the information we know about the "occurrence" are such that no conflict appears to exist between the interests of the insured and the interests of the indemnitee;

e. The indemnitee and the insured ask us to conduct and control the defense of that indemnitee against such "suit" and agree that we can assign the same counsel to defend the insured and the indemnitee; and

f. The indemnitee:

(1) Agrees in writing to:

  (a) Cooperate with us in the investigation, settlement or defense of the "suit";

  (b) Immediately send us copies of any demands, notices, summonses or legal papers received in connection with the "suit";

  (c) Notify any other insurer whose coverage is available to the indemnitee; and

  (d) Cooperate with us with respect to coordinating other applicable insurance available to the indemnitee; and

(2) Provides us with written authorization to:

  (a) Obtain records and other information related to the "suit"; and

  (b) Conduct and control the defense of the indemnitee in such "suit".

So long as the above conditions are met, attorneys fees incurred by us in the defense of that indemnitee, necessary litigation expenses incurred by us and necessary litigation expenses incurred by the indemnitee at our request will be paid as Supplementary Payments. Notwithstanding the provisions of paragraph **2.b.(2)** of COVERAGE A - BODILY INJURY AND PROPERTY DAMAGE LIABILITY (Section I - Coverages), such payments will not be deemed to be damages for "bodily injury" and "property damage" and will not reduce the limits of insurance.

Our obligation to defend an insured's indemnitee and to pay for attorneys fees and necessary litigation expenses as Supplementary Payments ends when:

a. We have used up the applicable limit of insurance in the payment of judgments or settlements; or

b. The conditions set forth above, or the terms of the agreement described in paragraph **f.** above, are no longer met.

SECTION II - WHO IS AN INSURED

1. If you are designated in the Declarations as:

a. An individual, you and your spouse are insureds, but only with respect to the conduct of a business of which you are the sole owner.

b. A partnership or joint venture, you are an insured. Your members, your partners, and their spouses are also insureds, but only with respect to the conduct of your business.

c. A limited liability company, you are an insured. Your members are also insureds, but only with respect to the conduct of your business. Your managers are insureds, but only with respect to their duties as your managers.

d. An organization other than a partnership, joint venture or limited liability company, you are an insured. Your "executive officers" and directors are insureds, but only with respect to their duties as your officers or directors. Your stockholders are also insureds, but only with respect to their liability as stockholders.

2. Each of the following is also an insured:

a. Your "employees", other than either your "executive officers" (if you are an organization other than a partnership, joint venture or limited liability company) or your managers (if you are a limited liability company), but only for acts within the scope of their employment by you or while performing duties related to the conduct of your business. However, none of these "employees" is an insured for:

(1) "Bodily injury" or "personal injury":

  (a) To you, to your partners or members (if you are a partnership or joint venture), to your members (if you are a limited liability company), or to a co-"employee" while that co-"employee" is either in the course of his or her employment or while performing duties related to the conduct of your business;

(b) To the spouse, child, parent, brother or sister of that co-"employee" as a consequence of paragraph **(1)(a)** above;

(c) For which there is any obligation to share damages with or repay someone else who must pay damages because of the injury described in paragraphs **(1)(a)** or **(b)** above; or

(d) Arising out of his or her providing or failing to provide professional health care services.

(2) "Property damage" to property:

(a) Owned, occupied or used by,

(b) Rented to, in the care, custody or control of, or over which physical control is being exercised for any purpose by

you, any of your "employees", any partner or member (if you are a partnership or joint venture), or any member (if you are a limited liability company).

b. Any person (other than your "employee") or any organization while acting as your real estate manager.

c. Any person or organization having proper temporary custody of your property if you die, but only:

(1) With respect to liability arising out of the maintenance or use of that property; and

(2) Until your legal representative has been appointed.

d. Your legal representative if you die, but only with respect to duties as such. That representative will have all your rights and duties under this Coverage Part.

3. With respect to "mobile equipment" registered in your name under any motor vehicle registration law, any person is an insured while driving such equipment along a public highway with your permission. Any other person or organization responsible for the conduct of such person is also an insured, but only with respect to liability arising out of the operation of the equipment, and only if no other insurance of any kind is available to that person or organization for this liability. However, no person or organization is an insured with respect to:

a. "Bodily injury" to a co-"employee" of the person driving the equipment; or

b. "Property damage" to property owned by, rented to, in the charge of or occupied by you or the employer of any person who is an insured under this provision.

4. Any organization you newly acquire or form, other than a partnership, joint venture or limited liability company, and over which you maintain ownership or majority interest, will qualify as a Named Insured if there is no other similar insurance available to that organization. However:

a. Coverage under this provision is afforded only until the 90th day after you acquire or form the organization or the end of the policy period, whichever is earlier;

b. Coverage A does not apply to "bodily injury" or "property damage" that occurred before you acquired or formed the organization; and

c. Coverage B does not apply to "personal injury" or "advertising injury" arising out of an offense committed before you acquired or formed the organization.

No person or organization is an insured with respect to the conduct of any current or past partnership, joint venture or limited liability company that is not shown as a Named Insured in the Declarations.

SECTION III - LIMITS OF INSURANCE

1. The Limits of Insurance shown in the Declarations and the rules below fix the most we will pay regardless of the number of:

a. Insureds;

b. Claims made or "suits" brought; or

c. Persons or organizations making claims or bringing "suits".

2. The General Aggregate Limit is the most we will pay for the sum of:

a. Medical expenses under Coverage C;

b. Damages under Coverage A, except damages because of "bodily injury" or "property damage" included in the "products-completed operations hazard"; and

c. Damages under Coverage B.

       CG 00 02 01 96

3. The Products-Completed Operations Aggregate Limit is the most we will pay under Coverage A for damages because of "bodily injury" and "property damage" included in the "products-completed operations hazard".

4. Subject to **2.** above, the Personal and Advertising Injury Limit is the most we will pay under Coverage B for the sum of all damages because of all "personal injury" and all "advertising injury" sustained by any one person or organization.

5. Subject to **2.** or **3.** above, whichever applies, the Each Occurrence Limit is the most we will pay for the sum of:

   a. Damages under Coverage A; and

   b. Medical expenses under Coverage C

   because of all "bodily injury" and "property damage" arising out of any one "occurrence".

6. Subject to **5.** above, the Fire Damage Limit is the most we will pay under Coverage A for damages because of "property damage" to premises, while rented to you or temporarily occupied by you with permission of the owner, arising out of any one fire.

7. Subject to **5.** above, the Medical Expense Limit is the most we will pay under Coverage C for all medical expenses because of "bodily injury" sustained by any one person.

The Limits of Insurance of this Coverage Part apply separately to each consecutive annual period and to any remaining period of less than 12 months, starting with the beginning of the policy period shown in the Declarations, unless the policy period is extended after issuance for an additional period of less than 12 months. In that case, the additional period will be deemed part of the last preceding period for purposes of determining the Limits of Insurance.

SECTION IV - COMMERCIAL GENERAL LIABILITY CONDITIONS

1. Bankruptcy

Bankruptcy or insolvency of the insured or of the insured's estate will not relieve us of our obligations under this Coverage Part.

2. Duties In The Event Of Occurrence, Offense, Claim Or Suit

   a. You must see to it that we are notified as soon as practicable of an "occurrence" or offense which may result in a claim. To the extent possible, notice should include:

   (1) How, when and where the "occurrence" or offense took place;

   (2) The names and addresses of any injured persons and witnesses; and

   (3) The nature and location of any injury or damage arising out of the "occurrence" or offense.

   Notice of an "occurrence" or offense is not notice of a claim.

   b. If a claim is received by any insured, you must:

   (1) Immediately record the specifics of the claim and the date received; and

   (2) Notify us as soon as practicable.

   You must see to it that we receive written notice of the claim as soon as practicable.

   c. You and any other involved insured must:

   (1) Immediately send us copies of any demands, notices, summonses or legal papers received in connection with the claim or a "suit";

   (2) Authorize us to obtain records and other information;

   (3) Cooperate with us in the investigation or settlement of the claim or defense against the "suit"; and

   (4) Assist us, upon our request, in the enforcement of any right against any person or organization which may be liable to the insured because of injury or damage to which this insurance may also apply.

   d. No insured will, except at that insured's own cost, voluntarily make a payment, assume any obligation, or incur any expense, other than for first aid, without our consent.

3. Legal Action Against Us

No person or organization has a right under this Coverage Part:

   a. To join us as a party or otherwise bring us into a "suit" asking for damages from an insured; or

   b. To sue us on this Coverage Part unless all of its terms have been fully complied with.

A person or organization may sue us to recover on an agreed settlement or on a final judgment against an insured obtained after an actual trial; but we will not be liable for damages that are not payable under the terms of this Coverage Part or that are in excess of the applicable limit of insurance. An agreed settlement means a settlement and release of liability signed by us, the insured and the claimant or the claimant's legal representative.

4. Other Insurance

If other valid and collectible insurance is available to the insured for a loss we cover under Coverages A or B of this Coverage Part, our obligations are limited as follows:

a. Primary Insurance

This insurance is primary except when **b.** below applies. If this insurance is primary, our obligations are not affected unless any of the other insurance is also primary. Then, we will share with all that other insurance by the method described in **c.** below.

b. Excess Insurance

This insurance is excess over any of the other insurance. whether primary, excess, contingent or on any other basis:

(1) That is effective prior to the beginning of the policy period shown in the Declarations of this insurance and applies to "bodily injury" or "property damage" on other than a claims-made basis, if:

(a) No Retroactive Date is shown in the Declarations of this insurance; or

(b) The other insurance has a policy period which continues after the Retroactive Date shown in the Declarations of this insurance;

(2) That is Fire. Extended Coverage, Builders' Risk, Installation Risk or similar coverage for "your work";

(3) That is Fire insurance for premises rented to you or temporarily occupied by you with permission of the owner; or

(4) If the loss arises out of the maintenance or use of aircraft, "autos" or watercraft to the extent not subject to Exclusion **g.** of Coverage A (Section I).

When this insurance is excess, we will have no duty under Coverages A or B to defend the insured against any "suit" if any other insurer has a duty to defend the insured against that "suit". If no other insurer defends. we will undertake to do so, but we will be entitled to the insured's rights against all those other insurers.

When this insurance is excess over other insurance, we will pay only our share of the amount of the loss, if any, that exceeds the sum of:

(1) The total amount that all such other insurance would pay for the loss in the absence of this insurance; and

(2) The total of all deductible and self-insured amounts under all that other insurance.

We will share the remaining loss, if any, with any other insurance that is not described in this Excess Insurance provision and was not bought specifically to apply in excess of the Limits of Insurance shown in the Declarations of this Coverage Part.

c. Method of Sharing

If all of the other insurance permits contribution by equal shares, we will follow this method also. Under this approach each insurer contributes equal amounts until it has paid its applicable limit of insurance or none of the loss remains, whichever comes first.

If any of the other insurance does not permit contribution by equal shares, we will contribute by limits. Under this method, each insurer's share is based on the ratio of its applicable limit of insurance to the total applicable limits of insurance of all insurers.

5. Premium Audit

a. We will compute all premiums for this Coverage Part in accordance with our rules and rates.

b. Premium shown in this Coverage Part as advance premium is a deposit premium only. At the close of each audit period we will compute the earned premium for that period. Audit premiums are due and payable on notice to the first Named Insured. If the sum of the advance and audit premiums paid for the policy period is greater than the earned premium, we will return the excess to the first Named Insured.

c. The first Named Insured must keep records of the information we need for premium computation, and send us copies at such times as we may request.

6. Representations

By accepting this policy. you agree:

a. The statements in the Declarations are accurate and complete;

 CG 00 02 01 96

b. Those statements are based upon representations you made to us; and

c. We have issued this policy in reliance upon your representations.

7. Separation Of Insureds

Except with respect to the Limits of Insurance, and any rights or duties specifically assigned in this Coverage Part to the first Named Insured, this insurance applies:

a. As if each Named Insured were the only Named Insured; and

b. Separately to each insured against whom claim is made or "suit" is brought.

8. Transfer Of Rights Of Recovery Against Others To Us

If the insured has rights to recover all or part of any payment we have made under this Coverage Part, those rights are transferred to us. The insured must do nothing after loss to impair them. At our request, the insured will bring "suit" or transfer those rights to us and help us enforce them.

9. When We Do Not Renew

If we decide not to renew this Coverage Part, we will mail or deliver to the first Named Insured shown in the Declarations written notice of the nonrenewal not less than 30 days before the expiration date.

If notice is mailed, proof of mailing will be sufficient proof of notice.

10. Your Right to Claim and "Occurrence" Information

We will provide the first Named Insured shown in the Declarations the following information relating to this and any preceding general liability claims-made Coverage Part we have issued to you during the previous three years:

a. A list or other record of each "occurrence", not previously reported to any other insurer, of which we were notified in accordance with paragraph 2.a. of the DUTIES IN THE EVENT OF OCCURRENCE, OFFENSE, CLAIM OR SUIT Condition in COMMERCIAL GENERAL LIABILITY CONDITIONS (Section IV). We will include the date and brief description of the "occurrence" if that information was in the notice we received.

b. A summary by policy year, of payments made and amounts reserved, stated separately, under any applicable General Aggregate Limit and Products-Completed Operations Aggregate Limit.

Amounts reserved are based on our judgment. They are subject to change and should not be regarded as ultimate settlement values.

You must not disclose this information to any claimant or any claimant's representative without our consent.

If we cancel or elect not to renew this Coverage Part, we will provide such information no later than 30 days before the date of policy termination. In other circumstances, we will provide this information only if we receive a written request from the first Named Insured within 60 days after the end of the policy period. In this case, we will provide this information within 45 days of receipt of the request.

We compile claim and "occurrence" information for our own business purposes and exercise reasonable care in doing so. In providing this information to the first Named Insured, we make no representations or warranties to insureds, insurers, or others to whom this information is furnished by or on behalf of any insured. Cancellation or non-renewal will be effective even if we inadvertently provide inaccurate information.

SECTION V - EXTENDED REPORTING PERIODS

1. We will provide one or more Extended Reporting Periods, as described below, if:

a. This Coverage Part is cancelled or not renewed; or

b. We renew or replace this Coverage Part with insurance that:

(1) Has a Retroactive Date later than the date shown in the Declarations of this Coverage Part; or

(2) Does not apply to "bodily injury", "property damage", "personal injury" or "advertising injury" on a claims-made basis.

2. Extended Reporting Periods do not extend the policy period or change the scope of coverage provided. They apply only to claims for:

a. "Bodily injury" or "property damage" that occurs before the end of the policy period but not before the Retroactive Date, if any, shown in the Declarations; or

b. "Personal injury" or "advertising injury" caused by an offense committed before the end of the policy period but not before the Retroactive Date, if any, shown in the Declarations.

Once in effect, Extended Reporting Periods may not be cancelled.

3. A Basic Extended Reporting Period is automatically provided without additional charge. This period starts with the end of the policy period and lasts for:

a. Five years with respect to claims because of "bodily injury" and "property damage" arising out of an "occurrence" reported to us, not later than 60 days after the end of the policy period, in accordance with paragraph 2.a. of the DUTIES IN THE EVENT OF OCCURRENCE, OFFENSE, CLAIM OR SUIT Condition in COMMERCIAL GENERAL LIABILITY CONDITIONS (Section IV);

b. Five years with respect to claims because of "personal injury" and "advertising injury" arising out of an offense reported to us, not later than 60 days after the end of the policy period, in accordance with paragraph 2.a. of the DUTIES IN THE EVENT OF OCCURRENCE, OFFENSE, CLAIM OR SUIT Condition in COMMERCIAL GENERAL LIABILITY CONDITIONS (Section IV); and

c. Sixty days with respect to claims arising from "occurrences" or offenses not previously reported to us.

The Basic Extended Reporting Period does not apply to claims that are covered under any subsequent insurance you purchase, or that would be covered but for exhaustion of the amount of insurance applicable to such claims.

4. The Basic Extended Reporting Period does not reinstate or increase the Limits of Insurance.

5. A Supplemental Extended Reporting Period of unlimited duration is available, but only by an endorsement and for an extra charge. This supplemental period starts when the Basic Extended Reporting Period, set forth in paragraph 3. above, ends.

You must give us a written request for the endorsement within 60 days after the end of the policy period. The Supplemental Extended Reporting Period will not go into effect unless you pay the additional premium promptly when due.

We will determine the additional premium in accordance with our rules and rates. In doing so, we may take into account the following:

a. The exposures insured;

b. Previous types and amounts of insurance;

c. Limits of Insurance available under this Coverage Part for future payment of damages; and

d. Other related factors.

The additional premium will not exceed 200% of the annual premium for this Coverage Part.

This endorsement shall set forth the terms, not inconsistent with this Section, applicable to the Supplemental Extended Reporting Period, including a provision to the effect that the insurance afforded for claims first received during such period is excess over any other valid and collectible insurance available under policies in force after the Supplemental Extended Reporting Period starts.

6. If the Supplemental Extended Reporting Period is in effect, we will provide the supplemental aggregate limits of insurance described below, but only for claims first received and recorded during the Supplemental Extended Reporting Period.

The supplemental aggregate limits of insurance will be equal to the dollar amount shown in the Declarations in effect at the end of the policy period for such of the following limits of insurance for which a dollar amount has been entered:

General Aggregate Limit
Products-Completed Operations Aggregate Limit

Paragraphs 2. and 3. of LIMITS OF INSURANCE (Section III) will be amended accordingly. The Personal and Advertising Injury Limit, the Each Occurrence Limit and the Fire Damage Limit shown in the Declarations will then continue to apply, as set forth in paragraphs 4., 5. and 6. of that Section.

SECTION VI - DEFINITIONS

1. "Advertising injury" means injury arising out of one or more of the following offenses:

a. Oral or written publication of material that slanders or libels a person or organization or disparages a person's or organization's goods, products or services;

b. Oral or written publication of material that violates a person's right of privacy;

c. Misappropriation of advertising ideas or style of doing business; or

d. Infringement of copyright, title or slogan.

2. "Auto" means a land motor vehicle, trailer or semitrailer designed for travel on public roads, including any attached machinery or equipment. But "auto" does not include "mobile equipment".

3. "Bodily injury" means bodily injury, sickness or disease sustained by a person, including death resulting from any of these at any time.

       CG 00 02 01 96

4. "Coverage territory" means:

  a. The United States of America (including its territories and possessions), Puerto Rico and Canada;

  b. International waters or airspace, provided the injury or damage does not occur in the course of travel or transportation to or from any place not included in **a.** above; or

  c. All parts of the world if:

    (1) The injury or damage arises out of:

      (a) Goods or products made or sold by you in the territory described in **a.** above; or

      (b) The activities of a person whose home is in the territory described in **a.** above, but is away for a short time on your business; and

    (2) The insured's responsibility to pay damages is determined in a "suit" on the merits, in the territory described in **a.** above or in a settlement we agree to.

5. "Employee" includes a "leased worker". "Employee" does not include a "temporary worker".

6. "Executive officer" means a person holding any of the officer positions created by your charter, constitution, by-laws or any other similar governing document.

7. "Impaired property" means tangible property, other than "your product" or "your work", that cannot be used or is less useful because:

  a. It incorporates "your product" or "your work" that is known or thought to be defective, deficient, inadequate or dangerous; or

  b. You have failed to fulfill the terms of a contract or agreement:

  if such property can be restored to use by:

  a. The repair, replacement, adjustment or removal of "your product" or "your work"; or

  b. Your fulfilling the terms of the contract or agreement.

8. "Insured contract" means:

  a. A contract for a lease of premises. However, that portion of the contract for a lease of premises that indemnifies any person or organization for damage by fire to premises while rented to you or temporarily occupied by you with permission of the owner is not an "insured contract";

  b. A sidetrack agreement;

  c. Any easement or license agreement, except in connection with construction or demolition operations on or within 50 feet of a railroad;

  d. An obligation, as required by ordinance, to indemnify a municipality, except in connection with work for a municipality;

  e. An elevator maintenance agreement;

  f. That part of any other contract or agreement pertaining to your business (including an indemnification of a municipality in connection with work performed for a municipality) under which you assume the tort liability of another party to pay for "bodily injury" or "property damage" to a third person or organization. Tort liability means a liability that would be imposed by law in the absence of any contract or agreement.

  Paragraph f. does not include that part of any contract or agreement:

  (1) That indemnifies a railroad for "bodily injury" or "property damage" arising out of construction or demolition operations within 50 feet of any railroad property and affecting any railroad bridge or trestle, tracks, road-beds, tunnel, underpass or crossing;

  (2) That indemnifies an architect, engineer or surveyor for injury or damage arising out of:

    (a) Preparing, approving, or failing to prepare or approve, maps, shop drawings, opinions, reports, surveys, field orders, change orders or drawings and specifications; or

    (b) Giving directions or instructions, or failing to give them, if that is the primary cause of the injury or damage; or

  (3) Under which the insured, if an architect, engineer or surveyor, assumes liability for an injury or damage arising out of the insured's rendering or failure to render professional services, including those listed in (2) above and supervisory, inspection, architectural or engineering activities.

9. "Leased worker" means a person leased to you by a labor leasing firm under an agreement between you and the labor leasing firm, to perform duties related to the conduct of your business. "Leased worker" does not include a "temporary worker".

10. "Loading or unloading" means the handling of property:

   a. After it is moved from the place where it is accepted for movement into or onto an aircraft, watercraft or "auto";

   b. While it is in or on an aircraft, watercraft or "auto"; or

   c. While it is being moved from an aircraft, watercraft or "auto" to the place where it is finally delivered;

   but "loading or unloading" does not include the movement of property by means of a mechanical device, other than a hand truck, that is not attached to the aircraft, watercraft or "auto".

11. "Mobile equipment" means any of the following types of land vehicles, including any attached machinery or equipment:

   a. Bulldozers, farm machinery, forklifts and other vehicles designed for use principally off public roads;

   b. Vehicles maintained for use solely on or next to premises you own or rent;

   c. Vehicles that travel on crawler treads;

   d. Vehicles, whether self-propelled or not, maintained primarily to provide mobility to permanently mounted:

      (1) Power cranes, shovels, loaders, diggers or drills: or

      (2) Road construction or resurfacing equipment such as graders, scrapers or rollers;

   e. Vehicles not described in a., b., c. or d. above that are not self-propelled and are maintained primarily to provide mobility to permanently attached equipment of the following types:

      (1) Air compressors, pumps and generators, including spraying, welding, building cleaning, geophysical exploration, lighting and well servicing equipment; or

      (2) Cherry pickers and similar devices used to raise or lower workers;

   f. Vehicles not described in a., b., c. or d. above maintained primarily for purposes other than the transportation of persons or cargo.

   However, self-propelled vehicles with the following types of permanently attached equipment are not "mobile equipment" but will be considered "autos":

   (1) Equipment designed primarily for:

      (a) Snow removal;

      (b) Road maintenance, but not construction or resurfacing; or

      (c) Street cleaning;

   (2) Cherry pickers and similar devices mounted on automobile or truck chassis and used to raise or lower workers; and

   (3) Air compressors, pumps and generators, including spraying, welding, building cleaning, geophysical exploration, lighting and well servicing equipment.

12. "Occurrence" means an accident, including continuous or repeated exposure to substantially the same general harmful conditions.

13. "Personal injury" means injury, other than "bodily injury", arising out of one or more of the following offenses:

   a. False arrest, detention or imprisonment;

   b. Malicious prosecution;

   c. The wrongful eviction from, wrongful entry into, or invasion of the right of private occupancy of a room, dwelling or premises that a person occupies by or on behalf of its owner, landlord or lessor;

   d. Oral or written publication of material that slanders or libels a person or organization or disparages a person's or organization's goods, products or services; or

   e. Oral or written publication of material that violates a person's right of privacy.

14. "Products-completed operations hazard":

   a. Includes all "bodily injury" and "property damage" occurring away from premises you own or rent and arising out of "your product" or "your work" except:

   (1) Products that are still in your physical possession; or

   (2) Work that has not yet been completed or abandoned. However, "your work" will be deemed completed at the earliest of the following times:

      (a) When all of the work called for in your contract has been completed.

      (b) When all of the work to be done at the job site has been completed if your contract calls for work at more than one job site.

(c) When that part of the work done at a job site has been put to its intended use by any person or organization other than another contractor or subcontractor working on the same project.

Work that may need service, maintenance, correction, repair or replacement, but which is otherwise complete, will be treated as completed.

b. Does not include "bodily injury" or "property damage" arising out of:

(1) The transportation of property, unless the injury or damage arises out of a condition in or on a vehicle not owned or operated by you, and that condition was created by the "loading or unloading" of that vehicle by any insured;

(2) The existence of tools, uninstalled equipment or abandoned or unused materials; or

(3) Products or operations for which the classification, listed in the Declarations or in a policy schedule, states that products-completed operations are subject to the General Aggregate Limit.

15. "Property damage" means:

a. Physical injury to tangible property, including all resulting loss of use of that property. All such loss of use shall be deemed to occur at the time of the physical injury that caused it; or

b. Loss of use of tangible property that is not physically injured. All such loss of use shall be deemed to occur at the time of the "occurrence" that caused it.

16. "Suit" means a civil proceeding in which damages because of "bodily injury", "property damage", "personal injury" or "advertising injury" to which this insurance applies are alleged. "Suit" includes:

a. An arbitration proceeding in which such damages are claimed and to which the insured must submit or does submit with our consent; or

b. Any other alternative dispute resolution proceeding in which such damages are claimed and to which the insured submits with our consent.

17. "Temporary worker" means a person who is furnished to you to substitute for a permanent "employee" on leave or to meet seasonal or short-term workload conditions.

18. "Your product" means:

a. Any goods or products, other than real property, manufactured, sold, handled, distributed or disposed of by:

(1) You;

(2) Others trading under your name; or

(3) A person or organization whose business or assets you have acquired; and

b. Containers (other than vehicles), materials, parts or equipment furnished in connection with such goods or products.

"Your product" includes:

a. Warranties or representations made at any time with respect to the fitness, quality, durability, performance or use of "your product"; and

b. The providing of or failure to provide warnings or instructions.

"Your product" does not include vending machines or other property rented to or located for the use of others but not sold.

19. "Your work" means:

a. Work or operations performed by you or on your behalf; and

b. Materials, parts or equipment furnished in connection with such work or operations.

"Your work" includes:

a. Warranties or representations made at any time with respect to the fitness, quality, durability, performance or use of "your work"; and

b. The providing of or failure to provide warnings or instructions.

COMMERCIAL GENERAL LIABILITY
CG 00 01 07 98

COMMERCIAL GENERAL LIABILITY COVERAGE FORM

Various provisions in this policy restrict coverage. Read the entire policy carefully to determine rights, duties and what is and is not covered.

Throughout this policy the words "you" and "your" refer to the Named Insured shown in the Declarations, and any other person or organization qualifying as a Named Insured under this policy. The words "we", "us" and "our" refer to the company providing this insurance.

The word "insured" means any person or organization qualifying as such under Section **II** – Who Is An Insured.

Other words and phrases that appear in quotation marks have special meaning. Refer to Section **V** – Definitions.

SECTION I – COVERAGES

COVERAGE A BODILY INJURY AND PROPERTY DAMAGE LIABILITY

1. Insuring Agreement

a. We will pay those sums that the insured becomes legally obligated to pay as damages because of "bodily injury" or "property damage" to which this insurance applies. We will have the right and duty to defend the insured against any "suit" seeking those damages. However, we will have no duty to defend the insured against any "suit" seeking damages for "bodily injury" or "property damage" to which this insurance does not apply. We may, at our discretion, investigate any "occurrence" and settle any claim or "suit" that may result. But:

(1) The amount we will pay for damages is limited as described in Section **III** – Limits Of Insurance; and

(2) Our right and duty to defend end when we have used up the applicable limit of insurance in the payment of judgments or settlements under Coverages **A** or **B** or medical expenses under Coverage **C**.

No other obligation or liability to pay sums or perform acts or services is covered unless explicitly provided for under Supplementary Payments – Coverages **A** and **B**.

b. This insurance applies to "bodily injury" and "property damage" only if:

(1) The "bodily injury" or "property damage" is caused by an "occurrence" that takes place in the "coverage territory"; and

(2) The "bodily injury" or "property damage" occurs during the policy period.

c. Damages because of "bodily injury" include damages claimed by any person or organization for care, loss of services or death resulting at any time from the "bodily injury".

2. Exclusions

This insurance does not apply to:

a. Expected Or Intended Injury

"Bodily injury" or "property damage" expected or intended from the standpoint of the insured. This exclusion does not apply to "bodily injury" resulting from the use of reasonable force to protect persons or property.

b. Contractual Liability

"Bodily injury" or "property damage" for which the insured is obligated to pay damages by reason of the assumption of liability in a contract or agreement. This exclusion does not apply to liability for damages:

(1) That the insured would have in the absence of the contract or agreement; or

(2) Assumed in a contract or agreement that is an "insured contract", provided the "bodily injury" or "property damage" occurs subsequent to the execution of the contract or agreement. Solely for the purposes of liability assumed in an "insured contract", reasonable attorney fees and necessary litigation expenses incurred by or for a party other than an insured are deemed to be damages because of "bodily injury" or "property damage", provided:

(a) Liability to such party for, or for the cost of, that party's defense has also been assumed in the same "insured contract"; and

(b) Such attorney fees and litigation expenses are for defense of that party against a civil or alternative dispute resolution proceeding in which damages to which this insurance applies are alleged.

c. Liquor Liability

"Bodily injury" or "property damage" for which any insured may be held liable by reason of:

(1) Causing or contributing to the intoxication of any person;

(2) The furnishing of alcoholic beverages to a person under the legal drinking age or under the influence of alcohol; or

(3) Any statute, ordinance or regulation relating to the sale, gift, distribution or use of alcoholic beverages.

This exclusion applies only if you are in the business of manufacturing, distributing, selling, serving or furnishing alcoholic beverages.

d. Workers' Compensation And Similar Laws

Any obligation of the insured under a workers' compensation, disability benefits or unemployment compensation law or any similar law.

e. Employer's Liability

"Bodily injury" to:

(1) An "employee" of the insured arising out of and in the course of:

   (a) Employment by the insured; or

   (b) Performing duties related to the conduct of the insured's business; or

(2) The spouse, child, parent, brother or sister of that "employee" as a consequence of Paragraph **(1)** above.

This exclusion applies:

(1) Whether the insured may be liable as an employer or in any other capacity; and

(2) To any obligation to share damages with or repay someone else who must pay damages because of the injury.

This exclusion does not apply to liability assumed by the insured under an "insured contract".

f. Pollution

(1) "Bodily injury" or "property damage" arising out of the actual, alleged or threatened discharge, dispersal, seepage, migration, release or escape of "pollutants":

   (a) At or from any premises, site or location which is or was at any time owned or occupied by, or rented or loaned to, any insured. However, this subparagraph does not apply to:

      (i) "Bodily injury" if sustained within a building and caused by smoke, fumes, vapor or soot from equipment used to heat that building;

      (ii) "Bodily injury" or "property damage" for which you may be held liable, if you are a contractor and the owner or lessee of such premises, site or location has been added to your policy as an additional insured with respect to your ongoing operations performed for that additional insured at that premises, site or location and such premises, site or location is not and never was owned or occupied by, or rented or loaned to, any insured, other than that additional insured; or

      (iii) "Bodily injury" or "property damage" arising out of heat, smoke or fumes from a "hostile fire";

   (b) At or from any premises, site or location which is or was at any time used by or for any insured or others for the handling, storage, disposal, processing or treatment of waste;

   (c) Which are or were at any time transported, handled, stored, treated, disposed of, or processed as waste by or for any insured or any person or organization for whom you may be legally responsible; or

(d) At or from any premises, site or location on which any insured or any contractors or subcontractors working directly or indirectly on any insured's behalf are performing operations if the "pollutants" are brought on or to the premises, site or location in connection with such operations by such insured, contractor or subcontractor. However, this subparagraph does not apply to:

(i) "Bodily injury" or "property damage" arising out of the escape of fuels, lubricants or other operating fluids which are needed to perform the normal electrical, hydraulic or mechanical functions necessary for the operation of "mobile equipment" or its parts, if such fuels, lubricants or other operating fluids escape from a vehicle part designed to hold, store or receive them. This exception does not apply if the "bodily injury" or "property damage" arises out of the intentional discharge, dispersal or release of the fuels, lubricants or other operating fluids, or if such fuels, lubricants or other operating fluids are brought on or to the premises, site or location with the intent that they be discharged, dispersed or released as part of the operations being performed by such insured, contractor or subcontractor;

(ii) "Bodily injury" or "property damage" sustained within a building and caused by the release of gases, fumes or vapors from materials brought into that building in connection with operations being performed by you or on your behalf by a contractor or subcontractor; or

(iii) "Bodily injury" or "property damage" arising out of heat, smoke or fumes from a "hostile fire".

(e) At or from any premises, site or location on which any insured or any contractors or subcontractors working directly or indirectly on any insured's behalf are performing operations if the operations are to test for, monitor, clean up, remove, contain, treat, detoxify or neutralize, or in any way respond to, or assess the effects of, "pollutants".

(2) Any loss, cost or expense arising out of any:

(a) Request, demand, order or statutory or regulatory requirement that any insured or others test for, monitor, clean up, remove, contain, treat, detoxify or neutralize, or in any way respond to, or assess the effects of, "pollutants"; or

(b) Claim or suit by or on behalf of a governmental authority for damages because of testing for, monitoring, cleaning up, removing, containing, treating, detoxifying or neutralizing, or in any way responding to, or assessing the effects of, "pollutants".

However, this paragraph does not apply to liability for damages because of "property damage" that the insured would have in the absence of such request, demand, order or statutory or regulatory requirement, or such claim or "suit" by or on behalf of a governmental authority.

g. Aircraft, Auto Or Watercraft

"Bodily injury" or "property damage" arising out of the ownership, maintenance, use or entrustment to others of any aircraft, "auto" or watercraft owned or operated by or rented or loaned to any insured. Use includes operation and "loading or unloading".

This exclusion does not apply to:

(1) A watercraft while ashore on premises you own or rent;

(2) A watercraft you do not own that is:

(a) Less than 26 feet long; and

(b) Not being used to carry persons or property for a charge;

(3) Parking an "auto" on, or on the ways next to, premises you own or rent, provided the "auto" is not owned by or rented or loaned to you or the insured;

(4) Liability assumed under any "insured contract" for the ownership, maintenance or use of aircraft or watercraft; or

(5) "Bodily injury" or "property damage" arising out of the operation of any of the equipment listed in Paragraph **f.(2)** or **f.(3)** of the definition of "mobile equipment".

h. Mobile Equipment

"Bodily injury" or "property damage" arising out of:

(1) The transportation of "mobile equipment" by an "auto" owned or operated by or rented or loaned to any insured; or

(2) The use of "mobile equipment" in, or while in practice for, or while being prepared for, any prearranged racing, speed, demolition, or stunting activity.

i. War

"Bodily injury" or "property damage" due to war, whether or not declared, or any act or condition incident to war. War includes civil war, insurrection, rebellion or revolution. This exclusion applies only to liability assumed under a contract or agreement.

j. Damage To Property

"Property damage" to:

(1) Property you own, rent, or occupy;

(2) Premises you sell, give away or abandon, if the "property damage" arises out of any part of those premises;

(3) Property loaned to you;

(4) Personal property in the care, custody or control of the insured;

(5) That particular part of real property on which you or any contractors or subcontractors working directly or indirectly on your behalf are performing operations, if the "property damage" arises out of those operations; or

(6) That particular part of any property that must be restored, repaired or replaced because "your work" was incorrectly performed on it.

Paragraphs **(1)**, **(3)** and **(4)** of this exclusion do not apply to "property damage" (other than damage by fire) to premises, including the contents of such premises, rented to you for a period of 7 or fewer consecutive days. A separate limit of insurance applies to Damage To Premises Rented To You as described in Section **III** – Limits Of Insurance.

Paragraph **(2)** of this exclusion does not apply if the premises are "your work" and were never occupied, rented or held for rental by you.

Paragraphs **(3)**, **(4)**, **(5)** and **(6)** of this exclusion do not apply to liability assumed under a sidetrack agreement.

Paragraph **(6)** of this exclusion does not apply to "property damage" included in the "products-completed operations hazard".

k. Damage To Your Product

"Property damage" to "your product" arising out of it or any part of it.

l. Damage To Your Work

"Property damage" to "your work" arising out of it or any part of it and included in the "products-completed operations hazard".

This exclusion does not apply if the damaged work or the work out of which the damage arises was performed on your behalf by a subcontractor.

m. Damage To Impaired Property Or Property Not Physically Injured

"Property damage" to "impaired property" or property that has not been physically injured, arising out of:

(1) A defect, deficiency, inadequacy or dangerous condition in "your product" or "your work"; or

(2) A delay or failure by you or anyone acting on your behalf to perform a contract or agreement in accordance with its terms.

This exclusion does not apply to the loss of use of other property arising out of sudden and accidental physical injury to "your product" or "your work" after it has been put to its intended use.

n. Recall Of Products, Work Or Impaired Property

Damages claimed for any loss, cost or expense incurred by you or others for the loss of use, withdrawal, recall, inspection, repair, replacement, adjustment, removal or disposal of:

(1) "Your product";

(2) "Your work"; or

(3) "Impaired property";

if such product, work, or property is withdrawn or recalled from the market or from use by any person or organization because of a known or suspected defect, deficiency, inadequacy or dangerous condition in it.

o. Personal And Advertising Injury

"Bodily injury" arising out of "personal and advertising injury".

Exclusions **c.** through **n.** do not apply to damage by fire to premises while rented to you or temporarily occupied by you with permission of the owner. A separate limit of insurance applies to this coverage as described in Section **III** – Limits Of Insurance.

       CG 00 01 07 98   ☐

COVERAGE B PERSONAL AND ADVERTISING INJURY LIABILITY

1. Insuring Agreement

a. We will pay those sums that the insured becomes legally obligated to pay as damages because of "personal and advertising injury" to which this insurance applies. We will have the right and duty to defend the insured against any "suit" seeking those damages. However, we will have no duty to defend the insured against any "suit" seeking damages for "personal and advertising injury" to which this insurance does not apply. We may, at our discretion, investigate any offense and settle any claim or "suit" that may result. But:

(1) The amount we will pay for damages is limited as described in Section **III** – Limits Of Insurance ; and

(2) Our right and duty to defend end when we have used up the applicable limit of insurance in the payment of judgments or settlements under Coverages **A** or **B** or medical expenses under Coverage **C.**

No other obligation or liability to pay sums or perform acts or services is covered unless explicitly provided for under Supplementary Payments – Coverages **A** and **B.**

b. This insurance applies to "personal and advertising injury" caused by an offense arising out of your business but only if the offense was committed in the "coverage territory" during the policy period.

2. Exclusions

This insurance does not apply to:

a. "Personal and advertising injury":

(1) Caused by or at the direction of the insured with the knowledge that the act would violate the rights of another and would inflict "personal and advertising injury";

(2) Arising out of oral or written publication of material, if done by or at the direction of the insured with knowledge of its falsity;

(3) Arising out of oral or written publication of material whose first publication took place before the beginning of the policy period;

(4) Arising out of a criminal act committed by or at the direction of any insured;

(5) For which the insured has assumed liability in a contract or agreement. This exclusion does not apply to liability for damages that the insured would have in the absence of the contract or agreement;

(6) Arising out of a breach of contract, except an implied contract to use another's advertising idea in your "advertisement";

(7) Arising out of the failure of goods, products or services to conform with any statement of quality or performance made in your "advertisement";

(8) Arising out of the wrong description of the price of goods, products or services stated in your "advertisement";

(9) Committed by an insured whose business is advertising, broadcasting, publishing or telecasting. However, this exclusion does not apply to Paragraphs **14.a., b.** and **c.** of "personal and advertising injury" under the Definitions Section; or

(10) Arising out of the actual, alleged or threatened discharge, dispersal, seepage, migration, release or escape of "pollutants" at any time.

b. Any loss, cost or expense arising out of any:

(1) Request, demand or order that any insured or others test for, monitor, clean up, remove, contain, treat, detoxify or neutralize, or in any way respond to, or assess the effects of, "pollutants"; or

(2) Claim or suit by or on behalf of a governmental authority for damages because of testing for, monitoring, cleaning up, removing, containing, treating, detoxifying or neutralizing, or in any way responding to, or assessing the effects of, "pollutants".

COVERAGE C MEDICAL PAYMENTS

1. Insuring Agreement

a. We will pay medical expenses as described below for "bodily injury" caused by an accident:

(1) On premises you own or rent;

(2) On ways next to premises you own or rent; or

(3) Because of your operations;

provided that:

(1) The accident takes place in the "coverage territory" and during the policy period;

(2) The expenses are incurred and reported to us within one year of the date of the accident; and

(3) The injured person submits to examination, at our expense, by physicians of our choice as often as we reasonably require.

b. We will make these payments regardless of fault. These payments will not exceed the applicable limit of insurance. We will pay reasonable expenses for:

(1) First aid administered at the time of an accident;

(2) Necessary medical, surgical, x-ray and dental services, including prosthetic devices; and

(3) Necessary ambulance, hospital, professional nursing and funeral services.

2. Exclusions

We will not pay expenses for "bodily injury":

a. To any insured.

b. To a person hired to do work for or on behalf of any insured or a tenant of any insured.

c. To a person injured on that part of premises you own or rent that the person normally occupies.

d. To a person, whether or not an "employee" of any insured, if benefits for the "bodily injury" are payable or must be provided under a workers' compensation or disability benefits law or a similar law.

e. To a person injured while taking part in athletics.

f. Included within the "products-completed operations hazard".

g. Excluded under Coverage **A.**

h. Due to war, whether or not declared, or any act or condition incident to war. War includes civil war, insurrection, rebellion or revolution.

SUPPLEMENTARY PAYMENTS – COVERAGES A AND B

1. We will pay, with respect to any claim we investigate or settle, or any "suit" against an insured we defend:

a. All expenses we incur.

b. Up to $250 for cost of bail bonds required because of accidents or traffic law violations arising out of the use of any vehicle to which the Bodily Injury Liability Coverage applies. We do not have to furnish these bonds.

c. The cost of bonds to release attachments, but only for bond amounts within the applicable limit of insurance. We do not have to furnish these bonds.

d. All reasonable expenses incurred by the insured at our request to assist us in the investigation or defense of the claim or "suit", including actual loss of earnings up to $250 a day because of time off from work.

e. All costs taxed against the insured in the "suit".

f. Prejudgment interest awarded against the insured on that part of the judgment we pay. If we make an offer to pay the applicable limit of insurance, we will not pay any prejudgment interest based on that period of time after the offer.

g. All interest on the full amount of any judgment that accrues after entry of the judgment and before we have paid, offered to pay, or deposited in court the part of the judgment that is within the applicable limit of insurance.

These payments will not reduce the limits of insurance.

2. If we defend an insured against a "suit" and an indemnitee of the insured is also named as a party to the "suit", we will defend that indemnitee if all of the following conditions are met:

a. The "suit" against the indemnitee seeks damages for which the insured has assumed the liability of the indemnitee in a contract or agreement that is an "insured contract";

b. This insurance applies to such liability assumed by the insured;

c. The obligation to defend, or the cost of the defense of, that indemnitee, has also been assumed by the insured in the same "insured contract";

d. The allegations in the "suit" and the information we know about the "occurrence" are such that no conflict appears to exist between the interests of the insured and the interests of the indemnitee;

e. The indemnitee and the insured ask us to conduct and control the defense of that indemnitee against such "suit" and agree that we can assign the same counsel to defend the insured and the indemnitee; and

f. The indemnitee:

(1) Agrees in writing to:

(a) Cooperate with us in the investigation, settlement or defense of the "suit";

(b) Immediately send us copies of any demands, notices, summonses or legal papers received in connection with the "suit";

(c) Notify any other insurer whose coverage is available to the indemnitee; and

(d) Cooperate with us with respect to coordinating other applicable insurance available to the indemnitee; and

Copyright, Insurance Services Office, Inc., 1997   CG 00 01 07 98   ☐

(2) Provides us with written authorization to:

(a) Obtain records and other information related to the "suit"; and

(b) Conduct and control the defense of the indemnitee in such "suit".

So long as the above conditions are met, attorneys' fees incurred by us in the defense of that indemnitee, necessary litigation expenses incurred by us and necessary litigation expenses incurred by the indemnitee at our request will be paid as Supplementary Payments. Notwithstanding the provisions of Paragraph **2.b.(2)** of Section **I** – Coverage **A** – Bodily Injury And Property Damage Liability, such payments will not be deemed to be damages for "bodily injury" and "property damage" and will not reduce the limits of insurance.

Our obligation to defend an insured's indemnitee and to pay for attorneys' fees and necessary litigation expenses as Supplementary Payments ends when:

a. We have used up the applicable limit of insurance in the payment of judgments or settlements; or

b. The conditions set forth above, or the terms of the agreement described in Paragraph **f.** above, are no longer met.

SECTION II – WHO IS AN INSURED

1. If you are designated in the Declarations as:

a. An individual, you and your spouse are insureds, but only with respect to the conduct of a business of which you are the sole owner.

b. A partnership or joint venture, you are an insured. Your members, your partners, and their spouses are also insureds, but only with respect to the conduct of your business.

c. A limited liability company, you are an insured. Your members are also insureds, but only with respect to the conduct of your business. Your managers are insureds, but only with respect to their duties as your managers.

d. An organization other than a partnership, joint venture or limited liability company, you are an insured. Your "executive officers" and directors are insureds, but only with respect to their duties as your officers or directors. Your stockholders are also insureds, but only with respect to their liability as stockholders.

2. Each of the following is also an insured:

a. Your "employees", other than either your "executive officers" (if you are an organization other than a partnership, joint venture or limited liability company) or your managers (if you are a limited liability company), but only for acts within the scope of their employment by you or while performing duties related to the conduct of your business. However, none of these "employees" is an insured for:

(1) "Bodily injury" or "personal and advertising injury":

(a) To you, to your partners or members (if you are a partnership or joint venture), to your members (if you are a limited liability company), or to a co-"employee" while that co-"employee" is either in the course of his or her employment or performing duties related to the conduct of your business;

(b) To the spouse, child, parent, brother or sister of that co-"employee" as a consequence of Paragraph **(1)(a)** above;

(c) For which there is any obligation to share damages with or repay someone else who must pay damages because of the injury described in Paragraphs **(1)(a)** or **(b)** above; or

(d) Arising out of his or her providing or failing to provide professional health care services.

(2) "Property damage" to property:

(a) Owned, occupied or used by,

(b) Rented to, in the care, custody or control of, or over which physical control is being exercised for any purpose by

you, any of your "employees", any partner or member (if you are a partnership or joint venture), or any member (if you are a limited liability company).

b. Any person (other than your "employee"), or any organization while acting as your real estate manager.

c. Any person or organization having proper temporary custody of your property if you die, but only:

(1) With respect to liability arising out of the maintenance or use of that property; and

(2) Until your legal representative has been appointed.

d. Your legal representative if you die, but only with respect to duties as such. That representative will have all your rights and duties under this Coverage Part.

3. With respect to "mobile equipment" registered in your name under any motor vehicle registration law, any person is an insured while driving such equipment along a public highway with your permission. Any other person or organization responsible for the conduct of such person is also an insured, but only with respect to liability arising out of the operation of the equipment, and only if no other insurance of any kind is available to that person or organization for this liability. However, no person or organization is an insured with respect to:

a. "Bodily injury" to a co-"employee" of the person driving the equipment; or

b. "Property damage" to property owned by, rented to, in the charge of or occupied by you or the employer of any person who is an insured under this provision.

4. Any organization you newly acquire or form, other than a partnership, joint venture or limited liability company, and over which you maintain ownership or majority interest, will qualify as a Named Insured if there is no other similar insurance available to that organization. However:

a. Coverage under this provision is afforded only until the 90th day after you acquire or form the organization or the end of the policy period, whichever is earlier;

b. Coverage **A** does not apply to "bodily injury" or "property damage" that occurred before you acquired or formed the organization; and

c. Coverage **B** does not apply to "personal and advertising injury" arising out of an offense committed before you acquired or formed the organization.

No person or organization is an insured with respect to the conduct of any current or past partnership, joint venture or limited liability company that is not shown as a Named Insured in the Declarations.

SECTION III – LIMITS OF INSURANCE

1. The Limits of Insurance shown in the Declarations and the rules below fix the most we will pay regardless of the number of:

a. Insureds;

b. Claims made or "suits" brought; or

c. Persons or organizations making claims or bringing "suits".

2. The General Aggregate Limit is the most we will pay for the sum of:

a. Medical expenses under Coverage **C**;

b. Damages under Coverage **A,** except damages because of "bodily injury" or "property damage" included in the "products-completed operations hazard"; and

c. Damages under Coverage **B.**

3. The Products-Completed Operations Aggregate Limit is the most we will pay under Coverage **A** for damages because of "bodily injury" and "property damage" included in the "products-completed operations hazard".

4. Subject to **2.** above, the Personal and Advertising Injury Limit is the most we will pay under Coverage **B** for the sum of all damages because of all "personal and advertising injury" sustained by any one person or organization.

5. Subject to **2.** or **3.** above, whichever applies, the Each Occurrence Limit is the most we will pay for the sum of:

a. Damages under Coverage **A;** and

b. Medical expenses under Coverage **C**

because of all "bodily injury" and "property damage" arising out of any one "occurrence".

6. Subject to **5.** above, the Damage To Premises Rented To You Limit is the most we will pay under Coverage **A** for damages because of "property damage" to any one premises, while rented to you, or in the case of damage by fire, while rented to you or temporarily occupied by you with permission of the owner.

7. Subject to **5.** above, the Medical Expense Limit is the most we will pay under Coverage **C** for all medical expenses because of "bodily injury" sustained by any one person.

The Limits of Insurance of this Coverage Part apply separately to each consecutive annual period and to any remaining period of less than 12 months, starting with the beginning of the policy period shown in the Declarations, unless the policy period is extended after issuance for an additional period of less than 12 months. In that case, the additional period will be deemed part of the last preceding period for purposes of determining the Limits of Insurance.

SECTION IV – COMMERCIAL GENERAL LIABILITY CONDITIONS

1. Bankruptcy

Bankruptcy or insolvency of the insured or of the insured's estate will not relieve us of our obligations under this Coverage Part.

2. Duties In The Event Of Occurrence, Offense, Claim Or Suit

a. You must see to it that we are notified as soon as practicable of an "occurrence" or an offense which may result in a claim. To the extent possible, notice should include:

(1) How, when and where the "occurrence" or offense took place;

(2) The names and addresses of any injured persons and witnesses; and

(3) The nature and location of any injury or damage arising out of the "occurrence" or offense.

b. If a claim is made or "suit" is brought against any insured, you must:

(1) Immediately record the specifics of the claim or "suit" and the date received; and

(2) Notify us as soon as practicable.

You must see to it that we receive written notice of the claim or "suit" as soon as practicable.

c. You and any other involved insured must:

(1) Immediately send us copies of any demands, notices, summonses or legal papers received in connection with the claim or "suit";

(2) Authorize us to obtain records and other information;

(3) Cooperate with us in the investigation or settlement of the claim or defense against the "suit"; and

(4) Assist us, upon our request, in the enforcement of any right against any person or organization which may be liable to the insured because of injury or damage to which this insurance may also apply.

d. No insured will, except at that insured's own cost, voluntarily make a payment, assume any obligation, or incur any expense, other than for first aid, without our consent.

3. Legal Action Against Us

No person or organization has a right under this Coverage Part:

a. To join us as a party or otherwise bring us into a "suit" asking for damages from an insured; or

b. To sue us on this Coverage Part unless all of its terms have been fully complied with.

A person or organization may sue us to recover on an agreed settlement or on a final judgment against an insured obtained after an actual trial; but we will not be liable for damages that are not payable under the terms of this Coverage Part or that are in excess of the applicable limit of insurance. An agreed settlement means a settlement and release of liability signed by us, the insured and the claimant or the claimant's legal representative.

4. Other Insurance

If other valid and collectible insurance is available to the insured for a loss we cover under Coverages **A** or **B** of this Coverage Part, our obligations are limited as follows:

a. Primary Insurance

This insurance is primary except when **b.** below applies. If this insurance is primary, our obligations are not affected unless any of the other insurance is also primary. Then, we will share with all that other insurance by the method described in **c.** below.

b. Excess Insurance

This insurance is excess over:

(1) Any of the other insurance, whether primary, excess, contingent or on any other basis:

(a) That is Fire, Extended Coverage, Builder's Risk, Installation Risk or similar coverage for "your work";

(b) That is Fire insurance for premises rented to you or temporarily occupied by you with permission of the owner;

(c) That is insurance purchased by you to cover your liability as a tenant for "property damage" to premises rented to you or temporarily occupied by you with permission of the owner; or

(d) If the loss arises out of the maintenance or use of aircraft, "autos" or watercraft to the extent not subject to Exclusion **g.** of Section I – Coverage **A** – Bodily Injury And Property Damage Liability.

(2) Any other primary insurance available to you covering liability for damages arising out of the premises or operations for which you have been added as an additional insured by attachment of an endorsement.

When this insurance is excess, we will have no duty under Coverages **A** or **B** to defend the insured against any "suit" if any other insurer has a duty to defend the insured against that "suit". If no other insurer defends, we will undertake to do so, but we will be entitled to the insured's rights against all those other insurers.

When this insurance is excess over other insurance, we will pay only our share of the amount of the loss, if any, that exceeds the sum of:

(1) The total amount that all such other insurance would pay for the loss in the absence of this insurance; and

(2) The total of all deductible and self-insured amounts under all that other insurance.

We will share the remaining loss, if any, with any other insurance that is not described in this Excess Insurance provision and was not bought specifically to apply in excess of the Limits of Insurance shown in the Declarations of this Coverage Part.

c. Method Of Sharing

If all of the other insurance permits contribution by equal shares, we will follow this method also. Under this approach each insurer contributes equal amounts until it has paid its applicable limit of insurance or none of the loss remains, whichever comes first.

If any of the other insurance does not permit contribution by equal shares, we will contribute by limits. Under this method, each insurer's share is based on the ratio of its applicable limit of insurance to the total applicable limits of insurance of all insurers.

5. Premium Audit

a. We will compute all premiums for this Coverage Part in accordance with our rules and rates.

b. Premium shown in this Coverage Part as advance premium is a deposit premium only. At the close of each audit period we will compute the earned premium for that period. Audit premiums are due and payable on notice to the first Named Insured. If the sum of the advance and audit premiums paid for the policy period is greater than the earned premium, we will return the excess to the first Named Insured.

c. The first Named Insured must keep records of the information we need for premium computation, and send us copies at such times as we may request.

6. Representations

By accepting this policy, you agree:

a. The statements in the Declarations are accurate and complete;

b. Those statements are based upon representations you made to us; and

c. We have issued this policy in reliance upon your representations.

7. Separation Of Insureds

Except with respect to the Limits of Insurance, and any rights or duties specifically assigned in this Coverage Part to the first Named Insured, this insurance applies:

a. As if each Named Insured were the only Named Insured; and

b. Separately to each insured against whom claim is made or "suit" is brought.

8. Transfer Of Rights Of Recovery Against Others To Us

If the insured has rights to recover all or part of any payment we have made under this Coverage Part, those rights are transferred to us. The insured must do nothing after loss to impair them. At our request, the insured will bring "suit" or transfer those rights to us and help us enforce them.

9. When We Do Not Renew

If we decide not to renew this Coverage Part, we will mail or deliver to the first Named Insured shown in the Declarations written notice of the nonrenewal not less than 30 days before the expiration date.

If notice is mailed, proof of mailing will be sufficient proof of notice.

SECTION V – DEFINITIONS

1. "Advertisement" means a notice that is broadcast or published to the general public or specific market segments about your goods, products or services for the purpose of attracting customers or supporters.

2. "Auto" means a land motor vehicle, trailer or semitrailer designed for travel on public roads, including any attached machinery or equipment. But "auto" does not include "mobile equipment".

3. "Bodily injury" means bodily injury, sickness or disease sustained by a person, including death resulting from any of these at any time.

4. "Coverage territory" means:

a. The United States of America (including its territories and possessions), Puerto Rico and Canada;

b. International waters or airspace, provided the injury or damage does not occur in the course of travel or transportation to or from any place not included in **a.** above; or

c. All parts of the world if:

    (1) The injury or damage arises out of:

        (a) Goods or products made or sold by you in the territory described in **a.** above; or

        (b) The activities of a person whose home is in the territory described in **a.** above, but is away for a short time on your business; and

    (2) The insured's responsibility to pay damages is determined in a "suit" on the merits, in the territory described in **a.** above or in a settlement we agree to.

5. "Employee" includes a "leased worker". "Employee" does not include a "temporary worker".

6. "Executive officer" means a person holding any of the officer positions created by your charter, constitution, by-laws or any other similar governing document.

7. "Hostile fire" means one which becomes uncontrollable or breaks out from where it was intended to be.

8. "Impaired property" means tangible property, other than "your product" or "your work", that cannot be used or is less useful because:

a. It incorporates "your product" or "your work" that is known or thought to be defective, deficient, inadequate or dangerous; or

b. You have failed to fulfill the terms of a contract or agreement;

if such property can be restored to use by:

a. The repair, replacement, adjustment or removal of "your product" or "your work"; or

b. Your fulfilling the terms of the contract or agreement.

9. "Insured contract" means:

a. A contract for a lease of premises. However, that portion of the contract for a lease of premises that indemnifies any person or organization for damage by fire to premises while rented to you or temporarily occupied by you with permission of the owner is not an "insured contract";

b. A sidetrack agreement;

c. Any easement or license agreement, except in connection with construction or demolition operations on or within 50 feet of a railroad;

d. An obligation, as required by ordinance, to indemnify a municipality, except in connection with work for a municipality;

e. An elevator maintenance agreement;

f. That part of any other contract or agreement pertaining to your business (including an indemnification of a municipality in connection with work performed for a municipality) under which you assume the tort liability of another party to pay for "bodily injury" or "property damage" to a third person or organization. Tort liability means a liability that would be imposed by law in the absence of any contract or agreement.

Paragraph **f.** does not include that part of any contract or agreement:

(1) That indemnifies a railroad for "bodily injury" or "property damage" arising out of construction or demolition operations, within 50 feet of any railroad property and affecting any railroad bridge or trestle, tracks, road-beds, tunnel, underpass or crossing;

(2) That indemnifies an architect, engineer or surveyor for injury or damage arising out of:

    (a) Preparing, approving, or failing to prepare or approve, maps, shop drawings, opinions, reports, surveys, field orders, change orders or drawings and specifications; or

    (b) Giving directions or instructions, or failing to give them, if that is the primary cause of the injury or damage; or

(3) Under which the insured, if an architect, engineer or surveyor, assumes liability for an injury or damage arising out of the insured's rendering or failure to render professional services, including those listed in **(2)** above and supervisory, inspection, architectural or engineering activities.

10. "Leased worker" means a person leased to you by a labor leasing firm under an agreement between you and the labor leasing firm, to perform duties related to the conduct of your business. "Leased worker" does not include a "temporary worker".

11. "Loading or unloading" means the handling of property:

a. After it is moved from the place where it is accepted for movement into or onto an aircraft, watercraft or "auto";

b. While it is in or on an aircraft, watercraft or "auto"; or

c. While it is being moved from an aircraft, watercraft or "auto" to the place where it is finally delivered;

but "loading or unloading" does not include the movement of property by means of a mechanical device, other than a hand truck, that is not attached to the aircraft, watercraft or "auto".

12. "Mobile equipment" means any of the following types of land vehicles, including any attached machinery or equipment:

a. Bulldozers, farm machinery, forklifts and other vehicles designed for use principally off public roads;

b. Vehicles maintained for use solely on or next to premises you own or rent;

c. Vehicles that travel on crawler treads;

d. Vehicles, whether self-propelled or not, maintained primarily to provide mobility to permanently mounted:

   (1) Power cranes, shovels, loaders, diggers or drills; or

   (2) Road construction or resurfacing equipment such as graders, scrapers or rollers;

e. Vehicles not described in **a.**, **b.**, **c.** or **d.** above that are not self-propelled and are maintained primarily to provide mobility to permanently attached equipment of the following types:

   (1) Air compressors, pumps and generators, including spraying, welding, building cleaning, geophysical exploration, lighting and well servicing equipment; or

   (2) Cherry pickers and similar devices used to raise or lower workers;

f. Vehicles not described in **a.**, **b.**, **c.** or **d.** above maintained primarily for purposes other than the transportation of persons or cargo.

However, self-propelled vehicles with the following types of permanently attached equipment are not "mobile equipment" but will be considered "autos":

   (1) Equipment designed primarily for:

     (a) Snow removal;

     (b) Road maintenance, but not construction or resurfacing; or

     (c) Street cleaning;

   (2) Cherry pickers and similar devices mounted on automobile or truck chassis and used to raise or lower workers; and

   (3) Air compressors, pumps and generators, including spraying, welding, building cleaning, geophysical exploration, lighting and well servicing equipment.

13. "Occurrence" means an accident, including continuous or repeated exposure to substantially the same general harmful conditions.

14. "Personal and advertising injury" means injury, including consequential "bodily injury", arising out of one or more of the following offenses:

a. False arrest, detention or imprisonment;

b. Malicious prosecution;

c. The wrongful eviction from, wrongful entry into, or invasion of the right of private occupancy of a room, dwelling or premises that a person occupies, committed by or on behalf of its owner, landlord or lessor;

d. Oral or written publication of material that slanders or libels a person or organization or disparages a person's or organization's goods, products or services;

e. Oral or written publication of material that violates a person's right of privacy;

f. The use of another's advertising idea in your "advertisement"; or

g. Infringing upon another's copyright, trade dress or slogan in your "advertisement".

15. "Pollutants" mean any solid, liquid, gaseous or thermal irritant or contaminant, including smoke, vapor, soot, fumes, acids, alkalis, chemicals and waste. Waste includes materials to be recycled, reconditioned or reclaimed.

16. "Products-completed operations hazard":

a. Includes all "bodily injury" and "property damage" occurring away from premises you own or rent and arising out of "your product" or "your work" except:

   (1) Products that are still in your physical possession; or

   (2) Work that has not yet been completed or abandoned. However, "your work" will be deemed completed at the earliest of the following times:

     (a) When all of the work called for in your contract has been completed.

     (b) When all of the work to be done at the job site has been completed if your contract calls for work at more than one job site.

     (c) When that part of the work done at a job site has been put to its intended use by any person or organization other than another contractor or subcontractor working on the same project.

Work that may need service, maintenance, correction, repair or replacement, but which is otherwise complete, will be treated as completed.

b. Does not include "bodily injury" or "property damage" arising out of:

  (1) The transportation of property, unless the injury or damage arises out of a condition in or on a vehicle not owned or operated by you, and that condition was created by the "loading or unloading" of that vehicle by any insured;

  (2) The existence of tools, uninstalled equipment or abandoned or unused materials; or

  (3) Products or operations for which the classification, listed in the Declarations or in a policy schedule, states that products-completed operations are subject to the General Aggregate Limit.

17. "Property damage" means:

a. Physical injury to tangible property, including all resulting loss of use of that property. All such loss of use shall be deemed to occur at the time of the physical injury that caused it; or

b. Loss of use of tangible property that is not physically injured. All such loss of use shall be deemed to occur at the time of the "occurrence" that caused it.

18. "Suit" means a civil proceeding in which damages because of "bodily injury", "property damage" or "personal and advertising injury" to which this insurance applies are alleged. "Suit" includes:

a. An arbitration proceeding in which such damages are claimed and to which the insured must submit or does submit with our consent; or

b. Any other alternative dispute resolution proceeding in which such damages are claimed and to which the insured submits with our consent.

19. "Temporary worker" means a person who is furnished to you to substitute for a permanent "employee" on leave or to meet seasonal or short-term workload conditions.

20. "Your product" means:

a. Any goods or products, other than real property, manufactured, sold, handled, distributed or disposed of by:

  (1) You;

  (2) Others trading under your name; or

  (3) A person or organization whose business or assets you have acquired; and

b. Containers (other than vehicles), materials, parts or equipment furnished in connection with such goods or products.

"Your product" includes:

a. Warranties or representations made at any time with respect to the fitness, quality, durability, performance or use of "your product"; and

b. The providing of or failure to provide warnings or instructions.

"Your product" does not include vending machines or other property rented to or located for the use of others but not sold.

21. "Your work" means:

a. Work or operations performed by you or on your behalf; and

b. Materials, parts or equipment furnished in connection with such work or operations.

"Your work" includes:

a. Warranties or representations made at any time with respect to the fitness, quality, durability, performance or use of "your work"; and

b. The providing of or failure to provide warnings or instructions.

COMMERCIAL GENERAL LIABILITY COVERAGE FORM

COVERAGES A AND B PROVIDE
CLAIMS-MADE COVERAGE
PLEASE READ THE ENTIRE FORM CAREFULLY

Various provisions in this policy restrict coverage. Read the entire policy carefully to determine rights, duties and what is and is not covered.

Throughout this policy the words "you" and "your" refer to the Named Insured shown in the Declarations, and any other person or organization qualifying as a Named Insured under this policy. The words "we", "us" and "our" refer to the Company providing this insurance.

The word "insured" means any person or organization qualifying as such under Section **II** – Who Is An Insured.

Other words and phrases that appear in quotation marks have special meaning. Refer to Section **VI** – Definitions.

SECTION I – COVERAGES

COVERAGE A BODILY INJURY AND PROPERTY DAMAGE LIABILITY

1. Insuring Agreement

a. We will pay those sums that the insured becomes legally obligated to pay as damages because of "bodily injury" or "property damage" to which this insurance applies. We will have the right and duty to defend the insured against any "suit" seeking those damages. However, we will have no duty to defend the insured against any "suit" seeking damages for "bodily injury" or "property damage" to which this insurance does not apply. We may, at our discretion, investigate any "occurrence" and settle any claim or "suit" that may result. But:

  (1) The amount we will pay for damages is limited as described in Section **III** – Limits Of Insurance; and

  (2) Our right and duty to defend end when we have used up the applicable limit of insurance in the payment of judgments or settlements under Coverages **A** or **B** or medical expenses under Coverage **C**.

No other obligation or liability to pay sums or perform acts or services is covered unless explicitly provided for under Supplementary Payments – Coverages **A** and **B**.

b. This insurance applies to "bodily injury" and "property damage" only if:

  (1) The "bodily injury" or "property damage" is caused by an "occurrence" that takes place in the "coverage territory";

  (2) The "bodily injury" or "property damage" did not occur before the Retroactive Date, if any, shown in the Declarations or after the end of the policy period; and

  (3) A claim for damages because of the "bodily injury" or "property damage" is first made against any insured, in accordance with Paragraph **c.** below, during the policy period or any Extended Reporting Period we provide under Section **V** – Extended Reporting Periods.

c. A claim by a person or organization seeking damages will be deemed to have been made at the earlier of the following times:

  (1) When notice of such claim is received and recorded by any insured or by us, whichever comes first; or

  (2) When we make settlement in accordance with Paragraph **1.a.** above.

All claims for damages because of "bodily injury" to the same person, including damages claimed by any person or organization for care, loss of services, or death resulting at any time from the "bodily injury", will be deemed to have been made at the time the first of those claims is made against any insured.

All claims for damages because of "property damage" causing loss to the same person or organization will be deemed to have been made at the time the first of those claims is made against any insured.

2. Exclusions

This insurance does not apply to:

a. **Expected Or Intended Injury**

"Bodily injury" or "property damage" expected or intended from the standpoint of the insured. This exclusion does not apply to "bodily injury" resulting from the use of reasonable force to protect persons or property.

b. Contractual Liability

"Bodily injury" or "property damage" for which the insured is obligated to pay damages by reason of the assumption of liability in a contract or agreement. This exclusion does not apply to liability for damages:

(1) That the insured would have in the absence of the contract or agreement; or

(2) Assumed in a contract or agreement that is an "insured contract", provided the "bodily injury" or "property damage" occurs subsequent to the execution of the contract or agreement. Solely for the purposes of liability assumed in an "insured contract", reasonable attorney fees and necessary litigation expenses incurred by or for a party other than an insured are deemed to be damages because of "bodily injury" or "property damage", provided:

(a) Liability to such party for, or for the cost of, that party's defense has also been assumed in the same "insured contract"; and

(b) Such attorney fees and litigation expenses are for defense of that party against a civil or alternative dispute resolution proceeding in which damages to which this insurance applies are alleged.

c. Liquor Liability

"Bodily injury" or "property damage" for which any insured may be held liable by reason of:

(1) Causing or contributing to the intoxication of any person;

(2) The furnishing of alcoholic beverages to a person under the legal drinking age or under the influence of alcohol; or

(3) Any statute, ordinance or regulation relating to the sale, gift, distribution or use of alcoholic beverages.

This exclusion applies only if you are in the business of manufacturing, distributing, selling, serving or furnishing alcoholic beverages.

d. Workers' Compensation And Similar Laws

Any obligation of the insured under a workers' compensation, disability benefits or unemployment compensation law or any similar law.

e. Employer's Liability

"Bodily injury" to:

(1) An "employee" of the insured arising out of and in the course of:

(a) Employment by the insured; or

(b) Performing duties related to the conduct of the insured's business; or

(2) The spouse, child, parent, brother or sister of that "employee" as a consequence of Paragraph (1) above.

This exclusion applies:

(1) Whether the insured may be liable as an employer or in any other capacity; and

(2) To any obligation to share damages with or repay someone else who must pay damages because of the injury.

This exclusion does not apply to liability assumed by the insured under an "insured contract".

f. Pollution

(1) "Bodily injury" or "property damage" arising out of the actual, alleged or threatened discharge, dispersal, seepage, migration, release or escape of "pollutants":

(a) At or from any premises, site or location which is or was at any time owned or occupied by, or rented or loaned to, any insured. However, this subparagraph does not apply to:

(i) "Bodily injury" if sustained within a building and caused by smoke, fumes, vapor or soot from equipment used to heat that building;

(ii) "Bodily injury" or "property damage" for which you may be held liable, if you are a contractor and the owner or lessee of such premises, site or location has been added to your policy as an additional insured with respect to your ongoing operations performed for that additional insured at that premises, site or location and such premises, site or location is not or never was owned or occupied by, or rented or loaned to, any insured, other than that additional insured; or

(iii) "Bodily injury" or "property damage" arising out of heat, smoke or fumes from a "hostile fire";

(b) At or from any premises, site or location which is or was at any time used by or for any insured or others for the handling, storage, disposal, processing or treatment of waste;

(c) Which are or were at any time transported, handled, stored, treated, disposed of, or processed as waste by or for any insured or any person or organization for whom you may be legally responsible; or

(d) At or from any premises, site or location on which any insured or any contractors or subcontractors working directly or indirectly on any insured's behalf are performing operations if the "pollutants" are brought on or to the premises, site or location in connection with such operations by such insured, contractor or subcontractor. However, this subparagraph does not apply to:

(i) "Bodily injury" or "property damage" arising out of the escape of fuels, lubricants or other operating fluids which are needed to perform the normal electrical, hydraulic or mechanical functions necessary for the operation of "mobile equipment" or its parts, if such fuels, lubricants or other operating fluids escape from a vehicle part designed to hold, store or receive them. This exception does not apply if the "bodily injury" or "property damage" arises out of the intentional discharge, dispersal or release of the fuels, lubricants or other operating fluids, or if such fuels, lubricants or other operating fluids are brought on or to the premises, site or location with the intent that they be discharged, dispersed or released as part of the operations being performed by such insured, contractor or subcontractor;

(ii) "Bodily injury" or "property damage" sustained within a building and caused by the release of gases, fumes or vapors from materials brought into that building in connection with operations being performed by you or on your behalf by a contractor or subcontractor; or

(iii) "Bodily injury" or "property damage" arising out of heat, smoke or fumes from a "hostile fire".

(e) At or from any premises, site or location on which any insured or any contractors or subcontractors working directly or indirectly on any insured's behalf are performing operations if the operations are to test for, monitor, clean up, remove, contain, treat, detoxify or neutralize, or in any way respond to, or assess the effects of, "pollutants".

(2) Any loss, cost or expense arising out of any:

(a) Request, demand, order or statutory or regulatory requirement that any insured or others test for, monitor, clean up, remove, contain, treat, detoxify or neutralize, or in any way respond to, or assess the effects of, "pollutants"; or

(b) Claim or suit by or on behalf of a governmental authority for damages because of testing for, monitoring, cleaning up, removing, containing, treating, detoxifying or neutralizing, or in any way responding to, or assessing the effects of, "pollutants".

However, this paragraph does not apply to liability for damages because of "property damage" that the insured would have in the absence of such request, demand, order or statutory or regulatory requirement, or such claim or "suit" by or on behalf of a governmental authority.

g. Aircraft, Auto Or Watercraft

"Bodily injury" or "property damage" arising out of the ownership, maintenance, use or entrustment to others of any aircraft, "auto" or watercraft owned or operated by or rented or loaned to any insured. Use includes operation and "loading or unloading".

This exclusion does not apply to:

(1) A watercraft while ashore on premises you own or rent;

(2) A watercraft you do not own that is:

(a) Less than 26 feet long; and

(b) Not being used to carry persons or property for a charge;

(3) Parking an "auto" on, or on the ways next to, premises you own or rent, provided the "auto" is not owned by or rented or loaned to you or the insured;

(4) Liability assumed under any "insured contract" for the ownership, maintenance or use of aircraft or watercraft; or

(5) "Bodily injury" or "property damage" arising out of the operation of any of the equipment listed in Paragraph **f.(2)** or **f.(3)** of the definition of "mobile equipment".

h. Mobile Equipment

"Bodily injury" or "property damage" arising out of:

(1) The transportation of "mobile equipment" by an "auto" owned or operated by or rented or loaned to any insured; or

(2) The use of "mobile equipment" in, or while in practice for, or while being prepared for, any prearranged racing, speed, demolition, or stunting activity.

i. War

"Bodily injury" or "property damage" due to war, whether or not declared, or any act or condition incident to war. War includes civil war, insurrection, rebellion or revolution. This exclusion applies only to liability assumed under a contract or agreement.

j. Damage To Property

"Property damage" to:

(1) Property you own, rent, or occupy;

(2) Premises you sell, give away or abandon, if the "property damage" arises out of any part of those premises;

(3) Property loaned to you;

(4) Personal property in the care, custody or control of the insured;

(5) That particular part of real property on which you or any contractors or subcontractors working directly or indirectly on your behalf are performing operations, if the "property damage" arises out of those operations; or

(6) That particular part of any property that must be restored, repaired or replaced because "your work" was incorrectly performed on it.

Paragraphs **(1)**, **(3)** and **(4)** of this exclusion do not apply to "property damage" (other than damage by fire) to premises, including the contents of such premises, rented to you for a period of 7 or fewer consecutive days. A separate limit of insurance applies to Damage To Premises Rented To You as described in Section III – Limits Of Insurance.

Paragraph **(2)** of this exclusion does not apply if the premises are "your work" and were never occupied, rented or held for rental by you.

Paragraphs **(3)**, **(4)**, **(5)** and **(6)** of this exclusion do not apply to liability assumed under a sidetrack agreement.

Paragraph **(6)** of this exclusion does not apply to "property damage" included in the "products-completed operations hazard".

k. Damage To Your Product

"Property damage" to "your product" arising out of it or any part of it.

l. Damage To Your Work

"Property damage" to "your work" arising out of it or any part of it and included in the "products-completed operations hazard".

This exclusion does not apply if the damaged work or the work out of which the damage arises was performed on your behalf by a subcontractor.

m. Damage To Impaired Property Or Property Not Physically Injured

"Property damage" to "impaired property" or property that has not been physically injured, arising out of:

(1) A defect, deficiency, inadequacy or dangerous condition in "your product" or "your work"; or

(2) A delay or failure by you or anyone acting on your behalf to perform a contract or agreement in accordance with its terms.

This exclusion does not apply to the loss of use of other property arising out of sudden and accidental physical injury to "your product" or "your work" after it has been put to its intended use.

n. Recall Of Products, Work Or Impaired Property

Damages claimed for any loss, cost or expense incurred by you or others for the loss of use, withdrawal, recall, inspection, repair, replacement, adjustment, removal or disposal of:

(1) "Your product";

(2) "Your work"; or

(3) "Impaired property";

if such product, work, or property is withdrawn or recalled from the market or from use by any person or organization because of a known or suspected defect, deficiency, inadequacy or dangerous condition in it.

o. Personal And Advertising Injury

"Bodily injury" arising out of "personal and advertising injury".

Exclusions **c.** through **n.** do not apply to damage by fire to premises while rented to you or temporarily occupied by you with permission of the owner. A separate limit of insurance applies to this coverage as described in Section III – Limits Of Insurance.

COVERAGE B PERSONAL AND ADVERTISING INJURY LIABILITY

1. Insuring Agreement

a. We will pay those sums that the insured becomes legally obligated to pay as damages because of "personal and advertising injury" to which this insurance applies. We will have the right and duty to defend the insured against any "suit" seeking those damages. However, we will have no duty to defend the insured against any "suit" seeking damages for "personal and advertising injury" to which this insurance does not apply. We may, at our discretion, investigate any offense and settle any claim or "suit" that may result. But:

(1) The amount we will pay for damages is limited as described in Section **III** – Limits Of Insurance; and

(2) Our right and duty to defend end when we have used up the applicable limit of insurance in the payment of judgments or settlements under Coverages **A** or **B** or medical expenses under Coverage **C**.

No other obligation or liability to pay sums or perform acts or services is covered unless explicitly provided for under Supplementary Payments – Coverages **A** and **B**.

b. This insurance applies to "personal and advertising injury" caused by an offense arising out of your business, but only if:

(1) The offense was committed in the "coverage territory";

(2) The offense was not committed before the Retroactive Date, if any, shown in the Declarations or after the end of the policy period; and

(3) A claim for damages because of the "personal and advertising injury" is first made against any insured, in accordance with Paragraph **c.** below, during the policy period or any Extended Reporting Period we provide under Section **V** – Extended Reporting Periods.

c. A claim made by a person or organization seeking damages will be deemed to have been made at the earlier of the following times:

(1) When notice of such claim is received and recorded by any insured or by us, whichever comes first; or

(2) When we make settlement in accordance with Paragraph **1.a.** above.

All claims for damages because of "personal injury and advertising injury" to the same person or organization as a result of an offense will be deemed to have been made at the time the first of those claims is made against any insured.

2. Exclusions

This insurance does not apply to:

a. "Personal and advertising injury":

(1) Caused by or at the direction of the insured with the knowledge that the act would violate the rights of another and would inflict "personal and advertising injury";

(2) Arising out of oral or written publication of material, if done by or at the direction of the insured with knowledge of its falsity;

(3) Arising out of oral or written publication of material whose first publication took place before the Retroactive Date, if any, shown in the Declarations;

(4) Arising out of a criminal act committed by or at the direction of any insured;

(5) For which the insured has assumed liability in a contract or agreement. This exclusion does not apply to liability for damages that the insured would have in the absence of the contract or agreement;

(6) Arising out of a breach of contract, except an implied contract to use another's advertising idea in your "advertisement";

(7) Arising out of the failure of goods, products or services to conform with any statement of quality or performance made in your "advertisement";

(8) Arising out of the wrong description of the price of goods, products or services stated in your "advertisement";

(9) Committed by an insured whose business is advertising, broadcasting, publishing or telecasting. However, this exclusion does not apply to Paragraphs **14.a., b.** and **c.** of "personal and advertising injury" under the Definitions Section; or

(10) Arising out of the actual, alleged or threatened discharge, dispersal, seepage, migration, release or escape of pollutants at any time.

b. Any loss, cost or expense arising out of any:

(1) Request, demand or order that any insured or others test for, monitor, clean up, remove, contain, treat, detoxify or neutralize, or in any way respond to, or assess the effects of, "pollutants"; or

(2) Claim or suit by or on behalf of a governmental authority for damages because of testing for, monitoring, cleaning up, removing, containing, treating, detoxifying or neutralizing, or in any way responding to, or assessing the effects of, "pollutants".

COVERAGE C MEDICAL PAYMENTS

1. Insuring Agreement

a. We will pay medical expenses as described below for "bodily injury" caused by an accident:

(1) On premises you own or rent;

(2) On ways next to premises you own or rent; or

(3) Because of your operations;

provided that:

(1) The accident takes place in the "coverage territory" and during the policy period;

(2) The expenses are incurred and reported to us within one year of the date of the accident; and

(3) The injured person submits to examination, at our expense, by physicians of our choice as often as we reasonably require.

b. We will make these payments regardless of fault. These payments will not exceed the applicable limit of insurance. We will pay reasonable expenses for:

(1) First aid administered at the time of an accident;

(2) Necessary medical, surgical, x-ray and dental services, including prosthetic devices; and

(3) Necessary ambulance, hospital, professional nursing and funeral services.

2. Exclusions

We will not pay expenses for "bodily injury":

a. To any insured.

b. To a person hired to do work for or on behalf of any insured or a tenant of any insured.

c. To a person injured on that part of premises you own or rent that the person normally occupies.

d. To a person, whether or not an "employee" of any insured, if benefits for the "bodily injury" are payable or must be provided under a workers' compensation or disability benefits law or a similar law.

e. To a person injured while taking part in athletics.

f. Included within the "products-completed operations hazard".

g. Excluded under Coverage A.

h. Due to war, whether or not declared, or any act or condition incident to war. War includes civil war, insurrection, rebellion or revolution.

SUPPLEMENTARY PAYMENTS – COVERAGES A AND B

1. We will pay, with respect to any claim we investigate or settle or any "suit" against an insured we defend:

a. All expenses we incur.

b. Up to $250 for cost of bail bonds required because of accidents or traffic law violations arising out of the use of any vehicle to which the Bodily Injury Liability Coverage applies. We do not have to furnish these bonds.

c. The cost of bonds to release attachments, but only for bond amounts within the applicable limit of insurance. We do not have to furnish these bonds.

d. All reasonable expenses incurred by the insured at our request to assist us in the investigation or defense of the claim or "suit", including actual loss of earnings up to $250 a day because of time off from work.

e. All costs taxed against the insured in the "suit".

f. Prejudgment interest awarded against the insured on that part of the judgment we pay. If we make an offer to pay the applicable limit of insurance, we will not pay any prejudgment interest based on that period of time after the offer.

g. All interest on the full amount of any judgment that accrues after entry of the judgment and before we have paid, offered to pay, or deposited in court the part of the judgment that is within the applicable limit of insurance.

These payments will not reduce the limits of insurance.

2. If we defend an insured against a "suit" and an indemnitee of the insured is also named as a party to the "suit", we will defend that indemnitee if all of the following conditions are met:

   a. The "suit" against the indemnitee seeks damages for which the insured has assumed the liability of the indemnitee in a contract or agreement that is an "insured contract";

   b. This insurance applies to such liability assumed by the insured;

   c. The obligation to defend, or the cost of the defense of, that indemnitee, has also been assumed by the insured in the same "insured contract";

   d. The allegations in the "suit" and the information we know about the "occurrence" are such that no conflict appears to exist between the interests of the insured and the interests of the indemnitee;

   e. The indemnitee and the insured ask us to conduct and control the defense of that indemnitee against such "suit" and agree that we can assign the same counsel to defend the insured and the indemnitee; and

   f. The indemnitee:

      (1) Agrees in writing to:

         (a) Cooperate with us in the investigation, settlement or defense of the "suit";

         (b) Immediately send us copies of any demands, notices, summonses or legal papers received in connection with the "suit";

         (c) Notify any other insurer whose coverage is available to the indemnitee; and

         (d) Cooperate with us with respect to coordinating other applicable insurance available to the indemnitee; and

      (2) Provides us with written authorization to:

         (a) Obtain records and other information related to the "suit"; and

         (b) Conduct and control the defense of the indemnitee in such "suit".

So long as the above conditions are met, attorneys' fees incurred by us in the defense of that indemnitee, necessary litigation expenses incurred by us and necessary litigation expenses incurred by the indemnitee at our request will be paid as Supplementary Payments. Notwithstanding the provisions of Paragraph **2.b.(2)** of Section I – Coverage **A** – Bodily Injury And Property Damage Liability, such payments will not be deemed to be damages for "bodily injury" and "property damage" and will not reduce the limits of insurance.

Our obligation to defend an insured's indemnitee and to pay for attorneys' fees and necessary litigation expenses as Supplementary Payments ends when:

   a. We have used up the applicable limit of insurance in the payment of judgments or settlements; or

   b. The conditions set forth above, or the terms of the agreement described in Paragraph **f.** above, are no longer met.

SECTION II – WHO IS AN INSURED

1. If you are designated in the Declarations as:

   a. An individual, you and your spouse are insureds, but only with respect to the conduct of a business of which you are the sole owner.

   b. A partnership or joint venture, you are an insured. Your members, your partners, and their spouses are also insureds, but only with respect to the conduct of your business.

   c. A limited liability company, you are an insured. Your members are also insureds, but only with respect to the conduct of your business. Your managers are insureds, but only with respect to their duties as your managers.

   d. An organization other than a partnership, joint venture or limited liability company, you are an insured. Your "executive officers" and directors are insureds, but only with respect to their duties as your officers or directors. Your stockholders are also insureds, but only with respect to their liability as stockholders.

2. Each of the following is also an insured:

   a. Your "employees", other than either your "executive officers" (if you are an organization other than a partnership, joint venture or limited liability company) or your managers (if you are a limited liability company), but only for acts within the scope of their employment by you or while performing duties related to the conduct of your business. However, none of these "employees" is an insured for:

      (1) "Bodily injury" or "personal and advertising injury":

         (a) To you, to your partners or members (if you are a partnership or joint venture), to your members (if you are a limited liability company), or to a co-"employee" while that co-"employee" is either in the course of his or her employment or while performing duties related to the conduct of your business;

         (b) To the spouse, child, parent, brother or sister of that co-"employee" as a consequence of Paragraph **(1)(a)** above;

(c) For which there is any obligation to share damages with or repay someone else who must pay damages because of the injury described in Paragraphs **(1)(a)** or **(b)** above; or

(d) Arising out of his or her providing or failing to provide professional health care services.

(2) "Property damage" to property:

(a) Owned, occupied or used by,

(b) Rented to, in the care, custody or control of, or over which physical control is being exercised for any purpose by

you, any of your "employees", any partner or member (if you are a partnership or joint venture), or any member (if you are a limited liability company).

b. Any person (other than your "employee") or any organization while acting as your real estate manager.

c. Any person or organization having proper temporary custody of your property if you die, but only:

(1) With respect to liability arising out of the maintenance or use of that property; and

(2) Until your legal representative has been appointed.

d. Your legal representative if you die, but only with respect to duties as such. That representative will have all your rights and duties under this Coverage Part.

3. With respect to "mobile equipment" registered in your name under any motor vehicle registration law, any person is an insured while driving such equipment along a public highway with your permission. Any other person or organization responsible for the conduct of such person is also an insured, but only with respect to liability arising out of the operation of the equipment, and only if no other insurance of any kind is available to that person or organization for this liability. However, no person or organization is an insured with respect to:

a. "Bodily injury" to a co-"employee" of the person driving the equipment; or

b. "Property damage" to property owned by, rented to, in the charge of or occupied by you or the employer of any person who is an insured under this provision.

4. Any organization you newly acquire or form, other than a partnership, joint venture or limited liability company, and over which you maintain ownership or majority interest, will qualify as a Named Insured if there is no other similar insurance available to that organization. However:

a. Coverage under this provision is afforded only until the 90th day after you acquire or form the organization or the end of the policy period, whichever is earlier;

b. Coverage **A** does not apply to "bodily injury" or "property damage" that occurred before you acquired or formed the organization; and

c. Coverage **B** does not apply to "personal and advertising injury" arising out of an offense committed before you acquired or formed the organization.

No person or organization is an insured with respect to the conduct of any current or past partnership, joint venture or limited liability company that is not shown as a Named Insured in the Declarations.

SECTION III – LIMITS OF INSURANCE

1. The Limits of Insurance shown in the Declarations and the rules below fix the most we will pay regardless of the number of:

a. Insureds;

b. Claims made or "suits" brought; or

c. Persons or organizations making claims or bringing "suits".

2. The General Aggregate Limit is the most we will pay for the sum of:

a. Medical expenses under Coverage **C**;

b. Damages under Coverage **A,** except damages because of "bodily injury" or "property damage" included in the "products-completed operations hazard"; and

c. Damages under Coverage **B**.

3. The Products-Completed Operations Aggregate Limit is the most we will pay under Coverage **A** for damages because of "bodily injury" and "property damage" included in the "products-completed operations hazard".

4. Subject to **2.** above, the Personal and Advertising Injury Limit is the most we will pay under Coverage **B** for the sum of all damages because of all "personal and advertising injury" sustained by any one person or organization.

         CG 00 02 07 98

5. Subject to **2.** or **3.** above, whichever applies, the Each Occurrence Limit is the most we will pay for the sum of:

   a. Damages under Coverage **A**; and

   b. Medical expenses under Coverage **C**

   because of all "bodily injury" and "property damage" arising out of any one "occurrence".

6. Subject to **5.** above, the Damage To Premises Rented To You Limit is the most we will pay under Coverage **A** for damages because of "property damage" to any one premises, while rented to you, or in the case of damage by fire, while rented to you or temporarily occupied by you with permission of the owner.

7. Subject to **5.** above, the Medical Expense Limit is the most we will pay under Coverage **C** for all medical expenses because of "bodily injury" sustained by any one person.

The Limits of Insurance of this Coverage Part apply separately to each consecutive annual period and to any remaining period of less than 12 months, starting with the beginning of the policy period shown in the Declarations, unless the policy period is extended after issuance for an additional period of less than 12 months. In that case, the additional period will be deemed part of the last preceding period for purposes of determining the Limits of Insurance.

SECTION IV – COMMERCIAL GENERAL LIABILITY CONDITIONS

1. Bankruptcy

Bankruptcy or insolvency of the insured or of the insured's estate will not relieve us of our obligations under this Coverage Part.

2. Duties In The Event Of Occurrence, Offense, Claim Or Suit

   a. You must see to it that we are notified as soon as practicable of an "occurrence" or offense which may result in a claim. To the extent possible, notice should include:

   (1) How, when and where the "occurrence" or offense took place;

   (2) The names and addresses of any injured persons and witnesses; and

   (3) The nature and location of any injury or damage arising out of the "occurrence" or offense.

   Notice of an "occurrence" or offense is not notice of a claim.

   b. If a claim is received by any insured, you must:

   (1) Immediately record the specifics of the claim and the date received; and

   (2) Notify us as soon as practicable.

   You must see to it that we receive written notice of the claim as soon as practicable.

   c. You and any other involved insured must:

   (1) Immediately send us copies of any demands, notices, summonses or legal papers received in connection with the claim or a "suit";

   (2) Authorize us to obtain records and other information;

   (3) Cooperate with us in the investigation or settlement of the claim or defense against the "suit"; and

   (4) Assist us, upon our request, in the enforcement of any right against any person or organization which may be liable to the insured because of injury or damage to which this insurance may also apply.

   d. No insured will, except at that insured's own cost, voluntarily make a payment, assume any obligation, or incur any expense, other than for first aid, without our consent.

3. Legal Action Against Us

No person or organization has a right under this Coverage Part:

   a. To join us as a party or otherwise bring us into a "suit" asking for damages from an insured; or

   b. To sue us on this Coverage Part unless all of its terms have been fully complied with.

A person or organization may sue us to recover on an agreed settlement or on a final judgment against an insured obtained after an actual trial; but we will not be liable for damages that are not payable under the terms of this Coverage Part or that are in excess of the applicable limit of insurance. An agreed settlement means a settlement and release of liability signed by us, the insured and the claimant or the claimant's legal representative.

4. Other Insurance

If other valid and collectible insurance is available to the insured for a loss we cover under Coverages **A** or **B** of this Coverage Part, our obligations are limited as follows:

   a. **Primary Insurance**

   This insurance is primary except when **b.** below applies. If this insurance is primary, our obligations are not affected unless any of the other insurance is also primary. Then, we will share with all that other insurance by the method described in **c.** below.

b. Excess Insurance

This insurance is excess over:

(1) Any of the other insurance, whether primary, excess, contingent or on any other basis:

(a) That is effective prior to the beginning of the policy period shown in the Declarations of this insurance and applies to "bodily injury" or "property damage" on other than a claims-made basis, if:

(i) No Retroactive Date is shown in the Declarations of this insurance; or

(ii) The other insurance has a policy period which continues after the Retroactive Date shown in the Declarations of this insurance;

(b) That is Fire, Extended Coverage, Builders' Risk, Installation Risk or similar coverage for "your work";

(c) That is Fire insurance for premises rented to you or temporarily occupied by you with permission of the owner;

(d) That is insurance purchased by you to cover your liability as a tenant for "property damage" to premises rented to you or temporarily occupied by you with permission of the owner; or

(e) If the loss arises out of the maintenance or use of aircraft, "autos" or watercraft to the extent not subject to Exclusion **g.** of Section **I** – Coverage **A** – Bodily Injury And Property Damage Liability.

(2) Any other primary insurance available to you covering liability for damages arising out of the premises or operations for which you have been added as an additional insured by attachment of an endorsement.

When this insurance is excess, we will have no duty under Coverages **A** or **B** to defend the insured against any "suit" if any other insurer has a duty to defend the insured against that "suit". If no other insurer defends, we will undertake to do so, but we will be entitled to the insured's rights against all those other insurers.

When this insurance is excess over other insurance, we will pay only our share of the amount of the loss, if any, that exceeds the sum of:

(1) The total amount that all such other insurance would pay for the loss in the absence of this insurance; and

(2) The total of all deductible and self-insured amounts under all that other insurance.

We will share the remaining loss, if any, with any other insurance that is not described in this Excess Insurance provision and was not bought specifically to apply in excess of the Limits of Insurance shown in the Declarations of this Coverage Part.

c. Method Of Sharing

If all of the other insurance permits contribution by equal shares, we will follow this method also. Under this approach each insurer contributes equal amounts until it has paid its applicable limit of insurance or none of the loss remains, whichever comes first.

If any of the other insurance does not permit contribution by equal shares, we will contribute by limits. Under this method, each insurer's share is based on the ratio of its applicable limit of insurance to the total applicable limits of insurance of all insurers.

5. Premium Audit

a. We will compute all premiums for this Coverage Part in accordance with our rules and rates.

b. Premium shown in this Coverage Part as advance premium is a deposit premium only. At the close of each audit period we will compute the earned premium for that period. Audit premiums are due and payable on notice to the first Named Insured. If the sum of the advance and audit premiums paid for the policy period is greater than the earned premium, we will return the excess to the first Named Insured.

c. The first Named Insured must keep records of the information we need for premium computation, and send us copies at such times as we may request.

6. Representations

By accepting this policy, you agree:

a. The statements in the Declarations are accurate and complete;

b. Those statements are based upon representations you made to us; and

c. We have issued this policy in reliance upon your representations.

7. Separation Of Insureds

Except with respect to the Limits of Insurance, and any rights or duties specifically assigned in this Coverage Part to the first Named Insured, this insurance applies:

a. As if each Named Insured were the only Named Insured; and

b. Separately to each insured against whom claim is made or "suit" is brought.

       CG 00 02 07 98   ☐

8. Transfer Of Rights Of Recovery Against Others To Us

If the insured has rights to recover all or part of any payment we have made under this Coverage Part, those rights are transferred to us. The insured must do nothing after loss to impair them. At our request, the insured will bring "suit" or transfer those rights to us and help us enforce them.

9. When We Do Not Renew

If we decide not to renew this Coverage Part, we will mail or deliver to the first Named Insured shown in the Declarations written notice of the nonrenewal not less than 30 days before the expiration date.

If notice is mailed, proof of mailing will be sufficient proof of notice.

10. Your Right To Claim And "Occurrence" Information

We will provide the first Named Insured shown in the Declarations the following information relating to this and any preceding general liability claims-made Coverage Part we have issued to you during the previous three years:

a. A list or other record of each "occurrence", not previously reported to any other insurer, of which we were notified in accordance with Paragraph **2.a.** of the Section **IV** – Duties In The Event Of Occurrence, Offense, Claim Or Suit Condition. We will include the date and brief description of the "occurrence" if that information was in the notice we received.

b. A summary by policy year, of payments made and amounts reserved, stated separately, under any applicable General Aggregate Limit and Products-Completed Operations Aggregate Limit.

Amounts reserved are based on our judgment. They are subject to change and should not be regarded as ultimate settlement values.

You must not disclose this information to any claimant or any claimant's representative without our consent.

If we cancel or elect not to renew this Coverage Part, we will provide such information no later than 30 days before the date of policy termination. In other circumstances, we will provide this information only if we receive a written request from the first Named Insured within 60 days after the end of the policy period. In this case, we will provide this information within 45 days of receipt of the request.

We compile claim and "occurrence" information for our own business purposes and exercise reasonable care in doing so. In providing this information to the first Named Insured, we make no representations or warranties to insureds, insurers, or others to whom this information is furnished by or on behalf of any insured. Cancellation or non-renewal will be effective even if we inadvertently provide inaccurate information.

SECTION V – EXTENDED REPORTING PERIODS

1. We will provide one or more Extended Reporting Periods, as described below, if:

a. This Coverage Part is canceled or not renewed; or

b. We renew or replace this Coverage Part with insurance that:

(1) Has a Retroactive Date later than the date shown in the Declarations of this Coverage Part; or

(2) Does not apply to "bodily injury", "property damage" or "personal and advertising injury" on a claims-made basis.

2. Extended Reporting Periods do not extend the policy period or change the scope of coverage provided. They apply only to claims for:

a. "Bodily injury" or "property damage" that occurs before the end of the policy period but not before the Retroactive Date, if any, shown in the Declarations; or

b. "Personal injury and advertising injury" caused by an offense committed before the end of the policy period but not before the Retroactive Date, if any, shown in the Declarations.

Once in effect, Extended Reporting Periods may not be canceled.

3. A Basic Extended Reporting Period is automatically provided without additional charge. This period starts with the end of the policy period and lasts for:

a. Five years with respect to claims because of "bodily injury" and "property damage" arising out of an "occurrence" reported to us, not later than 60 days after the end of the policy period, in accordance with Paragraph **2.a.** of the Section **IV** – Duties In The Event Of Occurrence, Offense, Claim Or Suit Condition;

b. Five years with respect to claims because of "personal and advertising injury" arising out of an offense reported to us, not later than 60 days after the end of the policy period, in accordance with Paragraph **2.a.** of the Section **IV** – Duties In The Event Of Occurrence, Offense, Claim Or Suit Condition; and

c. Sixty days with respect to claims arising from "occurrences" or offenses not previously reported to us.

The Basic Extended Reporting Period does not apply to claims that are covered under any subsequent insurance you purchase, or that would be covered but for exhaustion of the amount of insurance applicable to such claims.

4. The Basic Extended Reporting Period does not reinstate or increase the Limits of Insurance.

5. A Supplemental Extended Reporting Period of unlimited duration is available, but only by an endorsement and for an extra charge. This supplemental period starts when the Basic Extended Reporting Period, set forth in Paragraph **3.** above, ends.

You must give us a written request for the endorsement within 60 days after the end of the policy period. The Supplemental Extended Reporting Period will not go into effect unless you pay the additional premium promptly when due.

We will determine the additional premium in accordance with our rules and rates. In doing so, we may take into account the following:

a. The exposures insured;

b. Previous types and amounts of insurance;

c. Limits of Insurance available under this Coverage Part for future payment of damages; and

d. Other related factors.

The additional premium will not exceed 200% of the annual premium for this Coverage Part.

This endorsement shall set forth the terms, not inconsistent with this Section, applicable to the Supplemental Extended Reporting Period, including a provision to the effect that the insurance afforded for claims first received during such period is excess over any other valid and collectible insurance available under policies in force after the Supplemental Extended Reporting Period starts.

6. If the Supplemental Extended Reporting Period is in effect, we will provide the supplemental aggregate limits of insurance described below, but only for claims first received and recorded during the Supplemental Extended Reporting Period.

The supplemental aggregate limits of insurance will be equal to the dollar amount shown in the Declarations in effect at the end of the policy period for such of the following limits of insurance for which a dollar amount has been entered:

General Aggregate Limit
Products-Completed Operations Aggregate Limit

Paragraphs **2.** and **3.** of Section **III** – Limits Of Insurance will be amended accordingly. The Personal and Advertising Injury Limit, the Each Occurrence Limit and the Fire Damage Limit shown in the Declarations will then continue to apply, as set forth in Paragraphs **4.**, **5.** and **6.** of that Section.

SECTION VI – DEFINITIONS

1. "Advertisement" means a notice that is broadcast or published to the general public or specific market segments about your goods, products or services for the purpose of attracting customers or supporters.

2. "Auto" means a land motor vehicle, trailer or semitrailer designed for travel on public roads, including any attached machinery or equipment. But "auto" does not include "mobile equipment".

3. "Bodily injury" means bodily injury, sickness or disease sustained by a person, including death resulting from any of these at any time.

4. "Coverage territory" means:

   a. The United States of America (including its territories and possessions), Puerto Rico and Canada;

   b. International waters or airspace, provided the injury or damage does not occur in the course of travel or transportation to or from any place not included in **a.** above; or

   c. All parts of the world if:

      (1) The injury or damage arises out of:

         (a) Goods or products made or sold by you in the territory described in **a.** above; or

         (b) The activities of a person whose home is in the territory described in **a.** above, but is away for a short time on your business; and

      (2) The insured's responsibility to pay damages is determined in a "suit" on the merits, in the territory described in **a.** above or in a settlement we agree to.

5. "Employee" includes a "leased worker". "Employee" does not include a "temporary worker".

6. "Executive officer" means a person holding any of the officer positions created by your charter, constitution, by-laws or any other similar governing document.

7. "Hostile fire" means one which becomes uncontrollable or breaks out from where it was intended to be.

8. "Impaired property" means tangible property, other than "your product" or "your work", that cannot be used or is less useful because:

   a. It incorporates "your product" or "your work" that is known or thought to be defective, deficient, inadequate or dangerous; or

   b. You have failed to fulfill the terms of a contract or agreement;

   if such property can be restored to use by:

   a. The repair, replacement, adjustment or removal of "your product" or "your work"; or

   b. Your fulfilling the terms of the contract or agreement.

9. "Insured contract" means:

   a. A contract for a lease of premises. However, that portion of the contract for a lease of premises that indemnifies any person or organization for damage by fire to premises while rented to you or temporarily occupied by you with permission of the owner is not an "insured contract";

   b. A sidetrack agreement;

   c. Any easement or license agreement, except in connection with construction or demolition operations on or within 50 feet of a railroad;

   d. An obligation, as required by ordinance, to indemnify a municipality, except in connection with work for a municipality;

   e. An elevator maintenance agreement;

   f. That part of any other contract or agreement pertaining to your business (including an indemnification of a municipality in connection with work performed for a municipality) under which you assume the tort liability of another party to pay for "bodily injury" or "property damage" to a third person or organization. Tort liability means a liability that would be imposed by law in the absence of any contract or agreement.

   Paragraph f. does not include that part of any contract or agreement:

   (1) That indemnifies a railroad for "bodily injury" or "property damage" arising out of construction or demolition operations, within 50 feet of any railroad property and affecting any railroad bridge or trestle, tracks, road-beds, tunnel, underpass or crossing;

   (2) That indemnifies an architect, engineer or surveyor for injury or damage arising out of:

      (a) Preparing, approving, or failing to prepare or approve, maps, shop drawings, opinions, reports, surveys, field orders, change orders or drawings and specifications; or

      (b) Giving directions or instructions, or failing to give them, if that is the primary cause of the injury or damage; or

   (3) Under which the insured, if an architect, engineer or surveyor, assumes liability for an injury or damage arising out of the insured's rendering or failure to render professional services, including those listed in (2) above and supervisory, inspection, architectural or engineering activities.

10. "Leased worker" means a person leased to you by a labor leasing firm under an agreement between you and the labor leasing firm, to perform duties related to the conduct of your business. "Leased worker" does not include a "temporary worker".

11. "Loading or unloading" means the handling of property:

    a. After it is moved from the place where it is accepted for movement into or onto an aircraft, watercraft or "auto";

    b. While it is in or on an aircraft, watercraft or "auto"; or

    c. While it is being moved from an aircraft, watercraft or "auto" to the place where it is finally delivered;

    but "loading or unloading" does not include the movement of property by means of a mechanical device, other than a hand truck, that is not attached to the aircraft, watercraft or "auto".

12. "Mobile equipment" means any of the following types of land vehicles, including any attached machinery or equipment:

    a. Bulldozers, farm machinery, forklifts and other vehicles designed for use principally off public roads;

    b. Vehicles maintained for use solely on or next to premises you own or rent;

    c. Vehicles that travel on crawler treads;

    d. Vehicles, whether self-propelled or not, maintained primarily to provide mobility to permanently mounted:

       (1) Power cranes, shovels, loaders, diggers or drills; or

       (2) Road construction or resurfacing equipment such as graders, scrapers or rollers;

    e. Vehicles not described in a., b., c. or d. above that are not self-propelled and are maintained primarily to provide mobility to permanently attached equipment of the following types:

       (1) Air compressors, pumps and generators, including spraying, welding, building cleaning, geophysical exploration, lighting and well servicing equipment; or

       (2) Cherry pickers and similar devices used to raise or lower workers;

f. Vehicles not described in **a., b., c.** or **d.** above maintained primarily for purposes other than the transportation of persons or cargo.

However, self-propelled vehicles with the following types of permanently attached equipment are not "mobile equipment" but will be considered "autos":

(1) Equipment designed primarily for:

(a) Snow removal;

(b) Road maintenance, but not construction or resurfacing; or

(c) Street cleaning;

(2) Cherry pickers and similar devices mounted on automobile or truck chassis and used to raise or lower workers; and

(3) Air compressors, pumps and generators, including spraying, welding, building cleaning, geophysical exploration, lighting and well servicing equipment.

13. "Occurrence" means an accident, including continuous or repeated exposure to substantially the same general harmful conditions.

14. "Personal and advertising injury" means injury, including consequential "bodily injury", arising out of one or more of the following offenses:

a. False arrest, detention or imprisonment;

b. Malicious prosecution;

c. The wrongful eviction from, wrongful entry into, or invasion of the right of private occupancy of a room, dwelling or premises that a person occupies, committed by or on behalf of its owner, landlord or lessor;

d. Oral or written publication of material that slanders or libels a person or organization or disparages a person's or organization's goods, products or services;

e. Oral or written publication of material that violates a person's right of privacy;

f. The use of another's advertising idea in your "advertisement"; or

g. Infringing upon another's copyright, trade dress or slogan in your "advertisement".

15. "Pollutants" mean any solid, liquid, gaseous or thermal irritant or contaminant, including smoke, vapor, soot, fumes, acids, alkalis, chemicals and waste. Waste includes materials to be recycled, reconditioned or reclaimed.

16. "Products-completed operations hazard":

a. Includes all "bodily injury" and "property damage" occurring away from premises you own or rent and arising out of "your product" or "your work" except:

(1) Products that are still in your physical possession; or

(2) Work that has not yet been completed or abandoned. However, "your work" will be deemed completed at the earliest of the following times:

(a) When all of the work called for in your contract has been completed.

(b) When all of the work to be done at the job site has been completed if your contract calls for work at more than one job site.

(c) When that part of the work done at a job site has been put to its intended use by any person or organization other than another contractor or subcontractor working on the same project.

Work that may need service, maintenance, correction, repair or replacement, but which is otherwise complete, will be treated as completed.

b. Does not include "bodily injury" or "property damage" arising out of:

(1) The transportation of property, unless the injury or damage arises out of a condition in or on a vehicle not owned or operated by you, and that condition was created by the "loading or unloading" of that vehicle by any insured;

(2) The existence of tools, uninstalled equipment or abandoned or unused materials; or

(3) Products or operations for which the classification, listed in the Declarations or in a policy schedule, states that products-completed operations are subject to the General Aggregate Limit.

17. "Property damage" means:

a. Physical injury to tangible property, including all resulting loss of use of that property. All such loss of use shall be deemed to occur at the time of the physical injury that caused it; or

b. Loss of use of tangible property that is not physically injured. All such loss of use shall be deemed to occur at the time of the "occurrence" that caused it.

18. "Suit" means a civil proceeding in which damages because of "bodily injury", "property damage" or "personal and advertising injury" to which this insurance applies are alleged. "Suit" includes:

a. An arbitration proceeding in which such damages are claimed and to which the insured must submit or does submit with our consent; or

b. Any other alternative dispute resolution proceeding in which such damages are claimed and to which the insured submits with our consent.

19. "Temporary worker" means a person who is furnished to you to substitute for a permanent "employee" on leave or to meet seasonal or short-term workload conditions.

20. "Your product" means:

a. Any goods or products, other than real property, manufactured, sold, handled, distributed or disposed of by:

(1) You;

(2) Others trading under your name; or

(3) A person or organization whose business or assets you have acquired; and

b. Containers (other than vehicles), materials, parts or equipment furnished in connection with such goods or products.

"Your product" includes:

a. Warranties or representations made at any time with respect to the fitness, quality, durability, performance or use of "your product"; and

b. The providing of or failure to provide warnings or instructions.

"Your product" does not include vending machines or other property rented to or located for the use of others but not sold.

21. "Your work" means:

a. Work or operations performed by you or on your behalf; and

b. Materials, parts or equipment furnished in connection with such work or operations.

"Your work" includes:

a. Warranties or representations made at any time with respect to the fitness, quality, durability, performance or use of "your work"; and

b. The providing of or failure to provide warnings or instructions.

SAMPLE

COMMERCIAL GENERAL LIABILITY
CG 00 01 10 01

COMMERCIAL GENERAL LIABILITY COVERAGE FORM

Various provisions in this policy restrict coverage. Read the entire policy carefully to determine rights, duties and what is and is not covered.

Throughout this policy the words "you" and "your" refer to the Named Insured shown in the Declarations, and any other person or organization qualifying as a Named Insured under this policy. The words "we", "us" and "our" refer to the company providing this insurance.

The word "insured" means any person or organization qualifying as such under Section **II** – Who Is An Insured.

Other words and phrases that appear in quotation marks have special meaning. Refer to Section **V** – Definitions.

SECTION I – COVERAGES

COVERAGE A BODILY INJURY AND PROPERTY DAMAGE LIABILITY

1. Insuring Agreement

a. We will pay those sums that the insured becomes legally obligated to pay as damages because of "bodily injury" or "property damage" to which this insurance applies. We will have the right and duty to defend the insured against any "suit" seeking those damages. However, we will have no duty to defend the insured against any "suit" seeking damages for "bodily injury" or "property damage" to which this insurance does not apply. We may, at our discretion, investigate any "occurrence" and settle any claim or "suit" that may result. But:

(1) The amount we will pay for damages is limited as described in Section **III** – Limits Of Insurance; and

(2) Our right and duty to defend ends when we have used up the applicable limit of insurance in the payment of judgments or settlements under Coverages **A** or **B** or medical expenses under Coverage **C**.

No other obligation or liability to pay sums or perform acts or services is covered unless explicitly provided for under Supplementary Payments – Coverages **A** and **B**.

b. This insurance applies to "bodily injury" and "property damage" only if:

(1) The "bodily injury" or "property damage" is caused by an "occurrence" that takes place in the "coverage territory";

(2) The "bodily injury" or "property damage" occurs during the policy period; and

(3) Prior to the policy period, no insured listed under Paragraph **1.** of Section **II** – Who Is An Insured and no "employee" authorized by you to give or receive notice of an "occurrence" or claim, knew that the "bodily injury" or "property damage" had occurred, in whole or in part. If such a listed insured or authorized "employee" knew, prior to the policy period, that the "bodily injury" or "property damage" occurred, then any continuation, change or resumption of such "bodily injury" or "property damage" during or after the policy period will be deemed to have been known prior to the policy period.

c. "Bodily injury" or "property damage" which occurs during the policy period and was not, prior to the policy period, known to have occurred by any insured listed under Paragraph **1.** of Section **II** – Who Is An Insured or any "employee" authorized by you to give or receive notice of an "occurrence" or claim, includes any continuation, change or resumption of that "bodily injury" or "property damage" after the end of the policy period.

d. "Bodily injury" or "property damage" will be deemed to have been known to have occurred at the earliest time when any insured listed under Paragraph **1.** of Section **II** – Who Is An Insured or any "employee" authorized by you to give or receive notice of an "occurrence" or claim:

(1) Reports all, or any part, of the "bodily injury" or "property damage" to us or any other insurer;

(2) Receives a written or verbal demand or claim for damages because of the "bodily injury" or "property damage"; or

(3) Becomes aware by any other means that "bodily injury" or "property damage" has occurred or has begun to occur.

e. Damages because of "bodily injury" include damages claimed by any person or organization for care, loss of services or death resulting at any time from the "bodily injury".

2. Exclusions

This insurance does not apply to:

a. Expected Or Intended Injury

"Bodily injury" or "property damage" expected or intended from the standpoint of the insured. This exclusion does not apply to "bodily injury" resulting from the use of reasonable force to protect persons or property.

b. Contractual Liability

"Bodily injury" or "property damage" for which the insured is obligated to pay damages by reason of the assumption of liability in a contract or agreement. This exclusion does not apply to liability for damages:

(1) That the insured would have in the absence of the contract or agreement; or

(2) Assumed in a contract or agreement that is an "insured contract", provided the "bodily injury" or "property damage" occurs subsequent to the execution of the contract or agreement. Solely for the purposes of liability assumed in an "insured contract", reasonable attorney fees and necessary litigation expenses incurred by or for a party other than an insured are deemed to be damages because of "bodily injury" or "property damage", provided:

(a) Liability to such party for, or for the cost of, that party's defense has also been assumed in the same "insured contract"; and

(b) Such attorney fees and litigation expenses are for defense of that party against a civil or alternative dispute resolution proceeding in which damages to which this insurance applies are alleged.

c. Liquor Liability

"Bodily injury" or "property damage" for which any insured may be held liable by reason of:

(1) Causing or contributing to the intoxication of any person;

(2) The furnishing of alcoholic beverages to a person under the legal drinking age or under the influence of alcohol; or

(3) Any statute, ordinance or regulation relating to the sale, gift, distribution or use of alcoholic beverages.

This exclusion applies only if you are in the business of manufacturing, distributing, selling, serving or furnishing alcoholic beverages.

d. Workers' Compensation And Similar Laws

Any obligation of the insured under a workers' compensation, disability benefits or unemployment compensation law or any similar law.

e. Employer's Liability

"Bodily injury" to:

(1) An "employee" of the insured arising out of and in the course of:

(a) Employment by the insured; or

(b) Performing duties related to the conduct of the insured's business; or

(2) The spouse, child, parent, brother or sister of that "employee" as a consequence of Paragraph **(1)** above.

This exclusion applies:

(1) Whether the insured may be liable as an employer or in any other capacity; and

(2) To any obligation to share damages with or repay someone else who must pay damages because of the injury.

This exclusion does not apply to liability assumed by the insured under an "insured contract".

f. Pollution

(1) "Bodily injury" or "property damage" arising out of the actual, alleged or threatened discharge, dispersal, seepage, migration, release or escape of "pollutants":

(a) At or from any premises, site or location which is or was at any time owned or occupied by, or rented or loaned to, any insured. However, this subparagraph does not apply to:

(i) "Bodily injury" if sustained within a building and caused by smoke, fumes, vapor or soot from equipment used to heat that building;

(ii) "Bodily injury" or "property damage" for which you may be held liable, if you are a contractor and the owner or lessee of such premises, site or location has been added to your policy as an additional insured with respect to your ongoing operations performed for that additional insured at that premises, site or location and such premises, site or location is not and never was owned or occupied by, or rented or loaned to, any insured, other than that additional insured; or

(iii) "Bodily injury" or "property damage" arising out of heat, smoke or fumes from a "hostile fire";

(b) At or from any premises, site or location which is or was at any time used by or for any insured or others for the handling, storage, disposal, processing or treatment of waste;

(c) Which are or were at any time transported, handled, stored, treated, disposed of, or processed as waste by or for:

(i) Any insured; or

(ii) Any person or organization for whom you may be legally responsible; or

(d) At or from any premises, site or location on which any insured or any contractors or subcontractors working directly or indirectly on any insured's behalf are performing operations if the "pollutants" are brought on or to the premises, site or location in connection with such operations by such insured, contractor or subcontractor. However, this subparagraph does not apply to:

(i) "Bodily injury" or "property damage" arising out of the escape of fuels, lubricants or other operating fluids which are needed to perform the normal electrical, hydraulic or mechanical functions necessary for the operation of "mobile equipment" or its parts, if such fuels, lubricants or other operating fluids escape from a vehicle part designed to hold, store or receive them. This exception does not apply if the "bodily injury" or "property damage" arises out of the intentional discharge, dispersal or release of the fuels, lubricants or other operating fluids, or if such fuels, lubricants or other operating fluids are brought on or to the premises, site or location with the intent that they be discharged, dispersed or released as part of the operations being performed by such insured, contractor or subcontractor;

(ii) "Bodily injury" or "property damage" sustained within a building and caused by the release of gases, fumes or vapors from materials brought into that building in connection with operations being performed by you or on your behalf by a contractor or subcontractor; or

(iii) "Bodily injury" or "property damage" arising out of heat, smoke or fumes from a "hostile fire".

(e) At or from any premises, site or location on which any insured or any contractors or subcontractors working directly or indirectly on any insured's behalf are performing operations if the operations are to test for, monitor, clean up, remove, contain, treat, detoxify or neutralize, or in any way respond to, or assess the effects of, "pollutants".

(2) Any loss, cost or expense arising out of any:

(a) Request, demand, order or statutory or regulatory requirement that any insured or others test for, monitor, clean up, remove, contain, treat, detoxify or neutralize, or in any way respond to, or assess the effects of, "pollutants"; or

(b) Claim or "suit" by or on behalf of a governmental authority for damages because of testing for, monitoring, cleaning up, removing, containing, treating, detoxifying or neutralizing, or in any way responding to, or assessing the effects of, "pollutants".

However, this paragraph does not apply to liability for damages because of "property damage" that the insured would have in the absence of such request, demand, order or statutory or regulatory requirement, or such claim or "suit" by or on behalf of a governmental authority.

g. **Aircraft, Auto Or Watercraft**

"Bodily injury" or "property damage" arising out of the ownership, maintenance, use or entrustment to others of any aircraft, "auto" or watercraft owned or operated by or rented or loaned to any insured. Use includes operation and "loading or unloading".

This exclusion applies even if the claims against any insured allege negligence or other wrongdoing in the supervision, hiring, employment, training or monitoring of others by that insured, if the "occurrence" which caused the "bodily injury" or "property damage" involved the ownership, maintenance, use or entrustment to others of any aircraft, "auto" or watercraft that is owned or operated by or rented or loaned to any insured.

This exclusion does not apply to:

(1) A watercraft while ashore on premises you own or rent;

(2) A watercraft you do not own that is:

(a) Less than 26 feet long; and

(b) Not being used to carry persons or property for a charge;

(3) Parking an "auto" on, or on the ways next to, premises you own or rent, provided the "auto" is not owned by or rented or loaned to you or the insured;

(4) Liability assumed under any "insured contract" for the ownership, maintenance or use of aircraft or watercraft; or

(5) "Bodily injury" or "property damage" arising out of the operation of any of the equipment listed in Paragraph **f.(2)** or **f.(3)** of the definition of "mobile equipment".

h. **Mobile Equipment**

"Bodily injury" or "property damage" arising out of:

(1) The transportation of "mobile equipment" by an "auto" owned or operated by or rented or loaned to any insured; or

(2) The use of "mobile equipment" in, or while in practice for, or while being prepared for, any prearranged racing, speed, demolition, or stunting activity.

i. **War**

"Bodily injury" or "property damage" due to war, whether or not declared, or any act or condition incident to war. War includes civil war, insurrection, rebellion or revolution. This exclusion applies only to liability assumed under a contract or agreement.

j. **Damage To Property**

"Property damage" to:

(1) Property you own, rent, or occupy, including any costs or expenses incurred by you, or any other person, organization or entity, for repair, replacement, enhancement, restoration or maintenance of such property for any reason, including prevention of injury to a person or damage to another's property;

(2) Premises you sell, give away or abandon, if the "property damage" arises out of any part of those premises;

(3) Property loaned to you;

(4) Personal property in the care, custody or control of the insured;

(5) That particular part of real property on which you or any contractors or subcontractors working directly or indirectly on your behalf are performing operations, if the "property damage" arises out of those operations; or

(6) That particular part of any property that must be restored, repaired or replaced because "your work" was incorrectly performed on it.

Paragraphs **(1), (3)** and **(4)** of this exclusion do not apply to "property damage" (other than damage by fire) to premises, including the contents of such premises, rented to you for a period of 7 or fewer consecutive days. A separate limit of insurance applies to Damage To Premises Rented To You as described in Section **III** – Limits Of Insurance.

Paragraph **(2)** of this exclusion does not apply if the premises are "your work" and were never occupied, rented or held for rental by you.

Paragraphs **(3), (4), (5)** and **(6)** of this exclusion do not apply to liability assumed under a sidetrack agreement.

Paragraph **(6)** of this exclusion does not apply to "property damage" included in the "products-completed operations hazard".

k. Damage To Your Product

"Property damage" to "your product" arising out of it or any part of it.

l. Damage To Your Work

"Property damage" to "your work" arising out of it or any part of it and included in the "products-completed operations hazard".

This exclusion does not apply if the damaged work or the work out of which the damage arises was performed on your behalf by a subcontractor.

m. Damage To Impaired Property Or Property Not Physically Injured

"Property damage" to "impaired property" or property that has not been physically injured, arising out of:

(1) A defect, deficiency, inadequacy or dangerous condition in "your product" or "your work"; or

(2) A delay or failure by you or anyone acting on your behalf to perform a contract or agreement in accordance with its terms.

This exclusion does not apply to the loss of use of other property arising out of sudden and accidental physical injury to "your product" or "your work" after it has been put to its intended use.

n. Recall Of Products, Work Or Impaired Property

Damages claimed for any loss, cost or expense incurred by you or others for the loss of use, withdrawal, recall, inspection, repair, replacement, adjustment, removal or disposal of:

(1) "Your product";

(2) "Your work"; or

(3) "Impaired property";

if such product, work, or property is withdrawn or recalled from the market or from use by any person or organization because of a known or suspected defect, deficiency, inadequacy or dangerous condition in it.

o. Personal And Advertising Injury

"Bodily injury" arising out of "personal and advertising injury".

Exclusions **c.** through **n.** do not apply to damage by fire to premises while rented to you or temporarily occupied by you with permission of the owner. A separate limit of insurance applies to this coverage as described in Section **III** – Limits Of Insurance.

COVERAGE B PERSONAL AND ADVERTISING INJURY LIABILITY

1. Insuring Agreement

a. We will pay those sums that the insured becomes legally obligated to pay as damages because of "personal and advertising injury" to which this insurance applies. We will have the right and duty to defend the insured against any "suit" seeking those damages. However, we will have no duty to defend the insured against any "suit" seeking damages for "personal and advertising injury" to which this insurance does not apply. We may, at our discretion, investigate any offense and settle any claim or "suit" that may result. But:

(1) The amount we will pay for damages is limited as described in Section **III** – Limits Of Insurance ; and

(2) Our right and duty to defend end when we have used up the applicable limit of insurance in the payment of judgments or settlements under Coverages **A** or **B** or medical expenses under Coverage **C**.

No other obligation or liability to pay sums or perform acts or services is covered unless explicitly provided for under Supplementary Payments – Coverages **A** and **B**.

b. This insurance applies to "personal and advertising injury" caused by an offense arising out of your business but only if the offense was committed in the "coverage territory" during the policy period.

2. Exclusions

This insurance does not apply to:

a. Knowing Violation Of Rights Of Another

"Personal and advertising injury" caused by or at the direction of the insured with the knowledge that the act would violate the rights of another and would inflict "personal and advertising injury".

b. Material Published With Knowledge Of Falsity

"Personal and advertising injury" arising out of oral or written publication of material, if done by or at the direction of the insured with knowledge of its falsity.

c. Material Published Prior To Policy Period

"Personal and advertising injury" arising out of oral or written publication of material whose first publication took place before the beginning of the policy period.

d. Criminal Acts

"Personal and advertising injury" arising out of a criminal act committed by or at the direction of the insured.

e. Contractual Liability

"Personal and advertising injury" for which the insured has assumed liability in a contract or agreement. This exclusion does not apply to liability for damages that the insured would have in the absence of the contract or agreement.

f. Breach Of Contract

"Personal and advertising injury" arising out of a breach of contract, except an implied contract to use another's advertising idea in your "advertisement".

g. Quality Or Performance Of Goods – Failure To Conform To Statements

"Personal and advertising injury" arising out of the failure of goods, products or services to conform with any statement of quality or performance made in your "advertisement".

h. Wrong Description Of Prices

"Personal and advertising injury" arising out of the wrong description of the price of goods, products or services stated in your "advertisement".

i. Infringement Of Copyright, Patent, Trademark Or Trade Secret

"Personal and advertising injury" arising out of the infringement of copyright, patent, trademark, trade secret or other intellectual property rights.

However, this exclusion does not apply to infringement, in your "advertisement", of copyright, trade dress or slogan.

j. Insureds In Media And Internet Type Businesses

"Personal and advertising injury" committed by an insured whose business is:

(1) Advertising, broadcasting, publishing or telecasting;

(2) Designing or determining content of websites for others; or

(3) An Internet search, access, content or service provider.

However, this exclusion does not apply to Paragraphs **14.a., b.** and **c.** of "personal and advertising injury" under the Definitions Section.

For the purposes of this exclusion, the placing of frames, borders or links, or advertising, for you or others anywhere on the Internet, is not by itself, considered the business of advertising, broadcasting, publishing or telecasting.

k. Electronic Chatrooms Or Bulletin Boards

"Personal and advertising injury" arising out of an electronic chatroom or bulletin board the insured hosts, owns, or over which the insured exercises control.

     CG 00 01 10 01   ☐

l. Unauthorized Use Of Another's Name Or Product

"Personal and advertising injury" arising out of the unauthorized use of another's name or product in your e-mail address, domain name or metatag, or any other similar tactics to mislead another's potential customers.

m. Pollution

"Personal and advertising injury" arising out of the actual, alleged or threatened discharge, dispersal, seepage, migration, release or escape of "pollutants" at any time.

n. Pollution-Related

Any loss, cost or expense arising out of any:

(1) Request, demand or order that any insured or others test for, monitor, clean up, remove, contain, treat, detoxify or neutralize, or in any way respond to, or assess the effects of, "pollutants"; or

(2) Claim or suit by or on behalf of a governmental authority for damages because of testing for, monitoring, cleaning up, removing, containing, treating, detoxifying or neutralizing, or in any way responding to, or assessing the effects of, "pollutants".

COVERAGE C MEDICAL PAYMENTS

1. Insuring Agreement

a. We will pay medical expenses as described below for "bodily injury" caused by an accident:

(1) On premises you own or rent;

(2) On ways next to premises you own or rent; or

(3) Because of your operations;

provided that:

(1) The accident takes place in the "coverage territory" and during the policy period;

(2) The expenses are incurred and reported to us within one year of the date of the accident; and

(3) The injured person submits to examination, at our expense, by physicians of our choice as often as we reasonably require.

b. We will make these payments regardless of fault. These payments will not exceed the applicable limit of insurance. We will pay reasonable expenses for:

(1) First aid administered at the time of an accident;

(2) Necessary medical, surgical, x-ray and dental services, including prosthetic devices; and

(3) Necessary ambulance, hospital, professional nursing and funeral services.

2. Exclusions

We will not pay expenses for "bodily injury":

a. Any Insured

To any insured, except "volunteer workers".

b. Hired Person

To a person hired to do work for or on behalf of any insured or a tenant of any insured.

c. Injury On Normally Occupied Premises

To a person injured on that part of premises you own or rent that the person normally occupies.

d. Workers Compensation And Similar Laws

To a person, whether or not an "employee" of any insured, if benefits for the "bodily injury" are payable or must be provided under a workers' compensation or disability benefits law or a similar law.

e. Athletics Activities

To a person injured while taking part in athletics.

f. Products-Completed Operations Hazard

Included within the "products-completed operations hazard".

g. Coverage A Exclusions

Excluded under Coverage **A**.

h. War

Due to war, whether or not declared, or any act or condition incident to war. War includes civil war, insurrection, rebellion or revolution.

SUPPLEMENTARY PAYMENTS – COVERAGES A AND B

1. We will pay, with respect to any claim we investigate or settle, or any "suit" against an insured we defend:

a. All expenses we incur.

b. Up to $250 for cost of bail bonds required because of accidents or traffic law violations arising out of the use of any vehicle to which the Bodily Injury Liability Coverage applies. We do not have to furnish these bonds.

c. The cost of bonds to release attachments, but only for bond amounts within the applicable limit of insurance. We do not have to furnish these bonds.

d. All reasonable expenses incurred by the insured at our request to assist us in the investigation or defense of the claim or "suit", including actual loss of earnings up to $250 a day because of time off from work.

e. All costs taxed against the insured in the "suit".

f. Prejudgment interest awarded against the insured on that part of the judgment we pay. If we make an offer to pay the applicable limit of insurance, we will not pay any prejudgment interest based on that period of time after the offer.

g. All interest on the full amount of any judgment that accrues after entry of the judgment and before we have paid, offered to pay, or deposited in court the part of the judgment that is within the applicable limit of insurance.

These payments will not reduce the limits of insurance.

2. If we defend an insured against a "suit" and an indemnitee of the insured is also named as a party to the "suit", we will defend that indemnitee if all of the following conditions are met:

a. The "suit" against the indemnitee seeks damages for which the insured has assumed the liability of the indemnitee in a contract or agreement that is an "insured contract";

b. This insurance applies to such liability assumed by the insured;

c. The obligation to defend, or the cost of the defense of, that indemnitee, has also been assumed by the insured in the same "insured contract";

d. The allegations in the "suit" and the information we know about the "occurrence" are such that no conflict appears to exist between the interests of the insured and the interests of the indemnitee;

e. The indemnitee and the insured ask us to conduct and control the defense of that indemnitee against such "suit" and agree that we can assign the same counsel to defend the insured and the indemnitee; and

f. The indemnitee:

(1) Agrees in writing to:

(a) Cooperate with us in the investigation, settlement or defense of the "suit";

(b) Immediately send us copies of any demands, notices, summonses or legal papers received in connection with the "suit";

(c) Notify any other insurer whose coverage is available to the indemnitee; and

(d) Cooperate with us with respect to coordinating other applicable insurance available to the indemnitee; and

(2) Provides us with written authorization to:

(a) Obtain records and other information related to the "suit"; and

(b) Conduct and control the defense of the indemnitee in such "suit".

So long as the above conditions are met, attorneys' fees incurred by us in the defense of that indemnitee, necessary litigation expenses incurred by us and necessary litigation expenses incurred by the indemnitee at our request will be paid as Supplementary Payments. Notwithstanding the provisions of Paragraph **2.b.(2)** of Section I – Coverage **A** – Bodily Injury And Property Damage Liability, such payments will not be deemed to be damages for "bodily injury" and "property damage" and will not reduce the limits of insurance.

Our obligation to defend an insured's indemnitee and to pay for attorneys' fees and necessary litigation expenses as Supplementary Payments ends when:

a. We have used up the applicable limit of insurance in the payment of judgments or settlements; or

b. The conditions set forth above, or the terms of the agreement described in Paragraph **f.** above, are no longer met.

© ISO Properties, Inc., 2000   CG 00 01 10 01

SECTION II – WHO IS AN INSURED

1. If you are designated in the Declarations as:

   a. An individual, you and your spouse are insureds, but only with respect to the conduct of a business of which you are the sole owner.

   b. A partnership or joint venture, you are an insured. Your members, your partners, and their spouses are also insureds, but only with respect to the conduct of your business.

   c. A limited liability company, you are an insured. Your members are also insureds, but only with respect to the conduct of your business. Your managers are insureds, but only with respect to their duties as your managers.

   d. An organization other than a partnership, joint venture or limited liability company, you are an insured. Your "executive officers" and directors are insureds, but only with respect to their duties as your officers or directors. Your stockholders are also insureds, but only with respect to their liability as stockholders.

   e. A trust, you are an insured. Your trustees are also insureds, but only with respect to their duties as trustees.

2. Each of the following is also an insured:

   a. Your "volunteer workers" only while performing duties related to the conduct of your business, or your "employees", other than either your "executive officers" (if you are an organization other than a partnership, joint venture or limited liability company) or your managers (if you are a limited liability company), but only for acts within the scope of their employment by you or while performing duties related to the conduct of your business. However, none of these "employees" or "volunteer workers" are insureds for:

   (1) "Bodily injury" or "personal and advertising injury":

      (a) To you, to your partners or members (if you are a partnership or joint venture), to your members (if you are a limited liability company), to a co-"employee" while in the course of his or her employment or performing duties related to the conduct of your business, or to your other "volunteer workers" while performing duties related to the conduct of your business;

      (b) To the spouse, child, parent, brother or sister of that co-"employee" or "volunteer worker" as a consequence of Paragraph (1)(a) above;

      (c) For which there is any obligation to share damages with or repay someone else who must pay damages because of the injury described in Paragraphs (1)(a) or (b) above; or

      (d) Arising out of his or her providing or failing to provide professional health care services.

   (2) "Property damage" to property:

      (a) Owned, occupied or used by,

      (b) Rented to, in the care, custody or control of, or over which physical control is being exercised for any purpose by

      you, any of your "employees", "volunteer workers", any partner or member (if you are a partnership or joint venture), or any member (if you are a limited liability company).

   b. Any person (other than your "employee" or "volunteer worker"), or any organization while acting as your real estate manager.

   c. Any person or organization having proper temporary custody of your property if you die, but only:

   (1) With respect to liability arising out of the maintenance or use of that property; and

   (2) Until your legal representative has been appointed.

   d. Your legal representative if you die, but only with respect to duties as such. That representative will have all your rights and duties under this Coverage Part.

3. With respect to "mobile equipment" registered in your name under any motor vehicle registration law, any person is an insured while driving such equipment along a public highway with your permission. Any other person or organization responsible for the conduct of such person is also an insured, but only with respect to liability arising out of the operation of the equipment, and only if no other insurance of any kind is available to that person or organization for this liability. However, no person or organization is an insured with respect to:

   a. "Bodily injury" to a co-"employee" of the person driving the equipment; or

   b. "Property damage" to property owned by, rented to, in the charge of or occupied by you or the employer of any person who is an insured under this provision.

4. Any organization you newly acquire or form, other than a partnership, joint venture or limited liability company, and over which you maintain ownership or majority interest, will qualify as a Named Insured if there is no other similar insurance available to that organization. However:

   a. Coverage under this provision is afforded only until the 90th day after you acquire or form the organization or the end of the policy period, whichever is earlier;

   b. Coverage **A** does not apply to "bodily injury" or "property damage" that occurred before you acquired or formed the organization; and

   c. Coverage **B** does not apply to "personal and advertising injury" arising out of an offense committed before you acquired or formed the organization.

No person or organization is an insured with respect to the conduct of any current or past partnership, joint venture or limited liability company that is not shown as a Named Insured in the Declarations.

SECTION III – LIMITS OF INSURANCE

1. The Limits of Insurance shown in the Declarations and the rules below fix the most we will pay regardless of the number of:

   a. Insureds;

   b. Claims made or "suits" brought; or

   c. Persons or organizations making claims or bringing "suits".

2. The General Aggregate Limit is the most we will pay for the sum of:

   a. Medical expenses under Coverage **C**;

   b. Damages under Coverage **A**, except damages because of "bodily injury" or "property damage" included in the "products-completed operations hazard"; and

   c. Damages under Coverage **B**.

3. The Products-Completed Operations Aggregate Limit is the most we will pay under Coverage **A** for damages because of "bodily injury" and "property damage" included in the "products-completed operations hazard".

4. Subject to **2.** above, the Personal and Advertising Injury Limit is the most we will pay under Coverage **B** for the sum of all damages because of all "personal and advertising injury" sustained by any one person or organization.

5. Subject to **2.** or **3.** above, whichever applies, the Each Occurrence Limit is the most we will pay for the sum of:

   a. Damages under Coverage **A**; and

   b. Medical expenses under Coverage **C**

   because of all "bodily injury" and "property damage" arising out of any one "occurrence".

6. Subject to **5.** above, the Damage To Premises Rented To You Limit is the most we will pay under Coverage **A** for damages because of "property damage" to any one premises, while rented to you, or in the case of damage by fire, while rented to you or temporarily occupied by you with permission of the owner.

7. Subject to **5.** above, the Medical Expense Limit is the most we will pay under Coverage **C** for all medical expenses because of "bodily injury" sustained by any one person.

The Limits of Insurance of this Coverage Part apply separately to each consecutive annual period and to any remaining period of less than 12 months, starting with the beginning of the policy period shown in the Declarations, unless the policy period is extended after issuance for an additional period of less than 12 months. In that case, the additional period will be deemed part of the last preceding period for purposes of determining the Limits of Insurance.

SECTION IV – COMMERCIAL GENERAL LIABILITY CONDITIONS

1. **Bankruptcy**

   Bankruptcy or insolvency of the insured or of the insured's estate will not relieve us of our obligations under this Coverage Part.

2. **Duties In The Event Of Occurrence, Offense, Claim Or Suit**

   a. You must see to it that we are notified as soon as practicable of an "occurrence" or an offense which may result in a claim. To the extent possible, notice should include:

      (1) How, when and where the "occurrence" or offense took place;

      (2) The names and addresses of any injured persons and witnesses; and

      (3) The nature and location of any injury or damage arising out of the "occurrence" or offense.

b. If a claim is made or "suit" is brought against any insured, you must:

(1) Immediately record the specifics of the claim or "suit" and the date received; and

(2) Notify us as soon as practicable.

You must see to it that we receive written notice of the claim or "suit" as soon as practicable.

c. You and any other involved insured must:

(1) Immediately send us copies of any demands, notices, summonses or legal papers received in connection with the claim or "suit";

(2) Authorize us to obtain records and other information;

(3) Cooperate with us in the investigation or settlement of the claim or defense against the "suit"; and

(4) Assist us, upon our request, in the enforcement of any right against any person or organization which may be liable to the insured because of injury or damage to which this insurance may also apply.

d. No insured will, except at that insured's own cost, voluntarily make a payment, assume any obligation, or incur any expense, other than for first aid, without our consent.

3. Legal Action Against Us

No person or organization has a right under this Coverage Part:

a. To join us as a party or otherwise bring us into a "suit" asking for damages from an insured; or

b. To sue us on this Coverage Part unless all of its terms have been fully complied with.

A person or organization may sue us to recover on an agreed settlement or on a final judgment against an insured; but we will not be liable for damages that are not payable under the terms of this Coverage Part or that are in excess of the applicable limit of insurance. An agreed settlement means a settlement and release of liability signed by us, the insured and the claimant or the claimant's legal representative.

4. Other Insurance

If other valid and collectible insurance is available to the insured for a loss we cover under Coverages **A** or **B** of this Coverage Part, our obligations are limited as follows:

a. Primary Insurance

This insurance is primary except when **b.** below applies. If this insurance is primary, our obligations are not affected unless any of the other insurance is also primary. Then, we will share with all that other insurance by the method described in **c.** below.

b. Excess Insurance

This insurance is excess over:

(1) Any of the other insurance, whether primary, excess, contingent or on any other basis:

(a) That is Fire, Extended Coverage, Builder's Risk, Installation Risk or similar coverage for "your work";

(b) That is Fire insurance for premises rented to you or temporarily occupied by you with permission of the owner;

(c) That is insurance purchased by you to cover your liability as a tenant for "property damage" to premises rented to you or temporarily occupied by you with permission of the owner; or

(d) If the loss arises out of the maintenance or use of aircraft, "autos" or watercraft to the extent not subject to Exclusion **g.** of Section **I** – Coverage **A** – Bodily Injury And Property Damage Liability.

(2) Any other primary insurance available to you covering liability for damages arising out of the premises or operations for which you have been added as an additional insured by attachment of an endorsement.

When this insurance is excess, we will have no duty under Coverages **A** or **B** to defend the insured against any "suit" if any other insurer has a duty to defend the insured against that "suit". If no other insurer defends, we will undertake to do so, but we will be entitled to the insured's rights against all those other insurers.

When this insurance is excess over other insurance, we will pay only our share of the amount of the loss, if any, that exceeds the sum of:

(1) The total amount that all such other insurance would pay for the loss in the absence of this insurance; and

(2) The total of all deductible and self-insured amounts under all that other insurance.

We will share the remaining loss, if any, with any other insurance that is not described in this Excess Insurance provision and was not bought specifically to apply in excess of the Limits of Insurance shown in the Declarations of this Coverage Part.

c. Method Of Sharing

If all of the other insurance permits contribution by equal shares, we will follow this method also. Under this approach each insurer contributes equal amounts until it has paid its applicable limit of insurance or none of the loss remains, whichever comes first.

If any of the other insurance does not permit contribution by equal shares, we will contribute by limits. Under this method, each insurer's share is based on the ratio of its applicable limit of insurance to the total applicable limits of insurance of all insurers.

5. Premium Audit

a. We will compute all premiums for this Coverage Part in accordance with our rules and rates.

b. Premium shown in this Coverage Part as advance premium is a deposit premium only. At the close of each audit period we will compute the earned premium for that period and send notice to the first Named Insured. The due date for audit and retrospective premiums is the date shown as the due date on the bill. If the sum of the advance and audit premiums paid for the policy period is greater than the earned premium, we will return the excess to the first Named Insured.

c. The first Named Insured must keep records of the information we need for premium computation, and send us copies at such times as we may request.

6. Representations

By accepting this policy, you agree:

a. The statements in the Declarations are accurate and complete;

b. Those statements are based upon representations you made to us; and

c. We have issued this policy in reliance upon your representations.

7. Separation Of Insureds

Except with respect to the Limits of Insurance, and any rights or duties specifically assigned in this Coverage Part to the first Named Insured, this insurance applies:

a. As if each Named Insured were the only Named Insured; and

b. Separately to each insured against whom claim is made or "suit" is brought.

8. Transfer Of Rights Of Recovery Against Others To Us

If the insured has rights to recover all or part of any payment we have made under this Coverage Part, those rights are transferred to us. The insured must do nothing after loss to impair them. At our request, the insured will bring "suit" or transfer those rights to us and help us enforce them.

9. When We Do Not Renew

If we decide not to renew this Coverage Part, we will mail or deliver to the first Named Insured shown in the Declarations written notice of the nonrenewal not less than 30 days before the expiration date.

If notice is mailed, proof of mailing will be sufficient proof of notice.

SECTION V – DEFINITIONS

1. "Advertisement" means a notice that is broadcast or published to the general public or specific market segments about your goods, products or services for the purpose of attracting customers or supporters. For the purposes of this definition:

a. Notices that are published include material placed on the Internet or on similar electronic means of communication; and

b. Regarding web-sites, only that part of a website that is about your goods, products or services for the purposes of attracting customers or supporters is considered an advertisement.

2. "Auto" means a land motor vehicle, trailer or semitrailer designed for travel on public roads, including any attached machinery or equipment. But "auto" does not include "mobile equipment".

3. "Bodily injury" means bodily injury, sickness or disease sustained by a person, including death resulting from any of these at any time.

4. "Coverage territory" means:

a. The United States of America (including its territories and possessions), Puerto Rico and Canada;

b. International waters or airspace, but only if the injury or damage occurs in the course of travel or transportation between any places included in **a.** above; or

c. All other parts of the world if the injury or damage arises out of:

(1) Goods or products made or sold by you in the territory described in **a.** above;

(2) The activities of a person whose home is in the territory described in **a.** above, but is away for a short time on your business; or

(3) "Personal and advertising injury" offenses that take place through the Internet or similar electronic means of communication

provided the insured's responsibility to pay damages is determined in a "suit" on the merits, in the territory described in **a.** above or in a settlement we agree to.

5. "Employee" includes a "leased worker". "Employee" does not include a "temporary worker".

6. "Executive officer" means a person holding any of the officer positions created by your charter, constitution, by-laws or any other similar governing document.

7. "Hostile fire" means one which becomes uncontrollable or breaks out from where it was intended to be.

8. "Impaired property" means tangible property, other than "your product" or "your work", that cannot be used or is less useful because:

a. It incorporates "your product" or "your work" that is known or thought to be defective, deficient, inadequate or dangerous; or

b. You have failed to fulfill the terms of a contract or agreement;

if such property can be restored to use by:

a. The repair, replacement, adjustment or removal of "your product" or "your work"; or

b. Your fulfilling the terms of the contract or agreement.

9. "Insured contract" means:

a. A contract for a lease of premises. However, that portion of the contract for a lease of premises that indemnifies any person or organization for damage by fire to premises while rented to you or temporarily occupied by you with permission of the owner is not an "insured contract";

b. A sidetrack agreement;

c. Any easement or license agreement, except in connection with construction or demolition operations on or within 50 feet of a railroad;

d. An obligation, as required by ordinance, to indemnify a municipality, except in connection with work for a municipality;

e. An elevator maintenance agreement;

f. That part of any other contract or agreement pertaining to your business (including an indemnification of a municipality in connection with work performed for a municipality) under which you assume the tort liability of another party to pay for "bodily injury" or "property damage" to a third person or organization. Tort liability means a liability that would be imposed by law in the absence of any contract or agreement.

Paragraph **f.** does not include that part of any contract or agreement:

(1) That indemnifies a railroad for "bodily injury" or "property damage" arising out of construction or demolition operations, within 50 feet of any railroad property and affecting any railroad bridge or trestle, tracks, road-beds, tunnel, underpass or crossing;

(2) That indemnifies an architect, engineer or surveyor for injury or damage arising out of:

(a) Preparing, approving, or failing to prepare or approve, maps, shop drawings, opinions, reports, surveys, field orders, change orders or drawings and specifications; or

(b) Giving directions or instructions, or failing to give them, if that is the primary cause of the injury or damage; or

(3) Under which the insured, if an architect, engineer or surveyor, assumes liability for an injury or damage arising out of the insured's rendering or failure to render professional services, including those listed in **(2)** above and supervisory, inspection, architectural or engineering activities.

10. "Leased worker" means a person leased to you by a labor leasing firm under an agreement between you and the labor leasing firm, to perform duties related to the conduct of your business. "Leased worker" does not include a "temporary worker".

11. "Loading or unloading" means the handling of property:

a. After it is moved from the place where it is accepted for movement into or onto an aircraft, watercraft or "auto";

b. While it is in or on an aircraft, watercraft or "auto"; or

c. While it is being moved from an aircraft, watercraft or "auto" to the place where it is finally delivered;

but "loading or unloading" does not include the movement of property by means of a mechanical device, other than a hand truck, that is not attached to the aircraft, watercraft or "auto".

12. "Mobile equipment" means any of the following types of land vehicles, including any attached machinery or equipment:

a. Bulldozers, farm machinery, forklifts and other vehicles designed for use principally off public roads;

b. Vehicles maintained for use solely on or next to premises you own or rent;

c. Vehicles that travel on crawler treads;

d. Vehicles, whether self-propelled or not, maintained primarily to provide mobility to permanently mounted:

(1) Power cranes, shovels, loaders, diggers or drills; or

(2) Road construction or resurfacing equipment such as graders, scrapers or rollers;

e. Vehicles not described in **a., b., c.** or **d.** above that are not self-propelled and are maintained primarily to provide mobility to permanently attached equipment of the following types:

(1) Air compressors, pumps and generators, including spraying, welding, building cleaning, geophysical exploration, lighting and well servicing equipment; or

(2) Cherry pickers and similar devices used to raise or lower workers;

f. Vehicles not described in **a., b., c.** or **d.** above maintained primarily for purposes other than the transportation of persons or cargo.

However, self-propelled vehicles with the following types of permanently attached equipment are not "mobile equipment" but will be considered "autos":

(1) Equipment designed primarily for:

(a) Snow removal;

(b) Road maintenance, but not construction or resurfacing; or

(c) Street cleaning;

(2) Cherry pickers and similar devices mounted on automobile or truck chassis and used to raise or lower workers; and

(3) Air compressors, pumps and generators, including spraying, welding, building cleaning, geophysical exploration, lighting and well servicing equipment.

13. "Occurrence" means an accident, including continuous or repeated exposure to substantially the same general harmful conditions.

14. "Personal and advertising injury" means injury, including consequential "bodily injury", arising out of one or more of the following offenses:

a. False arrest, detention or imprisonment;

b. Malicious prosecution;

c. The wrongful eviction from, wrongful entry into, or invasion of the right of private occupancy of a room, dwelling or premises that a person occupies, committed by or on behalf of its owner, landlord or lessor;

d. Oral or written publication, in any manner, of material that slanders or libels a person or organization or disparages a person's or organization's goods, products or services;

e. Oral or written publication, in any manner, of material that violates a person's right of privacy;

f. The use of another's advertising idea in your "advertisement"; or

g. Infringing upon another's copyright, trade dress or slogan in your "advertisement".

15. "Pollutants" mean any solid, liquid, gaseous or thermal irritant or contaminant, including smoke, vapor, soot, fumes, acids, alkalis, chemicals and waste. Waste includes materials to be recycled, reconditioned or reclaimed.

16. "Products-completed operations hazard":

a. Includes all "bodily injury" and "property damage" occurring away from premises you own or rent and arising out of "your product" or "your work" except:

(1) Products that are still in your physical possession; or

(2) Work that has not yet been completed or abandoned. However, "your work" will be deemed completed at the earliest of the following times:

(a) When all of the work called for in your contract has been completed.

(b) When all of the work to be done at the job site has been completed if your contract calls for work at more than one job site.

(c) When that part of the work done at a job site has been put to its intended use by any person or organization other than another contractor or subcontractor working on the same project.

Work that may need service, maintenance, correction, repair or replacement, but which is otherwise complete, will be treated as completed.

b. Does not include "bodily injury" or "property damage" arising out of:

(1) The transportation of property, unless the injury or damage arises out of a condition in or on a vehicle not owned or operated by you, and that condition was created by the "loading or unloading" of that vehicle by any insured;

(2) The existence of tools, uninstalled equipment or abandoned or unused materials; or

(3) Products or operations for which the classification, listed in the Declarations or in a policy schedule, states that products-completed operations are subject to the General Aggregate Limit.

17. "Property damage" means:

a. Physical injury to tangible property, including all resulting loss of use of that property. All such loss of use shall be deemed to occur at the time of the physical injury that caused it; or

b. Loss of use of tangible property that is not physically injured. All such loss of use shall be deemed to occur at the time of the "occurrence" that caused it.

For the purposes of this insurance, electronic data is not tangible property.

As used in this definition, electronic data means information, facts or programs stored as or on, created or used on, or transmitted to or from computer software, including systems and applications software, hard or floppy disks, CD-ROMS, tapes, drives, cells, data processing devices or any other media which are used with electronically controlled equipment.

18. "Suit" means a civil proceeding in which damages because of "bodily injury", "property damage" or "personal and advertising injury" to which this insurance applies are alleged. "Suit" includes:

a. An arbitration proceeding in which such damages are claimed and to which the insured must submit or does submit with our consent; or

b. Any other alternative dispute resolution proceeding in which such damages are claimed and to which the insured submits with our consent.

19. "Temporary worker" means a person who is furnished to you to substitute for a permanent "employee" on leave or to meet seasonal or short-term workload conditions.

20. "Volunteer worker" means a person who is not your "employee", and who donates his or her work and acts at the direction of and within the scope of duties determined by you, and is not paid a fee, salary or other compensation by you or anyone else for their work performed for you.

21. "Your product":

a. Means:

(1) Any goods or products, other than real property, manufactured, sold, handled, distributed or disposed of by:

(a) You;

(b) Others trading under your name; or

(c) A person or organization whose business or assets you have acquired; and

(2) Containers (other than vehicles), materials, parts or equipment furnished in connection with such goods or products.

b. Includes

   (1) Warranties or representations made at any time with respect to the fitness, quality, durability, performance or use of "your product"; and

   (2) The providing of or failure to provide warnings or instructions.

c. Does not include vending machines or other property rented to or located for the use of others but not sold.

22. "Your work":

   a. Means:

   (1) Work or operations performed by you or on your behalf; and

   (2) Materials, parts or equipment furnished in connection with such work or operations.

   b. Includes

   (1) Warranties or representations made at any time with respect to the fitness, quality, durability, performance or use of "your work", and

   (2) The providing of or failure to provide warnings or instructions.

                 CG 00 01 10 01   ☐

COMMERCIAL GENERAL LIABILITY
CG 00 02 10 01

COMMERCIAL GENERAL LIABILITY COVERAGE FORM

**COVERAGES A AND B PROVIDE
CLAIMS-MADE COVERAGE
PLEASE READ THE ENTIRE FORM CAREFULLY**

Various provisions in this policy restrict coverage. Read the entire policy carefully to determine rights, duties and what is and is not covered.

Throughout this policy the words "you" and "your" refer to the Named Insured shown in the Declarations, and any other person or organization qualifying as a Named Insured under this policy. The words "we", "us" and "our" refer to the Company providing this insurance.

The word "insured" means any person or organization qualifying as such under Section **II** – Who Is An Insured.

Other words and phrases that appear in quotation marks have special meaning. Refer to Section **VI** – Definitions.

SECTION I – COVERAGES

COVERAGE A BODILY INJURY AND PROPERTY DAMAGE LIABILITY

1. Insuring Agreement

  a. We will pay those sums that the insured becomes legally obligated to pay as damages because of "bodily injury" or "property damage" to which this insurance applies. We will have the right and duty to defend the insured against any "suit" seeking those damages. However, we will have no duty to defend the insured against any "suit" seeking damages for "bodily injury" or "property damage" to which this insurance does not apply. We may, at our discretion, investigate any "occurrence" and settle any claim or "suit" that may result. But:

    (1) The amount we will pay for damages is limited as described in Section **III** – Limits Of Insurance; and

    (2) Our right and duty to defend ends when we have used up the applicable limit of insurance in the payment of judgments or settlements under Coverages **A** or **B** or medical expenses under Coverage **C**.

  No other obligation or liability to pay sums or perform acts or services is covered unless explicitly provided for under Supplementary Payments – Coverages **A** and **B**.

  b. This insurance applies to "bodily injury" and "property damage" only if:

    (1) The "bodily injury" or "property damage" is caused by an "occurrence" that takes place in the "coverage territory";

    (2) The "bodily injury" or "property damage" did not occur before the Retroactive Date, if any, shown in the Declarations or after the end of the policy period; and

    (3) A claim for damages because of the "bodily injury" or "property damage" is first made against any insured, in accordance with Paragraph **c.** below, during the policy period or any Extended Reporting Period we provide under Section **V** – Extended Reporting Periods.

  c. A claim by a person or organization seeking damages will be deemed to have been made at the earlier of the following times:

    (1) When notice of such claim is received and recorded by any insured or by us, whichever comes first; or

    (2) When we make settlement in accordance with Paragraph **1.a.** above.

  All claims for damages because of "bodily injury" to the same person, including damages claimed by any person or organization for care, loss of services, or death resulting at any time from the "bodily injury", will be deemed to have been made at the time the first of those claims is made against any insured.

  All claims for damages because of "property damage" causing loss to the same person or organization will be deemed to have been made at the time the first of those claims is made against any insured.

2. Exclusions

  This insurance does not apply to:

  a. Expected Or Intended Injury

  "Bodily injury" or "property damage" expected or intended from the standpoint of the insured. This exclusion does not apply to "bodily injury" resulting from the use of reasonable force to protect persons or property.

b. Contractual Liability

"Bodily injury" or "property damage" for which the insured is obligated to pay damages by reason of the assumption of liability in a contract or agreement. This exclusion does not apply to liability for damages:

(1) That the insured would have in the absence of the contract or agreement; or

(2) Assumed in a contract or agreement that is an "insured contract", provided the "bodily injury" or "property damage" occurs subsequent to the execution of the contract or agreement. Solely for the purposes of liability assumed in an "insured contract", reasonable attorney fees and necessary litigation expenses incurred by or for a party other than an insured are deemed to be damages because of "bodily injury" or "property damage", provided:

   (a) Liability to such party for, or for the cost of, that party's defense has also been assumed in the same "insured contract"; and

   (b) Such attorney fees and litigation expenses are for defense of that party against a civil or alternative dispute resolution proceeding in which damages to which this insurance applies are alleged.

c. Liquor Liability

"Bodily injury" or "property damage" for which any insured may be held liable by reason of:

(1) Causing or contributing to the intoxication of any person;

(2) The furnishing of alcoholic beverages to a person under the legal drinking age or under the influence of alcohol; or

(3) Any statute, ordinance or regulation relating to the sale, gift, distribution or use of alcoholic beverages.

This exclusion applies only if you are in the business of manufacturing, distributing, selling, serving or furnishing alcoholic beverages.

d. Workers' Compensation And Similar Laws

Any obligation of the insured under a workers' compensation, disability benefits or unemployment compensation law or any similar law.

e. Employer's Liability

"Bodily injury" to:

(1) An "employee" of the insured arising out of and in the course of:

   (a) Employment by the insured; or

   (b) Performing duties related to the conduct of the insured's business; or

(2) The spouse, child, parent, brother or sister of that "employee" as a consequence of Paragraph **(1)** above.

This exclusion applies:

(1) Whether the insured may be liable as an employer or in any other capacity; and

(2) To any obligation to share damages with or repay someone else who must pay damages because of the injury.

This exclusion does not apply to liability assumed by the insured under an "insured contract".

f. Pollution

(1) "Bodily injury" or "property damage" arising out of the actual, alleged or threatened discharge, dispersal, seepage, migration, release or escape of "pollutants":

   (a) At or from any premises, site or location which is or was at any time owned or occupied by, or rented or loaned to, any insured. However, this subparagraph does not apply to:

     (i) "Bodily injury" if sustained within a building and caused by smoke, fumes, vapor or soot from equipment used to heat that building;

     (ii) "Bodily injury" or "property damage" for which you may be held liable, if you are a contractor and the owner or lessee of such premises, site or location has been added to your policy as an additional insured with respect to your ongoing operations performed for that additional insured at that premises, site or location and such premises, site or location is not or never was owned or occupied by, or rented or loaned to, any insured, other than that additional insured; or

     (iii) "Bodily injury" or "property damage" arising out of heat, smoke or fumes from a "hostile fire";

   (b) At or from any premises, site or location which is or was at any time used by or for any insured or others for the handling, storage, disposal, processing or treatment of waste;

   (c) Which are or were at any time transported, handled, stored, treated, disposed of, or processed as waste by or for:

     (i) Any insured; or

　　　© ISO Properties, Inc., 2000

(ii) Any person or organization for whom you may be legally responsible; or

(d) At or from any premises, site or location on which any insured or any contractors or subcontractors working directly or indirectly on any insured's behalf are performing operations if the "pollutants" are brought on or to the premises, site or location in connection with such operations by such insured, contractor or subcontractor. However, this subparagraph does not apply to:

(i) "Bodily injury" or "property damage" arising out of the escape of fuels, lubricants or other operating fluids which are needed to perform the normal electrical, hydraulic or mechanical functions necessary for the operation of "mobile equipment" or its parts, if such fuels, lubricants or other operating fluids escape from a vehicle part designed to hold, store or receive them. This exception does not apply if the "bodily injury" or "property damage" arises out of the intentional discharge, dispersal or release of the fuels, lubricants or other operating fluids, or if such fuels, lubricants or other operating fluids are brought on or to the premises, site or location with the intent that they be discharged, dispersed or released as part of the operations being performed by such insured, contractor or subcontractor;

(ii) "Bodily injury" or "property damage" sustained within a building and caused by the release of gases, fumes or vapors from materials brought into that building in connection with operations being performed by you or on your behalf by a contractor or subcontractor; or

(iii) "Bodily injury" or "property damage" arising out of heat, smoke or fumes from a "hostile fire".

(e) At or from any premises, site or location on which any insured or any contractors or subcontractors working directly or indirectly on any insured's behalf are performing operations if the operations are to test for, monitor, clean up, remove, contain, treat, detoxify or neutralize, or in any way respond to, or assess the effects of, "pollutants".

(2) Any loss, cost or expense arising out of any:

(a) Request, demand, order or statutory or regulatory requirement that any insured or others test for, monitor, clean up, remove, contain, treat, detoxify or neutralize, or in any way respond to, or assess the effects of, "pollutants"; or

(b) Claim or suit by or on behalf of a governmental authority for damages because of testing for, monitoring, cleaning up, removing, containing, treating, detoxifying or neutralizing, or in any way responding to, or assessing the effects of, "pollutants".

However, this paragraph does not apply to liability for damages because of "property damage" that the insured would have in the absence of such request, demand, order or statutory or regulatory requirement, or such claim or "suit" by or on behalf of a governmental authority.

g. **Aircraft, Auto Or Watercraft**

"Bodily injury" or "property damage" arising out of the ownership, maintenance, use or entrustment to others of any aircraft, "auto" or watercraft owned or operated by or rented or loaned to any insured. Use includes operation and "loading or unloading".

This exclusion applies even if the claims against any insured allege negligence or other wrongdoing in the supervision, hiring, employment, training or monitoring of others by that insured, if the "occurrence" which caused the "bodily injury" or "property damage" involved the ownership, maintenance, use or entrustment to others of any aircraft, "auto" or watercraft that is owned or operated by or rented or loaned to any insured.

This exclusion does not apply to:

(1) A watercraft while ashore on premises you own or rent;

(2) A watercraft you do not own that is:

(a) Less than 26 feet long; and

(b) Not being used to carry persons or property for a charge;

(3) Parking an "auto" on, or on the ways next to, premises you own or rent, provided the "auto" is not owned by or rented or loaned to you or the insured;

(4) Liability assumed under any "insured contract" for the ownership, maintenance or use of aircraft or watercraft; or

(5) "Bodily injury" or "property damage" arising out of the operation of any of the equipment listed in Paragraph **f.(2)** or **f.(3)** of the definition of "mobile equipment".

h. Mobile Equipment

"Bodily injury" or "property damage" arising out of:

(1) The transportation of "mobile equipment" by an "auto" owned or operated by or rented or loaned to any insured; or

(2) The use of "mobile equipment" in, or while in practice for, or while being prepared for, any prearranged racing, speed, demolition, or stunting activity.

i. War

"Bodily injury" or "property damage" due to war, whether or not declared, or any act or condition incident to war. War includes civil war, insurrection, rebellion or revolution. This exclusion applies only to liability assumed under a contract or agreement.

j. Damage To Property

"Property damage" to:

(1) Property you own, rent, or occupy, including any costs or expenses incurred by you, or any other person, organization or entity, for repair, replacement, enhancement, restoration or maintenance of such property for any reason, including prevention of injury to a person or damage to another's property;

(2) Premises you sell, give away or abandon, if the "property damage" arises out of any part of those premises;

(3) Property loaned to you;

(4) Personal property in the care, custody or control of the insured;

(5) That particular part of real property on which you or any contractors or subcontractors working directly or indirectly on your behalf are performing operations, if the "property damage" arises out of those operations; or

(6) That particular part of any property that must be restored, repaired or replaced because "your work" was incorrectly performed on it.

Paragraphs **(1)**, **(3)** and **(4)** of this exclusion do not apply to "property damage" (other than damage by fire) to premises, including the contents of such premises, rented to you for a period of 7 or fewer consecutive days. A separate limit of insurance applies to Damage To Premises Rented To You as described in Section **III** – Limits Of Insurance.

Paragraph **(2)** of this exclusion does not apply if the premises are "your work" and were never occupied, rented or held for rental by you.

Paragraphs **(3)**, **(4)**, **(5)** and **(6)** of this exclusion do not apply to liability assumed under a sidetrack agreement.

Paragraph **(6)** of this exclusion does not apply to "property damage" included in the "products-completed operations hazard".

k. Damage To Your Product

"Property damage" to "your product" arising out of it or any part of it.

l. Damage To Your Work

"Property damage" to "your work" arising out of it or any part of it and included in the "products-completed operations hazard".

This exclusion does not apply if the damaged work or the work out of which the damage arises was performed on your behalf by a subcontractor.

m. Damage To Impaired Property Or Property Not Physically Injured

"Property damage" to "impaired property" or property that has not been physically injured, arising out of:

(1) A defect, deficiency, inadequacy or dangerous condition in "your product" or "your work"; or

(2) A delay or failure by you or anyone acting on your behalf to perform a contract or agreement in accordance with its terms.

This exclusion does not apply to the loss of use of other property arising out of sudden and accidental physical injury to "your product" or "your work" after it has been put to its intended use.

n. Recall Of Products, Work Or Impaired Property

Damages claimed for any loss, cost or expense incurred by you or others for the loss of use, withdrawal, recall, inspection, repair, replacement, adjustment, removal or disposal of:

(1) "Your product";

(2) "Your work"; or

(3) "Impaired property";

if such product, work, or property is withdrawn or recalled from the market or from use by any person or organization because of a known or suspected defect, deficiency, inadequacy or dangerous condition in it.

o. Personal And Advertising Injury

"Bodily injury" arising out of "personal and advertising injury".

Exclusions **c.** through **n.** do not apply to damage by fire to premises while rented to you or temporarily occupied by you with permission of the owner. A separate limit of insurance applies to this coverage as described in Section **III** – Limits Of Insurance.

COVERAGE B PERSONAL AND ADVERTISING INJURY LIABILITY

1. Insuring Agreement

a. We will pay those sums that the insured becomes legally obligated to pay as damages because of "personal and advertising injury" to which this insurance applies. We will have the right and duty to defend the insured against any "suit" seeking those damages. However, we will have no duty to defend the insured against any "suit" seeking damages for "personal and advertising injury" to which this insurance does not apply. We may, at our discretion, investigate any offense and settle any claim or "suit" that may result. But:

(1) The amount we will pay for damages is limited as described in Section **III** – Limits Of Insurance; and

(2) Our right and duty to defend end when we have used up the applicable limit of insurance in the payment of judgments or settlements under Coverages **A** or **B** or medical expenses under Coverage **C**.

No other obligation or liability to pay sums or perform acts or services is covered unless explicitly provided for under Supplementary Payments – Coverages **A** and **B**.

b. This insurance applies to "personal and advertising injury" caused by an offense arising out of your business, but only if:

(1) The offense was committed in the "coverage territory";

(2) The offense was not committed before the Retroactive Date, if any, shown in the Declarations or after the end of the policy period; and

(3) A claim for damages because of the "personal and advertising injury" is first made against any insured, in accordance with Paragraph **c.** below, during the policy period or any Extended Reporting Period we provide under Section **V** – Extended Reporting Periods.

c. A claim made by a person or organization seeking damages will be deemed to have been made at the earlier of the following times:

(1) When notice of such claim is received and recorded by any insured or by us, whichever comes first; or

(2) When we make settlement in accordance with Paragraph **1.a.** above.

All claims for damages because of "personal and advertising injury" to the same person or organization as a result of an offense will be deemed to have been made at the time the first of those claims is made against any insured.

2. Exclusions

This insurance does not apply to:

a. Knowing Violation Of Rights Of Another

"Personal and advertising injury" caused by or at the direction of the insured with the knowledge that the act would violate the rights of another and would inflict "personal and advertising injury".

b. Material Published With Knowledge Of Falsity

"Personal and advertising injury" arising out of oral or written publication of material, if done by or at the direction of the insured with knowledge of its falsity.

c. Material Published Prior To Policy Period

"Personal and advertising injury" arising out of oral or written publication of material whose first publication took place before the Retroactive Date, if any, shown in the Declarations.

d. Criminal Acts

"Personal and advertising injury" arising out of a criminal act committed by or at the direction of the insured.

e. Contractual Liability

"Personal and advertising injury" for which the insured has assumed liability in a contract or agreement. This exclusion does not apply to liability for damages that the insured would have in the absence of the contract or agreement.

f. Breach Of Contract

"Personal and advertising injury" arising out of a breach of contract, except an implied contract to use another's advertising idea in your "advertisement".

g. Quality Or Performance Of Goods – Failure To Conform To Statements

"Personal and advertising injury" arising out of the failure of goods, products or services to conform with any statement of quality or performance made in your "advertisement".

h. Wrong Description Of Prices

"Personal and advertising injury" arising out of the wrong description of the price of goods, products or services stated in your "advertisement".

i. Infringement Of Copyright, Patent, Trademark Or Trade Secret

"Personal and advertising injury" arising out of the infringement of copyright, patent, trademark, trade secret or other intellectual property rights.

However, this exclusion does not apply to infringement, in your "advertisement", of copyright, trade dress or slogan.

j. Insureds In Media And Internet Type Businesses

"Personal and advertising injury" committed by an insured whose business is:

(1) Advertising, broadcasting, publishing or telecasting;

(2) Designing or determining content of websites for others; or

(3) An Internet search, access, content or service provider.

However, this exclusion does not apply to Paragraphs **14.a.**, **b.** and **c.** of "personal and advertising injury" under the Definitions Section.

For the purposes of this exclusion, the placing of frames, borders or links, or advertising, for you or others anywhere on the Internet, is not by itself, considered the business of advertising, broadcasting, publishing or telecasting.

k. Electronic Chatrooms Or Bulletin Boards

"Personal and advertising injury" arising out of an electronic chatroom or bulletin board the insured hosts, owns, or over which the insured exercises control.

l. Unauthorized Use Of Another's Name Or Product

"Personal and advertising injury" arising out of the unauthorized use of another's name or product in your e-mail address, domain name or metatag, or any other similar tactics to mislead another's potential customers.

m. Pollution

"Personal and advertising injury" arising out of the actual, alleged or threatened discharge, dispersal, seepage, migration, release or escape of "pollutants" at any time.

n. Pollution-Related

Any loss, cost or expense arising out of any:

(1) Request, demand or order that any insured or others test for, monitor, clean up, remove, contain, treat, detoxify or neutralize, or in any way respond to, or assess the effects of, "pollutants"; or

(2) Claim or suit by or on behalf of a governmental authority for damages because of testing for, monitoring, cleaning up, removing, containing, treating, detoxifying or neutralizing, or in any way responding to, or assessing the effects of, "pollutants".

COVERAGE C MEDICAL PAYMENTS

1. Insuring Agreement

a. We will pay medical expenses as described below for "bodily injury" caused by an accident:

(1) On premises you own or rent;

(2) On ways next to premises you own or rent; or

(3) Because of your operations;

provided that:

(1) The accident takes place in the "coverage territory" and during the policy period;

(2) The expenses are incurred and reported to us within one year of the date of the accident; and

(3) The injured person submits to examination, at our expense, by physicians of our choice as often as we reasonably require.

b. We will make these payments regardless of fault. These payments will not exceed the applicable limit of insurance. We will pay reasonable expenses for:

(1) First aid administered at the time of an accident;

(2) Necessary medical, surgical, x-ray and dental services, including prosthetic devices; and

(3) Necessary ambulance, hospital, professional nursing and funeral services.

2. Exclusions

We will not pay expenses for "bodily injury":

a. Any Insured

To any insured, except "volunteer workers".

b. Hired Person

To a person hired to do work for or on behalf of any insured or a tenant of any insured.

c. Injury On Normally Occupied Premises

To a person injured on that part of premises you own or rent that the person normally occupies.

d. Workers Compensation And Similar Laws

To a person, whether or not an "employee" of any insured, if benefits for the "bodily injury" are payable or must be provided under a workers' compensation or disability benefits law or a similar law.

e. Athletics Activities

To a person injured while taking part in athletics.

f. Products-Completed Operations Hazard

Included within the "products-completed operations hazard".

g. Coverage A Exclusions

Excluded under Coverage **A**.

h. War

Due to war, whether or not declared, or any act or condition incident to war. War includes civil war, insurrection, rebellion or revolution.

SUPPLEMENTARY PAYMENTS – COVERAGES A AND B

1. We will pay, with respect to any claim we investigate or settle or any "suit" against an insured we defend:

   a. All expenses we incur.

   b. Up to $250 for cost of bail bonds required because of accidents or traffic law violations arising out of the use of any vehicle to which the Bodily Injury Liability Coverage applies. We do not have to furnish these bonds.

   c. The cost of bonds to release attachments, but only for bond amounts within the applicable limit of insurance. We do not have to furnish these bonds.

   d. All reasonable expenses incurred by the insured at our request to assist us in the investigation or defense of the claim or "suit", including actual loss of earnings up to $250 a day because of time off from work.

   e. All costs taxed against the insured in the "suit".

   f. Prejudgment interest awarded against the insured on that part of the judgment we pay. If we make an offer to pay the applicable limit of insurance, we will not pay any prejudgment interest based on that period of time after the offer.

   g. All interest on the full amount of any judgment that accrues after entry of the judgment and before we have paid, offered to pay, or deposited in court the part of the judgment that is within the applicable limit of insurance.

These payments will not reduce the limits of insurance.

2. If we defend an insured against a "suit" and an indemnitee of the insured is also named as a party to the "suit", we will defend that indemnitee if all of the following conditions are met:

   a. The "suit" against the indemnitee seeks damages for which the insured has assumed the liability of the indemnitee in a contract or agreement that is an "insured contract";

   b. This insurance applies to such liability assumed by the insured;

   c. The obligation to defend, or the cost of the defense of, that indemnitee, has also been assumed by the insured in the same "insured contract";

   d. The allegations in the "suit" and the information we know about the "occurrence" are such that no conflict appears to exist between the interests of the insured and the interests of the indemnitee;

   e. The indemnitee and the insured ask us to conduct and control the defense of that indemnitee against such "suit" and agree that we can assign the same counsel to defend the insured and the indemnitee; and

   f. The indemnitee:

      (1) Agrees in writing to:

         (a) Cooperate with us in the investigation, settlement or defense of the "suit";

         (b) Immediately send us copies of any demands, notices, summonses or legal papers received in connection with the "suit";

(c) Notify any other insurer whose coverage is available to the indemnitee; and

(d) Cooperate with us with respect to coordinating other applicable insurance available to the indemnitee; and

(2) Provides us with written authorization to:

(a) Obtain records and other information related to the "suit"; and

(b) Conduct and control the defense of the indemnitee in such "suit".

So long as the above conditions are met, attorneys' fees incurred by us in the defense of that indemnitee, necessary litigation expenses incurred by us and necessary litigation expenses incurred by the indemnitee at our request will be paid as Supplementary Payments. Notwithstanding the provisions of Paragraph **2.b.(2)** of Section **I** – Coverage **A** – Bodily Injury And Property Damage Liability, such payments will not be deemed to be damages for "bodily injury" and "property damage" and will not reduce the limits of insurance.

Our obligation to defend an insured's indemnitee and to pay for attorneys' fees and necessary litigation expenses as Supplementary Payments ends when:

a. We have used up the applicable limit of insurance in the payment of judgments or settlements; or

b. The conditions set forth above, or the terms of the agreement described in Paragraph **f.** above, are no longer met.

SECTION II – WHO IS AN INSURED

1. If you are designated in the Declarations as:

a. An individual, you and your spouse are insureds, but only with respect to the conduct of a business of which you are the sole owner.

b. A partnership or joint venture, you are an insured. Your members, your partners, and their spouses are also insureds, but only with respect to the conduct of your business.

c. A limited liability company, you are an insured. Your members are also insureds, but only with respect to the conduct of your business. Your managers are insureds, but only with respect to their duties as your managers.

d. An organization other than a partnership, joint venture or limited liability company, you are an insured. Your "executive officers" and directors are insureds, but only with respect to their duties as your officers or directors. Your stockholders are also insureds, but only with respect to their liability as stockholders.

e. A trust, you are an insured. Your trustees are also insureds, but only with respect to their duties as trustees.

2. Each of the following is also an insured:

a. Your "volunteer workers" only while performing duties related to the conduct of your business, or your "employees", other than either your "executive officers" (if you are an organization other than a partnership, joint venture or limited liability company) or your managers (if you are a limited liability company), but only for acts within the scope of their employment by you or while performing duties related to the conduct of your business. However, none of these "employees" or "volunteer workers" are insureds for:

(1) "Bodily injury" or "personal and advertising injury":

(a) To you, to your partners or members (if you are a partnership or joint venture), to your members (if you are a limited liability company), to a co-"employee" while in the course of his or her employment or performing duties related to the conduct of your business, or to your other "volunteer workers" while performing duties related to the conduct of your business;

(b) To the spouse, child, parent, brother or sister of that co-"employee" or "volunteer worker" as a consequence of Paragraph **(1)(a)** above;

(c) For which there is any obligation to share damages with or repay someone else who must pay damages because of the injury described in Paragraphs **(1)(a)** or **(b)** above; or

(d) Arising out of his or her providing or failing to provide professional health care services.

(2) "Property damage" to property:

(a) Owned, occupied or used by,

(b) Rented to, in the care, custody or control of, or over which physical control is being exercised for any purpose by

you, any of your "employees", "volunteer workers", any partner or member (if you are a partnership or joint venture), or any member (if you are a limited liability company).

b. Any person (other than your "employee" or "volunteer worker") or any organization while acting as your real estate manager.

SECTION II – WHO IS AN INSURED

1. If you are designated in the Declarations as:

   a. An individual, you and your spouse are insureds, but only with respect to the conduct of a business of which you are the sole owner.

   b. A partnership or joint venture, you are an insured. Your members, your partners, and their spouses are also insureds, but only with respect to the conduct of your business.

   c. A limited liability company, you are an insured. Your members are also insureds, but only with respect to the conduct of your business. Your managers are insureds, but only with respect to their duties as your managers.

   d. An organization other than a partnership, joint venture or limited liability company, you are an insured. Your "executive officers" and directors are insureds, but only with respect to their duties as your officers or directors. Your stockholders are also insureds, but only with respect to their liability as stockholders.

   e. A trust, you are an insured. Your trustees are also insureds, but only with respect to their duties as trustees.

2. Each of the following is also an insured:

   a. Your "volunteer workers" only while performing duties related to the conduct of your business, or your "employees", other than either your "executive officers" (if you are an organization other than a partnership, joint venture or limited liability company) or your managers (if you are a limited liability company), but only for acts within the scope of their employment by you or while performing duties related to the conduct of your business. However, none of these "employees" or "volunteer workers" are insureds for:

      (1) "Bodily injury" or "personal and advertising injury":

         (a) To you, to your partners or members (if you are a partnership or joint venture), to your members (if you are a limited liability company), to a co-"employee" while in the course of his or her employment or performing duties related to the conduct of your business, or to your other "volunteer workers" while performing duties related to the conduct of your business;

         (b) To the spouse, child, parent, brother or sister of that co-"employee" or "volunteer worker" as a consequence of Paragraph **(1)(a)** above;

         (c) For which there is any obligation to share damages with or repay someone else who must pay damages because of the injury described in Paragraphs **(1)(a)** or **(b)** above; or

         (d) Arising out of his or her providing or failing to provide professional health care services.

      (2) "Property damage" to property:

         (a) Owned, occupied or used by,

         (b) Rented to, in the care, custody or control of, or over which physical control is being exercised for any purpose by

         you, any of your "employees", "volunteer workers", any partner or member (if you are a partnership or joint venture), or any member (if you are a limited liability company).

   b. Any person (other than your "employee" or "volunteer worker"), or any organization while acting as your real estate manager.

   c. Any person or organization having proper temporary custody of your property if you die, but only:

      (1) With respect to liability arising out of the maintenance or use of that property; and

      (2) Until your legal representative has been appointed.

   d. Your legal representative if you die, but only with respect to duties as such. That representative will have all your rights and duties under this Coverage Part.

3. With respect to "mobile equipment" registered in your name under any motor vehicle registration law, any person is an insured while driving such equipment along a public highway with your permission. Any other person or organization responsible for the conduct of such person is also an insured, but only with respect to liability arising out of the operation of the equipment, and only if no other insurance of any kind is available to that person or organization for this liability. However, no person or organization is an insured with respect to:

   a. "Bodily injury" to a co-"employee" of the person driving the equipment; or

   b. "Property damage" to property owned by, rented to, in the charge of or occupied by you or the employer of any person who is an insured under this provision.

SECTION IV – COMMERCIAL GENERAL LIABILITY CONDITIONS

1. Bankruptcy

Bankruptcy or insolvency of the insured or of the insured's estate will not relieve us of our obligations under this Coverage Part.

2. Duties In The Event Of Occurrence, Offense, Claim Or Suit

a. You must see to it that we are notified as soon as practicable of an "occurrence" or offense which may result in a claim. To the extent possible, notice should include:

(1) How, when and where the "occurrence" or offense took place;

(2) The names and addresses of any injured persons and witnesses; and

(3) The nature and location of any injury or damage arising out of the "occurrence" or offense.

Notice of an "occurrence" or offense is not notice of a claim.

b. If a claim is received by any insured, you must:

(1) Immediately record the specifics of the claim and the date received; and

(2) Notify us as soon as practicable.

You must see to it that we receive written notice of the claim as soon as practicable.

c. You and any other involved insured must:

(1) Immediately send us copies of any demands, notices, summonses or legal papers received in connection with the claim or a "suit";

(2) Authorize us to obtain records and other information;

(3) Cooperate with us in the investigation or settlement of the claim or defense against the "suit"; and

(4) Assist us, upon our request, in the enforcement of any right against any person or organization which may be liable to the insured because of injury or damage to which this insurance may also apply.

d. No insured will, except at that insured's own cost, voluntarily make a payment, assume any obligation, or incur any expense, other than for first aid, without our consent.

3. Legal Action Against Us

No person or organization has a right under this Coverage Part:

a. To join us as a party or otherwise bring us into a "suit" asking for damages from an insured; or

b. To sue us on this Coverage Part unless all of its terms have been fully complied with.

A person or organization may sue us to recover on an agreed settlement or on a final judgment against an insured; but we will not be liable for damages that are not payable under the terms of this Coverage Part or that are in excess of the applicable limit of insurance. An agreed settlement means a settlement and release of liability signed by us, the insured and the claimant or the claimant's legal representative.

4. Other Insurance

If other valid and collectible insurance is available to the insured for a loss we cover under Coverages **A** or **B** of this Coverage Part, our obligations are limited as follows:

a. **Primary Insurance**

This insurance is primary except when **b.** below applies. If this insurance is primary, our obligations are not affected unless any of the other insurance is also primary. Then, we will share with all that other insurance by the method described in **c.** below.

b. **Excess Insurance**

This insurance is excess over:

(1) Any of the other insurance, whether primary, excess, contingent or on any other basis:

(a) That is effective prior to the beginning of the policy period shown in the Declarations of this insurance and applies to "bodily injury" or "property damage" on other than a claims-made basis, if:

(i) No Retroactive Date is shown in the Declarations of this insurance; or

(ii) The other insurance has a policy period which continues after the Retroactive Date shown in the Declarations of this insurance;

(b) That is Fire, Extended Coverage, Builders' Risk, Installation Risk or similar coverage for "your work";

(c) That is Fire insurance for premises rented to you or temporarily occupied by you with permission of the owner;

(d) That is insurance purchased by you to cover your liability as a tenant for "property damage" to premises rented to you or temporarily occupied by you with permission of the owner; or

(e) If the loss arises out of the maintenance or use of aircraft, "autos" or watercraft to the extent not subject to Exclusion **g.** of Section **I** – Coverage **A** – Bodily Injury And Property Damage Liability.

(2) Any other primary insurance available to you covering liability for damages arising out of the premises or operations for which you have been added as an additional insured by attachment of an endorsement.

When this insurance is excess, we will have no duty under Coverages **A** or **B** to defend the insured against any "suit" if any other insurer has a duty to defend the insured against that "suit". If no other insurer defends, we will undertake to do so, but we will be entitled to the insured's rights against all those other insurers.

When this insurance is excess over other insurance, we will pay only our share of the amount of the loss, if any, that exceeds the sum of:

(1) The total amount that all such other insurance would pay for the loss in the absence of this insurance; and

(2) The total of all deductible and self-insured amounts under all that other insurance.

We will share the remaining loss, if any, with any other insurance that is not described in this Excess Insurance provision and was not bought specifically to apply in excess of the Limits of Insurance shown in the Declarations of this Coverage Part.

c. Method Of Sharing

If all of the other insurance permits contribution by equal shares, we will follow this method also. Under this approach each insurer contributes equal amounts until it has paid its applicable limit of insurance or none of the loss remains, whichever comes first.

If any of the other insurance does not permit contribution by equal shares, we will contribute by limits. Under this method, each insurer's share is based on the ratio of its applicable limit of insurance to the total applicable limits of insurance of all insurers.

5. Premium Audit

a. We will compute all premiums for this Coverage Part in accordance with our rules and rates.

b. Premium shown in this Coverage Part as advance premium is a deposit premium only. At the close of each audit period we will compute the earned premium for that period and send notice to the first Named Insured. The due date for audit and retrospective premiums is the date shown as the due date on the bill. If the sum of the advance and audit premiums paid for the policy period is greater than the earned premium, we will return the excess to the first Named Insured.

c. The first Named Insured must keep records of the information we need for premium computation, and send us copies at such times as we may request.

6. Representations

By accepting this policy, you agree:

a. The statements in the Declarations are accurate and complete;

b. Those statements are based upon representations you made to us; and

c. We have issued this policy in reliance upon your representations.

7. Separation Of Insureds

Except with respect to the Limits of Insurance, and any rights or duties specifically assigned in this Coverage Part to the first Named Insured, this insurance applies:

a. As if each Named Insured were the only Named Insured; and

b. Separately to each insured against whom claim is made or "suit" is brought.

8. Transfer Of Rights Of Recovery Against Others To Us

If the insured has rights to recover all or part of any payment we have made under this Coverage Part, those rights are transferred to us. The insured must do nothing after loss to impair them. At our request, the insured will bring "suit" or transfer those rights to us and help us enforce them.

9. When We Do Not Renew

If we decide not to renew this Coverage Part, we will mail or deliver to the first Named Insured shown in the Declarations written notice of the nonrenewal not less than 30 days before the expiration date.

If notice is mailed, proof of mailing will be sufficient proof of notice.

10. Your Right To Claim And "Occurrence" Information

We will provide the first Named Insured shown in the Declarations the following information relating to this and any preceding general liability claims-made Coverage Part we have issued to you during the previous three years:

a. A list or other record of each "occurrence", not previously reported to any other insurer, of which we were notified in accordance with Paragraph **2.a.** of the Section **IV** – Duties In The Event Of Occurrence, Offense, Claim Or Suit Condition. We will include the date and brief description of the "occurrence" if that information was in the notice we received.

b. A summary by policy year, of payments made and amounts reserved, stated separately, under any applicable General Aggregate Limit and Products-Completed Operations Aggregate Limit.

Amounts reserved are based on our judgment. They are subject to change and should not be regarded as ultimate settlement values.

You must not disclose this information to any claimant or any claimant's representative without our consent.

If we cancel or elect not to renew this Coverage Part, we will provide such information no later than 30 days before the date of policy termination. In other circumstances, we will provide this information only if we receive a written request from the first Named Insured within 60 days after the end of the policy period. In this case, we will provide this information within 45 days of receipt of the request.

We compile claim and "occurrence" information for our own business purposes and exercise reasonable care in doing so. In providing this information to the first Named Insured, we make no representations or warranties to insureds, insurers, or others to whom this information is furnished by or on behalf of any insured. Cancellation or non-renewal will be effective even if we inadvertently provide inaccurate information.

SECTION V – EXTENDED REPORTING PERIODS

1. We will provide one or more Extended Reporting Periods, as described below, if:

a. This Coverage Part is canceled or not renewed; or

b. We renew or replace this Coverage Part with insurance that:

(1) Has a Retroactive Date later than the date shown in the Declarations of this Coverage Part; or

(2) Does not apply to "bodily injury", "property damage" or "personal and advertising injury" on a claims-made basis.

2. Extended Reporting Periods do not extend the policy period or change the scope of coverage provided. They apply only to claims for:

a. "Bodily injury" or "property damage" that occurs before the end of the policy period but not before the Retroactive Date, if any, shown in the Declarations; or

b. "Personal and advertising injury" caused by an offense committed before the end of the policy period but not before the Retroactive Date, if any, shown in the Declarations.

Once in effect, Extended Reporting Periods may not be canceled.

3. A Basic Extended Reporting Period is automatically provided without additional charge. This period starts with the end of the policy period and lasts for:

a. Five years with respect to claims because of "bodily injury" and "property damage" arising out of an "occurrence" reported to us, not later than 60 days after the end of the policy period, in accordance with Paragraph **2.a.** of the Section **IV** – Duties In The Event Of Occurrence, Offense, Claim Or Suit Condition;

b. Five years with respect to claims because of "personal and advertising injury" arising out of an offense reported to us, not later than 60 days after the end of the policy period, in accordance with Paragraph **2.a.** of the Section **IV** – Duties In The Event Of Occurrence, Offense, Claim Or Suit Condition; and

c. Sixty days with respect to claims arising from "occurrences" or offenses not previously reported to us.

The Basic Extended Reporting Period does not apply to claims that are covered under any subsequent insurance you purchase, or that would be covered but for exhaustion of the amount of insurance applicable to such claims.

4. The Basic Extended Reporting Period does not reinstate or increase the Limits of Insurance.

                   CG 00 02 10 01   ☐

5. A Supplemental Extended Reporting Period of unlimited duration is available, but only by an endorsement and for an extra charge. This supplemental period starts when the Basic Extended Reporting Period, set forth in Paragraph **3.** above, ends.

You must give us a written request for the endorsement within 60 days after the end of the policy period. The Supplemental Extended Reporting Period will not go into effect unless you pay the additional premium promptly when due.

We will determine the additional premium in accordance with our rules and rates. In doing so, we may take into account the following:

a. The exposures insured;

b. Previous types and amounts of insurance;

c. Limits of Insurance available under this Coverage Part for future payment of damages; and

d. Other related factors.

The additional premium will not exceed 200% of the annual premium for this Coverage Part.

This endorsement shall set forth the terms, not inconsistent with this Section, applicable to the Supplemental Extended Reporting Period, including a provision to the effect that the insurance afforded for claims first received during such period is excess over any other valid and collectible insurance available under policies in force after the Supplemental Extended Reporting Period starts.

6. If the Supplemental Extended Reporting Period is in effect, we will provide the supplemental aggregate limits of insurance described below, but only for claims first received and recorded during the Supplemental Extended Reporting Period.

The supplemental aggregate limits of insurance will be equal to the dollar amount shown in the Declarations in effect at the end of the policy period for such of the following limits of insurance for which a dollar amount has been entered:

General Aggregate Limit
Products-Completed Operations Aggregate Limit

Paragraphs **2.** and **3.** of Section **III** – Limits Of Insurance will be amended accordingly. The Personal and Advertising Injury Limit, the Each Occurrence Limit and the Damage To Premises Rented To You Limit shown in the Declarations will then continue to apply, as set forth in Paragraphs **4.**, **5.** and **6.** of that Section.

SECTION VI – DEFINITIONS

1. "Advertisement" means a notice that is broadcast or published to the general public or specific market segments about your goods, products or services for the purpose of attracting customers or supporters. For the purposes of this definition:

a. Notices that are published include material placed on the Internet or on similar electronic means of communication; and

b. Regarding web-sites, only that part of a web-site that is about your goods, products or services for the purposes of attracting customers or supporters is considered an advertisement.

2. "Auto" means a land motor vehicle, trailer or semitrailer designed for travel on public roads, including any attached machinery or equipment. But "auto" does not include "mobile equipment".

3. "Bodily injury" means bodily injury, sickness or disease sustained by a person, including death resulting from any of these at any time.

4. "Coverage territory" means:

a. The United States of America (including its territories and possessions), Puerto Rico and Canada;

b. International waters or airspace, but only if the injury or damage occurs in the course of travel or transportation between any places included in **a.** above; or

c. All other parts of the world if the injury or damage arises out of:

(1) Goods or products made or sold by you in the territory described in **a.** above;

(2) The activities of a person whose home is in the territory described in **a.** above, but is away for a short time on your business; or

(3) "Personal and advertising injury" offenses that take place through the Internet or similar electronic means of communication

provided the insured's responsibility to pay damages is determined in a "suit" on the merits, in the territory described in **a.** above or in a settlement we agree to.

5. "Employee" includes a "leased worker". "Employee" does not include a "temporary worker".

6. "Executive officer" means a person holding any of the officer positions created by your charter, constitution, by-laws or any other similar governing document.

7. "Hostile fire" means one which becomes uncontrollable or breaks out from where it was intended to be.

8. "Impaired property" means tangible property, other than "your product" or "your work", that cannot be used or is less useful because:

    a. It incorporates "your product" or "your work" that is known or thought to be defective, deficient, inadequate or dangerous; or

    b. You have failed to fulfill the terms of a contract or agreement;

if such property can be restored to use by:

    a. The repair, replacement, adjustment or removal of "your product" or "your work"; or

    b. Your fulfilling the terms of the contract or agreement.

9. "Insured contract" means:

    a. A contract for a lease of premises. However, that portion of the contract for a lease of premises that indemnifies any person or organization for damage by fire to premises while rented to you or temporarily occupied by you with permission of the owner is not an "insured contract";

    b. A sidetrack agreement;

    c. Any easement or license agreement, except in connection with construction or demolition operations on or within 50 feet of a railroad;

    d. An obligation, as required by ordinance, to indemnify a municipality, except in connection with work for a municipality;

    e. An elevator maintenance agreement;

    f. That part of any other contract or agreement pertaining to your business (including an indemnification of a municipality in connection with work performed for a municipality) under which you assume the tort liability of another party to pay for "bodily injury" or "property damage" to a third person or organization. Tort liability means a liability that would be imposed by law in the absence of any contract or agreement.

Paragraph **f.** does not include that part of any contract or agreement:

    (1) That indemnifies a railroad for "bodily injury" or "property damage" arising out of construction or demolition operations, within 50 feet of any railroad property and affecting any railroad bridge or trestle, tracks, road-beds, tunnel, underpass or crossing;

    (2) That indemnifies an architect, engineer or surveyor for injury or damage arising out of:

        (a) Preparing, approving, or failing to prepare or approve, maps, shop drawings, opinions, reports, surveys, field orders, change orders or drawings and specifications; or

        (b) Giving directions or instructions, or failing to give them, if that is the primary cause of the injury or damage; or

    (3) Under which the insured, if an architect, engineer or surveyor, assumes liability for an injury or damage arising out of the insured's rendering or failure to render professional services, including those listed in **(2)** above and supervisory, inspection, architectural or engineering activities.

10. "Leased worker" means a person leased to you by a labor leasing firm under an agreement between you and the labor leasing firm, to perform duties related to the conduct of your business. "Leased worker" does not include a "temporary worker".

11. "Loading or unloading" means the handling of property:

    a. After it is moved from the place where it is accepted for movement into or onto an aircraft, watercraft or "auto";

    b. While it is in or on an aircraft, watercraft or "auto"; or

    c. While it is being moved from an aircraft, watercraft or "auto" to the place where it is finally delivered;

but "loading or unloading" does not include the movement of property by means of a mechanical device, other than a hand truck, that is not attached to the aircraft, watercraft or "auto".

12. "Mobile equipment" means any of the following types of land vehicles, including any attached machinery or equipment:

   a. Bulldozers, farm machinery, forklifts and other vehicles designed for use principally off public roads;

   b. Vehicles maintained for use solely on or next to premises you own or rent;

   c. Vehicles that travel on crawler treads;

   d. Vehicles, whether self-propelled or not, maintained primarily to provide mobility to permanently mounted:

      (1) Power cranes, shovels, loaders, diggers or drills; or

      (2) Road construction or resurfacing equipment such as graders, scrapers or rollers;

   e. Vehicles not described in a., b., c. or d. above that are not self-propelled and are maintained primarily to provide mobility to permanently attached equipment of the following types:

      (1) Air compressors, pumps and generators, including spraying, welding, building cleaning, geophysical exploration, lighting and well servicing equipment; or

      (2) Cherry pickers and similar devices used to raise or lower workers;

   f. Vehicles not described in a., b., c. or d. above maintained primarily for purposes other than the transportation of persons or cargo.

      However, self-propelled vehicles with the following types of permanently attached equipment are not "mobile equipment" but will be considered "autos":

      (1) Equipment designed primarily for:

         (a) Snow removal;

         (b) Road maintenance, but not construction or resurfacing; or

         (c) Street cleaning;

      (2) Cherry pickers and similar devices mounted on automobile or truck chassis and used to raise or lower workers; and

      (3) Air compressors, pumps and generators, including spraying, welding, building cleaning, geophysical exploration, lighting and well servicing equipment.

13. "Occurrence" means an accident, including continuous or repeated exposure to substantially the same general harmful conditions.

14. "Personal and advertising injury" means injury, including consequential "bodily injury", arising out of one or more of the following offenses:

   a. False arrest, detention or imprisonment;

   b. Malicious prosecution;

   c. The wrongful eviction from, wrongful entry into, or invasion of the right of private occupancy of a room, dwelling or premises that a person occupies, committed by or on behalf of its owner, landlord or lessor;

   d. Oral or written publication, in any manner, of material that slanders or libels a person or organization or disparages a person's or organization's goods, products or services;

   e. Oral or written publication, in any manner, of material that violates a person's right of privacy;

   f. The use of another's advertising idea in your "advertisement"; or

   g. Infringing upon another's copyright, trade dress or slogan in your "advertisement".

15. "Pollutants" mean any solid, liquid, gaseous or thermal irritant or contaminant, including smoke, vapor, soot, fumes, acids, alkalis, chemicals and waste. Waste includes materials to be recycled, reconditioned or reclaimed.

16. "Products-completed operations hazard":

   a. Includes all "bodily injury" and "property damage" occurring away from premises you own or rent and arising out of "your product" or "your work" except:

      (1) Products that are still in your physical possession; or

      (2) Work that has not yet been completed or abandoned. However, "your work" will be deemed completed at the earliest of the following times:

         (a) When all of the work called for in your contract has been completed.

         (b) When all of the work to be done at the job site has been completed if your contract calls for work at more than one job site.

         (c) When that part of the work done at a job site has been put to its intended use by any person or organization other than another contractor or subcontractor working on the same project.

      Work that may need service, maintenance, correction, repair or replacement, but which is otherwise complete, will be treated as completed.

b. Does not include "bodily injury" or "property damage" arising out of:

   (1) The transportation of property, unless the injury or damage arises out of a condition in or on a vehicle not owned or operated by you, and that condition was created by the "loading or unloading" of that vehicle by any insured;

   (2) The existence of tools, uninstalled equipment or abandoned or unused materials; or

   (3) Products or operations for which the classification, listed in the Declarations or in a policy schedule, states that products-completed operations are subject to the General Aggregate Limit.

17. "Property damage" means:

   a. Physical injury to tangible property, including all resulting loss of use of that property. All such loss of use shall be deemed to occur at the time of the physical injury that caused it; or

   b. Loss of use of tangible property that is not physically injured. All such loss of use shall be deemed to occur at the time of the "occurrence" that caused it.

For the purposes of this insurance, electronic data is not tangible property.

As used in this definition, electronic data means information, facts or programs stored as or on, created or used on, or transmitted to or from, computer software, including systems and applications software, hard or floppy disks, CD-ROMS, tapes, drives, cells, data processing devices or any other media which are used with electronically controlled equipment.

18. "Suit" means a civil proceeding in which damages because of "bodily injury", "property damage" or "personal and advertising injury" to which this insurance applies are alleged. "Suit" includes:

   a. An arbitration proceeding in which such damages are claimed and to which the insured must submit or does submit with our consent; or

   b. Any other alternative dispute resolution proceeding in which such damages are claimed and to which the insured submits with our consent.

19. "Temporary worker" means a person who is furnished to you to substitute for a permanent "employee" on leave or to meet seasonal or short-term workload conditions.

20. "Volunteer worker" means a person who is not your "employee", and who donates his or her work and acts at the direction of and within the scope of duties determined by you, and is not paid a fee, salary or other compensation by you or anyone else for their work performed for you.

21. "Your product":

   a. Means:

     (1) Any goods or products, other than real property, manufactured, sold, handled, distributed or disposed of by:

       (a) You;

       (b) Others trading under your name; or

       (c) A person or organization whose business or assets you have acquired; and

     (2) Containers (other than vehicles), materials, parts or equipment furnished in connection with such goods or products.

   b. Includes:

     (1) Warranties or representations made at any time with respect to the fitness, quality, durability, performance or use of "your product"; and

     (2) The providing of or failure to provide warnings or instructions.

   c. Does not include vending machines or other property rented to or located for the use of others but not sold.

22. "Your work":

   a. Means:

     (1) Work or operations performed by you or on your behalf; and

     (2) Materials, parts or equipment furnished in connection with such work or operations.

   b. Includes:

     (1) Warranties or representations made at any time with respect to the fitness, quality, durability, performance or use of "your work" and

     (2) The providing of or failure to provide warnings or instructions.

COMMERCIAL GENERAL LIABILITY
CG 00 01 12 04

COMMERCIAL GENERAL LIABILITY COVERAGE FORM

Various provisions in this policy restrict coverage. Read the entire policy carefully to determine rights, duties and what is and is not covered.

Throughout this policy the words "you" and "your" refer to the Named Insured shown in the Declarations, and any other person or organization qualifying as a Named Insured under this policy. The words "we", "us" and "our" refer to the company providing this insurance.

The word "insured" means any person or organization qualifying as such under Section **II** – Who Is An Insured.

Other words and phrases that appear in quotation marks have special meaning. Refer to Section **V** – Definitions.

SECTION I – COVERAGES

COVERAGE A BODILY INJURY AND PROPERTY DAMAGE LIABILITY

1. Insuring Agreement

a. We will pay those sums that the insured becomes legally obligated to pay as damages because of "bodily injury" or "property damage" to which this insurance applies. We will have the right and duty to defend the insured against any "suit" seeking those damages. However, we will have no duty to defend the insured against any "suit" seeking damages for "bodily injury" or "property damage" to which this insurance does not apply. We may, at our discretion, investigate any "occurrence" and settle any claim or "suit" that may result. But:

(1) The amount we will pay for damages is limited as described in Section **III** – Limits Of Insurance; and

(2) Our right and duty to defend ends when we have used up the applicable limit of insurance in the payment of judgments or settlements under Coverages **A** or **B** or medical expenses under Coverage **C**.

No other obligation or liability to pay sums or perform acts or services is covered unless explicitly provided for under Supplementary Payments – Coverages **A** and **B**.

b. This insurance applies to "bodily injury" and "property damage" only if:

(1) The "bodily injury" or "property damage" is caused by an "occurrence" that takes place in the "coverage territory";

(2) The "bodily injury" or "property damage" occurs during the policy period; and

(3) Prior to the policy period, no insured listed under Paragraph **1.** of Section **II** – Who Is An Insured and no "employee" authorized by you to give or receive notice of an "occurrence" or claim, knew that the "bodily injury" or "property damage" had occurred, in whole or in part. If such a listed insured or authorized "employee" knew, prior to the policy period, that the "bodily injury" or "property damage" occurred, then any continuation, change or resumption of such "bodily injury" or "property damage" during or after the policy period will be deemed to have been known prior to the policy period.

c. "Bodily injury" or "property damage" which occurs during the policy period and was not, prior to the policy period, known to have occurred by any insured listed under Paragraph **1.** of Section **II** – Who Is An Insured or any "employee" authorized by you to give or receive notice of an "occurrence" or claim, includes any continuation, change or resumption of that "bodily injury" or "property damage" after the end of the policy period.

d. "Bodily injury" or "property damage" will be deemed to have been known to have occurred at the earliest time when any insured listed under Paragraph **1.** of Section **II** – Who Is An Insured or any "employee" authorized by you to give or receive notice of an "occurrence" or claim:

(1) Reports all, or any part, of the "bodily injury" or "property damage" to us or any other insurer;

(2) Receives a written or verbal demand or claim for damages because of the "bodily injury" or "property damage"; or

(3) Becomes aware by any other means that "bodily injury" or "property damage" has occurred or has begun to occur.

e. Damages because of "bodily injury" include damages claimed by any person or organization for care, loss of services or death resulting at any time from the "bodily injury".

2. Exclusions

This insurance does not apply to:

a. Expected Or Intended Injury

"Bodily injury" or "property damage" expected or intended from the standpoint of the insured. This exclusion does not apply to "bodily injury" resulting from the use of reasonable force to protect persons or property.

b. Contractual Liability

"Bodily injury" or "property damage" for which the insured is obligated to pay damages by reason of the assumption of liability in a contract or agreement. This exclusion does not apply to liability for damages:

(1) That the insured would have in the absence of the contract or agreement; or

(2) Assumed in a contract or agreement that is an "insured contract", provided the "bodily injury" or "property damage" occurs subsequent to the execution of the contract or agreement. Solely for the purposes of liability assumed in an "insured contract", reasonable attorney fees and necessary litigation expenses incurred by or for a party other than an insured are deemed to be damages because of "bodily injury" or "property damage", provided:

(a) Liability to such party for, or for the cost of, that party's defense has also been assumed in the same "insured contract"; and

(b) Such attorney fees and litigation expenses are for defense of that party against a civil or alternative dispute resolution proceeding in which damages to which this insurance applies are alleged.

c. Liquor Liability

"Bodily injury" or "property damage" for which any insured may be held liable by reason of:

(1) Causing or contributing to the intoxication of any person;

(2) The furnishing of alcoholic beverages to a person under the legal drinking age or under the influence of alcohol; or

(3) Any statute, ordinance or regulation relating to the sale, gift, distribution or use of alcoholic beverages.

This exclusion applies only if you are in the business of manufacturing, distributing, selling, serving or furnishing alcoholic beverages.

d. Workers' Compensation And Similar Laws

Any obligation of the insured under a workers' compensation, disability benefits or unemployment compensation law or any similar law.

e. Employer's Liability

"Bodily injury" to:

(1) An "employee" of the insured arising out of and in the course of:

(a) Employment by the insured; or

(b) Performing duties related to the conduct of the insured's business; or

(2) The spouse, child, parent, brother or sister of that "employee" as a consequence of Paragraph (1) above.

This exclusion applies:

(1) Whether the insured may be liable as an employer or in any other capacity; and

(2) To any obligation to share damages with or repay someone else who must pay damages because of the injury.

This exclusion does not apply to liability assumed by the insured under an "insured contract".

         CG 00 01 12 04   ☐

f. Pollution

(1) "Bodily injury" or "property damage" arising out of the actual, alleged or threatened discharge, dispersal, seepage, migration, release or escape of "pollutants":

(a) At or from any premises, site or location which is or was at any time owned or occupied by, or rented or loaned to, any insured. However, this subparagraph does not apply to:

(i) "Bodily injury" if sustained within a building and caused by smoke, fumes, vapor or soot produced by or originating from equipment that is used to heat, cool or dehumidify the building, or equipment that is used to heat water for personal use, by the building's occupants or their guests;

(ii) "Bodily injury" or "property damage" for which you may be held liable, if you are a contractor and the owner or lessee of such premises, site or location has been added to your policy as an additional insured with respect to your ongoing operations performed for that additional insured at that premises, site or location and such premises, site or location is not and never was owned or occupied by, or rented or loaned to, any insured, other than that additional insured; or

(iii) "Bodily injury" or "property damage" arising out of heat, smoke or fumes from a "hostile fire";

(b) At or from any premises, site or location which is or was at any time used by or for any insured or others for the handling, storage, disposal, processing or treatment of waste;

(c) Which are or were at any time transported, handled, stored, treated, disposed of, or processed as waste by or for:

(i) Any insured; or

(ii) Any person or organization for whom you may be legally responsible; or

(d) At or from any premises, site or location on which any insured or any contractors or subcontractors working directly or indirectly on any insured's behalf are performing operations if the "pollutants" are brought on or to the premises, site or location in connection with such operations by such insured, contractor or subcontractor. However, this subparagraph does not apply to:

(i) "Bodily injury" or "property damage" arising out of the escape of fuels, lubricants or other operating fluids which are needed to perform the normal electrical, hydraulic or mechanical functions necessary for the operation of "mobile equipment" or its parts, if such fuels, lubricants or other operating fluids escape from a vehicle part designed to hold, store or receive them. This exception does not apply if the "bodily injury" or "property damage" arises out of the intentional discharge, dispersal or release of the fuels, lubricants or other operating fluids, or if such fuels, lubricants or other operating fluids are brought on or to the premises, site or location with the intent that they be discharged, dispersed or released as part of the operations being performed by such insured, contractor or subcontractor;

(ii) "Bodily injury" or "property damage" sustained within a building and caused by the release of gases, fumes or vapors from materials brought into that building in connection with operations being performed by you or on your behalf by a contractor or subcontractor; or

(iii) "Bodily injury" or "property damage" arising out of heat, smoke or fumes from a "hostile fire".

(e) At or from any premises, site or location on which any insured or any contractors or subcontractors working directly or indirectly on any insured's behalf are performing operations if the operations are to test for, monitor, clean up, remove, contain, treat, detoxify or neutralize, or in any way respond to, or assess the effects of, "pollutants".

(2) Any loss, cost or expense arising out of any:

(a) Request, demand, order or statutory or regulatory requirement that any insured or others test for, monitor, clean up, remove, contain, treat, detoxify or neutralize, or in any way respond to, or assess the effects of, "pollutants"; or

(b) Claim or "suit" by or on behalf of a governmental authority for damages because of testing for, monitoring, cleaning up, removing, containing, treating, detoxifying or neutralizing, or in any way responding to, or assessing the effects of, "pollutants".

However, this paragraph does not apply to liability for damages because of "property damage" that the insured would have in the absence of such request, demand, order or statutory or regulatory requirement, or such claim or "suit" by or on behalf of a governmental authority.

g. Aircraft, Auto Or Watercraft

"Bodily injury" or "property damage" arising out of the ownership, maintenance, use or entrustment to others of any aircraft, "auto" or watercraft owned or operated by or rented or loaned to any insured. Use includes operation and "loading or unloading".

This exclusion applies even if the claims against any insured allege negligence or other wrongdoing in the supervision, hiring, employment, training or monitoring of others by that insured, if the "occurrence" which caused the "bodily injury" or "property damage" involved the ownership, maintenance, use or entrustment to others of any aircraft, "auto" or watercraft that is owned or operated by or rented or loaned to any insured.

This exclusion does not apply to:

(1) A watercraft while ashore on premises you own or rent;

(2) A watercraft you do not own that is:

(a) Less than 26 feet long; and

(b) Not being used to carry persons or property for a charge;

(3) Parking an "auto" on, or on the ways next to, premises you own or rent, provided the "auto" is not owned by or rented or loaned to you or the insured;

(4) Liability assumed under any "insured contract" for the ownership, maintenance or use of aircraft or watercraft; or

(5) "Bodily injury" or "property damage" arising out of:

(a) The operation of machinery or equipment that is attached to, or part of, a land vehicle that would qualify under the definition of "mobile equipment" if it were not subject to a compulsory or financial responsibility law or other motor vehicle insurance law in the state where it is licensed or principally garaged; or

(b) the operation of any of the machinery or equipment listed in Paragraph **f.(2)** or **f.(3)** of the definition of "mobile equipment".

h. Mobile Equipment

"Bodily injury" or "property damage" arising out of:

(1) The transportation of "mobile equipment" by an "auto" owned or operated by or rented or loaned to any insured; or

(2) The use of "mobile equipment" in, or while in practice for, or while being prepared for, any prearranged racing, speed, demolition, or stunting activity.

i. War

"Bodily injury" or "property damage", however caused, arising, directly or indirectly, out of:

(1) War, including undeclared or civil war;

(2) Warlike action by a military force, including action in hindering or defending against an actual or expected attack, by any government, sovereign or other authority using military personnel or other agents; or

(3) Insurrection, rebellion, revolution, usurped power, or action taken by governmental authority in hindering or defending against any of these.

j. Damage To Property

"Property damage" to:

(1) Property you own, rent, or occupy, including any costs or expenses incurred by you, or any other person, organization or entity, for repair, replacement, enhancement, restoration or maintenance of such property for any reason, including prevention of injury to a person or damage to another's property;

(2) Premises you sell, give away or abandon, if the "property damage" arises out of any part of those premises;

(3) Property loaned to you;

(4) Personal property in the care, custody or control of the insured;

(5) That particular part of real property on which you or any contractors or subcontractors working directly or indirectly on your behalf are performing operations, if the "property damage" arises out of those operations; or

(6) That particular part of any property that must be restored, repaired or replaced because "your work" was incorrectly performed on it.

Paragraphs **(1)**, **(3)** and **(4)** of this exclusion do not apply to "property damage" (other than damage by fire) to premises, including the contents of such premises, rented to you for a period of 7 or fewer consecutive days. A separate limit of insurance applies to Damage To Premises Rented To You as described in Section **III** – Limits Of Insurance.

Paragraph **(2)** of this exclusion does not apply if the premises are "your work" and were never occupied, rented or held for rental by you.

Paragraphs **(3)**, **(4)**, **(5)** and **(6)** of this exclusion do not apply to liability assumed under a sidetrack agreement.

Paragraph **(6)** of this exclusion does not apply to "property damage" included in the "products-completed operations hazard".

k. Damage To Your Product

"Property damage" to "your product" arising out of it or any part of it.

l. Damage To Your Work

"Property damage" to "your work" arising out of it or any part of it and included in the "products-completed operations hazard".

This exclusion does not apply if the damaged work or the work out of which the damage arises was performed on your behalf by a subcontractor.

m. Damage To Impaired Property Or Property Not Physically Injured

"Property damage" to "impaired property" or property that has not been physically injured, arising out of:

(1) A defect, deficiency, inadequacy or dangerous condition in "your product" or "your work"; or

(2) A delay or failure by you or anyone acting on your behalf to perform a contract or agreement in accordance with its terms.

This exclusion does not apply to the loss of use of other property arising out of sudden and accidental physical injury to "your product" or "your work" after it has been put to its intended use.

n. Recall Of Products, Work Or Impaired Property

Damages claimed for any loss, cost or expense incurred by you or others for the loss of use, withdrawal, recall, inspection, repair, replacement, adjustment, removal or disposal of:

(1) "Your product";

(2) "Your work"; or

(3) "Impaired property";

if such product, work, or property is withdrawn or recalled from the market or from use by any person or organization because of a known or suspected defect, deficiency, inadequacy or dangerous condition in it.

o. Personal And Advertising Injury

"Bodily injury" arising out of "personal and advertising injury".

p. Electronic Data

Damages arising out of the loss of, loss of use of, damage to, corruption of, inability to access, or inability to manipulate electronic data.

As used in this exclusion, electronic data means information, facts or programs stored as or on, created or used on, or transmitted to or from computer software, including systems and applications software, hard or floppy disks, CD-ROMS, tapes, drives, cells, data processing devices or any other media which are used with electronically controlled equipment.

Exclusions **c.** through **n.** do not apply to damage by fire to premises while rented to you or temporarily occupied by you with permission of the owner. A separate limit of insurance applies to this coverage as described in Section **III** – Limits Of Insurance.

COVERAGE B PERSONAL AND ADVERTISING INJURY LIABILITY

1. Insuring Agreement

a. We will pay those sums that the insured becomes legally obligated to pay as damages because of "personal and advertising injury" to which this insurance applies. We will have the right and duty to defend the insured against any "suit" seeking those damages. However, we will have no duty to defend the insured against any "suit" seeking damages for "personal and advertising injury" to which this insurance does not apply. We may, at our discretion, investigate any offense and settle any claim or "suit" that may result. But:

(1) The amount we will pay for damages is limited as described in Section **III** – Limits Of Insurance; and

(2) Our right and duty to defend end when we have used up the applicable limit of insurance in the payment of judgments or settlements under Coverages **A** or **B** or medical expenses under Coverage **C**.

No other obligation or liability to pay sums or perform acts or services is covered unless explicitly provided for under Supplementary Payments – Coverages **A** and **B**.

b. This insurance applies to "personal and advertising injury" caused by an offense arising out of your business but only if the offense was committed in the "coverage territory" during the policy period.

2. Exclusions

This insurance does not apply to:

a. Knowing Violation Of Rights Of Another

"Personal and advertising injury" caused by or at the direction of the insured with the knowledge that the act would violate the rights of another and would inflict "personal and advertising injury".

b. Material Published With Knowledge Of Falsity

"Personal and advertising injury" arising out of oral or written publication of material, if done by or at the direction of the insured with knowledge of its falsity.

c. Material Published Prior To Policy Period

"Personal and advertising injury" arising out of oral or written publication of material whose first publication took place before the beginning of the policy period.

d. Criminal Acts

"Personal and advertising injury" arising out of a criminal act committed by or at the direction of the insured.

e. Contractual Liability

"Personal and advertising injury" for which the insured has assumed liability in a contract or agreement. This exclusion does not apply to liability for damages that the insured would have in the absence of the contract or agreement.

f. Breach Of Contract

"Personal and advertising injury" arising out of a breach of contract, except an implied contract to use another's advertising idea in your "advertisement".

g. Quality Or Performance Of Goods – Failure To Conform To Statements

"Personal and advertising injury" arising out of the failure of goods, products or services to conform with any statement of quality or performance made in your "advertisement".

h. Wrong Description Of Prices

"Personal and advertising injury" arising out of the wrong description of the price of goods, products or services stated in your "advertisement".

i. Infringement Of Copyright, Patent, Trademark Or Trade Secret

"Personal and advertising injury" arising out of the infringement of copyright, patent, trademark, trade secret or other intellectual property rights.

However, this exclusion does not apply to infringement, in your "advertisement", of copyright, trade dress or slogan.

j. Insureds In Media And Internet Type Businesses

"Personal and advertising injury" committed by an insured whose business is:

(1) Advertising, broadcasting, publishing or telecasting;

(2) Designing or determining content of websites for others; or

(3) An Internet search, access, content or service provider.

However, this exclusion does not apply to Paragraphs **14.a., b.** and **c.** of "personal and advertising injury" under the Definitions Section.

For the purposes of this exclusion, the placing of frames, borders or links, or advertising, for you or others anywhere on the Internet, is not by itself, considered the business of advertising, broadcasting, publishing or telecasting.

k. Electronic Chatrooms Or Bulletin Boards

"Personal and advertising injury" arising out of an electronic chatroom or bulletin board the insured hosts, owns, or over which the insured exercises control.

l. Unauthorized Use Of Another's Name Or Product

"Personal and advertising injury" arising out of the unauthorized use of another's name or product in your e-mail address, domain name or metatag, or any other similar tactics to mislead another's potential customers.

     CG 00 01 12 04   □

m. Pollution

"Personal and advertising injury" arising out of the actual, alleged or threatened discharge, dispersal, seepage, migration, release or escape of "pollutants" at any time.

n. Pollution-Related

Any loss, cost or expense arising out of any:

(1) Request, demand, order or statutory or regulatory requirement that any insured or others test for, monitor, clean up, remove, contain, treat, detoxify or neutralize, or in any way respond to, or assess the effects of, "pollutants"; or

(2) Claim or suit by or on behalf of a governmental authority for damages because of testing for, monitoring, cleaning up, removing, containing, treating, detoxifying or neutralizing, or in any way responding to, or assessing the effects of, "pollutants".

o. War

"Personal and advertising injury", however caused, arising, directly or indirectly, out of:

(1) War, including undeclared or civil war;

(2) Warlike action by a military force, including action in hindering or defending against an actual or expected attack, by any government, sovereign or other authority using military personnel or other agents; or

(3) Insurrection, rebellion, revolution, usurped power, or action taken by governmental authority in hindering or defending against any of these.

COVERAGE C MEDICAL PAYMENTS

1. Insuring Agreement

a. We will pay medical expenses as described below for "bodily injury" caused by an accident:

(1) On premises you own or rent;

(2) On ways next to premises you own or rent; or

(3) Because of your operations;

provided that:

(1) The accident takes place in the "coverage territory" and during the policy period;

(2) The expenses are incurred and reported to us within one year of the date of the accident; and

(3) The injured person submits to examination, at our expense, by physicians of our choice as often as we reasonably require.

b. We will make these payments regardless of fault. These payments will not exceed the applicable limit of insurance. We will pay reasonable expenses for:

(1) First aid administered at the time of an accident;

(2) Necessary medical, surgical, x-ray and dental services, including prosthetic devices; and

(3) Necessary ambulance, hospital, professional nursing and funeral services.

2. Exclusions

We will not pay expenses for "bodily injury":

a. Any Insured

To any insured, except "volunteer workers".

b. Hired Person

To a person hired to do work for or on behalf of any insured or a tenant of any insured.

c. Injury On Normally Occupied Premises

To a person injured on that part of premises you own or rent that the person normally occupies.

d. Workers Compensation And Similar Laws

To a person, whether or not an "employee" of any insured, if benefits for the "bodily injury" are payable or must be provided under a workers' compensation or disability benefits law or a similar law.

e. Athletics Activities

To a person injured while practicing, instructing or participating in any physical exercises or games, sports, or athletic contests.

f. Products-Completed Operations Hazard

Included within the "products-completed operations hazard".

g. Coverage A Exclusions

Excluded under Coverage **A**.

SUPPLEMENTARY PAYMENTS – COVERAGES A AND B

1. We will pay, with respect to any claim we investigate or settle, or any "suit" against an insured we defend:

a. All expenses we incur.

b. Up to $250 for cost of bail bonds required because of accidents or traffic law violations arising out of the use of any vehicle to which the Bodily Injury Liability Coverage applies. We do not have to furnish these bonds.

c. The cost of bonds to release attachments, but only for bond amounts within the applicable limit of insurance. We do not have to furnish these bonds.

d. All reasonable expenses incurred by the insured at our request to assist us in the investigation or defense of the claim or "suit", including actual loss of earnings up to $250 a day because of time off from work.

e. All costs taxed against the insured in the "suit".

f. Prejudgment interest awarded against the insured on that part of the judgment we pay. If we make an offer to pay the applicable limit of insurance, we will not pay any prejudgment interest based on that period of time after the offer.

g. All interest on the full amount of any judgment that accrues after entry of the judgment and before we have paid, offered to pay, or deposited in court the part of the judgment that is within the applicable limit of insurance.

These payments will not reduce the limits of insurance.

2. If we defend an insured against a "suit" and an indemnitee of the insured is also named as a party to the "suit", we will defend that indemnitee if all of the following conditions are met:

a. The "suit" against the indemnitee seeks damages for which the insured has assumed the liability of the indemnitee in a contract or agreement that is an "insured contract";

b. This insurance applies to such liability assumed by the insured;

c. The obligation to defend, or the cost of the defense of, that indemnitee, has also been assumed by the insured in the same "insured contract";

d. The allegations in the "suit" and the information we know about the "occurrence" are such that no conflict appears to exist between the interests of the insured and the interests of the indemnitee;

e. The indemnitee and the insured ask us to conduct and control the defense of that indemnitee against such "suit" and agree that we can assign the same counsel to defend the insured and the indemnitee; and

f. The indemnitee:

(1) Agrees in writing to:

(a) Cooperate with us in the investigation, settlement or defense of the "suit";

(b) Immediately send us copies of any demands, notices, summonses or legal papers received in connection with the "suit";

(c) Notify any other insurer whose coverage is available to the indemnitee; and

(d) Cooperate with us with respect to coordinating other applicable insurance available to the indemnitee; and

(2) Provides us with written authorization to:

(a) Obtain records and other information related to the "suit"; and

(b) Conduct and control the defense of the indemnitee in such "suit".

So long as the above conditions are met, attorneys' fees incurred by us in the defense of that indemnitee, necessary litigation expenses incurred by us and necessary litigation expenses incurred by the indemnitee at our request will be paid as Supplementary Payments. Notwithstanding the provisions of Paragraph 2.b.(2) of Section I – Coverage A – Bodily Injury And Property Damage Liability, such payments will not be deemed to be damages for "bodily injury" and "property damage" and will not reduce the limits of insurance.

Our obligation to defend an insured's indemnitee and to pay for attorneys' fees and necessary litigation expenses as Supplementary Payments ends when:

a. We have used up the applicable limit of insurance in the payment of judgments or settlements; or

b. The conditions set forth above, or the terms of the agreement described in Paragraph f. above, are no longer met.

SECTION II – WHO IS AN INSURED

1. If you are designated in the Declarations as:

a. An individual, you and your spouse are insureds, but only with respect to the conduct of a business of which you are the sole owner.

b. A partnership or joint venture, you are an insured. Your members, your partners, and their spouses are also insureds, but only with respect to the conduct of your business.

c. A limited liability company, you are an insured. Your members are also insureds, but only with respect to the conduct of your business. Your managers are insureds, but only with respect to their duties as your managers.

d. An organization other than a partnership, joint venture or limited liability company, you are an insured. Your "executive officers" and directors are insureds, but only with respect to their duties as your officers or directors. Your stockholders are also insureds, but only with respect to their liability as stockholders.

e. A trust, you are an insured. Your trustees are also insureds, but only with respect to their duties as trustees.

2. Each of the following is also an insured:

a. Your "volunteer workers" only while performing duties related to the conduct of your business, or your "employees", other than either your "executive officers" (if you are an organization other than a partnership, joint venture or limited liability company) or your managers (if you are a limited liability company), but only for acts within the scope of their employment by you or while performing duties related to the conduct of your business. However, none of these "employees" or "volunteer workers" are insureds for:

(1) "Bodily injury" or "personal and advertising injury":

(a) To you, to your partners or members (if you are a partnership or joint venture), to your members (if you are a limited liability company), to a co-"employee" while in the course of his or her employment or performing duties related to the conduct of your business, or to your other "volunteer workers" while performing duties related to the conduct of your business;

(b) To the spouse, child, parent, brother or sister of that co-"employee" or "volunteer worker" as a consequence of Paragraph **(1)(a)** above;

(c) For which there is any obligation to share damages with or repay someone else who must pay damages because of the injury described in Paragraphs **(1)(a)** or **(b)** above; or

(d) Arising out of his or her providing or failing to provide professional health care services.

(2) "Property damage" to property:

(a) Owned, occupied or used by,

(b) Rented to, in the care, custody or control of, or over which physical control is being exercised for any purpose by

you, any of your "employees", "volunteer workers", any partner or member (if you are a partnership or joint venture), or any member (if you are a limited liability company).

b. Any person (other than your "employee" or "volunteer worker"), or any organization while acting as your real estate manager.

c. Any person or organization having proper temporary custody of your property if you die, but only:

(1) With respect to liability arising out of the maintenance or use of that property; and

(2) Until your legal representative has been appointed.

d. Your legal representative if you die, but only with respect to duties as such. That representative will have all your rights and duties under this Coverage Part.

3. Any organization you newly acquire or form, other than a partnership, joint venture or limited liability company, and over which you maintain ownership or majority interest, will qualify as a Named Insured if there is no other similar insurance available to that organization. However:

a. Coverage under this provision is afforded only until the 90th day after you acquire or form the organization or the end of the policy period, whichever is earlier;

b. Coverage **A** does not apply to "bodily injury" or "property damage" that occurred before you acquired or formed the organization; and

c. Coverage **B** does not apply to "personal and advertising injury" arising out of an offense committed before you acquired or formed the organization.

No person or organization is an insured with respect to the conduct of any current or past partnership, joint venture or limited liability company that is not shown as a Named Insured in the Declarations.

SECTION III – LIMITS OF INSURANCE

1. The Limits of Insurance shown in the Declarations and the rules below fix the most we will pay regardless of the number of:

a. Insureds;

b. Claims made or "suits" brought; or

c. Persons or organizations making claims or bringing "suits".

2. The General Aggregate Limit is the most we will pay for the sum of:

   a. Medical expenses under Coverage **C**;

   b. Damages under Coverage **A**, except damages because of "bodily injury" or "property damage" included in the "products-completed operations hazard"; and

   c. Damages under Coverage **B**.

3. The Products-Completed Operations Aggregate Limit is the most we will pay under Coverage **A** for damages because of "bodily injury" and "property damage" included in the "products-completed operations hazard".

4. Subject to **2.** above, the Personal and Advertising Injury Limit is the most we will pay under Coverage **B** for the sum of all damages because of all "personal and advertising injury" sustained by any one person or organization.

5. Subject to **2.** or **3.** above, whichever applies, the Each Occurrence Limit is the most we will pay for the sum of:

   a. Damages under Coverage **A**; and

   b. Medical expenses under Coverage **C**

because of all "bodily injury" and "property damage" arising out of any one "occurrence".

6. Subject to **5.** above, the Damage To Premises Rented To You Limit is the most we will pay under Coverage **A** for damages because of "property damage" to any one premises, while rented to you, or in the case of damage by fire, while rented to you or temporarily occupied by you with permission of the owner.

7. Subject to **5.** above, the Medical Expense Limit is the most we will pay under Coverage **C** for all medical expenses because of "bodily injury" sustained by any one person.

The Limits of Insurance of this Coverage Part apply separately to each consecutive annual period and to any remaining period of less than 12 months, starting with the beginning of the policy period shown in the Declarations, unless the policy period is extended after issuance for an additional period of less than 12 months. In that case, the additional period will be deemed part of the last preceding period for purposes of determining the Limits of Insurance.

SECTION IV – COMMERCIAL GENERAL LIABILITY CONDITIONS

1. Bankruptcy

Bankruptcy or insolvency of the insured or of the insured's estate will not relieve us of our obligations under this Coverage Part.

2. Duties In The Event Of Occurrence, Offense, Claim Or Suit

   a. You must see to it that we are notified as soon as practicable of an "occurrence" or an offense which may result in a claim. To the extent possible, notice should include:

      (1) How, when and where the "occurrence" or offense took place;

      (2) The names and addresses of any injured persons and witnesses; and

      (3) The nature and location of any injury or damage arising out of the "occurrence" or offense.

   b. If a claim is made or "suit" is brought against any insured, you must:

      (1) Immediately record the specifics of the claim or "suit" and the date received; and

      (2) Notify us as soon as practicable.

   You must see to it that we receive written notice of the claim or "suit" as soon as practicable.

   c. You and any other involved insured must:

      (1) Immediately send us copies of any demands, notices, summonses or legal papers received in connection with the claim or "suit";

      (2) Authorize us to obtain records and other information;

      (3) Cooperate with us in the investigation or settlement of the claim or defense against the "suit"; and

      (4) Assist us, upon our request, in the enforcement of any right against any person or organization which may be liable to the insured because of injury or damage to which this insurance may also apply.

   d. No insured will, except at that insured's own cost, voluntarily make a payment, assume any obligation, or incur any expense, other than for first aid, without our consent.

3. Legal Action Against Us

No person or organization has a right under this Coverage Part:

   a. To join us as a party or otherwise bring us into a "suit" asking for damages from an insured; or

b. To sue us on this Coverage Part unless all of its terms have been fully complied with.

A person or organization may sue us to recover on an agreed settlement or on a final judgment against an insured; but we will not be liable for damages that are not payable under the terms of this Coverage Part or that are in excess of the applicable limit of insurance. An agreed settlement means a settlement and release of liability signed by us, the insured and the claimant or the claimant's legal representative.

4. Other Insurance

If other valid and collectible insurance is available to the insured for a loss we cover under Coverages **A** or **B** of this Coverage Part, our obligations are limited as follows:

a. Primary Insurance

This insurance is primary except when **b.** below applies. If this insurance is primary, our obligations are not affected unless any of the other insurance is also primary. Then, we will share with all that other insurance by the method described in **c.** below.

b. Excess Insurance

This insurance is excess over:

(1) Any of the other insurance, whether primary, excess, contingent or on any other basis:

 (a) That is Fire, Extended Coverage, Builder's Risk, Installation Risk or similar coverage for "your work";

 (b) That is Fire insurance for premises rented to you or temporarily occupied by you with permission of the owner;

 (c) That is insurance purchased by you to cover your liability as a tenant for "property damage" to premises rented to you or temporarily occupied by you with permission of the owner; or

 (d) If the loss arises out of the maintenance or use of aircraft, "autos" or watercraft to the extent not subject to Exclusion **g.** of Section **I** – Coverage **A** – Bodily Injury And Property Damage Liability.

(2) Any other primary insurance available to you covering liability for damages arising out of the premises or operations, or the products and completed operations, for which you have been added as an additional insured by attachment of an endorsement.

When this insurance is excess, we will have no duty under Coverages **A** or **B** to defend the insured against any "suit" if any other insurer has a duty to defend the insured against that "suit". If no other insurer defends, we will undertake to do so, but we will be entitled to the insured's rights against all those other insurers.

When this insurance is excess over other insurance, we will pay only our share of the amount of the loss, if any, that exceeds the sum of:

(1) The total amount that all such other insurance would pay for the loss in the absence of this insurance; and

(2) The total of all deductible and self-insured amounts under all that other insurance.

We will share the remaining loss, if any, with any other insurance that is not described in this Excess Insurance provision and was not bought specifically to apply in excess of the Limits of Insurance shown in the Declarations of this Coverage Part.

c. Method Of Sharing

If all of the other insurance permits contribution by equal shares, we will follow this method also. Under this approach each insurer contributes equal amounts until it has paid its applicable limit of insurance or none of the loss remains, whichever comes first.

If any of the other insurance does not permit contribution by equal shares, we will contribute by limits. Under this method, each insurer's share is based on the ratio of its applicable limit of insurance to the total applicable limits of insurance of all insurers.

5. Premium Audit

a. We will compute all premiums for this Coverage Part in accordance with our rules and rates.

b. Premium shown in this Coverage Part as advance premium is a deposit premium only. At the close of each audit period we will compute the earned premium for that period and send notice to the first Named Insured. The due date for audit and retrospective premiums is the date shown as the due date on the bill. If the sum of the advance and audit premiums paid for the policy period is greater than the earned premium, we will return the excess to the first Named Insured.

c. The first Named Insured must keep records of the information we need for premium computation, and send us copies at such times as we may request.

6. Representations

By accepting this policy, you agree:

a. The statements in the Declarations are accurate and complete;

b. Those statements are based upon representations you made to us; and

c. We have issued this policy in reliance upon your representations.

7. Separation Of Insureds

Except with respect to the Limits of Insurance, and any rights or duties specifically assigned in this Coverage Part to the first Named Insured, this insurance applies:

a. As if each Named Insured were the only Named Insured; and

b. Separately to each insured against whom claim is made or "suit" is brought.

8. Transfer Of Rights Of Recovery Against Others To Us

If the insured has rights to recover all or part of any payment we have made under this Coverage Part, those rights are transferred to us. The insured must do nothing after loss to impair them. At our request, the insured will bring "suit" or transfer those rights to us and help us enforce them.

9. When We Do Not Renew

If we decide not to renew this Coverage Part, we will mail or deliver to the first Named Insured shown in the Declarations written notice of the nonrenewal not less than 30 days before the expiration date.

If notice is mailed, proof of mailing will be sufficient proof of notice.

SECTION V – DEFINITIONS

1. "Advertisement" means a notice that is broadcast or published to the general public or specific market segments about your goods, products or services for the purpose of attracting customers or supporters. For the purposes of this definition:

a. Notices that are published include material placed on the Internet or on similar electronic means of communication; and

b. Regarding web-sites, only that part of a website that is about your goods, products or services for the purposes of attracting customers or supporters is considered an advertisement.

2. "Auto" means:

a. A land motor vehicle, trailer or semitrailer designed for travel on public roads, including any attached machinery or equipment; or

b. Any other land vehicle that is subject to a compulsory or financial responsibility law or other motor vehicle insurance law in the state where it is licensed or principally garaged.

However, "auto" does not include "mobile equipment".

3. "Bodily injury" means bodily injury, sickness or disease sustained by a person, including death resulting from any of these at any time.

4. "Coverage territory" means:

a. The United States of America (including its territories and possessions), Puerto Rico and Canada;

b. International waters or airspace, but only if the injury or damage occurs in the course of travel or transportation between any places included in **a.** above; or

c. All other parts of the world if the injury or damage arises out of:

(1) Goods or products made or sold by you in the territory described in **a.** above;

(2) The activities of a person whose home is in the territory described in **a.** above, but is away for a short time on your business; or

(3) "Personal and advertising injury" offenses that take place through the Internet or similar electronic means of communication

provided the insured's responsibility to pay damages is determined in a "suit" on the merits, in the territory described in **a.** above or in a settlement we agree to.

5. "Employee" includes a "leased worker". "Employee" does not include a "temporary worker".

6. "Executive officer" means a person holding any of the officer positions created by your charter, constitution, by-laws or any other similar governing document.

7. "Hostile fire" means one which becomes uncontrollable or breaks out from where it was intended to be.

8. "Impaired property" means tangible property, other than "your product" or "your work", that cannot be used or is less useful because:

a. It incorporates "your product" or "your work" that is known or thought to be defective, deficient, inadequate or dangerous; or

b. You have failed to fulfill the terms of a contract or agreement;

if such property can be restored to use by:

a. The repair, replacement, adjustment or removal of "your product" or "your work"; or

b. Your fulfilling the terms of the contract or agreement.

9. "Insured contract" means:

a. A contract for a lease of premises. However, that portion of the contract for a lease of premises that indemnifies any person or organization for damage by fire to premises while rented to you or temporarily occupied by you with permission of the owner is not an "insured contract";

b. A sidetrack agreement;

c. Any easement or license agreement, except in connection with construction or demolition operations on or within 50 feet of a railroad;

d. An obligation, as required by ordinance, to indemnify a municipality, except in connection with work for a municipality;

e. An elevator maintenance agreement;

f. That part of any other contract or agreement pertaining to your business (including an indemnification of a municipality in connection with work performed for a municipality) under which you assume the tort liability of another party to pay for "bodily injury" or "property damage" to a third person or organization. Tort liability means a liability that would be imposed by law in the absence of any contract or agreement.

Paragraph **f.** does not include that part of any contract or agreement:

(1) That indemnifies a railroad for "bodily injury" or "property damage" arising out of construction or demolition operations, within 50 feet of any railroad property and affecting any railroad bridge or trestle, tracks, roadbeds, tunnel, underpass or crossing;

(2) That indemnifies an architect, engineer or surveyor for injury or damage arising out of:

(a) Preparing, approving, or failing to prepare or approve, maps, shop drawings, opinions, reports, surveys, field orders, change orders or drawings and specifications; or

(b) Giving directions or instructions, or failing to give them, if that is the primary cause of the injury or damage; or

(3) Under which the insured, if an architect, engineer or surveyor, assumes liability for an injury or damage arising out of the insured's rendering or failure to render professional services, including those listed in **(2)** above and supervisory, inspection, architectural or engineering activities.

10. "Leased worker" means a person leased to you by a labor leasing firm under an agreement between you and the labor leasing firm, to perform duties related to the conduct of your business. "Leased worker" does not include a "temporary worker".

11. "Loading or unloading" means the handling of property:

a. After it is moved from the place where it is accepted for movement into or onto an aircraft, watercraft or "auto";

b. While it is in or on an aircraft, watercraft or "auto"; or

c. While it is being moved from an aircraft, watercraft or "auto" to the place where it is finally delivered;

but "loading or unloading" does not include the movement of property by means of a mechanical device, other than a hand truck, that is not attached to the aircraft, watercraft or "auto".

12. "Mobile equipment" means any of the following types of land vehicles, including any attached machinery or equipment:

a. Bulldozers, farm machinery, forklifts and other vehicles designed for use principally off public roads;

b. Vehicles maintained for use solely on or next to premises you own or rent;

c. Vehicles that travel on crawler treads;

d. Vehicles, whether self-propelled or not, maintained primarily to provide mobility to permanently mounted:

(1) Power cranes, shovels, loaders, diggers or drills; or

(2) Road construction or resurfacing equipment such as graders, scrapers or rollers;

e. Vehicles not described in **a.**, **b.**, **c.** or **d.** above that are not self-propelled and are maintained primarily to provide mobility to permanently attached equipment of the following types:

(1) Air compressors, pumps and generators, including spraying, welding, building cleaning, geophysical exploration, lighting and well servicing equipment; or

(2) Cherry pickers and similar devices used to raise or lower workers;

f. Vehicles not described in **a.**, **b.**, **c.** or **d.** above maintained primarily for purposes other than the transportation of persons or cargo.

However, self-propelled vehicles with the following types of permanently attached equipment are not "mobile equipment" but will be considered "autos":

(1) Equipment designed primarily for:

  (a) Snow removal;

  (b) Road maintenance, but not construction or resurfacing; or

  (c) Street cleaning;

(2) Cherry pickers and similar devices mounted on automobile or truck chassis and used to raise or lower workers; and

(3) Air compressors, pumps and generators, including spraying, welding, building cleaning, geophysical exploration, lighting and well servicing equipment.

However, "mobile equipment" does not include any land vehicles that are subject to a compulsory or financial responsibility law or other motor vehicle insurance law in the state where it is licensed or principally garaged. Land vehicles subject to a compulsory or financial responsibility law or other motor vehicle insurance law are considered "autos".

13. "Occurrence" means an accident, including continuous or repeated exposure to substantially the same general harmful conditions.

14. "Personal and advertising injury" means injury, including consequential "bodily injury", arising out of one or more of the following offenses:

  a. False arrest, detention or imprisonment;

  b. Malicious prosecution;

  c. The wrongful eviction from, wrongful entry into, or invasion of the right of private occupancy of a room, dwelling or premises that a person occupies, committed by or on behalf of its owner, landlord or lessor;

  d. Oral or written publication, in any manner, of material that slanders or libels a person or organization or disparages a person's or organization's goods, products or services;

  e. Oral or written publication, in any manner, of material that violates a person's right of privacy;

  f. The use of another's advertising idea in your "advertisement"; or

  g. Infringing upon another's copyright, trade dress or slogan in your "advertisement".

15. "Pollutants" mean any solid, liquid, gaseous or thermal irritant or contaminant, including smoke, vapor, soot, fumes, acids, alkalis, chemicals and waste. Waste includes materials to be recycled, reconditioned or reclaimed.

16. "Products-completed operations hazard":

  a. Includes all "bodily injury" and "property damage" occurring away from premises you own or rent and arising out of "your product" or "your work" except:

  (1) Products that are still in your physical possession; or

  (2) Work that has not yet been completed or abandoned. However, "your work" will be deemed completed at the earliest of the following times:

  (a) When all of the work called for in your contract has been completed.

  (b) When all of the work to be done at the job site has been completed if your contract calls for work at more than one job site.

  (c) When that part of the work done at a job site has been put to its intended use by any person or organization other than another contractor or subcontractor working on the same project.

  Work that may need service, maintenance, correction, repair or replacement, but which is otherwise complete, will be treated as completed.

  b. Does not include "bodily injury" or "property damage" arising out of:

  (1) The transportation of property, unless the injury or damage arises out of a condition in or on a vehicle not owned or operated by you, and that condition was created by the "loading or unloading" of that vehicle by any insured;

  (2) The existence of tools, uninstalled equipment or abandoned or unused materials; or

  (3) Products or operations for which the classification, listed in the Declarations or in a policy schedule, states that products-completed operations are subject to the General Aggregate Limit.

17. "Property damage" means:

  a. Physical injury to tangible property, including all resulting loss of use of that property. All such loss of use shall be deemed to occur at the time of the physical injury that caused it; or

b. Loss of use of tangible property that is not physically injured. All such loss of use shall be deemed to occur at the time of the "occurrence" that caused it.

For the purposes of this insurance, electronic data is not tangible property.

As used in this definition, electronic data means information, facts or programs stored as or on, created or used on, or transmitted to or from computer software, including systems and applications software, hard or floppy disks, CD-ROMS, tapes, drives, cells, data processing devices or any other media which are used with electronically controlled equipment.

18. "Suit" means a civil proceeding in which damages because of "bodily injury", "property damage" or "personal and advertising injury" to which this insurance applies are alleged. "Suit" includes:

a. An arbitration proceeding in which such damages are claimed and to which the insured must submit or does submit with our consent; or

b. Any other alternative dispute resolution proceeding in which such damages are claimed and to which the insured submits with our consent.

19. "Temporary worker" means a person who is furnished to you to substitute for a permanent "employee" on leave or to meet seasonal or short-term workload conditions.

20. "Volunteer worker" means a person who is not your "employee", and who donates his or her work and acts at the direction of and within the scope of duties determined by you, and is not paid a fee, salary or other compensation by you or anyone else for their work performed for you.

21. "Your product":

a. Means:

(1) Any goods or products, other than real property, manufactured, sold, handled, distributed or disposed of by:

(a) You;

(b) Others trading under your name; or

(c) A person or organization whose business or assets you have acquired; and

(2) Containers (other than vehicles), materials, parts or equipment furnished in connection with such goods or products.

b. Includes

(1) Warranties or representations made at any time with respect to the fitness, quality, durability, performance or use of "your product"; and

(2) The providing of or failure to provide warnings or instructions.

c. Does not include vending machines or other property rented to or located for the use of others but not sold.

22. "Your work":

a. Means:

(1) Work or operations performed by you or on your behalf; and

(2) Materials, parts or equipment furnished in connection with such work or operations.

b. Includes

(1) Warranties or representations made at any time with respect to the fitness, quality, durability, performance or use of "your work", and

(2) The providing of or failure to provide warnings or instructions.

COMMERCIAL GENERAL LIABILITY COVERAGE FORM

**COVERAGES A AND B PROVIDE
CLAIMS-MADE COVERAGE
PLEASE READ THE ENTIRE FORM CAREFULLY**

Various provisions in this policy restrict coverage. Read the entire policy carefully to determine rights, duties and what is and is not covered.

Throughout this policy the words "you" and "your" refer to the Named Insured shown in the Declarations, and any other person or organization qualifying as a Named Insured under this policy. The words "we", "us" and "our" refer to the Company providing this insurance.

The word "insured" means any person or organization qualifying as such under Section **II** – Who Is An Insured.

Other words and phrases that appear in quotation marks have special meaning. Refer to Section **VI** – Definitions.

SECTION I – COVERAGES

COVERAGE A BODILY INJURY AND PROPERTY DAMAGE LIABILITY

1. Insuring Agreement

a. We will pay those sums that the insured becomes legally obligated to pay as damages because of "bodily injury" or "property damage" to which this insurance applies. We will have the right and duty to defend the insured against any "suit" seeking those damages. However, we will have no duty to defend the insured against any "suit" seeking damages for "bodily injury" or "property damage" to which this insurance does not apply. We may, at our discretion, investigate any "occurrence" and settle any claim or "suit" that may result. But:

(1) The amount we will pay for damages is limited as described in Section **III** – Limits Of Insurance; and

(2) Our right and duty to defend ends when we have used up the applicable limit of insurance in the payment of judgments or settlements under Coverages **A** or **B** or medical expenses under Coverage **C**.

No other obligation or liability to pay sums or perform acts or services is covered unless explicitly provided for under Supplementary Payments – Coverages **A** and **B**.

b. This insurance applies to "bodily injury" and "property damage" only if:

(1) The "bodily injury" or "property damage" is caused by an "occurrence" that takes place in the "coverage territory";

(2) The "bodily injury" or "property damage" did not occur before the Retroactive Date, if any, shown in the Declarations or after the end of the policy period; and

(3) A claim for damages because of the "bodily injury" or "property damage" is first made against any insured, in accordance with Paragraph **c.** below, during the policy period or any Extended Reporting Period we provide under Section **V** – Extended Reporting Periods.

c. A claim by a person or organization seeking damages will be deemed to have been made at the earlier of the following times:

(1) When notice of such claim is received and recorded by any insured or by us, whichever comes first; or

(2) When we make settlement in accordance with Paragraph **1.a.** above.

All claims for damages because of "bodily injury" to the same person, including damages claimed by any person or organization for care, loss of services, or death resulting at any time from the "bodily injury", will be deemed to have been made at the time the first of those claims is made against any insured.

All claims for damages because of "property damage" causing loss to the same person or organization will be deemed to have been made at the time the first of those claims is made against any insured.

2. Exclusions

This insurance does not apply to:

a. **Expected Or Intended Injury**

"Bodily injury" or "property damage" expected or intended from the standpoint of the insured. This exclusion does not apply to "bodily injury" resulting from the use of reasonable force to protect persons or property.

b. Contractual Liability

"Bodily injury" or "property damage" for which the insured is obligated to pay damages by reason of the assumption of liability in a contract or agreement. This exclusion does not apply to liability for damages:

(1) That the insured would have in the absence of the contract or agreement; or

(2) Assumed in a contract or agreement that is an "insured contract", provided the "bodily injury" or "property damage" occurs subsequent to the execution of the contract or agreement. Solely for the purposes of liability assumed in an "insured contract", reasonable attorney fees and necessary litigation expenses incurred by or for a party other than an insured are deemed to be damages because of "bodily injury" or "property damage", provided:

(a) Liability to such party for, or for the cost of, that party's defense has also been assumed in the same "insured contract"; and

(b) Such attorney fees and litigation expenses are for defense of that party against a civil or alternative dispute resolution proceeding in which damages to which this insurance applies are alleged.

c. Liquor Liability

"Bodily injury" or "property damage" for which any insured may be held liable by reason of:

(1) Causing or contributing to the intoxication of any person;

(2) The furnishing of alcoholic beverages to a person under the legal drinking age or under the influence of alcohol; or

(3) Any statute, ordinance or regulation relating to the sale, gift, distribution or use of alcoholic beverages.

This exclusion applies only if you are in the business of manufacturing, distributing, selling, serving or furnishing alcoholic beverages.

d. Workers' Compensation And Similar Laws

Any obligation of the insured under a workers' compensation, disability benefits or unemployment compensation law or any similar law.

e. Employer's Liability

"Bodily injury" to:

(1) An "employee" of the insured arising out of and in the course of:

(a) Employment by the insured; or

(b) Performing duties related to the conduct of the insured's business; or

(2) The spouse, child, parent, brother or sister of that "employee" as a consequence of Paragraph **(1)** above.

This exclusion applies:

(1) Whether the insured may be liable as an employer or in any other capacity; and

(2) To any obligation to share damages with or repay someone else who must pay damages because of the injury.

This exclusion does not apply to liability assumed by the insured under an "insured contract".

f. Pollution

(1) "Bodily injury" or "property damage" arising out of the actual, alleged or threatened discharge, dispersal, seepage, migration, release or escape of "pollutants":

(a) At or from any premises, site or location which is or was at any time owned or occupied by, or rented or loaned to, any insured. However, this subparagraph does not apply to:

(i) "Bodily injury" if sustained within a building and caused by smoke, fumes, vapor or soot produced by or originating from equipment that is used to heat, cool or dehumidify the building, or equipment that is used to heat water for personal use by the building's occupants or their guests;

(ii) "Bodily injury" or "property damage" for which you may be held liable, if you are a contractor and the owner or lessee of such premises, site or location has been added to your policy as an additional insured with respect to your ongoing operations performed for that additional insured at that premises, site or location and such premises, site or location is not or never was owned or occupied by, or rented or loaned to, any insured, other than that additional insured; or

(iii) "Bodily injury" or "property damage" arising out of heat, smoke or fumes from a "hostile fire";

(b) At or from any premises, site or location which is or was at any time used by or for any insured or others for the handling, storage, disposal, processing or treatment of waste;

          □

(c) Which are or were at any time transported, handled, stored, treated, disposed of, or processed as waste by or for:

  (i) Any insured; or

  (ii) Any person or organization for whom you may be legally responsible; or

(d) At or from any premises, site or location on which any insured or any contractors or subcontractors working directly or indirectly on any insured's behalf are performing operations if the "pollutants" are brought on or to the premises, site or location in connection with such operations by such insured, contractor or subcontractor. However, this subparagraph does not apply to:

  (i) "Bodily injury" or "property damage" arising out of the escape of fuels, lubricants or other operating fluids which are needed to perform the normal electrical, hydraulic or mechanical functions necessary for the operation of "mobile equipment" or its parts, if such fuels, lubricants or other operating fluids escape from a vehicle part designed to hold, store or receive them. This exception does not apply if the "bodily injury" or "property damage" arises out of the intentional discharge, dispersal or release of the fuels, lubricants or other operating fluids, or if such fuels, lubricants or other operating fluids are brought on or to the premises, site or location with the intent that they be discharged, dispersed or released as part of the operations being performed by such insured, contractor or subcontractor;

  (ii) "Bodily injury" or "property damage" sustained within a building and caused by the release of gases, fumes or vapors from materials brought into that building in connection with operations being performed by you or on your behalf by a contractor or subcontractor; or

  (iii) "Bodily injury" or "property damage" arising out of heat, smoke or fumes from a "hostile fire".

(e) At or from any premises, site or location on which any insured or any contractors or subcontractors working directly or indirectly on any insured's behalf are performing operations if the operations are to test for, monitor, clean up, remove, contain, treat, detoxify or neutralize, or in any way respond to, or assess the effects of, "pollutants".

(2) Any loss, cost or expense arising out of any:

(a) Request, demand, order or statutory or regulatory requirement that any insured or others test for, monitor, clean up, remove, contain, treat, detoxify or neutralize, or in any way respond to, or assess the effects of, "pollutants"; or

(b) Claim or suit by or on behalf of a governmental authority for damages because of testing for, monitoring, cleaning up, removing, containing, treating, detoxifying or neutralizing, or in any way responding to, or assessing the effects of, "pollutants".

However, this paragraph does not apply to liability for damages because of "property damage" that the insured would have in the absence of such request, demand, order or statutory or regulatory requirement, or such claim or "suit" by or on behalf of a governmental authority.

g. Aircraft, Auto Or Watercraft

"Bodily injury" or "property damage" arising out of the ownership, maintenance, use or entrustment to others of any aircraft, "auto" or watercraft owned or operated by or rented or loaned to any insured. Use includes operation and "loading or unloading".

This exclusion applies even if the claims against any insured allege negligence or other wrongdoing in the supervision, hiring, employment, training or monitoring of others by that insured, if the "occurrence" which caused the "bodily injury" or "property damage" involved the ownership, maintenance, use or entrustment to others of any aircraft, "auto" or watercraft that is owned or operated by or rented or loaned to any insured.

This exclusion does not apply to:

(1) A watercraft while ashore on premises you own or rent;

(2) A watercraft you do not own that is:

(a) Less than 26 feet long; and

(b) Not being used to carry persons or property for a charge;

(3) Parking an "auto" on, or on the ways next to, premises you own or rent, provided the "auto" is not owned by or rented or loaned to you or the insured;

(4) Liability assumed under any "insured contract" for the ownership, maintenance or use of aircraft or watercraft; or

(5) "Bodily injury" or "property damage" arising out of:

(a) The operation of machinery or equipment that is attached to, or part of, a land vehicle that would qualify under the definition of "mobile equipment" if it were not subject to a compulsory or financial responsibility law or other motor vehicle insurance law in the state where it is licensed or principally garaged; or

(b) The operation of any of the machinery or equipment listed in Paragraph **f.(2)** or **f.(3)** of the definition of "mobile equipment".

h. Mobile Equipment

"Bodily injury" or "property damage" arising out of:

(1) The transportation of "mobile equipment" by an "auto" owned or operated by or rented or loaned to any insured; or

(2) The use of "mobile equipment" in, or while in practice for, or while being prepared for, any prearranged racing, speed, demolition, or stunting activity.

i. War

"Bodily injury" or "property damage", however caused, arising, directly or indirectly, out of:

(1) War, including undeclared or civil war;

(2) Warlike action by a military force, including action in hindering or defending against an actual or expected attack, by any government, sovereign or other authority using military personnel or other agents; or

(3) Insurrection, rebellion, revolution, usurped power, or action taken by governmental authority in hindering or defending against any of these.

j. Damage To Property

"Property damage" to:

(1) Property you own, rent, or occupy, including any costs or expenses incurred by you, or any other person, organization or entity, for repair, replacement, enhancement, restoration or maintenance of such property for any reason, including prevention of injury to a person or damage to another's property;

(2) Premises you sell, give away or abandon, if the "property damage" arises out of any part of those premises;

(3) Property loaned to you;

(4) Personal property in the care, custody or control of the insured;

(5) That particular part of real property on which you or any contractors or subcontractors working directly or indirectly on your behalf are performing operations, if the "property damage" arises out of those operations; or

(6) That particular part of any property that must be restored, repaired or replaced because "your work" was incorrectly performed on it.

Paragraphs **(1)**, **(3)** and **(4)** of this exclusion do not apply to "property damage" (other than damage by fire) to premises, including the contents of such premises, rented to you for a period of 7 or fewer consecutive days. A separate limit of insurance applies to Damage To Premises Rented To You as described in Section **III** – Limits Of Insurance.

Paragraph **(2)** of this exclusion does not apply if the premises are "your work" and were never occupied, rented or held for rental by you.

Paragraphs **(3)**, **(4)**, **(5)** and **(6)** of this exclusion do not apply to liability assumed under a sidetrack agreement.

Paragraph **(6)** of this exclusion does not apply to "property damage" included in the "products-completed operations hazard".

k. Damage To Your Product

"Property damage" to "your product" arising out of it or any part of it.

l. Damage To Your Work

"Property damage" to "your work" arising out of it or any part of it and included in the "products-completed operations hazard".

CG 00 02 12 04   ☐

This exclusion does not apply if the damaged work or the work out of which the damage arises was performed on your behalf by a subcontractor.

m. Damage To Impaired Property Or Property Not Physically Injured

"Property damage" to "impaired property" or property that has not been physically injured, arising out of:

(1) A defect, deficiency, inadequacy or dangerous condition in "your product" or "your work"; or

(2) A delay or failure by you or anyone acting on your behalf to perform a contract or agreement in accordance with its terms.

This exclusion does not apply to the loss of use of other property arising out of sudden and accidental physical injury to "your product" or "your work" after it has been put to its intended use.

n. Recall Of Products, Work Or Impaired Property

Damages claimed for any loss, cost or expense incurred by you or others for the loss of use, withdrawal, recall, inspection, repair, replacement, adjustment, removal or disposal of:

(1) "Your product";

(2) "Your work"; or

(3) "Impaired property";

if such product, work, or property is withdrawn or recalled from the market or from use by any person or organization because of a known or suspected defect, deficiency, inadequacy or dangerous condition in it.

o. Personal And Advertising Injury

"Bodily injury" arising out of "personal and advertising injury".

p. Electronic Data

Damages arising out of the loss of, loss of use of, damage to, corruption of, inability to access, or inability to manipulate electronic data.

As used in this exclusion, electronic data means information, facts or programs stored as or on, created or used on, or transmitted to or from computer software, including systems and applications software, hard or floppy disks, CD-ROMS, tapes, drives, cells, data processing devices or any other media which are used with electronically controlled equipment.

Exclusions **c.** through **n.** do not apply to damage by fire to premises while rented to you or temporarily occupied by you with permission of the owner. A separate limit of insurance applies to this coverage as described in Section **III** – Limits Of Insurance.

COVERAGE B PERSONAL AND ADVERTISING INJURY LIABILITY

1. Insuring Agreement

a. We will pay those sums that the insured becomes legally obligated to pay as damages because of "personal and advertising injury" to which this insurance applies. We will have the right and duty to defend the insured against any "suit" seeking those damages. However, we will have no duty to defend the insured against any "suit" seeking damages for "personal and advertising injury" to which this insurance does not apply. We may, at our discretion, investigate any offense and settle any claim or "suit" that may result. But:

(1) The amount we will pay for damages is limited as described in Section **III** – Limits Of Insurance; and

(2) Our right and duty to defend end when we have used up the applicable limit of insurance in the payment of judgments or settlements under Coverages **A** or **B** or medical expenses under Coverage **C**.

No other obligation or liability to pay sums or perform acts or services is covered unless explicitly provided for under Supplementary Payments – Coverages **A** and **B**.

b. This insurance applies to "personal and advertising injury" caused by an offense arising out of your business, but only if:

(1) The offense was committed in the "coverage territory";

(2) The offense was not committed before the Retroactive Date, if any, shown in the Declarations or after the end of the policy period; and

(3) A claim for damages because of the "personal and advertising injury" is first made against any insured, in accordance with Paragraph **c.** below, during the policy period or any Extended Reporting Period we provide under Section **V** – Extended Reporting Periods.

c. A claim made by a person or organization seeking damages will be deemed to have been made at the earlier of the following times:

   (1) When notice of such claim is received and recorded by any insured or by us, whichever comes first; or

   (2) When we make settlement in accordance with Paragraph **1.a.** above.

   All claims for damages because of "personal and advertising injury" to the same person or organization as a result of an offense will be deemed to have been made at the time the first of those claims is made against any insured.

2. Exclusions

This insurance does not apply to:

a. Knowing Violation Of Rights Of Another

"Personal and advertising injury" caused by or at the direction of the insured with the knowledge that the act would violate the rights of another and would inflict "personal and advertising injury".

b. Material Published With Knowledge Of Falsity

"Personal and advertising injury" arising out of oral or written publication of material, if done by or at the direction of the insured with knowledge of its falsity.

c. Material Published Prior To Policy Period

"Personal and advertising injury" arising out of oral or written publication of material whose first publication took place before the Retroactive Date, if any, shown in the Declarations.

d. Criminal Acts

"Personal and advertising injury" arising out of a criminal act committed by or at the direction of the insured.

e. Contractual Liability

"Personal and advertising injury" for which the insured has assumed liability in a contract or agreement. This exclusion does not apply to liability for damages that the insured would have in the absence of the contract or agreement.

f. Breach Of Contract

"Personal and advertising injury" arising out of a breach of contract, except an implied contract to use another's advertising idea in your "advertisement".

g. Quality Or Performance Of Goods – Failure To Conform To Statements

"Personal and advertising injury" arising out of the failure of goods, products or services to conform with any statement of quality or performance made in your "advertisement".

h. Wrong Description Of Prices

"Personal and advertising injury" arising out of the wrong description of the price of goods, products or services stated in your "advertisement".

i. Infringement Of Copyright, Patent, Trademark Or Trade Secret

"Personal and advertising injury" arising out of the infringement of copyright, patent, trademark, trade secret or other intellectual property rights.

However, this exclusion does not apply to infringement, in your "advertisement", of copyright, trade dress or slogan.

j. Insureds In Media And Internet Type Businesses

"Personal and advertising injury" committed by an insured whose business is:

   (1) Advertising, broadcasting, publishing or telecasting;

   (2) Designing or determining content or websites for others; or

   (3) An Internet search, access, content or service provider.

However, this exclusion does not apply to Paragraphs **14.a., b.** and **c.** of "personal and advertising injury" under the Definitions Section.

For the purposes of this exclusion, the placing of frames, borders or links, or advertising, for you or others anywhere on the Internet, is not by itself, considered the business of advertising, broadcasting, publishing or telecasting.

k. Electronic Chatrooms Or Bulletin Boards

"Personal and advertising injury" arising out of an electronic chatroom or bulletin board the insured hosts, owns, or over which the insured exercises control.

     CG 00 02 12 04   □

l. Unauthorized Use Of Another's Name Or Product

"Personal and advertising injury" arising out of the unauthorized use of another's name or product in your e-mail address, domain name or metatag, or any other similar tactics to mislead another's potential customers.

m. Pollution

"Personal and advertising injury" arising out of the actual, alleged or threatened discharge, dispersal, seepage, migration, release or escape of "pollutants" at any time.

n. Pollution-Related

Any loss, cost or expense arising out of any:

(1) Request, demand, order or statutory or regulatory requirement that any insured or others test for, monitor, clean up, remove, contain, treat, detoxify or neutralize, or in any way respond to, or assess the effects of, "pollutants"; or

(2) Claim or suit by or on behalf of a governmental authority for damages because of testing for, monitoring, cleaning up, removing, containing, treating, detoxifying or neutralizing, or in any way responding to, or assessing the effects of, "pollutants".

o. War

"Personal and advertising injury", however caused, arising, directly or indirectly, out of:

(1) War, including undeclared or civil war;

(2) Warlike action by a military force, including action in hindering or defending against an actual or expected attack, by any government, sovereign or other authority using military personnel or other agents; or

(3) Insurrection, rebellion, revolution, usurped power, or action taken by governmental authority in hindering or defending against any of these.

COVERAGE C MEDICAL PAYMENTS

1. Insuring Agreement

a. We will pay medical expenses as described below for "bodily injury" caused by an accident:

(1) On premises you own or rent;

(2) On ways next to premises you own or rent; or

(3) Because of your operations;

provided that:

(1) The accident takes place in the "coverage territory" and during the policy period;

(2) The expenses are incurred and reported to us within one year of the date of the accident; and

(3) The injured person submits to examination, at our expense, by physicians of our choice as often as we reasonably require.

b. We will make these payments regardless of fault. These payments will not exceed the applicable limit of insurance. We will pay reasonable expenses for:

(1) First aid administered at the time of an accident;

(2) Necessary medical, surgical, x-ray and dental services, including prosthetic devices; and

(3) Necessary ambulance, hospital, professional nursing and funeral services.

2. Exclusions

We will not pay expenses for "bodily injury":

a. Any Insured

To any insured, except "volunteer workers".

b. Hired Person

To a person hired to do work for or on behalf of any insured or a tenant of any insured.

c. Injury On Normally Occupied Premises

To a person injured on that part of premises you own or rent that the person normally occupies.

d. Workers Compensation And Similar Laws

To a person, whether or not an "employee" of any insured, if benefits for the "bodily injury" are payable or must be provided under a workers' compensation or disability benefits law or a similar law.

e. Athletics Activities

To a person injured while practicing, instructing or participating in any physical exercises or games, sports, or athletic contests.

f. Products-Completed Operations Hazard

Included within the "products-completed operations hazard".

g. Coverage A Exclusions

Excluded under Coverage **A**.

SUPPLEMENTARY PAYMENTS – COVERAGES A AND B

1. We will pay, with respect to any claim we investigate or settle or any "suit" against an insured we defend:

   a. All expenses we incur.

   b. Up to $250 for cost of bail bonds required because of accidents or traffic law violations arising out of the use of any vehicle to which the Bodily Injury Liability Coverage applies. We do not have to furnish these bonds.

   c. The cost of bonds to release attachments, but only for bond amounts within the applicable limit of insurance. We do not have to furnish these bonds.

   d. All reasonable expenses incurred by the insured at our request to assist us in the investigation or defense of the claim or "suit", including actual loss of earnings up to $250 a day because of time off from work.

   e. All costs taxed against the insured in the "suit".

   f. Prejudgment interest awarded against the insured on that part of the judgment we pay. If we make an offer to pay the applicable limit of insurance, we will not pay any prejudgment interest based on that period of time after the offer.

   g. All interest on the full amount of any judgment that accrues after entry of the judgment and before we have paid, offered to pay, or deposited in court the part of the judgment that is within the applicable limit of insurance.

   These payments will not reduce the limits of insurance.

2. If we defend an insured against a "suit" and an indemnitee of the insured is also named as a party to the "suit", we will defend that indemnitee if all of the following conditions are met:

   a. The "suit" against the indemnitee seeks damages for which the insured has assumed the liability of the indemnitee in a contract or agreement that is an "insured contract";

   b. This insurance applies to such liability assumed by the insured;

   c. The obligation to defend, or the cost of the defense of, that indemnitee, has also been assumed by the insured in the same "insured contract";

   d. The allegations in the "suit" and the information we know about the "occurrence" are such that no conflict appears to exist between the interests of the insured and the interests of the indemnitee;

   e. The indemnitee and the insured ask us to conduct and control the defense of that indemnitee against such "suit" and agree that we can assign the same counsel to defend the insured and the indemnitee; and

   f. The indemnitee:

      (1) Agrees in writing to:

         (a) Cooperate with us in the investigation, settlement or defense of the "suit";

         (b) Immediately send us copies of any demands, notices, summonses or legal papers received in connection with the "suit";

         (c) Notify any other insurer whose coverage is available to the indemnitee; and

         (d) Cooperate with us with respect to coordinating other applicable insurance available to the indemnitee; and

      (2) Provides us with written authorization to:

         (a) Obtain records and other information related to the "suit"; and

         (b) Conduct and control the defense of the indemnitee in such "suit".

   So long as the above conditions are met, attorneys' fees incurred by us in the defense of that indemnitee, necessary litigation expenses incurred by us and necessary litigation expenses incurred by the indemnitee at our request will be paid as Supplementary Payments. Notwithstanding the provisions of Paragraph 2.b.(2) of Section I – Coverage **A** – Bodily Injury And Property Damage Liability, such payments will not be deemed to be damages for "bodily injury" and "property damage" and will not reduce the limits of insurance.

   Our obligation to defend an insured's indemnitee and to pay for attorneys' fees and necessary litigation expenses as Supplementary Payments ends when:

   a. We have used up the applicable limit of insurance in the payment of judgments or settlements; or

   b. The conditions set forth above, or the terms of the agreement described in Paragraph **f.** above, are no longer met.

SECTION II – WHO IS AN INSURED

1. If you are designated in the Declarations as:

   a. An individual, you and your spouse are insureds, but only with respect to the conduct of a business of which you are the sole owner.

   b. A partnership or joint venture, you are an insured. Your members, your partners, and their spouses are also insureds, but only with respect to the conduct of your business.

c. A limited liability company, you are an insured. Your members are also insureds, but only with respect to the conduct of your business. Your managers are insureds, but only with respect to their duties as your managers.

d. An organization other than a partnership, joint venture or limited liability company, you are an insured. Your "executive officers" and directors are insureds, but only with respect to their duties as your officers or directors. Your stockholders are also insureds, but only with respect to their liability as stockholders.

e. A trust, you are an insured. Your trustees are also insureds, but only with respect to their duties as trustees.

2. Each of the following is also an insured:

a. Your "volunteer workers" only while performing duties related to the conduct of your business, or your "employees", other than either your "executive officers" (if you are an organization other than a partnership, joint venture or limited liability company) or your managers (if you are a limited liability company), but only for acts within the scope of their employment by you or while performing duties related to the conduct of your business. However, none of these "employees" or "volunteer workers" are insureds for:

(1) "Bodily injury" or "personal and advertising injury":

(a) To you, to your partners or members (if you are a partnership or joint venture), to your members (if you are a limited liability company), to a co-"employee" while in the course of his or her employment or performing duties related to the conduct of your business, or to your other "volunteer workers" while performing duties related to the conduct of your business;

(b) To the spouse, child, parent, brother or sister of that co-"employee" or "volunteer worker" as a consequence of Paragraph **(1)(a)** above;

(c) For which there is any obligation to share damages with or repay someone else who must pay damages because of the injury described in Paragraphs **(1)(a)** or **(b)** above; or

(d) Arising out of his or her providing or failing to provide professional health care services.

(2) "Property damage" to property:

(a) Owned, occupied or used by,

(b) Rented to, in the care, custody or control of, or over which physical control is being exercised for any purpose by

you, any of your "employees", "volunteer workers", any partner or member (if you are a partnership or joint venture), or any member (if you are a limited liability company).

b. Any person (other than your "employee" or "volunteer worker") or any organization while acting as your real estate manager.

c. Any person or organization having proper temporary custody of your property if you die, but only:

(1) With respect to liability arising out of the maintenance or use of that property; and

(2) Until your legal representative has been appointed.

d. Your legal representative if you die, but only with respect to duties as such. That representative will have all your rights and duties under this Coverage Part.

3. Any organization you newly acquire or form, other than a partnership, joint venture or limited liability company, and over which you maintain ownership or majority interest, will qualify as a Named Insured if there is no other similar insurance available to that organization. However:

a. Coverage under this provision is afforded only until the 90th day after you acquire or form the organization or the end of the policy period, whichever is earlier;

b. Coverage **A** does not apply to "bodily injury" or "property damage" that occurred before you acquired or formed the organization; and

c. Coverage **B** does not apply to "personal and advertising injury" arising out of an offense committed before you acquired or formed the organization.

No person or organization is an insured with respect to the conduct of any current or past partnership, joint venture or limited liability company that is not shown as a Named Insured in the Declarations.

SECTION III – LIMITS OF INSURANCE

1. The Limits of Insurance shown in the Declarations and the rules below fix the most we will pay regardless of the number of:

a. Insureds;

b. Claims made or "suits" brought; or

c. Persons or organizations making claims or bringing "suits".

2. The General Aggregate Limit is the most we will pay for the sum of:

   a. Medical expenses under Coverage **C**;

   b. Damages under Coverage **A**, except damages because of "bodily injury" or "property damage" included in the "products-completed operations hazard"; and

   c. Damages under Coverage **B**.

3. The Products-Completed Operations Aggregate Limit is the most we will pay under Coverage **A** for damages because of "bodily injury" and "property damage" included in the "products-completed operations hazard".

4. Subject to **2.** above, the Personal and Advertising Injury Limit is the most we will pay under Coverage **B** for the sum of all damages because of all "personal and advertising injury" sustained by any one person or organization.

5. Subject to **2.** or **3.** above, whichever applies, the Each Occurrence Limit is the most we will pay for the sum of:

   a. Damages under Coverage **A**; and

   b. Medical expenses under Coverage **C**

   because of all "bodily injury" and "property damage" arising out of any one "occurrence".

6. Subject to **5.** above, the Damage To Premises Rented To You Limit is the most we will pay under Coverage **A** for damages because of "property damage" to any one premises, while rented to you, or in the case of damage by fire, while rented to you or temporarily occupied by you with permission of the owner.

7. Subject to **5.** above, the Medical Expense Limit is the most we will pay under Coverage **C** for all medical expenses because of "bodily injury" sustained by any one person.

The Limits of Insurance of this Coverage Part apply separately to each consecutive annual period and to any remaining period of less than 12 months, starting with the beginning of the policy period shown in the Declarations, unless the policy period is extended after issuance for an additional period of less than 12 months. In that case, the additional period will be deemed part of the last preceding period for purposes of determining the Limits of Insurance.

SECTION IV – COMMERCIAL GENERAL LIABILITY CONDITIONS

1. Bankruptcy

Bankruptcy or insolvency of the insured or of the insured's estate will not relieve us of our obligations under this Coverage Part.

2. Duties In The Event Of Occurrence, Offense, Claim Or Suit

   a. You must see to it that we are notified as soon as practicable of an "occurrence" or offense which may result in a claim. To the extent possible, notice should include:

   (1) How, when and where the "occurrence" or offense took place;

   (2) The names and addresses of any injured persons and witnesses; and

   (3) The nature and location of any injury or damage arising out of the "occurrence" or offense.

   Notice of an "occurrence" or offense is not notice of a claim.

   b. If a claim is received by any insured, you must:

   (1) Immediately record the specifics of the claim and the date received; and

   (2) Notify us as soon as practicable.

   You must see to it that we receive written notice of the claim as soon as practicable.

   c. You and any other involved insured must:

   (1) Immediately send us copies of any demands, notices, summonses or legal papers received in connection with the claim or a "suit";

   (2) Authorize us to obtain records and other information;

   (3) Cooperate with us in the investigation or settlement of the claim or defense against the "suit"; and

   (4) Assist us, upon our request, in the enforcement of any right against any person or organization which may be liable to the insured because of injury or damage to which this insurance may also apply.

   d. No insured will, except at that insured's own cost, voluntarily make a payment, assume any obligation, or incur any expense, other than for first aid, without our consent.

3. Legal Action Against Us

No person or organization has a right under this Coverage Part:

   a. To join us as a party or otherwise bring us into a "suit" asking for damages from an insured; or

   b. To sue us on this Coverage Part unless all of its terms have been fully complied with.

 CG 00 02 12 04 □

A person or organization may sue us to recover on an agreed settlement or on a final judgment against an insured; but we will not be liable for damages that are not payable under the terms of this Coverage Part or that are in excess of the applicable limit of insurance. An agreed settlement means a settlement and release of liability signed by us, the insured and the claimant or the claimant's legal representative.

4. Other Insurance

If other valid and collectible insurance is available to the insured for a loss we cover under Coverages **A** or **B** of this Coverage Part, our obligations are limited as follows:

a. Primary Insurance

This insurance is primary except when **b.** below applies. If this insurance is primary, our obligations are not affected unless any of the other insurance is also primary. Then, we will share with all that other insurance by the method described in **c.** below.

b. Excess Insurance

This insurance is excess over:

(1) Any of the other insurance, whether primary, excess, contingent or on any other basis:

(a) That is effective prior to the beginning of the policy period shown in the Declarations of this insurance and applies to "bodily injury" or "property damage" on other than a claims-made basis, if:

(i) No Retroactive Date is shown in the Declarations of this insurance; or

(ii) The other insurance has a policy period which continues after the Retroactive Date shown in the Declarations of this insurance;

(b) That is Fire, Extended Coverage, Builders' Risk, Installation Risk or similar coverage for "your work";

(c) That is Fire insurance for premises rented to you or temporarily occupied by you with permission of the owner;

(d) That is insurance purchased by you to cover your liability as a tenant for "property damage" to premises rented to you or temporarily occupied by you with permission of the owner; or

(e) If the loss arises out of the maintenance or use of aircraft, "autos" or watercraft to the extent not subject to Exclusion **g.** of Section **I** – Coverage **A** – Bodily Injury And Property Damage Liability.

(2) Any other primary insurance available to you covering liability for damages arising out of the premises or operations, or the products and completed operations, for which you have been added as an additional insured by attachment of an endorsement.

When this insurance is excess, we will have no duty under Coverages **A** or **B** to defend the insured against any "suit" if any other insurer has a duty to defend the insured against that "suit". If no other insurer defends, we will undertake to do so, but we will be entitled to the insured's rights against all those other insurers.

When this insurance is excess over other insurance, we will pay only our share of the amount of the loss, if any, that exceeds the sum of:

(1) The total amount that all such other insurance would pay for the loss in the absence of this insurance; and

(2) The total of all deductible and self-insured amounts under all that other insurance.

We will share the remaining loss, if any, with any other insurance that is not described in this Excess Insurance provision and was not bought specifically to apply in excess of the Limits of Insurance shown in the Declarations of this Coverage Part.

c. Method Of Sharing

If all of the other insurance permits contribution by equal shares, we will follow this method also. Under this approach each insurer contributes equal amounts until it has paid its applicable limit of insurance or none of the loss remains, whichever comes first.

If any of the other insurance does not permit contribution by equal shares, we will contribute by limits. Under this method, each insurer's share is based on the ratio of its applicable limit of insurance to the total applicable limits of insurance of all insurers.

5. Premium Audit

a. We will compute all premiums for this Coverage Part in accordance with our rules and rates.

b. Premium shown in this Coverage Part as advance premium is a deposit premium only. At the close of each audit period we will compute the earned premium for that period and send notice to the first Named Insured. The due date for audit and retrospective premiums is the date shown as the due date on the bill. If the sum of the advance and audit premiums paid for the policy period is greater than the earned premium, we will return the excess to the first Named Insured.

c. The first Named Insured must keep records of the information we need for premium computation, and send us copies at such times as we may request.

6. Representations

By accepting this policy, you agree:

a. The statements in the Declarations are accurate and complete;

b. Those statements are based upon representations you made to us; and

c. We have issued this policy in reliance upon your representations.

7. Separation Of Insureds

Except with respect to the Limits of Insurance, and any rights or duties specifically assigned in this Coverage Part to the first Named Insured, this insurance applies:

a. As if each Named Insured were the only Named Insured; and

b. Separately to each insured against whom claim is made or "suit" is brought.

8. Transfer Of Rights Of Recovery Against Others To Us

If the insured has rights to recover all or part of any payment we have made under this Coverage Part, those rights are transferred to us. The insured must do nothing after loss to impair them. At our request, the insured will bring "suit" or transfer those rights to us and help us enforce them.

9. When We Do Not Renew

If we decide not to renew this Coverage Part, we will mail or deliver to the first Named Insured shown in the Declarations written notice of the nonrenewal not less than 30 days before the expiration date.

If notice is mailed, proof of mailing will be sufficient proof of notice.

We will provide the first Named Insured shown in the Declarations the following information relating to this and any preceding general liability claims-made Coverage Part we have issued to you during the previous three years:

a. A list or other record of each "occurrence", not previously reported to any other insurer, of which we were notified in accordance with Paragraph 2.a. of the Section IV – Duties In The Event Of Occurrence, Offense, Claim Or Suit Condition. We will include the date and brief description of the "occurrence" if that information was in the notice we received.

b. A summary by policy year, of payments made and amounts reserved, stated separately, under any applicable General Aggregate Limit and Products-Completed Operations Aggregate Limit.

Amounts reserved are based on our judgment. They are subject to change and should not be regarded as ultimate settlement values.

You must not disclose this information to any claimant or any claimant's representative without our consent.

If we cancel or elect not to renew this Coverage Part, we will provide such information no later than 30 days before the date of policy termination. In other circumstances, we will provide this information only if we receive a written request from the first Named Insured within 60 days after the end of the policy period. In this case, we will provide this information within 45 days of receipt of the request.

We compile claim and "occurrence" information for our own business purposes and exercise reasonable care in doing so. In providing this information to the first Named Insured, we make no representations or warranties to insureds, insurers, or others to whom this information is furnished by or on behalf of any insured. Cancellation or non-renewal will be effective even if we inadvertently provide inaccurate information.

SECTION V – EXTENDED REPORTING PERIODS

1. We will provide one or more Extended Reporting Periods, as described below, if:

a. This Coverage Part is canceled or not renewed; or

b. We renew or replace this Coverage Part with insurance that:

(1) Has a Retroactive Date later than the date shown in the Declarations of this Coverage Part; or

         CG 00 02 12 04   □

(2) Does not apply to "bodily injury", "property damage" or "personal and advertising injury" on a claims-made basis.

2. Extended Reporting Periods do not extend the policy period or change the scope of coverage provided. They apply only to claims for:

a. "Bodily injury" or "property damage" that occurs before the end of the policy period but not before the Retroactive Date, if any, shown in the Declarations; or

b. "Personal and advertising injury" caused by an offense committed before the end of the policy period but not before the Retroactive Date, if any, shown in the Declarations.

Once in effect, Extended Reporting Periods may not be canceled.

3. A Basic Extended Reporting Period is automatically provided without additional charge. This period starts with the end of the policy period and lasts for:

a. Five years with respect to claims because of "bodily injury" and "property damage" arising out of an "occurrence" reported to us, not later than 60 days after the end of the policy period, in accordance with Paragraph **2.a.** of the Section **IV** – Duties In The Event Of Occurrence, Offense, Claim Or Suit Condition;

b. Five years with respect to claims because of "personal and advertising injury" arising out of an offense reported to us, not later than 60 days after the end of the policy period, in accordance with Paragraph **2.a.** of the Section **IV** – Duties In The Event Of Occurrence, Offense, Claim Or Suit Condition; and

c. Sixty days with respect to claims arising from "occurrences" or offenses not previously reported to us.

The Basic Extended Reporting Period does not apply to claims that are covered under any subsequent insurance you purchase, or that would be covered but for exhaustion of the amount of insurance applicable to such claims.

4. The Basic Extended Reporting Period does not reinstate or increase the Limits of Insurance.

5. A Supplemental Extended Reporting Period of unlimited duration is available, but only by an endorsement and for an extra charge. This supplemental period starts when the Basic Extended Reporting Period, set forth in Paragraph **3.** above, ends.

You must give us a written request for the endorsement within 60 days after the end of the policy period. The Supplemental Extended Reporting Period will not go into effect unless you pay the additional premium promptly when due.

We will determine the additional premium in accordance with our rules and rates. In doing so, we may take into account the following:

a. The exposures insured;

b. Previous types and amounts of insurance;

c. Limits of Insurance available under this Coverage Part for future payment of damages; and

d. Other related factors.

The additional premium will not exceed 200% of the annual premium for this Coverage Part.

This endorsement shall set forth the terms, not inconsistent with this Section, applicable to the Supplemental Extended Reporting Period, including a provision to the effect that the insurance afforded for claims first received during such period is excess over any other valid and collectible insurance available under policies in force after the Supplemental Extended Reporting Period starts.

6. If the Supplemental Extended Reporting Period is in effect, we will provide the supplemental aggregate limits of insurance described below, but only for claims first received and recorded during the Supplemental Extended Reporting Period.

The supplemental aggregate limits of insurance will be equal to the dollar amount shown in the Declarations in effect at the end of the policy period for such of the following limits of insurance for which a dollar amount has been entered:

General Aggregate Limit
Products-Completed Operations Aggregate Limit

Paragraphs **2.** and **3.** of Section **III** – Limits Of Insurance will be amended accordingly. The Personal and Advertising Injury Limit, the Each Occurrence Limit and the Damage To Premises Rented To You Limit shown in the Declarations will then continue to apply, as set forth in Paragraphs **4.**, **5.** and **6.** of that Section.

SECTION VI – DEFINITIONS

1. "Advertisement" means a notice that is broadcast or published to the general public or specific market segments about your goods, products or services for the purpose of attracting customers or supporters. For the purposes of this definition:

a. Notices that are published include material placed on the Internet or on similar electronic means of communication; and

b. Regarding web-sites, only that part of a web-site that is about your goods, products or services for the purposes of attracting customers or supporters is considered an advertisement.

2. "Auto" means:

a. A land motor vehicle, trailer or semitrailer designed for travel on public roads, including any attached machinery or equipment; or

b. Any other land vehicle that is subject to a compulsory or financial responsibility law or other motor vehicle insurance law in the state where it is licensed or principally garaged.

However, "auto" does not include "mobile equipment".

3. "Bodily injury" means bodily injury, sickness or disease sustained by a person, including death resulting from any of these at any time.

4. "Coverage territory" means:

a. The United States of America (including its territories and possessions), Puerto Rico and Canada;

b. International waters or airspace, but only if the injury or damage occurs in the course of travel or transportation between any places included in **a.** above; or

c. All other parts of the world if the injury or damage arises out of:

(1) Goods or products made or sold by you in the territory described in **a.** above;

(2) The activities of a person whose home is in the territory described in **a.** above, but is away for a short time on your business; or

(3) "Personal and advertising injury" offenses that take place through the Internet or similar electronic means of communication

provided the insured's responsibility to pay damages is determined in a "suit" on the merits, in the territory described in **a.** above or in a settlement we agree to.

5. "Employee" includes a "leased worker". "Employee" does not include a "temporary worker".

6. "Executive officer" means a person holding any of the officer positions created by your charter, constitution, by-laws or any other similar governing document.

7. "Hostile fire" means one which becomes uncontrollable or breaks out from where it was intended to be.

8. "Impaired property" means tangible property, other than "your product" or "your work", that cannot be used or is less useful because:

a. It incorporates "your product" or "your work" that is known or thought to be defective, deficient, inadequate or dangerous; or

b. You have failed to fulfill the terms of a contract or agreement;

if such property can be restored to use by:

a. The repair, replacement, adjustment or removal of "your product" or "your work"; or

b. Your fulfilling the terms of the contract or agreement.

9. "Insured contract" means:

a. A contract for a lease of premises. However, that portion of the contract for a lease of premises that indemnifies any person or organization for damage by fire to premises while rented to you or temporarily occupied by you with permission of the owner is not an "insured contract";

b. A sidetrack agreement;

c. Any easement or license agreement, except in connection with construction or demolition operations on or within 50 feet of a railroad;

d. An obligation, as required by ordinance, to indemnify a municipality, except in connection with work for a municipality;

e. An elevator maintenance agreement;

f. That part of any other contract or agreement pertaining to your business (including an indemnification of a municipality in connection with work performed for a municipality) under which you assume the tort liability of another party to pay for "bodily injury" or "property damage" to a third person or organization. Tort liability means a liability that would be imposed by law in the absence of any contract or agreement.

Paragraph **f.** does not include that part of any contract or agreement:

(1) That indemnifies a railroad for "bodily injury" or "property damage" arising out of construction or demolition operations, within 50 feet of any railroad property and affecting any railroad bridge or trestle, tracks, roadbeds, tunnel, underpass or crossing;

(2) That indemnifies an architect, engineer or surveyor for injury or damage arising out of:

    (a) Preparing, approving, or failing to prepare or approve, maps, shop drawings, opinions, reports, surveys, field orders, change orders or drawings and specifications; or

    (b) Giving directions or instructions, or failing to give them, if that is the primary cause of the injury or damage; or

(3) Under which the insured, if an architect, engineer or surveyor, assumes liability for an injury or damage arising out of the insured's rendering or failure to render professional services, including those listed in **(2)** above and supervisory, inspection, architectural or engineering activities.

10. "Leased worker" means a person leased to you by a labor leasing firm under an agreement between you and the labor leasing firm, to perform duties related to the conduct of your business. "Leased worker" does not include a "temporary worker".

11. "Loading or unloading" means the handling of property:

    a. After it is moved from the place where it is accepted for movement into or onto an aircraft, watercraft or "auto";

    b. While it is in or on an aircraft, watercraft or "auto"; or

    c. While it is being moved from an aircraft, watercraft or "auto" to the place where it is finally delivered;

but "loading or unloading" does not include the movement of property by means of a mechanical device, other than a hand truck, that is not attached to the aircraft, watercraft or "auto".

12. "Mobile equipment" means any of the following types of land vehicles, including any attached machinery or equipment:

    a. Bulldozers, farm machinery, forklifts and other vehicles designed for use principally off public roads;

    b. Vehicles maintained for use solely on or next to premises you own or rent;

    c. Vehicles that travel on crawler treads;

    d. Vehicles, whether self-propelled or not, maintained primarily to provide mobility to permanently mounted:

        (1) Power cranes, shovels, loaders, diggers or drills; or

        (2) Road construction or resurfacing equipment such as graders, scrapers or rollers;

    e. Vehicles not described in **a.**, **b.**, **c.** or **d.** above that are not self-propelled and are maintained primarily to provide mobility to permanently attached equipment of the following types:

        (1) Air compressors, pumps and generators, including spraying, welding, building cleaning, geophysical exploration, lighting and well servicing equipment; or

        (2) Cherry pickers and similar devices used to raise or lower workers;

    f. Vehicles not described in **a.**, **b.**, **c.** or **d.** above maintained primarily for purposes other than the transportation of persons or cargo.

    However, self-propelled vehicles with the following types of permanently attached equipment are not "mobile equipment" but will be considered "autos":

        (1) Equipment designed primarily for:

            (a) Snow removal;

            (b) Road maintenance, but not construction or resurfacing; or

            (c) Street cleaning;

        (2) Cherry pickers and similar devices mounted on automobile or truck chassis and used to raise or lower workers; and

        (3) Air compressors, pumps and generators, including spraying, welding, building cleaning, geophysical exploration, lighting and well servicing equipment.

    However, "mobile equipment" does not include land vehicles that are subject to a compulsory or financial responsibility law or other motor vehicle insurance law in the state where it is licensed or principally garaged. Land vehicles subject to a compulsory or financial responsibility law or other motor vehicle insurance law are considered "autos".

13. "Occurrence" means an accident, including continuous or repeated exposure to substantially the same general harmful conditions.

14. "Personal and advertising injury" means injury, including consequential "bodily injury", arising out of one or more of the following offenses:

    a. False arrest, detention or imprisonment;

    b. Malicious prosecution;

    c. The wrongful eviction from, wrongful entry into, or invasion of the right of private occupancy of a room, dwelling or premises that a person occupies, committed by or on behalf of its owner, landlord or lessor;

d. Oral or written publication, in any manner, of material that slanders or libels a person or organization or disparages a person's or organization's goods, products or services;

e. Oral or written publication, in any manner, of material that violates a person's right of privacy;

f. The use of another's advertising idea in your "advertisement"; or

g. Infringing upon another's copyright, trade dress or slogan in your "advertisement".

15. "Pollutants" mean any solid, liquid, gaseous or thermal irritant or contaminant, including smoke, vapor, soot, fumes, acids, alkalis, chemicals and waste. Waste includes materials to be recycled, reconditioned or reclaimed.

16. "Products-completed operations hazard":

a. Includes all "bodily injury" and "property damage" occurring away from premises you own or rent and arising out of "your product" or "your work" except:

(1) Products that are still in your physical possession; or

(2) Work that has not yet been completed or abandoned. However, "your work" will be deemed completed at the earliest of the following times:

(a) When all of the work called for in your contract has been completed.

(b) When all of the work to be done at the job site has been completed if your contract calls for work at more than one job site.

(c) When that part of the work done at a job site has been put to its intended use by any person or organization other than another contractor or subcontractor working on the same project.

Work that may need service, maintenance, correction, repair or replacement, but which is otherwise complete, will be treated as completed.

b. Does not include "bodily injury" or "property damage" arising out of:

(1) The transportation of property, unless the injury or damage arises out of a condition in or on a vehicle not owned or operated by you, and that condition was created by the "loading or unloading" of that vehicle by any insured;

(2) The existence of tools, uninstalled equipment or abandoned or unused materials; or

(3) Products or operations for which the classification, listed in the Declarations or in a policy schedule, states that products-completed operations are subject to the General Aggregate Limit.

17. "Property damage" means:

a. Physical injury to tangible property, including all resulting loss of use of that property. All such loss of use shall be deemed to occur at the time of the physical injury that caused it; or

b. Loss of use of tangible property that is not physically injured. All such loss of use shall be deemed to occur at the time of the "occurrence" that caused it.

For the purposes of this insurance, electronic data is not tangible property.

As used in this definition, electronic data means information, facts or programs stored as or on, created or used on, or transmitted to or from, computer software, including systems and applications software, hard or floppy disks, CD-ROMS, tapes, drives, cells, data processing devices or any other media which are used with electronically controlled equipment.

18. "Suit" means a civil proceeding in which damages because of "bodily injury", "property damage" or "personal and advertising injury" to which this insurance applies are alleged. "Suit" includes:

a. An arbitration proceeding in which such damages are claimed and to which the insured must submit or does submit with our consent; or

b. Any other alternative dispute resolution proceeding in which such damages are claimed and to which the insured submits with our consent.

19. "Temporary worker" means a person who is furnished to you to substitute for a permanent "employee" on leave or to meet seasonal or short-term workload conditions.

20. "Volunteer worker" means a person who is not your "employee", and who donates his or her work and acts at the direction of and within the scope of duties determined by you, and is not paid a fee, salary or other compensation by you or anyone else for their work performed for you.

21. "Your product":

a. Means:

(1) Any goods or products, other than real property, manufactured, sold, handled, distributed or disposed of by:

(a) You;

(b) Others trading under your name; or

(c) A person or organization whose business or assets you have acquired; and

(2) Containers (other than vehicles), materials, parts or equipment furnished in connection with such goods or products.

b. Includes:

(1) Warranties or representations made at any time with respect to the fitness, quality, durability, performance or use of "your product"; and

(2) The providing of or failure to provide warnings or instructions.

c. Does not include vending machines or other property rented to or located for the use of others but not sold.

22. "Your work":

a. Means:

(1) Work or operations performed by you or on your behalf; and

(2) Materials, parts or equipment furnished in connection with such work or operations.

b. Includes:

(1) Warranties or representations made at any time with respect to the fitness, quality, durability, performance or use of "your work" and

(2) The providing of or failure to provide warnings or instructions.

COMMERCIAL GENERAL LIABILITY
CG 00 01 12 07

COMMERCIAL GENERAL LIABILITY COVERAGE FORM

Various provisions in this policy restrict coverage. Read the entire policy carefully to determine rights, duties and what is and is not covered.

Throughout this policy the words "you" and "your" refer to the Named Insured shown in the Declarations, and any other person or organization qualifying as a Named Insured under this policy. The words "we", "us" and "our" refer to the company providing this insurance.

The word "insured" means any person or organization qualifying as such under Section II – Who Is An Insured.

Other words and phrases that appear in quotation marks have special meaning. Refer to Section V – Definitions.

SECTION I – COVERAGES

COVERAGE A BODILY INJURY AND PROPERTY DAMAGE LIABILITY

1. Insuring Agreement

  a. We will pay those sums that the insured becomes legally obligated to pay as damages because of "bodily injury" or "property damage" to which this insurance applies. We will have the right and duty to defend the insured against any "suit" seeking those damages. However, we will have no duty to defend the insured against any "suit" seeking damages for "bodily injury" or "property damage" to which this insurance does not apply. We may, at our discretion, investigate any "occurrence" and settle any claim or "suit" that may result. But:

    (1) The amount we will pay for damages is limited as described in Section III – Limits Of Insurance; and

    (2) Our right and duty to defend ends when we have used up the applicable limit of insurance in the payment of judgments or settlements under Coverages **A** or **B** or medical expenses under Coverage **C**.

  No other obligation or liability to pay sums or perform acts or services is covered unless explicitly provided for under Supplementary Payments – Coverages **A** and **B**.

  b. This insurance applies to "bodily injury" and "property damage" only if:

    (1) The "bodily injury" or "property damage" is caused by an "occurrence" that takes place in the "coverage territory";

    (2) The "bodily injury" or "property damage" occurs during the policy period; and

    (3) Prior to the policy period, no insured listed under Paragraph **1.** of Section II – Who Is An Insured and no "employee" authorized by you to give or receive notice of an "occurrence" or claim, knew that the "bodily injury" or "property damage" had occurred, in whole or in part. If such a listed insured or authorized "employee" knew, prior to the policy period, that the "bodily injury" or "property damage" occurred, then any continuation, change or resumption of such "bodily injury" or "property damage" during or after the policy period will be deemed to have been known prior to the policy period.

  c. "Bodily injury" or "property damage" which occurs during the policy period and was not, prior to the policy period, known to have occurred by any insured listed under Paragraph **1.** of Section II – Who Is An Insured or any "employee" authorized by you to give or receive notice of an "occurrence" or claim, includes any continuation, change or resumption of that "bodily injury" or "property damage" after the end of the policy period.

  d. "Bodily injury" or "property damage" will be deemed to have been known to have occurred at the earliest time when any insured listed under Paragraph **1.** of Section II – Who Is An Insured or any "employee" authorized by you to give or receive notice of an "occurrence" or claim:

    (1) Reports all, or any part, of the "bodily injury" or "property damage" to us or any other insurer;

    (2) Receives a written or verbal demand or claim for damages because of the "bodily injury" or "property damage"; or

    (3) Becomes aware by any other means that "bodily injury" or "property damage" has occurred or has begun to occur.

e. Damages because of "bodily injury" include damages claimed by any person or organization for care, loss of services or death resulting at any time from the "bodily injury".

2. Exclusions

This insurance does not apply to:

a. Expected Or Intended Injury

"Bodily injury" or "property damage" expected or intended from the standpoint of the insured. This exclusion does not apply to "bodily injury" resulting from the use of reasonable force to protect persons or property.

b. Contractual Liability

"Bodily injury" or "property damage" for which the insured is obligated to pay damages by reason of the assumption of liability in a contract or agreement. This exclusion does not apply to liability for damages:

(1) That the insured would have in the absence of the contract or agreement; or

(2) Assumed in a contract or agreement that is an "insured contract", provided the "bodily injury" or "property damage" occurs subsequent to the execution of the contract or agreement. Solely for the purposes of liability assumed in an "insured contract", reasonable attorney fees and necessary litigation expenses incurred by or for a party other than an insured are deemed to be damages because of "bodily injury" or "property damage", provided:

(a) Liability to such party for, or for the cost of, that party's defense has also been assumed in the same "insured contract"; and

(b) Such attorney fees and litigation expenses are for defense of that party against a civil or alternative dispute resolution proceeding in which damages to which this insurance applies are alleged.

c. Liquor Liability

"Bodily injury" or "property damage" for which any insured may be held liable by reason of:

(1) Causing or contributing to the intoxication of any person;

(2) The furnishing of alcoholic beverages to a person under the legal drinking age or under the influence of alcohol; or

(3) Any statute, ordinance or regulation relating to the sale, gift, distribution or use of alcoholic beverages.

This exclusion applies only if you are in the business of manufacturing, distributing, selling, serving or furnishing alcoholic beverages.

d. Workers' Compensation And Similar Laws

Any obligation of the insured under a workers' compensation, disability benefits or unemployment compensation law or any similar law.

e. Employer's Liability

"Bodily injury" to:

(1) An "employee" of the insured arising out of and in the course of:

(a) Employment by the insured; or

(b) Performing duties related to the conduct of the insured's business; or

(2) The spouse, child, parent, brother or sister of that "employee" as a consequence of Paragraph **(1)** above.

This exclusion applies whether the insured may be liable as an employer or in any other capacity and to any obligation to share damages with or repay someone else who must pay damages because of the injury.

This exclusion does not apply to liability assumed by the insured under an "insured contract".

f. Pollution

(1) "Bodily injury" or "property damage" arising out of the actual, alleged or threatened discharge, dispersal, seepage, migration, release or escape of "pollutants":

(a) At or from any premises, site or location which is or was at any time owned or occupied by, or rented or loaned to, any insured. However, this subparagraph does not apply to:

(i) "Bodily injury" if sustained within a building and caused by smoke, fumes, vapor or soot produced by or originating from equipment that is used to heat, cool or dehumidify the building, or equipment that is used to heat water for personal use, by the building's occupants or their guests;

(ii) "Bodily injury" or "property damage" for which you may be held liable, if you are a contractor and the owner or lessee of such premises, site or location has been added to your policy as an additional insured with respect to your ongoing operations performed for that additional insured at that premises, site or location and such premises, site or location is not and never was owned or occupied by, or rented or loaned to, any insured, other than that additional insured; or

(iii) "Bodily injury" or "property damage" arising out of heat, smoke or fumes from a "hostile fire";

(b) At or from any premises, site or location which is or was at any time used by or for any insured or others for the handling, storage, disposal, processing or treatment of waste;

(c) Which are or were at any time transported, handled, stored, treated, disposed of, or processed as waste by or for:

(i) Any insured; or

(ii) Any person or organization for whom you may be legally responsible; or

(d) At or from any premises, site or location on which any insured or any contractors or subcontractors working directly or indirectly on any insured's behalf are performing operations if the "pollutants" are brought on or to the premises, site or location in connection with such operations by such insured, contractor or subcontractor. However, this subparagraph does not apply to:

(i) "Bodily injury" or "property damage" arising out of the escape of fuels, lubricants or other operating fluids which are needed to perform the normal electrical, hydraulic or mechanical functions necessary for the operation of "mobile equipment" or its parts, if such fuels, lubricants or other operating fluids escape from a vehicle part designed to hold, store or receive them. This exception does not apply if the "bodily injury" or "property damage" arises out of the intentional discharge, dispersal or release of the fuels, lubricants or other operating fluids, or if such fuels, lubricants or other operating fluids are brought on or to the premises, site or location with the intent that they be discharged, dispersed or released as part of the operations being performed by such insured, contractor or subcontractor;

(ii) "Bodily injury" or "property damage" sustained within a building and caused by the release of gases, fumes or vapors from materials brought into that building in connection with operations being performed by you or on your behalf by a contractor or subcontractor; or

(iii) "Bodily injury" or "property damage" arising out of heat, smoke or fumes from a "hostile fire".

(e) At or from any premises, site or location on which any insured or any contractors or subcontractors working directly or indirectly on any insured's behalf are performing operations if the operations are to test for, monitor, clean up, remove, contain, treat, detoxify or neutralize, or in any way respond to, or assess the effects of, "pollutants".

(2) Any loss, cost or expense arising out of any:

(a) Request, demand, order or statutory or regulatory requirement that any insured or others test for, monitor, clean up, remove, contain, treat, detoxify or neutralize, or in any way respond to, or assess the effects of, "pollutants"; or

(b) Claim or "suit" by or on behalf of a governmental authority for damages because of testing for, monitoring, cleaning up, removing, containing, treating, detoxifying or neutralizing, or in any way responding to, or assessing the effects of, "pollutants".

However, this paragraph does not apply to liability for damages because of "property damage" that the insured would have in the absence of such request, demand, order or statutory or regulatory requirement, or such claim or "suit" by or on behalf of a governmental authority.

g. Aircraft, Auto Or Watercraft

"Bodily injury" or "property damage" arising out of the ownership, maintenance, use or entrustment to others of any aircraft, "auto" or watercraft owned or operated by or rented or loaned to any insured. Use includes operation and "loading or unloading".

This exclusion applies even if the claims against any insured allege negligence or other wrongdoing in the supervision, hiring, employment, training or monitoring of others by that insured, if the "occurrence" which caused the "bodily injury" or "property damage" involved the ownership, maintenance, use or entrustment to others of any aircraft, "auto" or watercraft that is owned or operated by or rented or loaned to any insured.

This exclusion does not apply to:

(1) A watercraft while ashore on premises you own or rent;

(2) A watercraft you do not own that is:

(a) Less than 26 feet long; and

(b) Not being used to carry persons or property for a charge;

(3) Parking an "auto" on, or on the ways next to, premises you own or rent, provided the "auto" is not owned by or rented or loaned to you or the insured;

(4) Liability assumed under any "insured contract" for the ownership, maintenance or use of aircraft or watercraft; or

(5) "Bodily injury" or "property damage" arising out of:

(a) The operation of machinery or equipment that is attached to, or part of, a land vehicle that would qualify under the definition of "mobile equipment" if it were not subject to a compulsory or financial responsibility law or other motor vehicle insurance law in the state where it is licensed or principally garaged; or

(b) the operation of any of the machinery or equipment listed in Paragraph **f.(2)** or **f.(3)** of the definition of "mobile equipment".

h. Mobile Equipment

"Bodily injury" or "property damage" arising out of:

(1) The transportation of "mobile equipment" by an "auto" owned or operated by or rented or loaned to any insured; or

(2) The use of "mobile equipment" in, or while in practice for, or while being prepared for, any prearranged racing, speed, demolition, or stunting activity.

i. War

"Bodily injury" or "property damage", however caused, arising, directly or indirectly, out of:

(1) War, including undeclared or civil war;

(2) Warlike action by a military force, including action in hindering or defending against an actual or expected attack, by any government, sovereign or other authority using military personnel or other agents; or

(3) Insurrection, rebellion, revolution, usurped power, or action taken by governmental authority in hindering or defending against any of these.

j. Damage To Property

"Property damage" to:

(1) Property you own, rent, or occupy, including any costs or expenses incurred by you, or any other person, organization or entity, for repair, replacement, enhancement, restoration or maintenance of such property for any reason, including prevention of injury to a person or damage to another's property;

(2) Premises you sell, give away or abandon, if the "property damage" arises out of any part of those premises;

(3) Property loaned to you;

(4) Personal property in the care, custody or control of the insured;

(5) That particular part of real property on which you or any contractors or subcontractors working directly or indirectly on your behalf are performing operations, if the "property damage" arises out of those operations; or

(6) That particular part of any property that must be restored, repaired or replaced because "your work" was incorrectly performed on it.

Paragraphs **(1)**, **(3)** and **(4)** of this exclusion do not apply to "property damage" (other than damage by fire) to premises, including the contents of such premises, rented to you for a period of 7 or fewer consecutive days. A separate limit of insurance applies to Damage To Premises Rented To You as described in Section **III** – Limits Of Insurance.

Paragraph **(2)** of this exclusion does not apply if the premises are "your work" and were never occupied, rented or held for rental by you.

Paragraphs **(3)**, **(4)**, **(5)** and **(6)** of this exclusion do not apply to liability assumed under a sidetrack agreement.

Paragraph **(6)** of this exclusion does not apply to "property damage" included in the "products-completed operations hazard".

k. Damage To Your Product

"Property damage" to "your product" arising out of it or any part of it.

l. Damage To Your Work

"Property damage" to "your work" arising out of it or any part of it and included in the "products-completed operations hazard".

This exclusion does not apply if the damaged work or the work out of which the damage arises was performed on your behalf by a subcontractor.

m. Damage To Impaired Property Or Property Not Physically Injured

"Property damage" to "impaired property" or property that has not been physically injured, arising out of:

(1) A defect, deficiency, inadequacy or dangerous condition in "your product" or "your work"; or

(2) A delay or failure by you or anyone acting on your behalf to perform a contract or agreement in accordance with its terms.

This exclusion does not apply to the loss of use of other property arising out of sudden and accidental physical injury to "your product" or "your work" after it has been put to its intended use.

n. Recall Of Products, Work Or Impaired Property

Damages claimed for any loss, cost or expense incurred by you or others for the loss of use, withdrawal, recall, inspection, repair, replacement, adjustment, removal or disposal of:

(1) "Your product";

(2) "Your work"; or

(3) "Impaired property";

if such product, work, or property is withdrawn or recalled from the market or from use by any person or organization because of a known or suspected defect, deficiency, inadequacy or dangerous condition in it.

o. Personal And Advertising Injury

"Bodily injury" arising out of "personal and advertising injury".

p. Electronic Data

Damages arising out of the loss of, loss of use of, damage to, corruption of, inability to access, or inability to manipulate electronic data.

As used in this exclusion, electronic data means information, facts or programs stored as or on, created or used on, or transmitted to or from computer software, including systems and applications software, hard or floppy disks, CD-ROMS, tapes, drives, cells, data processing devices or any other media which are used with electronically controlled equipment.

q. Distribution Of Material In Violation Of Statutes

"Bodily injury" or "property damage" arising directly or indirectly out of any action or omission that violates or is alleged to violate:

(1) The Telephone Consumer Protection Act (TCPA), including any amendment of or addition to such law; or

(2) The CAN-SPAM Act of 2003, including any amendment of or addition to such law; or

(3) Any statute, ordinance or regulation, other than the TCPA or CAN-SPAM Act of 2003, that prohibits or limits the sending, transmitting, communicating or distribution of material or information.

Exclusions **c.** through **n.** do not apply to damage by fire to premises while rented to you or temporarily occupied by you with permission of the owner. A separate limit of insurance applies to this coverage as described in Section **III** – Limits Of Insurance.

COVERAGE B PERSONAL AND ADVERTISING INJURY LIABILITY

1. Insuring Agreement

a. We will pay those sums that the insured becomes legally obligated to pay as damages because of "personal and advertising injury" to which this insurance applies. We will have the right and duty to defend the insured against any "suit" seeking those damages. However, we will have no duty to defend the insured against any "suit" seeking damages for "personal and advertising injury" to which this insurance does not apply. We may, at our discretion, investigate any offense and settle any claim or "suit" that may result. But:

(1) The amount we will pay for damages is limited as described in Section **III** – Limits Of Insurance; and

(2) Our right and duty to defend end when we have used up the applicable limit of insurance in the payment of judgments or settlements under Coverages **A** or **B** or medical expenses under Coverage **C**.

No other obligation or liability to pay sums or perform acts or services is covered unless explicitly provided for under Supplementary Payments – Coverages **A** and **B**.

b. This insurance applies to "personal and advertising injury" caused by an offense arising out of your business but only if the offense was committed in the "coverage territory" during the policy period.

2. Exclusions

This insurance does not apply to:

a. **Knowing Violation Of Rights Of Another**

"Personal and advertising injury" caused by or at the direction of the insured with the knowledge that the act would violate the rights of another and would inflict "personal and advertising injury".

b. **Material Published With Knowledge Of Falsity**

"Personal and advertising injury" arising out of oral or written publication of material, if done by or at the direction of the insured with knowledge of its falsity.

c. **Material Published Prior To Policy Period**

"Personal and advertising injury" arising out of oral or written publication of material whose first publication took place before the beginning of the policy period.

d. **Criminal Acts**

"Personal and advertising injury" arising out of a criminal act committed by or at the direction of the insured.

e. **Contractual Liability**

"Personal and advertising injury" for which the insured has assumed liability in a contract or agreement. This exclusion does not apply to liability for damages that the insured would have in the absence of the contract or agreement.

f. **Breach Of Contract**

"Personal and advertising injury" arising out of a breach of contract, except an implied contract to use another's advertising idea in your "advertisement".

g. **Quality Or Performance Of Goods – Failure To Conform To Statements**

"Personal and advertising injury" arising out of the failure of goods, products or services to conform with any statement of quality or performance made in your "advertisement".

h. **Wrong Description Of Prices**

"Personal and advertising injury" arising out of the wrong description of the price of goods, products or services stated in your "advertisement".

i. **Infringement Of Copyright, Patent, Trademark Or Trade Secret**

"Personal and advertising injury" arising out of the infringement of copyright, patent, trademark, trade secret or other intellectual property rights. Under this exclusion, such other intellectual property rights do not include the use of another's advertising idea in your "advertisement".

However, this exclusion does not apply to infringement, in your "advertisement", of copyright, trade dress or slogan.

j. **Insureds In Media And Internet Type Businesses**

"Personal and advertising injury" committed by an insured whose business is:

(1) Advertising, broadcasting, publishing or telecasting;

(2) Designing or determining content of websites for others; or

© ISO Properties, Inc., 2006

(3) An Internet search, access, content or service provider.

However, this exclusion does not apply to Paragraphs **14.a., b.** and **c.** of "personal and advertising injury" under the Definitions Section.

For the purposes of this exclusion, the placing of frames, borders or links, or advertising, for you or others anywhere on the Internet, is not by itself, considered the business of advertising, broadcasting, publishing or telecasting.

k. Electronic Chatrooms Or Bulletin Boards

"Personal and advertising injury" arising out of an electronic chatroom or bulletin board the insured hosts, owns, or over which the insured exercises control.

l. Unauthorized Use Of Another's Name Or Product

"Personal and advertising injury" arising out of the unauthorized use of another's name or product in your e-mail address, domain name or metatag, or any other similar tactics to mislead another's potential customers.

m. Pollution

"Personal and advertising injury" arising out of the actual, alleged or threatened discharge, dispersal, seepage, migration, release or escape of "pollutants" at any time.

n. Pollution-Related

Any loss, cost or expense arising out of any:

(1) Request, demand, order or statutory or regulatory requirement that any insured or others test for, monitor, clean up, remove, contain, treat, detoxify or neutralize, or in any way respond to, or assess the effects of, "pollutants"; or

(2) Claim or suit by or on behalf of a governmental authority for damages because of testing for, monitoring, cleaning up, removing, containing, treating, detoxifying or neutralizing, or in any way responding to, or assessing the effects of, "pollutants".

o. War

"Personal and advertising injury", however caused, arising, directly or indirectly, out of:

(1) War, including undeclared or civil war;

(2) Warlike action by a military force, including action in hindering or defending against an actual or expected attack, by any government, sovereign or other authority using military personnel or other agents; or

(3) Insurrection, rebellion, revolution, usurped power, or action taken by governmental authority in hindering or defending against any of these.

p. Distribution Of Material In Violation Of Statutes

"Personal and advertising injury" arising directly or indirectly out of any action or omission that violates or is alleged to violate:

(1) The Telephone Consumer Protection Act (TCPA), including any amendment of or addition to such law; or

(2) The CAN-SPAM Act of 2003, including any amendment of or addition to such law; or

(3) Any statute, ordinance or regulation, other than the TCPA or CAN-SPAM Act of 2003, that prohibits or limits the sending, transmitting, communicating or distribution of material or information.

COVERAGE C MEDICAL PAYMENTS

1. Insuring Agreement

a. We will pay medical expenses as described below for "bodily injury" caused by an accident:

(1) On premises you own or rent;

(2) On ways next to premises you own or rent; or

(3) Because of your operations;

provided that:

(a) The accident takes place in the "coverage territory" and during the policy period;

(b) The expenses are incurred and reported to us within one year of the date of the accident; and

(c) The injured person submits to examination, at our expense, by physicians of our choice as often as we reasonably require.

b. We will make these payments regardless of fault. These payments will not exceed the applicable limit of insurance. We will pay reasonable expenses for:

(1) First aid administered at the time of an accident;

(2) Necessary medical, surgical, x-ray and dental services, including prosthetic devices; and

(3) Necessary ambulance, hospital, professional nursing and funeral services.

2. Exclusions

We will not pay expenses for "bodily injury":

a. Any Insured

To any insured, except "volunteer workers".

b. Hired Person

To a person hired to do work for or on behalf of any insured or a tenant of any insured.

c. Injury On Normally Occupied Premises

To a person injured on that part of premises you own or rent that the person normally occupies.

d. Workers Compensation And Similar Laws

To a person, whether or not an "employee" of any insured, if benefits for the "bodily injury" are payable or must be provided under a workers' compensation or disability benefits law or a similar law.

e. Athletics Activities

To a person injured while practicing, instructing or participating in any physical exercises or games, sports, or athletic contests.

f. Products-Completed Operations Hazard

Included within the "products-completed operations hazard".

g. Coverage A Exclusions

Excluded under Coverage **A**.

SUPPLEMENTARY PAYMENTS – COVERAGES A AND B

1. We will pay, with respect to any claim we investigate or settle, or any "suit" against an insured we defend:

   a. All expenses we incur.

   b. Up to $250 for cost of bail bonds required because of accidents or traffic law violations arising out of the use of any vehicle to which the Bodily Injury Liability Coverage applies. We do not have to furnish these bonds.

   c. The cost of bonds to release attachments, but only for bond amounts within the applicable limit of insurance. We do not have to furnish these bonds.

   d. All reasonable expenses incurred by the insured at our request to assist us in the investigation or defense of the claim or "suit", including actual loss of earnings up to $250 a day because of time off from work.

   e. All court costs taxed against the insured in the "suit". However, these payments do not include attorneys' fees or attorneys' expenses taxed against the insured.

   f. Prejudgment interest awarded against the insured on that part of the judgment we pay. If we make an offer to pay the applicable limit of insurance, we will not pay any prejudgment interest based on that period of time after the offer.

   g. All interest on the full amount of any judgment that accrues after entry of the judgment and before we have paid, offered to pay, or deposited in court the part of the judgment that is within the applicable limit of insurance.

   These payments will not reduce the limits of insurance.

2. If we defend an insured against a "suit" and an indemnitee of the insured is also named as a party to the "suit", we will defend that indemnitee if all of the following conditions are met:

   a. The "suit" against the indemnitee seeks damages for which the insured has assumed the liability of the indemnitee in a contract or agreement that is an "insured contract";

   b. This insurance applies to such liability assumed by the insured;

   c. The obligation to defend, or the cost of the defense of, that indemnitee, has also been assumed by the insured in the same "insured contract";

   d. The allegations in the "suit" and the information we know about the "occurrence" are such that no conflict appears to exist between the interests of the insured and the interests of the indemnitee;

   e. The indemnitee and the insured ask us to conduct and control the defense of that indemnitee against such "suit" and agree that we can assign the same counsel to defend the insured and the indemnitee; and

   f. The indemnitee:

   (1) Agrees in writing to:

   (a) Cooperate with us in the investigation, settlement or defense of the "suit";

   (b) Immediately send us copies of any demands, notices, summonses or legal papers received in connection with the "suit";

   (c) Notify any other insurer whose coverage is available to the indemnitee; and

   (d) Cooperate with us with respect to coordinating other applicable insurance available to the indemnitee; and

   (2) Provides us with written authorization to:

   (a) Obtain records and other information related to the "suit"; and

(b) Conduct and control the defense of the indemnitee in such "suit".

So long as the above conditions are met, attorneys' fees incurred by us in the defense of that indemnitee, necessary litigation expenses incurred by us and necessary litigation expenses incurred by the indemnitee at our request will be paid as Supplementary Payments. Notwithstanding the provisions of Paragraph **2.b.(2)** of Section I – Coverage **A** – Bodily Injury And Property Damage Liability, such payments will not be deemed to be damages for "bodily injury" and "property damage" and will not reduce the limits of insurance.

Our obligation to defend an insured's indemnitee and to pay for attorneys' fees and necessary litigation expenses as Supplementary Payments ends when we have used up the applicable limit of insurance in the payment of judgments or settlements or the conditions set forth above, or the terms of the agreement described in Paragraph **f.** above, are no longer met.

SECTION II – WHO IS AN INSURED

1. If you are designated in the Declarations as:

   a. An individual, you and your spouse are insureds, but only with respect to the conduct of a business of which you are the sole owner.

   b. A partnership or joint venture, you are an insured. Your members, your partners, and their spouses are also insureds, but only with respect to the conduct of your business.

   c. A limited liability company, you are an insured. Your members are also insureds, but only with respect to the conduct of your business. Your managers are insureds, but only with respect to their duties as your managers.

   d. An organization other than a partnership, joint venture or limited liability company, you are an insured. Your "executive officers" and directors are insureds, but only with respect to their duties as your officers or directors. Your stockholders are also insureds, but only with respect to their liability as stockholders.

   e. A trust, you are an insured. Your trustees are also insureds, but only with respect to their duties as trustees.

2. Each of the following is also an insured:

   a. Your "volunteer workers" only while performing duties related to the conduct of your business, or your "employees", other than either your "executive officers" (if you are an organization other than a partnership, joint venture or limited liability company) or your managers (if you are a limited liability company), but only for acts within the scope of their employment by you or while performing duties related to the conduct of your business. However, none of these "employees" or "volunteer workers" are insureds for:

   (1) "Bodily injury" or "personal and advertising injury":

   (a) To you, to your partners or members (if you are a partnership or joint venture), to your members (if you are a limited liability company), to a co-"employee" while in the course of his or her employment or performing duties related to the conduct of your business, or to your other "volunteer workers" while performing duties related to the conduct of your business;

   (b) To the spouse, child, parent, brother or sister of that co-"employee" or "volunteer worker" as a consequence of Paragraph **(1)(a)** above;

   (c) For which there is any obligation to share damages with or repay someone else who must pay damages because of the injury described in Paragraphs **(1)(a)** or **(b)** above; or

   (d) Arising out of his or her providing or failing to provide professional health care services.

   (2) "Property damage" to property:

   (a) Owned, occupied or used by,

   (b) Rented to, in the care, custody or control of, or over which physical control is being exercised for any purpose by

   you, any of your "employees", "volunteer workers", any partner or member (if you are a partnership or joint venture), or any member (if you are a limited liability company).

b. Any person (other than your "employee" or "volunteer worker"), or any organization while acting as your real estate manager.

c. Any person or organization having proper temporary custody of your property if you die, but only:

   (1) With respect to liability arising out of the maintenance or use of that property; and

   (2) Until your legal representative has been appointed.

d. Your legal representative if you die, but only with respect to duties as such. That representative will have all your rights and duties under this Coverage Part.

3. Any organization you newly acquire or form, other than a partnership, joint venture or limited liability company, and over which you maintain ownership or majority interest, will qualify as a Named Insured if there is no other similar insurance available to that organization. However:

a. Coverage under this provision is afforded only until the 90th day after you acquire or form the organization or the end of the policy period, whichever is earlier;

b. Coverage **A** does not apply to "bodily injury" or "property damage" that occurred before you acquired or formed the organization; and

c. Coverage **B** does not apply to "personal and advertising injury" arising out of an offense committed before you acquired or formed the organization.

No person or organization is an insured with respect to the conduct of any current or past partnership, joint venture or limited liability company that is not shown as a Named Insured in the Declarations.

SECTION III – LIMITS OF INSURANCE

1. The Limits of Insurance shown in the Declarations and the rules below fix the most we will pay regardless of the number of:

a. Insureds;

b. Claims made or "suits" brought; or

c. Persons or organizations making claims or bringing "suits".

2. The General Aggregate Limit is the most we will pay for the sum of:

a. Medical expenses under Coverage **C**;

b. Damages under Coverage **A**, except damages because of "bodily injury" or "property damage" included in the "products-completed operations hazard"; and

c. Damages under Coverage **B**.

3. The Products-Completed Operations Aggregate Limit is the most we will pay under Coverage **A** for damages because of "bodily injury" and "property damage" included in the "products-completed operations hazard".

4. Subject to Paragraph **2.** above, the Personal and Advertising Injury Limit is the most we will pay under Coverage **B** for the sum of all damages because of all "personal and advertising injury" sustained by any one person or organization.

5. Subject to Paragraph **2.** or **3.** above, whichever applies, the Each Occurrence Limit is the most we will pay for the sum of:

a. Damages under Coverage **A**; and

b. Medical expenses under Coverage **C**

because of all "bodily injury" and "property damage" arising out of any one "occurrence".

6. Subject to Paragraph **5.** above, the Damage To Premises Rented To You Limit is the most we will pay under Coverage **A** for damages because of "property damage" to any one premises, while rented to you, or in the case of damage by fire, while rented to you or temporarily occupied by you with permission of the owner.

7. Subject to Paragraph **5.** above, the Medical Expense Limit is the most we will pay under Coverage **C** for all medical expenses because of "bodily injury" sustained by any one person.

The Limits of Insurance of this Coverage Part apply separately to each consecutive annual period and to any remaining period of less than 12 months, starting with the beginning of the policy period shown in the Declarations, unless the policy period is extended after issuance for an additional period of less than 12 months. In that case, the additional period will be deemed part of the last preceding period for purposes of determining the Limits of Insurance.

SECTION IV – COMMERCIAL GENERAL LIABILITY CONDITIONS

1. Bankruptcy

Bankruptcy or insolvency of the insured or of the insured's estate will not relieve us of our obligations under this Coverage Part.

2. Duties In The Event Of Occurrence, Offense, Claim Or Suit

a. You must see to it that we are notified as soon as practicable of an "occurrence" or an offense which may result in a claim. To the extent possible, notice should include:

   (1) How, when and where the "occurrence" or offense took place;

   (2) The names and addresses of any injured persons and witnesses; and

(3) The nature and location of any injury or damage arising out of the "occurrence" or offense.

b. If a claim is made or "suit" is brought against any insured, you must:

(1) Immediately record the specifics of the claim or "suit" and the date received; and

(2) Notify us as soon as practicable.

You must see to it that we receive written notice of the claim or "suit" as soon as practicable.

c. You and any other involved insured must:

(1) Immediately send us copies of any demands, notices, summonses or legal papers received in connection with the claim or "suit";

(2) Authorize us to obtain records and other information;

(3) Cooperate with us in the investigation or settlement of the claim or defense against the "suit"; and

(4) Assist us, upon our request, in the enforcement of any right against any person or organization which may be liable to the insured because of injury or damage to which this insurance may also apply.

d. No insured will, except at that insured's own cost, voluntarily make a payment, assume any obligation, or incur any expense, other than for first aid, without our consent.

3. Legal Action Against Us

No person or organization has a right under this Coverage Part:

a. To join us as a party or otherwise bring us into a "suit" asking for damages from an insured; or

b. To sue us on this Coverage Part unless all of its terms have been fully complied with.

A person or organization may sue us to recover on an agreed settlement or on a final judgment against an insured; but we will not be liable for damages that are not payable under the terms of this Coverage Part or that are in excess of the applicable limit of insurance. An agreed settlement means a settlement and release of liability signed by us, the insured and the claimant or the claimant's legal representative.

4. Other Insurance

If other valid and collectible insurance is available to the insured for a loss we cover under Coverages **A** or **B** of this Coverage Part, our obligations are limited as follows:

a. Primary Insurance

This insurance is primary except when Paragraph **b.** below applies. If this insurance is primary, our obligations are not affected unless any of the other insurance is also primary. Then, we will share with all that other insurance by the method described in Paragraph **c.** below.

b. Excess Insurance

(1) This insurance is excess over:

(a) Any of the other insurance, whether primary, excess, contingent or on any other basis:

(i) That is Fire, Extended Coverage, Builder's Risk, Installation Risk or similar coverage for "your work";

(ii) That is Fire insurance for premises rented to you or temporarily occupied by you with permission of the owner;

(iii) That is insurance purchased by you to cover your liability as a tenant for "property damage" to premises rented to you or temporarily occupied by you with permission of the owner; or

(iv) If the loss arises out of the maintenance or use of aircraft, "autos" or watercraft to the extent not subject to Exclusion **g.** of Section I – Coverage **A** – Bodily Injury And Property Damage Liability.

(b) Any other primary insurance available to you covering liability for damages arising out of the premises or operations, or the products and completed operations, for which you have been added as an additional insured by attachment of an endorsement.

(2) When this insurance is excess, we will have no duty under Coverages **A** or **B** to defend the insured against any "suit" if any other insurer has a duty to defend the insured against that "suit". If no other insurer defends, we will undertake to do so, but we will be entitled to the insured's rights against all those other insurers.

(3) When this insurance is excess over other insurance, we will pay only our share of the amount of the loss, if any, that exceeds the sum of:

(a) The total amount that all such other insurance would pay for the loss in the absence of this insurance; and

(b) The total of all deductible and self-insured amounts under all that other insurance.

(4) We will share the remaining loss, if any, with any other insurance that is not described in this Excess Insurance provision and was not bought specifically to apply in excess of the Limits of Insurance shown in the Declarations of this Coverage Part.

c. Method Of Sharing

If all of the other insurance permits contribution by equal shares, we will follow this method also. Under this approach each insurer contributes equal amounts until it has paid its applicable limit of insurance or none of the loss remains, whichever comes first.

If any of the other insurance does not permit contribution by equal shares, we will contribute by limits. Under this method, each insurer's share is based on the ratio of its applicable limit of insurance to the total applicable limits of insurance of all insurers.

5. Premium Audit

a. We will compute all premiums for this Coverage Part in accordance with our rules and rates.

b. Premium shown in this Coverage Part as advance premium is a deposit premium only. At the close of each audit period we will compute the earned premium for that period and send notice to the first Named Insured. The due date for audit and retrospective premiums is the date shown as the due date on the bill. If the sum of the advance and audit premiums paid for the policy period is greater than the earned premium, we will return the excess to the first Named Insured.

c. The first Named Insured must keep records of the information we need for premium computation, and send us copies at such times as we may request.

6. Representations

By accepting this policy, you agree:

a. The statements in the Declarations are accurate and complete;

b. Those statements are based upon representations you made to us; and

c. We have issued this policy in reliance upon your representations.

7. Separation Of Insureds

Except with respect to the Limits of Insurance, and any rights or duties specifically assigned in this Coverage Part to the first Named Insured, this insurance applies:

a. As if each Named Insured were the only Named Insured; and

b. Separately to each insured against whom claim is made or "suit" is brought.

8. Transfer Of Rights Of Recovery Against Others To Us

If the insured has rights to recover all or part of any payment we have made under this Coverage Part, those rights are transferred to us. The insured must do nothing after loss to impair them. At our request, the insured will bring "suit" or transfer those rights to us and help us enforce them.

9. When We Do Not Renew

If we decide not to renew this Coverage Part, we will mail or deliver to the first Named Insured shown in the Declarations written notice of the nonrenewal not less than 30 days before the expiration date.

If notice is mailed, proof of mailing will be sufficient proof of notice.

SECTION V – DEFINITIONS

1. "Advertisement" means a notice that is broadcast or published to the general public or specific market segments about your goods, products or services for the purpose of attracting customers or supporters. For the purposes of this definition:

a. Notices that are published include material placed on the Internet or on similar electronic means of communication; and

b. Regarding web-sites, only that part of a web-site that is about your goods, products or services for the purposes of attracting customers or supporters is considered an advertisement.

2. "Auto" means:

a. A land motor vehicle, trailer or semitrailer designed for travel on public roads, including any attached machinery or equipment; or

b. Any other land vehicle that is subject to a compulsory or financial responsibility law or other motor vehicle insurance law in the state where it is licensed or principally garaged.

However, "auto" does not include "mobile equipment".

3. "Bodily injury" means bodily injury, sickness or disease sustained by a person, including death resulting from any of these at any time.

4. "Coverage territory" means:

a. The United States of America (including its territories and possessions), Puerto Rico and Canada;

b. International waters or airspace, but only if the injury or damage occurs in the course of travel or transportation between any places included in Paragraph **a.** above; or

c. All other parts of the world if the injury or damage arises out of:

(1) Goods or products made or sold by you in the territory described in Paragraph **a.** above;

(2) The activities of a person whose home is in the territory described in Paragraph **a.** above, but is away for a short time on your business; or

(3) "Personal and advertising injury" offenses that take place through the Internet or similar electronic means of communication

provided the insured's responsibility to pay damages is determined in a "suit" on the merits, in the territory described in Paragraph **a.** above or in a settlement we agree to.

5. "Employee" includes a "leased worker". "Employee" does not include a "temporary worker".

6. "Executive officer" means a person holding any of the officer positions created by your charter, constitution, by-laws or any other similar governing document.

7. "Hostile fire" means one which becomes uncontrollable or breaks out from where it was intended to be.

8. "Impaired property" means tangible property, other than "your product" or "your work", that cannot be used or is less useful because:

a. It incorporates "your product" or "your work" that is known or thought to be defective, deficient, inadequate or dangerous; or

b. You have failed to fulfill the terms of a contract or agreement;

if such property can be restored to use by the repair, replacement, adjustment or removal of "your product" or "your work" or your fulfilling the terms of the contract or agreement.

9. "Insured contract" means:

a. A contract for a lease of premises. However, that portion of the contract for a lease of premises that indemnifies any person or organization for damage by fire to premises while rented to you or temporarily occupied by you with permission of the owner is not an "insured contract";

b. A sidetrack agreement;

c. Any easement or license agreement, except in connection with construction or demolition operations on or within 50 feet of a railroad;

d. An obligation, as required by ordinance, to indemnify a municipality, except in connection with work for a municipality;

e. An elevator maintenance agreement;

f. That part of any other contract or agreement pertaining to your business (including an indemnification of a municipality in connection with work performed for a municipality) under which you assume the tort liability of another party to pay for "bodily injury" or "property damage" to a third person or organization. Tort liability means a liability that would be imposed by law in the absence of any contract or agreement.

Paragraph **f.** does not include that part of any contract or agreement:

(1) That indemnifies a railroad for "bodily injury" or "property damage" arising out of construction or demolition operations, within 50 feet of any railroad property and affecting any railroad bridge or trestle, tracks, roadbeds, tunnel, underpass or crossing;

(2) That indemnifies an architect, engineer or surveyor for injury or damage arising out of:

(a) Preparing, approving, or failing to prepare or approve, maps, shop drawings, opinions, reports, surveys, field orders, change orders or drawings and specifications; or

(b) Giving directions or instructions, or failing to give them, if that is the primary cause of the injury or damage; or

(3) Under which the insured, if an architect, engineer or surveyor, assumes liability for an injury or damage arising out of the insured's rendering or failure to render professional services, including those listed in **(2)** above and supervisory, inspection, architectural or engineering activities.

10. "Leased worker" means a person leased to you by a labor leasing firm under an agreement between you and the labor leasing firm, to perform duties related to the conduct of your business. "Leased worker" does not include a "temporary worker".

11. "Loading or unloading" means the handling of property:

   a. After it is moved from the place where it is accepted for movement into or onto an aircraft, watercraft or "auto";

   b. While it is in or on an aircraft, watercraft or "auto"; or

   c. While it is being moved from an aircraft, watercraft or "auto" to the place where it is finally delivered;

   but "loading or unloading" does not include the movement of property by means of a mechanical device, other than a hand truck, that is not attached to the aircraft, watercraft or "auto".

12. "Mobile equipment" means any of the following types of land vehicles, including any attached machinery or equipment:

   a. Bulldozers, farm machinery, forklifts and other vehicles designed for use principally off public roads;

   b. Vehicles maintained for use solely on or next to premises you own or rent;

   c. Vehicles that travel on crawler treads;

   d. Vehicles, whether self-propelled or not, maintained primarily to provide mobility to permanently mounted:

      (1) Power cranes, shovels, loaders, diggers or drills; or

      (2) Road construction or resurfacing equipment such as graders, scrapers or rollers;

   e. Vehicles not described in Paragraph a., b., c. or d. above that are not self-propelled and are maintained primarily to provide mobility to permanently attached equipment of the following types:

      (1) Air compressors, pumps and generators, including spraying, welding, building cleaning, geophysical exploration, lighting and well servicing equipment; or

      (2) Cherry pickers and similar devices used to raise or lower workers;

   f. Vehicles not described in Paragraph a., b., c. or d. above maintained primarily for purposes other than the transportation of persons or cargo.

However, self-propelled vehicles with the following types of permanently attached equipment are not "mobile equipment" but will be considered "autos":

   (1) Equipment designed primarily for:

      (a) Snow removal;

      (b) Road maintenance, but not construction or resurfacing; or

      (c) Street cleaning;

   (2) Cherry pickers and similar devices mounted on automobile or truck chassis and used to raise or lower workers; and

   (3) Air compressors, pumps and generators, including spraying, welding, building cleaning, geophysical exploration, lighting and well servicing equipment.

However, "mobile equipment" does not include any land vehicles that are subject to a compulsory or financial responsibility law or other motor vehicle insurance law in the state where it is licensed or principally garaged. Land vehicles subject to a compulsory or financial responsibility law or other motor vehicle insurance law are considered "autos".

13. "Occurrence" means an accident, including continuous or repeated exposure to substantially the same general harmful conditions.

14. "Personal and advertising injury" means injury, including consequential "bodily injury", arising out of one or more of the following offenses:

   a. False arrest, detention or imprisonment;

   b. Malicious prosecution;

   c. The wrongful eviction from, wrongful entry into, or invasion of the right of private occupancy of a room, dwelling or premises that a person occupies, committed by or on behalf of its owner, landlord or lessor;

   d. Oral or written publication, in any manner, of material that slanders or libels a person or organization or disparages a person's or organization's goods, products or services;

   e. Oral or written publication, in any manner, of material that violates a person's right of privacy;

   f. The use of another's advertising idea in your "advertisement"; or

   g. Infringing upon another's copyright, trade dress or slogan in your "advertisement".

15. "Pollutants" mean any solid, liquid, gaseous or thermal irritant or contaminant, including smoke, vapor, soot, fumes, acids, alkalis, chemicals and waste. Waste includes materials to be recycled, reconditioned or reclaimed.

16. "Products-completed operations hazard":

a. Includes all "bodily injury" and "property damage" occurring away from premises you own or rent and arising out of "your product" or "your work" except:

(1) Products that are still in your physical possession; or

(2) Work that has not yet been completed or abandoned. However, "your work" will be deemed completed at the earliest of the following times:

(a) When all of the work called for in your contract has been completed.

(b) When all of the work to be done at the job site has been completed if your contract calls for work at more than one job site.

(c) When that part of the work done at a job site has been put to its intended use by any person or organization other than another contractor or subcontractor working on the same project.

Work that may need service, maintenance, correction, repair or replacement, but which is otherwise complete, will be treated as completed.

b. Does not include "bodily injury" or "property damage" arising out of:

(1) The transportation of property, unless the injury or damage arises out of a condition in or on a vehicle not owned or operated by you, and that condition was created by the "loading or unloading" of that vehicle by any insured;

(2) The existence of tools, uninstalled equipment or abandoned or unused materials; or

(3) Products or operations for which the classification, listed in the Declarations or in a policy schedule, states that products-completed operations are subject to the General Aggregate Limit.

17. "Property damage" means:

a. Physical injury to tangible property, including all resulting loss of use of that property. All such loss of use shall be deemed to occur at the time of the physical injury that caused it; or

b. Loss of use of tangible property that is not physically injured. All such loss of use shall be deemed to occur at the time of the "occurrence" that caused it.

For the purposes of this insurance, electronic data is not tangible property.

As used in this definition, electronic data means information, facts or programs stored as or on, created or used on, or transmitted to or from computer software, including systems and applications software, hard or floppy disks, CD-ROMS, tapes, drives, cells, data processing devices or any other media which are used with electronically controlled equipment.

18. "Suit" means a civil proceeding in which damages because of "bodily injury", "property damage" or "personal and advertising injury" to which this insurance applies are alleged. "Suit" includes:

a. An arbitration proceeding in which such damages are claimed and to which the insured must submit or does submit with our consent; or

b. Any other alternative dispute resolution proceeding in which such damages are claimed and to which the insured submits with our consent.

19. "Temporary worker" means a person who is furnished to you to substitute for a permanent "employee" on leave or to meet seasonal or short-term workload conditions.

20. "Volunteer worker" means a person who is not your "employee", and who donates his or her work and acts at the direction of and within the scope of duties determined by you, and is not paid a fee, salary or other compensation by you or anyone else for their work performed for you.

21. "Your product":

a. Means:

(1) Any goods or products, other than real property, manufactured, sold, handled, distributed or disposed of by:

(a) You;

(b) Others trading under your name; or

(c) A person or organization whose business or assets you have acquired; and

(2) Containers (other than vehicles), materials, parts or equipment furnished in connection with such goods or products.

b. Includes:

(1) Warranties or representations made at any time with respect to the fitness, quality, durability, performance or use of "your product"; and

(2) The providing of or failure to provide warnings or instructions.

c. Does not include vending machines or other property rented to or located for the use of others but not sold.

22. "Your work":

a. Means:

(1) Work or operations performed by you or on your behalf; and

(2) Materials, parts or equipment furnished in connection with such work or operations.

b. Includes:

(1) Warranties or representations made at any time with respect to the fitness, quality, durability, performance or use of "your work", and

(2) The providing of or failure to provide warnings or instructions.

COMMERCIAL GENERAL LIABILITY
CG 00 02 12 07

COMMERCIAL GENERAL LIABILITY COVERAGE FORM

**COVERAGES A AND B PROVIDE
CLAIMS-MADE COVERAGE
PLEASE READ THE ENTIRE FORM CAREFULLY**

Various provisions in this policy restrict coverage. Read the entire policy carefully to determine rights, duties and what is and is not covered.

Throughout this policy the words "you" and "your" refer to the Named Insured shown in the Declarations, and any other person or organization qualifying as a Named Insured under this policy. The words "we", "us" and "our" refer to the Company providing this insurance.

The word "insured" means any person or organization qualifying as such under Section II – Who Is An Insured.

Other words and phrases that appear in quotation marks have special meaning. Refer to Section VI – Definitions.

SECTION I – COVERAGES

COVERAGE A BODILY INJURY AND PROPERTY DAMAGE LIABILITY

1. Insuring Agreement

a. We will pay those sums that the insured becomes legally obligated to pay as damages because of "bodily injury" or "property damage" to which this insurance applies. We will have the right and duty to defend the insured against any "suit" seeking those damages. However, we will have no duty to defend the insured against any "suit" seeking damages for "bodily injury" or "property damage" to which this insurance does not apply. We may, at our discretion, investigate any "occurrence" and settle any claim or "suit" that may result. But:

(1) The amount we will pay for damages is limited as described in Section III – Limits Of Insurance; and

(2) Our right and duty to defend ends when we have used up the applicable limit of insurance in the payment of judgments or settlements under Coverages A or B or medical expenses under Coverage C.

No other obligation or liability to pay sums or perform acts or services is covered unless explicitly provided for under Supplementary Payments – Coverages A and B.

b. This insurance applies to "bodily injury" and "property damage" only if:

(1) The "bodily injury" or "property damage" is caused by an "occurrence" that takes place in the "coverage territory";

(2) The "bodily injury" or "property damage" did not occur before the Retroactive Date, if any, shown in the Declarations or after the end of the policy period; and

(3) A claim for damages because of the "bodily injury" or "property damage" is first made against any insured, in accordance with Paragraph **c.** below, during the policy period or any Extended Reporting Period we provide under Section V – Extended Reporting Periods.

c. A claim by a person or organization seeking damages will be deemed to have been made at the earlier of the following times:

(1) When notice of such claim is received and recorded by any insured or by us, whichever comes first; or

(2) When we make settlement in accordance with Paragraph **a.** above.

All claims for damages because of "bodily injury" to the same person, including damages claimed by any person or organization for care, loss of services, or death resulting at any time from the "bodily injury", will be deemed to have been made at the time the first of those claims is made against any insured.

All claims for damages because of "property damage" causing loss to the same person or organization will be deemed to have been made at the time the first of those claims is made against any insured.

2. Exclusions

This insurance does not apply to:

a. Expected Or Intended Injury

"Bodily injury" or "property damage" expected or intended from the standpoint of the insured. This exclusion does not apply to "bodily injury" resulting from the use of reasonable force to protect persons or property.

b. Contractual Liability

"Bodily injury" or "property damage" for which the insured is obligated to pay damages by reason of the assumption of liability in a contract or agreement. This exclusion does not apply to liability for damages:

(1) That the insured would have in the absence of the contract or agreement; or

(2) Assumed in a contract or agreement that is an "insured contract", provided the "bodily injury" or "property damage" occurs subsequent to the execution of the contract or agreement. Solely for the purposes of liability assumed in an "insured contract", reasonable attorney fees and necessary litigation expenses incurred by or for a party other than an insured are deemed to be damages because of "bodily injury" or "property damage", provided:

(a) Liability to such party for, or for the cost of, that party's defense has also been assumed in the same "insured contract"; and

(b) Such attorney fees and litigation expenses are for defense of that party against a civil or alternative dispute resolution proceeding in which damages to which this insurance applies are alleged.

c. Liquor Liability

"Bodily injury" or "property damage" for which any insured may be held liable by reason of:

(1) Causing or contributing to the intoxication of any person;

(2) The furnishing of alcoholic beverages to a person under the legal drinking age or under the influence of alcohol; or

(3) Any statute, ordinance or regulation relating to the sale, gift, distribution or use of alcoholic beverages.

This exclusion applies only if you are in the business of manufacturing, distributing, selling, serving or furnishing alcoholic beverages.

d. Workers' Compensation And Similar Laws

Any obligation of the insured under a workers' compensation, disability benefits or unemployment compensation law or any similar law.

e. Employer's Liability

"Bodily injury" to:

(1) An "employee" of the insured arising out of and in the course of:

(a) Employment by the insured; or

(b) Performing duties related to the conduct of the insured's business; or

(2) The spouse, child, parent, brother or sister of that "employee" as a consequence of Paragraph **(1)** above.

This exclusion applies whether the insured may be liable as an employer or in any other capacity and to any obligation to share damages with or repay someone else who must pay damages because of the injury.

This exclusion does not apply to liability assumed by the insured under an "insured contract".

f. Pollution

(1) "Bodily injury" or "property damage" arising out of the actual, alleged or threatened discharge, dispersal, seepage, migration, release or escape of "pollutants":

(a) At or from any premises, site or location which is or was at any time owned or occupied by, or rented or loaned to, any insured. However, this subparagraph does not apply to:

(i) "Bodily injury" if sustained within a building and caused by smoke, fumes, vapor or soot produced by or originating from equipment that is used to heat, cool or dehumidify the building, or equipment that is used to heat water for personal use by the building's occupants or their guests;

(ii) "Bodily injury" or "property damage" for which you may be held liable, if you are a contractor and the owner or lessee of such premises, site or location has been added to your policy as an additional insured with respect to your ongoing operations performed for that additional insured at that premises, site or location and such premises, site or location is not or never was owned or occupied by, or rented or loaned to, any insured, other than that additional insured; or

(iii) "Bodily injury" or "property damage" arising out of heat, smoke or fumes from a "hostile fire";

(b) At or from any premises, site or location which is or was at any time used by or for any insured or others for the handling, storage, disposal, processing or treatment of waste;

(c) Which are or were at any time transported, handled, stored, treated, disposed of, or processed as waste by or for:

(i) Any insured; or

(ii) Any person or organization for whom you may be legally responsible; or

(d) At or from any premises, site or location on which any insured or any contractors or subcontractors working directly or indirectly on any insured's behalf are performing operations if the "pollutants" are brought on or to the premises, site or location in connection with such operations by such insured, contractor or subcontractor. However, this subparagraph does not apply to:

(i) "Bodily injury" or "property damage" arising out of the escape of fuels, lubricants or other operating fluids which are needed to perform the normal electrical, hydraulic or mechanical functions necessary for the operation of "mobile equipment" or its parts, if such fuels, lubricants or other operating fluids escape from a vehicle part designed to hold, store or receive them. This exception does not apply if the "bodily injury" or "property damage" arises out of the intentional discharge, dispersal or release of the fuels, lubricants or other operating fluids, or if such fuels, lubricants or other operating fluids are brought on or to the premises, site or location with the intent that they be discharged, dispersed or released as part of the operations being performed by such insured, contractor or subcontractor;

(ii) "Bodily injury" or "property damage" sustained within a building and caused by the release of gases, fumes or vapors from materials brought into that building in connection with operations being performed by you or on your behalf by a contractor or subcontractor; or

(iii) "Bodily injury" or "property damage" arising out of heat, smoke or fumes from a "hostile fire".

(e) At or from any premises, site or location on which any insured or any contractors or subcontractors working directly or indirectly on any insured's behalf are performing operations if the operations are to test for, monitor, clean up, remove, contain, treat, detoxify or neutralize, or in any way respond to, or assess the effects of, "pollutants".

(2) Any loss, cost or expense arising out of any:

(a) Request, demand, order or statutory or regulatory requirement that any insured or others test for, monitor, clean up, remove, contain, treat, detoxify or neutralize, or in any way respond to, or assess the effects of, "pollutants"; or

(b) Claim or suit by or on behalf of a governmental authority for damages because of testing for, monitoring, cleaning up, removing, containing, treating, detoxifying or neutralizing, or in any way responding to, or assessing the effects of, "pollutants".

However, this paragraph does not apply to liability for damages because of "property damage" that the insured would have in the absence of such request, demand, order or statutory or regulatory requirement, or such claim or "suit" by or on behalf of a governmental authority.

g. Aircraft, Auto Or Watercraft

"Bodily injury" or "property damage" arising out of the ownership, maintenance, use or entrustment to others of any aircraft, "auto" or watercraft owned or operated by or rented or loaned to any insured. Use includes operation and "loading or unloading".

This exclusion applies even if the claims against any insured allege negligence or other wrongdoing in the supervision, hiring, employment, training or monitoring of others by that insured, if the "occurrence" which caused the "bodily injury" or "property damage" involved the ownership, maintenance, use or entrustment to others of any aircraft, "auto" or watercraft that is owned or operated by or rented or loaned to any insured.

This exclusion does not apply to:

(1) A watercraft while ashore on premises you own or rent;

(2) A watercraft you do not own that is:

   (a) Less than 26 feet long; and

   (b) Not being used to carry persons or property for a charge;

(3) Parking an "auto" on, or on the ways next to, premises you own or rent, provided the "auto" is not owned by or rented or loaned to you or the insured;

(4) Liability assumed under any "insured contract" for the ownership, maintenance or use of aircraft or watercraft; or

(5) "Bodily injury" or "property damage" arising out of:

   (a) The operation of machinery or equipment that is attached to, or part of, a land vehicle that would qualify under the definition of "mobile equipment" if it were not subject to a compulsory or financial responsibility law or other motor vehicle insurance law in the state where it is licensed or principally garaged; or

   (b) The operation of any of the machinery or equipment listed in Paragraph **f.(2)** or **f.(3)** of the definition of "mobile equipment".

h. Mobile Equipment

"Bodily injury" or "property damage" arising out of:

(1) The transportation of "mobile equipment" by an "auto" owned or operated by or rented or loaned to any insured; or

(2) The use of "mobile equipment" in, or while in practice for, or while being prepared for, any prearranged racing, speed, demolition, or stunting activity.

i. War

"Bodily injury" or "property damage", however caused, arising, directly or indirectly, out of:

(1) War, including undeclared or civil war;

(2) Warlike action by a military force, including action in hindering or defending against an actual or expected attack, by any government, sovereign or other authority using military personnel or other agents; or

(3) Insurrection, rebellion, revolution, usurped power, or action taken by governmental authority in hindering or defending against any of these.

j. Damage To Property

"Property damage" to:

(1) Property you own, rent, or occupy, including any costs or expenses incurred by you, or any other person, organization or entity, for repair, replacement, enhancement, restoration or maintenance of such property for any reason, including prevention of injury to a person or damage to another's property;

(2) Premises you sell, give away or abandon, if the "property damage" arises out of any part of those premises;

(3) Property loaned to you;

(4) Personal property in the care, custody or control of the insured;

(5) That particular part of real property on which you or any contractors or subcontractors working directly or indirectly on your behalf are performing operations, if the "property damage" arises out of those operations; or

(6) That particular part of any property that must be restored, repaired or replaced because "your work" was incorrectly performed on it.

Paragraphs **(1)**, **(3)** and **(4)** of this exclusion do not apply to "property damage" (other than damage by fire) to premises, including the contents of such premises, rented to you for a period of 7 or fewer consecutive days. A separate limit of insurance applies to Damage To Premises Rented To You as described in Section **III** – Limits Of Insurance.

Paragraph **(2)** of this exclusion does not apply if the premises are "your work" and were never occupied, rented or held for rental by you.

Paragraphs **(3)**, **(4)**, **(5)** and **(6)** of this exclusion do not apply to liability assumed under a sidetrack agreement.

Paragraph **(6)** of this exclusion does not apply to "property damage" included in the "products-completed operations hazard".

k. Damage To Your Product

"Property damage" to "your product" arising out of it or any part of it.

l. Damage To Your Work

"Property damage" to "your work" arising out of it or any part of it and included in the "products-completed operations hazard".

© ISO Properties, Inc., 2006

This exclusion does not apply if the damaged work or the work out of which the damage arises was performed on your behalf by a subcontractor.

m. Damage To Impaired Property Or Property Not Physically Injured

"Property damage" to "impaired property" or property that has not been physically injured, arising out of:

(1) A defect, deficiency, inadequacy or dangerous condition in "your product" or "your work"; or

(2) A delay or failure by you or anyone acting on your behalf to perform a contract or agreement in accordance with its terms.

This exclusion does not apply to the loss of use of other property arising out of sudden and accidental physical injury to "your product" or "your work" after it has been put to its intended use.

n. Recall Of Products, Work Or Impaired Property

Damages claimed for any loss, cost or expense incurred by you or others for the loss of use, withdrawal, recall, inspection, repair, replacement, adjustment, removal or disposal of:

(1) "Your product";

(2) "Your work"; or

(3) "Impaired property";

if such product, work, or property is withdrawn or recalled from the market or from use by any person or organization because of a known or suspected defect, deficiency, inadequacy or dangerous condition in it.

o. Personal And Advertising Injury

"Bodily injury" arising out of "personal and advertising injury".

p. Electronic Data

Damages arising out of the loss of, loss of use of, damage to, corruption of, inability to access, or inability to manipulate electronic data.

As used in this exclusion, electronic data means information, facts or programs stored as or on, created or used on, or transmitted to or from computer software, including systems and applications software, hard or floppy disks, CD-ROMS, tapes, drives, cells, data processing devices or any other media which are used with electronically controlled equipment.

q. Distribution Of Material In Violation Of Statutes

"Bodily injury" or "property damage" arising directly or indirectly out of any action or omission that violates or is alleged to violate:

(1) The Telephone Consumer Protection Act (TCPA), including any amendment of or addition to such law; or

(2) The CAN-SPAM Act of 2003, including any amendment of or addition to such law; or

(3) Any statute, ordinance or regulation, other than the TCPA or CAN-SPAM Act of 2003, that prohibits or limits the sending, transmitting, communicating or distribution of material or information.

Exclusions **c.** through **n.** do not apply to damage by fire to premises while rented to you or temporarily occupied by you with permission of the owner. A separate limit of insurance applies to this coverage as described in Section **III** – Limits Of Insurance.

COVERAGE B PERSONAL AND ADVERTISING INJURY LIABILITY

1. Insuring Agreement

a. We will pay those sums that the insured becomes legally obligated to pay as damages because of "personal and advertising injury" to which this insurance applies. We will have the right and duty to defend the insured against any "suit" seeking those damages. However, we will have no duty to defend the insured against any "suit" seeking damages for "personal and advertising injury" to which this insurance does not apply. We may, at our discretion, investigate any offense and settle any claim or "suit" that may result. But:

(1) The amount we will pay for damages is limited as described in Section **III** – Limits Of Insurance; and

(2) Our right and duty to defend end when we have used up the applicable limit of insurance in the payment of judgments or settlements under Coverages **A** or **B** or medical expenses under Coverage **C**.

No other obligation or liability to pay sums or perform acts or services is covered unless explicitly provided for under Supplementary Payments – Coverages **A** and **B**.

b. This insurance applies to "personal and advertising injury" caused by an offense arising out of your business, but only if:

(1) The offense was committed in the "coverage territory";

(2) The offense was not committed before the Retroactive Date, if any, shown in the Declarations or after the end of the policy period; and

(3) A claim for damages because of the "personal and advertising injury" is first made against any insured, in accordance with Paragraph **c.** below, during the policy period or any Extended Reporting Period we provide under Section **V** – Extended Reporting Periods.

c. A claim made by a person or organization seeking damages will be deemed to have been made at the earlier of the following times:

(1) When notice of such claim is received and recorded by any insured or by us, whichever comes first; or

(2) When we make settlement in accordance with Paragraph **a.** above.

All claims for damages because of "personal and advertising injury" to the same person or organization as a result of an offense will be deemed to have been made at the time the first of those claims is made against any insured.

2. Exclusions

This insurance does not apply to:

a. Knowing Violation Of Rights Of Another

"Personal and advertising injury" caused by or at the direction of the insured with the knowledge that the act would violate the rights of another and would inflict "personal and advertising injury".

b. Material Published With Knowledge Of Falsity

"Personal and advertising injury" arising out of oral or written publication of material, if done by or at the direction of the insured with knowledge of its falsity.

c. Material Published Prior To Policy Period

"Personal and advertising injury" arising out of oral or written publication of material whose first publication took place before the Retroactive Date, if any, shown in the Declarations.

d. Criminal Acts

"Personal and advertising injury" arising out of a criminal act committed by or at the direction of the insured.

e. Contractual Liability

"Personal and advertising injury" for which the insured has assumed liability in a contract or agreement. This exclusion does not apply to liability for damages that the insured would have in the absence of the contract or agreement.

f. Breach Of Contract

"Personal and advertising injury" arising out of a breach of contract, except an implied contract to use another's advertising idea in your "advertisement".

g. Quality Or Performance Of Goods – Failure To Conform To Statements

"Personal and advertising injury" arising out of the failure of goods, products or services to conform with any statement of quality or performance made in your "advertisement".

h. Wrong Description Of Prices

"Personal and advertising injury" arising out of the wrong description of the price of goods, products or services stated in your "advertisement".

i. Infringement Of Copyright, Patent, Trademark Or Trade Secret

"Personal and advertising injury" arising out of the infringement of copyright, patent, trademark, trade secret or other intellectual property rights. Under this exclusion, such other intellectual property rights do not include the use of another's advertising idea in your "advertisement".

However, this exclusion does not apply to infringement, in your "advertisement", of copyright, trade dress or slogan.

j. Insureds In Media And Internet Type Businesses

"Personal and advertising injury" committed by an insured whose business is:

(1) Advertising, broadcasting, publishing or telecasting;

(2) Designing or determining content or websites for others; or

(3) An Internet search, access, content or service provider.

However, this exclusion does not apply to Paragraphs **14.a.**, **b.** and **c.** of "personal and advertising injury" under the Definitions Section.

For the purposes of this exclusion, the placing of frames, borders or links, or advertising, for you or others anywhere on the Internet, is not by itself, considered the business of advertising, broadcasting, publishing or telecasting.

k. Electronic Chatrooms Or Bulletin Boards

"Personal and advertising injury" arising out of an electronic chatroom or bulletin board the insured hosts, owns, or over which the insured exercises control.

l. Unauthorized Use Of Another's Name Or Product

"Personal and advertising injury" arising out of the unauthorized use of another's name or product in your e-mail address, domain name or metatag, or any other similar tactics to mislead another's potential customers.

m. Pollution

"Personal and advertising injury" arising out of the actual, alleged or threatened discharge, dispersal, seepage, migration, release or escape of "pollutants" at any time.

n. Pollution-Related

Any loss, cost or expense arising out of any:

(1) Request, demand, order or statutory or regulatory requirement that any insured or others test for, monitor, clean up, remove, contain, treat, detoxify or neutralize, or in any way respond to, or assess the effects of, "pollutants"; or

(2) Claim or suit by or on behalf of a governmental authority for damages because of testing for, monitoring, cleaning up, removing, containing, treating, detoxifying or neutralizing, or in any way responding to, or assessing the effects of, "pollutants".

o. War

"Personal and advertising injury", however caused, arising, directly or indirectly, out of:

(1) War, including undeclared or civil war;

(2) Warlike action by a military force, including action in hindering or defending against an actual or expected attack, by any government, sovereign or other authority using military personnel or other agents; or

(3) Insurrection, rebellion, revolution, usurped power, or action taken by governmental authority in hindering or defending against any of these.

p. Distribution Of Material In Violation Of Statutes

"Personal and advertising injury" arising directly or indirectly out of any action or omission that violates or is alleged to violate:

(1) The Telephone Consumer Protection Act (TCPA), including any amendment of or addition to such law; or

(2) The CAN-SPAM Act of 2003, including any amendment of or addition to such law; or

(3) Any statute, ordinance or regulation, other than the TCPA or CAN-SPAM Act of 2003, that prohibits or limits the sending, transmitting, communicating or distribution of material or information.

COVERAGE C MEDICAL PAYMENTS

1. Insuring Agreement

a. We will pay medical expenses as described below for "bodily injury" caused by an accident:

(1) On premises you own or rent;

(2) On ways next to premises you own or rent; or

(3) Because of your operations;

provided that:

(a) The accident takes place in the "coverage territory" and during the policy period;

(b) The expenses are incurred and reported to us within one year of the date of the accident; and

(c) The injured person submits to examination, at our expense, by physicians of our choice as often as we reasonably require.

b. We will make these payments regardless of fault. These payments will not exceed the applicable limit of insurance. We will pay reasonable expenses for:

(1) First aid administered at the time of an accident;

(2) Necessary medical, surgical, x-ray and dental services, including prosthetic devices; and

(3) Necessary ambulance, hospital, professional nursing and funeral services.

2. Exclusions

We will not pay expenses for "bodily injury":

a. Any Insured

To any insured, except "volunteer workers".

b. Hired Person

To a person hired to do work for or on behalf of any insured or a tenant of any insured.

c. Injury On Normally Occupied Premises

To a person injured on that part of premises you own or rent that the person normally occupies.

d. Workers Compensation And Similar Laws

To a person, whether or not an "employee" of any insured, if benefits for the "bodily injury" are payable or must be provided under a workers' compensation or disability benefits law or a similar law.

e. Athletics Activities

To a person injured while practicing, instructing or participating in any physical exercises or games, sports, or athletic contests.

f. Products-Completed Operations Hazard

Included within the "products-completed operations hazard".

g. Coverage A Exclusions

Excluded under Coverage **A.**

SUPPLEMENTARY PAYMENTS – COVERAGES A AND B

1. We will pay, with respect to any claim we investigate or settle or any "suit" against an insured we defend:

   a. All expenses we incur.

   b. Up to $250 for cost of bail bonds required because of accidents or traffic law violations arising out of the use of any vehicle to which the Bodily Injury Liability Coverage applies. We do not have to furnish these bonds.

   c. The cost of bonds to release attachments, but only for bond amounts within the applicable limit of insurance. We do not have to furnish these bonds.

   d. All reasonable expenses incurred by the insured at our request to assist us in the investigation or defense of the claim or "suit", including actual loss of earnings up to $250 a day because of time off from work.

   e. All court costs taxed against the insured in the "suit". However, these payments do not include attorneys' fees or attorneys' expenses taxed against the insured.

   f. Prejudgment interest awarded against the insured on that part of the judgment we pay. If we make an offer to pay the applicable limit of insurance, we will not pay any prejudgment interest based on that period of time after the offer.

   g. All interest on the full amount of any judgment that accrues after entry of the judgment and before we have paid, offered to pay, or deposited in court the part of the judgment that is within the applicable limit of insurance.

These payments will not reduce the limits of insurance.

2. If we defend an insured against a "suit" and an indemnitee of the insured is also named as a party to the "suit", we will defend that indemnitee if all of the following conditions are met:

   a. The "suit" against the indemnitee seeks damages for which the insured has assumed the liability of the indemnitee in a contract or agreement that is an "insured contract";

   b. This insurance applies to such liability assumed by the insured;

   c. The obligation to defend, or the cost of the defense of, that indemnitee, has also been assumed by the insured in the same "insured contract";

   d. The allegations in the "suit" and the information we know about the "occurrence" are such that no conflict appears to exist between the interests of the insured and the interests of the indemnitee;

   e. The indemnitee and the insured ask us to conduct and control the defense of that indemnitee against such "suit" and agree that we can assign the same counsel to defend the insured and the indemnitee; and

   f. The indemnitee:

   (1) Agrees in writing to:

   (a) Cooperate with us in the investigation, settlement or defense of the "suit";

   (b) Immediately send us copies of any demands, notices, summonses or legal papers received in connection with the "suit";

   (c) Notify any other insurer whose coverage is available to the indemnitee; and

   (d) Cooperate with us with respect to coordinating other applicable insurance available to the indemnitee; and

   (2) Provides us with written authorization to:

   (a) Obtain records and other information related to the "suit"; and

   (b) Conduct and control the defense of the indemnitee in such "suit".

So long as the above conditions are met, attorneys' fees incurred by us in the defense of that indemnitee, necessary litigation expenses incurred by us and necessary litigation expenses incurred by the indemnitee at our request will be paid as Supplementary Payments. Notwithstanding the provisions of Paragraph **2.b.(2)** of Section **I** – Coverage **A** – Bodily Injury And Property Damage Liability, such payments will not be deemed to be damages for "bodily injury" and "property damage" and will not reduce the limits of insurance.

Our obligation to defend an insured's indemnitee and to pay for attorneys' fees and necessary litigation expenses as Supplementary Payments ends when we have used up the applicable limit of insurance in the payment of judgments or settlements or the conditions set forth above, or the terms of the agreement described in Paragraph **f.** above, are no longer met.

SECTION II – WHO IS AN INSURED

1. If you are designated in the Declarations as:

    a. An individual, you and your spouse are insureds, but only with respect to the conduct of a business of which you are the sole owner.

    b. A partnership or joint venture, you are an insured. Your members, your partners, and their spouses are also insureds, but only with respect to the conduct of your business.

    c. A limited liability company, you are an insured. Your members are also insureds, but only with respect to the conduct of your business. Your managers are insureds, but only with respect to their duties as your managers.

    d. An organization other than a partnership, joint venture or limited liability company, you are an insured. Your "executive officers" and directors are insureds, but only with respect to their duties as your officers or directors. Your stockholders are also insureds, but only with respect to their liability as stockholders.

    e. A trust, you are an insured. Your trustees are also insureds, but only with respect to their duties as trustees.

2. Each of the following is also an insured:

    a. Your "volunteer workers" only while performing duties related to the conduct of your business, or your "employees", other than either your "executive officers" (if you are an organization other than a partnership, joint venture or limited liability company) or your managers (if you are a limited liability company), but only for acts within the scope of their employment by you or while performing duties related to the conduct of your business. However, none of these "employees" or "volunteer workers" are insureds for:

    (1) "Bodily injury" or "personal and advertising injury":

    (a) To you, to your partners or members (if you are a partnership or joint venture), to your members (if you are a limited liability company), to a co-"employee" while in the course of his or her employment or performing duties related to the conduct of your business, or to your other "volunteer workers" while performing duties related to the conduct of your business;

    (b) To the spouse, child, parent, brother or sister of that co-"employee" or "volunteer worker" as a consequence of Paragraph **(a)** above;

    (c) For which there is any obligation to share damages with or repay someone else who must pay damages because of the injury described in Paragraphs **(a)** or **(b)** above; or

    (d) Arising out of his or her providing or failing to provide professional health care services.

    (2) "Property damage" to property:

    (a) Owned, occupied or used by,

    (b) Rented to, in the care, custody or control of, or over which physical control is being exercised for any purpose by

    you, any of your "employees", "volunteer workers", any partner or member (if you are a partnership or joint venture), or any member (if you are a limited liability company).

b. Any person (other than your "employee" or "volunteer worker") or any organization while acting as your real estate manager.

c. Any person or organization having proper temporary custody of your property if you die, but only:

(1) With respect to liability arising out of the maintenance or use of that property; and

(2) Until your legal representative has been appointed.

d. Your legal representative if you die, but only with respect to duties as such. That representative will have all your rights and duties under this Coverage Part.

3. Any organization you newly acquire or form, other than a partnership, joint venture or limited liability company, and over which you maintain ownership or majority interest, will qualify as a Named Insured if there is no other similar insurance available to that organization. However:

a. Coverage under this provision is afforded only until the 90th day after you acquire or form the organization or the end of the policy period, whichever is earlier;

b. Coverage A does not apply to "bodily injury" or "property damage" that occurred before you acquired or formed the organization; and

c. Coverage B does not apply to "personal and advertising injury" arising out of an offense committed before you acquired or formed the organization.

No person or organization is an insured with respect to the conduct of any current or past partnership, joint venture or limited liability company that is not shown as a Named Insured in the Declarations.

SECTION III – LIMITS OF INSURANCE

1. The Limits of Insurance shown in the Declarations and the rules below fix the most we will pay regardless of the number of:

a. Insureds;

b. Claims made or "suits" brought; or

c. Persons or organizations making claims or bringing "suits".

2. The General Aggregate Limit is the most we will pay for the sum of:

a. Medical expenses under Coverage C;

b. Damages under Coverage A, except damages because of "bodily injury" or "property damage" included in the "products-completed operations hazard"; and

c. Damages under Coverage B.

3. The Products-Completed Operations Aggregate Limit is the most we will pay under Coverage A for damages because of "bodily injury" and "property damage" included in the "products-completed operations hazard".

4. Subject to Paragraph 2. above, the Personal and Advertising Injury Limit is the most we will pay under Coverage B for the sum of all damages because of all "personal and advertising injury" sustained by any one person or organization.

5. Subject to Paragraph 2. or 3. above, whichever applies, the Each Occurrence Limit is the most we will pay for the sum of:

a. Damages under Coverage A; and

b. Medical expenses under Coverage C

because of all "bodily injury" and "property damage" arising out of any one "occurrence".

6. Subject to Paragraph 5. above, the Damage To Premises Rented To You Limit is the most we will pay under Coverage A for damages because of "property damage" to any one premises, while rented to you, or in the case of damage by fire, while rented to you or temporarily occupied by you with permission of the owner.

7. Subject to Paragraph 5. above, the Medical Expense Limit is the most we will pay under Coverage C for all medical expenses because of "bodily injury" sustained by any one person.

The Limits of Insurance of this Coverage Part apply separately to each consecutive annual period and to any remaining period of less than 12 months, starting with the beginning of the policy period shown in the Declarations, unless the policy period is extended after issuance for an additional period of less than 12 months. In that case, the additional period will be deemed part of the last preceding period for purposes of determining the Limits of Insurance.

SECTION IV – COMMERCIAL GENERAL LIABILITY CONDITIONS

1. Bankruptcy

Bankruptcy or insolvency of the insured or of the insured's estate will not relieve us of our obligations under this Coverage Part.

2. Duties In The Event Of Occurrence, Offense, Claim Or Suit

a. You must see to it that we are notified as soon as practicable of an "occurrence" or offense which may result in a claim. To the extent possible, notice should include:

(1) How, when and where the "occurrence" or offense took place;

(2) The names and addresses of any injured persons and witnesses; and

(3) The nature and location of any injury or damage arising out of the "occurrence" or offense.

Notice of an "occurrence" or offense is not notice of a claim.

b. If a claim is received by any insured, you must:

(1) Immediately record the specifics of the claim and the date received; and

(2) Notify us as soon as practicable.

You must see to it that we receive written notice of the claim as soon as practicable.

c. You and any other involved insured must:

(1) Immediately send us copies of any demands, notices, summonses or legal papers received in connection with the claim or a "suit";

(2) Authorize us to obtain records and other information;

(3) Cooperate with us in the investigation or settlement of the claim or defense against the "suit"; and

(4) Assist us, upon our request, in the enforcement of any right against any person or organization which may be liable to the insured because of injury or damage to which this insurance may also apply.

d. No insured will, except at that insured's own cost, voluntarily make a payment, assume any obligation, or incur any expense, other than for first aid, without our consent.

3. Legal Action Against Us

No person or organization has a right under this Coverage Part:

a. To join us as a party or otherwise bring us into a "suit" asking for damages from an insured; or

b. To sue us on this Coverage Part unless all of its terms have been fully complied with.

A person or organization may sue us to recover on an agreed settlement or on a final judgment against an insured; but we will not be liable for damages that are not payable under the terms of this Coverage Part or that are in excess of the applicable limit of insurance. An agreed settlement means a settlement and release of liability signed by us, the insured and the claimant or the claimant's legal representative.

4. Other Insurance

If other valid and collectible insurance is available to the insured for a loss we cover under Coverages **A** or **B** of this Coverage Part, our obligations are limited as follows:

a. Primary Insurance

This insurance is primary except when Paragraph **b.** below applies. If this insurance is primary, our obligations are not affected unless any of the other insurance is also primary. Then, we will share with all that other insurance by the method described in Paragraph **c.** below.

b. Excess Insurance

(1) This insurance is excess over:

(a) Any of the other insurance, whether primary, excess, contingent or on any other basis:

(i) That is effective prior to the beginning of the policy period shown in the Declarations of this insurance and applies to "bodily injury" or "property damage" on other than a claims-made basis, if:

i. No Retroactive Date is shown in the Declarations of this insurance; or

ii. The other insurance has a policy period which continues after the Retroactive Date shown in the Declarations of this insurance;

(ii) That is Fire, Extended Coverage, Builders' Risk, Installation Risk or similar coverage for "your work";

(iii) That is Fire insurance for premises rented to you or temporarily occupied by you with permission of the owner;

(iv) That is insurance purchased by you to cover your liability as a tenant for "property damage" to premises rented to you or temporarily occupied by you with permission of the owner; or

(v) If the loss arises out of the maintenance or use of aircraft, "autos" or watercraft to the extent not subject to Exclusion **g.** of Section **I** – Coverage **A** – Bodily Injury And Property Damage Liability.

(b) Any other primary insurance available to you covering liability for damages arising out of the premises or operations, or the products and completed operations, for which you have been added as an additional insured by attachment of an endorsement.

(2) When this insurance is excess, we will have no duty under Coverages **A** or **B** to defend the insured against any "suit" if any other insurer has a duty to defend the insured against that "suit". If no other insurer defends, we will undertake to do so, but we will be entitled to the insured's rights against all those other insurers.

(3) When this insurance is excess over other insurance, we will pay only our share of the amount of the loss, if any, that exceeds the sum of:

(a) The total amount that all such other insurance would pay for the loss in the absence of this insurance; and

(b) The total of all deductible and self-insured amounts under all that other insurance.

(4) We will share the remaining loss, if any, with any other insurance that is not described in this Excess Insurance provision and was not bought specifically to apply in excess of the Limits of Insurance shown in the Declarations of this Coverage Part.

c. Method Of Sharing

If all of the other insurance permits contribution by equal shares, we will follow this method also. Under this approach each insurer contributes equal amounts until it has paid its applicable limit of insurance or none of the loss remains, whichever comes first.

If any of the other insurance does not permit contribution by equal shares, we will contribute by limits. Under this method, each insurer's share is based on the ratio of its applicable limit of insurance to the total applicable limits of insurance of all insurers.

5. Premium Audit

a. We will compute all premiums for this Coverage Part in accordance with our rules and rates.

b. Premium shown in this Coverage Part as advance premium is a deposit premium only. At the close of each audit period we will compute the earned premium for that period and send notice to the first Named Insured. The due date for audit and retrospective premiums is the date shown as the due date on the bill. If the sum of the advance and audit premiums paid for the policy period is greater than the earned premium, we will return the excess to the first Named Insured.

c. The first Named Insured must keep records of the information we need for premium computation, and send us copies at such times as we may request.

6. Representations

By accepting this policy, you agree:

a. The statements in the Declarations are accurate and complete;

b. Those statements are based upon representations you made to us; and

c. We have issued this policy in reliance upon your representations.

7. Separation Of Insureds

Except with respect to the Limits of Insurance, and any rights or duties specifically assigned in this Coverage Part to the first Named Insured, this insurance applies:

a. As if each Named Insured were the only Named Insured; and

b. Separately to each insured against whom claim is made or "suit" is brought.

8. Transfer Of Rights Of Recovery Against Others To Us

If the insured has rights to recover all or part of any payment we have made under this Coverage Part, those rights are transferred to us. The insured must do nothing after loss to impair them. At our request, the insured will bring "suit" or transfer those rights to us and help us enforce them.

9. When We Do Not Renew

If we decide not to renew this Coverage Part, we will mail or deliver to the first Named Insured shown in the Declarations written notice of the nonrenewal not less than 30 days before the expiration date.

If notice is mailed, proof of mailing will be sufficient proof of notice.

10. Your Right To Claim And "Occurrence" Information

We will provide the first Named Insured shown in the Declarations the following information relating to this and any preceding general liability claims-made Coverage Part we have issued to you during the previous three years:

a. A list or other record of each "occurrence", not previously reported to any other insurer, of which we were notified in accordance with Paragraph **2.a.** of the Section **IV – Duties In The Event Of Occurrence, Offense, Claim Or Suit Condition.** We will include the date and brief description of the "occurrence" if that information was in the notice we received.

b. A summary by policy year, of payments made and amounts reserved, stated separately, under any applicable General Aggregate Limit and Products-Completed Operations Aggregate Limit.

Amounts reserved are based on our judgment. They are subject to change and should not be regarded as ultimate settlement values.

You must not disclose this information to any claimant or any claimant's representative without our consent.

If we cancel or elect not to renew this Coverage Part, we will provide such information no later than 30 days before the date of policy termination. In other circumstances, we will provide this information only if we receive a written request from the first Named Insured within 60 days after the end of the policy period. In this case, we will provide this information within 45 days of receipt of the request.

We compile claim and "occurrence" information for our own business purposes and exercise reasonable care in doing so. In providing this information to the first Named Insured, we make no representations or warranties to insureds, insurers, or others to whom this information is furnished by or on behalf of any insured. Cancellation or non-renewal will be effective even if we inadvertently provide inaccurate information.

SECTION V – EXTENDED REPORTING PERIODS

1. We will provide one or more Extended Reporting Periods, as described below, if:

a. This Coverage Part is canceled or not renewed; or

b. We renew or replace this Coverage Part with insurance that:

(1) Has a Retroactive Date later than the date shown in the Declarations of this Coverage Part; or

(2) Does not apply to "bodily injury", "property damage" or "personal and advertising injury" on a claims-made basis.

2. Extended Reporting Periods do not extend the policy period or change the scope of coverage provided. They apply only to claims for:

a. "Bodily injury" or "property damage" that occurs before the end of the policy period but not before the Retroactive Date, if any, shown in the Declarations; or

b. "Personal and advertising injury" caused by an offense committed before the end of the policy period but not before the Retroactive Date, if any, shown in the Declarations.

Once in effect, Extended Reporting Periods may not be canceled.

3. A Basic Extended Reporting Period is automatically provided without additional charge. This period starts with the end of the policy period and lasts for:

a. Five years with respect to claims because of "bodily injury" and "property damage" arising out of an "occurrence" reported to us, not later than 60 days after the end of the policy period, in accordance with Paragraph **2.a.** of the Section **IV – Duties In The Event Of Occurrence, Offense, Claim Or Suit Condition;**

b. Five years with respect to claims because of "personal and advertising injury" arising out of an offense reported to us, not later than 60 days after the end of the policy period, in accordance with Paragraph **2.a.** of the Section **IV – Duties In The Event Of Occurrence, Offense, Claim Or Suit Condition; and**

c. Sixty days with respect to claims arising from "occurrences" or offenses not previously reported to us.

The Basic Extended Reporting Period does not apply to claims that are covered under any subsequent insurance you purchase, or that would be covered but for exhaustion of the amount of insurance applicable to such claims.

4. The Basic Extended Reporting Period does not reinstate or increase the Limits of Insurance.

5. A Supplemental Extended Reporting Period of unlimited duration is available, but only by an endorsement and for an extra charge. This supplemental period starts when the Basic Extended Reporting Period, set forth in Paragraph **3.** above, ends.

You must give us a written request for the endorsement within 60 days after the end of the policy period. The Supplemental Extended Reporting Period will not go into effect unless you pay the additional premium promptly when due.

We will determine the additional premium in accordance with our rules and rates. In doing so, we may take into account the following:

a. The exposures insured;

b. Previous types and amounts of insurance;

c. Limits of Insurance available under this Coverage Part for future payment of damages; and

d. Other related factors.

The additional premium will not exceed 200% of the annual premium for this Coverage Part.

This endorsement shall set forth the terms, not inconsistent with this Section, applicable to the Supplemental Extended Reporting Period, including a provision to the effect that the insurance afforded for claims first received during such period is excess over any other valid and collectible insurance available under policies in force after the Supplemental Extended Reporting Period starts.

6. If the Supplemental Extended Reporting Period is in effect, we will provide the supplemental aggregate limits of insurance described below, but only for claims first received and recorded during the Supplemental Extended Reporting Period.

The supplemental aggregate limits of insurance will be equal to the dollar amount shown in the Declarations in effect at the end of the policy period for such of the following limits of insurance for which a dollar amount has been entered:

General Aggregate Limit
Products-Completed Operations Aggregate Limit

Paragraphs **2.** and **3.** of Section **III** – Limits Of Insurance will be amended accordingly. The Personal and Advertising Injury Limit, the Each Occurrence Limit and the Damage To Premises Rented To You Limit shown in the Declarations will then continue to apply, as set forth in Paragraphs **4.**, **5.** and **6.** of that Section.

SECTION VI – DEFINITIONS

1. "Advertisement" means a notice that is broadcast or published to the general public or specific market segments about your goods, products or services for the purpose of attracting customers or supporters. For the purposes of this definition:

a. Notices that are published include material placed on the Internet or on similar electronic means of communication; and

b. Regarding web-sites, only that part of a web-site that is about your goods, products or services for the purposes of attracting customers or supporters is considered an advertisement.

2. "Auto" means:

a. A land motor vehicle, trailer or semitrailer designed for travel on public roads, including any attached machinery or equipment; or

b. Any other land vehicle that is subject to a compulsory or financial responsibility law or other motor vehicle insurance law in the state where it is licensed or principally garaged.

However, "auto" does not include "mobile equipment".

3. "Bodily injury" means bodily injury, sickness or disease sustained by a person, including death resulting from any of these at any time.

4. "Coverage territory" means:

a. The United States of America (including its territories and possessions), Puerto Rico and Canada;

b. International waters or airspace, but only if the injury or damage occurs in the course of travel or transportation between any places included in Paragraph **a.** above; or

c. All other parts of the world if the injury or damage arises out of:

(1) Goods or products made or sold by you in the territory described in Paragraph **a.** above;

(2) The activities of a person whose home is in the territory described in Paragraph **a.** above, but is away for a short time on your business; or

(3) "Personal and advertising injury" offenses that take place through the Internet or similar electronic means of communication

provided the insured's responsibility to pay damages is determined in a "suit" on the merits, in the territory described in Paragraph **a.** above or in a settlement we agree to.

5. "Employee" includes a "leased worker". "Employee" does not include a "temporary worker".

6. "Executive officer" means a person holding any of the officer positions created by your charter, constitution, by-laws or any other similar governing document.

7. "Hostile fire" means one which becomes uncontrollable or breaks out from where it was intended to be.

8. "Impaired property" means tangible property, other than "your product" or "your work", that cannot be used or is less useful because:

a. It incorporates "your product" or "your work" that is known or thought to be defective, deficient, inadequate or dangerous; or

b. You have failed to fulfill the terms of a contract or agreement;

if such property can be restored to use by the repair, replacement, adjustment or removal of "your product" or "your work" or your fulfilling the terms of the contract or agreement.

9. "Insured contract" means:

a. A contract for a lease of premises. However, that portion of the contract for a lease of premises that indemnifies any person or organization for damage by fire to premises while rented to you or temporarily occupied by you with permission of the owner is not an "insured contract";

b. A sidetrack agreement;

c. Any easement or license agreement, except in connection with construction or demolition operations on or within 50 feet of a railroad;

d. An obligation, as required by ordinance, to indemnify a municipality, except in connection with work for a municipality;

e. An elevator maintenance agreement;

f. That part of any other contract or agreement pertaining to your business (including an indemnification of a municipality in connection with work performed for a municipality) under which you assume the tort liability of another party to pay for "bodily injury" or "property damage" to a third person or organization. Tort liability means a liability that would be imposed by law in the absence of any contract or agreement.

Paragraph **f.** does not include that part of any contract or agreement:

(1) That indemnifies a railroad for "bodily injury" or "property damage" arising out of construction or demolition operations, within 50 feet of any railroad property and affecting any railroad bridge or trestle, tracks, roadbeds, tunnel, underpass or crossing;

(2) That indemnifies an architect, engineer or surveyor for injury or damage arising out of:

(a) Preparing, approving, or failing to prepare or approve, maps, shop drawings, opinions, reports, surveys, field orders, change orders or drawings and specifications; or

(b) Giving directions or instructions, or failing to give them, if that is the primary cause of the injury or damage; or

(3) Under which the insured, if an architect, engineer or surveyor, assumes liability for an injury or damage arising out of the insured's rendering or failure to render professional services, including those listed in Paragraph **(2)** above and supervisory, inspection, architectural or engineering activities.

10. "Leased worker" means a person leased to you by a labor leasing firm under an agreement between you and the labor leasing firm, to perform duties related to the conduct of your business. "Leased worker" does not include a "temporary worker".

11. "Loading or unloading" means the handling of property:

a. After it is moved from the place where it is accepted for movement into or onto an aircraft, watercraft or "auto";

b. While it is in or on an aircraft, watercraft or "auto"; or

c. While it is being moved from an aircraft, watercraft or "auto" to the place where it is finally delivered;

but "loading or unloading" does not include the movement of property by means of a mechanical device, other than a hand truck, that is not attached to the aircraft, watercraft or "auto".

12. "Mobile equipment" means any of the following types of land vehicles, including any attached machinery or equipment:

a. Bulldozers, farm machinery, forklifts and other vehicles designed for use principally off public roads;

b. Vehicles maintained for use solely on or next to premises you own or rent;

c. Vehicles that travel on crawler treads;

d. Vehicles, whether self-propelled or not, maintained primarily to provide mobility to permanently mounted:

(1) Power cranes, shovels, loaders, diggers or drills; or

(2) Road construction or resurfacing equipment such as graders, scrapers or rollers;

e. Vehicles not described in Paragraph **a., b., c.** or **d.** above that are not self-propelled and are maintained primarily to provide mobility to permanently attached equipment of the following types:

(1) Air compressors, pumps and generators, including spraying, welding, building cleaning, geophysical exploration, lighting and well servicing equipment; or

(2) Cherry pickers and similar devices used to raise or lower workers;

f. Vehicles not described in Paragraph **a.**, **b.**, **c.** or **d.** above maintained primarily for purposes other than the transportation of persons or cargo.

However, self-propelled vehicles with the following types of permanently attached equipment are not "mobile equipment" but will be considered "autos":

(1) Equipment designed primarily for:

(a) Snow removal;

(b) Road maintenance, but not construction or resurfacing; or

(c) Street cleaning;

(2) Cherry pickers and similar devices mounted on automobile or truck chassis and used to raise or lower workers; and

(3) Air compressors, pumps and generators, including spraying, welding, building cleaning, geophysical exploration, lighting and well servicing equipment.

However, "mobile equipment" does not include land vehicles that are subject to a compulsory or financial responsibility law or other motor vehicle insurance law in the state where it is licensed or principally garaged. Land vehicles subject to a compulsory or financial responsibility law or other motor vehicle insurance law are considered "autos".

13. "Occurrence" means an accident, including continuous or repeated exposure to substantially the same general harmful conditions.

14. "Personal and advertising injury" means injury, including consequential "bodily injury", arising out of one or more of the following offenses:

a. False arrest, detention or imprisonment;

b. Malicious prosecution;

c. The wrongful eviction from, wrongful entry into, or invasion of the right of private occupancy of a room, dwelling or premises that a person occupies, committed by or on behalf of its owner, landlord or lessor;

d. Oral or written publication, in any manner, of material that slanders or libels a person or organization or disparages a person's or organization's goods, products or services;

e. Oral or written publication, in any manner, of material that violates a person's right of privacy;

f. The use of another's advertising idea in your "advertisement"; or

g. Infringing upon another's copyright, trade dress or slogan in your "advertisement".

15. "Pollutants" mean any solid, liquid, gaseous or thermal irritant or contaminant, including smoke, vapor, soot, fumes, acids, alkalis, chemicals and waste. Waste includes materials to be recycled, reconditioned or reclaimed.

16. "Products-completed operations hazard":

a. Includes all "bodily injury" and "property damage" occurring away from premises you own or rent and arising out of "your product" or "your work" except:

(1) Products that are still in your physical possession; or

(2) Work that has not yet been completed or abandoned. However, "your work" will be deemed completed at the earliest of the following times:

(a) When all of the work called for in your contract has been completed.

(b) When all of the work to be done at the job site has been completed if your contract calls for work at more than one job site.

(c) When that part of the work done at a job site has been put to its intended use by any person or organization other than another contractor or subcontractor working on the same project.

Work that may need service, maintenance, correction, repair or replacement, but which is otherwise complete, will be treated as completed.

b. Does not include "bodily injury" or "property damage" arising out of:

(1) The transportation of property, unless the injury or damage arises out of a condition in or on a vehicle not owned or operated by you, and that condition was created by the "loading or unloading" of that vehicle by any insured;

(2) The existence of tools, uninstalled equipment or abandoned or unused materials; or

(3) Products or operations for which the classification, listed in the Declarations or in a policy schedule, states that products-completed operations are subject to the General Aggregate Limit.

17. "Property damage" means:

a. Physical injury to tangible property, including all resulting loss of use of that property. All such loss of use shall be deemed to occur at the time of the physical injury that caused it; or

b. Loss of use of tangible property that is not physically injured. All such loss of use shall be deemed to occur at the time of the "occurrence" that caused it.

For the purposes of this insurance, electronic data is not tangible property.

As used in this definition, electronic data means information, facts or programs stored as or on, created or used on, or transmitted to or from, computer software, including systems and applications software, hard or floppy disks, CD-ROMS, tapes, drives, cells, data processing devices or any other media which are used with electronically controlled equipment.

18. "Suit" means a civil proceeding in which damages because of "bodily injury", "property damage" or "personal and advertising injury" to which this insurance applies are alleged. "Suit" includes:

a. An arbitration proceeding in which such damages are claimed and to which the insured must submit or does submit with our consent; or

b. Any other alternative dispute resolution proceeding in which such damages are claimed and to which the insured submits with our consent.

19. "Temporary worker" means a person who is furnished to you to substitute for a permanent "employee" on leave or to meet seasonal or short-term workload conditions.

20. "Volunteer worker" means a person who is not your "employee", and who donates his or her work and acts at the direction of and within the scope of duties determined by you, and is not paid a fee, salary or other compensation by you or anyone else for their work performed for you.

21. "Your product":

a. Means:

(1) Any goods or products, other than real property, manufactured, sold, handled, distributed or disposed of by:

(a) You;

(b) Others trading under your name; or

(c) A person or organization whose business or assets you have acquired; and

(2) Containers (other than vehicles), materials, parts or equipment furnished in connection with such goods or products.

b. Includes:

(1) Warranties or representations made at any time with respect to the fitness, quality, durability, performance or use of "your product"; and

(2) The providing of or failure to provide warnings or instructions.

c. Does not include vending machines or other property rented to or located for the use of others but not sold.

22. "Your work":

a. Means:

(1) Work or operations performed by you or on your behalf; and

(2) Materials, parts or equipment furnished in connection with such work or operations.

b. Includes:

(1) Warranties or representations made at any time with respect to the fitness, quality, durability, performance or use of "your work" and

(2) The providing of or failure to provide warnings or instructions.

COMMERCIAL GENERAL LIABILITY
CG 00 01 04 13

COMMERCIAL GENERAL LIABILITY COVERAGE FORM

Various provisions in this policy restrict coverage. Read the entire policy carefully to determine rights, duties and what is and is not covered.

Throughout this policy the words "you" and "your" refer to the Named Insured shown in the Declarations, and any other person or organization qualifying as a Named Insured under this policy. The words "we", "us" and "our" refer to the company providing this insurance.

The word "insured" means any person or organization qualifying as such under Section II – Who Is An Insured.

Other words and phrases that appear in quotation marks have special meaning. Refer to Section V – Definitions.

SECTION I – COVERAGES

COVERAGE A – BODILY INJURY AND PROPERTY DAMAGE LIABILITY

1. Insuring Agreement

a. We will pay those sums that the insured becomes legally obligated to pay as damages because of "bodily injury" or "property damage" to which this insurance applies. We will have the right and duty to defend the insured against any "suit" seeking those damages. However, we will have no duty to defend the insured against any "suit" seeking damages for "bodily injury" or "property damage" to which this insurance does not apply. We may, at our discretion, investigate any "occurrence" and settle any claim or "suit" that may result. But:

(1) The amount we will pay for damages is limited as described in Section III – Limits Of Insurance; and

(2) Our right and duty to defend ends when we have used up the applicable limit of insurance in the payment of judgments or settlements under Coverages **A** or **B** or medical expenses under Coverage **C**.

No other obligation or liability to pay sums or perform acts or services is covered unless explicitly provided for under Supplementary Payments – Coverages **A** and **B**.

b. This insurance applies to "bodily injury" and "property damage" only if:

(1) The "bodily injury" or "property damage" is caused by an "occurrence" that takes place in the "coverage territory";

(2) The "bodily injury" or "property damage" occurs during the policy period; and

(3) Prior to the policy period, no insured listed under Paragraph 1. of Section II – Who Is An Insured and no "employee" authorized by you to give or receive notice of an "occurrence" or claim, knew that the "bodily injury" or "property damage" had occurred, in whole or in part. If such a listed insured or authorized "employee" knew, prior to the policy period, that the "bodily injury" or "property damage" occurred, then any continuation, change or resumption of such "bodily injury" or "property damage" during or after the policy period will be deemed to have been known prior to the policy period.

c. "Bodily injury" or "property damage" which occurs during the policy period and was not, prior to the policy period, known to have occurred by any insured listed under Paragraph 1. of Section II – Who Is An Insured or any "employee" authorized by you to give or receive notice of an "occurrence" or claim, includes any continuation, change or resumption of that "bodily injury" or "property damage" after the end of the policy period.

d. "Bodily injury" or "property damage" will be deemed to have been known to have occurred at the earliest time when any insured listed under Paragraph 1. of Section II – Who Is An Insured or any "employee" authorized by you to give or receive notice of an "occurrence" or claim:

(1) Reports all, or any part, of the "bodily injury" or "property damage" to us or any other insurer;

(2) Receives a written or verbal demand or claim for damages because of the "bodily injury" or "property damage"; or

(3) Becomes aware by any other means that "bodily injury" or "property damage" has occurred or has begun to occur.

e. Damages because of "bodily injury" include damages claimed by any person or organization for care, loss of services or death resulting at any time from the "bodily injury".

2. Exclusions

This insurance does not apply to:

a. Expected Or Intended Injury

"Bodily injury" or "property damage" expected or intended from the standpoint of the insured. This exclusion does not apply to "bodily injury" resulting from the use of reasonable force to protect persons or property.

b. Contractual Liability

"Bodily injury" or "property damage" for which the insured is obligated to pay damages by reason of the assumption of liability in a contract or agreement. This exclusion does not apply to liability for damages:

(1) That the insured would have in the absence of the contract or agreement; or

(2) Assumed in a contract or agreement that is an "insured contract", provided the "bodily injury" or "property damage" occurs subsequent to the execution of the contract or agreement. Solely for the purposes of liability assumed in an "insured contract", reasonable attorneys' fees and necessary litigation expenses incurred by or for a party other than an insured are deemed to be damages because of "bodily injury" or "property damage", provided:

(a) Liability to such party for, or for the cost of, that party's defense has also been assumed in the same "insured contract"; and

(b) Such attorneys' fees and litigation expenses are for defense of that party against a civil or alternative dispute resolution proceeding in which damages to which this insurance applies are alleged.

c. Liquor Liability

"Bodily injury" or "property damage" for which any insured may be held liable by reason of:

(1) Causing or contributing to the intoxication of any person;

(2) The furnishing of alcoholic beverages to a person under the legal drinking age or under the influence of alcohol; or

(3) Any statute, ordinance or regulation relating to the sale, gift, distribution or use of alcoholic beverages.

This exclusion applies even if the claims against any insured allege negligence or other wrongdoing in:

(a) The supervision, hiring, employment, training or monitoring of others by that insured; or

(b) Providing or failing to provide transportation with respect to any person that may be under the influence of alcohol;

if the "occurrence" which caused the "bodily injury" or "property damage", involved that which is described in Paragraph **(1)**, **(2)** or **(3)** above.

However, this exclusion applies only if you are in the business of manufacturing, distributing, selling, serving or furnishing alcoholic beverages. For the purposes of this exclusion, permitting a person to bring alcoholic beverages on your premises, for consumption on your premises, whether or not a fee is charged or a license is required for such activity, is not by itself considered the business of selling, serving or furnishing alcoholic beverages.

d. Workers' Compensation And Similar Laws

Any obligation of the insured under a workers' compensation, disability benefits or unemployment compensation law or any similar law.

e. Employer's Liability

"Bodily injury" to:

(1) An "employee" of the insured arising out of and in the course of:

(a) Employment by the insured; or

(b) Performing duties related to the conduct of the insured's business; or

(2) The spouse, child, parent, brother or sister of that "employee" as a consequence of Paragraph **(1)** above.

This exclusion applies whether the insured may be liable as an employer or in any other capacity and to any obligation to share damages with or repay someone else who must pay damages because of the injury.

This exclusion does not apply to liability assumed by the insured under an "insured contract".

f. Pollution

(1) "Bodily injury" or "property damage" arising out of the actual, alleged or threatened discharge, dispersal, seepage, migration, release or escape of "pollutants":

(a) At or from any premises, site or location which is or was at any time owned or occupied by, or rented or loaned to, any insured. However, this subparagraph does not apply to:

(i) "Bodily injury" if sustained within a building and caused by smoke, fumes, vapor or soot produced by or originating from equipment that is used to heat, cool or dehumidify the building, or equipment that is used to heat water for personal use, by the building's occupants or their guests;

(ii) "Bodily injury" or "property damage" for which you may be held liable, if you are a contractor and the owner or lessee of such premises, site or location has been added to your policy as an additional insured with respect to your ongoing operations performed for that additional insured at that premises, site or location and such premises, site or location is not and never was owned or occupied by, or rented or loaned to, any insured, other than that additional insured; or

(iii) "Bodily injury" or "property damage" arising out of heat, smoke or fumes from a "hostile fire";

(b) At or from any premises, site or location which is or was at any time used by or for any insured or others for the handling, storage, disposal, processing or treatment of waste;

(c) Which are or were at any time transported, handled, stored, treated, disposed of, or processed as waste by or for:

(i) Any insured; or

(ii) Any person or organization for whom you may be legally responsible; or

(d) At or from any premises, site or location on which any insured or any contractors or subcontractors working directly or indirectly on any insured's behalf are performing operations if the "pollutants" are brought on or to the premises, site or location in connection with such operations by such insured, contractor or subcontractor. However, this subparagraph does not apply to:

(i) "Bodily injury" or "property damage" arising out of the escape of fuels, lubricants or other operating fluids which are needed to perform the normal electrical, hydraulic or mechanical functions necessary for the operation of "mobile equipment" or its parts, if such fuels, lubricants or other operating fluids escape from a vehicle part designed to hold, store or receive them. This exception does not apply if the "bodily injury" or "property damage" arises out of the intentional discharge, dispersal or release of the fuels, lubricants or other operating fluids, or if such fuels, lubricants or other operating fluids are brought on or to the premises, site or location with the intent that they be discharged, dispersed or released as part of the operations being performed by such insured, contractor or subcontractor;

(ii) "Bodily injury" or "property damage" sustained within a building and caused by the release of gases, fumes or vapors from materials brought into that building in connection with operations being performed by you or on your behalf by a contractor or subcontractor; or

(iii) "Bodily injury" or "property damage" arising out of heat, smoke or fumes from a "hostile fire".

(e) At or from any premises, site or location on which any insured or any contractors or subcontractors working directly or indirectly on any insured's behalf are performing operations if the operations are to test for, monitor, clean up, remove, contain, treat, detoxify or neutralize, or in any way respond to, or assess the effects of, "pollutants".

(2) Any loss, cost or expense arising out of any:

(a) Request, demand, order or statutory or regulatory requirement that any insured or others test for, monitor, clean up, remove, contain, treat, detoxify or neutralize, or in any way respond to, or assess the effects of, "pollutants"; or

(b) Claim or suit by or on behalf of a governmental authority for damages because of testing for, monitoring, cleaning up, removing, containing, treating, detoxifying or neutralizing, or in any way responding to, or assessing the effects of, "pollutants".

However, this paragraph does not apply to liability for damages because of "property damage" that the insured would have in the absence of such request, demand, order or statutory or regulatory requirement, or such claim or "suit" by or on behalf of a governmental authority.

g. Aircraft, Auto Or Watercraft

"Bodily injury" or "property damage" arising out of the ownership, maintenance, use or entrustment to others of any aircraft, "auto" or watercraft owned or operated by or rented or loaned to any insured. Use includes operation and "loading or unloading".

This exclusion applies even if the claims against any insured allege negligence or other wrongdoing in the supervision, hiring, employment, training or monitoring of others by that insured, if the "occurrence" which caused the "bodily injury" or "property damage" involved the ownership, maintenance, use or entrustment to others of any aircraft, "auto" or watercraft that is owned or operated by or rented or loaned to any insured.

This exclusion does not apply to:

(1) A watercraft while ashore on premises you own or rent;

(2) A watercraft you do not own that is:

(a) Less than 26 feet long; and

(b) Not being used to carry persons or property for a charge;

(3) Parking an "auto" on, or on the ways next to, premises you own or rent, provided the "auto" is not owned by or rented or loaned to you or the insured;

(4) Liability assumed under any "insured contract" for the ownership, maintenance or use of aircraft or watercraft; or

(5) "Bodily injury" or "property damage" arising out of:

(a) The operation of machinery or equipment that is attached to, or part of, a land vehicle that would qualify under the definition of "mobile equipment" if it were not subject to a compulsory or financial responsibility law or other motor vehicle insurance law where it is licensed or principally garaged; or

(b) The operation of any of the machinery or equipment listed in Paragraph **f.(2)** or **f.(3)** of the definition of "mobile equipment".

h. Mobile Equipment

"Bodily injury" or "property damage" arising out of:

(1) The transportation of "mobile equipment" by an "auto" owned or operated by or rented or loaned to any insured; or

(2) The use of "mobile equipment" in, or while in practice for, or while being prepared for, any prearranged racing, speed, demolition, or stunting activity.

i. War

"Bodily injury" or "property damage", however caused, arising, directly or indirectly, out of:

(1) War, including undeclared or civil war;

(2) Warlike action by a military force, including action in hindering or defending against an actual or expected attack, by any government, sovereign or other authority using military personnel or other agents; or

(3) Insurrection, rebellion, revolution, usurped power, or action taken by governmental authority in hindering or defending against any of these.

j. Damage To Property

"Property damage" to:

(1) Property you own, rent, or occupy, including any costs or expenses incurred by you, or any other person, organization or entity, for repair, replacement, enhancement, restoration or maintenance of such property for any reason, including prevention of injury to a person or damage to another's property;

(2) Premises you sell, give away or abandon, if the "property damage" arises out of any part of those premises;

(3) Property loaned to you;

(4) Personal property in the care, custody or control of the insured;

(5) That particular part of real property on which you or any contractors or subcontractors working directly or indirectly on your behalf are performing operations, if the "property damage" arises out of those operations; or

(6) That particular part of any property that must be restored, repaired or replaced because "your work" was incorrectly performed on it.

Paragraphs **(1)**, **(3)** and **(4)** of this exclusion do not apply to "property damage" (other than damage by fire) to premises, including the contents of such premises, rented to you for a period of seven or fewer consecutive days. A separate limit of insurance applies to Damage To Premises Rented To You as described in Section **III** – Limits Of Insurance.

Paragraph **(2)** of this exclusion does not apply if the premises are "your work" and were never occupied, rented or held for rental by you.

Paragraphs **(3)**, **(4)**, **(5)** and **(6)** of this exclusion do not apply to liability assumed under a sidetrack agreement.

Paragraph **(6)** of this exclusion does not apply to "property damage" included in the "products-completed operations hazard".

k. Damage To Your Product

"Property damage" to "your product" arising out of it or any part of it.

l. Damage To Your Work

"Property damage" to "your work" arising out of it or any part of it and included in the "products-completed operations hazard".

This exclusion does not apply if the damaged work or the work out of which the damage arises was performed on your behalf by a subcontractor.

m. Damage To Impaired Property Or Property Not Physically Injured

"Property damage" to "impaired property" or property that has not been physically injured, arising out of:

(1) A defect, deficiency, inadequacy or dangerous condition in "your product" or "your work"; or

(2) A delay or failure by you or anyone acting on your behalf to perform a contract or agreement in accordance with its terms.

This exclusion does not apply to the loss of use of other property arising out of sudden and accidental physical injury to "your product" or "your work" after it has been put to its intended use.

n. Recall Of Products, Work Or Impaired Property

Damages claimed for any loss, cost or expense incurred by you or others for the loss of use, withdrawal, recall, inspection, repair, replacement, adjustment, removal or disposal of:

(1) "Your product";

(2) "Your work"; or

(3) "Impaired property";

if such product, work, or property is withdrawn or recalled from the market or from use by any person or organization because of a known or suspected defect, deficiency, inadequacy or dangerous condition in it.

o. Personal And Advertising Injury

"Bodily injury" arising out of "personal and advertising injury".

p. Electronic Data

Damages arising out of the loss of, loss of use of, damage to, corruption of, inability to access, or inability to manipulate electronic data.

However, this exclusion does not apply to liability for damages because of "bodily injury".

As used in this exclusion, electronic data means information, facts or programs stored as or on, created or used on, or transmitted to or from computer software, including systems and applications software, hard or floppy disks, CD-ROMs, tapes, drives, cells, data processing devices or any other media which are used with electronically controlled equipment.

q. Recording And Distribution Of Material Or Information In Violation Of Law

"Bodily injury" or "property damage" arising directly or indirectly out of any action or omission that violates or is alleged to violate:

(1) The Telephone Consumer Protection Act (TCPA), including any amendment of or addition to such law;

(2) The CAN-SPAM Act of 2003, including any amendment of or addition to such law;

(3) The Fair Credit Reporting Act (FCRA), and any amendment of or addition to such law, including the Fair and Accurate Credit Transactions Act (FACTA); or

(4) Any federal, state or local statute, ordinance or regulation, other than the TCPA, CAN-SPAM Act of 2003 or FCRA and their amendments and additions, that addresses, prohibits, or limits the printing, dissemination, disposal, collecting, recording, sending, transmitting, communicating or distribution of material or information.

Exclusions **c.** through **n.** do not apply to damage by fire to premises while rented to you or temporarily occupied by you with permission of the owner. A separate limit of insurance applies to this coverage as described in Section **III** – Limits Of Insurance.

COVERAGE B – PERSONAL AND ADVERTISING INJURY LIABILITY

1. Insuring Agreement

a. We will pay those sums that the insured becomes legally obligated to pay as damages because of "personal and advertising injury" to which this insurance applies. We will have the right and duty to defend the insured against any "suit" seeking those damages. However, we will have no duty to defend the insured against any "suit" seeking damages for "personal and advertising injury" to which this insurance does not apply. We may, at our discretion, investigate any offense and settle any claim or "suit" that may result. But:

(1) The amount we will pay for damages is limited as described in Section **III** – Limits Of Insurance; and

(2) Our right and duty to defend end when we have used up the applicable limit of insurance in the payment of judgments or settlements under Coverages **A** or **B** or medical expenses under Coverage **C.**

No other obligation or liability to pay sums or perform acts or services is covered unless explicitly provided for under Supplementary Payments – Coverages **A** and **B.**

b. This insurance applies to "personal and advertising injury" caused by an offense arising out of your business but only if the offense was committed in the "coverage territory" during the policy period.

2. Exclusions

This insurance does not apply to:

a. Knowing Violation Of Rights Of Another

"Personal and advertising injury" caused by or at the direction of the insured with the knowledge that the act would violate the rights of another and would inflict "personal and advertising injury".

b. Material Published With Knowledge Of Falsity

"Personal and advertising injury" arising out of oral or written publication, in any manner, of material, if done by or at the direction of the insured with knowledge of its falsity.

c. Material Published Prior To Policy Period

"Personal and advertising injury" arising out of oral or written publication, in any manner, of material whose first publication took place before the beginning of the policy period.

d. Criminal Acts

"Personal and advertising injury" arising out of a criminal act committed by or at the direction of the insured.

e. Contractual Liability

"Personal and advertising injury" for which the insured has assumed liability in a contract or agreement. This exclusion does not apply to liability for damages that the insured would have in the absence of the contract or agreement.

f. Breach Of Contract

"Personal and advertising injury" arising out of a breach of contract, except an implied contract to use another's advertising idea in your "advertisement".

g. Quality Or Performance Of Goods – Failure To Conform To Statements

"Personal and advertising injury" arising out of the failure of goods, products or services to conform with any statement of quality or performance made in your "advertisement".

h. Wrong Description Of Prices

"Personal and advertising injury" arising out of the wrong description of the price of goods, products or services stated in your "advertisement".

         CG 00 01 04 13

i. Infringement Of Copyright, Patent, Trademark Or Trade Secret

"Personal and advertising injury" arising out of the infringement of copyright, patent, trademark, trade secret or other intellectual property rights. Under this exclusion, such other intellectual property rights do not include the use of another's advertising idea in your "advertisement".

However, this exclusion does not apply to infringement, in your "advertisement", of copyright, trade dress or slogan.

j. Insureds In Media And Internet Type Businesses

"Personal and advertising injury" committed by an insured whose business is:

(1) Advertising, broadcasting, publishing or telecasting;

(2) Designing or determining content of web sites for others; or

(3) An Internet search, access, content or service provider.

However, this exclusion does not apply to Paragraphs **14.a., b.** and **c.** of "personal and advertising injury" under the Definitions section.

For the purposes of this exclusion, the placing of frames, borders or links, or advertising, for you or others anywhere on the Internet, is not by itself, considered the business of advertising, broadcasting, publishing or telecasting.

k. Electronic Chatrooms Or Bulletin Boards

"Personal and advertising injury" arising out of an electronic chatroom or bulletin board the insured hosts, owns, or over which the insured exercises control.

l. Unauthorized Use Of Another's Name Or Product

"Personal and advertising injury" arising out of the unauthorized use of another's name or product in your e-mail address, domain name or metatag, or any other similar tactics to mislead another's potential customers.

m. Pollution

"Personal and advertising injury" arising out of the actual, alleged or threatened discharge, dispersal, seepage, migration, release or escape of "pollutants" at any time.

n. Pollution-related

Any loss, cost or expense arising out of any:

(1) Request, demand, order or statutory or regulatory requirement that any insured or others test for, monitor, clean up, remove, contain, treat, detoxify or neutralize, or in any way respond to, or assess the effects of, "pollutants"; or

(2) Claim or suit by or on behalf of a governmental authority for damages because of testing for, monitoring, cleaning up, removing, containing, treating, detoxifying or neutralizing, or in any way responding to, or assessing the effects of, "pollutants".

o. War

"Personal and advertising injury", however caused, arising, directly or indirectly, out of:

(1) War, including undeclared or civil war;

(2) Warlike action by a military force, including action in hindering or defending against an actual or expected attack, by any government, sovereign or other authority using military personnel or other agents; or

(3) Insurrection, rebellion, revolution, usurped power, or action taken by governmental authority in hindering or defending against any of these.

p. Recording And Distribution Of Material Or Information In Violation Of Law

"Personal and advertising injury" arising directly or indirectly out of any action or omission that violates or is alleged to violate:

(1) The Telephone Consumer Protection Act (TCPA), including any amendment of or addition to such law;

(2) The CAN-SPAM Act of 2003, including any amendment of or addition to such law;

(3) The Fair Credit Reporting Act (FCRA), and any amendment of or addition to such law, including the Fair and Accurate Credit Transactions Act (FACTA); or

(4) Any federal, state or local statute, ordinance or regulation, other than the TCPA, CAN-SPAM Act of 2003 or FCRA and their amendments and additions, that addresses, prohibits, or limits the printing, dissemination, disposal, collecting, recording, sending, transmitting, communicating or distribution of material or information.

COVERAGE C – MEDICAL PAYMENTS

1. Insuring Agreement

a. We will pay medical expenses as described below for "bodily injury" caused by an accident:

(1) On premises you own or rent;

(2) On ways next to premises you own or rent; or

(3) Because of your operations;

provided that:

(a) The accident takes place in the "coverage territory" and during the policy period;

(b) The expenses are incurred and reported to us within one year of the date of the accident; and

(c) The injured person submits to examination, at our expense, by physicians of our choice as often as we reasonably require.

b. We will make these payments regardless of fault. These payments will not exceed the applicable limit of insurance. We will pay reasonable expenses for:

(1) First aid administered at the time of an accident;

(2) Necessary medical, surgical, X-ray and dental services, including prosthetic devices; and

(3) Necessary ambulance, hospital, professional nursing and funeral services.

2. Exclusions

We will not pay expenses for "bodily injury":

a. **Any Insured**

To any insured, except "volunteer workers".

b. **Hired Person**

To a person hired to do work for or on behalf of any insured or a tenant of any insured.

c. **Injury On Normally Occupied Premises**

To a person injured on that part of premises you own or rent that the person normally occupies.

d. **Workers' Compensation And Similar Laws**

To a person, whether or not an "employee" of any insured, if benefits for the "bodily injury" are payable or must be provided under a workers' compensation or disability benefits law or a similar law.

e. **Athletics Activities**

To a person injured while practicing, instructing or participating in any physical exercises or games, sports, or athletic contests.

f. **Products-Completed Operations Hazard**

Included within the "products-completed operations hazard".

g. **Coverage A Exclusions**

Excluded under Coverage **A**.

SUPPLEMENTARY PAYMENTS – COVERAGES A AND B

1. We will pay, with respect to any claim we investigate or settle, or any "suit" against an insured we defend:

a. All expenses we incur.

b. Up to $250 for cost of bail bonds required because of accidents or traffic law violations arising out of the use of any vehicle to which the Bodily Injury Liability Coverage applies. We do not have to furnish these bonds.

c. The cost of bonds to release attachments, but only for bond amounts within the applicable limit of insurance. We do not have to furnish these bonds.

d. All reasonable expenses incurred by the insured at our request to assist us in the investigation or defense of the claim or "suit", including actual loss of earnings up to $250 a day because of time off from work.

e. All court costs taxed against the insured in the "suit". However, these payments do not include attorneys' fees or attorneys' expenses taxed against the insured.

f. Prejudgment interest awarded against the insured on that part of the judgment we pay. If we make an offer to pay the applicable limit of insurance, we will not pay any prejudgment interest based on that period of time after the offer.

   CG 00 01 04 13

g. All interest on the full amount of any judgment that accrues after entry of the judgment and before we have paid, offered to pay, or deposited in court the part of the judgment that is within the applicable limit of insurance.

These payments will not reduce the limits of insurance.

2. If we defend an insured against a "suit" and an indemnitee of the insured is also named as a party to the "suit", we will defend that indemnitee if all of the following conditions are met:

a. The "suit" against the indemnitee seeks damages for which the insured has assumed the liability of the indemnitee in a contract or agreement that is an "insured contract";

b. This insurance applies to such liability assumed by the insured;

c. The obligation to defend, or the cost of the defense of, that indemnitee, has also been assumed by the insured in the same "insured contract";

d. The allegations in the "suit" and the information we know about the "occurrence" are such that no conflict appears to exist between the interests of the insured and the interests of the indemnitee;

e. The indemnitee and the insured ask us to conduct and control the defense of that indemnitee against such "suit" and agree that we can assign the same counsel to defend the insured and the indemnitee; and

f. The indemnitee:

(1) Agrees in writing to:

(a) Cooperate with us in the investigation, settlement or defense of the "suit";

(b) Immediately send us copies of any demands, notices, summonses or legal papers received in connection with the "suit";

(c) Notify any other insurer whose coverage is available to the indemnitee; and

(d) Cooperate with us with respect to coordinating other applicable insurance available to the indemnitee; and

(2) Provides us with written authorization to:

(a) Obtain records and other information related to the "suit"; and

(b) Conduct and control the defense of the indemnitee in such "suit".

So long as the above conditions are met, attorneys' fees incurred by us in the defense of that indemnitee, necessary litigation expenses incurred by us and necessary litigation expenses incurred by the indemnitee at our request will be paid as Supplementary Payments. Notwithstanding the provisions of Paragraph **2.b.(2)** of Section **I** – Coverage **A** – Bodily Injury And Property Damage Liability, such payments will not be deemed to be damages for "bodily injury" and "property damage" and will not reduce the limits of insurance.

Our obligation to defend an insured's indemnitee and to pay for attorneys' fees and necessary litigation expenses as Supplementary Payments ends when we have used up the applicable limit of insurance in the payment of judgments or settlements or the conditions set forth above, or the terms of the agreement described in Paragraph **f.** above, are no longer met.

SECTION II – WHO IS AN INSURED

1. If you are designated in the Declarations as:

a. An individual, you and your spouse are insureds, but only with respect to the conduct of a business of which you are the sole owner.

b. A partnership or joint venture, you are an insured. Your members, your partners, and their spouses are also insureds, but only with respect to the conduct of your business.

c. A limited liability company, you are an insured. Your members are also insureds, but only with respect to the conduct of your business. Your managers are insureds, but only with respect to their duties as your managers.

d. An organization other than a partnership, joint venture or limited liability company, you are an insured. Your "executive officers" and directors are insureds, but only with respect to their duties as your officers or directors. Your stockholders are also insureds, but only with respect to their liability as stockholders.

e. A trust, you are an insured. Your trustees are also insureds, but only with respect to their duties as trustees.

2. Each of the following is also an insured:

   a. Your "volunteer workers" only while performing duties related to the conduct of your business, or your "employees", other than either your "executive officers" (if you are an organization other than a partnership, joint venture or limited liability company) or your managers (if you are a limited liability company), but only for acts within the scope of their employment by you or while performing duties related to the conduct of your business. However, none of these "employees" or "volunteer workers" are insureds for:

      (1) "Bodily injury" or "personal and advertising injury":

         (a) To you, to your partners or members (if you are a partnership or joint venture), to your members (if you are a limited liability company), to a co-"employee" while in the course of his or her employment or performing duties related to the conduct of your business, or to your other "volunteer workers" while performing duties related to the conduct of your business;

         (b) To the spouse, child, parent, brother or sister of that co-"employee" or "volunteer worker" as a consequence of Paragraph (1)(a) above;

         (c) For which there is any obligation to share damages with or repay someone else who must pay damages because of the injury described in Paragraph (1)(a) or (b) above; or

         (d) Arising out of his or her providing or failing to provide professional health care services.

      (2) "Property damage" to property:

         (a) Owned, occupied or used by;

         (b) Rented to, in the care, custody or control of, or over which physical control is being exercised for any purpose by;

         you, any of your "employees", "volunteer workers", any partner or member (if you are a partnership or joint venture), or any member (if you are a limited liability company).

   b. Any person (other than your "employee" or "volunteer worker"), or any organization while acting as your real estate manager.

   c. Any person or organization having proper temporary custody of your property if you die, but only:

      (1) With respect to liability arising out of the maintenance or use of that property; and

      (2) Until your legal representative has been appointed.

   d. Your legal representative if you die, but only with respect to duties as such. That representative will have all your rights and duties under this Coverage Part.

3. Any organization you newly acquire or form, other than a partnership, joint venture or limited liability company, and over which you maintain ownership or majority interest, will qualify as a Named Insured if there is no other similar insurance available to that organization. However:

   a. Coverage under this provision is afforded only until the 90th day after you acquire or form the organization or the end of the policy period, whichever is earlier;

   b. Coverage A does not apply to "bodily injury" or "property damage" that occurred before you acquired or formed the organization; and

   c. Coverage B does not apply to "personal and advertising injury" arising out of an offense committed before you acquired or formed the organization.

No person or organization is an insured with respect to the conduct of any current or past partnership, joint venture or limited liability company that is not shown as a Named Insured in the Declarations.

SECTION III – LIMITS OF INSURANCE

1. The Limits of Insurance shown in the Declarations and the rules below fix the most we will pay regardless of the number of:

   a. Insureds;

   b. Claims made or "suits" brought; or

   c. Persons or organizations making claims or bringing "suits".

2. The General Aggregate Limit is the most we will pay for the sum of:

   a. Medical expenses under Coverage C;

   b. Damages under Coverage A, except damages because of "bodily injury" or "property damage" included in the "products-completed operations hazard"; and

   c. Damages under Coverage B.

© Insurance Services Office, Inc., 2012

3. The Products-Completed Operations Aggregate Limit is the most we will pay under Coverage **A** for damages because of "bodily injury" and "property damage" included in the "products-completed operations hazard".

4. Subject to Paragraph **2.** above, the Personal And Advertising Injury Limit is the most we will pay under Coverage **B** for the sum of all damages because of all "personal and advertising injury" sustained by any one person or organization.

5. Subject to Paragraph **2.** or **3.** above, whichever applies, the Each Occurrence Limit is the most we will pay for the sum of:

   a. Damages under Coverage **A**; and

   b. Medical expenses under Coverage **C**

   because of all "bodily injury" and "property damage" arising out of any one "occurrence".

6. Subject to Paragraph **5.** above, the Damage To Premises Rented To You Limit is the most we will pay under Coverage **A** for damages because of "property damage" to any one premises, while rented to you, or in the case of damage by fire, while rented to you or temporarily occupied by you with permission of the owner.

7. Subject to Paragraph **5.** above, the Medical Expense Limit is the most we will pay under Coverage **C** for all medical expenses because of "bodily injury" sustained by any one person.

The Limits of Insurance of this Coverage Part apply separately to each consecutive annual period and to any remaining period of less than 12 months, starting with the beginning of the policy period shown in the Declarations, unless the policy period is extended after issuance for an additional period of less than 12 months. In that case, the additional period will be deemed part of the last preceding period for purposes of determining the Limits of Insurance.

SECTION IV – COMMERCIAL GENERAL LIABILITY CONDITIONS

1. **Bankruptcy**

   Bankruptcy or insolvency of the insured or of the insured's estate will not relieve us of our obligations under this Coverage Part.

2. **Duties In The Event Of Occurrence, Offense, Claim Or Suit**

   a. You must see to it that we are notified as soon as practicable of an "occurrence" or an offense which may result in a claim. To the extent possible, notice should include:

      (1) How, when and where the "occurrence" or offense took place;

      (2) The names and addresses of any injured persons and witnesses; and

      (3) The nature and location of any injury or damage arising out of the "occurrence" or offense.

   b. If a claim is made or "suit" is brought against any insured, you must:

      (1) Immediately record the specifics of the claim or "suit" and the date received; and

      (2) Notify us as soon as practicable.

      You must see to it that we receive written notice of the claim or "suit" as soon as practicable.

   c. You and any other involved insured must:

      (1) Immediately send us copies of any demands, notices, summonses or legal papers received in connection with the claim or "suit";

      (2) Authorize us to obtain records and other information;

      (3) Cooperate with us in the investigation or settlement of the claim or defense against the "suit"; and

      (4) Assist us, upon our request, in the enforcement of any right against any person or organization which may be liable to the insured because of injury or damage to which this insurance may also apply.

   d. No insured will, except at that insured's own cost, voluntarily make a payment, assume any obligation, or incur any expense, other than for first aid, without our consent.

3. **Legal Action Against Us**

   No person or organization has a right under this Coverage Part:

   a. To join us as a party or otherwise bring us into a "suit" asking for damages from an insured; or

   b. To sue us on this Coverage Part unless all of its terms have been fully complied with.

   A person or organization may sue us to recover on an agreed settlement or on a final judgment against an insured; but we will not be liable for damages that are not payable under the terms of this Coverage Part or that are in excess of the applicable limit of insurance. An agreed settlement means a settlement and release of liability signed by us, the insured and the claimant or the claimant's legal representative.

4. Other Insurance

If other valid and collectible insurance is available to the insured for a loss we cover under Coverages **A** or **B** of this Coverage Part, our obligations are limited as follows:

a. Primary Insurance

This insurance is primary except when Paragraph **b.** below applies. If this insurance is primary, our obligations are not affected unless any of the other insurance is also primary. Then, we will share with all that other insurance by the method described in Paragraph **c.** below.

b. Excess Insurance

(1) This insurance is excess over:

(a) Any of the other insurance, whether primary, excess, contingent or on any other basis:

(i) That is Fire, Extended Coverage, Builder's Risk, Installation Risk or similar coverage for "your work";

(ii) That is Fire insurance for premises rented to you or temporarily occupied by you with permission of the owner;

(iii) That is insurance purchased by you to cover your liability as a tenant for "property damage" to premises rented to you or temporarily occupied by you with permission of the owner; or

(iv) If the loss arises out of the maintenance or use of aircraft, "autos" or watercraft to the extent not subject to Exclusion **g.** of Section I – Coverage **A** – Bodily Injury And Property Damage Liability.

(b) Any other primary insurance available to you covering liability for damages arising out of the premises or operations, or the products and completed operations, for which you have been added as an additional insured.

(2) When this insurance is excess, we will have no duty under Coverages **A** or **B** to defend the insured against any "suit" if any other insurer has a duty to defend the insured against that "suit". If no other insurer defends, we will undertake to do so, but we will be entitled to the insured's rights against all those other insurers.

(3) When this insurance is excess over other insurance, we will pay only our share of the amount of the loss, if any, that exceeds the sum of:

(a) The total amount that all such other insurance would pay for the loss in the absence of this insurance; and

(b) The total of all deductible and self-insured amounts under all that other insurance.

(4) We will share the remaining loss, if any, with any other insurance that is not described in this Excess Insurance provision and was not bought specifically to apply in excess of the Limits of Insurance shown in the Declarations of this Coverage Part.

c. Method Of Sharing

If all of the other insurance permits contribution by equal shares, we will follow this method also. Under this approach each insurer contributes equal amounts until it has paid its applicable limit of insurance or none of the loss remains, whichever comes first.

If any of the other insurance does not permit contribution by equal shares, we will contribute by limits. Under this method, each insurer's share is based on the ratio of its applicable limit of insurance to the total applicable limits of insurance of all insurers.

5. Premium Audit

a. We will compute all premiums for this Coverage Part in accordance with our rules and rates.

b. Premium shown in this Coverage Part as advance premium is a deposit premium only. At the close of each audit period we will compute the earned premium for that period and send notice to the first Named Insured. The due date for audit and retrospective premiums is the date shown as the due date on the bill. If the sum of the advance and audit premiums paid for the policy period is greater than the earned premium, we will return the excess to the first Named Insured.

c. The first Named Insured must keep records of the information we need for premium computation, and send us copies at such times as we may request.

6. Representations

By accepting this policy, you agree:

a. The statements in the Declarations are accurate and complete;

b. Those statements are based upon representations you made to us; and

c. We have issued this policy in reliance upon your representations.

7. Separation Of Insureds

Except with respect to the Limits of Insurance, and any rights or duties specifically assigned in this Coverage Part to the first Named Insured, this insurance applies:

a. As if each Named Insured were the only Named Insured; and

b. Separately to each insured against whom claim is made or "suit" is brought.

8. Transfer Of Rights Of Recovery Against Others To Us

If the insured has rights to recover all or part of any payment we have made under this Coverage Part, those rights are transferred to us. The insured must do nothing after loss to impair them. At our request, the insured will bring "suit" or transfer those rights to us and help us enforce them.

9. When We Do Not Renew

If we decide not to renew this Coverage Part, we will mail or deliver to the first Named Insured shown in the Declarations written notice of the nonrenewal not less than 30 days before the expiration date.

If notice is mailed, proof of mailing will be sufficient proof of notice.

SECTION V – DEFINITIONS

1. "Advertisement" means a notice that is broadcast or published to the general public or specific market segments about your goods, products or services for the purpose of attracting customers or supporters. For the purposes of this definition:

a. Notices that are published include material placed on the Internet or on similar electronic means of communication; and

b. Regarding web sites, only that part of a web site that is about your goods, products or services for the purposes of attracting customers or supporters is considered an advertisement.

2. "Auto" means:

a. A land motor vehicle, trailer or semitrailer designed for travel on public roads, including any attached machinery or equipment; or

b. Any other land vehicle that is subject to a compulsory or financial responsibility law or other motor vehicle insurance law where it is licensed or principally garaged.

However, "auto" does not include "mobile equipment".

3. "Bodily injury" means bodily injury, sickness or disease sustained by a person, including death resulting from any of these at any time.

4. "Coverage territory" means:

a. The United States of America (including its territories and possessions), Puerto Rico and Canada;

b. International waters or airspace, but only if the injury or damage occurs in the course of travel or transportation between any places included in Paragraph **a.** above; or

c. All other parts of the world if the injury or damage arises out of:

(1) Goods or products made or sold by you in the territory described in Paragraph **a.** above;

(2) The activities of a person whose home is in the territory described in Paragraph **a.** above, but is away for a short time on your business; or

(3) "Personal and advertising injury" offenses that take place through the Internet or similar electronic means of communication;

provided the insured's responsibility to pay damages is determined in a "suit" on the merits, in the territory described in Paragraph **a.** above or in a settlement we agree to.

5. "Employee" includes a "leased worker". "Employee" does not include a "temporary worker".

6. "Executive officer" means a person holding any of the officer positions created by your charter, constitution, bylaws or any other similar governing document.

7. "Hostile fire" means one which becomes uncontrollable or breaks out from where it was intended to be.

8. "Impaired property" means tangible property, other than "your product" or "your work", that cannot be used or is less useful because:

a. It incorporates "your product" or "your work" that is known or thought to be defective, deficient, inadequate or dangerous; or

b. You have failed to fulfill the terms of a contract or agreement;

if such property can be restored to use by the repair, replacement, adjustment or removal of "your product" or "your work" or your fulfilling the terms of the contract or agreement.

9. "Insured contract" means:

a. A contract for a lease of premises. However, that portion of the contract for a lease of premises that indemnifies any person or organization for damage by fire to premises while rented to you or temporarily occupied by you with permission of the owner is not an "insured contract";

b. A sidetrack agreement;

c. Any easement or license agreement, except in connection with construction or demolition operations on or within 50 feet of a railroad;

d. An obligation, as required by ordinance, to indemnify a municipality, except in connection with work for a municipality;

e. An elevator maintenance agreement;

f. That part of any other contract or agreement pertaining to your business (including an indemnification of a municipality in connection with work performed for a municipality) under which you assume the tort liability of another party to pay for "bodily injury" or "property damage" to a third person or organization. Tort liability means a liability that would be imposed by law in the absence of any contract or agreement.

Paragraph f. does not include that part of any contract or agreement:

(1) That indemnifies a railroad for "bodily injury" or "property damage" arising out of construction or demolition operations, within 50 feet of any railroad property and affecting any railroad bridge or trestle, tracks, road-beds, tunnel, underpass or crossing;

(2) That indemnifies an architect, engineer or surveyor for injury or damage arising out of:

(a) Preparing, approving, or failing to prepare or approve, maps, shop drawings, opinions, reports, surveys, field orders, change orders or drawings and specifications; or

(b) Giving directions or instructions, or failing to give them, if that is the primary cause of the injury or damage; or

(3) Under which the insured, if an architect, engineer or surveyor, assumes liability for an injury or damage arising out of the insured's rendering or failure to render professional services, including those listed in (2) above and supervisory, inspection, architectural or engineering activities.

10. "Leased worker" means a person leased to you by a labor leasing firm under an agreement between you and the labor leasing firm, to perform duties related to the conduct of your business. "Leased worker" does not include a "temporary worker".

11. "Loading or unloading" means the handling of property:

a. After it is moved from the place where it is accepted for movement into or onto an aircraft, watercraft or "auto";

b. While it is in or on an aircraft, watercraft or "auto"; or

c. While it is being moved from an aircraft, watercraft or "auto" to the place where it is finally delivered;

but "loading or unloading" does not include the movement of property by means of a mechanical device, other than a hand truck, that is not attached to the aircraft, watercraft or "auto".

12. "Mobile equipment" means any of the following types of land vehicles, including any attached machinery or equipment:

a. Bulldozers, farm machinery, forklifts and other vehicles designed for use principally off public roads;

b. Vehicles maintained for use solely on or next to premises you own or rent;

c. Vehicles that travel on crawler treads;

d. Vehicles, whether self-propelled or not, maintained primarily to provide mobility to permanently mounted:

(1) Power cranes, shovels, loaders, diggers or drills; or

(2) Road construction or resurfacing equipment such as graders, scrapers or rollers;

e. Vehicles not described in Paragraph a., b., c. or d. above that are not self-propelled and are maintained primarily to provide mobility to permanently attached equipment of the following types:

(1) Air compressors, pumps and generators, including spraying, welding, building cleaning, geophysical exploration, lighting and well servicing equipment; or

(2) Cherry pickers and similar devices used to raise or lower workers;

f. Vehicles not described in Paragraph a., b., c. or d. above maintained primarily for purposes other than the transportation of persons or cargo.

   CG 00 01 04 13

However, self-propelled vehicles with the following types of permanently attached equipment are not "mobile equipment" but will be considered "autos":

(1) Equipment designed primarily for:

    (a) Snow removal;

    (b) Road maintenance, but not construction or resurfacing; or

    (c) Street cleaning;

(2) Cherry pickers and similar devices mounted on automobile or truck chassis and used to raise or lower workers; and

(3) Air compressors, pumps and generators, including spraying, welding, building cleaning, geophysical exploration, lighting and well servicing equipment.

However, "mobile equipment" does not include any land vehicles that are subject to a compulsory or financial responsibility law or other motor vehicle insurance law where it is licensed or principally garaged. Land vehicles subject to a compulsory or financial responsibility law or other motor vehicle insurance law are considered "autos".

13. "Occurrence" means an accident, including continuous or repeated exposure to substantially the same general harmful conditions.

14. "Personal and advertising injury" means injury, including consequential "bodily injury", arising out of one or more of the following offenses:

a. False arrest, detention or imprisonment;

b. Malicious prosecution;

c. The wrongful eviction from, wrongful entry into, or invasion of the right of private occupancy of a room, dwelling or premises that a person occupies, committed by or on behalf of its owner, landlord or lessor;

d. Oral or written publication, in any manner, of material that slanders or libels a person or organization or disparages a person's or organization's goods, products or services;

e. Oral or written publication, in any manner, of material that violates a person's right of privacy;

f. The use of another's advertising idea in your "advertisement"; or

g. Infringing upon another's copyright, trade dress or slogan in your "advertisement".

15. "Pollutants" mean any solid, liquid, gaseous or thermal irritant or contaminant, including smoke, vapor, soot, fumes, acids, alkalis, chemicals and waste. Waste includes materials to be recycled, reconditioned or reclaimed.

16. "Products-completed operations hazard":

a. Includes all "bodily injury" and "property damage" occurring away from premises you own or rent and arising out of "your product" or "your work" except:

    (1) Products that are still in your physical possession; or

    (2) Work that has not yet been completed or abandoned. However, "your work" will be deemed completed at the earliest of the following times:

        (a) When all of the work called for in your contract has been completed.

        (b) When all of the work to be done at the job site has been completed if your contract calls for work at more than one job site.

        (c) When that part of the work done at a job site has been put to its intended use by any person or organization other than another contractor or subcontractor working on the same project.

    Work that may need service, maintenance, correction, repair or replacement, but which is otherwise complete, will be treated as completed.

b. Does not include "bodily injury" or "property damage" arising out of:

    (1) The transportation of property, unless the injury or damage arises out of a condition in or on a vehicle not owned or operated by you, and that condition was created by the "loading or unloading" of that vehicle by any insured;

    (2) The existence of tools, uninstalled equipment or abandoned or unused materials; or

    (3) Products or operations for which the classification, listed in the Declarations or in a policy Schedule, states that products-completed operations are subject to the General Aggregate Limit.

17. "Property damage" means:

a. Physical injury to tangible property, including all resulting loss of use of that property. All such loss of use shall be deemed to occur at the time of the physical injury that caused it; or

b. Loss of use of tangible property that is not physically injured. All such loss of use shall be deemed to occur at the time of the "occurrence" that caused it.

For the purposes of this insurance, electronic data is not tangible property.

As used in this definition, electronic data means information, facts or programs stored as or on, created or used on, or transmitted to or from computer software, including systems and applications software, hard or floppy disks, CD-ROMs, tapes, drives, cells, data processing devices or any other media which are used with electronically controlled equipment.

18. "Suit" means a civil proceeding in which damages because of "bodily injury", "property damage" or "personal and advertising injury" to which this insurance applies are alleged. "Suit" includes:

   a. An arbitration proceeding in which such damages are claimed and to which the insured must submit or does submit with our consent; or

   b. Any other alternative dispute resolution proceeding in which such damages are claimed and to which the insured submits with our consent.

19. "Temporary worker" means a person who is furnished to you to substitute for a permanent "employee" on leave or to meet seasonal or short-term workload conditions.

20. "Volunteer worker" means a person who is not your "employee", and who donates his or her work and acts at the direction of and within the scope of duties determined by you, and is not paid a fee, salary or other compensation by you or anyone else for their work performed for you.

21. "Your product":

   a. Means:

      (1) Any goods or products, other than real property, manufactured, sold, handled, distributed or disposed of by:

         (a) You;

         (b) Others trading under your name; or

         (c) A person or organization whose business or assets you have acquired; and

      (2) Containers (other than vehicles), materials, parts or equipment furnished in connection with such goods or products.

   b. Includes:

      (1) Warranties or representations made at any time with respect to the fitness, quality, durability, performance or use of "your product"; and

      (2) The providing of or failure to provide warnings or instructions.

   c. Does not include vending machines or other property rented to or located for the use of others but not sold.

22. "Your work":

   a. Means:

      (1) Work or operations performed by you or on your behalf; and

      (2) Materials, parts or equipment furnished in connection with such work or operations.

   b. Includes:

      (1) Warranties or representations made at any time with respect to the fitness, quality, durability, performance or use of "your work"; and

      (2) The providing of or failure to provide warnings or instructions.

     CG 00 01 04 13

COMMERCIAL GENERAL LIABILITY COVERAGE FORM

COVERAGES A AND B PROVIDE CLAIMS-MADE COVERAGE.
PLEASE READ THE ENTIRE FORM CAREFULLY.

Various provisions in this policy restrict coverage. Read the entire policy carefully to determine rights, duties and what is and is not covered.

Throughout this policy the words "you" and "your" refer to the Named Insured shown in the Declarations, and any other person or organization qualifying as a Named Insured under this policy. The words "we", "us" and "our" refer to the company providing this insurance.

The word "insured" means any person or organization qualifying as such under Section II – Who Is An Insured.

Other words and phrases that appear in quotation marks have special meaning. Refer to Section VI – Definitions.

SECTION I – COVERAGES

COVERAGE A – BODILY INJURY AND PROPERTY DAMAGE LIABILITY

1. Insuring Agreement

a. We will pay those sums that the insured becomes legally obligated to pay as damages because of "bodily injury" or "property damage" to which this insurance applies. We will have the right and duty to defend the insured against any "suit" seeking those damages. However, we will have no duty to defend the insured against any "suit" seeking damages for "bodily injury" or "property damage" to which this insurance does not apply. We may, at our discretion, investigate any "occurrence" and settle any claim or "suit" that may result. But:

(1) The amount we will pay for damages is limited as described in Section III – Limits Of Insurance; and

(2) Our right and duty to defend ends when we have used up the applicable limit of insurance in the payment of judgments or settlements under Coverages A or B or medical expenses under Coverage C.

No other obligation or liability to pay sums or perform acts or services is covered unless explicitly provided for under Supplementary Payments – Coverages A and B.

b. This insurance applies to "bodily injury" and "property damage" only if:

(1) The "bodily injury" or "property damage" is caused by an "occurrence" that takes place in the "coverage territory";

(2) The "bodily injury" or "property damage" did not occur before the Retroactive Date, if any, shown in the Declarations or after the end of the policy period; and

(3) A claim for damages because of the "bodily injury" or "property damage" is first made against any insured, in accordance with Paragraph c. below, during the policy period or any Extended Reporting Period we provide under Section V – Extended Reporting Periods.

c. A claim by a person or organization seeking damages will be deemed to have been made at the earlier of the following times:

(1) When notice of such claim is received and recorded by any insured or by us, whichever comes first; or

(2) When we make settlement in accordance with Paragraph a. above.

All claims for damages because of "bodily injury" to the same person, including damages claimed by any person or organization for care, loss of services, or death resulting at any time from the "bodily injury", will be deemed to have been made at the time the first of those claims is made against any insured.

All claims for damages because of "property damage" causing loss to the same person or organization will be deemed to have been made at the time the first of those claims is made against any insured.

2. Exclusions

This insurance does not apply to:

a. **Expected Or Intended Injury**

"Bodily injury" or "property damage" expected or intended from the standpoint of the insured. This exclusion does not apply to "bodily injury" resulting from the use of reasonable force to protect persons or property.

b. Contractual Liability

"Bodily injury" or "property damage" for which the insured is obligated to pay damages by reason of the assumption of liability in a contract or agreement. This exclusion does not apply to liability for damages:

(1) That the insured would have in the absence of the contract or agreement; or

(2) Assumed in a contract or agreement that is an "insured contract", provided the "bodily injury" or "property damage" occurs subsequent to the execution of the contract or agreement. Solely for the purposes of liability assumed in an "insured contract", reasonable attorneys' fees and necessary litigation expenses incurred by or for a party other than an insured are deemed to be damages because of "bodily injury" or "property damage", provided:

(a) Liability to such party for, or for the cost of, that party's defense has also been assumed in the same "insured contract"; and

(b) Such attorneys' fees and litigation expenses are for defense of that party against a civil or alternative dispute resolution proceeding in which damages to which this insurance applies are alleged.

c. Liquor Liability

"Bodily injury" or "property damage" for which any insured may be held liable by reason of:

(1) Causing or contributing to the intoxication of any person;

(2) The furnishing of alcoholic beverages to a person under the legal drinking age or under the influence of alcohol; or

(3) Any statute, ordinance or regulation relating to the sale, gift, distribution or use of alcoholic beverages.

This exclusion applies even if the claims against any insured allege negligence or other wrongdoing in:

(a) The supervision, hiring, employment, training or monitoring of others by that insured; or

(b) Providing or failing to provide transportation with respect to any person that may be under the influence of alcohol;

if the "occurrence" which caused the "bodily injury" or "property damage", involved that which is described in Paragraph **(1)**, **(2)** or **(3)** above.

However, this exclusion applies only if you are in the business of manufacturing, distributing, selling, serving or furnishing alcoholic beverages. For the purposes of this exclusion, permitting a person to bring alcoholic beverages on your premises, for consumption on your premises, whether or not a fee is charged or a license is required for such activity, is not by itself considered the business of selling, serving or furnishing alcoholic beverages.

d. Workers' Compensation And Similar Laws

Any obligation of the insured under a workers' compensation, disability benefits or unemployment compensation law or any similar law.

e. Employer's Liability

"Bodily injury" to:

(1) An "employee" of the insured arising out of and in the course of:

(a) Employment by the insured; or

(b) Performing duties related to the conduct of the insured's business; or

(2) The spouse, child, parent, brother or sister of that "employee" as a consequence of Paragraph **(1)** above.

This exclusion applies whether the insured may be liable as an employer or in any other capacity and to any obligation to share damages with or repay someone else who must pay damages because of the injury.

This exclusion does not apply to liability assumed by the insured under an "insured contract".

f. Pollution

(1) "Bodily injury" or "property damage" arising out of the actual, alleged or threatened discharge, dispersal, seepage, migration, release or escape of "pollutants":

(a) At or from any premises, site or location which is or was at any time owned or occupied by, or rented or loaned to, any insured. However, this subparagraph does not apply to:

(i) "Bodily injury" if sustained within a building and caused by smoke, fumes, vapor or soot produced by or originating from equipment that is used to heat, cool or dehumidify the building, or equipment that is used to heat water for personal use by the building's occupants or their guests;

(ii) "Bodily injury" or "property damage" for which you may be held liable, if you are a contractor and the owner or lessee of such premises, site or location has been added to your policy as an additional insured with respect to your ongoing operations performed for that additional insured at that premises, site or location and such premises, site or location is not and never was owned or occupied by, or rented or loaned to, any insured, other than that additional insured; or

(iii) "Bodily injury" or "property damage" arising out of heat, smoke or fumes from a "hostile fire";

(b) At or from any premises, site or location which is or was at any time used by or for any insured or others for the handling, storage, disposal, processing or treatment of waste;

(c) Which are or were at any time transported, handled, stored, treated, disposed of, or processed as waste by or for:

(i) Any insured; or

(ii) Any person or organization for whom you may be legally responsible; or

(d) At or from any premises, site or location on which any insured or any contractors or subcontractors working directly or indirectly on any insured's behalf are performing operations if the "pollutants" are brought on or to the premises, site or location in connection with such operations by such insured, contractor or subcontractor. However, this subparagraph does not apply to:

(i) "Bodily injury" or "property damage" arising out of the escape of fuels, lubricants or other operating fluids which are needed to perform the normal electrical, hydraulic or mechanical functions necessary for the operation of "mobile equipment" or its parts, if such fuels, lubricants or other operating fluids escape from a vehicle part designed to hold, store or receive them. This exception does not apply if the "bodily injury" or "property damage" arises out of the intentional discharge, dispersal or release of the fuels, lubricants or other operating fluids, or if such fuels, lubricants or other operating fluids are brought on or to the premises, site or location with the intent that they be discharged, dispersed or released as part of the operations being performed by such insured, contractor or subcontractor;

(ii) "Bodily injury" or "property damage" sustained within a building and caused by the release of gases, fumes or vapors from materials brought into that building in connection with operations being performed by you or on your behalf by a contractor or subcontractor; or

(iii) "Bodily injury" or "property damage" arising out of heat, smoke or fumes from a "hostile fire".

(e) At or from any premises, site or location on which any insured or any contractors or subcontractors working directly or indirectly on any insured's behalf are performing operations if the operations are to test for, monitor, clean up, remove, contain, treat, detoxify or neutralize, or in any way respond to, or assess the effects of, "pollutants".

(2) Any loss, cost or expense arising out of any:

(a) Request, demand, order or statutory or regulatory requirement that any insured or others test for, monitor, clean up, remove, contain, treat, detoxify or neutralize, or in any way respond to, or assess the effects of, "pollutants"; or

(b) Claim or suit by or on behalf of a governmental authority for damages because of testing for, monitoring, cleaning up, removing, containing, treating, detoxifying or neutralizing, or in any way responding to, or assessing the effects of, "pollutants".

However, this paragraph does not apply to liability for damages because of "property damage" that the insured would have in the absence of such request, demand, order or statutory or regulatory requirement, or such claim or "suit" by or on behalf of a governmental authority.

g. Aircraft, Auto Or Watercraft

"Bodily injury" or "property damage" arising out of the ownership, maintenance, use or entrustment to others of any aircraft, "auto" or watercraft owned or operated by or rented or loaned to any insured. Use includes operation and "loading or unloading".

This exclusion applies even if the claims against any insured allege negligence or other wrongdoing in the supervision, hiring, employment, training or monitoring of others by that insured, if the "occurrence" which caused the "bodily injury" or "property damage" involved the ownership, maintenance, use or entrustment to others of any aircraft, "auto" or watercraft that is owned or operated by or rented or loaned to any insured.

This exclusion does not apply to:

(1) A watercraft while ashore on premises you own or rent;

(2) A watercraft you do not own that is:

(a) Less than 26 feet long; and

(b) Not being used to carry persons or property for a charge;

(3) Parking an "auto" on, or on the ways next to, premises you own or rent, provided the "auto" is not owned by or rented or loaned to you or the insured;

(4) Liability assumed under any "insured contract" for the ownership, maintenance or use of aircraft or watercraft; or

(5) "Bodily injury" or "property damage" arising out of:

(a) The operation of machinery or equipment that is attached to, or part of, a land vehicle that would qualify under the definition of "mobile equipment" if it were not subject to a compulsory or financial responsibility law or other motor vehicle insurance law where it is licensed or principally garaged; or

(b) The operation of any of the machinery or equipment listed in Paragraph **f.(2)** or **f.(3)** of the definition of "mobile equipment".

h. Mobile Equipment

"Bodily injury" or "property damage" arising out of:

(1) The transportation of "mobile equipment" by an "auto" owned or operated by or rented or loaned to any insured; or

(2) The use of "mobile equipment" in, or while in practice for, or while being prepared for, any prearranged racing, speed, demolition, or stunting activity.

i. War

"Bodily injury" or "property damage", however caused, arising, directly or indirectly, out of:

(1) War, including undeclared or civil war;

(2) Warlike action by a military force, including action in hindering or defending against an actual or expected attack, by any government, sovereign or other authority using military personnel or other agents; or

(3) Insurrection, rebellion, revolution, usurped power, or action taken by governmental authority in hindering or defending against any of these.

j. Damage To Property

"Property damage" to:

(1) Property you own, rent, or occupy, including any costs or expenses incurred by you, or any other person, organization or entity, for repair, replacement, enhancement, restoration or maintenance of such property for any reason, including prevention of injury to a person or damage to another's property;

(2) Premises you sell, give away or abandon, if the "property damage" arises out of any part of those premises;

(3) Property loaned to you;

(4) Personal property in the care, custody or control of the insured;

(5) That particular part of real property on which you or any contractors or subcontractors working directly or indirectly on your behalf are performing operations, if the "property damage" arises out of those operations; or

(6) That particular part of any property that must be restored, repaired or replaced because "your work" was incorrectly performed on it.

Paragraphs **(1)**, **(3)** and **(4)** of this exclusion do not apply to "property damage" (other than damage by fire) to premises, including the contents of such premises, rented to you for a period of seven or fewer consecutive days. A separate limit of insurance applies to Damage To Premises Rented To You as described in Section III – Limits Of Insurance.

Paragraph **(2)** of this exclusion does not apply if the premises are "your work" and were never occupied, rented or held for rental by you.

Paragraphs **(3)**, **(4)**, **(5)** and **(6)** of this exclusion do not apply to liability assumed under a sidetrack agreement.

Paragraph **(6)** of this exclusion does not apply to "property damage" included in the "products-completed operations hazard".

k. Damage To Your Product

"Property damage" to "your product" arising out of it or any part of it.

l. Damage To Your Work

"Property damage" to "your work" arising out of it or any part of it and included in the "products-completed operations hazard".

This exclusion does not apply if the damaged work or the work out of which the damage arises was performed on your behalf by a subcontractor.

m. Damage To Impaired Property Or Property Not Physically Injured

"Property damage" to "impaired property" or property that has not been physically injured, arising out of:

(1) A defect, deficiency, inadequacy or dangerous condition in "your product" or "your work"; or

(2) A delay or failure by you or anyone acting on your behalf to perform a contract or agreement in accordance with its terms.

This exclusion does not apply to the loss of use of other property arising out of sudden and accidental physical injury to "your product" or "your work" after it has been put to its intended use.

n. Recall Of Products, Work Or Impaired Property

Damages claimed for any loss, cost or expense incurred by you or others for the loss of use, withdrawal, recall, inspection, repair, replacement, adjustment, removal or disposal of:

(1) "Your product";

(2) "Your work"; or

(3) "Impaired property";

if such product, work, or property is withdrawn or recalled from the market or from use by any person or organization because of a known or suspected defect, deficiency, inadequacy or dangerous condition in it.

o. Personal And Advertising Injury

"Bodily injury" arising out of "personal and advertising injury".

p. Electronic Data

Damages arising out of the loss of, loss of use of, damage to, corruption of, inability to access, or inability to manipulate electronic data.

However, this exclusion does not apply to liability for damages because of "bodily injury".

As used in this exclusion, electronic data means information, facts or programs stored as or on, created or used on, or transmitted to or from computer software, including systems and applications software, hard or floppy disks, CD-ROMs, tapes, drives, cells, data processing devices or any other media which are used with electronically controlled equipment.

q. Recording And Distribution Of Material In Violation Of Law

"Bodily injury" or "property damage" arising directly or indirectly out of any action or omission that violates or is alleged to violate:

(1) The Telephone Consumer Protection Act (TCPA), including any amendment of or addition to such law;

(2) The CAN-SPAM Act of 2003, including any amendment of or addition to such law;

(3) The Fair Credit Reporting Act (FCRA), and any amendment of or addition to such law, including the Fair and Accurate Credit Transactions Act (FACTA); or

(4) Any federal, state or local statute, ordinance or regulation, other than the TCPA, CAN-SPAM Act of 2003 or FCRA and their amendments and additions, that addresses, prohibits, or limits the printing, dissemination, disposal, collecting, recording, sending, transmitting, communicating or distribution of material or information.

Exclusions **c.** through **n.** do not apply to damage by fire to premises while rented to you or temporarily occupied by you with permission of the owner. A separate limit of insurance applies to this coverage as described in Section **III** – Limits Of Insurance.

COVERAGE B – PERSONAL AND ADVERTISING INJURY LIABILITY

1. Insuring Agreement

a. We will pay those sums that the insured becomes legally obligated to pay as damages because of "personal and advertising injury" to which this insurance applies. We will have the right and duty to defend the insured against any "suit" seeking those damages. However, we will have no duty to defend the insured against any "suit" seeking damages for "personal and advertising injury" to which this insurance does not apply. We may, at our discretion, investigate any offense and settle any claim or "suit" that may result. But:

(1) The amount we will pay for damages is limited as described in Section **III** – Limits Of Insurance; and

(2) Our right and duty to defend end when we have used up the applicable limit of insurance in the payment of judgments or settlements under Coverages **A** or **B** or medical expenses under Coverage **C.**

No other obligation or liability to pay sums or perform acts or services is covered unless explicitly provided for under Supplementary Payments – Coverages **A** and **B.**

b. This insurance applies to "personal and advertising injury" caused by an offense arising out of your business, but only if:

(1) The offense was committed in the "coverage territory";

(2) The offense was not committed before the Retroactive Date, if any, shown in the Declarations or after the end of the policy period; and

(3) A claim for damages because of the "personal and advertising injury" is first made against any insured, in accordance with Paragraph **c.** below, during the policy period or any Extended Reporting Period we provide under Section **V** – Extended Reporting Periods.

c. A claim made by a person or organization seeking damages will be deemed to have been made at the earlier of the following times:

(1) When notice of such claim is received and recorded by any insured or by us, whichever comes first; or

(2) When we make settlement in accordance with Paragraph **a.** above.

All claims for damages because of "personal and advertising injury" to the same person or organization as a result of an offense will be deemed to have been made at the time the first of those claims is made against any insured.

2. Exclusions

This insurance does not apply to:

a. Knowing Violation Of Rights Of Another

"Personal and advertising injury" caused by or at the direction of the insured with the knowledge that the act would violate the rights of another and would inflict "personal and advertising injury".

b. Material Published With Knowledge Of Falsity

"Personal and advertising injury" arising out of oral or written publication, in any manner, of material, if done by or at the direction of the insured with knowledge of its falsity.

c. Material Published Prior To Policy Period

"Personal and advertising injury" arising out of oral or written publication, in any manner, of material whose first publication took place before the Retroactive Date, if any, shown in the Declarations.

d. Criminal Acts

"Personal and advertising injury" arising out of a criminal act committed by or at the direction of the insured.

                       CG 00 02 04 13

e. Contractual Liability

"Personal and advertising injury" for which the insured has assumed liability in a contract or agreement. This exclusion does not apply to liability for damages that the insured would have in the absence of the contract or agreement.

f. Breach Of Contract

"Personal and advertising injury" arising out of a breach of contract, except an implied contract to use another's advertising idea in your "advertisement".

g. Quality Or Performance Of Goods – Failure To Conform To Statements

"Personal and advertising injury" arising out of the failure of goods, products or services to conform with any statement of quality or performance made in your "advertisement".

h. Wrong Description Of Prices

"Personal and advertising injury" arising out of the wrong description of the price of goods, products or services stated in your "advertisement".

i. Infringement Of Copyright, Patent, Trademark Or Trade Secret

"Personal and advertising injury" arising out of the infringement of copyright, patent, trademark, trade secret or other intellectual property rights. Under this exclusion, such other intellectual property rights do not include the use of another's advertising idea in your "advertisement".

However, this exclusion does not apply to infringement, in your "advertisement", of copyright, trade dress or slogan.

j. Insureds In Media And Internet Type Businesses

"Personal and advertising injury" committed by an insured whose business is:

(1) Advertising, broadcasting, publishing or telecasting;

(2) Designing or determining content of web sites for others; or

(3) An Internet search, access, content or service provider.

However, this exclusion does not apply to Paragraphs **14.a., b.** and **c.** of "personal and advertising injury" under the Definitions section.

For the purposes of this exclusion, the placing of frames, borders or links, or advertising, for you or others anywhere on the Internet, is not by itself, considered the business of advertising, broadcasting, publishing or telecasting.

k. Electronic Chatrooms Or Bulletin Boards

"Personal and advertising injury" arising out of an electronic chatroom or bulletin board the insured hosts, owns, or over which the insured exercises control.

l. Unauthorized Use Of Another's Name Or Product

"Personal and advertising injury" arising out of the unauthorized use of another's name or product in your e-mail address, domain name or metatag, or any other similar tactics to mislead another's potential customers.

m. Pollution

"Personal and advertising injury" arising out of the actual, alleged or threatened discharge, dispersal, seepage, migration, release or escape of "pollutants" at any time.

n. Pollution-related

Any loss, cost or expense arising out of any:

(1) Request, demand, order or statutory or regulatory requirement that any insured or others test for, monitor, clean up, remove, contain, treat, detoxify or neutralize, or in any way respond to, or assess the effects of, "pollutants"; or

(2) Claim or suit by or on behalf of a governmental authority for damages because of testing for, monitoring, cleaning up, removing, containing, treating, detoxifying or neutralizing, or in any way responding to, or assessing the effects of, "pollutants".

o. War

"Personal and advertising injury", however caused, arising, directly or indirectly, out of:

(1) War, including undeclared or civil war;

(2) Warlike action by a military force, including action in hindering or defending against an actual or expected attack, by any government, sovereign or other authority using military personnel or other agents; or

(3) Insurrection, rebellion, revolution, usurped power, or action taken by governmental authority in hindering or defending against any of these.

p. Recording And Distribution Of Material In Violation Of Law

"Personal and advertising injury" arising directly or indirectly out of any action or omission that violates or is alleged to violate:

(1) The Telephone Consumer Protection Act (TCPA), including any amendment of or addition to such law;

(2) The CAN-SPAM Act of 2003, including any amendment of or addition to such law;

(3) The Fair Credit Reporting Act (FCRA), and any amendment of or addition to such law, including the Fair and Accurate Credit Transactions Act (FACTA); or

(4) Any federal, state or local statute, ordinance or regulation, other than the TCPA, CAN-SPAM Act of 2003 or FCRA and their amendments and additions, that addresses, prohibits, or limits the printing, dissemination, disposal, collecting, recording, sending, transmitting, communicating or distribution of material or information.

COVERAGE C – MEDICAL PAYMENTS

1. Insuring Agreement

a. We will pay medical expenses as described below for "bodily injury" caused by an accident:

(1) On premises you own or rent;

(2) On ways next to premises you own or rent; or

(3) Because of your operations;

provided that:

(a) The accident takes place in the "coverage territory" and during the policy period;

(b) The expenses are incurred and reported to us within one year of the date of the accident; and

(c) The injured person submits to examination, at our expense, by physicians of our choice as often as we reasonably require.

b. We will make these payments regardless of fault. These payments will not exceed the applicable limit of insurance. We will pay reasonable expenses for:

(1) First aid administered at the time of an accident;

(2) Necessary medical, surgical, X-ray and dental services, including prosthetic devices; and

(3) Necessary ambulance, hospital, professional nursing and funeral services.

2. Exclusions

We will not pay expenses for "bodily injury":

a. Any Insured

To any insured, except "volunteer workers".

b. Hired Person

To a person hired to do work for or on behalf of any insured or a tenant of any insured.

c. Injury On Normally Occupied Premises

To a person injured on that part of premises you own or rent that the person normally occupies.

d. Workers' Compensation And Similar Laws

To a person, whether or not an "employee" of any insured, if benefits for the "bodily injury" are payable or must be provided under a workers' compensation or disability benefits law or a similar law.

e. Athletics Activities

To a person injured while practicing, instructing or participating in any physical exercises or games, sports, or athletic contests.

f. Products-Completed Operations Hazard

Included within the "products-completed operations hazard".

g. Coverage A Exclusions

Excluded under Coverage **A**.

SUPPLEMENTARY PAYMENTS – COVERAGES A AND B

1. We will pay, with respect to any claim we investigate or settle or any "suit" against an insured we defend:

a. All expenses we incur.

b. Up to $250 for cost of bail bonds required because of accidents or traffic law violations arising out of the use of any vehicle to which the Bodily Injury Liability Coverage applies. We do not have to furnish these bonds.

c. The cost of bonds to release attachments, but only for bond amounts within the applicable limit of insurance. We do not have to furnish these bonds.

d. All reasonable expenses incurred by the insured at our request to assist us in the investigation or defense of the claim or "suit", including actual loss of earnings up to $250 a day because of time off from work.

e. All court costs taxed against the insured in the "suit". However, these payments do not include attorneys' fees or attorneys' expenses taxed against the insured.

f. Prejudgment interest awarded against the insured on that part of the judgment we pay. If we make an offer to pay the applicable limit of insurance, we will not pay any prejudgment interest based on that period of time after the offer.

g. All interest on the full amount of any judgment that accrues after entry of the judgment and before we have paid, offered to pay, or deposited in court the part of the judgment that is within the applicable limit of insurance.

These payments will not reduce the limits of insurance.

2. If we defend an insured against a "suit" and an indemnitee of the insured is also named as a party to the "suit", we will defend that indemnitee if all of the following conditions are met:

a. The "suit" against the indemnitee seeks damages for which the insured has assumed the liability of the indemnitee in a contract or agreement that is an "insured contract";

b. This insurance applies to such liability assumed by the insured;

c. The obligation to defend, or the cost of the defense of, that indemnitee, has also been assumed by the insured in the same "insured contract";

d. The allegations in the "suit" and the information we know about the "occurrence" are such that no conflict appears to exist between the interests of the insured and the interests of the indemnitee;

e. The indemnitee and the insured ask us to conduct and control the defense of that indemnitee against such "suit" and agree that we can assign the same counsel to defend the insured and the indemnitee; and

f. The indemnitee:

(1) Agrees in writing to:

(a) Cooperate with us in the investigation, settlement or defense of the "suit";

(b) Immediately send us copies of any demands, notices, summonses or legal papers received in connection with the "suit";

(c) Notify any other insurer whose coverage is available to the indemnitee; and

(d) Cooperate with us with respect to coordinating other applicable insurance available to the indemnitee; and

(2) Provides us with written authorization to:

(a) Obtain records and other information related to the "suit"; and

(b) Conduct and control the defense of the indemnitee in such "suit".

So long as the above conditions are met, attorneys' fees incurred by us in the defense of that indemnitee, necessary litigation expenses incurred by us and necessary litigation expenses incurred by the indemnitee at our request will be paid as Supplementary Payments. Notwithstanding the provisions of Paragraph **2.b.(2)** of Section I – Coverage **A** – Bodily Injury And Property Damage Liability, such payments will not be deemed to be damages for "bodily injury" and "property damage" and will not reduce the limits of insurance.

Our obligation to defend an insured's indemnitee and to pay for attorneys' fees and necessary litigation expenses as Supplementary Payments ends when we have used up the applicable limit of insurance in the payment of judgments or settlements or the conditions set forth above, or the terms of the agreement described in Paragraph **f.** above, are no longer met.

SECTION II – WHO IS AN INSURED

1. If you are designated in the Declarations as:

a. An individual, you and your spouse are insureds, but only with respect to the conduct of a business of which you are the sole owner.

b. A partnership or joint venture, you are an insured. Your members, your partners, and their spouses are also insureds, but only with respect to the conduct of your business.

c. A limited liability company, you are an insured. Your members are also insureds, but only with respect to the conduct of your business. Your managers are insureds, but only with respect to their duties as your managers.

d. An organization other than a partnership, joint venture or limited liability company, you are an insured. Your "executive officers" and directors are insureds, but only with respect to their duties as your officers or directors. Your stockholders are also insureds, but only with respect to their liability as stockholders.

e. A trust, you are an insured. Your trustees are also insureds, but only with respect to their duties as trustees.

2. Each of the following is also an insured:

a. Your "volunteer workers" only while performing duties related to the conduct of your business, or your "employees", other than either your "executive officers" (if you are an organization other than a partnership, joint venture or limited liability company) or your managers (if you are a limited liability company), but only for acts within the scope of their employment by you or while performing duties related to the conduct of your business. However, none of these "employees" or "volunteer workers" are insureds for:

(1) "Bodily injury" or "personal and advertising injury":

(a) To you, to your partners or members (if you are a partnership or joint venture), to your members (if you are a limited liability company), to a co-"employee" while in the course of his or her employment or performing duties related to the conduct of your business, or to your other "volunteer workers" while performing duties related to the conduct of your business;

(b) To the spouse, child, parent, brother or sister of that co-"employee" or "volunteer worker" as a consequence of Paragraph (a) above;

(c) For which there is any obligation to share damages with or repay someone else who must pay damages because of the injury described in Paragraph (a) or (b) above; or

(d) Arising out of his or her providing or failing to provide professional health care services.

(2) "Property damage" to property:

(a) Owned, occupied or used by;

(b) Rented to, in the care, custody or control of, or over which physical control is being exercised for any purpose by;

you, any of your "employees", "volunteer workers", any partner or member (if you are a partnership or joint venture), or any member (if you are a limited liability company).

b. Any person (other than your "employee" or "volunteer worker") or any organization while acting as your real estate manager.

c. Any person or organization having proper temporary custody of your property if you die, but only:

(1) With respect to liability arising out of the maintenance or use of that property; and

(2) Until your legal representative has been appointed.

d. Your legal representative if you die, but only with respect to duties as such. That representative will have all your rights and duties under this Coverage Part.

3. Any organization you newly acquire or form, other than a partnership, joint venture or limited liability company, and over which you maintain ownership or majority interest, will qualify as a Named Insured if there is no other similar insurance available to that organization. However:

a. Coverage under this provision is afforded only until the 90th day after you acquire or form the organization or the end of the policy period, whichever is earlier;

b. Coverage A does not apply to "bodily injury" or "property damage" that occurred before you acquired or formed the organization; and

c. Coverage B does not apply to "personal and advertising injury" arising out of an offense committed before you acquired or formed the organization.

No person or organization is an insured with respect to the conduct of any current or past partnership, joint venture or limited liability company that is not shown as a Named Insured in the Declarations.

SECTION III – LIMITS OF INSURANCE

1. The Limits of Insurance shown in the Declarations and the rules below fix the most we will pay regardless of the number of:

a. Insureds;

b. Claims made or "suits" brought; or

c. Persons or organizations making claims or bringing "suits".

2. The General Aggregate Limit is the most we will pay for the sum of:

    a. Medical expenses under Coverage **C**;

    b. Damages under Coverage **A**, except damages because of "bodily injury" or "property damage" included in the "products-completed operations hazard"; and

    c. Damages under Coverage **B**.

3. The Products-Completed Operations Aggregate Limit is the most we will pay under Coverage **A** for damages because of "bodily injury" and "property damage" included in the "products-completed operations hazard".

4. Subject to Paragraph **2.** above, the Personal And Advertising Injury Limit is the most we will pay under Coverage **B** for the sum of all damages because of all "personal and advertising injury" sustained by any one person or organization.

5. Subject to Paragraph **2.** or **3.** above, whichever applies, the Each Occurrence Limit is the most we will pay for the sum of:

    a. Damages under Coverage **A**; and

    b. Medical expenses under Coverage **C**

    because of all "bodily injury" and "property damage" arising out of any one "occurrence".

6. Subject to Paragraph **5.** above, the Damage To Premises Rented To You Limit is the most we will pay under Coverage **A** for damages because of "property damage" to any one premises, while rented to you, or in the case of damage by fire, while rented to you or temporarily occupied by you with permission of the owner.

7. Subject to Paragraph **5.** above, the Medical Expense Limit is the most we will pay under Coverage **C** for all medical expenses because of "bodily injury" sustained by any one person.

The Limits of Insurance of this Coverage Part apply separately to each consecutive annual period and to any remaining period of less than 12 months, starting with the beginning of the policy period shown in the Declarations, unless the policy period is extended after issuance for an additional period of less than 12 months. In that case, the additional period will be deemed part of the last preceding period for purposes of determining the Limits of Insurance.

SECTION IV – COMMERCIAL GENERAL LIABILITY CONDITIONS

1. Bankruptcy

Bankruptcy or insolvency of the insured or of the insured's estate will not relieve us of our obligations under this Coverage Part.

2. Duties In The Event Of Occurrence, Offense, Claim Or Suit

    a. You must see to it that we are notified as soon as practicable of an "occurrence" or offense which may result in a claim. To the extent possible, notice should include:

      (1) How, when and where the "occurrence" or offense took place;

      (2) The names and addresses of any injured persons and witnesses; and

      (3) The nature and location of any injury or damage arising out of the "occurrence" or offense.

    Notice of an "occurrence" or offense is not notice of a claim.

    b. If a claim is received by any insured, you must:

      (1) Immediately record the specifics of the claim and the date received; and

      (2) Notify us as soon as practicable.

    You must see to it that we receive written notice of the claim as soon as practicable.

    c. You and any other involved insured must:

      (1) Immediately send us copies of any demands, notices, summonses or legal papers received in connection with the claim or a "suit";

      (2) Authorize us to obtain records and other information;

      (3) Cooperate with us in the investigation or settlement of the claim or defense against the "suit"; and

      (4) Assist us, upon our request, in the enforcement of any right against any person or organization which may be liable to the insured because of injury or damage to which this insurance may also apply.

    d. No insured will, except at that insured's own cost, voluntarily make a payment, assume any obligation, or incur any expense, other than for first aid, without our consent.

3. Legal Action Against Us

No person or organization has a right under this Coverage Part:

    a. To join us as a party or otherwise bring us into a "suit" asking for damages from an insured; or

    b. To sue us on this Coverage Part unless all of its terms have been fully complied with.

A person or organization may sue us to recover on an agreed settlement or on a final judgment against an insured; but we will not be liable for damages that are not payable under the terms of this Coverage Part or that are in excess of the applicable limit of insurance. An agreed settlement means a settlement and release of liability signed by us, the insured and the claimant or the claimant's legal representative.

4. Other Insurance

If other valid and collectible insurance is available to the insured for a loss we cover under Coverages **A** or **B** of this Coverage Part, our obligations are limited as follows:

a. Primary Insurance

This insurance is primary except when Paragraph **b.** below applies. If this insurance is primary, our obligations are not affected unless any of the other insurance is also primary. Then, we will share with all that other insurance by the method described in Paragraph **c.** below.

b. Excess Insurance

(1) This insurance is excess over:

(a) Any of the other insurance, whether primary, excess, contingent or on any other basis:

(i) That is effective prior to the beginning of the policy period shown in the Declarations of this insurance and applies to "bodily injury" or "property damage" on other than a claims-made basis, if:

i. No Retroactive Date is shown in the Declarations of this insurance; or

ii. The other insurance has a policy period which continues after the Retroactive Date shown in the Declarations of this insurance;

(ii) That is Fire, Extended Coverage, Builders' Risk, Installation Risk or similar coverage for "your work";

(iii) That is Fire insurance for premises rented to you or temporarily occupied by you with permission of the owner;

(iv) That is insurance purchased by you to cover your liability as a tenant for "property damage" to premises rented to you or temporarily occupied by you with permission of the owner; or

(v) If the loss arises out of the maintenance or use of aircraft, "autos" or watercraft to the extent not subject to Exclusion **g.** of Section **I** – Coverage **A** – Bodily Injury And Property Damage Liability.

(b) Any other primary insurance available to you covering liability for damages arising out of the premises or operations, or the products and completed operations, for which you have been added as an additional insured.

(2) When this insurance is excess, we will have no duty under Coverages **A** or **B** to defend the insured against any "suit" if any other insurer has a duty to defend the insured against that "suit". If no other insurer defends, we will undertake to do so, but we will be entitled to the insured's rights against all those other insurers.

(3) When this insurance is excess over other insurance, we will pay only our share of the amount of the loss, if any, that exceeds the sum of:

(a) The total amount that all such other insurance would pay for the loss in the absence of this insurance; and

(b) The total of all deductible and self-insured amounts under all that other insurance.

(4) We will share the remaining loss, if any, with any other insurance that is not described in this Excess Insurance provision and was not bought specifically to apply in excess of the Limits of Insurance shown in the Declarations of this Coverage Part.

c. Method Of Sharing

If all of the other insurance permits contribution by equal shares, we will follow this method also. Under this approach each insurer contributes equal amounts until it has paid its applicable limit of insurance or none of the loss remains, whichever comes first.

If any of the other insurance does not permit contribution by equal shares, we will contribute by limits. Under this method, each insurer's share is based on the ratio of its applicable limit of insurance to the total applicable limits of insurance of all insurers.

 CG 00 02 04 13

5. Premium Audit

   a. We will compute all premiums for this Coverage Part in accordance with our rules and rates.

   b. Premium shown in this Coverage Part as advance premium is a deposit premium only. At the close of each audit period we will compute the earned premium for that period and send notice to the first Named Insured. The due date for audit and retrospective premiums is the date shown as the due date on the bill. If the sum of the advance and audit premiums paid for the policy period is greater than the earned premium, we will return the excess to the first Named Insured.

   c. The first Named Insured must keep records of the information we need for premium computation, and send us copies at such times as we may request.

6. Representations

By accepting this policy, you agree:

   a. The statements in the Declarations are accurate and complete;

   b. Those statements are based upon representations you made to us; and

   c. We have issued this policy in reliance upon your representations.

7. Separation Of Insureds

Except with respect to the Limits of Insurance, and any rights or duties specifically assigned in this Coverage Part to the first Named Insured, this insurance applies:

   a. As if each Named Insured were the only Named Insured; and

   b. Separately to each insured against whom claim is made or "suit" is brought.

8. Transfer Of Rights Of Recovery Against Others To Us

If the insured has rights to recover all or part of any payment we have made under this Coverage Part, those rights are transferred to us. The insured must do nothing after loss to impair them. At our request, the insured will bring "suit" or transfer those rights to us and help us enforce them.

9. When We Do Not Renew

If we decide not to renew this Coverage Part, we will mail or deliver to the first Named Insured shown in the Declarations written notice of the nonrenewal not less than 30 days before the expiration date.

If notice is mailed, proof of mailing will be sufficient proof of notice.

10. Your Right To Claim And Occurrence Information

We will provide the first Named Insured shown in the Declarations the following information relating to this and any preceding general liability claims-made Coverage Part we have issued to you during the previous three years:

   a. A list or other record of each "occurrence", not previously reported to any other insurer, of which we were notified in accordance with Paragraph **2.a.** of the Section **IV** – Duties In The Event Of Occurrence, Offense, Claim Or Suit Condition. We will include the date and brief description of the "occurrence" if that information was in the notice we received.

   b. A summary by policy year, of payments made and amounts reserved, stated separately, under any applicable General Aggregate Limit and Products-Completed Operations Aggregate Limit.

Amounts reserved are based on our judgment. They are subject to change and should not be regarded as ultimate settlement values.

You must not disclose this information to any claimant or any claimant's representative without our consent.

If we cancel or elect not to renew this Coverage Part, we will provide such information no later than 30 days before the date of policy termination. In other circumstances, we will provide this information only if we receive a written request from the first Named Insured within 60 days after the end of the policy period. In this case, we will provide this information within 45 days of receipt of the request.

We compile claim and "occurrence" information for our own business purposes and exercise reasonable care in doing so. In providing this information to the first Named Insured, we make no representations or warranties to insureds, insurers, or others to whom this information is furnished by or on behalf of any insured. Cancellation or nonrenewal will be effective even if we inadvertently provide inaccurate information.

SECTION V – EXTENDED REPORTING PERIODS

1. We will provide one or more Extended Reporting Periods, as described below, if:

   a. This Coverage Part is canceled or not renewed; or

   b. We renew or replace this Coverage Part with insurance that:

     (1) Has a Retroactive Date later than the date shown in the Declarations of this Coverage Part; or

(2) Does not apply to "bodily injury", "property damage" or "personal and advertising injury" on a claims-made basis.

2. Extended Reporting Periods do not extend the policy period or change the scope of coverage provided. They apply only to claims for:

a. "Bodily injury" or "property damage" that occurs before the end of the policy period but not before the Retroactive Date, if any, shown in the Declarations; or

b. "Personal and advertising injury" caused by an offense committed before the end of the policy period but not before the Retroactive Date, if any, shown in the Declarations.

Once in effect, Extended Reporting Periods may not be canceled.

3. A Basic Extended Reporting Period is automatically provided without additional charge. This period starts with the end of the policy period and lasts for:

a. Five years with respect to claims because of "bodily injury" and "property damage" arising out of an "occurrence" reported to us, not later than 60 days after the end of the policy period, in accordance with Paragraph **2.a.** of the Section **IV** – Duties In The Event Of Occurrence, Offense, Claim Or Suit Condition;

b. Five years with respect to claims because of "personal and advertising injury" arising out of an offense reported to us, not later than 60 days after the end of the policy period, in accordance with Paragraph **2.a.** of the Section **IV** – Duties In The Event Of Occurrence, Offense, Claim Or Suit Condition; and

c. Sixty days with respect to claims arising from "occurrences" or offenses not previously reported to us.

The Basic Extended Reporting Period does not apply to claims that are covered under any subsequent insurance you purchase, or that would be covered but for exhaustion of the amount of insurance applicable to such claims.

4. The Basic Extended Reporting Period does not reinstate or increase the Limits of Insurance.

5. A Supplemental Extended Reporting Period of unlimited duration is available, but only by an endorsement and for an extra charge. This supplemental period starts when the Basic Extended Reporting Period, set forth in Paragraph **3.** above, ends.

You must give us a written request for the endorsement within 60 days after the end of the policy period. The Supplemental Extended Reporting Period will not go into effect unless you pay the additional premium promptly when due.

We will determine the additional premium in accordance with our rules and rates. In doing so, we may take into account the following:

a. The exposures insured;

b. Previous types and amounts of insurance;

c. Limits of Insurance available under this Coverage Part for future payment of damages; and

d. Other related factors.

The additional premium will not exceed 200% of the annual premium for this Coverage Part.

This endorsement shall set forth the terms, not inconsistent with this section, applicable to the Supplemental Extended Reporting Period, including a provision to the effect that the insurance afforded for claims first received during such period is excess over any other valid and collectible insurance available under policies in force after the Supplemental Extended Reporting Period starts.

6. If the Supplemental Extended Reporting Period is in effect, we will provide the supplemental aggregate limits of insurance described below, but only for claims first received and recorded during the Supplemental Extended Reporting Period.

The supplemental aggregate limits of insurance will be equal to the dollar amount shown in the Declarations in effect at the end of the policy period for such of the following limits of insurance for which a dollar amount has been entered:

General Aggregate Limit
Products-Completed Operations Aggregate Limit

Paragraphs **2.** and **3.** of Section **III** – Limits Of Insurance will be amended accordingly. The Personal and Advertising Injury Limit, the Each Occurrence Limit and the Damage To Premises Rented To You Limit shown in the Declarations will then continue to apply, as set forth in Paragraphs **4.**, **5.** and **6.** of that section.

SECTION VI – DEFINITIONS

1. "Advertisement" means a notice that is broadcast or published to the general public or specific market segments about your goods, products or services for the purpose of attracting customers or supporters. For the purposes of this definition:

a. Notices that are published include material placed on the Internet or on similar electronic means of communication; and

b. Regarding web sites, only that part of a web site that is about your goods, products or services for the purposes of attracting customers or supporters is considered an advertisement.

2. "Auto" means:

   a. A land motor vehicle, trailer or semitrailer designed for travel on public roads, including any attached machinery or equipment; or

   b. Any other land vehicle that is subject to a compulsory or financial responsibility law or other motor vehicle insurance law where it is licensed or principally garaged.

   However, "auto" does not include "mobile equipment".

3. "Bodily injury" means bodily injury, sickness or disease sustained by a person, including death resulting from any of these at any time.

4. "Coverage territory" means:

   a. The United States of America (including its territories and possessions), Puerto Rico and Canada;

   b. International waters or airspace, but only if the injury or damage occurs in the course of travel or transportation between any places included in Paragraph a. above; or

   c. All other parts of the world if the injury or damage arises out of:

      (1) Goods or products made or sold by you in the territory described in Paragraph a. above;

      (2) The activities of a person whose home is in the territory described in Paragraph a. above, but is away for a short time on your business; or

      (3) "Personal and advertising injury" offenses that take place through the Internet or similar electronic means of communication;

      provided the insured's responsibility to pay damages is determined in a "suit" on the merits, in the territory described in Paragraph a. above or in a settlement we agree to.

5. "Employee" includes a "leased worker". "Employee" does not include a "temporary worker".

6. "Executive officer" means a person holding any of the officer positions created by your charter, constitution, bylaws or any other similar governing document.

7. "Hostile fire" means one which becomes uncontrollable or breaks out from where it was intended to be.

8. "Impaired property" means tangible property, other than "your product" or "your work", that cannot be used or is less useful because:

   a. It incorporates "your product" or "your work" that is known or thought to be defective, deficient, inadequate or dangerous; or

   b. You have failed to fulfill the terms of a contract or agreement;

   if such property can be restored to use by the repair, replacement, adjustment or removal of "your product" or "your work" or your fulfilling the terms of the contract or agreement.

9. "Insured contract" means:

   a. A contract for a lease of premises. However, that portion of the contract for a lease of premises that indemnifies any person or organization for damage by fire to premises while rented to you or temporarily occupied by you with permission of the owner is not an "insured contract";

   b. A sidetrack agreement;

   c. Any easement or license agreement, except in connection with construction or demolition operations on or within 50 feet of a railroad;

   d. An obligation, as required by ordinance, to indemnify a municipality, except in connection with work for a municipality;

   e. An elevator maintenance agreement;

   f. That part of any other contract or agreement pertaining to your business (including an indemnification of a municipality in connection with work performed for a municipality) under which you assume the tort liability of another party to pay for "bodily injury" or "property damage" to a third person or organization. Tort liability means a liability that would be imposed by law in the absence of any contract or agreement.

   Paragraph f. does not include that part of any contract or agreement:

      (1) That indemnifies a railroad for "bodily injury" or "property damage" arising out of construction or demolition operations, within 50 feet of any railroad property and affecting any railroad bridge or trestle, tracks, road-beds, tunnel, underpass or crossing;

      (2) That indemnifies an architect, engineer or surveyor for injury or damage arising out of:

         (a) Preparing, approving, or failing to prepare or approve, maps, shop drawings, opinions, reports, surveys, field orders, change orders or drawings and specifications; or

         (b) Giving directions or instructions, or failing to give them, if that is the primary cause of the injury or damage; or

(3) Under which the insured, if an architect, engineer or surveyor, assumes liability for an injury or damage arising out of the insured's rendering or failure to render professional services, including those listed in Paragraph **(2)** above and supervisory, inspection, architectural or engineering activities.

10. "Leased worker" means a person leased to you by a labor leasing firm under an agreement between you and the labor leasing firm, to perform duties related to the conduct of your business. "Leased worker" does not include a "temporary worker".

11. "Loading or unloading" means the handling of property:

   a. After it is moved from the place where it is accepted for movement into or onto an aircraft, watercraft or "auto";

   b. While it is in or on an aircraft, watercraft or "auto"; or

   c. While it is being moved from an aircraft, watercraft or "auto" to the place where it is finally delivered;

   but "loading or unloading" does not include the movement of property by means of a mechanical device, other than a hand truck, that is not attached to the aircraft, watercraft or "auto".

12. "Mobile equipment" means any of the following types of land vehicles, including any attached machinery or equipment:

   a. Bulldozers, farm machinery, forklifts and other vehicles designed for use principally off public roads;

   b. Vehicles maintained for use solely on or next to premises you own or rent;

   c. Vehicles that travel on crawler treads;

   d. Vehicles, whether self-propelled or not, maintained primarily to provide mobility to permanently mounted:

   (1) Power cranes, shovels, loaders, diggers or drills; or

   (2) Road construction or resurfacing equipment such as graders, scrapers or rollers;

   e. Vehicles not described in Paragraph **a., b., c.** or **d.** above that are not self-propelled and are maintained primarily to provide mobility to permanently attached equipment of the following types:

   (1) Air compressors, pumps and generators, including spraying, welding, building cleaning, geophysical exploration, lighting and well servicing equipment; or

   (2) Cherry pickers and similar devices used to raise or lower workers;

   f. Vehicles not described in Paragraph **a., b., c.** or **d.** above maintained primarily for purposes other than the transportation of persons or cargo.

   However, self-propelled vehicles with the following types of permanently attached equipment are not "mobile equipment" but will be considered "autos":

   (1) Equipment designed primarily for:

   (a) Snow removal;

   (b) Road maintenance, but not construction or resurfacing; or

   (c) Street cleaning;

   (2) Cherry pickers and similar devices mounted on automobile or truck chassis and used to raise or lower workers; and

   (3) Air compressors, pumps and generators, including spraying, welding, building cleaning, geophysical exploration, lighting and well servicing equipment.

   However, "mobile equipment" does not include land vehicles that are subject to a compulsory or financial responsibility law or other motor vehicle insurance law where it is licensed or principally garaged. Land vehicles subject to a compulsory or financial responsibility law or other motor vehicle insurance law are considered "autos".

13. "Occurrence" means an accident, including continuous or repeated exposure to substantially the same general harmful conditions.

14. "Personal and advertising injury" means injury, including consequential "bodily injury", arising out of one or more of the following offenses:

   a. False arrest, detention or imprisonment;

   b. Malicious prosecution;

   c. The wrongful eviction from, wrongful entry into, or invasion of the right of private occupancy of a room, dwelling or premises that a person occupies, committed by or on behalf of its owner, landlord or lessor;

   d. Oral or written publication, in any manner, of material that slanders or libels a person or organization or disparages a person's or organization's goods, products or services;

   e. Oral or written publication, in any manner, of material that violates a person's right of privacy;

   f. The use of another's advertising idea in your "advertisement"; or

g. Infringing upon another's copyright, trade dress or slogan in your "advertisement".

15. "Pollutants" mean any solid, liquid, gaseous or thermal irritant or contaminant, including smoke, vapor, soot, fumes, acids, alkalis, chemicals and waste. Waste includes materials to be recycled, reconditioned or reclaimed.

16. "Products-completed operations hazard":

a. Includes all "bodily injury" and "property damage" occurring away from premises you own or rent and arising out of "your product" or "your work" except:

(1) Products that are still in your physical possession; or

(2) Work that has not yet been completed or abandoned. However, "your work" will be deemed completed at the earliest of the following times:

(a) When all of the work called for in your contract has been completed.

(b) When all of the work to be done at the job site has been completed if your contract calls for work at more than one job site.

(c) When that part of the work done at a job site has been put to its intended use by any person or organization other than another contractor or subcontractor working on the same project.

Work that may need service, maintenance, correction, repair or replacement, but which is otherwise complete, will be treated as completed.

b. Does not include "bodily injury" or "property damage" arising out of:

(1) The transportation of property, unless the injury or damage arises out of a condition in or on a vehicle not owned or operated by you, and that condition was created by the "loading or unloading" of that vehicle by any insured;

(2) The existence of tools, uninstalled equipment or abandoned or unused materials; or

(3) Products or operations for which the classification, listed in the Declarations or in a policy Schedule, states that products-completed operations are subject to the General Aggregate Limit.

17. "Property damage" means:

a. Physical injury to tangible property, including all resulting loss of use of that property. All such loss of use shall be deemed to occur at the time of the physical injury that caused it; or

b. Loss of use of tangible property that is not physically injured. All such loss of use shall be deemed to occur at the time of the "occurrence" that caused it.

For the purposes of this insurance, electronic data is not tangible property.

As used in this definition, electronic data means information, facts or programs stored as or on, created or used on, or transmitted to or from, computer software, including systems and applications software, hard or floppy disks, CD-ROMs, tapes, drives, cells, data processing devices or any other media which are used with electronically controlled equipment.

18. "Suit" means a civil proceeding in which damages because of "bodily injury", "property damage" or "personal and advertising injury" to which this insurance applies are alleged. "Suit" includes:

a. An arbitration proceeding in which such damages are claimed and to which the insured must submit or does submit with our consent; or

b. Any other alternative dispute resolution proceeding in which such damages are claimed and to which the insured submits with our consent.

19. "Temporary worker" means a person who is furnished to you to substitute for a permanent "employee" on leave or to meet seasonal or short-term workload conditions.

20. "Volunteer worker" means a person who is not your "employee", and who donates his or her work and acts at the direction of and within the scope of duties determined by you, and is not paid a fee, salary or other compensation by you or anyone else for their work performed for you.

21. "Your product":

a. Means:

(1) Any goods or products, other than real property, manufactured, sold, handled, distributed or disposed of by:

(a) You;

(b) Others trading under your name; or

(c) A person or organization whose business or assets you have acquired; and

(2) Containers (other than vehicles), materials, parts or equipment furnished in connection with such goods or products.

b. Includes:

(1) Warranties or representations made at any time with respect to the fitness, quality, durability, performance or use of "your product"; and

(2) The providing of or failure to provide warnings or instructions.

c. Does not include vending machines or other property rented to or located for the use of others but not sold.

22. "Your work":

a. Means:

(1) Work or operations performed by you or on your behalf; and

(2) Materials, parts or equipment furnished in connection with such work or operations.

b. Includes:

(1) Warranties or representations made at any time with respect to the fitness, quality, durability, performance or use of "your work"; and

(2) The providing of or failure to provide warnings or instructions.

POLICY NUMBER:

COMMERCIAL GENERAL LIABILITY
CG DS 01 10 01

COMMERCIAL GENERAL LIABILITY DECLARATIONS

COMPANY NAME AREA	**PRODUCER NAME AREA**

NAMED INSURED: _____

MAILING ADDRESS: _____

_____

POLICY PERIOD: FROM _____ TO _____ AT 12:01 A.M. TIME AT
YOUR MAILING ADDRESS SHOWN ABOVE

IN RETURN FOR THE PAYMENT OF THE PREMIUM, AND SUBJECT TO ALL THE TERMS OF THIS POLICY, WE AGREE WITH YOU TO PROVIDE THE INSURANCE AS STATED IN THIS POLICY.

LIMITS OF INSURANCE		
EACH OCCURRENCE LIMIT	$ _____	
DAMAGE TO PREMISES RENTED TO YOU LIMIT	$ _____	Any one premises
MEDICAL EXPENSE LIMIT	$ _____	Any one person
PERSONAL & ADVERTISING INJURY LIMIT	$ _____	Any one person or organization
GENERAL AGGREGATE LIMIT	$ _____	
PRODUCTS/COMPLETED OPERATIONS AGGREGATE LIMIT	$ _____	

RETROACTIVE DATE (CG 00 02 ONLY)

THIS INSURANCE DOES NOT APPLY TO "BODILY INJURY", "PROPERTY DAMAGE" OR "PERSONAL AND ADVERTISING INJURY" WHICH OCCURS BEFORE THE RETROACTIVE DATE, IF ANY, SHOWN BELOW.

RETROACTIVE DATE: _____

(ENTER DATE OR "NONE" IF NO RETROACTIVE DATE APPLIES)

DESCRIPTION OF BUSINESS

FORM OF BUSINESS:

☐ INDIVIDUAL   ☐ PARTNERSHIP   ☐ JOINT VENTURE   ☐ TRUST

☐ LIMITED LIABILITY COMPANY   ☐ ORGANIZATION, INCLUDING A CORPORATION (BUT NOT IN-CLUDING A PARTNERSHIP, JOINT VENTURE OR LIMITED LIABILITY COMPANY)

BUSINESS DESCRIPTION: _____

ALL PREMISES YOU OWN, RENT OR OCCUPY	
LOCATION NUMBER	ADDRESS OF ALL PREMISES YOU OWN, RENT OR OCCUPY

CLASSIFICATION AND PREMIUM							
LOCATION NUMBER	CLASSIFICATION	CODE NO.	PREMIUM BASE	RATE		ADVANCE PREMIUM	
				Prem/ Ops	Prod/Comp Ops	Prem/ Ops	Prod/Comp Ops
			$	$	$	$	$

	STATE TAX OR OTHER (if applicable)	$ _____
	TOTAL PREMIUM (SUBJECT TO AUDIT)	$ _____
PREMIUM SHOWN IS PAYABLE:	AT INCEPTION	$ _____
	AT EACH ANNIVERSARY	$ _____
	(IF POLICY PERIOD IS MORE THAN ONE YEAR AND PREMIUM IS PAID IN ANNUAL INSTALLMENTS)	

AUDIT PERIOD (IF APPLICABLE)	☐ ANNUALLY	☐ SEMI-ANNUALLY	☐ QUARTERLY	☐ MONTHLY

ENDORSEMENTS
ENDORSEMENTS ATTACHED TO THIS POLICY:
_____
_____
_____

THESE DECLARATIONS, TOGETHER WITH THE COMMON POLICY CONDITIONS AND COVERAGE FORM(S) AND ANY ENDORSEMENT(S), COMPLETE THE ABOVE NUMBERED POLICY.

Countersigned:	By:
(Date)	(Authorized Representative)

NOTE

OFFICERS' FACSIMILE SIGNATURES MAY BE INSERTED HERE, ON THE POLICY COVER OR ELSEWHERE AT THE COMPANY'S OPTION.

IL 00 17 11 98

COMMON POLICY CONDITIONS

All Coverage Parts included in this policy are subject to the following conditions.

A. Cancellation

1. The first Named Insured shown in the Declarations may cancel this policy by mailing or delivering to us advance written notice of cancellation.

2. We may cancel this policy by mailing or delivering to the first Named Insured written notice of cancellation at least:

   a. 10 days before the effective date of cancellation if we cancel for nonpayment of premium; or

   b. 30 days before the effective date of cancellation if we cancel for any other reason.

3. We will mail or deliver our notice to the first Named Insured's last mailing address known to us.

4. Notice of cancellation will state the effective date of cancellation. The policy period will end on that date.

5. If this policy is cancelled, we will send the first Named Insured any premium refund due. If we cancel, the refund will be pro rata. If the first Named Insured cancels, the refund may be less than pro rata. The cancellation will be effective even if we have not made or offered a refund.

6. If notice is mailed, proof of mailing will be sufficient proof of notice.

B. Changes

This policy contains all the agreements between you and us concerning the insurance afforded. The first Named Insured shown in the Declarations is authorized to make changes in the terms of this policy with our consent. This policy's terms can be amended or waived only by endorsement issued by us and made a part of this policy.

C. Examination Of Your Books And Records

We may examine and audit your books and records as they relate to this policy at any time during the policy period and up to three years afterward.

D. Inspections And Surveys

1. We have the right to:

   a. Make inspections and surveys at any time;

   b. Give you reports on the conditions we find; and

   c. Recommend changes.

2. We are not obligated to make any inspections, surveys, reports or recommendations and any such actions we do undertake relate only to insurability and the premiums to be charged. We do not make safety inspections. We do not undertake to perform the duty of any person or organization to provide for the health or safety of workers or the public. And we do not warrant that conditions:

   a. Are safe or healthful; or

   b. Comply with laws, regulations, codes or standards.

3. Paragraphs 1. and 2. of this condition apply not only to us, but also to any rating, advisory, rate service or similar organization which makes insurance inspections, surveys, reports or recommendations.

4. Paragraph 2. of this condition does not apply to any inspections, surveys, reports or recommendations we may make relative to certification, under state or municipal statutes, ordinances or regulations, of boilers, pressure vessels or elevators.

E. Premiums

The first Named Insured shown in the Declarations:

1. Is responsible for the payment of all premiums; and

2. Will be the payee for any return premiums we pay.

F. Transfer Of Your Rights And Duties Under This Policy

Your rights and duties under this policy may not be transferred without our written consent except in the case of death of an individual named insured.

If you die, your rights and duties will be transferred to your legal representative but only while acting within the scope of duties as your legal representative. Until your legal representative is appointed, anyone having proper temporary custody of your property will have your rights and duties but only with respect to that property.

COMMERCIAL LIABILITY UMBRELLA COVERAGE FORM

Various provisions in this policy restrict coverage. Read the entire policy carefully to determine rights, duties and what is and is not covered.

Throughout this policy the words "you" and "your" refer to the Named Insured shown in the Declarations, and any other person or organization qualifying as a Named Insured under this policy. The words "we", "us" and "our" refer to the company providing this insurance.

The word "insured" means any person or organization qualifying as such under Section II – Who Is An Insured.

Other words and phrases that appear in quotation marks have special meaning. Refer to Section V – Definitions.

SECTION I – COVERAGES

COVERAGE A – BODILY INJURY AND PROPERTY DAMAGE LIABILITY

1. Insuring Agreement

a. We will pay on behalf of the insured the "ultimate net loss" in excess of the "retained limit" because of "bodily injury" or "property damage" to which this insurance applies. We will have the right and duty to defend the insured against any "suit" seeking damages for such "bodily injury" or "property damage" when the "underlying insurance" does not provide coverage or the limits of "underlying insurance" have been exhausted. When we have no duty to defend, we will have the right to defend, or to participate in the defense of, the insured against any other "suit" seeking damages to which this insurance may apply. However, we will have no duty to defend the insured against any "suit" seeking damages for "bodily injury" or "property damage" to which this insurance does not apply. At our discretion, we may investigate any "occurrence" that may involve this insurance and settle any resultant claim or "suit" for which we have the duty to defend. But:

(1) The amount we will pay for the "ultimate net loss" is limited as described in Section III – Limits Of Insurance; and

(2) Our right and duty to defend ends when we have used up the applicable limit of insurance in the payment of judgments or settlements under Coverages **A** or **B**.

No other obligation or liability to pay sums or perform acts or services is covered unless explicitly provided for under Supplementary Payments – Coverages **A** and **B**.

b. This insurance applies to "bodily injury" or "property damage" that is subject to an applicable "retained limit". If any other limit, such as a sublimit, is specified in the "underlying insurance", this insurance does not apply to "bodily injury" or "property damage" arising out of that exposure unless that limit is specified in the Declarations under the Schedule of "underlying insurance".

c. This insurance applies to "bodily injury" and "property damage" only if:

(1) The "bodily injury" or "property damage" is caused by an "occurrence" that takes place in the "coverage territory";

(2) The "bodily injury" or "property damage" occurs during the policy period; and

(3) Prior to the policy period, no insured listed under Paragraph **1.a.** of Section II – Who Is An Insured and no "employee" authorized by you to give or receive notice of an "occurrence" or claim, knew that the "bodily injury" or "property damage" had occurred, in whole or in part. If such a listed insured or authorized "employee" knew, prior to the policy period, that the "bodily injury" or "property damage" occurred, then any continuation, change or resumption of such "bodily injury" or "property damage" during or after the policy period will be deemed to have been known prior to the policy period.

d. "Bodily injury" or "property damage" which occurs during the policy period and was not, prior to the policy period, known to have occurred by any insured listed under Paragraph **1.a.** of Section II – Who Is An Insured or any "employee" authorized by you to give or receive notice of an "occurrence" or claim, includes any continuation, change or resumption of that "bodily injury" or "property damage" after the end of the policy period.

e. "Bodily injury" or "property damage" will be deemed to have been known to have occurred at the earliest time when any insured listed under Paragraph **1.a.** of Section **II** – Who Is An Insured or any "employee" authorized by you to give or receive notice of an "occurrence" or claim:

  (1) Reports all, or any part, of the "bodily injury" or "property damage" to us or any other insurer;

  (2) Receives a written or verbal demand or claim for damages because of the "bodily injury" or "property damage"; or

  (3) Becomes aware by any other means that "bodily injury" or "property damage" has occurred or has begun to occur.

f. Damages because of "bodily injury" include damages claimed by any person or organization for care, loss of services or death resulting at any time from the "bodily injury".

2. Exclusions

This insurance does not apply to:

a. Expected Or Intended Injury

"Bodily injury" or "property damage" expected or intended from the standpoint of the insured. This exclusion does not apply to "bodily injury" resulting from the use of reasonable force to protect persons or property.

b. Contractual Liability

"Bodily injury" or "property damage" for which the insured is obligated to pay damages by reason of the assumption of liability in a contract or agreement. This exclusion does not apply to liability for damages:

  (1) That the insured would have in the absence of the contract or agreement; or

  (2) Assumed in a contract or agreement that is an "insured contract", provided the "bodily injury" or "property damage" occurs subsequent to the execution of the contract or agreement. Solely for the purposes of liability assumed in an "insured contract", reasonable attorneys' fees and necessary litigation expenses incurred by or for a party other than an insured are deemed to be damages because of "bodily injury" or "property damage", provided:

    (a) Liability to such party for, or for the cost of, that party's defense has also been assumed in the same "insured contract"; and

    (b) Such attorneys' fees and litigation expenses are for defense of that party against a civil or alternative dispute resolution proceeding in which damages to which this insurance applies are alleged.

c. Liquor Liability

"Bodily injury" or "property damage" for which any insured may be held liable by reason of:

  (1) Causing or contributing to the intoxication of any person;

  (2) The furnishing of alcoholic beverages to a person under the legal drinking age or under the influence of alcohol; or

  (3) Any statute, ordinance or regulation relating to the sale, gift, distribution or use of alcoholic beverages.

This exclusion applies even if the claims against any insured allege negligence or other wrongdoing in:

  (a) The supervision, hiring, employment, training or monitoring of others by that insured; or

  (b) Providing or failing to provide transportation with respect to any person that may be under the influence of alcohol;

if the "occurrence" which caused the "bodily injury" or "property damage" involved that which is described in Paragraph **(1)**, **(2)** or **(3)** above.

However, this exclusion applies only if you are in the business of manufacturing, distributing, selling, serving or furnishing alcoholic beverages. For the purposes of this exclusion, permitting a person to bring alcoholic beverages on your premises, for consumption on your premises, whether or not a fee is charged or a license is required for such activity, is not by itself considered the business of selling, serving or furnishing alcoholic beverages.

This exclusion does not apply to the extent that valid "underlying insurance" for the liquor liability risks described above exists or would have existed but for the exhaustion of underlying limits for "bodily injury" and "property damage". To the extent this exclusion does not apply, the insurance provided under this Coverage Part for the liquor liability risks described above will follow the same provisions, exclusions and limitations that are contained in the applicable "underlying insurance", unless otherwise directed by this insurance.

d. Workers' Compensation And Similar Laws

Any obligation of the insured under a workers' compensation, disability benefits or unemployment compensation law or any similar law.

e. ERISA

Any obligation of the insured under the Employee Retirement Income Security Act of 1974 (ERISA), and any amendments thereto or any similar federal, state or local statute.

f. Auto Coverages

(1) "Bodily injury" or "property damage" arising out of the ownership, maintenance or use of any "auto" which is not a "covered auto"; or

(2) Any loss, cost or expense payable under or resulting from any first-party physical damage coverage; no-fault law; personal injury protection or auto medical payments coverage; or uninsured or underinsured motorist law.

g. Employer's Liability

"Bodily injury" to:

(1) An "employee" of the insured arising out of and in the course of:

(a) Employment by the insured; or

(b) Performing duties related to the conduct of the insured's business; or

(2) The spouse, child, parent, brother or sister of that "employee" as a consequence of Paragraph **(1)** above.

This exclusion applies whether the insured may be liable as an employer or in any other capacity, and to any obligation to share damages with or repay someone else who must pay damages because of the injury.

This exclusion does not apply to liability assumed by the insured under an "insured contract".

With respect to injury arising out of a "covered auto", this exclusion does not apply to "bodily injury" to domestic "employees" not entitled to workers' compensation benefits. For the purposes of this insurance, a domestic "employee" is a person engaged in household or domestic work performed principally in connection with a residence premises.

This exclusion does not apply to the extent that valid "underlying insurance" for the employer's liability risks described above exists or would have existed but for the exhaustion of underlying limits for "bodily injury". To the extent this exclusion does not apply, the insurance provided under this Coverage Part for the employer's liability risks described above will follow the same provisions, exclusions and limitations that are contained in the applicable "underlying insurance", unless otherwise directed by this insurance.

h. Employment-related Practices

"Bodily injury" to:

(1) A person arising out of any:

(a) Refusal to employ that person;

(b) Termination of that person's employment; or

(c) Employment-related practices, policies, acts or omissions, such as coercion, demotion, evaluation, reassignment, discipline, defamation, harassment, humiliation, discrimination or malicious prosecution directed at that person; or

(2) The spouse, child, parent, brother or sister of that person as a consequence of "bodily injury" to that person at whom any of the employment-related practices described in Paragraph **(a)**, **(b)**, or **(c)** above is directed.

This exclusion applies whether the injury-causing event described in Paragraph **(a)**, **(b)** or **(c)** above occurs before employment, during employment or after employment of that person.

This exclusion applies whether the insured may be liable as an employer or in any other capacity, and to any obligation to share damages with or repay someone else who must pay damages because of the injury.

i. Pollution

(1) "Bodily injury" or "property damage" which would not have occurred in whole or part but for the actual, alleged or threatened discharge, dispersal, seepage, migration, release or escape of "pollutants" at any time; or

(2) "Pollution cost or expense".

This exclusion does not apply if valid "underlying insurance" for the pollution liability risks described above exists or would have existed but for the exhaustion of underlying limits for "bodily injury" and "property damage". To the extent this exclusion does not apply, the insurance provided under this Coverage Part for the pollution risks described above will follow the same provisions, exclusions and limitations that are contained in the applicable "underlying insurance", unless otherwise directed by this insurance.

j. Aircraft Or Watercraft

"Bodily injury" or "property damage" arising out of the ownership, maintenance, use or entrustment to others of any aircraft or watercraft owned or operated by or rented or loaned to any insured. Use includes operation and "loading or unloading".

This exclusion applies even if the claims against any insured allege negligence or other wrongdoing in the supervision, hiring, employment, training or monitoring of others by that insured, if the "occurrence" which caused the "bodily injury" or "property damage" involved the ownership, maintenance, use or entrustment to others of any aircraft or watercraft that is owned or operated by or rented or loaned to any insured.

This exclusion does not apply to:

(1) A watercraft while ashore on premises you own or rent;

(2) A watercraft you do not own that is:

  (a) Less than 50 feet long; and

  (b) Not being used to carry persons or property for a charge;

(3) Liability assumed under any "insured contract" for the ownership, maintenance or use of aircraft or watercraft;

(4) The extent that valid "underlying insurance" for the aircraft or watercraft liability risks described above exists or would have existed but for the exhaustion of underlying limits for "bodily injury" or "property damage". To the extent this exclusion does not apply, the insurance provided under this Coverage Part for the aircraft or watercraft risks described above will follow the same provisions, exclusions and limitations that are contained in the "underlying insurance", unless otherwise directed by this insurance; or

(5) Aircraft that is:

  (a) Chartered by, loaned to, or hired by you with a paid crew; and

  (b) Not owned by any insured.

k. Racing Activities

"Bodily injury" or "property damage" arising out of the use of "mobile equipment" or "autos" in, or while in practice for, or while being prepared for, any prearranged professional or organized racing, speed, demolition, or stunting activity or contest.

l. War

"Bodily injury" or "property damage", however caused, arising, directly or indirectly, out of:

(1) War, including undeclared or civil war;

(2) Warlike action by a military force, including action in hindering or defending against an actual or expected attack, by any government, sovereign or other authority using military personnel or other agents; or

(3) Insurrection, rebellion, revolution, usurped power, or action taken by governmental authority in hindering or defending against any of these.

m. Damage To Property

"Property damage" to:

(1) Property:

  (a) You own, rent, or occupy, including any costs or expenses incurred by you, or any other person, organization or entity, for repair, replacement, enhancement, restoration or maintenance of such property for any reason, including prevention of injury to a person or damage to another's property; or

  (b) Owned or transported by the insured and arising out of the ownership, maintenance or use of a "covered auto".

(2) Premises you sell, give away or abandon, if the "property damage" arises out of any part of those premises;

(3) Property loaned to you;

(4) Personal property in the care, custody or control of the insured;

(5) That particular part of real property on which you or any contractors or subcontractors working directly or indirectly on your behalf are performing operations, if the "property damage" arises out of those operations; or

(6) That particular part of any property that must be restored, repaired or replaced because "your work" was incorrectly performed on it.

Paragraph (2) of this exclusion does not apply if the premises are "your work" and were never occupied, rented or held for rental by you.

Paragraphs (1)(b), (3), (4), (5) and (6) of this exclusion do not apply to liability assumed under a sidetrack agreement.

Paragraphs (3) and (4) of this exclusion do not apply to liability assumed under a written Trailer Interchange agreement.

Paragraph (6) of this exclusion does not apply to "property damage" included in the "products-completed operations hazard".

n. Damage To Your Product

"Property damage" to "your product" arising out of it or any part of it.

o. Damage To Your Work

"Property damage" to "your work" arising out of it or any part of it and included in the "products-completed operations hazard".

This exclusion does not apply if the damaged work or the work out of which the damage arises was performed on your behalf by a subcontractor.

p. Damage To Impaired Property Or Property Not Physically Injured

"Property damage" to "impaired property" or property that has not been physically injured, arising out of:

(1) A defect, deficiency, inadequacy or dangerous condition in "your product" or "your work"; or

(2) A delay or failure by you or anyone acting on your behalf to perform a contract or agreement in accordance with its terms.

This exclusion does not apply to the loss of use of other property arising out of sudden and accidental physical injury to "your product" or "your work" after it has been put to its intended use.

q. Recall Of Products, Work Or Impaired Property

Damages claimed for any loss, cost or expense incurred by you or others for the loss of use, withdrawal, recall, inspection, repair, replacement, adjustment, removal or disposal of:

(1) "Your product";

(2) "Your work"; or

(3) "Impaired property";

if such product, work, or property is withdrawn or recalled from the market or from use by any person or organization because of a known or suspected defect, deficiency, inadequacy or dangerous condition in it.

r. Personal And Advertising Injury

"Bodily injury" arising out of "personal and advertising injury".

s. Professional Services

"Bodily injury" or "property damage" due to rendering of or failure to render any professional service. This includes but is not limited to:

(1) Legal, accounting or advertising services;

(2) Preparing, approving, or failing to prepare or approve, maps, shop drawings, opinions, reports, surveys, field orders, change orders or drawings or specifications;

(3) Inspection, supervision, quality control, architectural or engineering activities done by or for you on a project on which you serve as construction manager;

(4) Engineering services, including related supervisory or inspection services;

(5) Medical, surgical, dental, X-ray or nursing services treatment, advice or instruction;

(6) Any health or therapeutic service treatment, advice or instruction;

(7) Any service, treatment, advice or instruction for the purpose of appearance or skin enhancement, hair removal or replacement, or personal grooming or therapy;

(8) Any service, treatment, advice or instruction relating to physical fitness, including service, treatment, advice or instruction in connection with diet, cardiovascular fitness, bodybuilding or physical training programs;

(9) Optometry or optical or hearing aid services including the prescribing, preparation, fitting, demonstration or distribution of ophthalmic lenses and similar products or hearing aid devices;

(10) Body piercing services;

(11) Services in the practice of pharmacy;

(12) Law enforcement or firefighting services; and

(13) Handling, embalming, disposal, burial, cremation or disinterment of dead bodies.

This exclusion applies even if the claims against any insured allege negligence or other wrongdoing in the supervision, hiring, employment, training or monitoring of others by that insured, if the "occurrence" which caused the "bodily injury" or "property damage", involved the rendering of or failure to render any professional service.

t. Electronic Data

Damages arising out of the loss of, loss of use of, damage to, corruption of, inability to access or inability to manipulate electronic data.

However, this exclusion does not apply to liability for damages because of "bodily injury".

As used in this exclusion, electronic data means information, facts or programs stored as or on, created or used on, or transmitted to or from computer software, including systems and applications software, hard or floppy disks, CD-ROMs, tapes, drives, cells, data processing devices or any other media which are used with electronically controlled equipment.

This exclusion does not apply if valid "underlying insurance" for the electronic data risks described above exists or would have existed but for the exhaustion of underlying limits for "bodily injury" and "property damage". The insurance provided under this Coverage Part will follow the same provisions, exclusions and limitations that are contained in the applicable "underlying insurance", unless otherwise directed by this insurance.

u. Recording And Distribution Of Material Or Information In Violation Of Law

"Bodily injury" or "property damage" arising directly or indirectly out of any action or omission that violates or is alleged to violate:

(1) The Telephone Consumer Protection Act (TCPA), including any amendment of or addition to such law;

(2) The CAN-SPAM Act of 2003, including any amendment of or addition to such law;

(3) The Fair Credit Reporting Act (FCRA), and any amendment of or addition to such law, including the Fair and Accurate Credit Transactions Act (FACTA); or

(4) Any federal, state or local statute, ordinance or regulation, other than the TCPA, CAN-SPAM Act of 2003 or FCRA and their amendments and additions, that addresses, prohibits, or limits the printing, dissemination, disposal, collecting, recording, sending, transmitting, communicating or distribution of material or information.

COVERAGE B – PERSONAL AND ADVERTISING INJURY LIABILITY

1. Insuring Agreement

a. We will pay on behalf of the insured the "ultimate net loss" in excess of the "retained limit" because of "personal and advertising injury" to which this insurance applies. We will have the right and duty to defend the insured against any "suit" seeking damages for such "personal and advertising injury" when the "underlying insurance" does not provide coverage or the limits of "underlying insurance" have been exhausted. When we have no duty to defend, we will have the right to defend, or to participate in the defense of, the insured against any other "suit" seeking damages to which this insurance may apply. However, we will have no duty to defend the insured against any "suit" seeking damages for "personal and advertising injury" to which this insurance does not apply. At our discretion, we may investigate any offense that may involve this insurance and settle any resultant claim or "suit" for which we have the duty to defend. But:

(1) The amount we will pay for the "ultimate net loss" is limited as described in Section III – Limits Of Insurance; and

(2) Our right and duty to defend end when we have used up the applicable limit of insurance in the payment of judgments or settlements under Coverages **A** or **B**.

No other obligation or liability to pay sums or perform acts or services is covered unless explicitly provided for under Supplementary Payments – Coverages **A** and **B**.

b. This insurance applies to "personal and advertising injury" that is subject to an applicable "retained limit". If any other limit, such as a sublimit, is specified in the "underlying insurance", this insurance does not apply to "personal and advertising injury" arising out of that exposure unless that limit is specified in the Declarations under the Schedule of "underlying insurance".

c. This insurance applies to "personal and advertising injury" caused by an offense arising out of your business but only if the offense was committed in the "coverage territory" during the policy period.

             CU 00 01 04 13

2. Exclusions

This insurance does not apply to:

a. "Personal and advertising injury":

(1) Knowing Violation Of Rights Of Another

Caused by or at the direction of the insured with the knowledge that the act would violate the rights of another and would inflict "personal and advertising injury".

(2) Material Published With Knowledge Of Falsity

Arising out of oral or written publication, in any manner, of material, if done by or at the direction of the insured with knowledge of its falsity.

(3) Material Published Prior To Policy Period

Arising out of oral or written publication, in any manner, of material whose first publication took place before the beginning of the policy period.

(4) Criminal Acts

Arising out of a criminal act committed by or at the direction of the insured.

(5) Contractual Liability

For which the insured has assumed liability in a contract or agreement. This exclusion does not apply to:

(a) Liability for damages that the insured would have in the absence of the contract or agreement.

(b) Liability for false arrest, detention or imprisonment assumed in a contract or agreement.

(6) Breach Of Contract

Arising out of a breach of contract, except an implied contract to use another's advertising idea in your "advertisement".

(7) Quality Or Performance Of Goods – Failure To Conform To Statements

Arising out of the failure of goods, products or services to conform with any statement of quality or performance made in your "advertisement".

(8) Wrong Description Of Prices

Arising out of the wrong description of the price of goods, products or services stated in your "advertisement".

(9) Infringement Of Copyright, Patent, Trademark Or Trade Secret

Arising out of the infringement of copyright, patent, trademark, trade secret or other intellectual property rights. Under this exclusion, such other intellectual property rights do not include the use of another's advertising idea in your "advertisement".

However, this exclusion does not apply to infringement, in your "advertisement", of copyright, trade dress or slogan.

(10) Insureds In Media And Internet Type Businesses

Committed by an insured whose business is:

(a) Advertising, broadcasting, publishing or telecasting;

(b) Designing or determining content of web sites for others; or

(c) An Internet search, access, content or service provider.

However, this exclusion does not apply to Paragraphs 14.a., b. and c. of "personal and advertising injury" under the Definitions section.

For the purposes of this exclusion, the placing of frames, borders or links, or advertising, for you or others anywhere on the Internet, is not by itself, considered the business of advertising, broadcasting, publishing or telecasting.

(11) Electronic Chatrooms Or Bulletin Boards

Arising out of an electronic chatroom or bulletin board the insured hosts, owns, or over which the insured exercises control.

(12) Unauthorized Use Of Another's Name Or Product

Arising out of the unauthorized use of another's name or product in your e-mail address, domain name or metatag, or any other similar tactics to mislead another's potential customers.

(13) Pollution

Arising out of the actual, alleged or threatened discharge, dispersal, seepage, migration, release or escape of "pollutants" at any time.

(14) Employment-related Practices

To:

(a) A person arising out of any:

(i) Refusal to employ that person;

(ii) Termination of that person's employment; or

(iii) Employment-related practices, policies, acts or omissions, such as coercion, demotion, evaluation, reassignment, discipline, defamation, harassment, humiliation, discrimination or malicious prosecution directed at that person; or

(b) The spouse, child, parent, brother or sister of that person as a consequence of "personal and advertising injury" to that person at whom any of the employment-related practices described in Paragraph **(i)**, **(ii)** or **(iii)** above is directed.

This exclusion applies whether the injury-causing event described in Paragraph **(i)**, **(ii)** or **(iii)** above occurs before employment, during employment or after employment of that person.

This exclusion applies whether the insured may be liable as an employer or in any other capacity, and to any obligation to share damages with or repay someone else who must pay damages because of the injury.

(15) Professional Services

Arising out of the rendering of or failure to render any professional service. This includes but is not limited to:

(a) Legal, accounting or advertising services;

(b) Preparing, approving, or failing to prepare or approve, maps, shop drawings, opinions, reports, surveys, field orders, change orders or drawings or specifications;

(c) Inspection, supervision, quality control, architectural or engineering activities done by or for you on a project on which you serve as construction manager;

(d) Engineering services, including related supervisory or inspection services;

(e) Medical, surgical, dental, X-ray or nursing services treatment, advice or instruction;

(f) Any health or therapeutic service treatment, advice or instruction;

(g) Any service, treatment, advice or instruction for the purpose of appearance or skin enhancement, hair removal or replacement, or personal grooming or therapy;

(h) Any service, treatment, advice or instruction relating to physical fitness, including service, treatment, advice or instruction in connection with diet, cardiovascular fitness, bodybuilding or physical training programs;

(i) Optometry or optical or hearing aid services including the prescribing, preparation, fitting, demonstration or distribution of ophthalmic lenses and similar products or hearing aid devices;

(j) Body piercing services;

(k) Services in the practice of pharmacy;

(l) Law enforcement or firefighting services; and

(m) Handling, embalming, disposal, burial, cremation or disinterment of dead bodies.

This exclusion applies even if the claims against any insured allege negligence or other wrongdoing in the supervision, hiring, employment, training or monitoring of others by that insured, if the offense which caused the "personal and advertising injury", involved the rendering of or failure to render any professional service.

(16) War

However caused, arising, directly or indirectly, out of:

(a) War, including undeclared or civil war;

(b) Warlike action by a military force, including action in hindering or defending against an actual or expected attack, by any government, sovereign or other authority using military personnel or other agents; or

(c) Insurrection, rebellion, revolution, usurped power, or action taken by governmental authority in hindering or defending against any of these.

(17) Recording And Distribution Of Material Or Information In Violation Of Law

Arising directly or indirectly out of any action or omission that violates or is alleged to violate:

(a) The Telephone Consumer Protection Act (TCPA), including any amendment of or addition to such law;

(b) The CAN-SPAM Act of 2003, including any amendment of or addition to such law;

(c) The Fair Credit Reporting Act (FCRA), and any amendment of or addition to such law, including the Fair and Accurate Credit Transactions Act (FACTA); or

(d) Any federal, state or local statute, ordinance or regulation, other than the TCPA, CAN-SPAM Act of 2003 or FCRA and their amendments and additions, that addresses, prohibits, or limits the printing, dissemination, disposal, collecting, recording, sending, transmitting, communicating or distribution of material or information.

b. "Pollution cost or expense".

SUPPLEMENTARY PAYMENTS – COVERAGES A AND B

1. We will pay, with respect to any claim we investigate or settle, or any "suit" against an insured we defend, when the duty to defend exists:

a. All expenses we incur.

b. Up to $2,000 for cost of bail bonds (including bonds for related traffic law violations) required because of an "occurrence" we cover. We do not have to furnish these bonds.

c. The cost of bonds to release attachments, but only for bond amounts within the applicable limit of insurance. We do not have to furnish these bonds.

d. All reasonable expenses incurred by the insured at our request to assist us in the investigation or defense of the claim or "suit", including actual loss of earnings up to $250 a day because of time off from work.

e. All court costs taxed against the insured in the "suit". However, these payments do not include attorneys' fees or attorneys' expenses taxed against the insured.

f. Prejudgment interest awarded against the insured on that part of the judgment we pay. If we make an offer to pay the applicable limit of insurance, we will not pay any prejudgment interest based on that period of time after the offer.

g. All interest on the full amount of any judgment that accrues after entry of the judgment and before we have paid, offered to pay, or deposited in court the part of the judgment that is within the applicable limit of insurance.

These payments will not reduce the limits of insurance.

2. When we have the right but not the duty to defend the insured and elect to participate in the defense, we will pay our own expenses but will not contribute to the expenses of the insured or the "underlying insurer".

3. If we defend an insured against a "suit" and an indemnitee of the insured is also named as a party to the "suit", we will defend that indemnitee if all of the following conditions are met:

a. The "suit" against the indemnitee seeks damages for which the insured has assumed the liability of the indemnitee in a contract or agreement that is an "insured contract";

b. This insurance applies to such liability assumed by the insured;

c. The obligation to defend, or the cost of the defense of, that indemnitee, has also been assumed by the insured in the same "insured contract";

d. The allegations in the "suit" and the information we know about the "occurrence" are such that no conflict appears to exist between the interests of the insured and the interests of the indemnitee;

e. The indemnitee and the insured ask us to conduct and control the defense of that indemnitee against such "suit" and agree that we can assign the same counsel to defend the insured and the indemnitee; and

f. The indemnitee:

(1) Agrees in writing to:

(a) Cooperate with us in the investigation, settlement or defense of the "suit";

(b) Immediately send us copies of any demands, notices, summonses or legal papers received in connection with the "suit";

(c) Notify any other insurer whose coverage is available to the indemnitee; and

(d) Cooperate with us with respect to coordinating other applicable insurance available to the indemnitee; and

(2) Provides us with written authorization to:

(a) Obtain records and other information related to the "suit"; and

(b) Conduct and control the defense of the indemnitee in such "suit".

So long as the above conditions are met, attorneys' fees incurred by us in the defense of that indemnitee, necessary litigation expenses incurred by us and necessary litigation expenses incurred by the indemnitee at our request will be paid as Supplementary Payments. Notwithstanding the provisions of Paragraph **2.b.(2)** of Section **I** – Coverage **A** – Bodily Injury And Property Damage Liability, such payments will not be deemed to be damages for "bodily injury" and "property damage" and will not reduce the limits of insurance.

Our obligation to defend an insured's indemnitee and to pay for attorneys' fees and necessary litigation expenses as Supplementary Payments ends when we have used up the applicable limit of insurance in the payment of judgments or settlements or the conditions set forth above, or the terms of the agreement described in Paragraph **f.** above, are no longer met.

SECTION II – WHO IS AN INSURED

1. Except for liability arising out of the ownership, maintenance or use of "covered autos":

a. If you are designated in the Declarations as:

(1) An individual, you and your spouse are insureds, but only with respect to the conduct of a business of which you are the sole owner.

(2) A partnership or joint venture, you are an insured. Your members, your partners, and their spouses are also insureds, but only with respect to the conduct of your business.

(3) A limited liability company, you are an insured. Your members are also insureds, but only with respect to the conduct of your business. Your managers are insureds, but only with respect to their duties as your managers.

(4) An organization other than a partnership, joint venture or limited liability company, you are an insured. Your "executive officers" and directors are insureds, but only with respect to their duties as your officers or directors. Your stockholders are also insureds, but only with respect to their liability as stockholders.

(5) A trust, you are an insured. Your trustees are also insureds, but only with respect to their duties as trustees.

b. Each of the following is also an insured:

(1) Your "volunteer workers" only while performing duties related to the conduct of your business, or your "employees", other than either your "executive officers" (if you are an organization other than a partnership, joint venture or limited liability company) or your managers (if you are a limited liability company), but only for acts within the scope of their employment by you or while performing duties related to the conduct of your business. However, none of these "employees" or "volunteer workers" are insureds for:

(a) "Bodily injury" or "personal and advertising injury":

(i) To you, to your partners or members (if you are a partnership or joint venture), to your members (if you are a limited liability company), to a co-"employee" in the course of his or her employment or performing duties related to the conduct of your business or to your other "volunteer workers" while performing duties related to the conduct of your business;

(ii) To the spouse, child, parent, brother or sister of that co-"employee" or "volunteer worker" as a consequence of Paragraph **(a)(i)** above; or

(iii) For which there is any obligation to share damages with or repay someone else who must pay damages because of the injury described in Paragraph **(a)(i)** or **(ii)** above.

(b) "Property damage" to property:

(i) Owned, occupied or used by;

(ii) Rented to, in the care, custody or control of, or over which physical control is being exercised for any purpose by;

you, any of your "employees", "volunteer workers", any partner or member (if you are a partnership or joint venture), or any member (if you are a limited liability company).

(2) Any person (other than your "employee" or "volunteer worker"), or any organization while acting as your real estate manager.

(3) Any person or organization having proper temporary custody of your property if you die, but only:

    (a) With respect to liability arising out of the maintenance or use of that property; and

    (b) Until your legal representative has been appointed.

(4) Your legal representative if you die, but only with respect to duties as such. That representative will have all your rights and duties under this Coverage Part.

c. Any organization you newly acquire or form, other than a partnership, joint venture or limited liability company, and over which you maintain ownership or majority interest, will qualify as a Named Insured if there is no other similar insurance available to that organization. However:

(1) Coverage under this provision is afforded only until the 90th day after you acquire or form the organization or the end of the policy period, whichever is earlier;

(2) Coverage **A** does not apply to "bodily injury" or "property damage" that occurred before you acquired or formed the organization; and

(3) Coverage **B** does not apply to "personal and advertising injury" arising out of an offense committed before you acquired or formed the organization.

2. Only with respect to liability arising out of the ownership, maintenance or use of "covered autos":

a. You are an insured.

b. Anyone else while using with your permission a "covered auto" you own, hire or borrow is also an insured except:

(1) The owner or anyone else from whom you hire or borrow a "covered auto". This exception does not apply if the "covered auto" is a trailer or semitrailer connected to a "covered auto" you own.

(2) Your "employee" if the "covered auto" is owned by that "employee" or a member of his or her household.

(3) Someone using a "covered auto" while he or she is working in a business of selling, servicing, repairing, parking or storing "autos" unless that business is yours.

(4) Anyone other than your "employees", partners (if you are a partnership), members (if you are a limited liability company), or a lessee or borrower or any of their "employees", while moving property to or from a "covered auto".

(5) A partner (if you are a partnership), or a member (if you are a limited liability company) for a "covered auto" owned by him or her or a member of his or her household.

(6) "Employees" with respect to "bodily injury" to:

    (a) Any fellow "employee" of the insured arising out of and in the course of the fellow "employee's" employment or while performing duties related to the conduct of your business; or

    (b) The spouse, child, parent, brother or sister of that fellow "employee" as a consequence of Paragraph **(a)** above.

c. Anyone liable for the conduct of an insured described above is also an insured, but only to the extent of that liability.

3. Any additional insured under any policy of "underlying insurance" will automatically be an insured under this insurance.

Subject to Section **III** – Limits Of Insurance, if coverage provided to the additional insured is required by a contract or agreement, the most we will pay on behalf of the additional insured is the amount of insurance:

a. Required by the contract or agreement, less any amounts payable by any "underlying insurance"; or

b. Available under the applicable Limits of Insurance shown in the Declarations;

whichever is less.

Additional insured coverage provided by this insurance will not be broader than coverage provided by the "underlying insurance".

No person or organization is an insured with respect to the conduct of any current or past partnership, joint venture or limited liability company that is not shown as a Named Insured in the Declarations.

SECTION III – LIMITS OF INSURANCE

1. The Limits of Insurance shown in the Declarations and the rules below fix the most we will pay regardless of the number of:

   a. Insureds;

   b. Claims made, "suits" brought, or number of vehicles involved; or

   c. Persons or organizations making claims or bringing "suits".

2. The Aggregate Limit is the most we will pay for the sum of all "ultimate net loss" under:

   a. Coverage **A,** except "ultimate net loss" because of "bodily injury" or "property damage" arising out of the ownership, maintenance or use of a "covered auto"; and

   b. Coverage **B.**

3. Subject to Paragraph **2.** above, the Each Occurrence Limit is the most we will pay for the sum of all "ultimate net loss" under Coverage **A** because of all "bodily injury" and "property damage" arising out of any one "occurrence".

4. Subject to Paragraph **2.** above, the Personal And Advertising Injury Limit is the most we will pay under Coverage **B** for the sum of all "ultimate net loss" because of all "personal and advertising injury" sustained by any one person or organization.

5. If there is "underlying insurance" with a policy period that is nonconcurrent with the policy period of this Commercial Liability Umbrella Coverage Part, the "retained limit(s)" will only be reduced or exhausted by payments for:

   a. "Bodily injury" or "property damage" which occurs during the policy period of this Coverage Part; or

   b. "Personal and advertising injury" for offenses that are committed during the policy period of this Coverage Part.

   However, if any "underlying insurance" is written on a claims-made basis, the "retained limit(s)" will only be reduced or exhausted by claims for that insurance that are made during the policy period, or any Extended Reporting Period, of this Coverage Part.

The Aggregate Limit, as described in Paragraph **2.** above, applies separately to each consecutive annual period and to any remaining period of less than 12 months, starting with the beginning of the policy period shown in the Declarations, unless the policy period is extended after issuance for an additional period of less than 12 months. In that case, the additional period will be deemed part of the last preceding period for purposes of determining the Limits of Insurance.

SECTION IV – CONDITIONS

1. **Appeals**

   If the "underlying insurer" or insured elects not to appeal a judgment in excess of the "retained limit", we may do so at our own expense. We will also pay for taxable court costs, pre- and postjudgment interest and disbursements associated with such appeal. In no event will this provision increase our liability beyond the applicable Limits of Insurance described in Section **III** – Limits Of Insurance.

2. **Bankruptcy**

   a. **Bankruptcy Of Insured**

      Bankruptcy or insolvency of the insured or of the insured's estate will not relieve us of our obligations under this Coverage Part.

   b. **Bankruptcy Of Underlying Insurer**

      Bankruptcy or insolvency of the "underlying insurer" will not relieve us of our obligations under this Coverage Part.

   However, this insurance will not replace the "underlying insurance" in the event of bankruptcy or insolvency of the "underlying insurer". This insurance will apply as if the "underlying insurance" were in full effect.

3. **Duties In The Event Of Occurrence, Offense, Claim Or Suit**

   a. You must see to it that we are notified as soon as practicable of an "occurrence" or an offense, regardless of the amount, which may result in a claim. To the extent possible, notice should include:

      (1) How, when and where the "occurrence" or offense took place;

      (2) The names and addresses of any injured persons and witnesses; and

      (3) The nature and location of any injury or damage arising out of the "occurrence" or offense.

   b. If a claim is made or "suit" is brought against any insured, you must:

      (1) Immediately record the specifics of the claim or "suit" and the date received; and

      (2) Notify us as soon as practicable.

      You must see to it that we receive written notice of the claim or "suit" as soon as practicable.

   c. You and any other involved insured must:

      (1) Immediately send us copies of any demands, notices, summonses or legal papers received in connection with the claim or "suit";

(2) Authorize us to obtain records and other information;

(3) Cooperate with us in the investigation or settlement of the claim or defense against the "suit"; and

(4) Assist us, upon our request, in the enforcement of any right against any person or organization which may be liable to the insured because of injury or damage to which this insurance may also apply.

d. No insured will, except at that insured's own cost, voluntarily make a payment, assume any obligation, or incur any expense, other than for first aid, without our consent.

4. Legal Action Against Us

No person or organization has a right under this Coverage Part:

a. To join us as a party or otherwise bring us into a "suit" asking for damages from an insured; or

b. To sue us on this Coverage Part unless all of its terms have been fully complied with.

A person or organization may sue us to recover on an agreed settlement or on a final judgment against an insured; but we will not be liable for damages that are not payable under the terms of this Coverage Part or that are in excess of the applicable limit of insurance. An agreed settlement means a settlement and release of liability signed by us, the insured and the claimant or the claimant's legal representative.

5. Other Insurance

a. This insurance is excess over, and shall not contribute with any of the other insurance, whether primary, excess, contingent or on any other basis. This condition will not apply to insurance specifically written as excess over this Coverage Part.

When this insurance is excess, we will have no duty under Coverages **A** or **B** to defend the insured against any "suit" if any other insurer has a duty to defend the insured against that "suit". If no other insurer defends, we will undertake to do so, but we will be entitled to the insured's rights against all those other insurers.

b. When this insurance is excess over other insurance, we will pay only our share of the "ultimate net loss" that exceeds the sum of:

(1) The total amount that all such other insurance would pay for the loss in the absence of the insurance provided under this Coverage Part; and

(2) The total of all deductible and self-insured amounts under all that other insurance.

6. Premium Audit

a. We will compute all premiums for this Coverage Part in accordance with our rules and rates.

b. Premium shown in this Coverage Part as advance premium is a deposit premium only. At the close of each audit period we will compute the earned premium for that period and send notice to the first Named Insured. The due date for audit and retrospective premiums is the date shown as the due date on the bill. If the sum of the advance and audit premiums paid for the policy period is greater than the earned premium, we will return the excess to the first Named Insured.

c. The first Named Insured must keep records of the information we need for premium computation, and send us copies at such times as we may request.

7. Representations Or Fraud

By accepting this policy, you agree:

a. The statements in the Declarations are accurate and complete;

b. Those statements are based upon representations you made to us;

c. We have issued this policy in reliance upon your representations; and

d. This policy is void in any case of fraud by you as it relates to this policy or any claim under this policy.

8. Separation Of Insureds

Except with respect to the Limits of Insurance, and any rights or duties specifically assigned in this Coverage Part to the first Named Insured, this insurance applies:

a. As if each Named Insured were the only Named Insured; and

b. Separately to each insured against whom claim is made or "suit" is brought.

9. Transfer Of Rights Of Recovery Against Others To Us

If the insured has rights to recover all or part of any payment we have made under this Coverage Part, those rights are transferred to us. The insured must do nothing after loss to impair them. At our request, the insured will bring "suit" or transfer those rights to us and help us enforce them.

10. When We Do Not Renew

If we decide not to renew this Coverage Part, we will mail or deliver to the first Named Insured shown in the Declarations written notice of the nonrenewal not less than 30 days before the expiration date.

If notice is mailed, proof of mailing will be sufficient proof of notice.

11. Loss Payable

Liability under this Coverage Part does not apply to a given claim unless and until:

a. The insured or insured's "underlying insurer" has become obligated to pay the "retained limit"; and

b. The obligation of the insured to pay the "ultimate net loss" in excess of the "retained limit" has been determined by a final settlement or judgment or written agreement among the insured, claimant and us.

12. Transfer Of Defense

When the underlying limits of insurance have been used up in the payment of judgments or settlements, the duty to defend will be transferred to us. We will cooperate in the transfer of control to us of any outstanding claims or "suits" seeking damages to which this insurance applies which would have been covered by the "underlying insurance" had the applicable limit not been used up.

13. Maintenance Of/Changes To Underlying Insurance

Any "underlying insurance" must be maintained in full effect without reduction of coverage or limits except for the reduction of the aggregate limit in accordance with the provisions of such "underlying insurance" that results from payment of claims, settlement or judgments to which this insurance applies.

Such exhaustion or reduction is not a failure to maintain "underlying insurance". Failure to maintain "underlying insurance" will not invalidate insurance provided under this Coverage Part, but insurance provided under this Coverage Part will apply as if the "underlying insurance" were in full effect.

If there is an increase in the scope of coverage of any "underlying insurance" during the term of this policy, our liability will be no more than it would have been if there had been no such increase.

You must notify us in writing, as soon as practicable, if any "underlying insurance" is cancelled, not renewed, replaced or otherwise terminated, or if the limits or scope of coverage of any "underlying insurance" is changed.

14. Expanded Coverage Territory

a. If a "suit" is brought in a part of the "coverage territory" that is outside the United States of America (including its territories and possessions), Puerto Rico or Canada, and we are prevented by law, or otherwise, from defending the insured, the insured will initiate a defense of the "suit". We will reimburse the insured, under Supplementary Payments, for any reasonable and necessary expenses incurred for the defense of a "suit" seeking damages to which this insurance applies, that we would have paid had we been able to exercise our right and duty to defend.

If the insured becomes legally obligated to pay sums because of damages to which this insurance applies in a part of the "coverage territory" that is outside the United States of America (including its territories and possessions), Puerto Rico or Canada, and we are prevented by law, or otherwise, from paying such sums on the insured's behalf, we will reimburse the insured for such sums.

b. All payments or reimbursements we make for damages because of judgments or settlements will be made in U.S. currency at the prevailing exchange rate at the time the insured became legally obligated to pay such sums. All payments or reimbursements we make for expenses under Supplementary Payments will be made in U.S. currency at the prevailing exchange rate at the time the expenses were incurred.

c. Any disputes between you and us as to whether there is coverage under this policy must be filed in the courts of the United States of America (including its territories and possessions), Canada or Puerto Rico.

d. The insured must fully maintain any coverage required by law, regulation or other governmental authority during the policy period, except for reduction of the aggregate limits due to payments of claims, judgments or settlements.

Failure to maintain such coverage required by law, regulation or other governmental authority will not invalidate this insurance. However, this insurance will apply as if the required coverage by law, regulation or other governmental authority was in full effect.

                   CU 00 01 04 13

SECTION V – DEFINITIONS

1. "Advertisement" means a notice that is broadcast or published to the general public or specific market segments about your goods, products or services for the purpose of attracting customers or supporters. For the purposes of this definition:

   a. Notices that are published include material placed on the Internet or on similar electronic means of communication; and

   b. Regarding web sites, only that part of a web site that is about your goods, products or services for the purposes of attracting customers or supporters is considered an advertisement.

2. "Auto" means:

   a. A land motor vehicle, trailer or semitrailer designed for travel on public roads, including any attached machinery or equipment; or

   b. Any other land vehicle that is subject to a compulsory or financial responsibility law or other motor vehicle insurance law where it is licensed or principally garaged.

   However, "auto" does not include "mobile equipment".

3. "Bodily injury" means bodily injury, disability, sickness or disease sustained by a person, including death resulting from any of these at any time. "Bodily injury" includes mental anguish or other mental injury resulting from "bodily injury".

4. "Coverage territory" means anywhere in the world with the exception of any country or jurisdiction which is subject to trade or other economic sanction or embargo by the United States of America.

5. "Covered auto" means only those "autos" to which "underlying insurance" applies.

6. "Employee" includes a "leased worker". "Employee" does not include a "temporary worker".

7. "Executive officer" means a person holding any of the officer positions created by your charter, constitution, bylaws or any other similar governing document.

8. "Impaired property" means tangible property, other than "your product" or "your work", that cannot be used or is less useful because:

   a. It incorporates "your product" or "your work" that is known or thought to be defective, deficient, inadequate or dangerous; or

   b. You have failed to fulfill the terms of a contract or agreement;

if such property can be restored to use by the repair, replacement, adjustment or removal of "your product" or "your work", or your fulfilling the terms of the contract or agreement.

9. "Insured contract" means:

   a. A contract for a lease of premises. However that portion of the contract for a lease of premises that indemnifies any person or organization for damage by fire to premises while rented to you or temporarily occupied by you with permission of the owner is not an "insured contract";

   b. A sidetrack agreement;

   c. Any easement or license agreement, except in connection with construction or demolition operations on or within 50 feet of a railroad;

   d. An obligation, as required by ordinance, to indemnify a municipality, except in connection with work for a municipality;

   e. An elevator maintenance agreement;

   f. That part of any contract or agreement entered into, as part of your business, pertaining to the rental or lease, by you or any of your "employees", of any "auto". However, such contract or agreement shall not be considered an "insured contract" to the extent that it obligates you or any of your "employees" to pay for "property damage" to any "auto" rented or leased by you or any of your "employees".

   g. That part of any other contract or agreement pertaining to your business (including an indemnification of a municipality in connection with work performed for a municipality) under which you assume the tort liability of another party to pay for "bodily injury" or "property damage" to a third person or organization. Tort liability means a liability that would be imposed by law in the absence of any contract or agreement.

   Paragraphs f. and g. do not include that part of any contract or agreement:

   (1) That indemnifies a railroad for "bodily injury" or "property damage" arising out of construction or demolition operations, within 50 feet of any railroad property and affecting any railroad bridge or trestle, tracks, road-beds, tunnel, underpass or crossing;

   (2) That pertains to the loan, lease or rental of an "auto" to you or any of your "employees", if the "auto" is loaned, leased or rented with a driver; or

(3) That holds a person or organization engaged in the business of transporting property by "auto" for hire harmless for your use of a "covered auto" over a route or territory that person or organization is authorized to serve by public authority.

10. "Leased worker" means a person leased to you by a labor leasing firm under an agreement between you and the labor leasing firm, to perform duties related to the conduct of your business. "Leased worker" does not include a "temporary worker".

11. "Loading or unloading" means the handling of property:

a. After it is moved from the place where it is accepted for movement into or onto an aircraft, watercraft or "auto";

b. While it is in or on an aircraft, watercraft or "auto"; or

c. While it is being moved from an aircraft, watercraft or "auto" to the place where it is finally delivered;

but "loading or unloading" does not include the movement of property by means of a mechanical device, other than a hand truck, that is not attached to the aircraft, watercraft or "auto".

12. "Mobile equipment" means any of the following types of land vehicles, including any attached machinery or equipment:

a. Bulldozers, farm machinery, forklifts and other vehicles designed for use principally off public roads;

b. Vehicles maintained for use solely on or next to premises you own or rent;

c. Vehicles that travel on crawler treads;

d. Vehicles, whether self-propelled or not, maintained primarily to provide mobility to permanently mounted:

(1) Power cranes, shovels, loaders, diggers or drills; or

(2) Road construction or resurfacing equipment such as graders, scrapers or rollers;

e. Vehicles not described in Paragraph **a.**, **b.**, **c.** or **d.** above that are not self-propelled and are maintained primarily to provide mobility to permanently attached equipment of the following types:

(1) Air compressors, pumps and generators, including spraying, welding, building cleaning, geophysical exploration, lighting and well servicing equipment; or

(2) Cherry pickers and similar devices used to raise or lower workers;

f. Vehicles not described in Paragraph **a.**, **b.**, **c.** or **d.** above maintained primarily for purposes other than the transportation of persons or cargo.

However, self-propelled vehicles with the following types of permanently attached equipment are not "mobile equipment" but will be considered "autos":

(1) Equipment designed primarily for:

(a) Snow removal;

(b) Road maintenance, but not construction or resurfacing; or

(c) Street cleaning;

(2) Cherry pickers and similar devices mounted on automobile or truck chassis and used to raise or lower workers; and

(3) Air compressors, pumps and generators, including spraying, welding, building cleaning, geophysical exploration, lighting and well servicing equipment.

However, "mobile equipment" does not include land vehicles that are subject to a compulsory or financial responsibility law or other motor vehicle insurance law where it is licensed or principally garaged. Land vehicles subject to a compulsory or financial responsibility law or other motor vehicle insurance law are considered "autos".

13. "Occurrence" means an accident, including continuous or repeated exposure to substantially the same general harmful conditions.

14. "Personal and advertising injury" means injury, including consequential "bodily injury", arising out of one or more of the following offenses:

a. False arrest, detention or imprisonment;

b. Malicious prosecution;

c. The wrongful eviction from, wrongful entry into, or invasion of the right of private occupancy of a room, dwelling or premises that a person occupies, committed by or on behalf of its owner, landlord or lessor;

d. Oral or written publication, in any manner, of material that slanders or libels a person or organization or disparages a person's or organization's goods, products or services;

e. Oral or written publication, in any manner, of material that violates a person's right of privacy;

f. The use of another's advertising idea in your "advertisement"; or

g. Infringing upon another's copyright, trade dress or slogan in your "advertisement".

15. "Pollutants" mean any solid, liquid, gaseous or thermal irritant or contaminant, including smoke, vapor, soot, fumes, acids, alkalis, chemicals and waste. Waste includes materials to be recycled, reconditioned or reclaimed.

16. "Pollution cost or expense" means any loss, cost or expense arising out of any:

a. Request, demand, order or statutory or regulatory requirement that any insured or others test for, monitor, clean up, remove, contain, treat, detoxify or neutralize, or in any way respond to, or assess the effects of, "pollutants"; or

b. Claim or suit by or on behalf of a governmental authority for damages because of testing for, monitoring, cleaning up, removing, containing, treating, detoxifying or neutralizing, or in any way responding to, or assessing the effects of, "pollutants".

17. "Products-completed operations hazard":

a. Includes all "bodily injury" and "property damage" occurring away from premises you own or rent and arising out of "your product" or "your work" except:

(1) Products that are still in your physical possession; or

(2) Work that has not yet been completed or abandoned. However, "your work" will be deemed completed at the earliest of the following times:

(a) When all of the work called for in your contract has been completed.

(b) When all of the work to be done at the job site has been completed if your contract calls for work at more than one job site.

(c) When that part of the work done at a job site has been put to its intended use by any person or organization other than another contractor or subcontractor working on the same project.

Work that may need service, maintenance, correction, repair or replacement, but which is otherwise complete, will be treated as completed.

b. Does not include "bodily injury" or "property damage" arising out of:

(1) The transportation of property, unless the injury or damage arises out of a condition in or on a vehicle not owned or operated by you, and that condition was created by the "loading or unloading" of that vehicle by any insured; or

(2) The existence of tools, uninstalled equipment or abandoned or unused materials.

18. "Property damage" means:

a. Physical injury to tangible property, including all resulting loss of use of that property. All such loss of use shall be deemed to occur at the time of the physical injury that caused it; or

b. Loss of use of tangible property that is not physically injured. All such loss of use shall be deemed to occur at the time of the "occurrence" that caused it.

With respect to the ownership, maintenance or use of "covered autos", property damage also includes "pollution cost or expense", but only to the extent that coverage exists under the "underlying insurance" or would have existed but for the exhaustion of the underlying limits.

For the purposes of this insurance, with respect to other than the ownership, maintenance or use of "covered autos", electronic data is not tangible property.

As used in this definition, electronic data means information, facts or programs stored as or on, created or used on, or transmitted to or from computer software (including systems and applications software), hard or floppy disks, CD-ROMs, tapes, drives, cells, data processing devices or any other media which are used with electronically controlled equipment.

19. "Retained limit" means the available limits of "underlying insurance" scheduled in the Declarations or the "self-insured retention", whichever applies.

20. "Self-insured retention" means the dollar amount listed in the Declarations that will be paid by the insured before this insurance becomes applicable only with respect to "occurrences" or offenses not covered by the "underlying insurance". The "self-insured retention" does not apply to "occurrences" or offenses which would have been covered by "underlying insurance" but for the exhaustion of applicable limits.

21. "Suit" means a civil proceeding in which damages because of "bodily injury", "property damage" or "personal and advertising injury" to which this insurance applies are alleged. "Suit" includes:

a. An arbitration proceeding in which such damages are claimed and to which the insured must submit or does submit with our consent; or

b. Any other alternative dispute resolution proceeding in which such damages are claimed and to which the insured submits with our consent or the "underlying insurer's" consent.

22. "Temporary worker" means a person who is furnished to you to substitute for a permanent "employee" on leave or to meet seasonal or short-term workload conditions.

23. "Ultimate net loss" means the total sum, after reduction for recoveries or salvages collectible, that the insured becomes legally obligated to pay as damages by reason of settlement or judgments or any arbitration or other alternate dispute method entered into with our consent or the "underlying insurer's" consent.

24. "Underlying insurance" means any policies of insurance listed in the Declarations under the Schedule of "underlying insurance".

25. "Underlying insurer" means any insurer who provides any policy of insurance listed in the Schedule of "underlying insurance".

26. "Volunteer worker" means a person who is not your "employee", and who donates his or her work and acts at the direction of and within the scope of duties determined by you, and is not paid a fee, salary or other compensation by you or anyone else for their work performed for you.

27. "Your product":

  a. Means:

    (1) Any goods or products, other than real property, manufactured, sold, handled, distributed or disposed of by:

      (a) You;

      (b) Others trading under your name; or

      (c) A person or organization whose business or assets you have acquired; and

    (2) Containers (other than vehicles), materials, parts or equipment furnished in connection with such goods or products.

b. Includes:

  (1) Warranties or representations made at any time with respect to the fitness, quality, durability, performance or use of "your product"; and

  (2) The providing of or failure to provide warnings or instructions.

c. Does not include vending machines or other property rented to or located for the use of others but not sold.

28. "Your work":

  a. Means:

    (1) Work or operations performed by you or on your behalf; and

    (2) Materials, parts or equipment furnished in connection with such work or operations.

  b. Includes:

    (1) Warranties or representations made at any time with respect to the fitness, quality, durability, performance or use of "your work"; and

    (2) The providing of or failure to provide warnings or instructions.

COMMERCIAL EXCESS LIABILITY COVERAGE FORM

Various provisions in this policy restrict coverage. Read the entire policy carefully to determine rights, duties and what is and is not covered.

Throughout this policy the words "you" and "your" refer to the Named Insured shown in the Declarations, and any other person or organization qualifying as a Named Insured under this policy. The words "we", "us" and "our" refer to the company providing this insurance. The word "insured" means any person or organization qualifying as such under the "controlling underlying insurance".

Other words and phrases that appear in quotation marks in this Coverage Part have special meaning. Refer to Section **IV** – Definitions. Other words and phrases that are not defined under this Coverage Part but defined in the "controlling underlying insurance" will have the meaning described in the policy of "controlling underlying insurance".

The insurance provided under this Coverage Part will follow the same provisions, exclusions and limitations that are contained in the applicable "controlling underlying insurance", unless otherwise directed by this insurance. To the extent such provisions differ or conflict, the provisions of this Coverage Part will apply. However, the coverage provided under this Coverage Part will not be broader than that provided by the applicable "controlling underlying insurance".

There may be more than one "controlling underlying insurance" listed in the Declarations and provisions in those policies conflict, and which are not superseded by the provisions of this Coverage Part. In such a case, the provisions, exclusions and limitations of the "controlling underlying insurance" applicable to the particular "event" for which a claim is made or suit is brought will apply.

SECTION I – COVERAGES

1. Insuring Agreement

  a. We will pay on behalf of the insured the "ultimate net loss" in excess of the "retained limit" because of "injury or damage" to which insurance provided under this Coverage Part applies.

    We will have the right and duty to defend the insured against any suit seeking damages for such "injury or damage" when the applicable limits of "controlling underlying insurance" have been exhausted in accordance with the provisions of such "controlling underlying insurance".

When we have no duty to defend, we will have the right to defend, or to participate in the defense of, the insured against any other suit seeking damages for "injury or damage".

However, we will have no duty to defend the insured against any suit seeking damages for which insurance under this policy does not apply.

At our discretion, we may investigate any "event" that may involve this insurance and settle any resultant claim or suit, for which we have the duty to defend.

But:

  (1) The amount we will pay for "ultimate net loss" is limited as described in Section **II** – Limits Of Insurance; and

  (2) Our right and duty to defend ends when we have used up the applicable limit of insurance in the payment of judgments or settlements under this Coverage Part. However, if the policy of "controlling underlying insurance" specifies that limits are reduced by defense expenses, our right and duty to defend ends when we have used up the applicable limit of insurance in the payment of defense expenses, judgments or settlements under this Coverage Part.

  b. This insurance applies to "injury or damage" that is subject to an applicable "retained limit". If any other limit, such as, a sublimit, is specified in the "controlling underlying insurance", this insurance does not apply to "injury or damage" arising out of that exposure unless that limit is specified in the Declarations under the Schedule of "controlling underlying insurance".

  c. If the "controlling underlying insurance" requires, for a particular claim, that the "injury or damage" occur during its policy period in order for that coverage to apply, then this insurance will only apply to that "injury or damage" if it occurs during the policy period of this Coverage Part. If the "controlling underlying insurance" requires that the "event" causing the particular "injury or damage" takes place during its policy period in order for that coverage to apply, then this insurance will apply to the claim only if the "event" causing that "injury or damage" takes place during the policy period of this Coverage Part.

d. Any additional insured under any policy of "controlling underlying insurance" will automatically be an additional insured under this insurance. If coverage provided to the additional insured is required by a contract or agreement, the most we will pay on behalf of the additional insured is the amount of insurance required by the contract, less any amounts payable by any "controlling underlying insurance".

Additional insured coverage provided by this insurance will not be broader than coverage provided by the "controlling underlying insurance".

2. Exclusions

The following exclusions, and any other exclusions added by endorsement, apply to this Coverage Part. In addition, the exclusions applicable to any "controlling underlying insurance" apply to this insurance unless superseded by the following exclusions, or superseded by any other exclusions added by endorsement to this Coverage Part.

Insurance provided under this Coverage Part does not apply to:

a. Medical Payments

Medical payments coverage or expenses that are provided without regard to fault, whether or not provided by the applicable "controlling underlying insurance".

b. Auto

Any loss, cost or expense payable under or resulting from any of the following auto coverages:

(1) First-party physical damage coverage;

(2) No-fault coverage;

(3) Personal injury protection or auto medical payments coverage; or

(4) Uninsured or underinsured motorists coverage.

c. Pollution

(1) "Injury or damage" which would not have occurred, in whole or in part, but for the actual, alleged or threatened discharge, dispersal, seepage, migration, release or escape of pollutants at any time.

(2) Any loss, cost or expense arising out of any:

(a) Request, demand, order or statutory or regulatory requirement that any insured or others test for, monitor, clean up, remove, contain, treat, detoxify or neutralize, or in any way respond to, or assess the effects of, pollutants; or

(b) Claim or suit by or on behalf of a governmental authority for damages because of testing for, monitoring, cleaning up, removing, containing, treating, detoxifying or neutralizing, or in any way responding to, or assessing the effects of, pollutants.

This exclusion does not apply to the extent that valid "controlling underlying insurance" for the pollution liability risks described above exists or would have existed but for the exhaustion of underlying limits for "injury or damage".

d. Workers' Compensation And Similar Laws

Any obligation of the insured under a workers' compensation, disability benefits or unemployment compensation law or any similar law.

SECTION II – LIMITS OF INSURANCE

1. The Limits of Insurance shown in the Declarations, and the rules below fix the most we will pay regardless of the number of:

a. Insureds;

b. Claims made or suits brought, or number of vehicles involved;

c. Persons or organizations making claims or bringing suits; or

d. Limits available under any "controlling underlying insurance".

2. The Limits of Insurance of this Coverage Part will apply as follows:

a. This insurance only applies in excess of the "retained limit".

b. The Aggregate Limit is the most we will pay for the sum of all "ultimate net loss", for all "injury or damage" covered under this Coverage Part.

However, this Aggregate Limit only applies to "injury or damage" that is subject to an aggregate limit of insurance under the "controlling underlying insurance".

c. Subject to Paragraph **2.b.** above, the Each Occurrence Limit is the most we will pay for the sum of all "ultimate net loss" under this insurance because of all "injury or damage" arising out of any one "event".

d. If the Limits of Insurance of the "controlling underlying insurance" are reduced by defense expenses by the terms of that policy, any payments for defense expenses we make will reduce our applicable Limits of Insurance in the same manner.

     CX 00 01 04 13

3. If any "controlling underlying insurance" has a policy period that is different from the policy period of this Coverage Part then, for the purposes of this insurance, the "retained limit" will only be reduced or exhausted by payments made for "injury or damage" covered under this insurance.

The Aggregate Limit of this Coverage Part applies separately to each consecutive annual period of this Coverage Part and to any remaining period of this Coverage Part of less than 12 months, starting with the beginning of the policy period shown in the Declarations, unless the policy period is extended after issuance for an additional period of less than 12 months. In that case, the additional period will be deemed part of the last preceding period for purposes of determining the Limits of Insurance.

SECTION III – CONDITIONS

The following conditions apply. In addition, the conditions applicable to any "controlling underlying insurance" are also applicable to the coverage provided under this insurance unless superseded by the following conditions.

1. Appeals

If the "controlling underlying insurer" or insured elects not to appeal a judgment in excess of the amount of the "retained limit", we may do so at our own expense. We will also pay for taxable court costs, pre- and postjudgment interest and disbursements associated with such appeal. In no event will this provision increase our liability beyond the applicable Limits of Insurance described in Section II – Limits Of Insurance.

2. Bankruptcy

a. Bankruptcy Of Insured

Bankruptcy or insolvency of the insured or of the insured's estate will not relieve us of our obligations under this Coverage Part.

b. Bankruptcy Of Controlling Underlying Insurer

Bankruptcy or insolvency of the "controlling underlying insurer" will not relieve us of our obligations under this Coverage Part.

However, insurance provided under this Coverage Part will not replace any "controlling underlying insurance" in the event of bankruptcy or insolvency of the "controlling underlying insurer". The insurance provided under this Coverage Part will apply as if the "controlling underlying insurance" were in full effect and recoverable.

3. Duties In The Event Of An Event, Claim Or Suit

a. You must see to it that we are notified as soon as practicable of an "event", regardless of the amount, which may result in a claim under this insurance. To the extent possible, notice should include:

(1) How, when and where the "event" took place;

(2) The names and addresses of any injured persons and witnesses; and

(3) The nature and location of any "injury or damage" arising out of the "event".

b. If a claim is made or suit is brought against any insured, you must:

(1) Immediately record the specifics of the claim or suit and the date received; and

(2) Notify us as soon as practicable.

You must see to it that we receive written notice of the claim or suit as soon as practicable.

c. You and any other insured involved must:

(1) Immediately send us copies of any demands, notices, summonses or legal papers received in connection with the claim or suit;

(2) Authorize us to obtain records and other information;

(3) Cooperate with us in the investigation or settlement of the claim or defense against the suit; and

(4) Assist us, upon our request, in the enforcement of any right against any person or organization which may be liable to the insured because of "injury or damage" to which this insurance may also apply.

d. No insured will, except at that insured's own cost, voluntarily make a payment, assume any obligation, or incur any expense, other than for first aid, without our consent.

4. First Named Insured Duties

The first Named Insured is the person or organization first named in the Declarations and is responsible for the payment of all premiums. The first Named Insured will act on behalf of all other Named Insureds for giving and receiving of notice of cancellation or the receipt of any return premium that may become payable.

At our request, the first Named Insured will furnish us, as soon as practicable, with a complete copy of any "controlling underlying insurance" and any subsequently issued endorsements or policies which may in any way affect the insurance provided under this Coverage Part.

5. Cancellation

 a. The first Named Insured shown in the Declarations may cancel this policy by mailing or delivering to us advance written notice of cancellation.

 b. We may cancel this policy by mailing or delivering to the first Named Insured written notice of cancellation at least:

  (1) 10 days before the effective date of cancellation if we cancel for nonpayment of premium; or

  (2) 30 days before the effective date of cancellation if we cancel for any other reason.

 c. We will mail or deliver our notice to the first Named Insured's last mailing address known to us.

 d. Notice of cancellation will state the effective date of cancellation. The policy period will end on that date.

 e. If this policy is cancelled, we will send the first Named Insured any premium refund due. If we cancel, the refund will be pro rata. If the first Named Insured cancels, the refund may be less than pro rata. The cancellation will be effective even if we have not made or offered a refund.

 f. If notice is mailed, proof of mailing will be sufficient proof of notice.

6. Changes

This Coverage Part contains all the agreements between you and us concerning the insurance afforded. The first Named Insured is authorized by all other insureds to make changes in the terms of this Coverage Part with our consent. This Coverage Part's terms can be amended or waived only by endorsement.

7. Maintenance Of/Changes To Controlling Underlying Insurance

Any "controlling underlying insurance" must be maintained in full effect without reduction of coverage or limits except for the reduction of aggregate limits in accordance with the provisions of such "controlling underlying insurance" that results from "injury or damage" to which this insurance applies.

Such exhaustion or reduction is not a failure to maintain "controlling underlying insurance". Failure to maintain "controlling underlying insurance" will not invalidate insurance provided under this Coverage Part, but insurance provided under this Coverage Part will apply as if the "controlling underlying insurance" were in full effect.

The first Named Insured must notify us in writing, as soon as practicable, if any "controlling underlying insurance" is cancelled, not renewed, replaced or otherwise terminated, or if the limits or scope of coverage of any "controlling underlying insurance" is changed.

8. Other Insurance

 a. This insurance is excess over, and shall not contribute with any of the other insurance, whether primary, excess, contingent or on any other basis. This condition will not apply to insurance specifically written as excess over this Coverage Part.

  When this insurance is excess, if no other insurer defends, we may undertake to do so, but we will be entitled to the insured's rights against all those other insurers.

 b. When this insurance is excess over other insurance, we will pay only our share of the "ultimate net loss" that exceeds the sum of:

  (1) The total amount that all such other insurance would pay for the loss in the absence of the insurance provided under this Coverage Part; and

  (2) The total of all deductible and self-insured amounts under all that other insurance.

9. Premium Audit

 a. We will compute all premiums for this Coverage Part in accordance with our rules and rates.

 b. If this policy is auditable, the premium shown in this Coverage Part as advance premium is a deposit premium only. At the close of each audit period, we will compute the earned premium for that period and send notice to the first Named Insured. The due date for audit premium is the date shown as the due date on the bill. If the sum of the advance and audit premiums paid for the policy period is greater than the earned premium, we will return the excess to the first Named Insured.

 c. The first Named Insured must keep records of the information we need for premium computation, and send us copies at such times as we may request.

10. Loss Payable

Liability under this Coverage Part does not apply to a given claim unless and until:

a. The insured or insured's "controlling underlying insurer" has become obligated to pay the "retained limit"; and

b. The obligation of the insured to pay the "ultimate net loss" in excess of the "retained limit" has been determined by a final settlement or judgment or written agreement among the insured, claimant, "controlling underlying insurer" (or a representative of one or more of these) and us.

11. Legal Action Against Us

No person or organization has a right under this Coverage Part:

a. To join us as a party or otherwise bring us into a suit asking for damages from an insured; or

b. To sue us on this Coverage Part unless all of its terms have been fully complied with.

A person or organization may sue us to recover on an agreed settlement or on a final judgment against an insured; but we will not be liable for damages that are not payable under the terms of this Coverage Part or that are in excess of the applicable limit of insurance. An agreed settlement means a settlement and release of liability signed by us, the insured, "controlling underlying insurer" and the claimant or the claimant's legal representative.

12. Transfer Of Defense

a. Defense Transferred To Us

When the limits of "controlling underlying insurance" have been exhausted, in accordance with the provisions of "controlling underlying insurance", we may elect to have the defense transferred to us. We will cooperate in the transfer of control to us of any outstanding claims or suits seeking damages to which this insurance applies and which would have been covered by the "controlling underlying insurance" had the applicable limit not been exhausted.

b. Defense Transferred By Us

When our limits of insurance have been exhausted our duty to provide a defense will cease.

We will cooperate in the transfer of control of defense to any insurer specifically written as excess over this Coverage Part of any outstanding claims or suits seeking damages to which this insurance applies and which would have been covered by the "controlling underlying insurance" had the applicable limit not been exhausted.

In the event that there is no insurance written as excess over this Coverage Part, we will cooperate in the transfer of control to the insured and its designated representative.

13. When We Do Not Renew

If we decide not to renew this Coverage Part, we will mail or deliver to the first Named Insured shown in the Declarations written notice of the nonrenewal not less than 30 days before the expiration date.

If notice is mailed, proof of mailing will be sufficient proof of notice.

SECTION IV – DEFINITIONS

The definitions applicable to any "controlling underlying insurance" also apply to this insurance. In addition, the following definitions apply.

1. "Controlling underlying insurance" means any policy of insurance or self-insurance listed in the Declarations under the Schedule of "controlling underlying insurance".

2. "Controlling underlying insurer" means any insurer who provides any policy of insurance listed in the Declarations under the Schedule of "controlling underlying insurance".

3. "Event" means an occurrence, offense, accident, act, or other event, to which the applicable "controlling underlying insurance" applies.

4. "Injury or damage" means any injury or damage, covered in the applicable "controlling underlying insurance" arising from an "event".

5. "Retained limit" means the available limits of "controlling underlying insurance" applicable to the claim.

6. "Ultimate net loss" means the total sum, after reduction for recoveries, or salvages collectible, that the insured becomes legally obligated to pay as damages by reason of:

   a. Settlements, judgments, binding arbitration; or

   b. Other binding alternate dispute resolution proceeding entered into with our consent.

   "Ultimate net loss" includes defense expenses if the "controlling underlying insurance" specifies that limits are reduced by defense expenses.

Index

Case Index

This revised case index lists cases according to subject matter. Note that some cited cases are not found in this coverage guide but are listed for the reader's information.

Additional Insured

Bodily Injury

Building/Structure

Care, Custody or Control

Claims-Made

Coverage Territory

Damages

Defamation

Defense Costs

Endorsements

ERPL

Exclusions

False Publication

Faulty Workmanship

Impaired Property

Inspections

Insurance Agreement

Insured Contract

Joint Ventures

Liquor Liability

Loss of Use

Malicious Prosecution

Meaning of Loading/Unloading

Meaning of Occurrence

Meaning of That Particular Part

Mobile Equipment

Policy Date

Pollution Exclusion

Private Occupancy

Professional Liability

Progressive Injury

Railroad Protective

Reimbursement of Defense Costs

Sistership Exclusion

Supplementary Payments

What is Property Damage

Who is an Insured

Wrongful Eviction

Your Product

Your Work